# HTML, CSS, & JavaScript®

## ALL-IN-ONE

## by Paul McFedries

A Wiley Brand

## HTML, CSS, & JavaScript® All-in-One For Dummies®

Published by: **John Wiley & Sons, Inc.**, 111 River Street, Hoboken, NJ 07030-5774, www.wiley.com

Copyright © 2023 by John Wiley & Sons, Inc., Hoboken, New Jersey

Published simultaneously in Canada

For general information on our other products and services, please contact our Customer Care Department within the U.S. at 877-762-2974, outside the U.S. at 317-572-3993, or fax 317-572-4002. For technical support, please visit https://hub.wiley.com/community/support/dummies.

Wiley publishes in a variety of print and electronic formats and by print-on-demand. Some material included with standard print versions of this book may not be included in e-books or in print-on-demand. If this book refers to media such as a CD or DVD that is not included in the version you purchased, you may download this material at http://booksupport.wiley.com. For more information about Wiley products, visit www.wiley.com.

Library of Congress Control Number: 2023940485

ISBN 978-1-394-16468-4 (pbk); ISBN 978-1-394-16497-4 (ebk); ISBN 978-1-394-16472-1 (ebk)

SKY10050345_070523

# Contents at a Glance

# Table of Contents

# Introduction

Let me start off this book by letting you in on a little secret. If you talk to or read things written by people who make websites for a living, it's all "HTML this" and "CSS that." They go on and on about "tags" and "properties" and "collapsing margins" and blah blah blah. It can be more than a little intimidating, so you can easily come away with the idea that crafting a web page is *really* hard. You may end up believing that creating stuff for the web is a for-geeks-with-CS-graduate-degrees-only business.

Okay, it's time for that secret I just promised you. Ready? Come closer. Closer. Okay:

*whispers* *Learning how to build web pages is not hard.*

Sure, it *sounds* hard; and if you've ever taken a peek at some web page code, it certainly *looks* hard; and, I'll admit, building a huge and insanely complex site like Amazon or Instagram really *is* hard. But creating a personal website? Not hard. Fabricating a site to showcase a hobby? Not hard. Crafting some pages for a local charity, team, or small business? You got it: Not hard!

Still don't believe me? That's okay, I get it: HTML, CSS, and JavaScript — the technologies that enable anyone to assemble web pages — have a reputation problem. After all, so the thinking goes, people have used HTML, CSS, and Java-Script to sculpt some truly sensational sites, so *of course* such sophistication must come with a near-vertical learning curve. Duh.

For years now I've talked to many smart people who believed all that and who therefore wouldn't even dream of building a web page from scratch. How many awesome websites never got built because their would-be builders thought HTML, CSS, and JavaScript were well beyond their capabilities? Why is no one talking about how accessible these technologies really are?

After asking myself these questions over and over, I finally decided to do something about it. I decided to write this book, the aim of which is to prove to everyone — yes, even skeptical you — that the technologies behind the web are approachable, straightforward, and readily learnable.

# About This Book

Welcome, then, to *HTML, CSS, and JavaScript All-in-One For Dummies*. This book gives you a complete education on the technologies that enable anyone to craft professional-looking web pages. You learn how to set up the tools you need, how to use HTML and CSS to design and build your site, and how to use JavaScript to program your pages. My goal is to show you that these technologies aren't hard to learn, and that even the greenest rookie web designer can learn how to put together pages that will amaze their family and friends (and themselves).

If you're looking for lots of programming history, computer science theory, and long-winded explanations of concepts, I'm sorry, but you won't find it here. My philosophy throughout this book comes from Linus Torvalds, the creator of the Linux operating system: "Talk is cheap. Show me the code." I explain what needs to be explained and then I move on without further ado (or, most of the time, without any ado at all) to examples and scripts that do more to illuminate a concept that any verbose explanations I could muster (and believe me, I can muster verbosity with the best of them).

## Getting started with the book

How you approach this book depends on your current level of web coding expertise (or lack thereof):

>> If you're just starting out, begin at the beginning with Book 1 and work at your own pace sequentially through to Books 2 and 3. This will give you all the knowledge you need to pick and choose what you want to learn throughout the rest of the book.

>> If you know HTML and CSS, you can probably get away with taking a fast look at Books 2 and 3, and then settle in with Book 4 and beyond.

>> If you've done some JavaScript coding already, I suggest working quickly through the material in Book 4, and then exploring the rest of the minibooks as you see fit.

## My "No AI" guarantee

As I began updating this edition of the book, the world was awash in posts and talk and endless speculation about artificial intelligence, to the point where it seemed we'd soon be welcoming our new AI overlords. That's not likely to happen anytime soon, but AI is here to stay and has already established itself as a significant part of many people's workday routines.

I've been as enamored of ChatGPT and its ilk as the biggest AI boosters. I use AI for entertainment and curiosity, but I don't use it for work. That is to say that not one word of the text, code, or examples used in this book has been generated by AI. Everything you read here is, for good or ill, the product of my warped-from-birth brain.

# Foolish Assumptions

This book is not a primer on the internet or on using the World Wide Web. This is a book on building web pages, pure and simple. This means I assume the following:

>> You know how to operate a basic text editor, and how to get around the operating system and file system on your computer.

>> You have an internet connection.

>> You know how to use your web browser.

Yep, that's it.

I should mention here that this book is all about coding what web nerds call the *front end*, which means the stuff you see in your web browser. The web also has a *back end*, which refers to what happens on the web server. I don't get into any back-end coding in this book. If you're interested in that part of the web, may I not-so-humbly suggest my book *Web Coding and Development All-in-One For Dummies* (Wiley).

# Icons Used in This Book

This icon points out juicy tidbits that are likely to be repeatedly useful to you — so please don't forget them.

**REMEMBER**

Think of these icons as the fodder of advice columns. They offer (hopefully) wise advice or a bit more information about a topic under discussion.

**TIP**

**WARNING**

Look out! In this book, you see this icon when I'm trying to help you avoid mistakes that can cost you time, money, or embarrassment.

**TECHNICAL STUFF**

When you see this icon, you've come across material that isn't critical to understand but will satisfy the curious. Think "inquiring minds want to know" when you see this icon.

# Beyond the Book

Some extra content for this book is available on the web. Go online to find the following:

>> **The examples used in the book:** You can find these in either of the following places:

- **My website:** https://paulmcfedries.com/htmlcssjsfd

- **GitHub:** https://github.com/paulmcfe/html-css-js-fd

The examples are organized by book and then by chapter within each minibook. For each example, you can view the code, copy it to your computer's clipboard, and run the code in the browser.

>> **The Web Dev Workbench:** To try your own HTML, CSS, and JavaScript code and see instant results, fire up the following site:

   https://webdevworkshop.io/wb

You won't break anything, so feel free to use the site to run some experiments and play around with HTML, CSS, and JavaScript.

>> **Bonus chapters:** I had much more to tell you than I could fit in this book, so go to www.dummies.com/go/htmlcss&javascriptaiofd to download additional chapters that will show you some amazingly powerful techniques and animations to raise your CSS game.

>> **Cheat Sheet:** Go to www.dummies.com and search *HTML, CSS, & JavaScript All-in-One For Dummies* to find the Cheat Sheet for this book. Here you'll find a ready-to-roll HTML template for a basic web page, a set of 15 essential CSS selectors, and ten powerful JavaScript debugging strategies.

# 1

# Getting Started

# Contents at a Glance

# Chapter **1**

# Getting Acquainted with HTML, CSS, and JavaScript

*Well begun is half done.*

— ANCIENT GREEK PROVERB

In the early days of the internet in general and of the web in particular, people often used the abbreviation RTFM, which stood for (in the bowdlerized version), *read the freaking manual*. In days of yore, software programs came with little booklets — called *manuals* — that described the workings of the program. Look-before-you-leap types would carefully read the manual and would therefore know how to use the program. But a sizable proportion of the population would rather leap than look, meaning they would just start using the software, poking around willy-nilly to try to make things happen. Those dedicated leapers would inevitably end up on message boards or forums, desperately seeking solutions to the problems their haphazard experimenting caused them. The answer, more than often than not, was a simple one: "RTFM!"

This book is a sort of manual writ large for using HTML, CSS, and JavaScript. However, and this is particularly true if you're just getting started with coding web pages, if there's any part of the book that fits the RTFM credo, it's this chapter. *Everything* you learn in this chapter acts as a kind of home base for the explorations that come later, especially in Book 2 and beyond.

In this chapter, you learn the basic concepts behind HTML, CSS, and JavaScript, get a better understanding of how they work, and get started exploring these powerful technologies.

# What Do HTML, CSS, and JavaScript Do, Exactly?

If you're new to the world of weaving web pages, you may be asking yourself a very basic — but a very *astute* — question about HTML, CSS, and JavaScript: What do they do?

The bird's-eye view is that HTML, CSS, and JavaScript are the technologies behind what appears when you visit a page on the web. Sure, your trusty web browser shows you the page text and images, but the way in which the text and images are presented to you is a function of the page's underlying HTML, CSS, and JavaScript code. These technologies have three separate but interrelated functions:

>> **Structure:** The basic scaffolding of the page, such as the page headings, the text paragraphs, and where the images appear. This is the realm of HTML.

>> **Style:** How the page looks, including the fonts, colors, and margins. This is the bailiwick of CSS.

>> **Dynamism:** Extras that make the page perform actions such as interacting with the user, "listening" for mouse clicks and keypresses, and writing content to the page based on certain conditions. This is the job of JavaScript.

That's the big picture. I get into all this in a bit more detail later in this chapter (starting with HTML in the "Adding Structure with HTML" section).

# Why Learn HTML, CSS, and JavaScript?

I mention in the Introduction that learning HTML, CSS, and JavaScript isn't hard. That's still true, but I must admit that it doesn't tell the entire story. Yes, learning these technologies isn't hard, but it's certainly not trivial, either. Although you could probably memorize every element of HTML in an afternoon, both CSS and JavaScript are huge topics that take time to master. And although the basics of HTML, CSS, and JavaScript have a pleasingly gentle learning curve, after you get past these ABCs you quickly run into quite a few quirks and gotchas that steepen the ascent.

So, it's reasonable to ask a basic question right up front: Why may you want to go to the trouble to learn HTML, CSS, and JavaScript? After all, there's no shortage of templates, web page generators, content management systems, and web designers out there that — with varying degrees of ease, cost, and success — can convert your words and images into honest-to-goodness web pages. Why not take one of these easier paths to putting up a web presence?

Good question. And it just may be the case that, if you're chronically short on time or motivation, one of these let-someone-else-do-most-of-the-work solutions may be the right one for you. For everyone else, here are my reasons — call them the Four Cs — for learning HTML, CSS, and JavaScript to handcraft your own web pages:

>> **Carte blanche:** When you build web pages with your bare hands using HTML, CSS, and JavaScript, you have complete freedom over every aspect of your creation: content, colors, fonts, layout, the whole shebang. A new web page is a *tabula rasa* that you can fill up in whatever way you like.

>> **Creativity:** Forging your own web pages means you have the final say (not to mention the first, second, and third say) over not only what you say, but *how* you say it. You don't have one hand tied behind your back in the form of someone else's design or vision. Instead, you can express yourself in whatever way you want to show the world.

>> **Customization:** Almost any prefab web page is a rigid construct that offers only the most minimal customizations at creation time, and often no further customizing after the page is published. Forget that! When your pages are handmade, every possibility is open to you from the start and, of course, your pages are always infinitely customizable.

>> **Cost:** It may surprise you to learn that the cost of producing your own web pages using HTML, CSS, and JavaScript is effectively nothing. That's right: zero (0) dollars (or euros or pesos or whatever). How can that be? Because, as I discuss in the section that follows, all you really need to handmake a web page is a text editor, and most of those are free. Yep, you'll usually need to pay someone to host your pages on the web (check out Book 1, Chapter 3 for the details), but forging those pages is free.

# Seeing How It All Works

You know the web. You've browsed until your fingers are blue. You've experienced the wonder of those websites that are truly spectacular. Now, as you're about to embark on the journey of learning how to create your own web pages, you may believe that to achieve those amazing effects you need some fancy software. Perhaps a big-time page layout program or maybe a high-end word processor with special add-ins and templates for doing web pages. Or maybe you need a hideously complex and expensive "web page processor" app that offers the requisite bells and whistles needed to crank out perfect and professional-looking pages.

Well, it gives me great pleasure to report that you don't need any of those things. The only thing you really need to start banging out web pages is a humble text editor. All you have is Windows' Notepad or the Mac's TextEdit? Yup, either one will do. (Thankfully, you don't have to use either of these lowly programs because the world is awash in editors that are designed to make entering and editing HTML, CSS, and JavaScript — and, of course, text — a snap. And most of them are free! Refer to Book 1, Chapter 2 for more info.)

I see by your raised eyebrow that needing only a text editor surprises you. How is it possible, you ask, that the web's awesome web pages could even remotely be the product of an ignoble text editor? How do you get the magnificence of the web from the mundanity of pure text?

The answer to these questions lies with the app you use to surf the web: the browser. Most web pages are just text with strategically placed HTML (for structure), CSS (for style), and JavaScript (for dynamism) code. In simplest terms, when you navigate to a page, the web browser grabs the page's text file and dissects the file to look for its HTML, CSS, and JavaScript markings. The browser then uses that code to display — or, as the web geeks say, *render* — the page accordingly.

For example, you can add special codes inside a text file to specify that you want a particular collection of words or phrases to appear as a bulleted list. When the web browser comes to that part of the file, it dutifully renders those items as a list, bullets and all. The person browsing your page doesn't get the "render these items as a bulleted list" code; they just get the bulleted list. The web browser performs these and many other transformations behind the scenes. As long as you have the right HTML, CSS, and JavaScript markings in the right places, the browser will render your page the way you want.

# To get started, launch a new text file

So, to get to the point at long last, your first step whenever you want to create a web page is to start a new text file. To do that, not surprisingly, you need to fire up your favorite text editor:

» **Notepad (Windows):** In Windows 11, choose Start⇨All Apps⇨Notepad. Notepad displays a brand-new text file automatically when you start the program. You can also fire up a new document by choosing File⇨New.

» **TextEdit (Mac):** Click Search (the magnifying glass) in the menu bar, start typing **textedit**, and then click TextEdit as soon as it shows up in the search results. In the dialog box that appears, click New Document. You can launch a new text file any time you need one by choosing File⇨New.

» **Something else:** If you have another text editor, launch it the way you normally do and create a new file.

**WARNING**

What about using a word processor instead? Well, technically, you could use something like Microsoft Word or Apple Pages, but I don't recommend it. These programs tend to produce complicated web page files with extra files that do who-knows-what. Do yourself a favor and keep things simple by using a text editor.

**TIP**

If you'd prefer to start playing around right away without having to create any files, there are online tools you can use to mess around with HTML, CSS, and JavaScript without any fuss. Check out the final section of Book 1, Chapter 2 to learn how to do web coding online.

## Notes about saving HTML files

While slaving away on the text file that will become your web page, make sure you practice safe computing. That is, make sure you save your work regularly. However, going by the thousands of notes I've received from readers, I can tell you that the number-one thing that trips up wet-behind-the-ears webmeisters is improperly saving their HTML files.

To help you easily leap these saving hurdles, here are a few notes to pore over:

» **The Save command:** You save a file by choosing File⇨Save. The first time you do this with a new file, the Save As dialog box shows up for work. You use this dialog box to specify three things: the filename, the file type, and the file's location on your hard disk. The next few notes discuss some tidbits about the name and type.

- **Use the right file extension:** For garden-variety web pages, your file names must end with either the `.htm` or the `.html` file extension (for example, `mypage.html`). Therefore, when you name your file, be sure to specify either `.htm` or `.html`.

**REMEMBER**

Many new HTMLers get confused about whether to use `.htm` or `.html` when naming their files. Actually, you're free to use either one because it doesn't make any difference. That said, most people go with the `.html` extension. Either way, in this chapter and throughout this book, I refer to such files as "HTML files."

- **Use lowercase filenames:** The majority of web servers (computers that store web pages) are downright finicky when it comes to uppercase letters versus lowercase letters. For example, the typical server thinks that `index.html` and `INDEX.HTML` are two different files. It's dumb, I know. So to be safe, always enter your filenames using only lowercase letters.

- **Don't use spaces:** Windows and macOS are happy to deal with filenames that include spaces. However, web servers and web browsers can get confused if they come upon a filename that has one or more spaces. So don't use spaces in your filenames. If you want to separate words in file and directory names, use an underscore (_) or a hyphen (-).

- **Use the right file type:** While in the Save As dialog box, you need to select the correct file type for your HTML file. How you do this depends on what program you're using. In most programs (including TextEdit), you use the File Format (or Save As Type) list to select Web Page (`.html`) or something similar, as shown in Figure 1-1. If you're using Notepad, use the Save As Type list to select All Files (*.*). This ensures that Notepad uses your `.htm` or `.html` extension (and not its normal `.txt` extension).

- **Save it:** When you've completed your chores in the Save As dialog box, click Save to save the file.

## This book in four words: Edit. Save. Reload. Repeat.

By now you've probably figured out the biggest problem associated with fashioning a web page out of a text file: There's no way to know what the page will look like after it has been foisted on to the web! Fortunately, all is not lost. Most browsers are more than happy to let you load a text file right from the confines of your computer's hard disk (or whatever location you've used to save your file). This means you can test drive your page without first having to put it on the web. Nice.

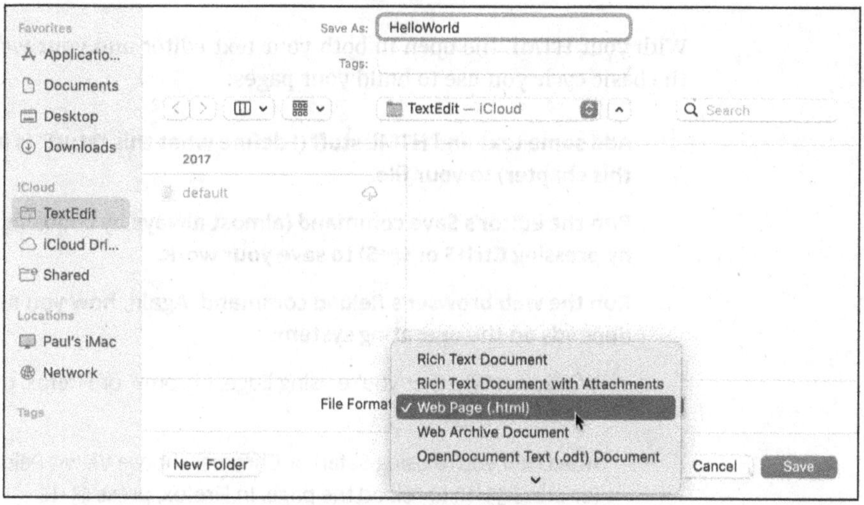

**FIGURE 1-1:**
Most text editors
enable you to
choose the Web
Page file type.

So, assuming that you've already creating and saved your HTML file as I describe in the previous section, your first task is to open the HTML file in your text editor and in your web browser:

>> **Text editor:** Run the Open command (almost always by choosing File⇨Open or by pressing Ctrl+O or ⌘+O) to open the HTML file you want to work with (if it's not open already, that is).

When you run the Open command, the Open dialog box that appears may not show your HTML files because, by default, the editor shows only regular text files that use the .txt extension. To make your HTML files show up, use the Files of Type list to select All Documents (*.*) or All Files (*.*).

>> **Web browser:** Run the Open command to load the same HTML file that you have open in your text editor. Finding the Open command is either trivial or tricky, depending on your operating system:

• **Windows:** Whether you're using Edge, Chrome, or Firefox, press Ctrl+O to display the Open dialog box; then select the HTML file and click Open.

• **macOS:** Whether you're using Safari, Chrome, or Firefox, choose File⇨Open File (or press ⌘+O) to display the Open dialog; then select the HTML file and click Open.

To open the HTML file in your computer's default web browser, locate the HTML file in File Explorer (Windows) or Finder (macOS) and then double-click the file.

With your HTML file open in both your text editor and your web browser, here's the basic cycle you use to build your pages:

1. **Add some text and HTML stuff (I define what this "stuff" is in the rest of this chapter) to your file.**

2. **Run the editor's Save command (almost always by choosing File⇨Save or by pressing Ctrl+S or ⌘+S) to save your work.**

3. **Run the web browser's Reload command. Again, how you invoke Reload depends on the operating system:**

   - **Windows:** Whether you're using Edge, Chrome, or Firefox, press Ctrl+R to reload the page.

   - **macOS:** If you're using Safari or Chrome, choose View⇨Reload Page (or press ⌘+R) to reload the page. In Firefox, press ⌘+R.

TIP

All web browsers have a Reload button somewhere in their toolbar. In almost all cases, the Reload button is a circular arrow, similar to the one shown in the margin.

The web browser reloads the page and displays whatever changes you made to the HTML file in Step 1.

4. **Repeat Steps 1 through 3 as often as you like.**

# Adding Structure with HTML

When it comes to building stuff for the web, it's no exaggeration to say that the one indispensable thing, the *sine qua non* for those of you who studied Latin in school, is HTML. That's because absolutely everything else you make as a web developer — your CSS rules and even your JavaScript code — can't hang its hat anywhere but on some HTML. These other web development technologies don't even make sense outside of an HTML context.

So, in a sense, this section and the chapters in Book 2 are the most important for you as a web coder because all the rest of the book depends to a greater or lesser degree on the HTML know-how found in those pages. If that sounds intimidating, not to worry: One of the great things about HTML is that it's not a huge topic, so you can get up to full HTML speed without a massive investment of time and effort.

Because HTML is so important, you'll be happy to know that I don't rush things. You'll get a thorough grounding in all things HTML, and when you're done, you'll be more than ready to tackle the rest of your web development education.

## What is HTML?

Building a web page from scratch using your bare hands may seem like a daunting task. It doesn't help that the codes you use to set up, configure, and format a web page are called the HyperText Markup Language (HTML for short), a name that could only warm the cockles of a geek's heart. Here's a mercifully brief look at each term:

>> **HyperText:** In prehistoric times — that is, the 1980s — tall-forehead types referred to any text that, when selected, takes you to a different document as *hypertext*. So this is just an oblique reference to the links that are the defining characteristic of web pages.

>> **Markup:** These are the instructions that specify how the content of a web page should be displayed in the web browser.

>> **Language:** This word refers to the set of codes that comprise all the markup possibilities for a page.

But even though the name HTML is intimidating, the codes used by HTML aren't even close to being hard to learn. There are only a few of them, and in many cases they even make sense!

## Getting the hang of HTML elements and tags

At its most basic, HTML is nothing more than a collection of markup codes — called *elements* — that specify the structure of your web page. In HTML, "structure" is a rubbery concept that can refer to anything from the overall layout of the page all the way down to a single word or even just a character or two.

For most of your HTML chores, you create a kind of container. What types of things can reside in this container? Mostly text, although often they will be entire chunks of the web page and even other elements.

Most HTML containers use the following generic format:

```
<element>content</element>
```

What you have here are a couple of codes that define the container for a particular HTML element. Many elements are one- or two-letter abbreviations, but sometimes they're entire words. You always surround these elements with angle brackets <>; the brackets tell the web browser that it's dealing with a chunk of HTML and not just some random text. An element surrounded by angle brackets is called a *tag*.

**REMEMBER**

An HTML code by itself is called an *element*; the element surrounded by angle brackets is known as a *tag*.

The first of these codes — ⟨element⟩ — is called the *start tag* and it marks the opening of the container; the second of the codes — ⟨/element⟩ — is called the *end tag* and it marks the closing of the container. (Note the extra slash (/) that appears in the end tag.)

In between the start and end tags, you have the *content*, which refers to whatever is contained in the tag. For example, here's a simple sentence that may appear in a web page:

```
This is a web page with something important to say.
```

Figure 1-2 shows how this may look in a web browser.

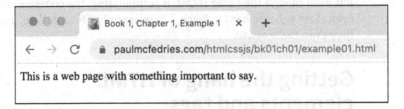

**FIGURE 1-2:**
The sample sentence as it appears in a web browser.

Ho hum, right? Suppose you want to punch this up a bit by emphasizing "important." In HTML, the element for emphasis is em, so you'd modify your sentence like so:

```
This is a web page with something <em>important</em> to say.
```

Notice how I've surrounded the word important with ⟨em⟩ and ⟨/em⟩? The first ⟨em⟩ is the start tag and it says to the browser, "Yo, Browser Boy! You know the text that comes after this? Be a good fellow and treat it as emphasized text." This continues until the browser reaches the end tag ⟨/em⟩, which lets the browser know that it's supposed to stop what it's doing. So the ⟨/em⟩ tells the browser, "Okay, okay, that's enough with the emphasis already!"

All web browsers display emphasized text in italics, so that's how the word now appears, as you can eyeball in Figure 1-3.

FIGURE 1-3:
The sentence
revised to
italicize the word
important.

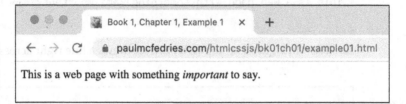

Book 1, Chapter 1, Example 1

paulmcfedries.com/htmlcssjs/bk01ch01/example01.html

This is a web page with something *important* to say.

There are tags for lots of other structures, including important text, paragraphs, headings, page titles, links, and lists. HTML is just the sum total of all these tags.

**WARNING**

One of the most common mistakes rookie web weavers make is to forget the slash (/) that identifies an end tag. If your page looks wrong when you view it in a browser, look for a missing slash. Also look for a backslash (\) instead of a slash, which is another common error.

## Understanding tag attributes

You'll often use tags straight up, but all tags are capable of being modified in various ways. The modification may be as simple as supplying a unique identifier to the tag for use in a script or a style, or it may be a way to change how the tag operates. Either way, you modify a tag by adding one or more *attributes* to the start tag. Most attributes use the following generic syntax:

```
<tag attribute="value">
```

Here, you replace `attribute` with the name of the attribute you want to apply to the tag, and you replace `value` with the value you want to assign the attribute. Surround the value with either double quotation marks (`attribute="value"`) or single quotation marks (`attribute='value'`). If you add two or more attributes to a tag, be sure to separate each with a space.

**TECHNICAL
STUFF**

Technically, you can omit the quotation marks around the attribute value as long as the value doesn't contain any spaces or any of the following characters: " ' ` = < or >. Also, if the value is the empty string (""), you can just write the attribute name by itself (that is, instead of `attribute=""`, you can write just `attribute`).

For example, the `<hr>` tag adds a horizontal line across the web page (hr stands for *horizontal rule*). You use only the start tag in this case (as a simple line, it can't "contain" anything, so no end tag is needed), as demonstrated in the following example (in this book's example files, check out bk01ch01/example01.html):

```
This is a web page with something <em>important</em> to say.
<hr>
```

As shown in Figure 1-4, the web browser draws a line right across the page.

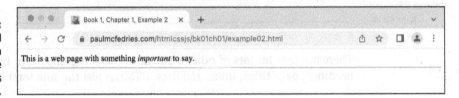

FIGURE 1-4:
When you add the <hr> tag, a horizontal line appears across the page.

You can also add the `width` attribute to the `<hr>` tag and specify the width you prefer. For example, if you want the line to traverse only half the page width, set the `width` attribute to "50%". Similarly, to make sure that the smaller line is aligned with the left side of the page, set the `align` attribute to "left". Here's how the code looks now (refer to bk01ch01/example02.html):

```
This is a web page with something <em>important</em> to say.
<hr align="left" width="50%">
```

As Figure 1-5 shows, the web browser obeys your command and draws a line that aligns with the left side of the page and takes up only half the width of the page.

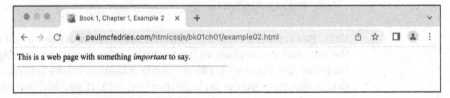

FIGURE 1-5:
The aligned and halved hr element.

# A barebones HTML page

In this section, I show you the tags that serve as the basic blueprint you'll use for all your web pages.

Your HTML files will always lead off with the following tag:

```
<!DOCTYPE html>
```

This tag (it has no end tag) is the so-called *Doctype declaration,* and it has an eye-glazingly abstruse technical meaning that, happily, you can safely ignore. All I'll say about it is that you have to include this tag at the top of all your HTML files to make sure that your pages render properly. (Also, I tend to write DOCTYPE in uppercase letters out of habit, but writing it as doctype is perfectly legal.)

Next up, you add the <html lang="en"> tag. This tag doesn't do a whole lot except tell any web browser that tries to read the file that it's dealing with a file that contains HTML doodads. It also uses the lang attribute to specify the document's language, which in this case is English.

Similarly, the last line in your document will always be the corresponding end tag: </html>. You can think of this tag as the HTML equivalent for "The End." So, each of your web pages will include this on the second line:

```
<html lang="en">
```

and this on the last line:

```
</html>
```

The next items serve to divide the page into two sections: the head and the body. The head section is like an introduction to the page. Web browsers use the head to glean various types of information about the page. A number of items can appear in the head section, but the only one that makes any real sense at this early stage is the title of the page, which I talk about in the next section, "Giving your page a title."

To define the head, add <head> and </head> tags immediately below the <html> tag you typed in earlier. So, your web page should now look like this:

```
<!DOCTYPE html>
<html lang="en">
    <head>
    </head>
</html>
```

**REMEMBER**

Although technically it makes no difference if you enter your tag names in upper-case or lowercase letters, the HTML powers-that-be recommend HTML tags in lowercase letters, so that's the style I use in this book, and I encourage you to do the same.

REMEMBER

Notice that I indented the <head> and </head> tags a bit (by four spaces, actually). This indentation is good practice whenever you have HTML tags that reside within another HTML container because it makes your code easier to read and easier to troubleshoot.

While you're in the head section, here's an added head-scratcher:

```
<meta charset="utf-8">
```

You place this element between the <head> and </head> tags (indented another four spaces for easier reading). It tells the web browser that your web page uses the UTF-8 character set, which you can mostly ignore except to know that UTF-8 contains almost every character (domestic and foreign), punctuation mark, and symbol known to humankind.

The body section is where you enter the text and other fun stuff that the browser will actually display. To define the body, place <body> and </body> tags after the head section (that is, below the </head> tag):

```
<!DOCTYPE html>
<html lang="en">
    <head>
        <meta charset="utf-8">
    </head>
    <body>
    </body>
</html>
```

WARNING

A common page error is to include two or more copies of these basic tags, particularly the <body> tag. For best results, be sure you use each of these five basic structural tags — <!DOCTYPE>, <html>, <head>, <meta>, and <body> — only one time on each page.

## Giving your page a title

When you surf the web, you've probably noticed that your browser displays some text in the current tab. That tab text is the web page title, which is a short (or sometimes long) phrase that gives the page a name. You can give your own web page a name by adding the <title> tag to the page's head section.

To define a title, surround the title text with the <title> and </title> tags. For example, if you want the title of your page to be "My Home Sweet Home Page," enter it as follows:

```
<title>My Home Sweet Home Page</title>
```

Note that you always place the title inside the head section, so your basic HTML document now looks like this (check out bk01ch01/example03.html):

```
<!DOCTYPE html>
<html lang="en">
    <head>
        <meta charset="utf-8">
        <title>My Home Sweet Home Page</title>
    </head>
    <body>
    </body>
</html>
```

Figure 1-6 shows this HTML file loaded into a web browser. Notice how the title appears in the browser's tab bar.

**FIGURE 1-6:**
The text you insert into the `<title>` tag shows up in the browser tab.

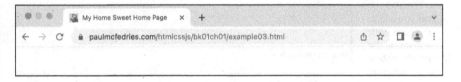

Here are a few things to keep in mind when thinking of a title for your page:

>> Be sure your title describes what the page is all about.

>> Don't make your title too long. If you do, the browser may chop it off because the tab doesn't have enough room to display it. Fifty or 60 characters are usually the max.

>> Use titles that make sense when someone views them out of context. For example, if someone really likes your page, that person may add it to their list of favorites or bookmarks. The browser displays the page title in the Favorites list, so it's important that the title makes sense when a viewer looks at the bookmarks later on.

>> Don't use cryptic or vague titles. Titling a page "Link #42" or "My Web Page" may make sense to you, but your visitors will almost certainly be scratching their heads.

## Adding some text

Now it's time to put some flesh on your web page's bones by entering the text you want to appear in the body of the page. For the most part, you can type the text between the `<body>` and `</body>` tags, like this (refer to bk01ch01/example04. html)):

```
<!DOCTYPE html>
<html lang="en">
    <head>
        <meta charset="utf-8">
        <title>My Home Sweet Home Page</title>
    </head>
    <body>
        Hello HTML World!
    </body>
</html>
```

Figure 1-7 shows how a web browser displays this HTML.

FIGURE 1-7:
Text you add to the page body appears in the browser's content window.

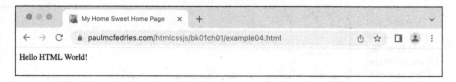

Before you start typing, however, there are a few things you should know:

>> You may think you can line things up and create some interesting effects by stringing together two or more spaces. Ha! Web browsers chew up all those extra spaces and spit them out into the nether regions of cyberspace. Why? Well, the philosophy of the web is that you can use only HTML elements to lay out a document. So, a run of multiple spaces (or *white space,* as it's called) is ignored.

>> Tabs also fall under the rubric of white space. You can enter tabs all day long, but the browser ignores them completely.

>> Browsers also like to ignore the carriage return. It may sound reasonable to the likes of you and me that pressing Enter (or Return on a Mac) starts a new paragraph, but that's not so in the HTML world.

>> If you want to separate two chunks of text, you have multiple ways to go, but here are the two easiest:

   ● **For no space between the texts:** Place a `<br>` (for line break) tag between the two bits of text.

   ● **For some breathing room between the texts:** Surround each chunk of text with the `<p>` and `</p>` (for paragraph) tags.

>> If HTML documents are just plain text, does that mean you're out of luck if you need to use characters such as © and €? Luckily, no. For the most part, you can just add these characters to your file. However, HTML also has special codes for these kinds of characters. I talk about them a bit in Book 2, Chapter 2.

>> If, for some reason, you're using a word processor instead of a text editor, know that it won't help to format your text using the program's built-in commands. The browser cheerfully ignores even the most elaborate formatting jobs because browsers understand only HTML (and CSS and JavaScript). And besides, a document with formatting is, by definition, not a pure text file, so a browser may have trouble loading it.

## Some notes on structure versus style

One of the key points of front-end web development is to separate the structure of the web page from its styling. This makes the page faster to build, easier to maintain, and more predictable across a range of browsers and operating systems. HTML provides the structure side, while CSS handles the styling.

That's fine as far as it goes, but HTML performs its structural duties with a couple of quirks you need to understand:

>> **This isn't your father's idea of structure.** That is, when you think of the structure of a document, you probably think of larger chunks such as articles, sections, and paragraphs. HTML does all that, but it also deals with structure at the level of sentences, words, and even characters.

>> **HTML's structures often come with some styling attached.** Or, I should say, all web browsers come with predefined styling that they use when they render some HTML tags. Yes, I know I just said that it's best to separate structure and style, so this can be a tad confusing. Think of it this way: When you build a new deck using cedar, your completed deck has a natural "cedar" look to it, but you're free to apply a coat of varnish or paint. HTML is the cedar, whereas CSS is the paint.

I mention these quirks because they can help to answer some questions that may arise as you work with HTML tags.

**REMEMBER**

Another key to understanding why HTML does what it does is that much of HTML — especially its most recent incarnation, HTML5 — has been set up so that a web page is "understandable" to an extent by software that analyzes the page. One important example is a screen reader used by some visually impaired surfers. If a screen reader can easily figure out the entire structure of the page from its HTML tags, it can present the page properly to the user. Similarly, software that seeks to index, read, or otherwise analyze the page will be able to do this successfully only if the page's HTML tags are a faithful representation of the page's intended structure.

# Adding Style with CSS

One of the things that makes web coding with HTML so addictive is that you can slap up a page using a few basic tags and find that it usually works pretty good when you examine the result in the browser. A work of art it's not, but it won't make your eyes sore. That basic functionality and appearance are baked in courtesy of the default formatting that all web browsers apply to various HTML elements. For example, `<strong>` text appears in a bold font, there's a bit of vertical space between `<p>` (paragraph) elements, and `<h1>` (heading level 1) text shows up quite a bit larger than regular text.

The browsers' default formatting means that even a basic page looks reasonable, but I'm betting you're reading this book because you want to shoot for something more than reasonable. In this section, you discover that the secret to creating great-looking pages is to override the default browser formatting with your own. You do that by augmenting your pages with some CSS.

## Figuring out cascading style sheets

If you want to control the look of your web pages, the royal road to that goal is a web-coding technology called *cascading style sheets,* or *CSS*. As I mention in the previous section, your design goal should always be to separate structure and formatting when you build any web project. HTML's job is to take care of the structure part, but to handle the formatting of the page, you must turn to CSS. Before getting to the specifics, I answer three simple questions: What's a style? What's a sheet? What's a cascade?

### Styles: Bundles of formatting options

If you've ever used a fancy-schmancy word processor such as Microsoft Word, Google Docs, or Apple Pages, you've probably stumbled over a style or two in your travels. In a nutshell, a *style* is a bundle of formatting options rolled into one nice, neat package. For example, you may have a "Title" style that combines four formatting options: bold, centered, 24-point type size, and a Verdana typeface. You can then "apply" this style to any text, and the program dutifully formats the text with all four options. If you change your mind later and decide that your titles should use an 18-point font, all you have to do is redefine the Title style. The program then automatically trudges through the entire document and updates each bit of text that uses the Title style.

In a web page, a style performs a similar function. That is, it enables you to define a series of formatting options for a given page element, such as a tag like `<div>` or `<h1>`. Like word processor styles, web page styles offer two main advantages:

» They save time because you create the definition of the style's formatting once, and the browser applies that formatting each time you use the corresponding page element.

» They make your pages easier to modify because all you need to do is edit the style definition, and then all the places where the style is used within the page get updated automatically.

For example, Figure 1-8 shows some `<h1>` text as it appears with the web browser's default formatting (check out bk01ch01/example05.html). Figure 1-9 shows the same `<h1>` text, but now I've souped up the text with several styles, including a border, a font size of 72 pixels, the Verdana typeface, and page centering (refer to bk01ch01/example06.html).

**FIGURE 1-8:**
An `<h1>` heading that appears with the web browser's default formatting.

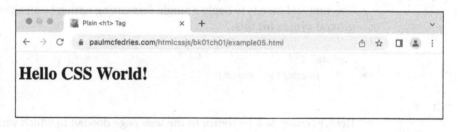

**FIGURE 1-9:**
The same text from Figure 1-8, except now with added styles.

## Sheets: Collections of styles

So far, so good, but what the heck is a sheet? The term *style sheet* harkens back to the days of yore when old-timey publishing firms would keep track of their preferences for things like typefaces, type sizes, margins, and so on. All these so-called "house styles" were stored in a manual known as a *style sheet*. On the web, a style sheet is similar: It's a collection styles that you can apply to a web page.

## Cascading: How styles propagate

The "cascading" part of the name *cascading style sheets* is a bit technical, but it refers to a mechanism that's built into CSS for propagating styles between elements. For example, suppose you want all your page text to be blue instead of the default black. Does that mean you have to create a "display as blue" CSS instruction for every single text-related tag on your page? No, thank goodness! Instead, you apply it just once, to, say, the ‹body› tag, and CSS makes sure that every text tag in the ‹body› tag gets displayed as blue. This is called *cascading* a style.

# Getting the hang of CSS rules and declarations

Before I show you how to actually use CSS in your web pages, take a second to get a grip on just what a style looks like.

The simplest case is to apply a single formatting option to an element. Here's the general syntax for this:

```
element {
    property: value;
}
```

Here, `element` is a reference to the web page doodad to which you want the style applied. This reference is often a tag name (such as `h1` or `div`), but CSS has a powerful toolbox of ways you can reference things, which I discuss in Book 3, Chapter 2.

The *property* part is the name of the CSS property you want to apply. CSS offers a large collection of properties, each of which is a short, alphabetic keyword, such as `font-family` for the typeface, `color` for the text color, and `border-width` for the thickness of a border. The property name is followed by a colon (`:`), a space for readability, the *value* you want to assign to the property, and then a semicolon (`;`). This line of code is known in the trade as a *CSS declaration* (although the description *property-value pair* is quite common, as well).

**REMEMBER**

Always enter the *property* name using lowercase letters. If the *value* includes any characters other than letters or a hyphen, you need to surround the value with quotation marks (single or double).

Notice, too, that the declaration is surrounded by braces ({ and }). You can place multiple declarations between the braces, and that collection is known as a *declaration block*. A declaration block applied to a page item (such as an HTML element) is called a *style rule*.

For example, the following rule applies a 72-pixel (indicated by the px unit) font size to the ‹h1› tag:

```
h1 {
    font-size: 72px;
}
```

The following example shows the rule I used to style the h1 element as shown earlier in Figure 1-9 (again, this code appears in bk01ch01/example06.html):

```
h1 {
    border-width: 1px;
    border-style: solid;
    border-color: black;
    font-family: Verdana;
    font-size: 72px;
    text-align: center;
}
```

**REMEMBER**

Note that the declaration block is most easily read if you indent the declarations with a tab or with either two or four spaces. The order of the declarations isn't crucial; some developers use alphabetical order, whereas others group related properties together.

Besides applying multiple styles to a single item, it's also possible to apply a single style to multiple items. You set up the style in the usual way, but instead of a single item at the beginning of the rule, you list all the items that you want to style, separated by commas. In the following example, a yellow background color is applied to the ‹header›, ‹aside›, and ‹footer› elements:

```
header,
aside,
footer {
    background-color: yellow;
}
```

## Adding styles to a page

With HTML tags, you just plop the tag where you want it to appear on the page, but styles aren't quite so straightforward. In fact, there are three main ways to get your web page styled: inline styles, internal style sheets, and external style sheets.

### Inserting inline styles

An *inline style* is a style rule that you insert directly into whatever tag you want to format. Here's the general syntax to use:

```
<element style="property1: value1; property2: value2; ...">
```

That is, you add the style attribute to your tag, and then set it equal to one or more declarations, separated by semicolons.

For example, to apply 72-pixel type to an <h1> heading, you could add an inline style that uses the font-size CSS property:

```
<h1 style="font-size: 72px;">
```

**REMEMBER**

Note that an inline style gets applied only to the tag within which it appears. Consider the following code (check out bk01ch01/example07.html):

```
<h1 style="font-size: 72px;">The Big Cheese</h1>
<h1>Just How Big Is This Cheese?</h1>
<h1>And Why Cheese, Of All Things?</h1>
```

As shown in Figure 1-10, the larger type size gets applied only to the first <h1> tag, whereas the other two h1 elements appear in the browser's default size.

### Embedding an internal style sheet

Inline styles are a useful tool, but because they get shoehorned inside tags, they tend to be difficult to maintain because they end up scattered all over the page's HTML code. You're also more likely to want a particular style rule applied to multiple page items.

For easier maintenance of your styles, and to take advantage of the many ways that CSS offers to apply a single style rule to multiple page items, you need to turn to style sheets, which can be either internal (as I discuss here) or external (as I discuss in the next section).

**FIGURE 1-10:**
Only the top ‹h1›
tag has the inline
style, so only its
text is styled
at 72 pixels.

An *internal style sheet* is a style sheet that resides within the same file as the page's
HTML code. Specifically, the style sheet is embedded between the ‹style› and
‹/style› tags in the page's head section, like so:

```
<!DOCTYPE html>
<html lang="en">
    <head>
        <style>
            Your style rules go here
        </style>
    </head>
    <body>
. . .
```

Here's the general syntax to use:

```
<style>
    itemA {
        propertyA1: valueA1;
        propertyA2: valueA2;
        . . .
    }
    itemB {
        propertyB1: valueB1;
        propertyB2: valueB2;
        . . .
    }
    . . .
</style>
```

As the preceding code shows, an internal style sheet consists of one or more style rules embedded within a `<style>` tag, which is why an internal style sheet is also sometimes called an *embedded style sheet*.

In the following code (refer to bk01ch01/example08.html), I apply border styles to the h1 and h2 elements: solid and dotted, respectively. Figure 1-11 shows the result.

HTML:

```
<h1>solid adj. having no break or interruption</h1>
<h2>dotty adj. 1. crazy or eccentric.</h2>
<h2>dotty adj. 2. feeble or unsteady.</h2>
<h2>dotty adj. 3. enthusiastic.</h2>
```

CSS:

```
<style>
    h1 {
        border-width: 2px;
        border-style: solid;
        border-color: black;
    }
    h2 {
        border-width: 2px;
        border-style: dotted;
        border-color: black;
    }
</style>
```

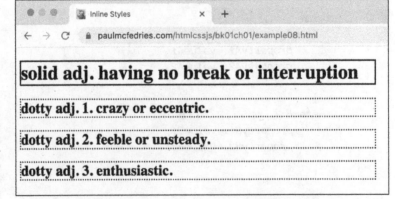

**FIGURE 1-11:** An internal style sheet that applies different border styles to the h1 (top) and h2 elements.

Note, in particular, that my single style rule for the h2 element gets applied to all the ‹h2› tags in the web page. That's the power of a style sheet: You need only a single rule to apply one or more style declarations to every instance of a particular element.

The internal style sheet method is best when you want to apply a particular set of style rules to just a single web page. If you have rules that you want applied to multiple pages, you need to go the external style sheet route.

## Linking to an external style sheet

Style sheets get insanely powerful when you use an *external style sheet*, which is a separate file that contains your style rules. To use these rules within any web page, you add a special ‹link› tag inside the page head. This tag specifies the name of the external style sheet file, and the browser then uses that file to grab the style rules.

Here are the steps you need to follow to set up an external style sheet:

**1.** **Use your favorite text editor to create a shiny new text file.**

**2.** **Add your style rules to this file.**

Note that you don't need the ‹style› tag or any other HTML tags.

**3.** **Save the file.**

It's traditional to save external style sheet files using a .css extension (for example, styles.css), which helps you remember down the road that this is a style sheet file. You can either save the file in the same folder as your HTML file, or you can create a subfolder (named, say, css or styles).

**4.** **For every page in which you want to use the styles, add a ‹link› tag inside the page's head section.**

Here's the general format to use (where *filename*.css is the name of your external style sheet file):

```
<link rel="stylesheet" href="filename.css">
```

If you created a subfolder for your CSS files, be sure to add the subfolder to the href value (for example, href="styles/filename.css").

For example, suppose you create a style sheet file named styles.css, and that file includes the following style rules:

```
h1 {
    color: blue;
}
p {
    font-size: 24px;
}
```

You then refer to that file by using the ‹link› tag, as shown here (check out bk01ch01/example09.html):

```
<!DOCTYPE html>
<html lang="en">
    <head>
        <link rel="stylesheet" href="styles.css">
    </head>
    <body>
        <h1>This Heading Will Appear Blue</h1>
        <p>This text will be displayed in a 24-pixel font.</p>
    </body>
</html>
```

Why is this use of a style sheet so powerful? You can add the same ‹link› tag to any number of web pages and they'll all use the same style rules, making it a breeze to create a consistent look and feel for your site. And if you decide that your ‹h1› text should be green instead, all you have to do is edit the style sheet file (styles.css). Automatically, every single one of your pages that link to this file will be updated with the new style!

# Adding Dynamism with JavaScript

JavaScript is (and has been for a while) universal on the web. Sure, there are plenty of barebones home pages out there that are nothing but HTML and a sprinkling of CSS, but everything else — from humble personal blogs to fancy-pants designer portfolios to big-time corporate e-commerce operations — relies on JavaScript to make things look good and work the way they're supposed to (most of the time, anyway).

# What is JavaScript?

When a web browser is confronted with an HTML file, it goes through a simple but tedious process: It reads the file one line at a time, starting from (usually) the <html> tag at the top and finishing with the </html> tag at the bottom. Along the way, it may have to break out of this line-by-line monotony to perform some action based on what it has read. For example, if it stumbles over the <img> tag, the browser will immediately ask the web server to ship out a copy of the graphics file specified in the src attribute (check out Book 2, Chapter 3).

The point here is that, at its core, a web browser is really just a page-reading machine that doesn't know how to do much of anything else besides follow the instructions (the markup) in an HTML file. (For my own convenience, I'm ignoring the browser's other capabilities, such as saving bookmarks.)

One of the reasons that many folks get hooked on creating web pages is that they realize from the very beginning that they have control over this page-reading machine. Slap some text between a <b> tag and its corresponding </b> end tag and the browser dutifully displays the text as bold. Create a CSS grid structure (check out Book 5, Chapter 3) and the browser displays your formerly haphazard text in nice, neat rows and columns, no questions asked. These two examples show that, instead of just viewing pages from the outside, you now have a key to get *inside* the machine and start working its controls. *That* is the hook that grabs people and gets them seriously interested in web page design.

Imagine if you could take this idea of controlling the page-reading machine to the next level. Imagine if, instead of ordering the machine to process mere tags and rules, you could issue much more sophisticated commands that could actually control the inner workings of the page-reading machine. Who wouldn't want that?

Well, that's the premise behind JavaScript. It's essentially just a collection of commands that you can wield to control the browser. Like HTML tags, JavaScript commands are inserted directly into the web page file. When the browser does its line-by-line reading of the file and it comes across a JavaScript command, it executes that command, just like that.

However, the key here is that the amount of control JavaScript gives you over the page-reading machine is much greater than what you get with HTML tags. The reason is that JavaScript is a full-fledged *programming language*. The "L" in HTML may stand for "language," but there isn't even the tiniest hint of a programming language associated with HTML. JavaScript, though, is the real programming deal.

## Adding a script to a page

Okay, that's more than enough theory. It's time to roll up your sleeves, crack your knuckles, and start coding. This section describes the standard procedure for constructing and testing a script and takes you through a couple of examples.

### The <script> tag

The basic container for a script is, naturally enough, the HTML <script> tag and its associated </script> end tag:

```
<script>
    JavaScript statements go here
</script>
```

**TECHNICAL STUFF**

In HTML5 you can use <script> without any attributes, but before HTML5 the tag would look like this:

```
<script type="text/javascript">
```

The type attribute told the browser the programming language being used in the script, but JavaScript is the default now, so you no longer need it. You still come across the <script> tag with the type attribute used on a ton of pages, so I thought I'd better let you know what it means.

### Where do you put the <script> tag?

With certain exceptions, it doesn't matter a great deal where you put your <script> tag. Some people place the tag between the page's </head> and <body> tags. The HTML standard recommends placing the <script> tag within the page header (that is, between <head> and </head>), so that's the style I use in this book:

```
<!DOCTYPE html>
<html lang="en">
    <head>
        <meta charset="utf-8">
        <title>Where do you put the script tag?</title>
        <script>
            JavaScript statements go here
        </script>
    </head>
    <body>
        </body>
</html>
```

Here are the exceptions to the put-your-script-anywhere technique:

>> If your script is designed to write data to the page, the <script> tag must be positioned within the page body (that is, between the <body> and </body> tags) in the exact position where you want the text to appear.

>> If your script refers to an item on the page (such as a form object), the script must be placed *after* that item.

>> With many HTML tags, you can add one or more JavaScript statements as attributes directly within the tag.

**REMEMBER**

It's perfectly acceptable to insert multiple <script> tags within a single page, as long as each one has a corresponding </script> end tag, and as long as you don't put one <script> block within another one.

# Example #1: Displaying a message to the user

You're now ready to construct and try out your first script. This example shows you the simplest of all JavaScript actions: displaying a basic message to the user. The following code shows the script within an HTML file (refer to bk01ch01/example10.html):

```
<!DOCTYPE html>
<html lang="en">
    <head>
        <meta charset="utf-8">
        <title>Displaying a Message to the User</title>
        <script>
            alert("Hello JavaScript World!");
        </script>
    </head>
    <body>
    </body>
</html>
```

As shown in here, place the script within the header of a page, save the file, and then open the HTML file within your browser.

This script consists of just a single line:

```
alert("Hello JavaScript World!");
```

This is called a *statement,* and each statement is designed to perform a single JavaScript task. Your scripts will range from simple programs with just a few statements to huge projects consisting of hundreds of statements.

You may be wondering about the semicolon (;) that appears at the end of the statement. Good eye. You use the semicolon to mark the end of each of your JavaScript statements.

In the example, the statement runs the JavaScript alert() method, which displays to the user whatever message is enclosed within the parentheses (which could be a welcome message, an announcement of new features on your site, an advertisement for a promotion, and so on). Figure 1-12 shows the message that appears when you open the file.

TECHNICAL STUFF

A *method* is a special kind of JavaScript feature that you use to specify an action that you want your code to perform.

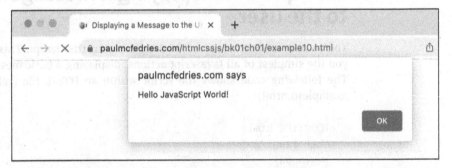

**FIGURE 1-12:** This "alert" message appears when you open the HTML file containing the example script.

How did the browser know to run the JavaScript statement? When a browser processes (*parses,* in the vernacular) a page, it basically starts at the beginning of the HTML file and works its way down, one line at a time, as I mention earlier. If it trips over a <script> tag, it knows one or more JavaScript statements are coming, and it automatically executes those statements, in order, as soon as it reads them. The exception is when JavaScript statements are enclosed within a *function,* which I explain in Book 4, Chapter 5.

WARNING

One of the cardinal rules of JavaScript programming is "one statement, one line." That is, each statement must appear on only a single line, and there should be no more than one statement on each line. I said "should" in the second part of the previous sentence because it is possible to put multiple statements on a single line, as long as you separate each statement with a semicolon (;). There are rare times when it's necessary to have two or more statements on one line, but you should avoid it for the bulk of your programming because multiple-statement lines are difficult to read and to troubleshoot.

# Example #2: Writing text to the page

One of JavaScript's most powerful features is the capability to write text and even HTML tags and CSS rules to the web page on-the-fly. That is, the text (or whatever) gets inserted into the page when a web browser loads the page. What good is that? For one thing, it's ideal for time-sensitive data. For example, you may want to display the date and time that a web page was last modified so that visitors know how old (or new) the page is. Here's some code that shows just such a script (check out bk01ch01/example11.html):

```
<!DOCTYPE html>
<html lang="en">
    <head>
        <meta charset="utf-8">
        <title>Writing Data to the Page</title>
    </head>
    <body>
        This is a regular line of text.<br>
        <script>
            document.write("Last modified: " + document.
  lastModified)
        </script>
        <br>This is another line of regular text.
    </body>
</html>
```

Notice how the script appears within the body of the HTML document, which is necessary whenever you want to write data to the page. Figure 1-13 shows the result.

**FIGURE 1-13:**
When you open the file, the text displays the date and time the file was last modified.

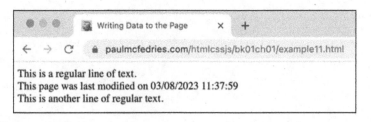

This script makes use of the document *object*, which is a built-in JavaScript construct that refers to whatever HTML file (document) the script resides in (check out Book 4, Chapter 6 for more about the document object). The document.write() statement tells the browser to insert whatever is within the parentheses to the web page. The document.lastModified portion returns the date and time the file was last changed and saved.

IN THIS CHAPTER

» Installing a variety of web browsers for testing

» Setting up your folders

» Learning what to look for in a good text editor

» Making sure you have everything you need

» Constructing code using the WebDev Workbench

# Chapter **2**

# Getting Ready to Code

*Beware of enterprises that require new clothes.*

— HENRY DAVID THOREAU

One of the things that can quickly dishearten a person taking up a new hobby or pastime is the early realization that to do the thing right, you need quite a bit of new stuff: new tools, new materials, and, yes, perhaps even new clothes. It's enough to nip a newfound fascination with baking or running or macramé in the bud.

One of the most attractive features of learning to build web pages using HTML, CSS, and JavaScript is that you don't need an expensive or complicated setup to get started. In fact, you may not need anything new at all because, if you have a Windows PC or a Mac, it's almost certainly the case that you already have everything you need. Sweet!

That said, there are a few basic chores you ought to run through to ensure that you're off to the best possible start, and in this chapter, you explore everything that's involved with that mercifully brief to-do list. You also delve into the surprisingly deep world of text editors and learn how to choose one that suits your style, just in case your default Windows or Mac text editor isn't getting the job done for you. Finally, this chapter also introduces you to a very useful online tool for painlessly testing HTML, CSS, and JavaScript code. Ready?

# Setting Up Your Test Browsers

In Book 1, Chapter 1, I talk about the "edit, save, reload" cycle, in which you make and save changes to your code, and then reload the file in a web browser to examine how everything looks. That's a good habit to get into, but I also want to urge you to practice that habit with a variety of web browsers. Why? Because although today's modern desktop browsers generally render web pages similarly, that's not always the case. The larger and more complex the page, the greater the likelihood that it will look noticeably different in one or more web browsers.

In most cases, the different look won't be a deal breaker and will be something you can live with. In some instances, however, the difference may have a significant effect on how your page looks or operates, in which case you'll need to find a workaround or alternative to solve the problem.

The good news is that you don't need to test your pages on every one of the dozens of web browsers that are available for Windows and macOS. Instead, it's sufficient to install and use the following "big four" browsers, which, combined, account for more than 90 percent of the desktop browser market:

>> **Google Chrome:** `https://www.google.com/chrome/`

>> **Apple Safari (macOS only):** `https://support.apple.com/downloads/safari`

>> **Microsoft Edge:** `https://support.microsoft.com/microsoft-edge`

>> **Mozilla Firefox:** `https://www.mozilla.org/firefox/new/`

What about smartphone and tablet browsers? Yep, they're important, too, but I hold off on them until you can put your pages on the web. I talk about testing your pages in detail in Book 1, Chapter 4.

# Creating Your Local Folders

You may want to create just a single web page, in which case you don't have to worry all that much about where you store the HTML file on your computer. Pop the file into your user account's Documents folder, for example, and you're good to go.

However, your purchase of this rather large book tells me that you're not a one-page-and-move-on-to-the-next-hobby type of person. No, you're in this to create a *bunch* of pages, am I right? If so, then long before you get started, you need to give some thought as to how you want to store your web stuff locally (that is, on your computer).

# First, create the local root folder

You begin by creating a folder that will act as the home base for all your web projects. In the web development trade, this folder is called the *root* because all your web projects "branch off" from this folder.

It really doesn't matter all that much where you create this root folder or what name you give it. Here are a couple of things to consider:

>> **Make it easy to find.** The folder should be relatively easy to navigate to, which generally means not burying it too deeply in your hard drive's folder hierarchy. Creating the root as a subfolder off your user account's Documents folder is a good way to go.

>> **Give it a memorable name.** The name should be descriptive enough that you know immediately that it's your web page root. The name `public_html` is very common because (as you learn in Book 1, Chapter 3) that's the name that many web hosting providers automatically assign to your root directory on the server. Another common root folder name is `htdocs` (short for *hypertext documents*).

# Now create the local subfolders, if any

What you do from here depends on the number of web development projects you're going to build, and the number of files in each project:

>> **A single web development project consisting of just a few files.** In this case, just put all the files into the root folder.

>> **A single web development project consisting of many files.** The more likely scenario for a typical web development project is to have multiple HTML, CSS, and JavaScript files, plus lots of ancillary files such as images and fonts. Although it's okay to place all your HTML files in the root folder, do yourself a favor and organize all your other files into subfolders by file type: a `css` subfolder for CSS files, a `js` subfolder for JavaScript files, an `images` folder for graphics, and so on.

>> **Multiple web development projects.** As a web developer, you'll almost certainly create tons of web projects, so it's crucial to organize them. The ideal way to do that is to create a separate root subfolder for each project. Then within each of these subfolders, you can create sub-subfolders for file types such as CSS, JavaScript, images, and so on.

# Choosing Your Text Editor

One of the truly amazing things about front-end web development is that all you ever work with are basic text files. (I'm ignoring here files such as images, videos, and fonts.) But surely all the structure you add with HTML tags requires some obscure and complex file type? No way, José: It's text all the way down. What about all that formatting stuff associated with CSS? Nope: nothing but text. JavaScript? Text.

What this text-only landscape means is that you don't need any highfalutin, high-priced software to develop for the web. A humble text editor is all you require to dip a toe or two in the web-coding waters.

However, saying that all you need to code is a text editor is like saying that all you need to live is food: It's certainly true, but more than a little short on specifics. After all, to a large extent the quality of your life depends on the food you eat. If you survive on nothing but bread and water, well, "surviving" is all you're doing. What you really need is a balanced diet that supplies all the nutrients your body needs. And pie.

The bread-and-water version of a text editor is the bare-bones program that came with your computer: Notepad if you run Windows, or TextEdit if you have a Mac. You can survive as a web developer using these programs, but that's not living, if you ask me. You need the editing equivalent of vitamins and minerals (and, yes, pie) if you want to flourish as a web coder. These nutrients are the features and tools that are crucial to being an efficient and organized developer:

>> **Syntax highlighting:** *Syntax* refers to the arrangement of characters and symbols that create correct programming code, and *syntax highlighting* is an editing feature that color-codes certain syntax elements for easier reading. For example, whereas regular text may appear black, all the HTML tags may be shown in blue and the CSS properties may appear red. The best text editors let you choose the syntax colors, either by offering prefab themes or by letting you apply custom colors.

>> **Line numbers:** It may seem like a small thing, but having a text editor that numbers each line, as shown in Figure 2-1 (which shows Visual Studio Code, a popular text editor), can be a major time-saver. When the web browser alerts you to an error in your code (refer to Book 4, Chapter 10), it gives you an error message and, crucially, the line number of the error. This information enables you to quickly locate the culprit and (fingers crossed) fix the problem pronto.

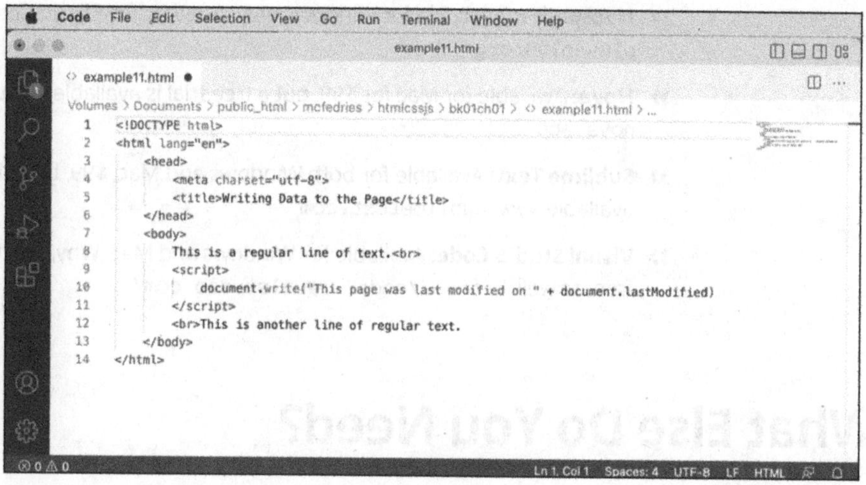

**FIGURE 2-1:**
Line numbers, as
seen here down
the left side of
the window, are a
crucial text editor
feature.

```
 1   <!DOCTYPE html>
 2   <html lang="en">
 3       <head>
 4           <meta charset="utf-8">
 5           <title>Writing Data to the Page</title>
 6       </head>
 7       <body>
 8           This is a regular line of text.<br>
 9           <script>
10               document.write("This page was last modified on " + document.lastModified)
11           </script>
12           <br>This is another line of regular text.
13       </body>
14   </html>
```

>> **Code previews:** A good text editor will let you get a preview of how your code will look in a web browser. The preview may appear in the same window as your code, or in a separate window, and it should update automatically as you modify and save your code.

>> **Code completion:** This is a handy feature that, when you start typing something, displays a list of possible code items that complete your typing. You can then select the one you want and press Tab or Enter to add it to your code without having to type the whole thing.

>> **Spell checking:** You always want to put your best web foot forward, which in part means posting pages that don't contain any typos or misspellings. A good text editor has a built-in spell checker that will catch your gaffes before you put your pages on the web.

>> **Text processing:** The best text editors offer a selection of text processing features, such as automatic indentation of code blocks, converting tabs to spaces and vice-versa, shifting chunks of code right or left, removing unneeded spaces at the end of lines, hiding blocks of code, and more.

The good news is that there's no shortage of text editors that support all these features and many more. That's also the bad news, because it means you have a huge range of programs to choose from. To help you get started, here, in alphabetical order, are a few editors to take for test drives:

>> **Atom:** Available for Windows and Mac. Free! http://atom.io

>> **Brackets:** Available for Windows and Mac. Also free! http://brackets.io/

>> **Notepad++:** Available for Windows only. Another freebie. https://notepad-plus-plus.org/

>> **Nova:** Available for Mac for $99, but a free trial is available. https://nova.app

>> **Sublime Text:** Available for both Windows and Mac. $99, but a free trial is available. www.sublimetext.com

>> **Visual Studio Code:** Available for Windows and Mac. Why, yes, this one is free, as well. https://code.visualstudio.com/

# What Else Do You Need?

Although it's true that all you need is a text editor to write web-page code, you may need a few other things before you can cross "Publish a web page" off your bucket list:

>> **Photo editor:** If you plan on including your own photos on your web pages (check out Book 2, Chapter 3 to learn how to reference images in your HTML files), you may need some photo-editing software to perform basic photo improvement tasks such as cropping out unwanted portions, enhancing colors, and adding special effects. You may also need to add annotations, adjust the image size, and change the image file format to JPEG. The Photos apps that come with Windows and macOS can perform basic chores, but for more serious work, you'll want a higher-end app such as Adobe Photoshop (big bucks; https://www.adobe.com/products/photoshop.html) or GIMP (free; https://www.gimp.org/).

>> **Design software:** If you want to create your own images to use on your web pages, you'll need a design app that has the tools you require to realize your visions. You can use Windows Paint for basic imagery, but for more ambitious work, you'll want a full-featured app such as Adobe Illustrator (big bucks; https://www.adobe.com/products/illustrator.html) or Inkscape (free; https://inkscape.org/).

>> **FTP client:** Many web-hosting services require you to upload your files to the server, and that almost always means using an FTP (File Transfer Protocol) program. For more about FTP and FTP clients, refer to Book 1, Chapter 3.

# Using the WebDev Workbench

The edit-save-reload workflow for building web pages in HTML, CSS, and Java-Script works great, but sometimes you just want to try a quick experiment or tweak. Nothing wrong with that. (On the contrary, the best way to learn HTML, CSS, and JavaScript is to run frequent experiments and to make small adjustments to your code to find out what happens.) However, cranking up a new HTML file, saving it, and then loading it into a browser may feel like overkill, depending on the size of your experiment or tweak.

Whenever you just want to try a quick web-coding thing, it's often best to use an online environment that enables you to type in your tags, rules, or scripts and then get the results immediately. CodePen (`https://codepen.io/`) is a popular online web development tool. However, may I also humbly suggest an interactive online development sandbox that I built myself? It's called WebDev Workbench, and you can find it here:

`https://webdevworkshop.io/wb" https://webdevworkshop.io/wb`

As shown in Figure 2-2, the WebDev Workbench consists of three tabs:

>> **HTML:** Use this tab to type your text and HTML tags. Note that the "page" infrastructure — that is, the `<html>` and `</html>` tags, the entire head section, and the `<body>` and `</body>` tags reside behind the scenes, as it were, so you use the HTML tab to enter just what you'd put in the body of the page.

>> **CSS:** Use this tab to type your CSS rules. The rules are added to the "page" header within `<style>` and `</style>` tags, all of which happens invisibly.

>> **JavaScript:** Use this tab to type your JavaScript statements. The statements are added (behind the scenes, as it were) to the "page" header within `<script>` and `</script>` tags.

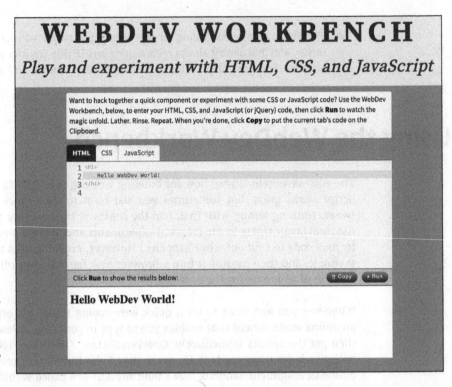

**FIGURE 2-2:**
The WebDev
Workbench is
an online web
coding sandbox
you can play
around in.

When you're ready to put your handiwork into action, click the Run button, and the WebDev Workbench renders the HTML, CSS, and JavaScript results in the bottom box (as shown in Figure 2-2).

If you write some code you want to keep, display the tab that contains the code and then click the Copy button to place the tab's code on your computer's Clipboard. You can then paste the copied code into your text editor.

IN THIS CHAPTER

» **Understanding web hosting providers**

» **Examining the various choices for hosting your site**

» **Choosing the host that's right for you**

» **Looking around your new web home**

» **Getting your site files to your web host**

# Chapter **3**

# Finding and Setting Up a Web Host

*Nothing stinks like a pile of unpublished writing.*

— SYLVIA PLATH

Y ou build your web pages from the comfort of your Mac or PC, and if you've chosen your text editor well (as I describe in Book 1, Chapter 2), you can even use your computer to preview how your web pages will look in a browser. That's fine and dandy, but I think you'll agree that the whole point of building a web page is to, you know, put it on the web! First, you need to subject your code to the wilds of the wider web to make sure it works out there. Even if it seems to be running like a champ on your local server, you can't give it the seal of approval until you've proven that it runs champ-like on a remote server. Second, after your code is ready, the only way the public can appreciate your handiwork is to get it out where they can surf to it.

Whether you're testing or shipping your code, you need somewhere to put it, and that's what this chapter is about. Here you explore the wide and sometimes wacky world of web hosts. You delve into what they offer, investigate ways to choose a good one, and then take a tour of your web home away from home.

# Understanding Web Hosting Providers

A common question posed by web development newcomers is "Where the heck do I put my web page when it's done?" If you've asked that question, you're doing okay because it means you're clued in to something crucial: Just because you've created a web page and you have an internet connection doesn't mean your site is automatically a part of the web. After all, people on the web have no way of getting to your computer. You're working in splendid isolation because no one either on your network or on the internet can access your web-page files.

In other words, your computer isn't set up to hand out documents (such as web pages) to remote visitors who ask for them. Computers that can do this are called *servers* (because they "serve" stuff out to the web), and computers that special-ize in distributing web pages are called *web servers*. So, your web page isn't on the web until you store it on a remote web server. Because this computer is, in effect, playing "host" to your pages, such machines are also called *web hosts*. Companies that run these web hosts are called *webhosting providers*. Now, just how do you go about finding a web host? Well, the answer to that depends on a bunch of factors, including the type of site you have, how you connect to the internet in the first place, and how much money (if any) you're willing to fork out for the privilege. In the end, you have three choices:

>> Your existing internet provider

>> A free hosting provider

>> A commercial hosting provider

## Using your existing internet provider

If you access the internet via a corporate or educational network, your institution may have its own web server that you can use. If you get online via an inter-net service provider (ISP), phone or email its customer service department to ask whether the company has a web server available. Almost all ISPs provide space so that their customers can put up personal pages free of charge.

## Finding a free hosting provider

If cash is in short supply, a few hosting providers will bring your website in from the cold out of the goodness of their hearts. In some cases, these services are open only to specific groups such as students, artists, nonprofit organizations, and so on. However, plenty of providers put up personal sites free of charge. What's the catch? Well, there are almost always restrictions both on how much data you can store and on the type of data you can store (no ads, no dirty pictures, and so on). You may also be required to display some kind of "banner" advertisement for the hosting provider on your pages. Alternatively, there are quite a few sites around that will host your pages at no charge and without annoying banner ads. The catch is that these sites host only "static" files, which means HTML, CSS, and JavaScript files that don't require a server for data. Here are some totally free static site hosts to check out:

» **Cloudflare Pages:** https://pages.cloudflare.com/

» **GitHub Pages:** https://pages.github.com/"https://pages.github.com/

» **Netlify:** https://www.netlify.com/

## Signing up with a commercial hosting provider

For personal and business-related websites, many web artisans end up renting a chunk of a web server from a commercial hosting provider. You normally hand over a setup fee to get your account going and then you're looking at a monthly fee. Why shell out all that dough when there are so many free sites lying around? Because, as with most things in life, you get what you pay for. By paying for your host, you generally get more features, better service, and fewer annoyances (such as the ads that some free sites display).

# A Buyer's Guide to Web Hosting

Unfortunately, choosing a web host isn't as straightforward as you may like it to be. For one thing, hundreds of hosts are out there clamoring for your business; for another, the pitches and come-ons your average web host employs are strewn with jargon and technical terms. I can't help you by reducing the number of web hosts, but I can help you understand what those hosts are yammering on about. Here's a list of the terms you're most likely to come across when researching web hosts:

» **Storage space:** Refers to the amount of room allotted to you on the host's web server to store your files. The amount of acreage you get determines the amount of data you can store. For example, if you get a 1MB (1 megabyte) limit, you can't store more than 1MB's worth of files on the server. HTML files don't take up much real estate, but large graphics sure do, so you need to watch your limit. For example, you could probably store about 200 pages in 1MB of storage (assuming about 5KB per page), but only about 20 images (assuming about 50KB per image). Generally speaking, the more you pay for a host, the more storage space you get.

» **Bandwidth:** A measure of how much of your data the server serves. For example, suppose the HTML file for your page is 1KB (1 kilobyte) and the graphics associated with the page consume 9KB. If someone accesses your page, the server ships out a total of 10KB; if 10 people access the page (either at the same time or over a period of time), the total bandwidth is 100KB. Most hosts give you a bandwidth limit (or "cap"), which is most often a certain number of megabytes or gigabytes per month. (A gigabyte is equal to about 1,000 megabytes.) Again, the more you pay, the greater the bandwidth you get.

**WARNING**

If you exceed your bandwidth limit, users will usually still be able to get to your pages (although some hosts shut down access to an offending site). However, almost all web hosts charge you an extra fee for exceeding your bandwidth, so check out this possibility before signing up. The usual penalty is a set fee per every megabyte or gigabyte over your cap.

» **Domain name:** A general internet address, such as wiley.com or whitehouse.gov. They tend to be easier to remember than the long-winded addresses most web hosts supply you by default, so they're a popular feature. Two types of domain names are available:

- A regular domain name (such as *yourdomain*.com or *yourdomain*.org)

- A subdomain name (such as *yourdomain.webhostdomain*.com)

To get a regular domain, you either need to use one of the many domain registration services such as GoDaddy (https://www.godaddy.com/) or Register.com (https://www.register.com/). A more convenient route is to choose a web hosting provider that will do this for you. Either way, it will usually cost you $35 per year (although some hosts offer cheap domains as a "loss leader" and recoup their costs with hosting fees; also, discount domain registrars such as GoDaddy offer domains for as little as $9.99 per year). If you go the direct route, almost all web hosts will host your domain, which means that people who use your domain name will get directed to your website on the host's web server. For this to work, you must tweak the domain settings on the registrar. This usually involves changing the Domain Name System (DNS; this system translates domain names into the actual addresses of resources on the internet) servers associated with the domain so that they point at the web host's domain name servers. Your web host will give you instructions on how to do this.

With a subdomain name, "webhostdomain.com" is the domain name of the web hosting company, and it tacks on whatever name you want to the beginning. Many web hosts will provide you with this type of domain, often for free.

>> **Email addresses:** Most hosts offer you one or more email addresses along with your web space. The more you pay, the more mailboxes you get. Some hosts offer *email forwarding,* which enables you to have messages that are sent to your web host address rerouted to some other email address.

>> **Shared server:** If the host offers a *shared server* (or *virtual server*), it means that you'll be sharing the server with other websites — dozens or even hundreds of them. The web host takes care of all the highly technical server-management chores, so all you have to do is maintain your site. This is by far the best (and cheapest of the commercial options) choice for individuals or small business types.

>> **Dedicated server:** You get your very own server computer on the host. That may sound like a good thing, but it's usually up to you to manage the server, which can be a dauntingly technical task. Also, dedicated servers are much more expensive than shared servers.

>> **Operating system:** The operating system on the web server. You usually have two choices: Unix (or Linux) and Windows Server. Unix systems have the reputation of being very reliable and fast, even under heavy traffic loads, so they're usually the best choice for a shared server. Windows systems are a better choice for dedicated servers because they're easier to administer than their Unix brethren. Note, too, that Unix servers are case sensitive in terms of file and directory names; Windows servers are not.

>> **Databases:** The number of databases you get to create with your account. Unix systems usually offer MySQL databases, whereas Windows servers offer SQL Server databases.

>> **Administration interface:** This is the host app that you use to perform tasks on the server, such as uploading files or creating users. Many hosts offer the excellent cPanel interface, and most Unix-based systems offer the phpMyAdmin app for managing your MySQL data.

>> **Ad requirements:** A few free web hosts require you to display some type of advertising on your pages. This could be a banner ad across the top of the page, a "pop-up" ad that appears each time a person accesses your pages, or a "watermark" ad, usually a semitransparent logo that hovers over your page. Fortunately, free hosts that insist on ads are rare these days.

>> **Uptime:** The percentage of time the host's server is up and serving. There's no such thing as 100 percent uptime because all servers require maintenance and upgrades at some point. However, the best hosts have uptime numbers of over 99 percent. (If a host doesn't advertise its uptime, it's probably because it's very low. Be sure to ask before committing yourself.)

>> **Tech support:** If you have problems setting up or accessing your site, you want to know that help — in the form of *tech support* — is just around the corner. The best hosts offer 24/7 tech support, which means you can contact the company — by phone, chat, or email — 24 hours a day, seven days a week.

>> **FTP support:** You usually use the internet's *FTP* service to transfer your files from your computer to the web host. If a host offers *FTP access* (some hosts have their own method for transferring files), be sure you can use it anytime you want and have no restrictions on the amount of data you can transfer at one time.

>> **Website statistics:** Tell you things such as how many people have visited your site, which pages are the most popular, how much bandwidth your pages are consuming, which browsers and browser versions surfers are using, and more. Most decent hosts offer a ready-made stats package, but the best ones also give you access to the "raw" log files so that you can play with the data yourself.

>> **E-commerce:** Some hosts offer a service that lets you set up a web "store" so that you can sell stuff on your site. That service usually includes a "shopping script," access to credit card authorization and other payment systems, and the ability to set up a secure connection. You usually get this capability only in the more expensive hosting packages, and you'll most often have to pay a setup fee to get your store built.

>> **Scalability:** The host can modify your site's features as required. For example, if your site becomes very popular, you may need to increase your bandwidth limit. If the host is scalable, it can easily change your limit (or any other feature of your site).

# Finding a Web Host

Okay, you're ready to start researching the hosts to find one that suits your web style. As I mentioned earlier, there are hundreds, perhaps even thousands, of hosts, so how is a body supposed to whittle them down to some kind of short list? Here are some ideas:

>> **Ask your friends and colleagues.** The best way to find a good host is that old standby, word of mouth. If someone you trust says a host is good, chances are you won't be disappointed. This is assuming you and your pal have similar hosting needs. If you want a full-blown e-commerce site, don't solicit recommendations from someone who has only a humble home page.

>> **Solicit host reviews from experts.** Ask existing webmasters and other people "in the know" about which hosts they recommend or have heard good things about. A good place to find such experts is Web Hosting Talk (www.webhostingtalk.com), a collection of forums related to web hosting.

>> **Contact web host customers.** Visit sites that use a particular web host and send an email message to the webmaster asking what they think of the host's service.

>> **Peruse the lists of web hosts.** A number of sites track and compare web hosts, so they're an easy way to get in a lot of research. Careful, though, because there are a lot of sketchy lists out there that are only trying to make a buck by getting you to click ads. Here are some reputable places to start:

- **CNET Web Hosting Solutions:** www.cnet.com/web-hosting

- **PC Magazine Web Site Hosting Services Reviews:** www.pcmag.com/reviews/web-hosting-services

- **Review Hell:** www.reviewhell.com

- **Review Signal Web Hosting Reviews:** http://reviewsignal.com/webhosting

# Finding Your Way around Your New Web Home

After you sign up with a web hosting provider and your account is established, the web administrator creates two things for you: a directory on the server you can use to store your website files, and your very own web address. (This is also true if you're using a web server associated with your corporate or school network.) The directory — which is known in the biz as your *root directory* — usually takes one of the following forms:

```
/yourname/
/home/yourname/
/yourname/public_html/
```

In each case, *yourname* is the login name (or username) the provider assigns to you, or it may be your domain name (with or without the .com part). Remember, your root directory is a slice of the host's web server, and this slice is yours to monkey around with as you see fit. This usually means you can do all or most of the following to the root:

>> Add files to the directory.

>> Add subdirectories to the directory.

>> Move or copy files from one directory to another.

>> Rename files or directories.

>> Delete files from the directory.

Your web address normally takes one of the following shapes:

```
https://provider/yourname/
https://yourname.provider/
https://www.yourname.com/
```

Here, *provider* is the host name of your provider (for example, www.hostcompany.com or just hostcompany.com), and *yourname* is your login name or domain name. Here are some examples:

```
https://www.hostcompany.com/mywebsite/
https://mywebsite.hostcompany.com/
https://www.mywebsite.com/
```

## Your directory and your web address

There's a direct and important relationship between your server directory and your address. That is, your address actually "points to" your directory and enables other people to view the files you store in that directory. For example, suppose I decide to store a file named thingamajig.html in my directory and my main address is http://mywebsite.hostcompany.com/. This means someone else can view that page by typing the following URL into a web browser:

```
https://mywebsite.hostcompany.com/thingamajig.html
```

Similarly, suppose I create a subdirectory named stuff and use it to store a file named index.html. A surfer can view that file by convincing a web browser to head for the following URL:

```
https://mywebsite.hostcompany.com/stuff/index.html"
    https://mywebsite.hostcompany.com/stuff/index.html
```

In other words, folks can surf to your files and directories by strategically tacking on the appropriate filenames and directory names after your main web address.

## Making your hard disk mirror your web home

As a web developer, one of the key ways to keep your projects organized is to set up your directories on your computer (as I describe in Book 1, Chapter 2) and then mirror those directories on your web host. Believe me, this will make your uploading duties immeasurably easier.

REMEMBER

Moving a file from your computer to a remote location (such as your web host's server) is known in the file transfer trade as *uploading.* This process begins at the root. On the web host, you already have a root directory assigned to you by the hosting provider. The root folder that you created on your computer is then the local mirror of the root directory.

TIP

To avoid confusion, consider renaming your local root folder to have the same name as your web host root directory. For example, if your web host assigned you a root directory named public_html, it's a good idea to rename your local root folder to public_html. To help you understand why mirroring your local and remote directory structures is so useful, suppose in your local root folder you set up a subfolder named graphics that you use to store your image files. To insert into your page a file named mydog.jpg from that folder, you'd use the following reference (refer to Book 2, Chapter 3):

```
graphics/mydog.jpg
```

When you send your HTML file to the server and you then display the file in a browser, it looks for mydog.jpg in the graphics subdirectory. If you don't have such a subdirectory — either you didn't create it or you used a different name, such as images — the browser won't find mydog.jpg and your image won't show. In other words, if you match the root subdirectories on your web server with the root subfolders on your computer, your page will work properly without modifications both at home and on the web.

WARNING

One common faux pas beginning web developers make is to include the local drive and all the folder names when referencing a file. Here's an example:

```
C:\users\paul\documents\public_html\graphics\mydog.jpg
```

This image will show up just fine when it's viewed from your computer, but it will fail miserably when you upload it to the server and view it on the web. That's because the C:\users\paul\documents\ part exists only on your computer.

**WARNING**

The Unix (or Linux) computers that play host to the vast majority of web servers are downright finicky when it comes to the uppercase and lowercase letters used in file and directory names. It's crucial that you check the file references in your code to be sure the file and directory names you use match the combination of uppercase and lowercase letters used on your server. For example, suppose you have a CSS file on your server that's named styles.css. If your HTML references that file as, say, STYLES.CSS, the server won't find the file and your styles won't get applied.

## Uploading your site files

When your web page or site is ready for its debut, it's time to get your files to your host's web server. If the server is on your company or school network, you send the files over the network to the directory set up by your system administrator. Otherwise, you upload the files to the root directory created for you on the hosting provider's web server. How you go about uploading your site files depends on the web host, but here are the four most common scenarios:

>> **Use an FTP program.** It's a rare web host that doesn't offer support for the File Transfer Protocol (FTP, for short), which is the internet's most popular method for transfer files from here to there. To use FTP, you usually need to get a piece of software called an *FTP client,* which enables you to connect to your web host's FTP server (your host can provide you with instructions for this) and offers an interface for standard file tasks, such as navigating and creating folders, uploading files, deleting and renaming files, and so on. Popular (and free!) FTP apps that have versions for both Windows and macOS are Cyberduck (https://cyberduck.io) and or FileZilla (https://filezilla-project.org).

>> **Use your text editor's file upload feature.** Some text editors come with an FTP client built-in, so you can edit a file and then immediately upload it with a single command. The Nova text editor (https://nova.app; for macOS only) supports this too-handy-for-words feature.

>> **Use the File Manager feature of cPanel.** I mention earlier that lots of web hosts offer an administration tool called cPanel that offers an interface for hosting tasks such as email and domain management. cPanel also offers a File Manager feature that you can use to upload files and perform other file management chores.

>> **Use the web host's proprietary upload tool.** For some reason, a few web hosts offer only their own proprietary interface for uploading and messing around with files and directories. Check out your host's Help or Support page for instructions.

## Making changes to your web files

What happens if you send a web development file to your web host and then realize you've made a typing gaffe or you spy a coding mistake? Or what if you have more information to add to one of your web pages? How do you make changes to the files you've already sent? Well, here's the short answer: You don't. That's right, after you've sent your files, you never have to bother with them again. That doesn't mean you can never update your site, however. Instead, you make your changes to the files that reside on your computer and then send these revised files to your web host. These files replace the old files, and your site is updated just like that.

WARNING

Be sure you send the updated file to the correct directory on the server. Otherwise, you may wonder why your changes don't appear when you refresh the page in your browser (and there's also the possibility that you may overwrite a file that happens to have the same name in some other directory).

Chapter **4**

# Testing and Validating Your Code

*Validate your HTML. Know what it means to have valid HTML markup . . . . More information is always better than less information. Why fly blind?*

— JEFF ATTWOOD

Have you ever heard of a *read-only user*? This play on *read-only memory* refers to someone whose use of the web goes only as far as reading things other people have created. I don't know if that moniker currently applies to you. If it does, it won't for much longer because by reading this book, you're arming yourself with the tools necessary to be one of the web's creators. Soon, all those other read-only users will be reading *your* words!

There's something almost *magical* about building your very own web page with your bare hands using nothing but HTML, CSS, and JavaScript. If you're feeling that magic, you're no doubt itching to get cracking and get something, *anything* up on the web to show off to your posse. I feel you. But, if you're serious about establishing a significant presence on the web, I also want to urge you to not rush headlong into just slapping up any old thing. By all means publish as much as you want, but as you publish, get into the habit of testing and validating your code to make sure you're putting out solid, well-built pages that will stand the test of time.

In this chapter, you explore the important topic of testing your web pages to make sure they look good and work well in a variety of web browsers. You also investigate the vital task of validating your HTML, CSS, and JavaScript code to make sure it passes muster. Yep, these are extra hurdles you have to leap over, but you'll learn that they take only a little extra time and are worth the effort.

# Cross-Browser Testing Your Code

One of the biggest mistakes that rookie web developers make is using a single web browser to check the progress of their pages. Most commonly, developers use Google Chrome running on Windows as the only testing browser. Of course, the page ends up looking great on Chrome, but then the developer is shocked when people using Firefox on the Mac or Safari on an iPad have problems with the page!

Sure, Chrome is the most popular web browser these days, but one of the distressing facts of being a web developer is that not everyone uses Chrome, and not everyone surfs using a desktop PC.

## Taking a look at browser market share

To prove that not everyone uses the Chrome browser or a desktop PC, Table 4-1 lists the top four browser market share values for the overall market and then categorized by desktop, tablet, and smartphone.

**TABLE 4-1** **Browser Market Share (March 2023)**

| Market | First | Second | Third | Fourth |
|---|---|---|---|---|
| Overall | Chrome (64.5%) | Safari (18.8%) | Edge (4.1%) | Firefox (3.4%) |
| Desktop | Chrome (65.8%) | Edge (11.1%) | Safari (10.9%) | Firefox (6.5%) |
| Tablet | Chrome (49.3%) | Safari (35.2%) | Android (13.3%) | Opera (0.7%) |
| Smartphone | Chrome (64.6%) | Safari (25.1%) | Samsung Internet (4.5%) | Opera (1.8%) |

*Source: StatCounter (*`https://gs.statcounter.com/browser-market-share`*)*

These numbers confirm Chrome's popularity, but they also show that Chrome decidedly does *not* dominate the web browser market. Yep, having about a two-thirds market share (overall, desktop, and smartphone) is impressive, but if you code only for Chrome, you're flying blind for fully one-third of your page visitors (and more than half of your tablet visitors).

## Your cross-browser testing suite

To ensure a positive experience for most of the people who come to your site, you need to expand your browser testing. A minimal testing suite would include the following:

» **Windows:** Chrome, Safari, Edge, and Firefox

» **Mac:** Chrome, Safari, and Firefox

» **iPadOS:** Chrome and Safari

» **Android tablet:** Chrome

» **iOS:** Chrome and Safari

» **Android smartphone:** Chrome

REMEMBER

Almost every Android web browser has been built using Chromium, which is the open-source version of Google Chrome. This means that all these browsers will load and render web pages as Chrome does, so you're fine just using Chrome as the Android test browser.

## Cross-browser testing online

Okay, I hear your *very* loud objections to the testing suite I propose in the previous section: Not everyone has both a Windows PC and a Mac! Not everyone has both an Apple and an Android tablet and smartphone! Heck, not everyone has both a tablet and a smartphone!

Valid objections all. So, what are you supposed to do if you really want to do extensive cross-browser testing but don't have access to a wide variety of browsers, operating systems, and devices?

Never fear: Online cross-browser testing is here! There are a bunch of online sites that will take your page URL and test it on a bunch of different (virtual) browsers, and then show you the results. Most of these sites require a paid subscription for heavy use, but they offer free access for a limited number of tests each month. Here are the most popular online cross-browser testing sites:

>> **BrowserStack:** www.browserstack.com/screenshots

>> **Comparium:** https://comparium.app/

>> **LambdaTest:** www.lamdatest.com

>> **Sauce Labs:** https://saucelabs.com

# Understanding Validation

*Validation* is an automated process that checks your code for errors and nonstandard syntax. Having valid HTML, CSS, and JavaScript code doesn't guarantee a flawless web page, but it does ensure that all modern web browsers can parse and interpret your code correctly. If your code is valid but your page is still wonky, you know the fault lies somewhere else (such as your overall design of the page).

Okay, so what do I mean by "valid" web page code? That depends on the language:

>> **HTML:** The Web Hypertext Application Technology Working Group (which is, mercifully, almost always shortened to the more reasonable WHATWG) maintains the so-called Living Standard for HTML, which some people also refer to as HTML5. The "living" part means that this standard is constantly evolving, so there are no big new releases and no sub-versions (such as 5.1 or 5.2.129). When you validate HTML, you're comparing your tags, attributes, and other HTML stuff with the specifications outlined in the Living Standard (which can be found here: https://html.spec.whatwg.org/; check out Figure 4-1).

**TIP**

How do you pronounce WHATWG. Let me count the ways! Some folks say *what-wig*; others say *what-double-you-gee*; some more eccentric types say *what-wee-gee*. More often than not, I say *what-working-group* for the extra clarity it provides.

>> **CSS:** The World Wide Web Consortium (W3C to those in the know) maintains a large collection of specifications for various aspects of CSS. These aspects — known as *modules* — cover CSS categories such as colors, fonts, selectors, and the box model. The current release is CSS 3, Revision 1. When you validate CSS, you're comparing your properties, declarations, and other CSS bric-a-brac with the specifications outlined in the W3C's standards (here's the starting point: https://www.w3.org/TR/CSS/#css; see Figure 4-2).

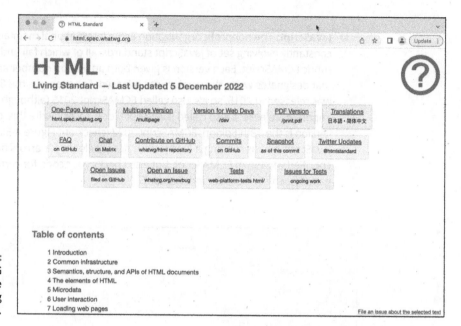

FIGURE 4-1:
WHATWG
maintains the
HTML Living
Standard.

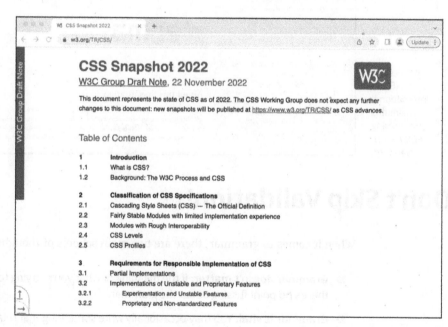

FIGURE 4-2:
The W3C
maintains the
CSS standards.

>> **JavaScript:** The nonprofit organization Ecma International maintains a constantly evolving set of JavaScript standards, all of which fall under the rubric ECMAScript. Each version is given both an edition number and a year that designates when the version was released. For example, the 6th Edition was released in 2015, so it's also called ECMAScript 2015 (although this important release is also called JavaScript 6 or JS 6). As I write this, the current version is the 13th Edition, ECMAScript 2022 (check out Figure 4-3). Validating JavaScript means running a *linter*, which not only looks for errors based on a specified version of ECMAScript, but also checks your code for certain stylistic gaffes (such as improper indentation).

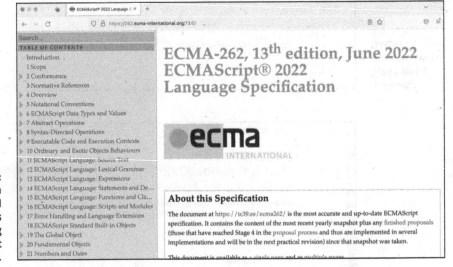

**FIGURE 4-3:** Ecma International maintains the evolving ECMAScript standard.

# Don't Skip Validation!

When it comes to grammar, there are two main schools of thought:

>> **Grammar doesn't matter:** If the meaning of what you're trying to say is clear, there's no point fussing about the grammar.

>> **Grammar is vital:** You may occasionally write something that retains its meaning despite having poor grammar, but the more likely result is writing that's difficult to parse, flat-out wrong, or off-putting to the reader.

In a sense, HTML and CSS code are like the grammar of your web page. That is, in the same way that writing is a bunch of text given some semblance of coherence and structure through its grammar, so too is a web page a bunch of text given coherence and structure through its HTML and CSS code.

As with grammar, there are also two schools of thought regarding validation:

>> **Validation doesn't matter:** If your web page renders properly, there's no point validating your code.

>> **Validation is vital:** Even if your web page appears to render properly, having invalid HTML or CSS code means that your overall structure is more fragile; programs that read your code (including search engine crawlers and assistive technologies such as screen readers) may have trouble parsing the code; and you may be providing a poor user experience for some visitors.

So, I think my bias here is clear: Your writing should be grammatical and your web pages should use validated HTML and CSS. The good news is that although writing perfectly grammatical sentences may be hard, publishing perfectly valid HTML and CSS code isn't even remotely difficult because, as you learn in the next few sections, there's an abundance of free tools available that can help.

# Validating Your HTML Code

HTML creates the structure for your web page, so if your tags are astray or your attributes are askew, there's a good chance your page will suffer for it. Fortunately, keeping your HTML code in apple-pie order is easier than you may think because you can validate your code either online or right within any reasonably powerful text editor that supports HTML files.

## Validating HTML online

The W3C operates an online app called the Markup Validation Service (check out Figure 4-4) that can check your HTML code for errors by comparing the code to the current HTML specifications. Best of all, this service is absolutely free!

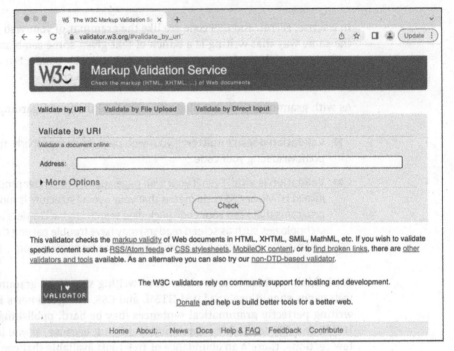

**FIGURE 4-4:**
The W3C's
Markup
Validation Service
lets you validate a
page by address,
file upload, or
code input.

The W3C's Markup Validation Service gives you three routes to validate your HTML code:

» **By address:** Type or paste the address of the page if you've already published the page to the web.

» **By file upload:** Upload your HTML file to the service.

» **By code input:** Type or paste your HTML code.

Here's how it works:

1. **Send your favorite web browser to** https://validator.w3.org.

   The Markup Validation Service appears.

2. **Tell the validator how you want to check your HTML:**

   • **By address:** Make sure the Validate By URI tab is selected (it should be by default), and then use the Address text box to type or paste the address of the page you want to validate.

   URI is short for Uniform Resource Identifier, which refers to any set of characters that identifies some resource used on the web. A URL (Uniform Resource Locator, a.k.a. a web address) is an example of a URI.

**TECHNICAL STUFF**

- **By file upload:** Click the Validate By File Upload tab, click Choose File, use the Open dialog box to select the HTML file you want to validate, and then click Open.

- **By code input:** Click the Validate By Direct Input tab; then use the big text box to type or paste the HTML code you want to validate.

3. **Click Check.**

   The Markup Validation Service digs in to your HTML code and then displays the results. If you dotted all your HTML *i*'s and crossed all your HTML *t*'s, you get the message No errors or warnings to show, as displayed in Figure 4-5. If, instead, something's amiss with your code, you get one or more error messages, as displayed in Figure 4-6. (In this example, the validator is complaining that the page's head section doesn't contain a title element.)

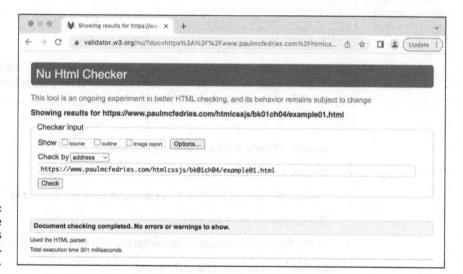

**FIGURE 4-5:**
This is the page that appears if your HTML checks out.

# Validating HTML in your text editor

I present a list of top-notch text editors in Book 1, Chapter 2. Most of those apps support extras — known as *add-ins* or *extensions* — that enable you to install features that aren't part of the app by default. One such feature is HTML validation, which checks your HTML code on the fly and lets you know right away when you've taken a wrong turn.

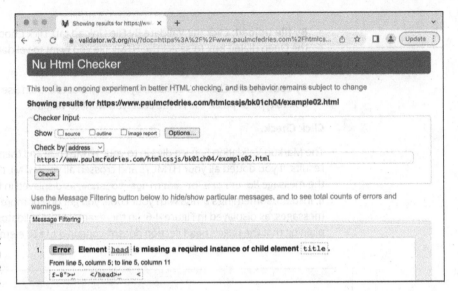

FIGURE 4-6:
If your HTML isn't
up to code, you
get one or more
error messages.

Refer to your editor's Help docs to learn how to install HTML validation. Because Visual Studio Code is the most popular editor for HTML these days, here are the steps to follow to install the HTMLHint extension, which is an HTML validation tool for VS Code:

1. **Launch VS Code if it's not already running.**

2. **Choose View ⇨ Extensions.**

   You can also press Ctrl+Shift+X (Windows) or ⌘+Shift+X (macOS).

   The Extensions pane appears.

3. **In the Search Extensions in Marketplace text box, type** htmlhint.

   VS Code displays a list of search results.

4. **In the results, click HTMLHint.**

   VS Code creates a new tab to display the info page for the HTMLHint extension, as shown in Figure 4-7.

5. **Click Install.**

   VS Code installs the HTMLHint extension.

6. **Click Close (X) in the Extension: HTMLHint tab.**

With the HTMLHint extension installed, VS Code now displays a squiggly line under any problematic tag. To find out what's going on, either hover the mouse pointer over the squiggly line or choose View ⇨ Problems (Ctrl+Shift+M or ⌘+Shift+M) to open the Problems panel, as shown in Figure 4-8.

FIGURE 4-7:
VS Code's info
page for the
HTMLHint
extension.

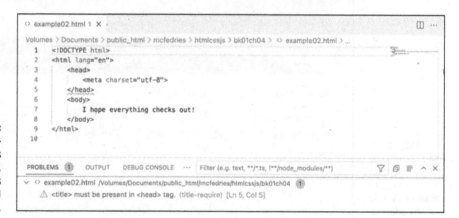

FIGURE 4-8:
When a squig-
gly line infests
your HTML code,
open VS Code's
Problems panel
to investigate.

# Validating Your CSS Code

If your web page is rendering weirdly or doesn't have the styling you expect, there's a good chance that some snag in your CSS is causing the problem. How can you tell? Well, you could double- or even triple-check your handiwork, but a much easier way is to validate your CSS code, which you can do either online or within a text editor that supports (or can add) CSS validation.

## Validating CSS online

The W3C offers an online tool called the CSS Validation Service (shown in Figure 4-9) that can compare your code to the current CSS specifications and then let you know if you've gone off the rails at any point. Oh, and did I mention that the CSS Validation Service is free? Sweet!

The CSS Validation Service gives you three ways to validate your CSS code (as shown in Figure 4-9):

» **By address:** Type or paste the address of an HTML file (if it contains your CSS) or a CSS file that you've already published to the web. (Note that the nerds at the W3C refer to a web address as a URI, which is short for Uniform Resource Identifier.)

» **By file upload:** Upload your HTML or CSS file to the service.

» **By code input:** Type or paste your CSS code.

**FIGURE 4-9:** You can use the CSS Validation Service to validate CSS code by address, file upload, or code input.

Here are the steps to follow:

1. **Using the nearest web browser, navigate to** https://jigsaw.w3.org/css-validator/.

   The Markup Validation Service appears.

2. **Tell the validator how you want to check your CSS:**

   • **By address:** Click the By URI tab and then use the Address text box to type or paste the address of the HTML file (if that's where your CSS resides) or CSS file you want to validate.

- **By file upload:** Click the By File Upload tab, click Choose File, use the Open dialog box to select the HTML file (if that's where your CSS resides) or CSS file you want to validate, and then click Open.

- **By code input:** Click the By Direct Input tab and then use the text box to type or paste the CSS code you want to validate.

3. **Click Check.**

The CSS Validation Service compares your CSS with the official specs and then displays the results. If your CSS rocks, you get the jaunty message Congratulations! No error found, as shown in Figure 4-10. If, sadly, your CSS sucks, you get one or more error messages, as shown in Figure 4-11.

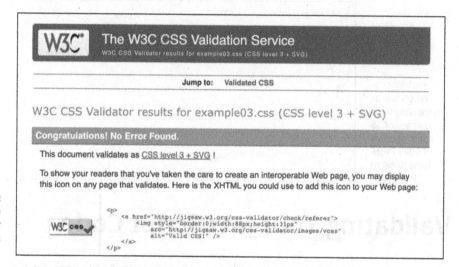

**FIGURE 4-10:** This page appears if your CSS code passes all the checks.

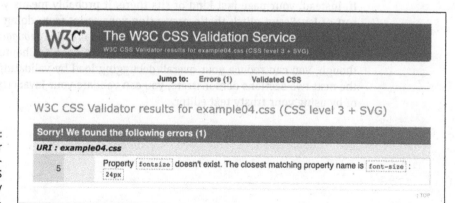

**FIGURE 4-11:** You get one or more error messages if your CSS code isn't ready for prime time.

## Validating CSS in your text editor

Most decent CSS-friendly text editors (such as the ones I mention in Book 1, Chapter 2) can validate your CSS code, either right out of the box or by installing an add-in or extension. Refer to your editor's Help docs to learn how to add or use CSS validation.

One editor that supports CSS validation by default is VS Code, which displays a wavy line under any CSS gaffes it finds. To find out what all the fuss is about, either hover the mouse pointer over the wavy line or choose View⇨Problems (Ctrl+Shift+M or ⌘+Shift+M) to open the Problems panel, as shown in Figure 4-12.

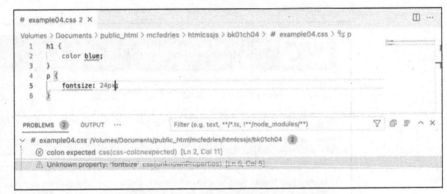

**FIGURE 4-12:** When one or more wavy lines mar your CSS code, open VS Code's Problems panel to learn why.

# Validating Your JavaScript Code

You add JavaScript code to a web page to make the page dynamic and interactive. If, instead, your page just kind of sits there, it probably means you've got some sort of JavaScript glitch that's preventing your script from doing its job. The art and science of tracking down programming errors is called *debugging*, and I devote an entire chapter to it later in the book (check out Book 4, Chapter 10). For now, though, you can reduce your overall debugging load by validating your code. As the next two sections demonstrate, you can validate your JavaScript either online or by using your trusty text editor.

# Validating JavaScript online

Quite a few free online tools are just sitting around waiting to validate your Java-Script code. One of the simplest and most popular is JSHint, which can validate directly typed or pasted code. Here's how it works:

**1.** **Send any handy web browser to** https://jshint.com.

The JS Hint page appears.

**2.** **Click Configure.**

JSHint displays a list of options you can configure. For the purposes of this book's code, you need to configure JSHint to support JavaScript features that were released with the 6th Edition (ECMAScript 2015 or ES6).

**3.** **Select the New JavaScript Features (ES6) option.**

**4.** **Click Configure.**

JSHint closes the list of options.

**5.** **In the left side of the window, type or paste the JavaScript code you want to validate.**

JSHint automatically scans and analyzes your code and, if it finds one or more things it can't figure out, it displays error messages to the right of the code, as shown in Figure 4-13.

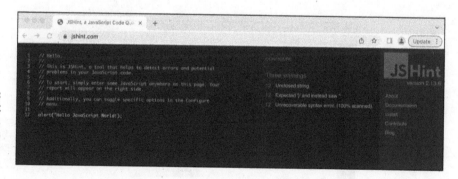

**FIGURE 4-13:**
If your JavaScript code has flaws, JSHint displays one or more error messages.

Testing and Validating Your Code

# Validating JavaScript in your text editor

Most JavaScript-savvy text editors (such as the ones I mention in Book 1, Chapter 2) can validate — or *lint* — your JavaScript statements, usually by installing an add-in or an extension. Refer to your editor's Help docs to learn how to add or use a JavaScript validator — or *linter*.

As an example, VS Code supports a popular extension called ESLint (the "ES" part is short for ECMAScript) that can find code errors and suggest edits for code that violates generally accepted programming principles. Here are the steps to follow to install ESLint in VS Code:

1. **Launch VS Code if it's not already running.**

2. **Choose View ⇨ Extensions.**

   You can also press Ctrl+Shift+X (Windows) or ⌘+Shift+X (macOS).

   The Extensions pane appears.

3. **In the Search Extensions in Marketplace text box, type** eslint.

   VS Code displays a list of search results.

4. **In the results, click ESLint.**

   VS Code creates a new tab to display the info page for the ESLint extension, as shown in Figure 4-14.

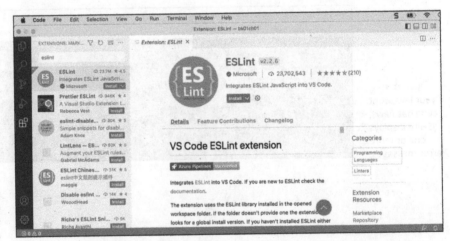

**FIGURE 4-14:**
VS Code's info page for the ESLint extension.

5. **Click Install.**

   VS Code installs the ESLint extension.

6. **Click Close (X) in the Extension: ESLint tab.**

With the ESLint extension installed, VS Code shows a squiggly line under any rogue code. To find out what's gone awry, either hover the mouse pointer over the squiggly line or choose View⇨Problems (Ctrl+Shift+M or ⌘+Shift+M) to open the Problems panel, as shown in Figure 4-15.

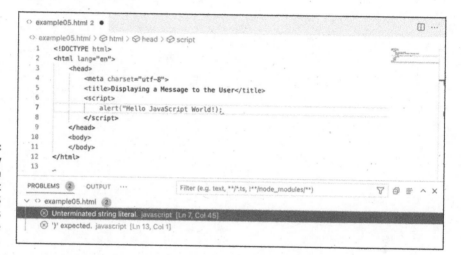

**FIGURE 4-15:** When a squiggly line appears in your JavaScript code, open VS Code's Problems panel to figure out what's wrong.

# Learning HTML Basics

2

# Contents at a Glance

IN THIS CHAPTER

» **Herding your text into paragraphs**

» **Organizing your page with headings**

» **Adding line breaks and horizontal rules**

» **Getting familiar with HTML's all-important semantic page tags**

» **Annotating your code with comments**

Chapter **1**

# Building Good Bones: Structuring the Page

*Together let us desire, conceive, and create the new structure of the future.*

— WALTER GROPIUS

I f you've ever shopped for a house — particularly if your budget skewed more to the bargain end of the asking-price scale — your Realtor most likely showed you a few places that, although clearly requiring some work, were still worth considering because they had "good bones." In Realtor-speak, *good bones* means the house has (among other attributes) a solid foundation, well-built framing, and a decent roof. In other words, the house has a strong overall structure.

When it comes to building web homes, you want your pages to have good bones, as well. Creating that solid structure is the province of HTML, particularly the elements used to convert plain text into the structural elements of the page.

In this chapter, you explore those foundational HTML tags that add the most basic structure to any page, including headings and paragraphs, articles and sections, and headers and footers. You also learn about a few other structure-related elements for creating things like line breaks and horizontal rules. What you learn in this chapter will form the basis of every web page project you undertake.

# Getting to Know HTML's Basic Structure Tags

One of the most important concepts you need to understand as you get started with HTML is that whatever text you shoehorn between the `<body>` and `</body>` tags has no inherent structure. To show you what I mean, I copied the first few headings and paragraphs of this section and pasted them into an HTML file. Figure 1-1 shows what happens when I open the HTML file in a web browser (check out bk02ch01/example01.html in this book's example files).

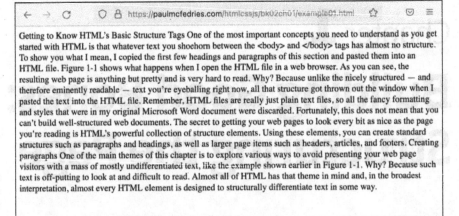

**FIGURE 1-1:**
Bare text has no structure in an HTML document.

The resulting web page is anything but pretty and is very hard to read. Why? Because unlike the nicely structured — and therefore eminently readable — text you're eyeballing right now, all that structure got thrown out the window when I pasted the text into the HTML file. Remember, HTML files are really just plain-text files, so all the fancy formatting and styles that were in my original Microsoft Word document were discarded.

Fortunately, this absence of formatting does *not* mean that you can't build well-structured web documents. The secret to getting your web pages to look every bit as nice as the page you're reading is HTML's powerful collection of structure elements. Using these elements, you can create standard structures such as paragraphs and headings, as well as larger page items such as headers, articles, and footers.

# Creating paragraphs

One of the main themes of this chapter is to explore various ways to avoid presenting your web page visitors with a mass of mostly undifferentiated text, like the example shown earlier in Figure 1-1. Why? Because such text is off-putting to look at and difficult to read.

Almost all of HTML has that theme in mind and, in the broadest interpretation, almost every HTML element is designed to structurally differentiate text in some way.

The simplest and most common example is the use of the p element, which turns any text surrounded by the `<p>` start tag and the `</p>` end tag into a paragraph:

```
<p>
    This is now a paragraph.
</p>
```

What does it mean to say that a chunk of text in a web page is a paragraph? At the most basic level, it just means that the text is rendered with a bit of space above and below. To demonstrate, I added p elements to the plain text shown earlier in Figure 1-1. The result (refer to bk02ch01/example02.html), shown in Figure 1-2, is that the text now is separated into paragraphs, which is already a big improvement.

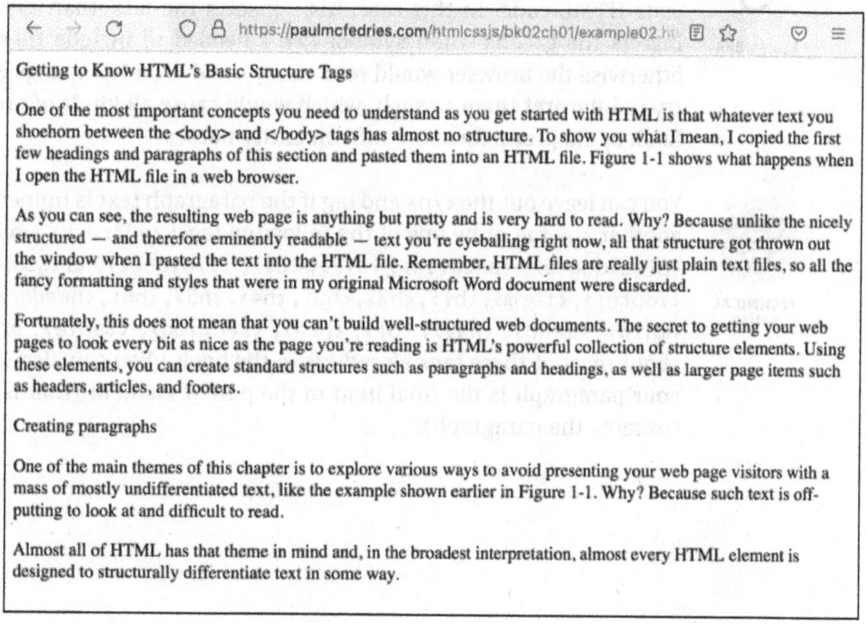

**FIGURE 1-2:**
The text from
Figure 1-1
separated into
paragraphs by
adding
`<p>` tags.

Getting to Know HTML's Basic Structure Tags

One of the most important concepts you need to understand as you get started with HTML is that whatever text you shoehorn between the <body> and </body> tags has almost no structure. To show you what I mean, I copied the first few headings and paragraphs of this section and pasted them into an HTML file. Figure 1-1 shows what happens when I open the HTML file in a web browser.

As you can see, the resulting web page is anything but pretty and is very hard to read. Why? Because unlike the nicely structured — and therefore eminently readable — text you're eyeballing right now, all that structure got thrown out the window when I pasted the text into the HTML file. Remember, HTML files are really just plain text files, so all the fancy formatting and styles that were in my original Microsoft Word document were discarded.

Fortunately, this does not mean that you can't build well-structured web documents. The secret to getting your web pages to look every bit as nice as the page you're reading is HTML's powerful collection of structure elements. Using these elements, you can create standard structures such as paragraphs and headings, as well as larger page items such as headers, articles, and footers.

Creating paragraphs

One of the main themes of this chapter is to explore various ways to avoid presenting your web page visitors with a mass of mostly undifferentiated text, like the example shown earlier in Figure 1-1. Why? Because such text is off-putting to look at and difficult to read.

Almost all of HTML has that theme in mind and, in the broadest interpretation, almost every HTML element is designed to structurally differentiate text in some way.

Here's what the first part of the body of the HTML file now looks like:

```
Getting to Know HTML's Basic Structure Tags
<p>
    One of the most important concepts you need to understand as
you get started with HTML is that whatever text you shoehorn
between the &lt;body&gt; and &lt;/body&gt; tags has almost no
structure. To show you what I mean, I copied the first few
headings and paragraphs of this section and pasted them into
an HTML file. Figure 1-1 shows what happens when I open the
HTML file in a web browser.
</p>
<p>
    The resulting web page is anything but pretty and is very
hard to read. Why? Because unlike the nicely structured — and
therefore eminently readable — text you're eyeballing right
now, all that structure got thrown out the window when I
pasted the text into the HTML file. Remember, HTML files are
really just plain text files, so all the fancy formatting and
styles that were in my original Microsoft Word document were
discarded.
</p>
```

**REMEMBER**

What's with the &lt; and &gt; gobbledygook in the first paragraph? These are examples of HTML entity names, which you use to insert special characters into your HTML code. In this case, &lt; inserts the less-than symbol (<) and &gt; inserts the greater-than symbol (>). I needed to include these inserts because otherwise the browser would read <body> and </body> as tags instead of text and try to interpret them as such, which would cause all kinds of problems. Check out Book 2, Chapter 2 for more info on entity names.

**TECHNICAL STUFF**

You can leave out the </p> end tag if the paragraph text is immediately followed by another <p> tag or by one of the following tags: <address>, <article>, <aside>, <blockquote>, <details>, <div>, <dl>, <fieldset>, <figcaption>, <figure>, <footer>, <form>, <h1>, <h2>, <h3>, <h4>, <h5>, <h6>, <header>, <hgroup>, <hr>, <main>, <menu>, <nav>, <ol>, <pre>, <section>, <table>, or <ul>. (You learn about most of these tags elsewhere in the book.) You can also skip the </p> tag if your paragraph is the final item in the parent element (that is, the element that contains the paragraph).

**TECHNICAL
STUFF**

## BLOCK-LEVEL ELEMENTS VERSUS INLINE ELEMENTS

One useful way to think about HTML elements is to separate them into two distinct categories:

- **Block-level element:** An element that carves out a rectangular area on the page. That area always starts on a new line and its width extends out to the full width of its containing element. By default, consecutive block-level elements are always stacked one on top of the other.

- **Inline-level element:** An element that takes up only the space between its start and end tags. By default, inline-level elements follow along with the flow of the surrounding text.

These are actually CSS distinctions, so I hold off on a more in-depth look until I talk about page layout starting in Book 5, Chapter 1. For now, though, note that most of the elements I discuss in this chapter — starting with the p element — are block-level elements.

## Dividing your text with headings

In Book 1, Chapter 1, I mention that you can give your web page a title using the aptly named `<title>` tag. However, that title appears only in the browser's tab. What if you want to add a title that appears in the body of the page? That's almost easier done than said because HTML comes with a few tags that enable you to define *headings*, which are bits of text that appear in a separate paragraph and usually stick out from the surrounding text by being bigger, appearing in a bold typeface, and so on.

There are six heading tags in all, ranging from `<h1>`, which uses the largest type size, down to `<h6>`, which uses the smallest size. Each of these start tags has a corresponding end tag, from `</h1>` down to `</h6>`.

Here's some web page code (check out bk02ch01/example03.html) that demonstrates the six heading tags, and Figure 1-3 shows how they look in a web browser:

```
<h1>This is Heading 1</h1>
<h2>This is Heading 2</h2>
<h3>This is Heading 3</h3>
<h4>This is Heading 4</h4>
<h5>This is Heading 5</h5>
<h6>This is Heading 6</h6>
```

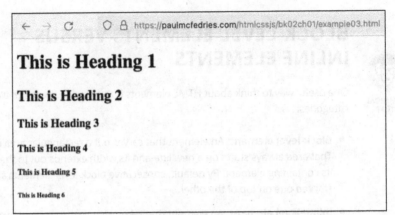

**FIGURE 1-3:**
The six HTML
heading tags.

What's up with all the different headings? The idea is that you use them to create a kind of outline for your web page. How you do this depends on the page, but here's one possibility:

>> Use <h1> for the overall page title.

>> Use <h2> for the page subtitle.

>> Use <h3> for the titles of the main sections of your page.

>> Use <h4> for the titles of the subsections of your page.

**REMEMBER**

Each web page you create should have only one h1 element. Technically, you're allowed to use multiple h1 elements, but it's considered a best practice to have only one.

**WARNING**

Don't skip heading levels. For example, if you use an h1 and then an h2, don't jump next to h4. Skipping levels like this can mess up programs that rely on a consistent use of headings to create things like a table of contents for your page.

For example, in the paragraph-enhanced web page shown earlier in Figure 1-2, the first line ("Getting to Know HTML's Basic Structure Tag") is the title of a main section, whereas the line by itself closer to the bottom ("Creating paragraphs") is the title of a subsection. I can turn these into headings, like so:

```
<h3>Getting to Know HTML's Basic Structure Tag</h3>
<h4>Creating paragraphs</h4>
```

Figure 1-4 shows the results (check out bk02ch01/example04.html).

> **Getting to Know HTML's Basic Structure Tags**
>
> One of the most important concepts you need to understand as you get started with HTML is that whatever text you shoehorn between the <body> and </body> tags has almost no structure. To show you what I mean, I copied the first few headings and paragraphs of this section and pasted them into an HTML file. Figure 1-1 shows what happens when I open the HTML file in a web browser.
>
> As you can see, the resulting web page is anything but pretty and is very hard to read. Why? Because unlike the nicely structured — and therefore eminently readable — text you're eyeballing right now, all that structure got thrown out the window when I pasted the text into the HTML file. Remember, HTML files are really just plain text files, so all the fancy formatting and styles that were in my original Microsoft Word document were discarded.
>
> Fortunately, this does not mean that you can't build well-structured web documents. The secret to getting your web pages to look every bit as nice as the page you're reading is HTML's powerful collection of structure elements. Using these elements, you can create standard structures such as paragraphs and headings, as well as larger page items such as headers, articles, and footers.
>
> **Creating paragraphs**
>
> One of the main themes of this chapter is to explore various ways to avoid presenting your web page visitors with a mass of mostly undifferentiated text, like the example shown earlier in Figure 1-1. Why? Because such text is off-putting to look at and difficult to read.
>
> Almost all of HTML has that theme in mind and, in the broadest interpretation, almost every HTML element is designed to structurally differentiate text in some way.

**FIGURE 1-4:**
The text from
Figure 1-2 with
headings added.

# Adding line breaks

If you look closely at the paragraphs and headings shown in Figure 1-4, one of the first things you may notice is that the browser renders the elements with a significant amount of space between them. That's a good thing, because it's that empty space that makes the page so much more readable than the all-crammed-together text from Figure 1-1.

However, with some forms of text, the "paragraphs" are single lines, such as address blocks, code listings, or poems. In these cases, you *don't* want all that white space between the lines. For example, Figure 1-5 shows what happens when I code the following limerick with <p> tags (refer to bk02ch01/example05.html):

```
<p>There once was woman named Elle,
<p>Who learned tons of HTML.
<p>Then she came to an ode
<p>That she just couldn't code,
<p>Now she lives in a white padded cell.
```

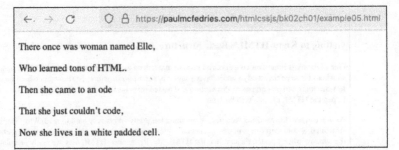

There once was woman named Elle,

Who learned tons of HTML.

Then she came to an ode

That she just couldn't code,

Now she lives in a white padded cell.

**FIGURE 1-5:**
A limerick that has each line as a paragraph.

It just doesn't look right, does it? Fortunately, the HTML powers-that-be thought of just this scenario and created a special element to handle it: br. This *line break* element does just that: it tells the web browser to start the next element on a new line, but without any space between the two lines. You place the <br> tag (it doesn't have an end tag) where you want the line break to occur, which is generally at the end of a line of text, as shown here (check out bk02ch01/example06.html):

```
There once was woman named Elle,<br>
Who learned tons of HTML.<br>
Then she came to an ode<br>
That she just couldn't code,<br>
Now she lives in a white padded cell.
```

Figure 1-6 shows the result. Ah, that's better!

There once was woman named Elle,
Who learned tons of HTML.
Then she came to an ode
That she just couldn't code,
Now she lives in a white padded cell.

**FIGURE 1-6:**
The limerick using line breaks instead of paragraphs.

## Separating stuff with a horizontal rule

HTML's structure tags are designed to help others make sense of your page. (These "others" are usually people, but sometimes they're special programs that process pages, such as for the visually impaired.) So, a typical page may have an <article> tag (refer to "Carving Up the Page," next), which then has one or more <section> tags (also covered in "Carving Up the Page"), which has one or more headings, which has one or more paragraphs.

So far, so sensible. However, one scenario is a bit tricky. Say you're working in a section of the page under a particular heading, and you come to a new paragraph where the text changes as follows:

» The change is big enough that it merits some kind of visual indicator (and not, say, just a new paragraph).

» The change isn't big enough to merit a new heading.

For example, the change may be a new theme based on the subject of the current section; a scene change in your narrative; or a transition leading up to a new topic.

For these kinds of *thematic breaks*, HTML offers the hr element. The name is short for *horizontal rule*, and the element does just what it says: It draws a horizontal rule (that's a line to the likes of you and me) clear across the page. The result? A nice, clean visual indication that the next paragraph is in some way a break from the previous one. Figure 1-7 offers an example where I've placed an <hr> tag between this paragraph and the next one (check out bk02ch01/example07.html).

Now it's time to take these page-structure ramblings to the next level with an in-depth look at HTML's so-called *semantic* page elements. After you've mastered the tags I cover in the next section, you'll know everything you need to know to build pages with good digital bones.

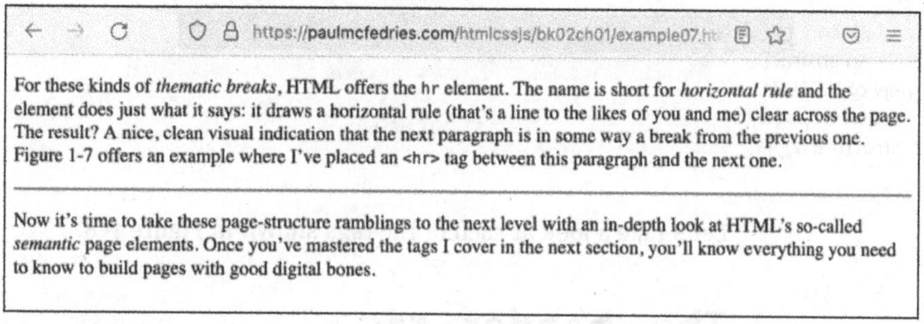

**FIGURE 1-7:**
With an <hr> tag between two paragraphs, HTML draws a horizontal rule to signal a thematic break in your text.

For these kinds of *thematic breaks*, HTML offers the hr element. The name is short for *horizontal rule* and the element does just what it says: it draws a horizontal rule (that's a line to the likes of you and me) clear across the page. The result? A nice, clean visual indication that the next paragraph is in some way a break from the previous one. Figure 1-7 offers an example where I've placed an <hr> tag between this paragraph and the next one.

Now it's time to take these page-structure ramblings to the next level with an in-depth look at HTML's so-called *semantic* page elements. Once you've mastered the tags I cover in the next section, you'll know everything you need to know to build pages with good digital bones.

# Carving Up the Page

Why is it important for your web pages to be well-structured? Well, think about the high-level structure of this book, which includes the front and back covers, the table of contents, an index, and six mini-books, each of which contains several chapters, which, in turn consist of many sections and paragraphs within those sections. It's all nice and neat and well-organized, if I do say so myself.

Now imagine, instead, that this entire book was just page after page of undifferentiated text: no minibooks, no chapters, no sections, no paragraphs, plus no table of contents or index. I've just described a book-reader's worst nightmare, and I'm sure I couldn't even pay you to read such a thing.

Your web pages will suffer from the same fate unless you add some structure to the body section. I talk about structural elements such as headings and paragraphs earlier in this chapter, but now I'm kicking things up a notch and talking about HTML's high-level structure tags.

The first thing to understand about these tags is that they're designed to infuse meaning — that is, semantics — into your page structures. You'll learn what this means as I introduce each tag, but for now, get a load of the abstract page shown in Figure 1-8.

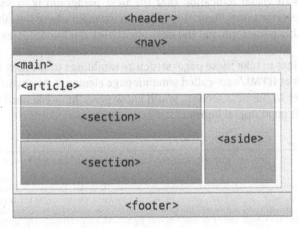

FIGURE 1-8:
An abstract view of HTML5's semantic page structure tags.

Let's take a look at each of the tags shown in Figure 1-8.

## The <header> tag

You use the <header> tag to create a *page header*, which is usually a strip across the top of the page that includes elements such as the site or page title and a logo. (Don't confuse this with the page's head section that appears between the <head> and </head> tags.)

Because the header almost always appears at the top of the page, the <header> tag is usually seen right after the <body> tag, as shown in the following example (and Figure 1-9; check out bk02ch01/example08.html):

```
<body>
    <header>
        <img src="iis-logo.png" alt="Isn't it Semantic?
company logo">
        <h1>Welcome to "Isn't it Semantic?"</h1>
        <hr>
    </header>
    ...
</body>
```

**REMEMBER**

Although the header element usually appears at the top of a web page, that's not the only place you can use it. For example, if you have section elements that begin with introductory content — for example, an icon, a section number, a link, or a date — you can add a header element at the beginning of each section.

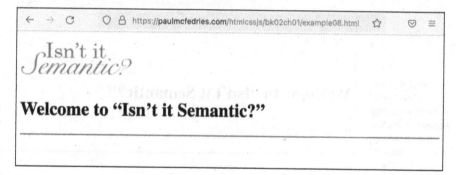

FIGURE 1-9:
A page header
with a logo,
title, and
horizontal rule.

## The <nav> tag

The <nav> tag defines a page section that includes a few elements that help visitors navigate your site. These elements could be links to the main sections of the site, links (check out Book 2, Chapter 2) to recently posted content, or a search feature. The <nav> section typically appears near the top of the page, just after the header, as shown here (and in Figure 1-10; refer to bk02ch01/example09.html):

```
<body>
    <header>
        <img src="iis-logo.png" alt="Isn't it Semantic?
company logo">
        <h1>Welcome to "Isn't it Semantic?"</h1>
        <hr>
    </header>
    <nav>
```

```
        <a href="/">Home</a>
        <a href="semantics.html">Semantics</a>
        <a href="contact.html">Contact</a>
        <a href="about.html">About</a>
    </nav>
    ...
</body>
```

**REMEMBER**

Feel free to use the nav element anywhere you have navigational links. Sitewide navigational links are almost always tucked into a nav element that appears just below the main page header. However, you may have navigational links specific to an article or section, and it's perfectly fine to put a nav element near the top of those elements.

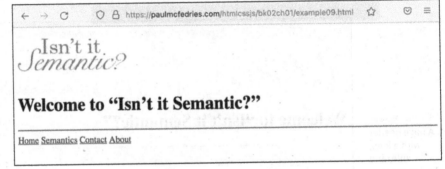

**FIGURE 1-10:**
The <nav>
section usually
appears just after
the <header>
section.

## The <main> tag

The <main> tag sets up a section to hold the content that is, in a sense, the point of the page. For example, if you're creating the page to tell everyone all that you know about Siamese Fighting Fish, your Siamese Fighting Fish text, images, links, and so on would go into the <main> section.

The <main> section usually comes right after the <head> and <nav> sections:

```
<body>
    <header>
        ...
    </header>
    <nav>
        ...
    </nav>
    <main>
```

```
            Main content goes here
        </main>
        ...
</body>
```

## The <article> tag

You use the `<article>` tag to create a page section that contains a complete composition of some sort: a blog post, an essay, a poem, a review, a diatribe, a jeremiad, and so on.

In most cases, you'll have a single `<article>` tag nested inside your page's `<main>` section:

```
<body>
    <header>
        ...
    </header>
    <nav>
        ...
    </nav>
    <main>
        <article>
            Article content goes here
        </article>
    </main>
    ...
</body>
```

However, it isn't a hard and fast rule that your page can have only one `<article>` tag. In fact, it isn't a rule at all. If you want to have two compositions in your page — and thus two `<article>` sections within your `<main>` tag — be my guest.

## The <section> tag

The `<section>` tag indicates a major part of page: usually a heading tag followed by some text. How do you know whether a chunk of the page is "major" or not? The easiest way is to imagine if your page had a table of contents. If you'd want a particular part of your page to be included in that table of contents, it's major enough to merit the `<section>` tag.

Most of the time, your `<section>` tags will appear within an `<article>` tag:

```
<main>
    <article>

<section>
        Section 1 heading goes here
        Section 1 text goes here
      </section>

<section>
        Section 2 heading goes here
        Section 2 text goes here
      </section>
      ...
    </article>
</main>
```

## The <aside> tag

You use the `<aside>` tag to cordon off a bit of the page for content that, although important or relevant for the site as a whole, is at best tangentially related to the page's `<main>` content. The `<aside>` is often a sidebar that includes site news or links to recent content, but it may also include links to other site pages that are related to current page.

The `<aside>` element most often appears within the `<main>` area, but after the `<article>` content.

```
<body>
    <header>
        ...
    </header>
    <nav>
        ...
    </nav>
    <main>
        <article>
            ...
        </article>
        <aside>
```

```
        Aside content goes here
        </aside>
    </main>
    ...
</body>
```

**TIP**

Another common use for the aside element is to display a pull-quote (that is, a quotation pulled from the web page text; head over to Book 5, Chapter 1 for an example).

## The <footer> tag

You use the ⟨footer⟩ tag to create a *page footer*, which is typically a strip across the bottom of the page that includes elements such as a copyright notice, contact info, and social media links.

Because the footer almost always appears at the bottom of the page, the ⟨footer⟩ tag is usually seen right before the ⟨/body⟩ end tag, as shown here:

```
<body>
    <header>
        ...
    </header>
    <nav>
        ...
    </nav>
    <main>
        <article>
            ...
        </article>
        <aside>
            ...
        </aside>
    </main>
    <footer>
        Footer content goes here
    </footer>
</body>
```

# Handling nonsemantic content with <div>

The <header>, <nav>, <main>, <article>, <section>, <aside>, and <footer> elements create meaningful structures within your page, which is why HTML nerds call these *semantic* elements. Even the humble <p> tag introduced earlier in this chapter is semantic in that it represents a single paragraph, usually within a <section> element.

But what's a would-be web weaver to do when they want to add a chunk of content that just doesn't fit any of the standard semantic tags? That happens a lot, and the solution is to slap that content inside a div (for "division") element. The <div> tag is a generic container that doesn't represent anything meaningful, so it's the perfect place for any nonsemantic stuff that needs a home:

```
<div>
    Non-semantic content goes right here
</div>
```

Here's an example (check out bk02ch01/example10.html):

```
<div>
    Requisite social media links:
</div>
<div>
    <a href="https://facebook.com/">Facebook</a>
    <a href="https://twitter.com/">Twitter</a>
    <a href="https://instagram.com/">Instagram</a>
    <a href="http://www.hbo.com/silicon-valley">Hooli</a>
</div>
```

Notice in Figure 1-11 that the browser renders the two <div> elements on separate lines.

FIGURE 1-11:
The browser renders each <div> section on a new line.

# Handling words and characters with <span>

If you want to do something with a small chunk of a larger piece of text, such as a phrase, a word, or even a character or three, you need to turn to a so-called *inline element,* which creates a container that exists within some larger element and flows along with the rest of the content in that larger element. The most common inline element to use is <span>, which creates a container around a bit of text (refer to bk02ch01/example11.html):

```
<p>
Notice how an <span style="font-variant: small-caps">
inline element</span> flows right along with the
rest of the text.
</p>
```

What's happening here is that the <span> tag is applying a style called *small caps* to the text between <span> and </span> (inline element). As shown in Figure 1-12, the <span> text flows along with the rest of the paragraph.

**FIGURE 1-12:**
Using <span>
makes the
container
flow with the
surrounding text.

Notice how an INLINE ELEMENT flows right along with the rest of the text.

# Commenting Your Code

HTML tags, with their angle brackets and attributes, take a bit of getting used to, but after you get the hang of them, reading and scanning your code become easier. Perusing a small web page that contains just a handful of HTML elements is usually straightforward, but that state of affairs won't last long. It seems that even the simplest web projects end up with dozens or, more likely, hundreds of lines of HTML.

Getting a grip on all that HTML is no easy task, particularly if you haven't looked at the code for a while. The questions usually come thick and fast at that point: What is that div element doing? Why did I put that nav element there? What's going on with that <hr> tag?

One way you can help to make your code more readable and understandable —
particularly if someone else is going to be looking at your code or if you want to
give yourself a hand when you return to the code six months from now — is to
add a generous helping of comments to the code. In an HTML file, a *comment* is
a bit of text that the web browser ignores completely when it renders the page.
That may sound utterly useless to you, but rest assured that comments have quite
a few uses:

» To add text that explains why a particular chunk of HTML is written the
way it is.

» To help differentiate parts of the HTML code that use similar tag structures.

» To mark sections of the HTML file that you or someone else needs to start
work on or complete.

To mark some text as a comment, precede the text with ‹!-- and follow the text
with --›. Here's an example:

```
<div>
    Requisite social media links:
</div>
<!--
    Each of the following links needs to be updated with the
    full address to our corresponding social media page.
    Thanks!
-->
<div>
    <a href="https://facebook.com/">Facebook</a>
    <a href="https://twitter.com/">Twitter</a>
    <a href="https://instagram.com/">Instagram</a>
    <a href="http://www.hbo.com/silicon-valley">Hooli</a>
</div>
```

# Chapter 2

# Adding Links, Lists, and Other Text Tidbits

*You see some blue underlined word and you click on it and it takes you somewhere else. That's the simplest definition of hypertext.*

— ROBERT CAILLIAU

In Book 2, Chapter 1, I go through the various HTML tags that enable you to give your web pages the "good bones" of a proper structure. But just as the foundation, framing, and plumbing don't make a house a home, structural elements such as main, article, and p don't make a web page a home page. Turning an empty house into a cozy home means adding personal touches such as furniture, carpeting, artwork, and a lava lamp or two. The web page equivalent is not only filling in your HTML structure with text but also taking advantage of the satisfyingly long list of elements that make your text do interesting things.

In this chapter, you investigate many of HTML's text-related tags. For example, you learn the elements that mark up text that you want emphasized in some way. You find out how to add quotations and how to turn any chunk of text into a link. You also explore the wonderful world of HTML list-making, which includes building both bulleted and numbered lists. Do you need to add characters such as © (copyright) and € (euro) to your pages? You learn how to add those and many other special symbols. Finally, I close the chapter with a quick look at more than a dozen other text-related tags that may come in handy as you furnish your web home away from home.

# Applying the Basic Text Tags

HTML has a few tags that enable you to add structure to text. Many web developers use these tags only for the built-in browser formatting that comes with them, but you really should try to use the tags *semantically*, as the geeks say, which means to use them based on the meaning you want the text to convey.

## Emphasizing text

One of the most common meanings you can attach to text is emphasis. By putting a little extra oomph on a word or phrase, you tell the reader to add stress to that text, which can subtly alter the meaning of your words. For example, consider the following sentence:

```
You'll never fit in there with that ridiculous thing on
    your head!
```

Now consider the same sentence with emphasis added to one word:

```
You'll never fit in there with that ridiculous thing on
    your head!
```

You emphasize text on a web page by surrounding that text with the <em> and </em> tags (refer to bk02ch02/example01.html in this book's example files):

```
You'll <em>never</em> fit in there with that ridiculous thing on
    your head!
```

All web browsers render the emphasized text in italics, as shown in Figure 2-1.

I should also mention that HTML has a closely related tag: <i>. The <i> tag's job is to mark up *alternative text*, which refers to any text that you want treated with a different mood or role than regular text. Common examples include book titles, technical terms, foreign words, or a person's thoughts. All web browsers render text between `<i>` and `</i>` in italics.

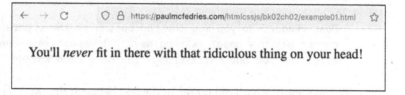
## Marking important text

One common meaning that you'll often want your text to convey is importance. It may be some significant step in a procedure, a vital prerequisite or condition for something, or a crucial passage within a longer text block. In each case, you're dealing with text that you don't want your readers to miss, so it needs to stand out from the regular prose that surrounds it. In HTML, you mark text as important by surrounding it with the `<strong>` and `</strong>` tags, as in this example (check out bk02ch02/example02.html):

```
Dear reader: Do you see the red button in the upper-right
corner of this page? <strong>Never click the red
button!</strong> You have been warned.
```

All web browsers render text marked up with the `<strong>` tag in bold, as shown in Figure 2-2.

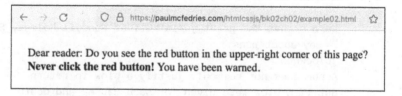

**FIGURE 2-2:**
The browser renders important text using bold.

Just to keep us all on our web development toes, HTML also offers a close cousin of the `<strong>` tag: the `<b>` tag. You use the `<b>` tag to mark up keywords in the text. A *keyword* is a term that you want to draw attention to because it plays a different role than the regular text. It could be a company name or a person's name (think of those famous "bold-faced names" that are the staple of celebrity gossip columns). The browser renders text between the `<b>` and `</b>` tags in a bold font.

## Nesting tags

It's perfectly legal — and often necessary — to combine multiple tag types by nesting one inside the other. For example, check out this code (bk02ch02/example03.html):

```
Dear reader: Do you see the red button in the upper-right
corner of this page? <strong>Never, I repeat <em>never</em>,
click the red button!</strong> You have been warned.
```

Did you notice what I did there? In the text between the `<strong>` and `</strong>` tags, I marked up a word with the `<em>` and `</em>` tags. The result? You got it: bold, italic text, as shown in Figure 2-3.

**FIGURE 2-3:** The browser usually combines nested tags, such as the bold, italic text shown here.

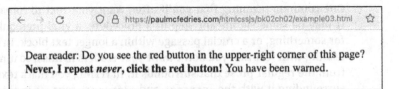

Dear reader: Do you see the red button in the upper-right corner of this page? **Never, I repeat *never*, click the red button!** You have been warned.

## Adding quotations

You may have noticed that each chapter of this book begins with a short, apt quotation because, hey, who doesn't love a good quote, right? The readers of your web pages will be quote-appreciators, too, I'm sure, so why not sprinkle your text with a few words from the wise? In HTML, you designate a passage of text as a quotation by using the `<blockquote>` tag. Here's an example (bk02ch02/example04.html):

```
Here's what the great jurist Oliver Wendell Holmes, Sr. had to
    say about puns:
<blockquote>
A pun does not commonly justify a blow in return.
But if a blow were given for such cause, and death
ensued, the jury would be judges both of the facts
and of the pun, and might, if the latter were of an
aggravated character, return a verdict of justifiable
homicide.
</blockquote>
Clearly, the dude was not a pun fan.
```

The web browser renders the text between `<blockquote>` and `</blockquote>` in its own paragraph that it also indents slightly from the left margin, as shown in Figure 2-4.

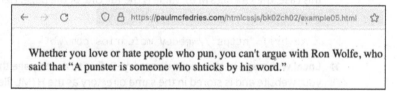

**FIGURE 2-4:**
The web browser renders `<blockquote>` text indented slighted from the left.

Here's what the great jurist Oliver Wendell Holmes, Sr. had to say about puns:

> A pun does not commonly justify a blow in return. But if a blow were given for such cause, and death ensued, the jury would be judges both of the facts and of the pun, and might, if the latter were of an aggravated character, return a verdict of justifiable homicide.

Clearly, the dude was not a pun fan.

I should also mention the closely related q element, which you can use to mark up a so-called *inline quotation*. You use an inline quotation for short quotes that can flow along with the regular text. Here's an example (bk02ch02/example05.html):

```
Whether you love or hate people who pun, you can't argue with
Ron Wolfe, who said that <q>A punster is someone who shticks
by his word.</q>
```

As shown in Figure 2-5, the web browser renders the quote between quotation marks.

**FIGURE 2-5:**
The web browser renders `<q>` text surrounded by quotation marks.

Whether you love or hate people who pun, you can't argue with Ron Wolfe, who said that "A punster is someone who shticks by his word."

**TIP**

The q element supports the `cite` attribute, which is a web address that designates the source of the quotation and is readable by screen readers and other assistive technologies. Here's an example (bk02ch02/example05a.html):

```
The WHATWG says that using the q element is optional and that
<q cite="https://html.spec.whatwg.org/#the-q-element"">using
explicit quotation punctuation without q elements is just as
correct.</q>
```

Adding Links, Lists, and
Other Text Tidbits

# Creating Links

When all is said and done (actually, long before that), your website will consist of anywhere from 2 to 102 pages (or even more, if you've got lots to say). Here's the thing, though: If you manage to cajole someone onto your home page, how do you get that person to your other pages? That really is what the web is all about, isn't it — getting folks from one page to another? And of course, you already know the answer to the question. You get visitors from your home page to your other pages by creating links that take people from here to there. In this section, you learn how to build your own links and how to finally put the "hypertext" into your HTML.

## Linking basics

The HTML tags that do the link thing are `<a>` and `</a>`. Here's how the `<a>` tag works:

```
<a href="address">
```

Here, `href` stands for *hypertext reference*, which is just a fancy-schmancy way of saying "address" or "URL." Your job is to replace *address* with the actual address of the web page you want to use for the link. And yes, you have to enclose the address in quotation marks. The form of `address` value you use depends on where the web page is located with respect to the page that has the link. There are three possibilities:

>> **Remote web page:** Refers to a web page that's not part of your website. In this case, the `<a>` tag's `href` value is the full URL of the page. Here's an example:

```
<a href="https://webdev.mcfedries.com/wb">
```

>> **Local web page in the same directory:** Refers to a web page that's part of your website and is stored in the same directory as the HTML file that has the link. In this case, the `<a>` tag's `href` value is the filename of the page. Here's an example:

```
<a href="rutabagas.html">
```

>> **Local web page in a different directory:** Refers to a web page that's part of your website and is stored in a directory other than the one used by the HTML file that has the link. In this case, the `<a>` tag's `href` value is a backslash (/), followed by the directory name, another backslash, and then the filename of the page. Here's an example:

```
<a href="/wordplay/puns.html">
```

You're not done yet, though, not by a long shot (insert groan of disappointment here). What are you missing? Right: You have to give the reader some descriptive link text to click. That's pretty straightforward because all you do is insert the text between the `<a>` and `</a>` tags, like this:

```
<a href="address">Link text</a>
```

Need an example? You got it (bk02ch02/example06.html):

```
To play with HTML and CSS, check out the
<a href="https://webdevworkshop.io/wb">
Web Dev Workbench</a>!
```

Figure 2-6 shows how it looks in a web browser. Notice how the browser colors and underlines the link text, and when I point my mouse at the link, the address I specified in the `<a>` tag appears in the lower-left corner of the browser window.

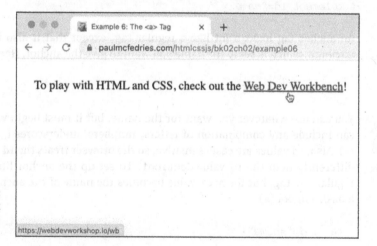

**FIGURE 2-6:**
How the link
appears in the
web browser.

## Anchors aweigh: Internal links

When a surfer clicks a standard link, the page loads and the browser displays the top part of the page. However, it's possible to set up a special kind of link that forces the browser to initially display some other part of the page, such as a section in the middle of the page. For these special links, I use the term *internal links*, because they take the reader directly to some inner part of the page.

When would you ever use an internal link? Most of your HTML pages will probably be short and sweet, and the web surfers who drop by will have no trouble navigating their way around. But if, like me, you suffer from a bad case of terminal verbosity combined with bouts of extreme long-windedness, you'll end up with web pages that are lengthy, to say the least. Rather than force your readers to scroll through your tome-like creations, you can set up links to various sections of the document. You can then assemble these links at the top of the page to form a sort of "hypertable of contents," as an example.

Internal links actually link to a specially marked section — called an *anchor* — that you've inserted somewhere in the same page. To understand how anchors work, think of how you may mark a spot in a book you're reading. You may dog-ear the page, attach a note, or place something between the pages, such as a bookmark or your cat's tail. An anchor performs the same function: It "marks" a particular spot in a web page, and you can then use a regular <a> tag to link to that spot. Here's the general format for an anchor tag:

```
<element id="name">
```

An anchor tag looks a lot like a regular tag, except that it also includes the id attribute, which is set to the name you want to give the anchor. Here's an example:

```
<section id="section1">
```

**REMEMBER**

You can use whatever you want for the name, but it must begin with a letter and can include any combination of letters, numbers, underscores (_), and hyphens (-). Also, id values are case-sensitive, so the browser treats the id value section1 differently than the id value Section1. To set up the anchor link, you create a regular <a> tag, but the href value becomes the name of the anchor, preceded by a hash symbol (#):

```
<a href="#name">
```

Here's an example that links to the anchor I showed earlier:

```
<a href="#section1">
```

Although you'll mostly use anchors to link to sections of the same web page, there's no law against using them to link to specific sections of other pages. What you do is add the appropriate anchor to the other page and then link to it by adding the anchor's name (preceded, as usual, by #) to the end of the page's filename. Here's an example:

```
<a href="chapter57.html#section1">
```

# Building Bulleted and Numbered Lists

For some reason, people love lists: Best (and Worst) Dressed lists, Top Ten lists, My All-Time Favorite *X* lists, where *X* is whatever you want it to be: movies, songs, books, *I Love Lucy* episodes — you name it. People like lists, for whatever reasons. Okay, so let's make some lists. Easy, right? Well, sure, any website jockey can just plop a Best Tootsie Roll Flavors Ever list on a page by typing each item, one after the other. Perhaps our list maker even gets a bit clever and inserts the ‹br› tag between each item, which displays them on separate lines. Ooooh.

Yes, you can make a list that way, and it works well enough, I suppose, but there's a better way. HTML has a few tags that are specially designed to give you much more control over your list-building chores. For example, you can create a bulleted list that actually has those little bullets out front of each item. Nice! Want a Top Ten list, instead? HTML has your back by offering special tags for numbered lists, too.

## Making your point with bulleted lists

A no-frills, ‹br›-separated list isn't very useful or readable because it doesn't come with any type of eye candy that helps differentiate one item from the next. An official, HTML-approved bulleted list solves that problem by leading off each item with a bullet — a cute little black dot. Bulleted lists use two types of tags:

» The entire list is surrounded by the ‹ul› and ‹/ul› tags. Why "ul"? Well, what the rest of the world calls a bulleted list, the HTML poohbahs call an *unordered list*.

» Each item in the list is preceded by the ‹li› (list item) tag and is closed with the ‹/li› end tag. (Technically, the ‹/li› end tag is optional as long as the next item is either another ‹li› tag or the ‹/ul› end tag.)

The general setup looks like this:

```
<ul>
    <li>Bullet text goes here</li>
    <li>And here</li>
    <li>And here</li>
    <li>You get the idea...</li>
</ul>
```

Notice that I've indented the list items by four spaces, which makes it easier to realize that they're part of a `<ul></ul>` container. Here's an example to chew on (bk02ch02/example07.html):

```html
<h3>My All-Time Favorite Oxymorons</h3>
<ul>
    <li>Pretty ugly</li>
    <li>Military intelligence</li>
    <li>Jumbo shrimp</li>
    <li>Original copy</li>
    <li>Random order</li>
    <li>Act naturally</li>
    <li>Tight slacks</li>
    <li>Freezer burn</li>
    <li>Sight unseen</li>
    <li>Microsoft Works</li>
</ul>
```

Figure 2-7 shows how the web browser renders this code, cute little bullets and all.

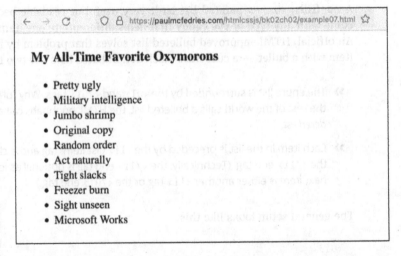

**FIGURE 2-7:**
A typical
bulleted list.

**TIP**

If your unordered list of items consists of commands that a page visitor can run, then a semantic alternative to `ul` is the `menu` element, which represents an unordered list of commands. You build your `menu` list in exactly the same way as a `ul` list. That is, your commands are each surrounded by `<li>` and `</li>` tags, and all of those are surrounded by `<menu>` and `</menu>`:

```
<menu>
    <li>Settings</li>
    <li>Account</li>
    <li>Help</li>
</menu>
```

## Numbered lists: Easy as one, two, three

If you want to include a numbered list of items — it could be a Top Ten list, bowling league standings, steps to follow, or any kind of ranking — don't bother inserting the numbers yourself. Instead, you can use an HTML *numbered list* to make the web browser generate the numbers for you. As do bulleted lists, numbered lists use two types of tags:

>> The entire list is surrounded by the <ol> and </ol> tags. The "ol" here is short for *ordered list,* because those HTML nerds just have to be different, don't they?

>> Each item in the list is surrounded by <li> and </li>.

Here's the general structure to use:

```
<ol>
    <li>First item</li>
    <li>Second item</li>
    <li>Third item</li>
    <li>You got this...</li>
</ol>
```

I've indented the list items by four spaces to make it easier to notice that they're inside an <ol></ol> container. Here's an example (bk02ch02/example08.html):

```
<h3>My Ten Favorite U.S. College Nicknames</h3>
<ol>
    <li>U.C. Santa Cruz Banana Slugs</li>
    <li>Delta State Fighting Okra</li>
    <li>Kent State Golden Flashes</li>
    <li>Evergreen State College Geoducks</li>
    <li>New Mexico Tech Pygmies</li>
    <li>South Carolina Fighting Gamecocks</li>
    <li>Southern Illinois Salukis</li>
    <li>Whittier Poets</li>
    <li>Western Illinois Leathernecks</li>
    <li>Delaware Fightin' Blue Hens</li>
</ol>
```

Notice that I didn't include any numbers before each list item. However, when I display this document in a browser (check out Figure 2-8), the numbers are automatically inserted. Pretty slick, huh?

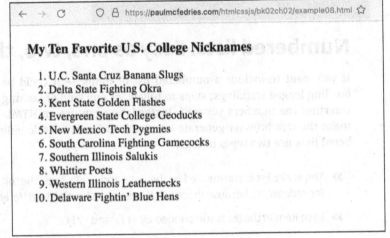

**FIGURE 2-8:**
When the web browser renders the ordered list, it's kind enough to add the numbers for you automatically.

**My Ten Favorite U.S. College Nicknames**

1. U.C. Santa Cruz Banana Slugs
2. Delta State Fighting Okra
3. Kent State Golden Flashes
4. Evergreen State College Geoducks
5. New Mexico Tech Pygmies
6. South Carolina Fighting Gamecocks
7. Southern Illinois Salukis
8. Whittier Poets
9. Western Illinois Leathernecks
10. Delaware Fightin' Blue Hens

# Inserting Special Characters

In Book 1, Chapter 1, I talk briefly about a special `<meta>` tag that goes into the head section:

```
<meta charset="utf-8">
```

It may not look like it, but that tag adds a bit of magic to your web page. The voodoo is that now you can add special characters such as © and ™ directly to your web page text, and the web browser will display them without complaint. The trick is how you add these characters directly to your text, and that depends on your operating system. First, if you're using Windows, you have two choices:

» Hold down the Alt key and then press the character's four-digit ASCII code using your keyboard's numeric keypad. For example, you type an em dash (—) by pressing Alt+0151.

» Paste the character from the Character Map application that comes with Windows.

If you're a Mac user, you also have two choices:

>> Type the character's special keyboard shortcut. For example, you type an em dash (—) by pressing Option+Shift+- (hyphen).

>> Paste the character from the Symbols Viewer that comes with macOS.

Having said all that, I should point out that there's another way to add special characters to a page. The web wizards who created HTML came up with special codes called *character entities* (which is surely a name only a true geek would love) that represent these oddball symbols. These codes come in two flavors: a *character reference* and an *entity name*. Character references are basically just numbers, and the entity names are friendlier symbols that describe the character you're trying to display. For example, you can display the registered trademark symbol (™) by using either the &#174; character reference or the &reg; entity name, as shown here:

```
Print-On-Non-Demand&#174;
```

or

```
Print-On-Non-Demand&reg;
```

Note that both character references and entity names begin with an ampersand (&) and end with a semicolon (;). Don't forget either character when using special symbols in your own pages.

**REMEMBER**

One very common use of character references is for displaying HTML tags without the web browser rendering them as tags. To do this, replace the tag's less-than sign (<) with &lt; (or &#060;) and the tag's greater-than sign (>) with &gt; (or &#062;).

# A Few More HTML Text Tags to Know

There's a pretty good chance that you may go the rest of your HTML career using only the HTML text elements that I've talked about so far in this chapter: em, i, strong, b, blockquote, q, a, ul, ol, and li. However, HTML offers quite a few more text-related tags. Sure, many of these tags are obscure and using most of them feels a bit like semantic overkill, but you never know when a particular element may be just the thing for a web project. With that spirit in mind, the next few sections take you through an extensive (but by no means complete) collection of text tags that are worth adding to your HTML toolbox.

In the sections that follow, I mention the default styling (if any) that web browsers apply to the text within each element. However, you're always free to override an element's default styling using CSS, so don't shun a particular tag just because you're not a fan of how the browser renders it by default.

## <abbr>: The abbreviation text tag

You use the abbr element to mark up an abbreviation or acronym. There are two ways to use this element:

```
<abbr>abbreviation</abbr> (expansion)
<abbr title="expansion">abbreviation</abbr>
```

In both cases, *abbreviation* is the abbreviation you're marking up and *expansion* is the full text expansion of the abbreviation. The first method puts the expansion right in the text for the user to read; the second method hides the expansion until the reader hovers the mouse pointer over the abbreviation, at which point the expansion appears in a tooltip, as shown in the following example and Figure 2-9 (bk02ch02/example09.html):

```
What happens to upwardly-mobile couples who have children
and then one spouse stops working to raise the kids?
Why, their life becomes a
<abbr title="single income, two children, oppressive
    mortgage">SITCOM</abbr>, of course.
```

**FIGURE 2-9:**
When you include the title attribute, hovering the mouse over the abbreviation displays the expansion in a tooltip.

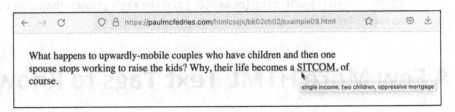

## <address>: The address text tag

Your web page — or some part of your web page, such as an article element — may have contact information, which could include an email address, a telephone number, and a postal address. You can mark up that contact information semantically by surrounding it with <address> and </address> tags, like so (bk02ch02/example10.html):

```
<p>
    Having a problem? Please "contact us" here:
</p>
<address>
    The Complaints Department<br>
    0 Black Hole Blvd, Suite -23<br>
    Nowheresville, BC N0N 0N0
</address>
```

As shown in Figure 2-10, browsers render `address` text in italics.

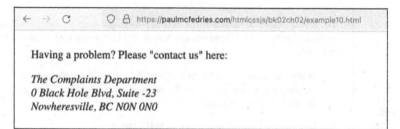

Having a problem? Please "contact us" here:

*The Complaints Department*
*0 Black Hole Blvd, Suite -23*
*Nowheresville, BC N0N 0N0*

FIGURE 2-10:
Contact info
marked up with
the <address>
tag is rendered
in italics.

## <cite>: The citation text tag

If your web page cites a creative work, you can semantically mark up a reference to that work using the `cite` element. You create this reference by surrounding the name of the work — or a link to the work where the link text is the work's name — with the `<cite>` and `</cite>` tags.

**REMEMBER**

For the purposes of the `cite` element, the phrase "creative work" takes a broad meaning that includes the following list supplied with this element's specification: a book, a paper, an essay, a poem, a score, a song, a script, a film, a TV show, a game, a sculpture, a painting, a theatre production, a play, an opera, a musical, an exhibition, a legal case report, a computer program. Here's an example (bk02ch02/example11.html):

```
<p>
    The HTML specs published by the WHAT Working Group
    are notoriously dry, fussy, and judge-sober.  However,
    every now and then some wag sneaks in a bit of humor:
</p>
<blockquote>
    A person's name is not the title of a work — even if
    people call that person a piece of work — and the element
    must therefore not be used to mark up people's names.
```

```
</blockquote>
<p>
    Source: <cite><a href="https://html.spec.whatwg.org/#the-
    cite-element">The cite element</a></cite>, published by
    WHATWG.
</p>
```

As shown in Figure 2-11, browsers render `cite` text in italics.

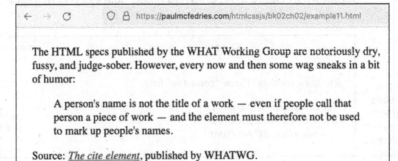

FIGURE 2-11:
Browsers use
italics to render
text marked
up with the
<cite> tag.

The HTML specs published by the WHAT Working Group are notoriously dry, fussy, and judge-sober. However, every now and then some wag sneaks in a bit of humor:

> A person's name is not the title of a work — even if people call that person a piece of work — and the element must therefore not be used to mark up people's names.

Source: *The cite element*, published by WHATWG.

**WARNING**

As the WHATWG quotation shown in Figure 2-11 makes clear, the specifications for the `cite` element are adamant that the element should include only the title of the creative work, not the name of the person who created it. By all means, give a shout-out to the creator, but just be sure to do it outside of the `cite` element (as I do in the preceding example).

# <code>: The code text tag

If your web page includes a word, phrase, or line of computer code — such as an HTML element name, a CSS declaration (property/value pair), or a JavaScript statement — you can wrap that code, appropriately enough, in the `code` element. Here's an example (bk02ch02/example12.html):

```
<p>
    Way back in 1994, someone at Netscape (one of the
    original web browsers) had the not-so-bright idea that
    text that blinked on and off would be a good thing. Thus
    the <code>&lt;blink&gt;</code> tag — the most reviled tag
    of all time — was born.
</p>
```

As Figure 2-12 shows, browsers render code text in a monospace font.

**FIGURE 2-12:**
Browsers display
code text in a
monospace font.

← → C     ○ 🔒 https://paulmcfedries.com/htmlcssjs/bk02ch02/example12.html

Way back in 1994, someone at Netscape (one of the original web browsers) had the not-so-bright idea that text that blinked on and off would be a good thing. Thus the `<blink>` tag — the most reviled tag of all time — was born.

**REMEMBER**

The `<code>` tag is an inline element, which means code text flows along with the surrounding text. If you want to include multiple lines of computer code on your page, you need to press the `<pre>` tag into service. Refer to "`<pre>`: The preformatted text tag," later in this chapter.

**TIP**

If your code includes a variable name, you can mark up that name semantically using the var (for "variable") element:

```
Given positive values of the variables <var>x</var> and
    <var>y</var>, what is the price of tea in China?
```

Web browsers render var text in italics.

**TIP**

A slightly different scenario is when you want to include in your web page some kind of sample output from a computer program (such as an error message). The HTML element-of-choice for this is the samp element (where "samp" is short for "sample output"):

```
Plugging in that URL produced the dreaded <samp>404 Not
    Found</samp> error.
```

# `<dfn>`: The definition text tag

The *defining instance* of a term is the usage of the term that's immediately followed by the term's definition. Did you notice what just happened? My use of "defining instance" was the defining instance of the term *defining instance*! The point of these linguistic shenanigans is that whenever you use a defining instance in a web page, you can mark it up semantically using the dfn element (bk02ch02/example13.html):

```
The <dfn>defining instance</dfn> of a term is the usage of
the term that's immediately followed by the term's
definition.
```

As Figure 2-13 shows, the browser renders dfn text in italics.

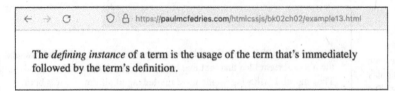

FIGURE 2-13:
Browsers render
dfn text in italics.

The *defining instance* of a term is the usage of the term that's immediately followed by the term's definition.

# <dl>: The description list text tag

Earlier in this chapter (refer to "Building Bulleted and Numbered Lists") I talk about two kinds of lists you can add to your web pages: bulleted lists and numbered lists. However, HTML also supports a third list type called a *description list*, where each entry is a name-value group. Originally, people used description lists for glossaries or dictionaries where each name-value group consisted of a term and the definition of the term. As you'll learn, though, description lists are useful for more than just definitions. To mark the name-value group for each entry in these lists, you need two different tags. The name is enclosed in a dt element, whereas the value is enclosed in a dd element, like this:

```
<dt>name</dt>
<dd>value</dd>
```

Repeat for each name-value group and surround the whole list with the <dl> and </dl> tags to complete your description list. Here's how the whole thing looks:

```
<dl>
    <dt>A name</dt>
    <dd>Its value</dd>
    <dt>Another name</dt>
    <dd>Another value</dd>
    <dt>Yet another name</dt>
    <dd>Yet another value</dd>
    <dt>Etc.</dt>
    <dd>Abbreviation of a Latin phrase that means "and so
 forth."</dd>
</dl>
```

Here's a more realistic example (bk02ch02/example14.html):

```
<h3>Some Insults Worth Hurling</h3>
<dl>
    <dt>disingenuflect</dt>
    <dd>To act in a servile or worshipful manner insincerely
        or hypocritically.</dd>
    <dt>dudefussing</dt>
    <dd>Making numerous small, needless adjustments as a
        pretense of effort, particularly by a man.</dd>
    <dt>escalefter</dt>
    <dd>A person who stands on the left side of a busy
        escalator, thus blocking those who would walk up or
        down.</dd>
    <dt>nerdsplaining</dt>
    <dd>Explaining in an overly intellectual, obsessively
        detailed way, particularly when the topic is obscure
        or highly technical.</dd>
    <dt>omnishambles</dt>
    <dd>A situation or person that is a mess in every
        possible way.</dd>
</dl>
```

Figure 2-14 shows how things look in the browser.

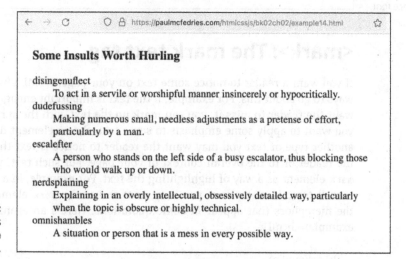

**FIGURE 2-14:**
A few definitions
arrayed in a
description list.

## <kbd>: The keyboard input text tag

If your web page includes instructions or steps that contain shortcut keys or similar keyboard input, you can mark up those keys semantically using the kbd element. Here's an example:

```
To abort the countdown and prevent detonation, press
    <kbd>Esc</kbd>.
```

For shortcut key combinations, you can mark up each key with the kbd element and then surround the combination itself with another set of <kbd>/</kbd> tags, like so (bk02ch02/example15.html):

```
Alternatively, you can restart the countdown by pressing
    <kbd><kbd>Ctrl</kbd>+<kbd>R</kbd></kbd>.
```

As shown in Figure 2-15, the browser renders your marked-up keys in a mono-space font.

**FIGURE 2-15:**
The web browser
kindly renders
kbd text in a
monospace font.

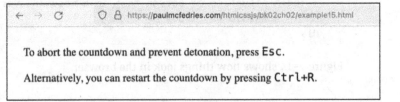

To abort the countdown and prevent detonation, press Esc.

Alternatively, you can restart the countdown by pressing Ctrl+R.

## <mark>: The mark text tag

If you want a reader to notice some text on your page, HTML gives you multiple ways to go about this. For example, if the text is important enough that you don't want the reader to miss it, you can mark up the text with the strong element. If you want to apply some emphasis to some text, the em element does the job. Yet another type of text you may want the reader to notice is text that's relevant to the reader or to the overall context of your page. For such text, you can use the mark element as a way of highlighting the text. For example, in a page where the overall topic is metaphors, you may want to use the mark element to mark up the metaphors that appear in some quotations. Here's an example (bk02ch02/example16.html):

```
<blockquote>
    If words, as Samuel Johnson said, are the <mark>'dress'
    of rational thought</mark>, a good vocabulary is
```

```
    <mark>the Wonderbra of intellect</mark>. —Hilary Bower
</blockquote>
<blockquote>
    Language is not just the spoken and written word, it is
    also <mark>the currency of conscious thought</mark>. What
    one cannot put into words is hard to even think about.
    —Nicholas Wade
</blockquote>
```

The browser displays mark element text with a yellow highlight.

# \<pre>: The preformatted text tag

Back in the section "<code>: The code text tag," I talk about using the code element to mark up a word or phrase of computer code. However, lots of code snippets are multi-line affairs, so to mark up these longer code blocks, you need to turn to the pre element. Why pre? Because it offers two useful characteristics that make it perfect for rendering code just so:

>> The web browser renders pre text using a monospace font.

>> The web browser includes multiple whitespace characters such a spaces in its rendering, rather than ignoring them, which is the default for most other tags.

The result? Your code is rendered exactly as it's written in your HTML file, with all your multi-space indentations that make the code easier to read. For example, here's some CSS code from Book 1, Chapter 1, marked up with the pre element (bk02ch02/example17.html):

```
<pre>
&lt;style&gt;
    h1 {
        border-width: 2px;
        border-style: solid;
        border-color: black;
    }
    h2 {
        border-width: 2px;
        border-style: dotted;
        border-color: black;
    }
&lt;/style&gt;
</pre>
```

As Figure 2-16 shows, the `pre` element faithfully renders all the spaces in the code.

```
https://paulmcfedries.com/htmlcssjs/bk02ch02/example17.html

<style>
    h1 {
        border-width: 2px;
        border-style: solid;
        border-color: black;
    }
    h2 {
        border-width: 2px;
        border-style: dotted;
        border-color: black;
    }
</style>
```

**FIGURE 2-16:**
The pre element displays text exactly as its written, multiple spaces and all.

**REMEMBER**

To add some semantic goodness to your computer code listings, surround the text with the `code` element, like so:

```
<pre><code>
Your code goes here
</code></pre>
```

# \<s>: The strikethrough text tag

After you publish your web page, some of the information on the page may become inaccurate or no longer relevant. Most of the time, you'll just fix the inaccuracy, remove the text, or update the text to make it relevant. However, in some situations, you may want to keep the old text while adding the new or updated text. Why would you do this? Usually, it's because you want the reader to be able to compare or contrast the old text with the new. For example, if a product now has a lower price, that reduced price packs a more powerful punch if the user can also read the older, higher price. In HTML, you represent text that's inaccurate or no longer relevant using the `s` element, as shown in the following example (bk02ch02/example18.html):

```
<h3>Who Needs Tickets?</h3>
<hr>
<h4>The Brazil Nutcracker</h4>
<p>
    <s>All performances: $950 per ticket</s>
```

```
</p>
<p>
    SOLD OUT!
</p>
<hr>
<h4>Sleeping Pill Beauty</h4>
<p>
    <s>All performances: $15,000 per ticket</s>
</p>
<p>
    Now $9.99!
</p>
<hr>
```

The result appears in Figure 2-17, where the web browser renders s element text using the strikethrough effect.

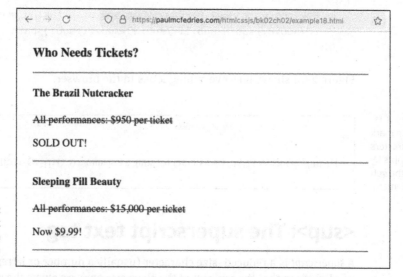

**Who Needs Tickets?**

---

**The Brazil Nutcracker**

~~All performances: $950 per ticket~~

SOLD OUT!

---

**Sleeping Pill Beauty**

~~All performances: $15,000 per ticket~~

Now $9.99!

---

FIGURE 2-17:
The s element
renders text with
a strikethrough
effect.

**REMEMBER**

You may be tempted to use the s element to indicate (perhaps ironically) text that has been deleted, like so:

```
What <s>idiot</s>person would pay that much money to attend a
    ballet?
```

However, the preferred method for this kind of markup is to use the del element, which is specifically designed to indicate deleted text (and also renders the text using the strikethrough effect):

```
What <del>idiot</del>person would pay that much money to attend
    a ballet?
```

## <sub>: The subscript text tag

If your web page includes mathematical formulas or chemical symbols (hey, it could happen), one or more of the terms may require a subscript. A *subscript* is a reduced-size character (usually a number or letter) that's shifted down slightly so that part of the character appears below the baseline of the text. For example: $H_2O$ (the chemical formula for water). You mark up a character or three as a subscript by using the sub element. Here's an example (bk02ch02/example19.html):

```
<p>
    Feeling up today? Perhaps your brain is taking a dopamine
    (C<sub>8</sub>H<sub>11</sub>NO<sub>2</sub>) bath.
</p>
```

Figure 2-18 shows how everything looks in the browser.

**FIGURE 2-18:** You can mark up characters as subscripts by using the sub element.

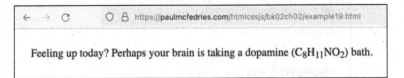

Feeling up today? Perhaps your brain is taking a dopamine ($C_8H_{11}NO_2$) bath.

## <sup>: The superscript text tag

A *superscript* is a reduced-size character (usually a number or letter) that's shifted up slightly so that the top part of the character appears above the regular text. For example: $e = mc^2$ (Einstein's famous formula showing the equivalence of mass and energy). Now, sure, your web pages may contain formulas such as this example, but a more common use of a subscript is to mark a footnote. Whether it's to designate a formula power or a footnote marker, you can tell the browser to display one or more characters as a superscript by using the sup element. Here's a footnote example (bk02ch02/example20.html):

```
<p>
    Everyone, from the factory worker to the faculty member,
    appreciates some aspect of language; everyone is, in one
    way or another, "bethump'd with words"<sup>1</sup>.
</p>
    <hr>
<p>
    <sup>1</sup>This phrase comes from Shakespeare:
    <blockquote>Zounds! I was never so bethump'd with words<br>
    Since I first call'd my brother's father dad.<br>
    —<i>King John</i>, 1596, Act ii, Scene 2
    </blockquote>
</p>
```

Note that I used a superscript both as a footnote marker in the text and to start the footnote itself. Figure 2-19 shows what the web browser does with this code.

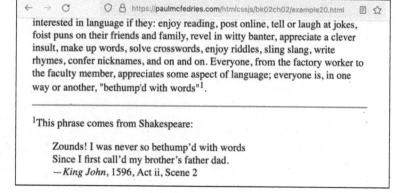

**FIGURE 2-19:** You can use the sup element to mark up your page with footnotes.

# Chapter **3**

# Working with Images, Video, and other Media

*Telling stories with visuals is an ancient art. We've been drawing pictures on cave walls for centuries. It's like what they say about the perfect picture book. The art and the text stand alone, but together, they create something even better.*

— DEBORAH WILES

I f you ever come across a very old web page — I'm talking about pages from the late 1990s and very early 2000s — chances are that page is a sea of text, with perhaps the odd island of a heading to rest your tired, swimming eyes. The lesson from those old pages is clear: A page that consists of nothing but text is not only an eyesore but also the cause of sore eyes.

To be clear, I'm not saying that having a boatload of text on a page is necessarily a bad thing. The real problem with those old pages is that they combine tons of text with poor typography, including ugly fonts, too-small text, busy backgrounds, and poor spacing. You learn all the principles of top-notch typography in Book 3, Chapter 7, so you'll be able to make your pages look good even if they sport a lot of text.

However, we live in a world that adores the visual, and the people who visit your pages will be looking for at least a bit of eye candy. In this chapter, you explore the visual side of HTML. You learn how to add photos, illustrations, and other images to your pages, and you delve into the art of embedding video clips and audio snippets into your pages. It's a veritable feast for the eyes and ears.

# Inserting Images

Whether you want to tell stories, give instructions, pontificate, or just plain rant about something, you can do all that and more by adding text to your page. But to make it more interesting for your readers, add a bit of imagery every now and then. To that end, there's an HTML tag you can use to add one or more images to your page.

## First, a mercifully brief look at image formats

Before getting too far into this picture business, I should tell you that, unfortunately, you can't use just any old image on a web page. Browsers are limited in the types of images they can display. There are, in fact, four main types of image formats you can use:

>> **GIF:** The original web graphics format (it's short for Graphics Interchange Format). GIF (pronounced "giff" or "jiff") is limited to 256 colors, so it's rarely used for static images. Instead, most folks nowadays use animated GIFs, which combine multiple image files into a single animation.

**TIP**

Want to create your own animated GIFs? Of course you do! The easiest way is to use one of the online sites that offer this service. Two popular sites are GIPHY (https://giphy.com/create/gifmaker) and Canva (www.canva.com/create/gif-maker/).

>> **JPEG:** Gets its name from the Joint Photographic Experts Group that invented it. JPEG (it's pronounced "jay-peg") supports complex images that have many millions of colors. The main advantage of JPEG files is that, given the same image, they're smaller than GIFs, so they take less time to download. Careful, though: JPEG uses *lossy* compression, which means that it makes the image smaller by discarding redundant pixels. The greater the compression, the more pixels that are discarded, and the less sharp the image will appear. That said, if you have a photo or similarly complex image, JPEG is almost always the best choice because it gives the smallest file size.

>> **PNG:** The Portable Network Graphics format supports millions of colors. PNG (pronounced "p-n-g" or "ping") is a compressed format, but unlike JPEGs, PNGs use *lossless* compression. This means that images retain sharpness, but the file sizes can get quite big. If you have an illustration or icon that uses solid colors, or a photo that contains large areas of near-solid color, PNG is a good choice. PNG also supports transparency.

>> **SVG:** With the Scalable Vector Graphics format, images are generated using *vectors* (mathematical formulas based on points and shapes on a grid) rather than pixels. Surprisingly, these vectors reside as a set of instructions in a special-text-based format, which means you can edit the image using a text editor! SVG is a good choice for illustrations, particularly if you have software that supports the SVG format, such as Inkscape or Adobe Illustrator.

## Inserting an image

Okay, enough of all that. It's time to start squeezing some images onto your web page. As mentioned earlier, there's an HTML code that tells a browser to display an image. It's the `<img>` tag, and here's how it works:

```
<img src="filename" alt="description" title="title">
```

Here, src is short for source; `filename` is the name (and often also the location) of the graphics file you want to display; `description` is a short description of the image (which is read by screen readers and seen by users who aren't displaying images or if the image fails to load); and `title` is a tooltip that appears when the user hovers the mouse pointer over the image. Note that there's no end tag to add here.

**WARNING**

The alt attribute is required, and your web page isn't valid HTML if you have images that don't have an alt value. That's because *alt text* (as the alt value is often called) is a crucial aspect of your page's accessibility; for much more about alt text and accessibility, refer to Book 2, Chapter 6. That said, if you use images that are purely ornamental, you don't need to describe them. In each such case, include the alt attribute in the `<img>` tag, but set its value to the null string (" " ), like so:

```
<img src="filename" alt="" title="title">
```

Here's an example to eyeball. Suppose you have an image named logo.png. To add it to your page, you use the following line:

```
<img src="logo.png" alt="The Logophilia Ltd. company logo"
    title="Logophilia Ltd.">
```

In effect, this tag says to the browser, "Excuse me? Would you be so kind as to go out and grab the image file named `logo.png` and insert it in the page right here where the `<img>` tag is?" Dutifully, the browser grabs the image from your web server and displays it in the page.

For this simple example to work, bear in mind that your HTML file and your graphics file need to be sitting in the same directory. Many webmasters create a subdirectory just for images, which keeps things neat and tidy. If you plan on doing this, be sure you study my instructions for using directories and subdirectories in Book 1, Chapter 2.

Here's an example of including an image in a web page, and Figure 3-1 shows how things appear in a web browser (refer to bk02ch03/example01.html in this book's example files):

```
To see a World in a Grain of Sand<br>
And a Heaven in a Wild Flower<br>
—William Blake<br>
<img src="images/flower-and-ant.jpg" alt="Macro photo showing an
    ant exploring a flower" title="Flower and Ant">
```

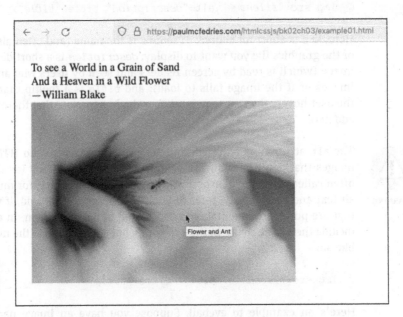

**FIGURE 3-1:**
A web page with an image thrown in.

# Inserting a figure with a caption

Throughout this book, when I want you to check out a nearby screen capture, I say something like "Figure 3-1 shows how things appear in a web browser." This is your cue to find the image that has "Figure 3-1" in the caption.

In general, a *figure* is an image that's referenced in some way in the main text of the document. You may not use figures all that often in your web pages, but for those times that you do, you'll be pleased to know that HTML has the figure element to add some semantic sheen to the img element. Need to add a caption to the image? HTML has your back with the figcaption element.

Here's the general syntax for designating that an image is a figure with a caption:

```
<figure>
    <img src="filename" alt="description" title="title">
    <figcaption>
        Insert your caption here
    </figcaption>
</figure>
```

Here's a full-fledged example, with the result shown (figure reference coming!) in Figure 3-2 (check out bk02ch03/example02.html):

```
<p>
    Checking out the source code of a web page isn't
    normally a "fun" experience. Most often, your goal is to get
    the name of a file or to figure out how the site
    performed some HTML or CSS magic. But every once in a
    very long while you can find a surprise, even a
    delightful one, waiting in the source code. As shown in
    Figure 1, I came across one such surprise the other day
    while viewing source on a page from <i>The Guardian</i>.
</p>
<figure>
    <img src="images/guardian-we-are-hiring.jpg"
    alt="Screenshot of the source code of The Guardian
    newspaper web page showing a developer want ad written in
    ASCII art" title="Source Code Want Ad">
    <figcaption>
        <b>Figure 1</b>—A want ad buried in the HTML source
        of <i>The Guardian</i> newspaper web page.
    </figcaption>
</figure>
```

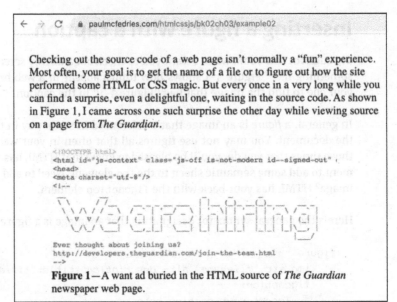

**FIGURE 3-2:**
A web page with
a figure and a
caption.

## Turning an image into a link

In Book 2, Chapter 2, I talk about using the a element to turn a word or phrase into an honest-to-goodness link. But your links don't always have to be text. If you have a logo, icon, or other picture that you want your readers to click to go to a different page, you can set up that image as a link.

Here's the general technique to use:

```
<a href="address"><img src="filename" alt="description"></a>
```

You set up the ‹a› tag in the usual way, but this time between ‹a› and ‹/a› you use an ‹img› tag instead of some text. Just like that, your image becomes a link that folks can click to jump to whatever page you specify in the href attribute.

Here's an example (bk02ch03/example03.html):

```
<header>
    <a href="/"><img src="images/iis-logo.png" alt="Isn't it
  Semantic? company logo"></a>
    <h1>Welcome to "Isn't it Semantic?"</h1>
    <hr>
</header>
```

# Controlling an image's vertical alignment

If you check back with the HTML code for Figure 3-1, you'll notice that I added a `<br>` tag just before the `<img>` tag:

```
—William Blake<br>
<img src="images/flower-and-ant.jpg" alt="Macro photo showing an
    ant exploring a flower" title="Flower and Ant">
```

I did that because otherwise the browser would have positioned the image inline with the text. Why? Because, perhaps surprisingly, `img` is an inline element, not a block element. Fortunately, if you do want an image to flow along with the text, you have some control over how the image and text align, but it requires a quick foray into CSS territory. To control the vertical alignment of an object, you use the `vertical-align` property:

```
selector {
    vertical-align: value;
}
```

Or, as an attribute:

```
style="vertical-align: value;"
```

For *value*, you can enter a length (in, say, pixels), where positive lengths shift the image up and negative lengths shift the image down. The `vertical-align` property also supports quite a few predefined values, of which the following are the ones you need to know:

» `baseline`: Vertically aligns the bottom of the image with the baseline of the line of text in which the image resides. (The *baseline* is the imaginary horizontal line that runs under the bottoms of letters such as c and i that don't have descenders.) This is the default value.

» `bottom`: Vertically aligns the bottom of the image with the bottom of the line of text in which the image resides. (The line *bottom* is the imaginary horizontal line that runs under the lowest parts of letters such as g and y. These below-the-baseline parts are known as *descenders*.)

» `middle`: Vertically aligns the middle of the image with the baseline of the line of text in which the image resides, plus half of the x-height of the current font. (A font's *x-height* is the height of letters that don't have ascenders or descenders, such as c and x.)

» top: Vertically aligns the top of the image with the top of the line of text in which the image resides. (The line *top* is the imaginary horizontal line that runs over the topmost parts of letters such as *h* and *t*. These above-the-x-height parts are known as *ascenders*.)

Here's an example, and Figure 3-3 shows how things look in the browser (bk02ch03/example04.html):

```html
<div>
    <img src="images/image01.jpg" alt="" style="vertical-align:
    baseline;">Baseline
</div>
<div>
    <img src="images/image02.jpg" alt="" style="vertical-align:
    bottom">Bottom
</div>
<div>
    <img src="images/image03.jpg" alt="" style="vertical-align:
    middle">Middle
</div>
<div>
    <img src="images/image04.jpg" alt="" style="vertical-align:
    top">Top
</div>
```

FIGURE 3-3:
The vertical-
align property
values in action.

Baseline   Bottom   Middle   Top

**REMEMBER**

Wondering how you define a background image for a page? I thought as much. That's done with CSS, and I go through the details in Book 3, Chapter 6.

# Embedding Videos

If a picture is worth the proverbial thousand words, what's a video worth? No idea, but it must be an awfully big number given the profusion of video content on the web. It seems that every Tom, Diego, and Harriette with a home page is serving up video fare. If you want to join their ranks, you've come to the right place.

How you embed a video into a web page depends on the type of video:

>> **Third-party video:** For videos from third-party sites such as YouTube, Vimeo, and Dailymotion, you insert some HTML code into your page that automatically plays the video from the third-party site.

>> **Your own video:** For video files that you create yourself, you upload the file to your server and then use the video element to insert the video into your page.

The next couple of sections provide the sometimes-gory details.

## Embedding a third-party video

By far the easiest way to liven up your web page with video content is to embed some HTML code that plays the video from a third-party online video provider, such as YouTube. This is the easy route because it means you don't have to worry about video formats, uploading video files, and dealing with the often-onerous bandwidth costs of serving videos.

Almost every online video provider offers a Share feature for each video, and that Share feature usually includes an Embed component that enables you to copy the required code to embed the video in your page. Here are the instructions for obtaining the required HTML code from three major online video providers:

>> **Dailymotion:** Go to dailymotion.com and locate the video you want to embed in your page. Click the Share icon (as shown in the margin) and then click Embed Video to display a dialog box that shows the required code. Click the Autoplay switch On or Off, as desired. (When Autoplay is on, it means the video starts automatically each time someone surfs to your page.) Select the code, press Ctrl+C (⌘+C in macOS) to copy the code, and then paste the code into your HTML file at the place where you want the video to appear.

>> **Vimeo:** Go to vimeo.com and display the video you want to embed in your page. Click the Share icon (it's the same as the Dailymotion icon shown in the margin). In the Share this Video dialog box that appears, the Embed box displays the required code. If you want, you can click Show Options to

customize the code to taste. Click the Embed box to select the code, press Ctrl+C (⌘+C in macOS) to copy the code, and then paste the code into your HTML file at the location where you want the video to appear.

» **YouTube:** Go to youtube.com and find the video you want to embed in your page. Click the Share button. In the Share dialog box that appears, click Embed to display the code, as shown in Figure 3-4. Adjust the options as needed, click Copy, and then paste the code into your HTML file at the spot where you want the video to appear.

**FIGURE 3-4:**
The embed code for a YouTube video.

**TECHNICAL STUFF**

If the HTML code you copy from most online video providers looks intimidatingly complex, that's because it is! The code usually consists of an ‹iframe› tag — the iframe element is used to embed another web page within the current page — with various attributes applied. These attributes include style (with various CSS properties specified), height, width, and the all-important src attribute, which specifies the online address of the video.

**WARNING**

Unless you really know what you're doing, you shouldn't edit or otherwise mess with the HTML code supplied by the online video provider. One false move and your embedded video won't work.

## Embedding your own videos

If you prefer (or need) to go the DIY-video route, I have both good news and bad news for you, but I'm afraid the ratio of the two leans much more to the bad news side of things.

The good news is that HTML provides the video element, which you use to embed a video player into a page, which in turn not only displays your video but also offers playback controls. The bad news is that web-friendly video file formats are a bit of a mishmash these days, so it's not always obvious which is the best way to go.

## Some notes about web media file formats

**TECHNICAL STUFF**

Before proceeding, you need to know that web media file formats have two important aspects:

>> **The container:** The file format of the media. Why is it called a *container*? Because it's an archive file — something akin to a Zip file — that contains multiple items required by the media, including the codecs (refer to the next item) and the metadata.

>> **The codec:** The algorithm used to encode and compress the media into a digital format, as well as to decode and decompress the media for playback. (So, *codec* is a blend word that combines *code/decode* and *compress/decompress*.)

What all this means is that every web media file comes in a specific media format, that format uses a particular container, and within that container are (among other things) all the codecs that the format supports. It's hideously complex, but matters are made much worse when you find out that there's no such thing as a standard video file format!

## The bad news: Web video formats

When you're dealing with embedding video in your pages, you have three main formats to deal with:

>> **MPEG-4:** Uses the MPEG-4 container, inside which is the H.264 video codec, as well as the AAC audio codec. This format is patented but free for end users. MPEG-4 video files use the file extension .mp4.

>> **Ogg:** Uses the Ogg container, inside which is the Theora video codec, as well as the Vorbis or Opus audio codec. This format is open source and royalty free. Ogg video files use the file extension: .ogg or .ogv.

>> **WebM:** Uses the WebM container, inside which is either the VP8 or VP9 video codec, as well as the Vorbis or Opus audio codec. This format is open source and royalty free. WebM video files use the file extension .webm.

**TIP**

There are tons of online tools available that will convert videos to the formats I list here. Two sites worth trying are Zamzar (www.zamzar.com) and Online-Convert (www.online-convert.com/).

I wish I could point to one of these formats and say, "Use that one exclusively." However, two things prevent me from doing that:

>> **Browser support:** Both MPEG-4 and WebM are fully supported by all the major browsers, but support for Ogg is not quite there yet.

>> **Royalties:** Both Ogg and WebM are royalty-free, but the patented MPEG-4 requires browser companies to pay a royalty to use it. The excellent quality of MPEG-4 videos means that all major browsers support it, but that may not always be the case in the future.

The bottom line is that although you're probably fine using MPEG-4 for your own video files, if you can also produce a WebM version, you should offer both file formats to your visitors. To learn how to do that, read on for the details of HTML's video element.

## The good news: The <video> tag

Given the complexity of the web video formats that I waxed unlyrical on in the previous section, it's a welcome relief to find out that actually embedding your own video into a web page is relatively straightforward thanks to the handy video element. How you use the video element depends on whether you're offering a single video file format or multiple formats.

First, here's the general video element syntax to use if you're dishing out just a single video file format:

```
<video src="source"
    poster="poster"
    width="width"
    height="height"
    autoplay
    controls
    loop
</video>
```

Here's what each attribute means:

>> src: The name of the video file, if the file is in the same location as the HTML file. If the video file resides in a different directory, you need to include that info so that the browser knows where to look for the file.

>> poster: The name (and directory, if needed) of an image that you want the browser to display before video playback begins. Most of the time you use a title frame or still frame from the video.

>> `width`: The width, in pixels, of the video playback window.

>> `height`: The height, in pixels, of the video playback window.

>> `autoplay`: Include this attribute to have the browser automatically start playing the video as soon as enough of the file has been downloaded for smooth playback. If you don't want the video to start automatically, omit the `autoplay` attribute.

>> `controls`: Include this attribute to have the browser display the playback controls in the video window. If you don't want your visitors to be able to control the playback, omit the `controls` attribute.

>> `loop`: Include this attribute to have the browser automatically begin playback from the beginning whenever the video ends. If you want the video to play only once, omit the `loop` attribute.

Here's an example of embedding video, and Figure 3-5 shows the video embedded in the web page (bk02ch03/example05.html).

```
<video src="videos/bear.mp4"
    poster="images/bear.png"
    width="640"
    height="480"
    autoplay
    controls
    loop
</video>
```

**FIGURE 3-5:**
An MPEG-4 video embedded in a web page.

If you want to offer multiple video formats, remove the src attribute from the `<video>` tag and add multiple source elements, one for each format you want to offer:

```
<video
    poster="filename"
    width="value"
    height="value"
    autoplay
    controls
    loop>
    <source src="filename"
            type='type; codecs="codecs"'>
    <source etc...
</video>
```

The video attributes are the same as I describe earlier, but here's what you need to know about the `<source>` tag's attributes:

>> src: The name of the video file, if the file is in the same location as the HTML file. If the video file resides in a different directory, you need to include that info so that the browser knows where to look for the file.

>> type: A string (surrounded by single quotation marks) that specifies the video format type, which is a comma-separated and double-quotation-mark-surrounded list of the format's video and audio codecs:

- *MPEG-4:* Use the following:

  ```
  type='video/mp4; codecs="avc1.4D401E, mp4a.40.2"'
  ```

- *Ogg:* Use one of the following:

  ```
  type='video/ogg; codecs="theora, vorbis"'
  type='video/ogg; codecs="theora, opus"'
  ```

- *WebM:* Use one of the following:

  ```
  type='video/webm; codecs="vp8, vorbis"'
  type='video/webm; codecs="vp9, vorbis"'
  type='video/webm; codecs="vp9, opus"'
  ```

The browser runs through the source elements in the order you specify them and plays the first compatible video format that it comes across.

Here's an example (bk02ch03/example06.html):

```
<video
    poster="images/bear.png"
    width="640"
    height="480"
    autoplay
    controls
    loop>
    <source src="videos/bear.mp4"
            type='video/mp4; codecs="avc1.4D401E, mp4a.40.2"'>
    <source src="videos/bear.webm"
            type='video/webm; codecs="vp8, vorbis"'>
    <source src="videos/bear.ogv"
            type='video/ogg; codecs="theora, vorbis"'>
</video>
```

# Embedding Audio Snippets

In modern web pages, embedded audio snippets aren't as popular as embedded videos, but you may have occasion to offer your visitors some kind of audio treat. As with video, how you embed audio into a web page depends on the type of audio:

>> **Third-party audio:** For audio files from third-party sites such as SoundCloud, Bandcamp, or Mixcloud, you insert some HTML code into your page that automatically plays the audio from the third-party site.

>> **Your own audio:** For audio files that you create yourself, you upload the file to your server and then use the audio element to insert the audio into your page.

The next couple of sections provide the details.

## Embedding third-party audio

You can get an audio snippet up and playing on your web page quickly by embedding some HTML code that plays the audio from a third-party online audio provider, such as SoundCloud.

Most online audio providers offer a Share feature for each audio that includes an Embed component. The Share feature enables you to copy the required code to embed the audio in your page. Here's how to obtain the required HTML code from three major online audio providers:

>> **Bandcamp:** Go to bandcamp.com and open the audio you want to embed in your page. Click the Share/Embed button, click Embed This Album, and then click a player style to display the code. Customize the player as needed and then copy the code that appears in the Embed text box. Then paste the code into your HTML file at the place where you want the audio player to appear.

>> **Mixcloud:** Go to mixcloud.com and display the audio you want to embed in your page. Click the Share button and, in the dialog box that appears, click the Embed Player tab. Click which style of audio widget you want to use, and then copy the code that appears in the dialog box. (You can also click More Options to customize your player.) Paste the code into your HTML file at the location where you want the audio widget to appear.

>> **SoundCloud:** Go to soundcloud.com and find the audio you want to embed in your page. Click the Share button and, in the dialog box that appears, click the Embed tab to display the code, as shown in Figure 3-6. Adjust the options as needed, copy the code from the Code text box, and then paste the code into your HTML file at the spot where you want the audio player to appear.

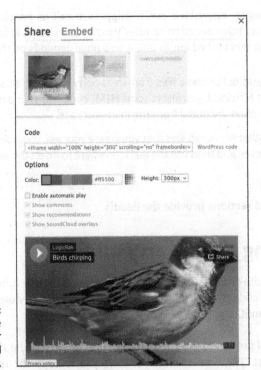

**FIGURE 3-6:**
The embed code and options for a SoundCloud audio track.

**WARNING** Unless you know what you're doing, don't edit the HTML code supplied by the online audio provider. One imprudent change is all it may take to prevent your embedded audio from playing.

## Embedding your own audio

Got your own audio file that you want to serve up to your page visitors? No problem! The audio file format is a bit saner than the video format world, and HTML offers the audio element for relatively pain-free audio embedding.

### Web audio formats

For web audio, you have the following formats to deal with:

>> **MP3:** This format is both the container and the audio codec. This format is patented but free for end users. These audio files use the file extension .mp3.

>> **WAV:** This format is both the container and the audio codec. These audio files use the file extension .wav.

>> **WebM:** This format uses the WebM container, inside which is the Vorbis or Opus audio codec. This format is open source and royalty free. These audio files use the file extension .webm.

>> **Ogg:** This format uses the Ogg container, inside which is the Vorbis or Opus audio codec. This format is open source and royalty free. These audio files use the file extension .ogg or .oga.

>> **MPEG-4:** This format uses the MPEG-4 container, inside which is the AAC audio codec. This format is patented but free for end users. These audio files use the file extension .m4a.

**TIP** There are lots of online tools for converting audio files to the formats I list here. Three sites worth trying are Zamzar (www.zamzar.com), Online-Convert (www.online-convert.com/), and Media.io (https://media.io).

**REMEMBER** All major browsers have long supported the MP3 format, so you can almost always get away with using just the MP3 file type.

## The &lt;audio&gt; tag

First, here's the general `audio` element syntax to use if you're dishing out just a single audio file format:

```
<audio src="source"
    autoplay
    controls
    loop
</audio>
```

Here's what each attribute means:

» `src`: The name of the audio file, if the file is in the same location as the HTML file. If the audio file resides in a different directory, you need to include that info so that the browser knows where to look for the file.

» `autoplay`: Include this attribute to have the browser automatically start playing the audio as soon as enough of the file has been downloaded for smooth playback. If you don't want the audio to start automatically, omit the `autoplay` attribute.

» `controls`: Include this attribute to have the browser display the playback controls in the audio window. If you don't want your visitors to be able to control the playback, omit the `controls` attribute.

» `loop`: Include this attribute to have the browser automatically begin playback from the beginning whenever the audio ends. If you want the audio to play only once, omit the `loop` attribute.

Here's an example of embedding audio, and Figure 3-7 shows the audio embedded in the web page (bk02ch03/example07.html).

```
<audio src="audio/jabberwocky.mp3"
    autoplay
    controls
    loop
</audio>
```

**FIGURE 3-7:**
An MP3 audio file embedded in a web page.

If you want to offer multiple audio formats, take out the ‹audio› tag's src attribute and add one source element for each format you want to offer:

```
<audio
    autoplay
    controls
    loop>
    <source src="filename"
            type="type">
    <source etc...
</video>
```

The audio attributes are the same as I describe earlier, but here's what you need to know about the ‹source› tag's attributes:

» src: The name of the audio file, if the file is in the same location as the HTML file. If the audio file resides in a different directory, you need to include that info so that the browser knows where to look for the file.

» type: The audio format type, such as audio/mp3 or audio/wav.

The browser runs through the source elements in the order you specify them and plays the first compatible audio format that it comes across.

Here's an example (bk02ch03/example08.html):

```
<audio
    autoplay
    controls
    loop
    <source src="audio/jabberwocky.mp3"
            type="audio/mp3">
    <source src="audio/jabberwocky.m4a"
            type="audio/mp4">
    <source src="audio/jabberwocky.webm"
            type="audio/webm">
    <source src="audio/jabberwocky.ogg"
            type="audio/ogg">
    <source src="audio/jabberwocky.wav"
            type="audio/wav">
</audio>
```

IN THIS CHAPTER

» **Learning why tables are useful**

» **Touring a typical table**

» **Creating simple tables**

» **Crafting ever-so-slightly advanced tables**

» **Making your tables stylish**

# Chapter **4**

# Building Tables with Your Bare Hands

*If a picture is worth 1,000 words, then surely a table is worth at least 500.*

— ANONYMOUS

Your web pages will mostly consist of text and a few images or other media. However, every now and then you'll need to offer some data to your page visitors. It may be the results of an experiment, some financial numbers, or an inventory of your cubic zirconia collection.

How you present that data depends on how much data there is and how it's structured. In many cases, data is best presented in a row-and-column format that's reminiscent of a spreadsheet or database. That sounds like it may require some advanced coding techniques, but HTML rides to the rescue here with a collection of elements that enable you to build a special web page structure called a table.

In this chapter, you learn a bit of web carpentry as I show you how to build and work with tables. Don't worry if you can't tell a hammer from a hacksaw; the tables you'll be dealing with are purely digital. An HTML table is a rectangular grid of rows and columns on a web page, into which you can enter all kinds of info, including text, numbers, links, and even images. This chapter tells you everything you need to know to build and style your own table specimens.

# What Is a Table?

An HTML *table* is a structure that presents data in a rectangular arrangement that consists of one or more columns and one or more rows. In that sense, you can think of a table as a kind of database: Each table column is the equivalent of a database field, which contains a single type of information, such as a name, address, or phone number; each row serves as the equivalent of a database record, which holds a set of associated field values, such as the information for a single contact. Figure 4-1 shows a typical table and points out a few key features (for the code, check out bk02ch04/example01.html in this book's example files).

FIGURE 4-1: An HTML table is a rectangular arrangement of data into rows, columns, and cells.

**Redefining "Humongous"**

World Records for Selected Fruits and Vegetables

| Crop | Weight (Imperial) | Weight (Metric) | Date Grown | Grower |
|---|---|---|---|---|
| apple | 4 lb. 1 oz. | 1.85 kg | Oct. 14, 2005 | Chisato Iwasaki |
| avocado | 5 lb. 9.6 oz. | 2.55 kg | Dec. 14, 2018 | Pokini family |
| beet | 52 lb. 14 oz. | 23.995 kg | May 23, 2019 | Fortey Family |
| cantaloupe | 67 lb. 1.8 oz. | 30.47 kg | Aug. 5, 2019 | William N. McCaslin |
| carrot | 22 lb. 7.04 oz. | 10.17 kg | Sept. 9, 2017 | Christopher Qualley |
| cauliflower | 60 lb. 9.3 oz. | 27.48 kg | April 21, 2014 | Peter Glazebrook |
| celery | 92 lb. 9 oz. | 42.0 kg | Sept. 29, 2018 | Gary Heeks |
| cucumber | 23 lb. 7 oz. | 12.9 kg | Sept. 26, 2015 | David Thomas |
| grapefruit | 7 lb. 14 oz. | 3.6 kg | Jan. 19, 2019 | Mary Beth Meyer, Douglas Meyer |
| green cabbage | 138 lb. 4 oz. | 62.71 kg | Aug. 31, 2012 | Scott A. Robb |
| kale | 105 lb. 14.5 oz. | 48.04 kg | Aug. 29, 2007 | Scott Robb |
| lemon | 11 lb. 9.7 oz. | 5.3 kg | Jan. 8, 2003 | Aharon Shemoel |
| peach | 1 lb. 12 oz. | 816.5 g | July 11, 2018 | Al Pearson, Lawton Pearson |
| pear | 6 lb. 8 oz. | 2.9 kg | Nov. 11, 2011 | JA Aichi Toyota Nashi Bukai |
| pineapple | 18 lb. 4 oz. | 8.28 kg | Nov. 30, 2011 | Christine McCallum |
| pomegranate | 5 lb. 11.68 oz. | 2.60 kg | Nov. 27, 2017 | Zhang Yuanpeng |
| potato | 24 lb. 14.4 oz. | 11.3 kg | Dec. 8, 2008 | Khalil Semhat |
| pumpkin | 2,702 lb. 13.9 oz. | 1,226 kg | Sept. 26, 2021 | Stefano Cutrupi |
| radish | 68 lb. 9 oz. | 31.1 kg | Feb. 9, 2003 | Manabu Oono |
| summer squash | 256 lb. 9.8 oz. | 116.4 kg | Sept. 23, 2021 | Vincent Sjodin |
| sweet potato | 81 lb. 9 oz. | 37 kg | March 8, 2004 | Manuel Pérez Pérez |
| tomato | 10 lb. 12.7 oz. | 4.9 kg | July 15, 2020 | Dan Sutherland |
| turnip | 63 lb. 14 oz. | 29 kg | Nov. 2, 2020 | Damien Allard |
| watermelon | 350 lb. 8 oz. | 159 kg | Oct. 4, 2013 | Christopher Kent |
| zucchini | 115 lb. | 52 kg | Sept. 28, 2020 | Ron Sholtz |

To make sure you understand what's going on (that is my job, after all), check out a bit of table lingo:

>> **Row:** A single "line" of data that runs across the table.

>> **Column:** A single vertical section of data. In the Figure 4-1 table, there are five columns.

>> **Cell:** The intersection of a row and column. The cells hold the individual items of data that you're using the table to present.

>> **Caption:** Text that appears (usually) above the table and is used to describe the contents of the table.

>> **Headers:** The first row of the table. The headers are optional, but many people use them to label each column.

Nothing too rocket science-y there. At this point, two questions may pop up in your mind. First, given that the pre element (refer to Book 2, Chapter 2) does a great job at making text line up all nice and neat, why use a table when pre can do a similar job? Good question. Here are just a few advantages that tables bring to the, uh, table:

>> **Aligning text is easy.** Getting text to line up using pre is frustrating at best, and a hair-pulling, head-pounding, curse-the-very-existence-of-the-@#$%&!-web chore at worst. With tables, though, you can get your text to line up like boot camp recruits with very little effort.

>> **Cells don't affect each other.** Each table cell is self-contained. You can edit and style the contents of a cell without disturbing the arrangement of the other table elements.

>> **Text wrapping works like buttah.** The text wraps inside each cell, making it a snap to create multiple-line entries.

>> **You can throw in the kitchen sink.** Tables can include not only text, but images and links as well (even other tables!).

>> **They look good.** Text wrapped inside a pre element uses a monospace font, which doesn't look great, but tables use the regular page font, which looks much nicer. And, as an added bonus, tables come with lots of CSS properties that you can take advantage of to make your tables look awesome.

Second, given that tables seem very good at positioning text just so, and given that tables support not only text but also images and other content, would it be possible to lay out my page using a giant table? Another great question! You're on a roll!

Let me start by saying that organizing page elements using tables was the standard layout technique for many years. However, nobody was a big fan of using tables this way because tables are too rigid, too unwieldy, and are difficult to render well on both large and small screens. These days, *nobody* uses tables to lay out a page, preferring newer and more powerful technologies such as Flexbox (refer to Book 5, Chapter 2) and Grid (refer to Book 5, Chapter 3).

# Web Woodworking: How to Build a Table

Okay, it's time to put the table pedal to the HTML metal and start cranking out some of these table things. The next few sections take you through the steps for building a basic table.

## The simplest case: a one-row table

As an example, I'm going to build a simple table of funny town names that are related to food. Why not? Tables always start with the following container:

```
<table>
</table>
```

All the other table tags fit between these two tags. Next, you add the container for the table body (that is, the rows and columns, not including the table header, which you'll get to a bit later).

```
<table>
    <tbody>
    </tbody>
</table>
```

After you've got this basic structure in place, most of your remaining table chores involve the following four-step process:

1. **Add a row.**

2. **Divide the row into the number of columns you want.**

3. **Insert data into each cell.**

4. **Repeat Steps 1 through 3 until done.**

To add a row, you toss a `<tr>` (table row) tag and a `</tr>` tag (its corresponding end tag) between `<tbody>` and `</tbody>`:

```
<table>
    <tbody>
        <tr>
        </tr>
    </tbody>
</table>
```

Now you divide that row into columns by placing the ‹td› (table data) and ‹/td› tags between ‹tr› and ‹/tr›. Each ‹td›‹/td› combination represents one column (or, more specifically, an individual cell in the row), so if, for example, you want a three-column table, you do this:

```
<table>
    <tbody>
        <tr>
            <td></td>
            <td></td>
            <td></td>
        </tr>
    </tbody>
</table>
```

Now you enter the row's cell data by typing text between each ‹td› tag and its ‹/td› end tag:

```
<table>
    <tbody>
        <tr>
            <td>Candy Kitchen</td>
            <td>New Mexico</td>
            <td>59</td>
        </tr>
    </tbody>
</table>
```

Figure 4-2 shows how things look so far.

FIGURE 4-2:
A simple
one-row table.

Remember that you can put any of the following within the ‹td› and ‹/td› tags:

» Text

» Links

» Lists

» Images and other media (such as video and audio)

» Another table

# Adding more rows

When your first row is firmly in place, you repeat the procedure for the other rows in the table. For my example table, here's the HTML that includes the data for all the rows:

```
<table>
    <tbody>
        <tr>
            <tr>
                <td>Candy Kitchen</td><td>New Mexico
</td><td>59</td>
            </tr>
            <tr>
                <td>Hot Coffee</td><td>Mississippi
</td><td>2,586</td>
            </tr>
            <tr>
                <td>Ketchuptown</td><td>South Carolina
</td><td>84</td>
            </tr>
            <tr>
                <td>Sandwich</td><td>New Hampshire
</td><td>1,354</td>
            </tr>
            <tr>
                <td>Two Egg</td><td>Florida
</td><td>3,683</td>
            </tr>
        </tr>
    </tbody>
</table>
```

To make the code a bit easier to read, I put the td elements for each row in a single line. Figure 4-3 shows the progress made so far (check out bk02ch04/example02.html).

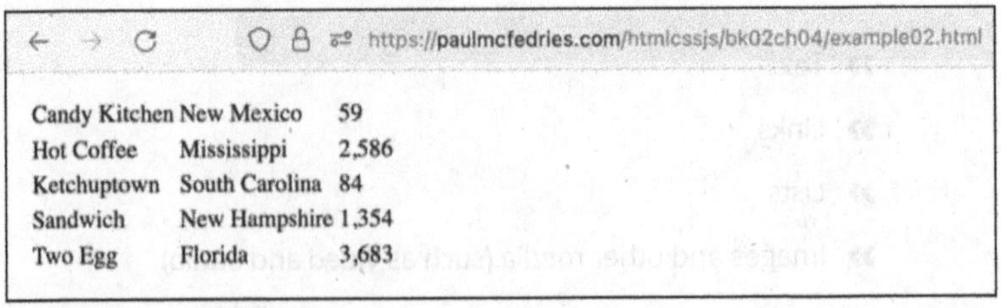

← → C          ○ 🔒 ⇄ https://paulmcfedries.com/htmlcssjs/bk02ch04/example02.html

Candy Kitchen New Mexico      59
Hot Coffee    Mississippi     2,586
Ketchuptown   South Carolina  84
Sandwich      New Hampshire   1,354
Two Egg       Florida         3,683

**FIGURE 4-3:**
The completed
table body.
Looking good!

# Adding More Table Elements

A table that has a body with one or more rows and one or more columns is a fully paid-up member of the HTML table club, so if that's all you need to present your data, you can move on to the next item on your web page to-do list. However, HTML tables offer quite a few more features that you may consider. For example, your table may need column or row headings (or both), a description of the table content, or a row that summarizes the table in some way. All these features are possible with a few extra table-related elements, as the next few sections show.

## Creating a header row

If your table displays stats, financial data, or numeric info, there's a good chance your readers won't be able to figure out the meaning of the contents of one or more columns. For example, look back at Figure 4-3. Do you know what the numbers in the third column represent? You may be able to guess, but you really don't want your readers to be making guesses about your data.

You can make your readers' lives easier by including labels at the top of each column that describe what's in the column. (You don't need a long-winded explanation; in most cases, a word or two should do the job.) To add these labels, you first create a new table section called the *head*:

```
<thead>
</thead>
```

Place this section just above the <tbody> tag.

Now you create a *header row*. This is similar to a regular row, except that you replace <td> and </td> with <th> (table header) and </th>, like this:

```
<thead>
    <tr>
        <th>First Column Header</th>
        <th>Second Column Header</th>
        <th>And So On, Ad Nauseum</th>
    </tr>
</thead>
```

As the code shows, the th element is a lot like the td element. The difference is that the browser displays text that appears between the <th> and </th> tags as bold and centered within the cell. This helps the reader differentiate the header from the rest of the table data. Remember, though, that headers are optional; you can bypass them if your table doesn't need them.

Okay, now add a head section and header row to your example table:

```
<table>
    <thead>
        <tr>
            <th>Town</th>
            <th>State</th>
            <th>Population</th>
        </tr>
    </thead>
    <tbody>
    etc.
```

Figure 4-4 shows the table with the column headings (bk02ch04/example03. html).

https://paulmcfedries.com/htmlcssjs/bk02ch04/example03.html 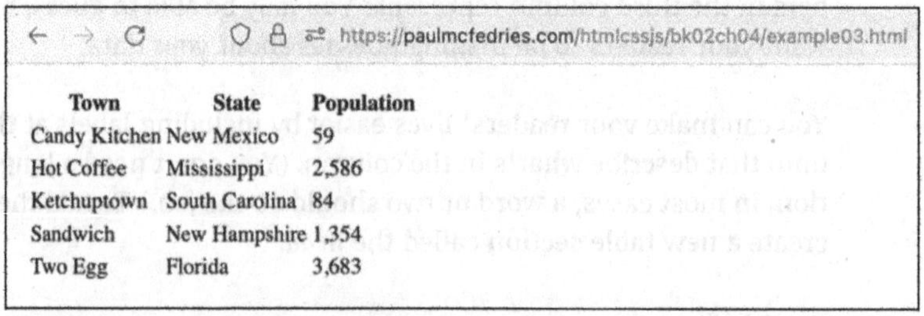

| Town | State | Population |
|------|-------|-----------|
| Candy Kitchen | New Mexico | 59 |
| Hot Coffee | Mississippi | 2,586 |
| Ketchuptown | South Carolina | 84 |
| Sandwich | New Hampshire | 1,354 |
| Two Egg | Florida | 3,683 |

**FIGURE 4-4:**
The example table, now with column headings.

## Including a caption

The next basic table element is the caption. A caption is a short description (a sentence or two) that tells the reader the purpose of the table. You define the caption with the caption element:

```
<caption>
    Caption text goes here
</caption>
```

You add the caption code just after the `<table>` tag. By default, the web browser displays the caption centered above the table, but you can change that default with a bit of CSS (check out "Changing the location of the caption," later in this chapter). Here's the first part of my table code with the caption added:

```
<table>
    <caption>
        Funny Food-Based Town Names
    </caption>
    <thead>
    etc.
```

Figure 4-5 shows the table with the caption now appearing above the header row (bk02ch04/example04.html).

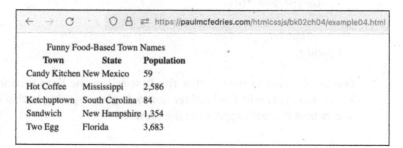

Funny Food-Based Town Names

| Town | State | Population |
|------|-------|-----------|
| Candy Kitchen | New Mexico | 59 |
| Hot Coffee | Mississippi | 2,586 |
| Ketchuptown | South Carolina | 84 |
| Sandwich | New Hampshire | 1,354 |
| Two Egg | Florida | 3,683 |

**FIGURE 4-5:** The example table with an added caption.

## Creating a header column

In some tables, the values in the first column act as labels that describe the contents of the rest of each row. HTML doesn't have a specific element for this kind of header column, but you can roll your own by replacing the <td> and </td> tags in the first column with <th> and </th> tags. This tells the browser to display the items in the first column in bold text and centered in the column. Here's an example (bk02ch04/example05.html):

```
<table>
    <caption>
        Fifth Quarter Sales By Category
    </caption>
    <thead>
        <tr>
            <th></th><th>Units Sold</th><th>Total Sales</th>
        </tr>
    </thead>
    <tbody>
        <tr>
            <th>Doodads</th><td>5,732</td><td>$28,603</td>
        </tr>
        <tr>
```

```
        <th>Doohickeys</th><td>8,502</td><td>$59,429</td>
    </tr>
    <tr>
        <th>Gizmos</th><td>10,468</td><td>$41,767</td>
    </tr>
    <tr>
        <th>Thingamajigs</th><td>4,498</td><td>$40,437</td>
    </tr>
    <tr>
        <th>Whatchamacallits</th><td>7,165</td>
<td>$57,248</td>
    </tr>
  </tbody>
</table>
```

One small point to note is that the first cell in the head section uses the code `<th></th>`. This tells the browser not to display anything in that cell. Figure 4-6 shows how the table appears in the browser.

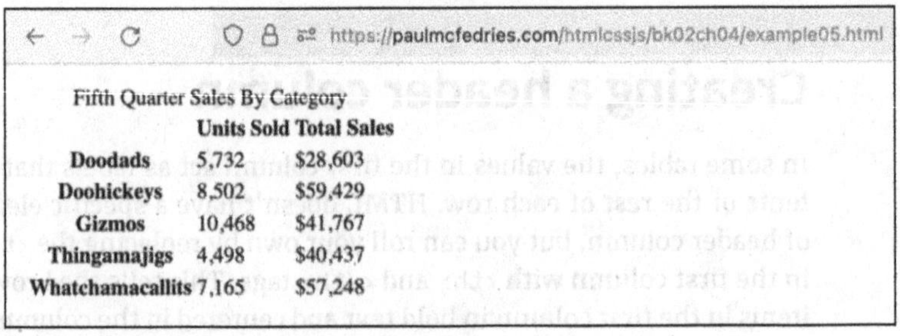

Fifth Quarter Sales By Category

| | Units Sold | Total Sales |
|---|---|---|
| Doodads | 5,732 | $28,603 |
| Doohickeys | 8,502 | $59,429 |
| Gizmos | 10,468 | $41,767 |
| Thingamajigs | 4,498 | $40,437 |
| Whatchamacallits | 7,165 | $57,248 |

**FIGURE 4-6:**
A table with a column header.

## Creating a table footer

If your table data lends itself to some kind of summary — for example, the sums or averages of one or more columns — you can place that summary in the table's foot section.

You begin with a container built out of the `<tfoot>` and `</tfoot>` tags:

```
<tfoot>
</tfoot>
```

Place this section just below the `</tbody>` tag.

Now you create a *footer row*. This is a regular row made with the `tr` element, plus whatever `td` (or `th`) elements you need:

```
<tfoot>
    <tr>
        <td>First Column Footer</td>
        <td>Second Column Footer</td>
        <td>Yet Another Column Footer</td>
    </tr>
</tfoot>
```

Insert the tfoot element just below the </tbody> tag, as shown in the following example (bk02ch04/example06.html):

```
<table>
    <caption>
        Fifth Quarter Sales By Category
    </caption>
    <thead>
        <tr>
            <th></th><th>Units Sold</th><th>Total Sales</th>
        </tr>
    </thead>
    <tbody>
        <tr>
            <th>Doodads</th><td>5,732</td><td>$28,603</td>
        </tr>
        <tr>
            <th>Doohickeys</th><td>8,502</td><td>$59,429</td>
        </tr>
        <tr>
            <th>Gizmos</th><td>10,468</td><td>$41,767</td>
        </tr>
        <tr>
            <th>Thingamajigs</th><td>4,498</td><td>$40,437</td>
        </tr>
        <tr>
            <th>Whatchamacallits</th><td>7,165</td>
    <td>$57,248</td>
        </tr>
    </tbody>
    <tfoot>
        <tr>
            <th>Totals</th><td>36,365</td><td>$227,484</td>
        </tr>
    </tfoot>
</table>
```

Figure 4-7 shows the table with the footer row added.

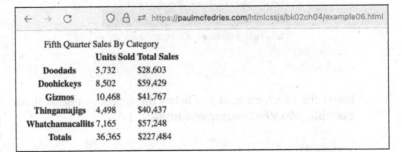

Fifth Quarter Sales By Category

| | Units Sold | Total Sales |
|---|---|---|
| Doodads | 5,732 | $28,603 |
| Doohickeys | 8,502 | $59,429 |
| Gizmos | 10,468 | $41,767 |
| Thingamajigs | 4,498 | $40,437 |
| Whatchamacallits | 7,165 | $57,248 |
| Totals | 36,365 | $227,484 |

**FIGURE 4-7:**
A table with a footer row.

# Table Refinishing: Styling Your Tables

The tags I discuss earlier in this chapter are enough to enable you to build tables that are sturdy, if not altogether flashy. If that's all you need, you can safely ignore the rest of the flapdoodle in this chapter. However, if you'd like a tad more control over the layout and look of your tables, the next few sections take you through some useful refinements that can give your tables that certain *je ne sais quoi*.

## Aligning text within cells

When it comes to aligning the data within your table cells, you have two possibilities to consider:

» **Horizontal alignment:** Refers to how cell text is aligned with respect to the left and right edges of the cell. The standard-issue horizontal alignment for table cells is left-aligned for data (td) cells and centered for header (th) cells.

» **Vertical alignment:** Refers to how cell text is aligned with respect to the top and bottom edges of the cell. The default vertical alignment for all table cells is in the middle of the cell (vertically speaking).

If you prefer to override these defaults for one or more cells, there are CSS properties that can get the job done. The next couple of sections explain how.

## Aligning cell text horizontally

You customize a cell's horizontal alignment by using the CSS text-align property:

```
selector {
    text-align: value;
}
```

Or, as an attribute:

```
style="text-align: value;"
```

For *value*, you can use any of the following:

» left: Aligns text with the left edge of the cell.

» center: Aligns text with the horizontal middle of the cell.

» right: Aligns text with the right edge of the cell.

» justify: Aligns text with both the left and right edges of the cell.

For example, if you want all your th elements to be left-aligned rather than centered, you add the following rule to your CSS:

```
th {
    text-align: left;
}
```

Here's a larger example that demonstrates all four text-align values (bk02ch04/example07.html):

```
<table>
    <thead>
        <tr>
            <th>Idiom</th><th>Part of Speech</th><th>First
    Used</th><th>Definition</th>
        </tr>
    </thead>
    <tbody>
        <tr>
            <td style="text-align: left;">
                goat cheese curtain
            </td>
            <td style="text-align: center;">
                noun
            </td>
            <td style="text-align: right;">
                2012
```

```
        </td>
        <td style="text-align: justify; width: 200px;">
            An imaginary boundary that separates urban
            sophisticates from those with simple,
            traditional, or uncultured tastes.
        </td>
    </tr>
    </tbody>
</table>
```

As shown in Figure 4-8, the first column is left-aligned, the second column is centered, the third column is right-aligned, and the fourth column is justified.

https://paulmcfedries.com/htmlcssjs/bk02ch04/example07.html

| Idiom | Part of Speech | First Used | Definition |
|---|---|---|---|
| goat cheese curtain | noun | 2012 | An imaginary boundary that separates urban sophisticates from those with simple, traditional, or uncultured tastes. |

**FIGURE 4-8:** The text-align values in action.

## TARGETING ENTIRE COLUMNS

**TECHNICAL STUFF**

Adding the style attribute to the <td> tag, as I do in the example, is fine for small tables, but if your table has dozens or even hundreds of rows, adding a style declaration to dozens or hundreds of <td> tags is nobody's idea of fun. Fortunately, you can use a special CSS selector to target a specific table column with a single rule:

```
td:nth-child(x) {
    declarations go here
}
```

Here, x is the number of the column you want to style. For example, the following rule applies the justify alignment to the entire fourth column of a table:

```
td:nth-child(4) {
    text-align: justify;
}
```

You learn more about the powerful nth-child selector in Book 3, Chapter 3.

**TECHNICAL STUFF**

Note that I added the declaration `width: 200px;` to the fourth `<td>` tag. If I didn't restrict the width, the column would just take up all the available width in the browser window, which wouldn't show the justify effect. Refer to Book 3, Chapter 1 to learn more about the `width` property. Note, too, that I added a border around each cell to make it easier to notice the alignment. Check out "Bring on the borders," later in this chapter, to learn how to work with table borders.

## Aligning cell text vertically

You can also align your text vertically within a cell. This comes in handy if one cell is quite large (because it contains either a truckload of text or a relatively large image) and you'd like to adjust the vertical position of the other cells in the same row. To control the vertical alignment within a cell, you use the CSS `vertical-align` property:

```
selector {
    vertical-align: value;
}
```

Or, as an attribute:

```
style="vertical-align: value;"
```

For *value*, the `vertical-align` property supports quite a few predefined keywords, of which the following are the ones you need to know:

>> `bottom`: Aligns text with the bottom of the cell.

>> `middle`: Aligns text with the vertical center of the cell. This is the default vertical alignment.

>> `top`: Aligns the text with the top of the cell.

For example, if you want all your `td` elements to align with the top of their cells rather than in the middle, you add the following rule to your CSS:

```
td {
    vertical-align: top;
}
```

**Building Tables with Your Bare Hands**

Here's a larger example that demonstrates all three `vertical-align` values (bk02ch04/example08.html):

```
<table>
    <thead>
        <tr>
            <th>Idiom</th><th>Part of Speech</th><th>First
    Used</th><th>Definition</th>
        </tr>
    </thead>
    <tbody>
        <tr>
            <td style=" vertical-align: top;">
                goat cheese curtain
            </td>
            <td style=" vertical-align: middle;">
                noun
            </td>
            <td style=" vertical-align: bottom;">
                2012
            </td>
            <td style="text-align: justify; width: 200px;">
                An imaginary boundary that separates urban
                sophisticates from those with simple,
                traditional, or uncultured tastes.
            </td>
        </tr>
    </tbody>
</table>
```

As shown in Figure 4-9, the first column is top-aligned, the second column is middle-aligned, and the third column is bottom-aligned.

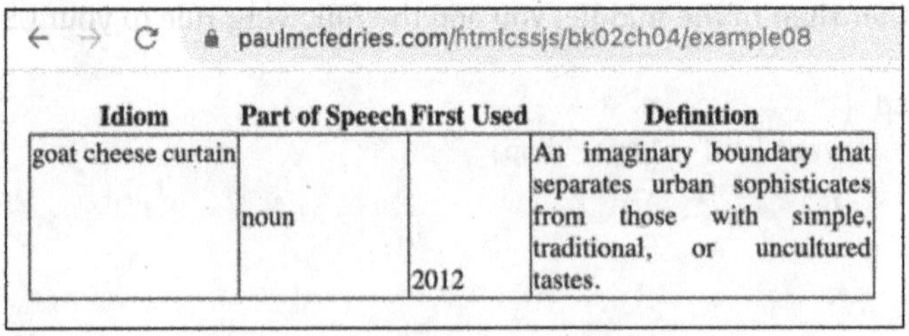

**FIGURE 4-9:**
A demo of the
`vertical-align`
values.

# Bring on the borders

By default, the web browser displays a table without any borders either around the table as a whole or between the rows and columns. That borderlessness isn't usually a deal-breaker because most tables have enough whitespace within the cells due to the different widths of the cell items.

However, if the table's items have a more or less uniform width within each column, the table can start to look awfully claustrophobic, as demonstrated in Figure 4-10 (bk02ch04/example09.html).

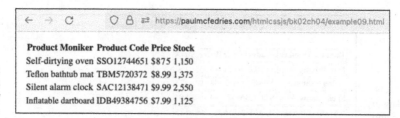

FIGURE 4-10:
Some tables
can look awfully
cramped.

One way to make such a table easier to read is to add borders both around the table itself and between each row and column. To build a border, you use CSS. Specifically, you can use the following simplified syntax for the border property:

```
selector {
    border: width style color;
}
```

Here, `selector` is the table element you want to style, and the border property takes the following values:

>> *width*: The thickness of the border, expressed in any CSS-friendly measurement unit (refer to Book 3, Chapter 5), such as px for pixels.

>> *style*: The type of border, which can be any of the following keywords: dotted, dashed, double, groove, ridge, inset, outset, or solid. I explain these keywords in Book 3, Chapter 1.

>> *color*: The color of the border, which can be any CSS color value, such as the keyword black. Refer to Book 3, Chapter 6 to get the full story on CSS colors.

REMEMBER

This simplified syntax for the border property will work for most of your table needs. If you want to get the full story on building big-time borders with CSS, tune in to Book 3, Chapter 1.

For example, to place a 1-pixel wide, solid, black border around a table's th and td elements, you add the following rule to your CSS (bk02ch04/example10.html):

```css
th, td {
    border: 1px solid black;
}
```

If you look carefully at the table shown in Figure 4-11, you'll notice a teeny-tiny gap between each row and column. Having that gap isn't awful, but I think you'll agree that it's not stunningly attractive, either. How do you get rid of it?

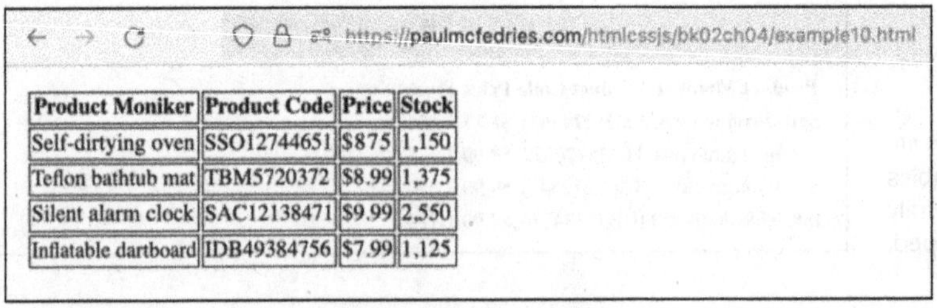

FIGURE 4-11:
Borders adding to the table's th and td elements.

The browser window shows the URL https://paulmcfedries.com/htmlcssjs/bk02ch04/example10.html and the following table:

| Product Moniker | Product Code | Price | Stock |
|---|---|---|---|
| Self-dirtying oven | SSO12744651 | $875 | 1,150 |
| Teflon bathtub mat | TBM5720372 | $8.99 | 1,375 |
| Silent alarm clock | SAC12138471 | $9.99 | 2,550 |
| Inflatable dartboard | IDB49384756 | $7.99 | 1,125 |

That gap comes from the *border spacing*, which is the space that the web browser adds between each row and column. You learn how to control the border spacing in the next section. You may think that you can solve the "gap problem" by setting the border spacing to zero. Yep, you can definitely do that, but it doesn't look good because all your inside borders become twice as thick. (The browser essentially just smooshes all the adjacent borders together.)

A better solution is to style the table element with the border-collapse CSS property and set it to collapse, like so:

```css
table {
    border-collapse: collapse;
}
```

As shown in Figure 4-12, those little gaps between the borders are now history (bk02ch04/example11.html).

| Product Moniker | Product Code | Price | Stock |
|---|---|---|---|
| Self-dirtying oven | SSO12744651 | $875 | 1,150 |
| Teflon bathtub mat | TBM5720372 | $8.99 | 1,375 |
| Silent alarm clock | SAC12138471 | $9.99 | 2,550 |
| Inflatable dartboard | IDB49384756 | $7.99 | 1,125 |

FIGURE 4-12:
No more
unsightly gaps
between the
borders!

## Putting your data in a padded cell

The table in Figure 4-12 is slightly easier to read (compared to the original table shown in Figure 4-9) thanks to the borders, but there's no denying that the table still looks uninvitingly cramped. That's because web browsers like to cram data into a cell as tightly as possible, so they leave next to no space between the contents of the cell and the cell border. This space is called the *cell padding*, and the good news is that you can control the amount of padding in your table cells with a bit of CSS magic.

To give your table data more room to breathe, use the following simplified syntax for the padding property:

```
selector {
    padding: value;
}
```

Here, *selector* is the table element you want to style, and *value* is the amount of the padding added around the cell text (above and below, and to the left and right), expressed in any CSS-approved measurement unit (refer to Book 3, Chapter 5), such as px for pixels.

REMEMBER

This simplified padding property syntax works just fine for most tables. To learn the full syntax for this property, head over to Book 3, Chapter 1.

For example, to pad a table's th and td elements with 5 pixels of space, you'd add the following rule to your CSS:

```
th, td {
    padding: 5px;
}
```

Figure 4-13 shows the updated table (bk02ch04/example12.html). Ah, that's better.

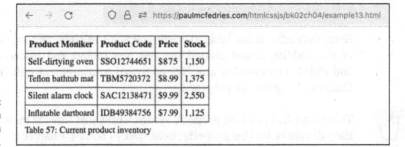

## Changing the location of the caption

If you adorn your table with a caption, then by default the web browser places the caption text above the table. If you prefer to have your table captions appear below the table instead, you can use the caption-side property to realize your goal:

```
caption {
    caption-side: bottom;
}
```

Figure 4-14 shows a table with a caption on the bottom (bk02ch04/example13. html).

IN THIS CHAPTER

» **Understanding web form basics**

» **Adding a button or two**

» **Inserting text boxes and text areas**

» **Adding checkboxes and radio buttons**

» **Working with lists and labels**

» **Putting a picker on your page**

# Chapter **5**

# Using Forms to Make a Page Interactive

*From humble beginnings, forms in HTML5 are now tremendously flexible and powerful, providing natively much of the functionality that we as developers have been adding in with JavaScript over the years.*

— PETER GASSTON

Publishing pages on the web is definitely an exhilarating experience. But after that initial excitement wears off, one post-publishing effect you may notice is that your pages just kind of sit there. True, sitting there isn't a terrible state for a page since the real point of publishing to the web is to put out info that other people want to read. In that case, having the page just sit there is a good thing.

Still, it would be nice if even some of your pages offered something more to the curious visitor. Instead of having people always just surf in, read your stuff for a while, and then surf out, wouldn't it be great if you also offered something that made them stick around a bit longer? What about coming up with some way to make your pages more interactive?

Ah, now you're talking, because HTML *does* offer a mechanism for turning a just-sitting-there web page into an interactive one: a web form. In this chapter, you explore all that web forms have to offer. After mastering the basics, you investigate the amazing features offered by HTML web forms, which can include not only standard knickknacks such as buttons, text boxes, and lists, but also more advanced controls for selecting things like dates and colors. It's a veritable forms smorgasbord, so get ready to tuck in!

# What Is a Web Form?

Most modern programs toss a dialog box in your face if they need to extract some information from you. For example, selecting a program's Print command most likely results in some kind of Print dialog box showing up. The purpose of this dialog box is to ask for info such as the number of copies you want, the pages you want to print, the printer you want to use, and so on.

A form is essentially the web page equivalent of a dialog box. It's a page section populated with text boxes, lists, checkboxes, command buttons, and other controls to get information from the user. For example, Figure 5-1 shows a form from my website. This is a form that people can use to send me a message. The form includes a text box for the person's name, another for their email address, a larger text area for the message, and a command button to send the data to my server.

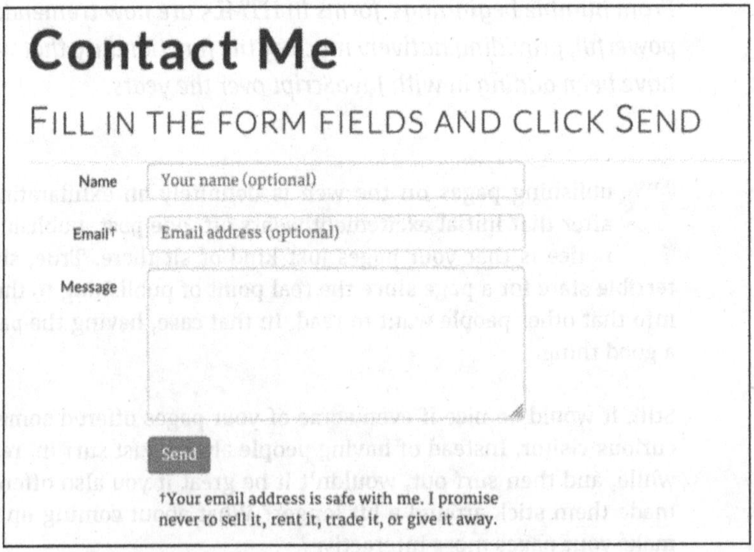

## Contact Me

FILL IN THE FORM FIELDS AND CLICK SEND

Name       Your name (optional)

Email†     Email address (optional)

Message

Send

†Your email address is safe with me. I promise
never to sell it, rent it, trade it, or give it away.

**FIGURE 5-1:**
A typical
web form.

A web form is a little data-gathering machine. What kinds of data can it gather? You name it:

>> Text, from a single word up to a long post

>> Numbers, dates, and times

>> Which item is (or items are) selected in a list

>> Whether a checkbox is selected

>> Which one of a group of radio buttons is selected

What happens to that data after you've gathered it? There are two roads the data can travel: Server Street and Local Lane.

## Cruising along Server Street

The Server Street route means that your web server gets in on the action. Here are the basic steps that occur:

1. The user clicks a button to submit the form.

2. Your JavaScript code gathers and readies the form data for sending.

3. The code sends the form data to a script on the server.

4. The server script extracts the form data.

5. The server script processes the form data in some way (say, by gathering info from a database).

6. The server script outputs either the requested data or some kind of code that indicates the result of the operation.

7. Your JavaScript code processes the data returned by the server and updates the web page accordingly.

If that all sounds intimidatingly complex, you're right: It is, and that's why it's well beyond the scope of this book.

**TIP**

If you're really interested in submitting form data to your server, I have another book that will tell you everything you need to know. It's called *Web Coding and Development All-in-One For Dummies* (Wiley).

## Taking a walk down Local Lane

The Local Lane route doesn't get the web server involved at all:

1. The user changes the form data in some way.

2. Your JavaScript code detects the changed data.

3. The JavaScript code associated with the changed form field updates the web page based on the changed data.

Ah, that's much simpler, isn't it? But what can you do with this more limited form processing? Lots of things, actually:

>> **Add filters:** If your page is really long, you can give your readers a form that enables them to filter the content.

>> **Hide and display content:** If your page contains lots of disclosure widgets (objects that, when clicked, display some hidden content; they're also called *accordions*), you can add buttons that display and hide all the hidden content at once.

>> **Customize the page:** You can offer a form that enables visitors to customize the look of the page in some way (say, by changing the colors or the font).

>> **Store user preferences:** You can use a form to elicit a visitor's personal information or preferences and store that data in the browser.

>> **Calculate something:** You can build a form that takes one or more inputs and then displays the result of a calculation (such as a mortgage payment or a conversion from an imperial unit to a metric unit).

>> **Enhance accessibility:** You can use a form that enables a visitor to activate certain accessibility features, such as high-contrast colors and a larger type size.

In this chapter, I stick to the slow pace of Local Lane and show you how to build forms that you can use locally. To learn how to handle form events, you need JavaScript, so I hold off on that until Book 4, Chapter 11.

# Building a Web Form

You build web forms with your bare hands using special HTML tags. The latest version of HTML — HTML5 — includes many new form goodies, most of which now have great browser support, so I show you both the oldie-but-goodie and the latest-and-greatest in the form world over the next few sections.

## Setting up the form

To get your form started, you wrap everything inside the `<form>` tag:

```
<form>
</form>
```

**REMEMBER**

Because you're using the form just to add local interaction to the web page and won't be submitting any form data to the server, technically you don't need the `<form>` tag at all. However, you should use one anyway most of the time because including the `<form>` tag enables the user to submit the form by pressing Enter or Return, and it also gets you a submit button (such as Go) in mobile browsers.

## Adding a form button

Most forms include a button that the user clicks when they've completed the form and wants to initiate the form's underlying action. This is known as *submitting* the form, and that term has traditionally meant sending the form data to a server-side script for processing. These days, however, and certainly in this book, "submitting" the form can also mean updating something on the web page without sending anything to the server. For example, clicking a button may set the page's background color.

The old style of submitting a form is to use an `<input>` tag where the `type` attribute is set to `submit`:

```
<input type="submit" value="buttonText">
```

The *buttonText* here is a placeholder for the text that appears on the button face.

For example:

```
<input type="submit" value="Submit Me!">
```

This style is rarely used in modern web development because it's a bit tricky to style such a button. For that reason, most web developers use the `<button>` tag, instead:

```
<button type="submit">buttonText</button>
```

The *buttonText* here again stands in for the text that appears on the button face.

For example:

```
<button type="submit">Ship It</button>
```

**TIP**

For better-looking buttons, use CSS to style the following:

>> **Rounded corners:** To control the roundness of the button corners, use the border-radius property set to either a measurement (in, say, pixels) or a percentage. For example:

```
button {
    border-radius: 15px;
}
```

>> **Drop shadow:** To add a drop shadow to a button, apply the box-shadow: *x y blur color* property, where *x* is the horizontal offset of the shadow, *y* is the vertical offset of the shadow, *blur* is the amount the shadow is blurred, and *color* is the shadow color. For example:

```
button {
    box-shadow: 3px 3px 5px grey;
}
```

## Working with text fields

Text-based fields are the most commonly used form elements, and most of them use the ‹input› tag:

```
<input type="textType" name="textName" value="textValue" placeho
lder="textPrompt">
```

>> *textType:* The kind of text field you want to use in your form.

>> *textName:* The name you assign to the field.

>> *textValue:* The initial value of the field, if any.

>> *textPrompt:* Text that appears temporarily in the field when the page first loads and is used to prompt the user about the required input. The place-holder text disappears as soon as the user starts typing in the field.

Here's a list of the available text-based types you can use for the type attribute:

>> text: Displays a text box into which the user types a line of text. Add the size attribute to specify the width of the field, in characters (the default is 20). Here's an example:

```
<input type="text" name="company" size="50">
```

» number: Displays a text box into which the user types a numeric value. Most browsers add a spin box that enables the user to increment or decrement the number by clicking the up or down arrow, respectively. Check out this example:

```
<input type="number" name="points" value="100">
```

I should also mention the range type, which displays a slider control that enables the user to click and drag to choose a numeric value between a specified minimum and maximum:

```
<input type="range" name="transparency" min="0" max="100"
    value="100">
```

» email: Displays a text box into which the user types an email address. Add the multiple attribute to allow the user to type two or more addresses, separated by commas. Add the size attribute to specify the width of the field, in characters. An example for you:

```
<input type="email" name="user-email" placeholder="you@
    yourdomain.com">
```

» url: Displays a text box into which the user types a URL. Add the size attribute to specify the width of the field, in characters. Here's a for instance:

```
<input type="url" name="homepage" placeholder="e.g.,
    http://domain.com/">
```

» tel: Displays a text box into which the user types a telephone number. Use the size attribute to specify the width of the field, in characters. Here's an example:

```
<input type="tel" name="mobile" placeholder="(xxx)
    xxx-xxxx">
```

» time: Displays a text box into which the user types a time, usually hours and minutes. For example:

```
<input type="time" name="start-time">
```

» password: Displays a text box into which the user types a password. The typed characters appear as dots ( · ). Add the autocomplete attribute to specify whether the user's browser or password management software can automatically enter the password. Set the attribute to current-password to allow password autocompletion, or to off to disallow autocompletion. Need an example? ·Done:

```
<input type="password" name="userpassword"
    autocomplete="current-password">
```

» search: Displays a text box into which the user types a search term. Add the size attribute to specify the width of the field, in characters. Why, yes, I do have an example:

```
<input type="search" name="q" placeholder="Type a search
    term">
```

» hidden: Adds an input field to the form, but doesn't display the field to the user. That sounds weird, I know, but it's a handy way to store a value that you want to include in the submit, but you don't want the user to notice or modify. Here's an example:

```
<input id="userSession" name="user-session" type="hidden"
    value="jwr274">
```

**REMEMBER**

Some older browsers don't get special text fields such as email and time, but you can still use them in your pages because those clueless browsers will ignore the type attribute and just display a standard text field.

That was a lot of text-related fields, but you're not done yet! There are two others you need to know about:

» <textarea>: This tag displays a text box into which the user can type multiple lines of text. Add the rows attribute to specify how many lines of text are displayed. If you want default text to appear in the text box, add the text between the <textarea> and </textarea> tags. Here's an example:

```
<textarea name="message" rows="5">
Default text goes here.
</textarea>
```

» <label>: Associates a label with a form field. There are two ways to use a label:

Method #1 — Surround the form field with <label> and </label> tags, and insert the label text before or after the field, like so:

```
<label>
Email:
<input type="email" name="user-email" placeholder="you@
    yourdomain.com">
</label>
```

Method #2 — Add an `id` value to the field's tag, set the `<label>` tag's for attribute to the same value, and insert the label text between the `<label>` and `</label>` tags, as I've done here:

```
<label for="useremail">Email:</label>
<input id="useremail" type="email" name="user-email"
    placeholder="you@yourdomain.com">
```

Figure 5-2 demonstrates each of these text fields (for the code, check out bk02ch05/example01.html in this book's example files).

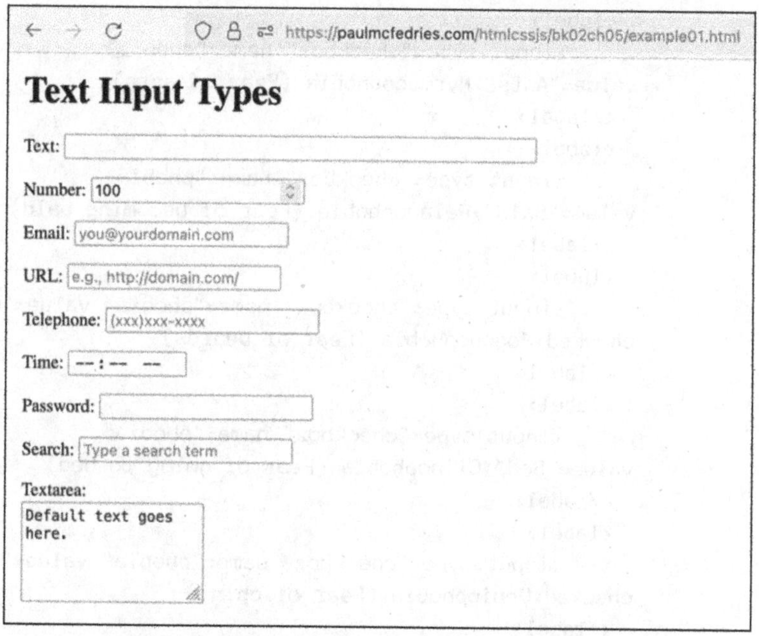

**FIGURE 5-2:** The various text input types you can use in your forms.

# Adding checkboxes

You use a checkbox in a web form to toggle a setting on (that is, the checkbox is selected) and off (the checkbox is deselected). You create a checkbox by including in your form the following version of the `<input>` tag:

```
<input type="checkbox" name="checkName" value="checkValue"
    [checked]>
```

» *checkName:* The name you want to assign to the checkbox.

» *checkValue:* The value you want to assign to the checkbox.

» checked: When this optional attribute is present, the checkbox is initially selected.

Here's an example (check out bk02ch05/example02.html):

```
<fieldset>
    <legend>
        What's your phobia? (Please check all that apply):
    </legend>
    <label>
        <input type="checkbox" name="phobia"
value="Ants">Myrmecophobia (Fear of ants)
    </label>
    <label>
        <input type="checkbox" name="phobia"
value="Bald">Peladophobia (Fear of becoming bald)
    </label>
    <label>
        <input type="checkbox" name="phobia" value="Beards"
checked>Pogonophobia (Fear of beards)
    </label>
    <label>
        <input type="checkbox" name="phobia"
value="Bed">Clinophobia (Fear of going to bed)
    </label>
    <label>
        <input type="checkbox" name="phobia" value="Chins"
checked>Geniophobia (Fear of chins)
    </label>
    <label>
        <input type="checkbox" name="phobia"
value="Flowers">Anthophobia (Fear of flowers)
    </label>
    <label>
        <input type="checkbox" name="phobia"
value="Flying">Aviatophobia (Fear of flying)
    </label>
    <label>
        <input type="checkbox" name="phobia"
value="Purple">Porphyrophobia (Fear of purple)
    </label>
```

```
     <label>
          <input type="checkbox" name="phobia" value="Teeth"
     checked>Odontophobia (Fear of teeth)
     </label>
     <label>
          <input type="checkbox" name="phobia"
     value="Thinking">Phronemophobia (Fear of thinking)
     </label>
     <label>
          <input type="checkbox" name="phobia" value="Vegetables">
     Lachanophobia (Fear of vegetables)
     </label>
     <label>
          <input type="checkbox" name="phobia" value="Fear"
     checked>Phobophobia (Fear of fear)
     </label>
     <label>
          <input type="checkbox" name="phobia"
     value="Everything">Pantophobia (Fear of everything)
     </label>
</fieldset>
```

Some notes about this code:

>> You use the `<fieldset>` tag to group a collection of related form
fields together.

>> You use the `<legend>` tag to create a caption for the parent `fieldset`
element. Figure 5-3 shows how this looks in the browser.

>> Because the `<input>` tags are wrapped in their respective `<label>` tags, the
user can select or deselect each checkbox by clicking the checkbox itself or by
clicking its label.

>> To get each checkbox on its own line, I added the declaration `display:`
`block` to the CSS for the `label` element. Check out Book 3, Chapter 1 to learn
how the `display` property works.

## Working with radio buttons

If you want to offer your users a collection of related options, only one of which
can be selected at a time, then radio buttons (sometimes called option buttons) are
the way to go. Form radio buttons congregate in groups of two or more, and only
one button in the group can be selected at any time. If the user clicks another button in that group, it becomes selected and the previously selected button becomes
deselected.

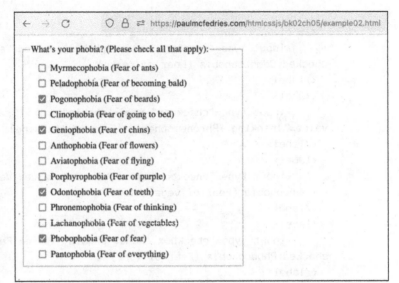

FIGURE 5-3:
Some checkbox
form fields,
wrapped in a
fieldset group
with a legend
element.

You create a radio button using the following variation of the `<input>` tag:

```
<input type="radio" name="radioGroup" value="radioValue"
  [checked]>
```

➤ *radioGroup:* The name you want to assign to the group of radio buttons. All the radio buttons that use the same name value belong to that group.

➤ *radioValue:* The value you want to assign to the radio button. If this radio button is selected when the form is submitted, this is the value that is sent.

➤ checked: When this optional attribute is present, the radio button is initially selected.

Here's an example, and Figure 5-4 shows what happens (bk02ch05/example03. html):

```
<fieldset>
    <legend>
        Select a delivery method
    </legend>
    <div>
        <input type="radio" id="carrier-pigeon" name="delivery"
value="pigeon" checked>
        <label for="carrier-pigeon">Carrier pigeon</label>
    </div>
    <div>
```

```
        <input type="radio" id="pony-express" name="delivery"
value="pony">
        <label for="pony-express">Pony express</label>
   </div>
   <div>
        <input type="radio" id="snail-mail" name="delivery"
value="postal">
        <label for="snail-mail">Snail mail</label>
   </div>
   <div>
        <input type="radio" id="some-punk" name="delivery"
value="bikecourier">
        <label for="some-punk">Some punk on a bike</label>
   </div>
</fieldset>
```

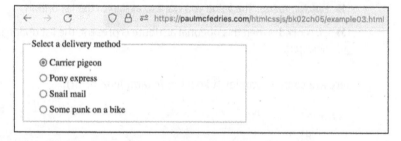

**FIGURE 5-4:**
Some radio
button form
fields.

## Adding selection lists

Selection lists are common sights in HTML forms because they enable the web developer to display a relatively large number of choices in a compact control that most users know how to operate. When deciding between a checkbox, radio button group, or selection list, here are some rough guidelines to follow:

>> If an option or setting has only two values that can be represented by on and off, use a checkbox.

>> If the option or setting has three or four values, use a group of three or four radio buttons.

>> If the option or setting has five or more values, use a selection list.

This section shows you how to create selection lists. As you work through this part, it'll help to remember that a selection list is really an amalgam of two types of fields: the list container and the options within that container. The former is a select element and the latter is a collection of option elements.

To create the list container, you use the `<select>` tag:

```
<select name="selectName" size="selectSize" [multiple]>
```

> » *selectName*: The name you want to assign to the selection list.

> » *selectSize*: The optional number of rows in the selection list box that are visible. If you omit this value, the browser displays the list as a drop-down box.

> » multiple: When this optional attribute is present, the user is allowed to select multiple options in the list.

For each item in the list, you add an `<option>` tag between the `<select>` and `</select>` tags:

```
<option value="optionValue" [selected]>
```

> » *optionValue*: The value you want to assign to the list option.

> » selected: When this optional attribute is present, the list option is initially selected.

Here are some examples (bk02ch05/example04.html):

```
<form>
    <div>
        <label for="hair-color">Select your hair color:
    </label><br>
        <select id="hair-color" name="hair-color">
            <option value="black">Black</option>
            <option value="blonde">Blonde</option>
            <option value="brunette" selected>Brunette</option>
            <option value="red">Red</option>
            <option value="neon">Something neon</option>
            <option value="none">None</option>
        </select>
    </div>
    <div>
        <label for="hair-style">Select your hair style:
    </label><br>
        <select id="hair-style" name="hair-style" size="4">
            <option value="bouffant">Bouffant</option>
            <option value="mohawk">Mohawk</option>
            <option value="page-boy">Page Boy</option>
            <option value="permed">Permed</option>
            <option value="shag">Shag</option>
```

```
        <option value="straight" selected>Straight</option>
        <option value="none">Style? What style?</option>
    </select>
  </div>
  <div>
      <label for="hair-products">Hair products used in the
last year:</label><br>
      <select id="hair-products" name="hair-products" size="5"
multiple>
        <option value="gel">Gel</option>
        <option value="grecian-formula">Grecian Formula
</option>
        <option value="mousse">Mousse</option>
        <option value="peroxide">Peroxide</option>
        <option value="shoe-black">Shoe black</option>
    </select>
  </div>
</form>
```

There are three lists here (refer to Figure 5-5):

» hair-color: This list doesn't specify a size, so the browser displays it as a drop-down list.

» hair-style: This list uses a size value of 4, so four options are visible in the list.

» hair-products: This list uses a size value of 5, so five options are visible in the list. Also, the multiple attribute is set, so you can select multiple options in the list.

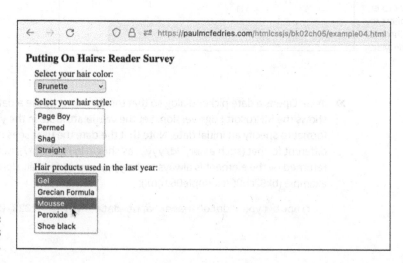

**FIGURE 5-5:**
Some examples
of selection lists.

# Bringing in pickers

HTML also offers a number of other `<input>` tag types that fall under a category I call "pickers," meaning that in each case the field displays a button that, when clicked, opens a control that enables the user to pick a value. Here's a quick look at the available pickers:

» `color`: Opens a color picker dialog that enables the user to choose a color. The color picker varies depending on the browser and operating system; Figure 5-6 shows the Google Chrome for the Mac version. Set the `value` attribute in the `#rrggbb` format to specify an initial color (the default is black: `#000000`). Here's an example (bk02ch05/example05.html):

```
<input type="color" name="bg-color" value="#4f5392">
```

» If the text `#rrggbb` is meaningless to you, not to worry: I explain it in satisfying detail in Book 3, Chapter 6.

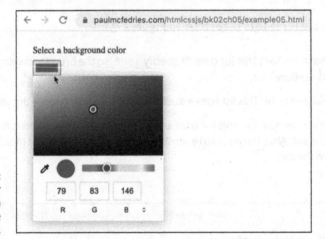

**FIGURE 5-6:** The color picker that appears in Google Chrome for the Mac.

» `date`: Opens a date picker dialog so that the user can choose a date. Figure 5-7 shows the Microsoft Edge version. Set the `value` attribute in the `yyyy-mm-dd` format to specify an initial date. Note that the date the user sees may use a different format (such as `mm/dd/yyyy`, as shown in Figure 5-7), but the value returned by the element is always in the `yyyy-mm-dd` format. Here's an example (bk02ch05/example06.html):

```
<input type="date" name="appt-date" value="2023-08-23">
```

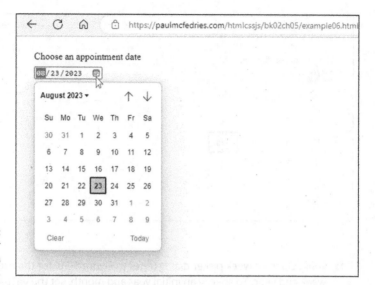

**FIGURE 5-7:**
The date picker
that appears in
Microsoft Edge.

>> `file`: Displays a Choose File button (refer to Figure 5-8) that, when clicked, opens the user's operating system's file picker dialog so that the user can select a file. You can add the `multiple` attribute to enable the user to select more than one file. Here's an example (bk02ch05/example07.html):

```
<input type="file" name="user-photo">
```

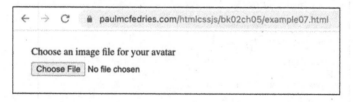

**FIGURE 5-8:**
The date picker
that appears in
Chrome.

>> `month`: Opens a month picker dialog (refer to Figure 5-9) to enable the user to choose a month and year. Set the `value` attribute in the yyyy–mm format to specify an initial month and year. The value the user sees may be in a different format (such as August 2023), but the value returned by the element is always in the yyyy–mm format. Here's an example (bk02ch05/example08.html):

```
<input type="month" name="birthday-month" value="2023-08">
```

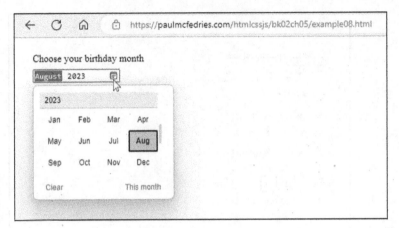

**FIGURE 5-9:**
The month picker
that appears in
Microsoft Edge.

» **week:** Opens a week picker dialog (refer to Figure 5-10) for the user to select a
week and year. To specify an initial year and month, set the `value` attribute
in the yyyy–W*nn* format, where *nn* is the two-digit week number. The value
shown to the user may be in another format (such as Week 34, 2023), but
the value returned by the element is always in the yyyy–W*nn* format. Here's an
example (bk02ch05/example09.html):

```
<input type="week" name="vacation-week" value="2023-W34">
```

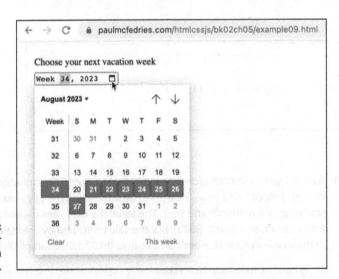

**FIGURE 5-10:**
The week picker
that appears in
Chrome.

# Chapter 6

# Making Your Web Pages Accessible

*The power of the Web is in its universality. Access by everyone regardless of disability is an essential aspect.*

— TIM BERNERS-LEE (INVENTOR OF THE WORLD WIDE WEB)

I f you're lucky enough to have good eyesight, adequate hearing, decent motor skills, and a brain that does its job well (most of the time, anyway), it's easy to fall into the trap that *everyone* who visits your website will have had the same luck in life. Falling into that trap means you'll build your site thinking that if it looks good and works well for you, it will also look good and work well for all your visitors.

In this chapter, I hope to convince you that no matter how good a hand you've drawn in life, it's thoughtful, ethical, and smart to remember that there are lots of people — I'm talking a *billion* people worldwide — who've been given tougher cards to play in the form of some kind of significant disability. In this chapter, I hope to convince you that your web pages, no matter how simple, are simply not done until you've made them accessible to everyone, regardless of their abilities. In this chapter, I hope to convince you that configuring your pages to make them accessible to every visitor is not only the right thing to do but also an easy thing to do.

# Why to Make Your Pages Accessible

If you were opening a brick-and-mortar retail operation, it's very unlikely you'd design your storefront with barbed wire blocking the door! Sure, certain agile or freakishly long-legged people might still be able to enter your store by leaping or stepping over the barbed wire, but why on earth would you design things to prevent everyone else from entering? You wouldn't, of course, because that level of inaccessibility is obviously counter-productive and, well, silly.

When you design a web page that looks good and works well only for people with able eyes and ears and sufficient control over their limbs and mind, you're essentially blocking access to your page with the digital equivalent of barbed wire.

## Accessibility is a right

The United Nations Convention on the Rights of Persons with Disabilities requires stakeholders to take measures to "promote access for persons with disabilities to new information and communications technologies and systems, including the Internet." In other words, access to the web is nothing less than a *fundamental human right*.

When planning a web page, the thoughtful developer remains aware at all times that the people who visit and use the page come with different abilities. When planning a web page, the ethical developer understands that even though every person is different, they all have an equal right to use the page. When you give everyone equal access to your web page, you're making your page *accessible*.

Accessibility, then, is not only a right, but it's also the right thing to do.

**REMEMBER**

In online discussions and essays, accessibility is often shortened to *a11y*: that is, the letter *a*, followed by the number *11*, and then the letter *y*. Why 11? Because that's how many letters there are between the *a* and *y* in *accessibility*. Also, *a11y* looks like the word *ally*, which underlines the idea that anyone who implements accessibility features is an ally to the people with disabilities.

## Accessibility brings other benefits

That it's morally and ethically correct to make your web pages accessible to all comers is, I'm sure, all the incentive you need. However, making your pages accessible does bring other benefits.

For example, a page built with accessibility in mind is also a search-engine-friendly page, meaning that your accessible page will rank higher in search results than a similar, nonaccessible page.

An accessible page also provides benefits for non-disabled groups, such as people who surf with images turned off or who have to deal with extremely slow internet speeds.

Finally, it's easy to make a business case for going accessible:

>> **Accessibility gives you instant access to a big market:** According to the World Health Organization, about 1.3 billion people have some form of significant disability, and it's estimated that those billion-plus people wield a spending power in excess of six trillion dollars. That's a lot of zeroes! If you want to sell things on your site, why exclude such a huge chunk of the market?

>> **Accessibility may also be the legally required thing to do:** In many jurisdictions, it's now illegal for commercial websites to be inaccessible. Most countries have policies in place that require businesses to offer equal access to all. If your business website has global reach, failing to make the site accessible subjects your company to huge legal risk.

>> **Accessibility makes you look good:** Making your business pages accessible to all creates goodwill, puts a shine on your brand, and makes you part of the solution, not part of the problem.

**REMEMBER**

Whatever motivates you to make your pages accessible is awesome. However, it's important to remember that making your website one hundred percent accessible to one hundred percent of your visitors, while perhaps a noble and worthy goal, is, practically speaking, pretty much impossible, as upcoming pages explain.

# Understanding Web Accessibility

Isn't it a burden to have to add features to your pages to make them accessible? Nope, not even close. As long as you build your pages with equal access in mind from the get-go, incorporating accessible features takes very little effort on your part.

As you see later in this chapter, web accessibility isn't hard or onerous to implement. Or, I should say, it's not hard or onerous to implement *if* you understand who requires accessible features and why they require them, and what types of assistive technologies are used by people with disabilities. The next couple of sections tell you everything you need to know.

## Understanding who needs accessibility

One of the main complaints about web innovation these days is that web developers are building apps and services that solve only the developers' own problems. Food-delivery, groceries-to-your-door, and pet-sitting services are just a few of the many examples. The problem here is thinking that if I have a problem that needs solved, everybody else in the world must also want that problem solved. More broadly, these apps are examples of a web developer assuming that everyone who uses a site is basically just like the developer.

**REMEMBER**

### ACCESSIBILITY ISN'T ONLY ABOUT THE DISABLED

Although the focus of your accessibility efforts should be on accommodating disabled users as best you can, it's important to remember that your accessibility tweaks also help a wide range of other users, including the following:

- Users who surf the web using nonstandard devices, such as smart TVs, smart watches, and game consoles. These devices often either lack mouse support altogether or offer only a rudimentary capability to move and click a pointer. So, in that sense, users of these devices have many of the same challenges as people with motor disabilities.

- Users with slow internet connections, restrictive bandwidth caps, or low-power computers may surf the web with images turned off, which makes sites load faster and uses less bandwidth. So, these users are similar to people with visual impairments in that they rely on your descriptions of your page images.

- Users who surf the web using mobile devices such as smartphones and tablets usually don't have access to a mouse. Therefore, site features that rely on, say, hovering a mouse pointer over a page object won't work for those users, which makes them similar to people who don't have the ability to use a mouse.

With these users in mind, you can see that "accessibility" can be defined in the broadest sense as making your website functional for as many people as possible.

To really *get* accessibility, the first step is to understand deeply one simple fact:

*Your users are not you.*

In particular, an alarmingly high portion (estimates range from 5 to 20 percent) of the people who visit your site will live with some form of disability to a varying degree.

What types of disability am I talking about? Planning for accessibility means taking the following conditions into account:

>> **Visual:** Includes full or partial blindness, color-blindness, and reduced vision.

>> **Auditory:** Includes full or partial deafness, difficulty hearing, the inability to hear sounds at certain frequencies, and tinnitus.

>> **Motor:** Includes the inability to use a pointing device such as a mouse, restricted movement, lack of fine motor control, excessive trembling or shaking, and slow reflexes or response times.

>> **Cognitive:** Includes learning disabilities, focusing problems, impaired memory, and extreme distractibility.

In each case, the disability may have been something present at birth, or it could have come about through disease or trauma. However, it's also important to remember that one or more of these disabilities may be the result of simply getting older. Folks who are no longer spring chickens (or even summer chickens, for that matter) could have reduced visual acuity, partial or complete deafness, reduced motor control, and mild to significant cognitive impairment. And because our populations (with just a few exceptions) are rapidly getting older, the number of people surfing the web with some form of disability is only going to grow.

## Learning about assistive technologies for web surfing

It's one thing to know that many people who visit your pages will have a disability of one kind or another. However, that knowledge doesn't do you much good unless you also know how that disability changes the web experience for those people. How does a person with limited eyesight "read" a web page? How does someone who can't control a mouse "click" a link?

The answer to these and similar questions is that most people with disabilities use some form of software or hardware tool to help them surf to, read, navigate, and interact with a web page. These tools fall under the rubric of *assistive technology* (AT), and knowing the tools that disabled users turn to is crucial in helping you design your web pages to be accessible.

## Assistive technologies for visual disabilities

People with limited eyesight use a variety of AT to make screen elements easier to see:

>> **Screen magnifier:** A hardware device or software utility that magnifies a portion of the screen. Windows offers the Magnifier program; macOS has the Zoom feature.

>> **The web browser's Zoom feature:** All the major web browsers offer a Zoom command that magnifies the entire page.

>> **Custom browser text size:** All major browsers enable users to set a custom text size.

For users who are blind or nearly blind, a screen reader is the AT of choice. A *screen reader* is a software program that reads aloud whatever text appears on a web page, including the following:

>> Headings

>> Page text

>> Link text

>> Descriptions of images and other media

There are third-party screen readers available, but all operating systems have built-in screen readers, including Narrator for Windows and VoiceOver for macOS. Having free access to the powerful screen reader in your operating system is great news because it means you can crank it up and try surfing the web with it to get a feel for how it works.

## Assistive technologies for auditory disabilities

People with poor hearing often use special headphones or hearing aids to boost sound input. For people who are deaf or nearly deaf, however, you can make a couple of accommodations:

>> If your page has video content, the video should include the capability to turn on captions.

>> If your page has audio content, you should provide a link to a transcript of the audio.

### Assistive technologies for motor disabilities

Some people with profound motor disabilities can surf the web (or use any computer function) only with a head-pointer device. However, for most people with a motor disability, the major problem is that they lack sufficient control to operate a mouse or trackpad. Instead, they rely on the keyboard to interact with web pages, so your pages need to be navigable via keyboard input. See "Making Your Pages Keyboard-Friendly," later in this chapter.

### Assistive technologies for cognitive disabilities

Some people with certain types of cognitive impairment use software tools to help them focus on the task at hand. You can also set up your web pages to help people focus and to avoid unnecessary confusion:

>> Don't add bling to your pages just for the sake of being flashy. Keep your page design as simple as possible.

>> Keep your navigation and layout consistent across all your pages.

>> Provide clear and simple instructions for tasks such as filling out forms.

>> Wherever possible, stick to web conventions such as underlined link text.

# Making Your Page Structure Accessible

By far the easiest way to get a big jump on making your web pages accessible is by baking accessibility into the HTML structure itself. Does this mean jumping through a bunch of new hoops and learning a bunch of new tags and attributes? Nope. Quite the opposite: It really means using headings and semantic sectioning elements just the way I talk about using them earlier in this book (see Book 2, Chapter 1).

## Using headings hierarchically

Users of screen readers often get a feel for a page by navigating through its headings. To assist such users, you should first ensure that your headings make sense when read aloud and accurately describe the contents of the section to follow. You should also use headings in a way that honors their built-in hierarchy:

>> **Use only one h1 element per page:** That h1 element should be the page title.

>> **Use h2 for headings:** For all the main headings on your page, use the h2 element.

» **Use h3 for subheadings, and so on:** Inside each h2 element, the main subheadings should be h3 elements. Similarly, within an h3 the main sub-subheadings should be h4 elements; within an h4 the main sub-sub-subheadings should be h5 elements, and within an h5 the main sub-sub-sub-subheadings should be h6 elements.

» **Don't skip headings:** Don't go, say, from an h2 to an h4 just because you feel like it or prefer the look of the text (see the next item).

» **Don't use headings for decorative purposes:** Don't use a heading just because you need something bold or because you like the size of that heading's text. That's what CSS is for.

## Using semantic sectioning elements

You certainly could build your page with nothing but styled div elements (and an alarming number of web coders do exactly that!), but the result is not only messy and unstructured, but it's also an accessibility nightmare. Why? Because a screen reader or other assistive tech has nothing to grab onto, so to speak. Sure, it will still speak (or whatever) the page content, but there will be no context.

Fortunately, it doesn't take you any longer to build your page using the semantic sectioning elements — such as header, nav, main, article, and footer — that I talk about in Book 2 Chapter 1. This approach not only provides welcome structure to the page layout, it also gives you accessibility for free because these so-called *landmarks* help assistive tech make sense of the page and screen readers will include the underlying semantic meaning as part of the readout.

For example, when a screen reader comes across a nav element, it will usually say "navigation," and when it comes across a header element, it will usually say "banner."

# Making Text Accessible

Almost all web pages are mostly text, so if you can make your text accessible, then you've gone a long way towards making your page accessible. Here are a few pointers to bear in mind:

» **Don't use absolute measurement units for text sizes:** One of the first things someone with difficulty seeing may do before surfing the web is customize their browser with larger default text size. If you then style your text with an absolute measurement unit such as pixels, you override that larger default size. You have suddenly become extremely unpopular with that person and with everyone else who has taken the trouble to adjust their browser's text. Accessible text starts with text sizes that use a relative measurement unit, such as em or rem. (Confused by all this? Don't worry: I go into CSS measurement units in just-this-side-of-excruciating detail in Book 3, Chapter 5.)

>> **Make sure the text is readable:** Don't make your text ridiculously small and make sure to provide sufficient contrast between the text color and the back-ground color (see "Ensuring Sufficient Color Contrast," later in this chapter).

>> **Make link text descriptive.** For each link on your page, the link text should describe what lies on the other side of the link. Screen readers speak link text aloud, so if your link just says "Click" or "Click here," you're not telling your visitor anything useful about where the link goes.

Do this:

```
<a href="kumquats.html">Learn more about kumquats</a>
```

Don't do this:

```
To learn more about kumquats, <a href="kumquats.html">click
    here</a>
```

>> **Don't hide text if you don't have to:** It's possible to use CSS or JavaScript to temporarily hide text that doesn't need to be displayed at the moment. For example, you can create tabs where the content of one tab is visible and the content of the other tabs is not. The standard way of making some text not visible is to hide it, but that plays havoc with screen readers, which don't see the hidden text. So, if you can help it, never hide your page text.

# Making Media Accessible

Web page text is inherently accessibility-friendly because screen readers speak it aloud by default and with a bit of care on your part you can make your text easier to read for people with less than perfect eyesight. Unfortunately, that friendliness doesn't apply to web page media, including images, videos, and audio snippets. These elements are harder to make accessible, but you can still do plenty to make sure that all your visitors can enjoy your page media elements.

# Specifying alt text for images

To help visually impaired users or users who are surfing with images turned off, you can use the `<img>` tag's `alt` attribute to provide a description for each significant image on your page. For the visually impaired, a screen reader reads aloud the value of every `<img>` tag's `alt` attribute, so important or structural images should include a brief description as the `alt` value:

```
<img src="twitter.png" alt="Icon for link to Twitter">
```

Here are some notes on writing useful `alt` text:

» Keep it short. Longwinded descriptions are rarely needed or useful.

» Say directly what the image represents.

» Include meaningful details from the image. Here, *meaningful* means relevant to the context of the page or surrounding text.

» Don't repeat any info that's already in the surrounding text.

» You don't need to add an `alt` value for purely decorative images, but you must include the `alt` tag (set to an empty string: `alt=""`) or your HTML code won't validate.

# Making other media accessible

Compared to images, video and audio content take a bit more work to make them accessible, which essentially means doing one of the following:

» **Audio content:** Users with auditory impairments can't hear content delivered via the `audio` element. You can support these users by making a transcript of the audio available.

» **Video content:** Users with visual impairments can't see content delivered via the `video` element, whereas users with auditory impairments can't hear the `video` element's audio track. For the latter, a transcript of the video's audio track should be made available. For the former, your video should have closed captions or subtitles that appear while the video is playing.

One way of making captions or subtitles appear while a video is playing is to create a Web Video Text Tracks (WebVTT) file, which is a text file that contains time cues and text to display during those cues.

**TIP**

The building of a WebVTT text file is straightforward, but it's beyond the scope of this book. Fortunately, there's an excellent description of the format on the Mozilla Developer Network: `https://developer.mozilla.org/en-US/docs/Web/API/WebVTT_API`

After you have your WebVTT file (which uses the `.vtt` extension), you then use the `track` element to let the browser know the file is available for a `video` element:

```
<track kind="type" src="filename">
```

>> kind: Specifies the type of track. For *value*, you can use any of the following keywords: `subtitles` (this is the default), `captions`, `descriptions` (descriptions of the video content), or `chapters` (chapter titles only).

>> src: The filename (and path, if the file resides in a directory other than the one that stores the HTML file) of the WebVTT file.

You insert the `<track>` tag between the `<video>` and `</video>` tags, like so:

```
<video
    src="/media/videos/kumquats.mp4"
    controls
    <track
        kind="captions"
        src="/media/cc/kumquats-captions.vtt">
</video>
```

# Buffing Up Your Page Accessibility Semantics

Whenever you're wearing your "Accessibility" hat, one of the key questions you need to ask yourself for each element on your page is, "What might an assistive technology need to know about this element?" That is, what information do you need to provide so that a screen reader or similar AT can determine the purpose of the element?

In other words, you want to make the *meaning* of each element clear, and the info you provide about the meaning of each element is referred to as *accessibility semantics*. Over the next few sections, I talk about a few ways that you can enhance the accessibility semantics of your pages.

## Adding form field labels

In Book 2, Chapter 5, I talk about the `label` element, which you can use to associate a text label or caption with a form field. There are two methods you can use:

» **Implicit label:** Surround the form field with `<label>` and `</label>` tags, and insert the label text either before or after the field. Here's an example:

```
<label>
    Favorite vegetable:
    <input type="text">
</label>
```

» **Explicit label:** Insert an `id` value into the field tag, set the `<label>` tag's `for` attribute to the same value, and insert the label text between the `<label>` and `</label>` tags. Here's a for instance:

```
<label for="fave-veg">Favorite vegetable:</label>
<input id="fave-veg" type="text">
```

Adding the `<label>` tag provides two accessibility wins:

» It enables the user to select the field by also clicking the label. This increases the target area for clicking, which helps users with unsteady hands.

» The label text is now associated with the field, which means a screen reader will read out the label text when the user selects the field.

Be sure to add a label for every `<input>` tag, as well as each `<select>` and `<textarea>` tag.

## Understanding ARIA roles, states, and properties

The World Wide Web Consortium is home to the Web Accessibility Initiative (WAI), which aims to make the web an accessible place for everyone. One of the key WAI technologies is Accessible Rich Internet Applications (ARIA), which is a collection of roles, states, and properties that are designed to bring accessibility semantics to every element of your web page's user interface:

>> **ARIA role:** A keyword that defines what type of user interface control a page element represents. For example, if you've coded a `div` element to look and work like a command button, that element's role is `button`. You assign a role to an element using the `role` attribute, like so:

```
<div role="button">Apply Changes</div>
```

>> **ARIA property:** A value that describes some aspect of the user interface control. For example, if you want to include placeholder text in an editable `div` element, you can let assistive technologies know about the placeholder by adding the `aria-placeholder` attribute:

```
<div
    contenteditable
    role="textbox"
    aria-placeholder="user@domain.com">
</div>
```

>> **ARIA state:** A keyboard or value that specifies the current condition of the user interface control. For example, if your web application uses a `div` element as an on/off switch, but that element is currently disabled, you can signal that disabled state to assistive technologies by setting the `aria-disabled` attribute to true:

```
<div role="switch" aria-disabled="true"></div>
```

There are three main categories of ARIA roles:

>> Landmark roles

>> Section structure roles

>> Widget roles

**REMEMBER**

I talk about the roles in each of these categories in the next few sections. However, it's important to understand that you don't need to use ARIA roles if you use semantic HTML elements because those elements have implicit roles that are understood by assistive technologies. For example, the `button` element has an implicit `button` role, so no need to include `role="button"` in the `<button>` tag. See `https://developer.mozilla.org/en-US/docs/Web/Accessibility/ARIA/Roles/` for a satisfyingly complete look at the ARIA roles.

## Landmark ARIA roles

*Landmark* ARIA roles identify major structural elements of the page and assistive technologies use these landmarks to enable the user to navigate quickly through the major sections of a page. Table 6-1 lists the landmark roles and their corresponding HTML semantic elements.

**TABLE 6-1**     Landmark ARIA Roles

| ARIA role | HTML Semantic Element |
|---|---|
| banner | header |
| complementary | aside |
| contentinfo | footer |
| form | form |
| main | main |
| navigation | nav |
| region | section |
| search | N/A |

The `search` role doesn't have an equivalent HTML element, but most of the time you'll use it within a `form` element, like this:

```
<form role="search">
    Your search controls go here
</form>
```

**WARNING**

The point of landmark roles (and their corresponding HTML sectioning elements) is to give assistive tech a forest-instead-of-the-trees view of the page. Therefore, don't overuse landmark roles or you run the risk of your page appearing to be nothing but trees!

## Section structure ARIA roles

*Section structure* ARIA roles identify sections of page content with a specific purpose. Most section structure ARIA roles have a semantic HTML equivalent, but a few don't, and I list those in Table 6-2.

**TABLE 6-2**

## Section Structure Roles without HTML Equivalents

| ARIA role | Description |
|-----------|-------------|
| feed | Identifies a scrollable list of items where new items are added as the user scrolls to the bottom of the list |
| math | Identifies a mathematical expression |
| none (or presentation) | Hides an element's implicit ARIA role from assistive technologies |
| note | Identifies a section with content that is ancillary to the main page topic |
| toolbar | Identifies a section with controls that are meant to be used as a toolbar |
| tooltip | Identifies text that appears when the user hovers the mouse pointer over an element or gives the element focus via the keyboard |

Table 6-3 lists the section structure ARIA roles that have semantic HTML equivalents. In each case, it's best to use the semantic HTML elements instead of the ARIA roles.

**TABLE 6-3**

## Section Structure Roles with HTML Equivalents

| ARIA role | HTML Semantic Element |
|-----------|----------------------|
| article | article |
| cell | td |
| definition | dfn |
| figure | figure |
| heading | h1 through h6 |
| img | img or picture |
| list | ol or ul |
| listitem | li |
| meter | meter |
| row | tr |
| rowgroup | tbody, thead, or tfoot |
| rowheader | th |
| table | table |
| term | dfn or dt |

## Widget ARIA roles

*Widget* ARIA roles identify interactive user interface elements. Table 6-4 lists those widget ARIA roles that don't have semantic HTML equivalents.

**TABLE 6-4**     **Widget Roles Without HTML Equivalents**

| ARIA role | Identifies |
|---|---|
| combobox | An input control that enables the user to either type a value or select a value from a list |
| menu | A control that enables the user to select an item from a list of choices |
| menubar | A control that contains a set of menu widgets |
| scrollbar | A page object that controls vertical or horizontal scrolling within a viewing region |
| searchbox | A text box control used specifically to input text for a search operation |
| slider | An input control that enables the user to choose from a range of values |
| spinbutton | An input control that enables the user to increment or decrement a value |
| switch | An input control that the user can alternate between the "on" and "off" states |
| tab | A control that, when selected, displays its associated tabpanel widget |
| tablist | A control that contains a set of tab widgets |
| tabpanel | A control that contains the content of the currently selected tab widget |
| tree | A widget that enables the user to select one or more items from a hierarchical set |
| treegrid | A tabular version of a tree widget |
| treeitem | An item in a tree widget |

A few widget ARIA roles also have semantic HTML equivalents, as I outline in Table 6-5. In each case, it's best to use the semantic HTML elements instead of the ARIA roles.

**TABLE 6-5**     **Widget Roles with HTML Equivalents**

| ARIA role | HTML Semantic Element |
|---|---|
| button | button |
| checkbox | input type="checkbox" |
| link | a |

| ARIA role | HTML Semantic Element |
|---|---|
| option | option |
| progressbar | progress |
| radio | input type="radio" |
| textbox | input type="text" |

## Differentiating semantic page elements of the same type

One problem you run into when trying to accommodate screen readers in your code is when you have multiple semantic page elements of the same type. For example, your page may have two nav elements: one in the page header, another in the page article, as shown here:

```
<header>
    <nav>
        <h3>Site Navigation</h3>
        Site navigation code goes here
    </nav>
</header>

<main>
    <article>
        <nav>
            <h3>Article Navigation</h3>
            Article navigation code goes here
        </nav>
    </article>
</main>
```

How can a screen reader user find out what each nav element does? One option is to navigate through the elements to see what each one contains, a process that's both time-consuming and burdensome. A better way is to add an id attribute to the h3 element within each nav element, then use the aria-labelledby attribute in the nav element to specify the id of the associated heading. Here's the updated example:

```
<header>
    <nav aria-labelledby="site-navigation">
        <h3 id="site-navigation">Site Navigation</h3>
        Site navigation code goes here
    </nav>
```

```
    </header>

    <main>
        <article>
            <nav aria-labelledby="article-navigation">
                <h3 id="article-navigation">Article Navigation</h3>
                Article navigation code goes here
            </nav>
        </article>
    </main>
```

For example, within the header element, the <h3> tag now has an id attribute with the value site-navigation. In the nav element, the aria-labelledby attribute is also given the value site-navigation. This tells the screen reader that the text Site Navigation describes this particular nav element.

What if your user interface doesn't have a handy h3 (or whatever) element to act as the label? No problem. You can use the aria-label attribute directly in the tag you want to label:

```
<header>
    <nav aria-label="Site Navigation">
        Site navigation code goes here
    </nav>
</header>

<main>
    <article>
        <nav aria-label="Article Navigation">
            Article navigation code goes here
        </nav>
    </article>
</main>
```

# Making Your Pages Keyboard-Friendly

Many users with disabilities lack the dexterity or the ability to use a mouse or other pointing device. Many of those users navigate and interact with web pages using the keyboard, so it's vital that your web pages be keyboard friendly.

Out of the box, HTML offers the following keyboard support:

» Form controls and links are navigable via the keyboard.

» All other HTML elements are *not* navigable via the keyboard.

» Pressing Tab moves the focus forward from the current element to the next navigable element, where "forward" refers to the direction that the elements appear in the HTML source code.

» Pressing Shift+Tab moves the focus backward from the current element to the previous navigable element, where "backward" refers to the reverse direction that the elements appear in the HTML source code.

» For navigable elements that have multiple components — such as a group of radio buttons or a selection list — after the user places the focus on the element, the user can navigate the components inside the element by pressing the arrow keys.

» Pressing the spacebar selects the current element. When a button element has the focus, for example, pressing the spacebar is the same as clicking the button; when a checkbox has the focus, pressing the spacebar toggles the checkbox between the selected (checked) and nonselected (unchecked) state.

The order in which the page elements receive the focus as you press Tab is called — no surprises here — the *tab order*. What *is* surprising is that the tab order isn't set in stone, meaning that you can both add elements to it and remove elements from it. The next two sections provide the details.

**TIP**

Another way you can ramp up the keyboard friendliness of your web page is to assign shortcut keys to user interface controls. Defining keyboard shortcuts falls under the spell of JavaScript, so I leave that solution to Book 4, Chapter 11.

## Adding an element to the tab order

If you stick with native HTML elements, you probably don't need to do anything extra for accessible keyboard access. However, what if you have, say, a div or span element that you want to be accessible by pressing Tab or Shift+Tab? That's no problem — just plop tabindex="0" into the tag, like this:

```
<div role="tablist" tabindex="0">
```

When the web browser sees tabindex="0" inside a tag, it automatically adds that element to the tab order, so users will be able to navigate to the element using Tab or Shift+Tab. How awesome is *that*?

# Removing an element from the tab order

Every once in a while, you may end up with a navigable page element that you *don't* want in the tab order. For example, if an element is disabled, then there's no point in having users navigate to it using Tab or Shift+Tab.

To remove an element from the tab order, insert `tabindex="-1"` into the element's tag, like so:

```
<button tabindex="-1">
    Can't touch this
</button>
```

When the web browser stumbles upon `tabindex="-1"` inside a tag, it removes that element from the tab order, so users pressing Tab or Shift+Tab will skip right over it.

# Ensuring Sufficient Color Contrast

Some people — even some people with decent eyesight have trouble reading web page text if there isn't sufficient contrast between the color of the text and the color of the background. For example, it's distressingly common these days to see either light gray text on a slightly lighter gray background (see Figure 6-1, left) or dark gray text on a slightly darker gray background (see Figure 6-1, right). Some web designers think this is "cool," but the rest of us may use some saltier language to describe it.

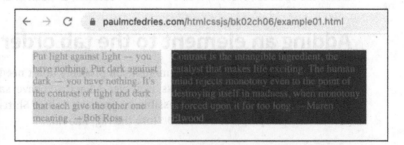

**FIGURE 6-1:**
Light text on a light background (left) and dark text on a dark background (right).

The examples in Figure 6-1 are a bit extreme, admittedly, but you shouldn't assume that just because you can easily read your text, everyone will have just as easy a time. Lots of people with either a visual impairment or aging eyes have trouble reading text that appears insufficiently darker or lighter than the background.

So, how do you know when the foreground and background colors you've chosen have enough color contrast? You can turn to a measurement called the *contrast ratio*, which compares the hue and luminance (brightness) of one color with the hue and luminance of another. The result is a number greater than or equal to one with the following properties:

» The lower the number, the lower the contrast between the two colors.

» The higher the number, the greater the contrast between the two colors.

» A contrast ratio of 1 means the two colors are the same (or close enough to being the same).

Okay, so what is *sufficient* color contrast? The world's web accessibility gurus have decreed that a contrast ratio of 4.5 or higher is what you need to shoot for. Happily, you don't have to worry about calculating contrast ratios yourself. Instead, you can use an online tool called WebAim (Web Accessibility In Mind) Contrast Checker, which is available here:

```
https://webaim.org/resources/contrastchecker/
```

In both the Foreground Color and Background Color boxes, either enter an RGB hex color code or click the color swatch to choose a color. Instantly, the page spits out the contrast ratio (see Figure 6-2).

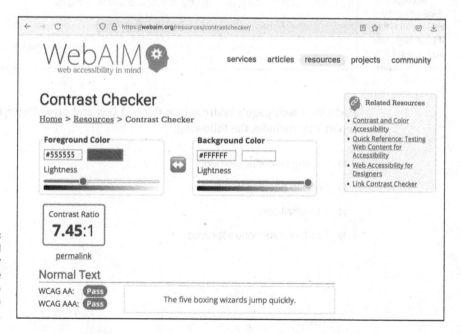

FIGURE 6-2: Use the WebAIM Contrast Checker to find out the contrast ratio between any two colors.

**TIP**

To learn what on earth "RGB hex color code" could possibly mean, see Book 3, Chapter 6.

# Validating the Accessibility of a Page

All the accessibility tweaks I've discussed in this chapter might seem like a lot to keep track of. What if you miss something? That's a legit concern, but the web can help. Once your page is on the web, you can check its accessibility by heading over to the Web Accessibility Evaluation Tool (WAVE) at `http://wave.webaim.org`, shown in Figure 6-3.

**WAVE Web Accessibility Evaluation Tools**

WAVE® is a suite of evaluation tools that helps authors make their web content more accessible to individuals with disabilities. WAVE can identify many accessibility and Web Content Accessibility Guideline (WCAG) errors, but also facilitates human evaluation of web content. Our philosophy is to focus on issues that we know impact end users, facilitate human evaluation, and to educate about web accessibility.

**FIGURE 6-3:**
The Web Accessibility Evaluation Tool will let you know if your page has any accessibility faux pas.

Paste your web page's address into the text box and press Enter/Return to see a report that includes the following:

» Missing semantic elements

» Skipped heading levels

» Too-small text

» Too-low color contrast ratios

# 3

# Learning CSS Basics

# Contents at a Glance

IN THIS CHAPTER

» **Wrapping your head around the CSS box model**

» **Giving elements room to breathe with padding**

» **Enclosing elements with borders**

» **Keeping other elements at bay with margins**

» **Setting the width and height of page elements**

Chapter **1**

# Figuring Out the CSS Box Model

*Every element in web design is a rectangular box. This was my ah-ha moment that helped me really start to understand CSS-based web design and accomplish the layouts I wanted to accomplish.*

— CHRIS COYIER

'm not going to lie to you: When you're just getting started with CSS, the elements on the page will sometimes seem to defy your every command. Like surly teenagers, they ignore your best advice and refuse to understand that you are — or you are supposed to be — the boss of them. Okay, I did lie to you a little: That can happen to even the most experienced web coders. Why the attitude? Because although web browsers are fine pieces of software for getting around the web, by default they're not very adept at laying out a web page. Like overly permissive grandparents, they just let the page elements do whatever they like. Your job as a parent, er, I mean, a web developer, is to introduce some discipline to the page.

Fortunately, CSS comes with a huge number of tools and techniques that you can wield to make stubborn page elements behave themselves. Those tools and techniques form the bulk of this book and are the topics of Books 2, 5, and 6. But just about everything you do as a CSS developer will in some way involve (or be influenced by) the CSS box model, which is the subject you delve into in this chapter. The box model is so fundamental to almost everything in CSS that you should consider this chapter to be the foundation for almost every other CSS topic in the book.

# Thinking Outside (but Also Inside) the Box Model

Every web page consists of a series of HTML tags, and each of those tags represents an element on the page. In the strange and geeky world known as Style Sheet Land, each of these elements is considered to have an invisible box around it (okay, it's a very strange world). That may not sound like a big deal, but those boxes are the royal road to CSS mastery.

## Understanding the components of the box model

Figure 1-1 shows what the aforementioned invisible box looks like in the abstract, and Figure 1-2 shows an actual page element.

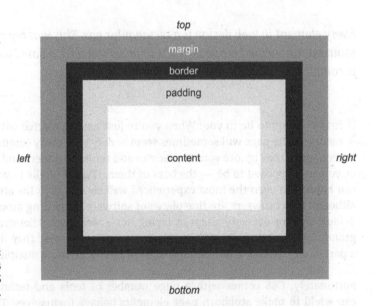

**FIGURE 1-1:**
The components of the CSS box model.

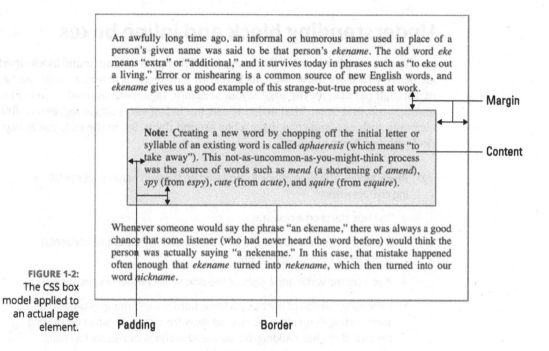

An awfully long time ago, an informal or humorous name used in place of a person's given name was said to be that person's *ekename*. The old word *eke* means "extra" or "additional," and it survives today in phrases such as "to eke out a living." Error or mishearing is a common source of new English words, and *ekename* gives us a good example of this strange-but-true process at work.

**Note:** Creating a new word by chopping off the initial letter or syllable of an existing word is called *aphaeresis* (which means "to take away"). This not-as-uncommon-as-you-might-think process was the source of words such as *mend* (a shortening of *amend*), *spy* (from *espy*), *cute* (from *acute*), and *squire* (from *esquire*).

Whenever someone would say the phrase "an ekename," there was always a good chance that some listener (who had never heard the word before) would think the person was actually saying "a nekename." In this case, that mistake happened often enough that *ekename* turned into *nekename*, which then turned into our word *nickname*.

Margin

Content

Padding

Border

**FIGURE 1-2:** The CSS box model applied to an actual page element.

Figures 1-1 and 1-2 show the following box components:

>> **Content:** The stuff inside the box, such as text, links, lists, images, and video. In other words, the content of all the boxes in your page is nothing more nor less than the actual content you've added to the page. The four sides of the content area — that is, its top, left, bottom, and right edges — define the *content box*.

>> **Padding:** The space that surrounds the content. That is, it's the space just outside the content, but inside the border (discussed next). Refer to "Adding Padding," later in this chapter, to find out more about messing around with the padding. The four sides of the padding area define the *padding box*.

>> **Border:** The space that surrounds the padding. That is, it's the space just outside the padding, but inside the margin (discussed next). Refer to "Putting a Border On It," later in this chapter, to get a good look at how you can manipulate borders with CSS. The four sides of the border define the *border box*.

>> **Margin:** The space that surrounds the border. That is, it's the space just outside the border. The four sides of the margin define the *margin box*.

Note that the padding, border, and margin are all "optional" in the sense that you can use CSS rules to shrink them down to nothing. Also, the top, left, bottom, and right edges of the padding box, border box, and margin box all have corresponding CSS properties that you can play around with.

# Understanding block and inline boxes

You may be tempted to think that these invisible boxes only surround block-level elements, which are those elements that start new sections of text: p, blockquote, h1 through h6, div, all the page layout semantic tags, such as header, article, and section, and so on. That makes sense, but in fact every single tag, even inline elements such as a and span, have a box around them. So, in the end, you always deal with two types of boxes:

» **Block boxes:** This type of box is rendered on the web page using the following characteristics:

- The box starts on a new line.

- If you don't set a width for the box, the box will fill the entire horizontal space of its containing element.

- If you set the width and height of the box, those properties get applied.

- Increasing the size of the box padding, borders, and margins causes surrounding elements to be pushed away from the box, while decreasing the size of the box padding, borders, and margins causes surrounding elements to be drawn closer to the box.

By definition, the default value for the display property of a block box is block:

```
display: block;
```

» **Inline boxes:** This type of box is rendered on the web page as follows:

- The box flows along with the surrounding content.

- The box will only be as wide as its content requires.

- If you set the width and height of the box, those properties do not get applied.

- Increasing or decreasing the size of the vertical padding, borders, and margins has no effect on the surrounding elements.

- Increasing the size of the horizontal padding, borders, and margins causes surrounding elements to be pushed away from the box, while decreasing the size of the horizontal padding, borders, and margins causes surrounding elements to be drawn closer to the box.

By definition, the default value for the display property of an inline box is inline:

```
display: inline;
```

# Changing the display type for a box

Just because an element such as h1 or div is a block box by default, and an element such as a or span is an inline box by default, it doesn't mean these elements can never change their display type. For example, when creating a set of navigation links, many developers place the links inside li (list) elements, which use a block box, and change those elements to an inline box so that the links run horizontally. I show you an example of this in just a second.

You can an element's display type using the display property:

```
selector {
    display: value;
}
```

» *selector*: A CSS selector that specifies the item (or items) you want to style.

» *value*: A keyword that specifies the display type. You can use any of the following:

- block: Changes the display type to a block box.

- inline: Changes the display type to an inline box.

- inline-block: Changes the display type to an inline box, but one where the web browser respects any changes you make to the element's width and height properties.

**REMEMBER**

A *selector* is a CSS feature that enables you to choose a page object by element name, class, HTML attribute, and much more. Check out Book 3, Chapters 2 and 3 for a detailed look at CSS selectors.

Here's an example that uses a selector to change the display type for the li element (check out bk03ch01/example01.html in this book's example files):

HTML:

```
<ul>
    <li>Home</li>
    <li>Blog</li>
    <li>Contact Us</li>
    <li>Surprise!</li>
    <li>Support</li>
</ul>
```

CSS:

```
li {
    display: inline;
    margin-right: 8px;
}
```

The HTML code defines an unordered list. In the CSS, the display property for the li element is set to inline, which causes the list items to display horizontally, as shown in Figure 1-3. (I added the margin-right: 8px declaration to give each li item a bit of space to its right; refer to "Manipulating Element Margins," later in this chapter.)

FIGURE 1-3:
The list items are
now displayed as
inline boxes.

← → C 🔒 paulmcfedries.com/htmlcssjs/bk03ch01/example01.html

Home  Blog  Contact Us  Surprise!  Support

REMEMBER

The display property has many other possible values. For example, if you want to temporarily hide an element, you can style the element with display: none. You also modify an element's display property when using Flexbox (covered in Book 5, Chapter 2) and Grid (covered in Book 5, Chapter 3).

## Eyeballing an element's box

The box that surrounds an element is invisible, so all this box stuff can feel a bit abstract. Also, as you discover in the rest of this chapter, there are tons of CSS properties you can use to change the size of the top, right, bottom, and left padding areas, borders, and margins. It's a lot to keep track of, so how can you be sure that your CSS is getting applied the way you want?

The best way is to use your web browser's development tools. I go into the CSS-related development tools in detail in Book 3, Chapter 4. For now, you can view an element in the development tools by right-clicking the element and then clicking Inspect (or Inspect Element, depending on the browser you're using). In the pane that appears, click the Computed tab that appears on the right side. As shown in Figure 1-4, this tab includes a representation of the selected element's box model. The inner box tells you the dimensions of the content box, and concentric boxes then display the size of each padding area, border, and margin.

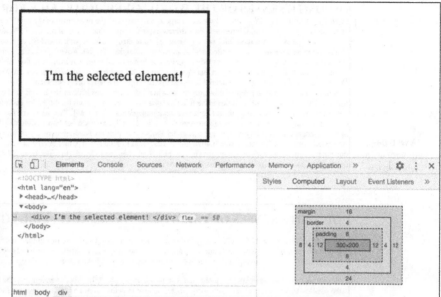

**FIGURE 1-4:**
The development tools' Computed tab shows the dimensions of the selected element's box model.

# A Brief Digression on Whitespace

A major web design concept is the notion of *whitespace:* blank, content-free chunks of the page. The whiteness of whitespace is optional: whitespace can be any color you like as long as it doesn't contain any content; it's the *blankness* of whitespace that does the heavy lifting, design-wise.

Why is whitespace so important? Because, when used generously and judiciously, whitespace opens up your page to make it more inviting, easier to navigate, and more pleasurable to read.

For example, take a look at the page shown in Figure 1-5. This page is almost devoid of blank areas, so it presents as just a wall of text. Who'd want to read that? Now compare that with the version of the same page shown in Figure 1-6. Ah, that's better. What made the difference? In the version of the page shown in Figure 1-5, I deliberately set all the margins to 0. In Figure 1-6, I removed that setting and let the browser style the content using its default rules, which include whitespace around most block elements.

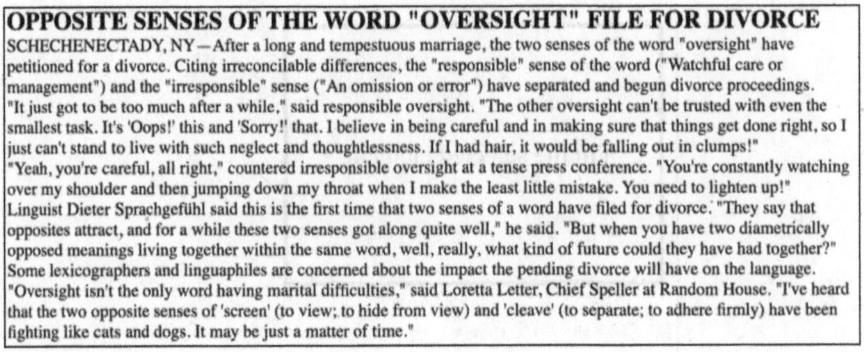

**OPPOSITE SENSES OF THE WORD "OVERSIGHT" FILE FOR DIVORCE**

SCHECHENECTADY, NY—After a long and tempestuous marriage, the two senses of the word "oversight" have petitioned for a divorce. Citing irreconcilable differences, the "responsible" sense of the word ("Watchful care or management") and the "irresponsible" sense ("An omission or error") have separated and begun divorce proceedings. "It just got to be too much after a while," said responsible oversight. "The other oversight can't be trusted with even the smallest task. It's 'Oops!' this and 'Sorry!' that. I believe in being careful and in making sure that things get done right, so I just can't stand to live with such neglect and thoughtlessness. If I had hair, it would be falling out in clumps!" "Yeah, you're careful, all right," countered irresponsible oversight at a tense press conference. "You're constantly watching over my shoulder and then jumping down my throat when I make the least little mistake. You need to lighten up!" Linguist Dieter Sprachgefühl said this is the first time that two senses of a word have filed for divorce. "They say that opposites attract, and for a while these two senses got along quite well," he said. "But when you have two diametrically opposed meanings living together within the same word, well, really, what kind of future could they have had together?" Some lexicographers and linguaphiles are concerned about the impact the pending divorce will have on the language. "Oversight isn't the only word having marital difficulties," said Loretta Letter, Chief Speller at Random House. "I've heard that the two opposite senses of 'screen' (to view; to hide from view) and 'cleave' (to separate; to adhere firmly) have been fighting like cats and dogs. It may be just a matter of time."

**FIGURE 1-5:**
A web page with very little whitespace.

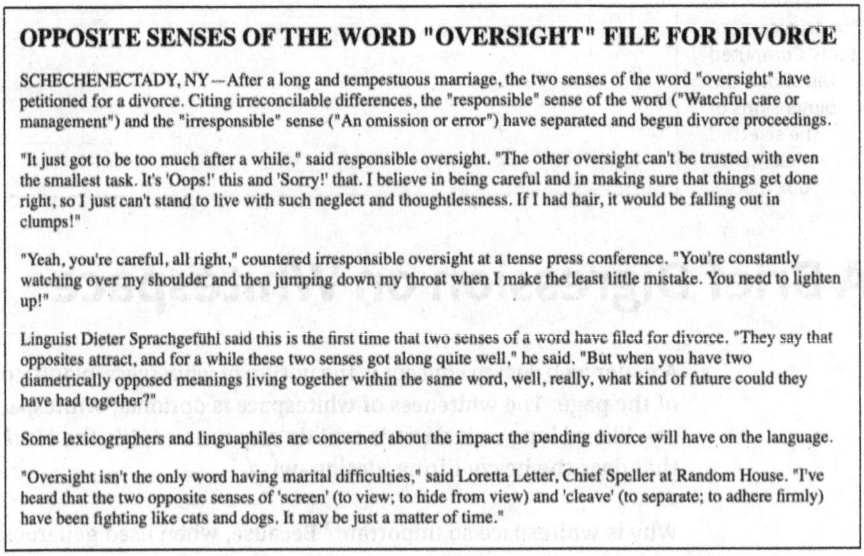

**OPPOSITE SENSES OF THE WORD "OVERSIGHT" FILE FOR DIVORCE**

SCHECHENECTADY, NY—After a long and tempestuous marriage, the two senses of the word "oversight" have petitioned for a divorce. Citing irreconcilable differences, the "responsible" sense of the word ("Watchful care or management") and the "irresponsible" sense ("An omission or error") have separated and begun divorce proceedings.

"It just got to be too much after a while," said responsible oversight. "The other oversight can't be trusted with even the smallest task. It's 'Oops!' this and 'Sorry!' that. I believe in being careful and in making sure that things get done right, so I just can't stand to live with such neglect and thoughtlessness. If I had hair, it would be falling out in clumps!"

"Yeah, you're careful, all right," countered irresponsible oversight at a tense press conference. "You're constantly watching over my shoulder and then jumping down my throat when I make the least little mistake. You need to lighten up!"

Linguist Dieter Sprachgefühl said this is the first time that two senses of a word have filed for divorce. "They say that opposites attract, and for a while these two senses got along quite well," he said. "But when you have two diametrically opposed meanings living together within the same word, well, really, what kind of future could they have had together?"

Some lexicographers and linguaphiles are concerned about the impact the pending divorce will have on the language.

"Oversight isn't the only word having marital difficulties," said Loretta Letter, Chief Speller at Random House. "I've heard that the two opposite senses of 'screen' (to view; to hide from view) and 'cleave' (to separate; to adhere firmly) have been fighting like cats and dogs. It may be just a matter of time."

**FIGURE 1-6:**
The same page, now with added whitespace!

How do you control whitespace in your pages? CSS actually has quite a few techniques you can turn to, but the following two will be your whitespace workhorses:

» **Controlling whitespace inside each element:** This means giving each element generous padding, which ensures that the element's content isn't crowded by its border.

» **Controlling whitespace outside each element:** This means giving each element generous margins, which ensures that the element isn't crowded by surrounding elements.

# Adding Padding

In the CSS box model, the *padding* is the space that surrounds the content out to the border.

There are four sections to the padding — above, to the right of, below, and to the left of the content — so CSS offers four corresponding properties for adding padding to an element:

```
selector {
    padding-top: top-value;
    padding-right: right-value;
    padding-bottom: bottom-value;
    padding-left: left-value;
}
```

» *selector*: A CSS selector that specifies the item (or items) you want to style.

» *top-value* (and so on): A number followed by a CSS measurement unit (such as px, em, rem, vw, or vh; refer to Book 3, Chapter 5 to find out what these units mean) or a percentage.

Figure 1-7 shows a chunk of text with a border, but no padding. The result is that the content is uncomfortably close to the border, making the text feel cramped.

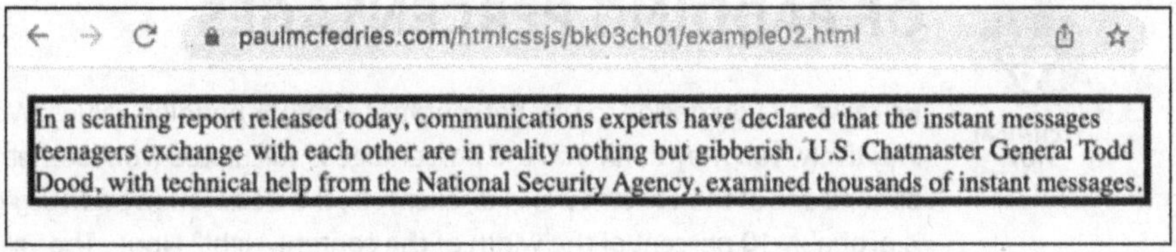

paulmcfedries.com/htmlcssjs/bk03ch01/example02.html

In a scathing report released today, communications experts have declared that the instant messages teenagers exchange with each other are in reality nothing but gibberish. U.S. Chatmaster General Todd Dood, with technical help from the National Security Agency, examined thousands of instant messages.

**FIGURE 1-7:**
Some text with a border, but no padding.

Figure 1-8 shows how much nicer the text looks when I apply the following rule to the text (which is inside a `<p>` tag; check out bk03ch01/example02.html):

```
p {
    padding-top: 16px;
    padding-right: 12px;
    padding-bottom: 16px;
    padding-left: 20px;
}
```

← → C 🔒 paulmcfedries.com/htmlcssjs/bk03ch01/example02.html

In a scathing report released today, communications experts have declared that the instant messages teenagers exchange with each other are in reality nothing but gibberish. U.S. Chatmaster General Todd Dood, with technical help from the National Security Agency, examined thousands of instant messages.

**FIGURE 1-8:**
The same text from Figure 1-7, with padding added.

CSS also offers a shorthand syntax that uses the `padding` property. There are four different syntaxes you can use with the `padding` property, and they're all listed in Table 1-1.

# GROKKING THE WEIRDNESS OF PADDING PERCENTAGES

**TECHNICAL STUFF**

Be careful if you decide to use percentages for your padding values. Why? Because, intuitively, you may think that the percentage is calculated from something like the dimensions of the content box. For example, the declaration `padding-right: 10%` is probably 10 percent of the width of the content, right? Nope. The value the browser would actually use is 10 percent of the width of the *parent* element (that is, whatever element contains the element you're styling)!

But wait, things get even weirder: If you set `padding-top` or `padding-bottom` to a percentage, the browser still calculates the percentage using the *width* of the parent element!

**TABLE 1-1**    The padding Shorthand Property

| Syntax | Description |
|---|---|
| padding: *value1*; | Applies *value1* to all four sides |
| padding: *value1 value2*; | Applies *value1* to the top and bottom and *value2* to the right and left |
| padding: *value1 value2 value3*; | Applies *value1* to the top, *value2* to the right and left, and *value3* to the bottom |
| padding: *value1 value2 value3 value4*; | Applies *value1* to the top, *value2* to the right, *value3* to the bottom, and *value4* to the left |

Here's how you'd rewrite the previous example using the padding shorthand:

```
p {
    padding: 16px 12px 16px 20px;
}
```

# Putting a Border on It

Modern web design eschews vertical and horizontal lines as a means of separating content, preferring instead to let copious amounts of whitespace do the job. However, that doesn't mean you should never use lines in your designs, particularly borders. An element's *border* is the notional set of lines that enclose the element's content and padding. Borders are an often useful way to make it clear than an element is separate from the surrounding elements in the page.

## Applying a border

There are four lines associated with an element's border — above, to the right of, below, and to the left of the padding — so CSS offers four properties for adding borders to an element:

```
selector {
    border-top: top-width top-style top-color;
    border-right: right-width right-style right-color;
    border-bottom: bottom-width bottom-style bottom-color;
    border-left: left-width left-style left-color;
}
```

Each border requires three values:

>> **Width:** The thickness of the border line, which you specify using a number followed by a CSS measurement unit (such as px, em, rem, vw, or vh). Note, however, that most border widths are measured in pixels, usually 1px. You can also specify one of the following keywords: thin, medium, or thick (although note that the thickness associated with each keyword isn't defined in the CSS standard, so your mileage may vary depending on the browser).

>> **Style:** The type of border line, which must be one of the following keywords:

* dotted: Displays the border as a series of dots.

* dashed: Displays the border as a series of dashes.

* solid: Displays the border as an uninterrupted line.

* double: Displays the border as two solid, parallel lines.

* groove: Displays the border as though it's carved into the page as a v-shaped trough (the opposite effect of ridge).

* ridge Displays the border as though it's raised from the page as a v-shaped extrusion (the opposite effect of groove).

* inset: Displays the border as though it was embedded into the page (the opposite effect of outset).

* outset: Displays the border as though it was embossed on the page (the opposite effect of inset).

Figure 1-9 shows an example of each style. (I used 24px as the border width for the groove, ridge, inset, and outset styles because their effects are hard to discern at smaller widths; check out bk03ch01/example03.html.)

**TIP**

>> **Color:** The color of the border line. You can use a color keyword, an rgb() function, an hsl() function, or an RGB code, as I describe in Book 3, Chapter 6.

Here's an example that adds a 1-pixel, dashed, red bottom border to the header element:

```
header {
    border-bottom: 1px dashed red;
}
```

At times in your CSS work, you may need to focus on a very specific part of the border. For example, you may want to work with just the style of the bottom border or the color of the left border. No problem!

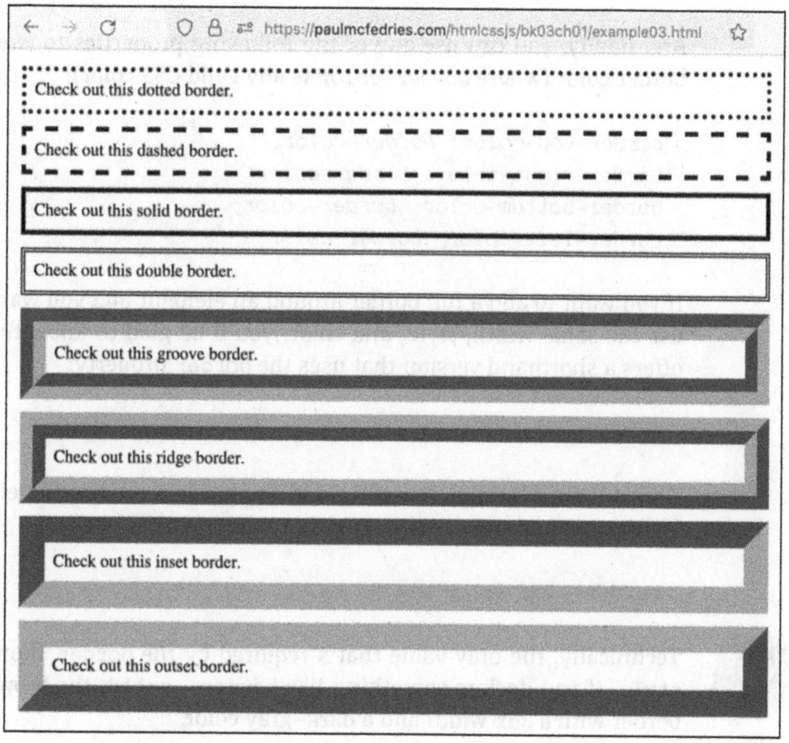

FIGURE 1-9:
The border style
keywords in
action.

You can use any of the following properties, for example, to work with a specific border width (where *border-width* is a width in any CSS measurement unit):

```
border-top-width: border-width;
border-right-width: border-width;
border-bottom-width: border-width;
border-left-width: border-width;
```

Similarly, you can use any of the following properties to work with a specific border style (where *border-style* is any valid border style keyword, such as solid or dashed):

```
border-top-style: border-style;
border-right-style: border-style;
border-bottom-style: border-style;
border-left-style: border-style;
```

And finally, you can use any of the following properties to work with a specific border color (where *border-color* is any valid CSS color):

```
border-top-color: border-color;
border-right-color: border-color;
border-bottom-color: border-color;
border-left-color: border-color;
```

If you want to add a full border around an element and you want all four sides to use the same width, style, and color, you'll be glad to know that CSS mercifully offers a shorthand version that uses the border property:

```
border: width style color;
```

Here's the declaration I used to add the borders around the elements shown in Figures 1-5 and 1-6:

```
border: 4px solid black;
```

Technically, the only value that's required by the border shorthand property is *style*. If you declare something like border: solid, the browser draws a solid border with a 3px width and a dark-gray color.

To help visualize your page's various boxes, you may think it's a good idea to add a border to some or all of the elements. However, that's not a great idea for two reasons. First, it's a lot of work. Second, adding a border affects the layout, so you're not really seeing your page in its true box model glory. A better solution is to take advantage of the outline property, which draws a line around the element's border but doesn't affect the page layout in any way. Set the outline property to three values: a size, a color, and a style (use the same style keywords as the border property). Here's an example that puts a 1-pixel, red, dashed outline around every page element (the * selector refers to everything on the page):

```
* {
    outline: 1px red dashed;
}
```

## Rounding your borders

The boxes in the box model are resolutely rectangular, but that doesn't mean you have to always settle for sharp corners when you add a border around an element. To give your borders a softer look, you can round them using the border-radius property, which can round one or more corners based on the arc of either a circle or an ellipse.

**TECHNICAL STUFF**

# RECOGNIZING INTERNATIONAL BORDERS

In CSS, the *writing mode* describes whether text is displayed on the page horizontally (as it is in English and Arabic) or vertically (as it is in Chinese and Japanese) and which direction block elements progress: top to bottom (as in English and Arabic); right to left (as in Chinese and Japanese); or left to right (as in Mongolian). CSS also recognizes the *directionality* of horizontal text, which can be left to right (as it is in English and most horizontal languages) or right to left (as it is in Arabic and Hebrew).

CSS reduces all these concepts into the following abstractions:

- *Inline dimension:* The dimension along which text flows in the current writing mode. In English, Arabic, and Hebrew, the inline dimension is horizontal; in Japanese and Chinese, the inline dimension is vertical.

- *Block dimension*: The dimension along which block elements progress. In English, Arabic, and Hebrew, the block dimension is vertical; in Japanese and Chinese, the block dimension is horizontal.

I mention all this to point out that, given all these possible writing modes and directions, using a property such as border-left is meaningful only for horizontal, left-to-right languages. That is, in, say, English, what border-left really refers to is "the border at the start of this element's inline dimension." However, in Hebrew, border-left would mean "the border at the *end* of this element's inline dimension."

So, if you're working with text that will appear in multiple languages, it makes no sense to use a property such as border-left because its meaning may change depending on the language. Instead, you can use the CSS *logical properties,* which eschew physical descriptors such as top, right, bottom, and left in favor of the following logical descriptors:

- inline: Refers to the inline dimension of the element.

- block: Refers to the block dimension of the element.

- inline-start: Refers to the beginning of the element's inline dimension (left in English, right in Arabic, top in Japanese).

- inline-end: Refers to the end of the element's inline dimension (right in English, left in Arabic, bottom in Japanese).

- block-start: Refers to the beginning of the element's block dimension (top in English and Arabic, right in Japanese).

- block-end: Refers to the end of the element's block dimension (bottom in English and Arabic, left in Japanese).

*(continued)*

(continued)

So, anywhere in your CSS code where you use, say, left, you can substitute the logical descriptor inline-start. This would mean that border-left becomes border-inline-start. Similarly, anywhere you use top, you can substitute the logical descriptor block-start, which means that, for example, border-top-style becomes border-block-start-style.

Note, too, that all this applies to not only borders but also padding, margins, and sizes.

## Rounding borders based on the arc of a circle

The most common and most straightforward way to round an element's border corners is to base the rounding on the arc of a circle with a specified radius. Here's the border-radius syntax to use for this case:

```
selector {
    border-radius: radius;
}
```

» *selector*: A CSS selector that specifies the item (or items) you want to style.

» *radius*: A value (expressed on one of the standard CSS measurement units, such as px, em, rem, vw, or vh) or a percentage.

The radius you're specifying here is the radius of a circle. Figure 1-10 shows how this works (bk03ch01/example04.html). The element on the left has no border radius, so it's got the default right-angled corners. The element on the right has a border radius of 100px set on the top-right corner. (I show you how to specify individual corners shortly.) Notice how the rounded corner of the border follows an arc of the inscribed circle. That circle has a radius of 100px. The bigger the radius value, the bigger the circle, so the more rounded the corner.

For example, suppose you have an aside element that has a border you want to round slightly. Here's some CSS that'll do it:

```
aside {
    border: 1px solid black;
    border-radius: 10px;
}
```

The preceding border-radius syntax is a shorthand version that applies a single radius value to all four corners. There are actually four different syntaxes you can use with the border-radius property, and they're all listed in Table 1-2.

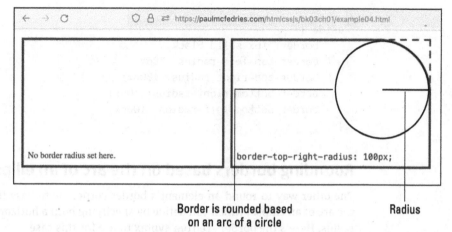

No border radius set here.

border-top-right-radius: 100px;

**FIGURE 1-10:**
How CSS rounds
a border based
on the arc
of a circle.

Border is rounded based
on an arc of a circle

Radius

**TABLE 1-2**    **The Extended** `border-radius` **Shorthand Property**

| Syntax | Description |
|---|---|
| `border-radius:` *radius1*; | Applies *radius1* to all four corners |
| `border-radius:` *radius1 radius2*; | Applies *radius1* to the top-left and bottom-right corners and *radius2* to the top-right and bottom-left corners |
| `border-radius:` *radius1 radius2 radius3*; | Applies *radius1* to the top-left corner, *radius2* to the top-right and bottom-left corners, and *radius3* to the bottom-right corner |
| `border-radius:` *radius1 radius2 radius3 radius4*; | Applies *radius1* to the top-left corner, *radius2* to the top-right corner, *radius3* to the bottom-right corner, and *radius4* to the bottom-left corner |

Alternatively, if you want to be more explicit, you can style individual corners using separate properties:

```
selector {
    border-top-left-radius: radiusTL;
    border-top-right-radius: radiusTR;
    border-bottom-right-radius: radiusBR;
    border-bottom-left-radius: radiusBL;
}
```

For example, the following two CSS rules do the same rounding job:

```
aside {
    border: 1px solid black;
    border-radius: 50px 100px 10px;
}
```

```
aside {
    border: 1px solid black;
    border-top-left-radius: 50px;
    border-top-right-radius: 100px;
    border-bottom-right-radius: 10px;
    border-bottom-left-radius: 100px;
}
```

## Rounding borders based on the arc of an ellipse

The other way to round an element's border corners is to base the rounding on the arc of an ellipse, which you define by specifying both a horizontal and vertical radius. Here's the border-radius syntax to use for this case:

```
selector {
    border-radius: horizontal vertical;
}
```

» *selector*: A CSS selector that specifies the item (or items) you want to style.

» *horizontal*: The horizontal radius as a value (expressed on one of the standard CSS measurement units, such as px, em, rem, vw, or vh) or a percentage (that is, a percentage of the element's width).

» *vertical*: The vertical radius as a value (expressed on one of the standard CSS measurement units, such as px, em, rem, vw, or vh) or a percentage (that is, a percentage of the element's height).

The horizontal and vertical radii define an ellipse. Figure 1-11 shows how this works (bk03ch01/example04.html). The element on the left has no border radius, so it's got the standard-issue right-angled corners. The element on the right has a border radius of 100px 50px set on the top-right corner. Notice how the rounded corner of the border follows an arc of the inscribed ellipse.

For example, suppose you have a div element that has a border you want to round slightly based on an ellipse. Here's some CSS that'll do it:

```
div {
    border: 3px outset darkgreen;
    border-radius: 10px 20px;
}
```

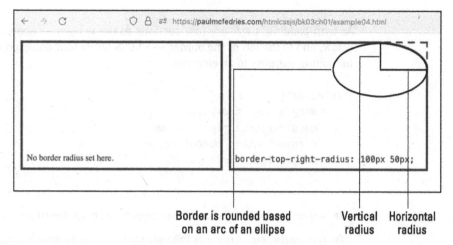

**FIGURE 1-11:**
How CSS rounds
a border based
on the arc
of an ellipse.

Border is rounded based
on an arc of an ellipse

Vertical
radius

Horizontal
radius

If you want to work with individual corners, the syntax is slightly different:

```
selector {
    border-top-left-radius: horizontalTL verticalTL;
    border-top-right-radius: horizontalTR verticalTR;
    border-bottom-right-radius: horizontalBR verticalBR;
    border-bottom-left-radius: horizontalBL verticalBL;
}
```

Here's an example:

```
aside {
    border: 5px dashed red;
    border-top-left-radius: 50px 75px;
    border-top-right-radius: 100px 50px;
    border-bottom-right-radius: 75px 100px;
    border-bottom-left-radius: 50px 25px;
}
```

# Manipulating Element Margins

The final component of the CSS box model is the *margin*, which is the space around the border of the box. Margins are an important detail in web design because they prevent elements from rubbing up against the edges of the browser content area, ensure that two elements don't overlap each other (unless you want them to), and create a pleasing amount of whitespace between elements.

As with padding, there are four sections to the margin — above, to the right of, below, and to the left of the border — so CSS offers four corresponding properties for adding margins to an element:

```
selector {
    margin-top: top-value;
    margin-right: right-value;
    margin-bottom: bottom-value;
    margin-left: left-value;
}
```

» *selector*: A CSS selector that specifies the item (or items) you want to style

» *top-value*, etc.: A number followed by a CSS measurement unit (such as px, em, rem, vw, or vh; refer to Book 3, Chapter 5 to find out what these units mean) or a percentage

Here's an example:

```
aside {
    margin-top: 16px;
    margin-right: 8px;
    margin-bottom: 32px;
    margin-left: 24px;
}
```

**WARNING**

Watch out if you use percentage values for your margins. Why? Because, any margin percentage you use is calculated based on the width of the *parent* element (that is, the element that contains the element you're styling). Note that the browser still uses the container element's width to calculate the percentage value even if you're styling the *top* or *bottom* margin, which takes some getting used to!

**TIP**

If you want to center a block element horizontally within its parent, you can do it with margins. First, you need to give the element a width (refer to "Styling Element Sizes," later in this chapter). Then add the following to a rule that targets the element:

```
margin-right: auto;
margin-left: auto;
```

As it does for padding, CSS also offers a shorthand syntax for the margin property. Table 1-3 lists the four syntaxes you can use with the margin property.

**TABLE 1-3**     The `margin` Shorthand Property

| Syntax | Description |
|---|---|
| margin: *value1*; | Applies *value1* to all four sides |
| margin: *value1 value2*; | Applies *value1* to the top and bottom and *value2* to the right and left |
| margin: *value1 value2 value3*; | Applies *value1* to the top, *value2* to the right and left, and *value3* to the bottom |
| margin: *value1 value2 value3 value4*; | Applies *value1* to the top, *value2* to the right, *value3* to the bottom, and *value4* to the left |

Here's the shorthand version of the previous example:

```css
aside {
    margin: 16px 8px 32px 24px;
}
```

## Taking advantage of negative margins

One interesting feature of the margin properties is that they accept *negative* values. What the heck does that mean? When you set, say, an element's `margin-top` property to a positive value, the effect is to push that element down, away from whatever element is above it. If you set the element's `margin-top` property to a negative value, the effect is to draw that element up, toward whatever element is above it. This effect can be useful if you want two elements to overlap or to butt up against each other in some sort of interesting way.

## Collapsing margins ahead!

CSS has no shortage of eccentricities, and you'll come across most of them in your web development career. Here's a look at one of the odder things that CSS does. First, here's some HTML and CSS code to chew over (bk03ch01/example05. html):

HTML:

```html
<header>
    <img src="images/notw.png" alt="News of the Word logo">
    <h1>News of the Word</h1>
    <h3>Language news you won't find anywhere else (for good
  reason!)</h3>
</header>
```

```
<nav>
    <a href="#">Home</a>
    <a href="#">What's New</a>
    <a href="#">What's Old</a>
    <a href="#">What's What</a>
</nav>
```

CSS:

```
nav {
    margin-top: 8px;
    padding: 12px;
    border: 1px solid black;
}
```

I'd like to draw your attention in particular to the margin-top: 8px declaration in the nav element's CSS rule. Figure 1-12 shows that, sure enough, the browser has rendered a small margin above the nav element.

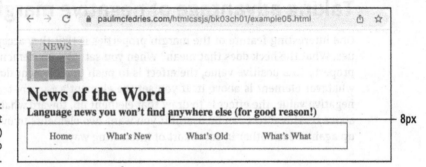

**FIGURE 1-12:** The nav element (with the border) has an 8px top border.

Suppose now I decide that I want a bit more space between the header and the nav elements, so I add a bottom margin to the header:

```
header {
    margin-bottom: 8px;
}
```

Figure 1-13 shows the result.

FIGURE 1-13:
The header
element with a
bottom margin
added (with the
border) has an
8px top border.

News of the Word

Language news you won't find anywhere else (for good reason!)

| Home | What's New | What's Old | What's What |

8px (still!)

No, you're not hallucinating: The space between the header and nav elements didn't change one iota! Welcome to the wacky world of CSS! In this case, the wackiness comes courtesy of a CSS "feature" called *collapsing margins*. When one element's bottom margin butts up against another element's top margin, common sense would dictate that the web browser would add the two margin values together. Hah; you wish! Instead, the browser uses the larger of the two margin values and throws out the smaller value. That is, it "collapses" the two margin values into a single value.

So, does that mean you're stuck? Not at all. To get some extra vertical space between two elements, you have four choices:

>> Increase the margin-top value of the bottom element.

>> Increase the margin-bottom value of the top element.

>> If you already have margin-top defined on the bottom element, and the top element doesn't use a border, add a padding-bottom value to the top element.

>> If you already have margin-bottom defined on the top element, and the bottom element doesn't use a border, add a padding-top value to the bottom element.

In the last two bullets, combining a top or bottom margin on one element with a bottom or top padding on the other element works because the browser doesn't collapse a margin/padding combo.

**REMEMBER** If you use floated or absolutely positioned elements (as I explain in Book 5, Chapter 1), the margins of those elements never collapse. Also, margins don't collapse in flex containers (check out Book 5, Chapter 2 to find out what a "flex container" is).

### Dealing with negative margins

Everything that I've said so far about collapsing margins applies to positive margin values, but what about negative margins? In that case, there are two scenarios to consider:

>> **Both margins are negative:** The browser collapses the margins and uses the "most negative" margin as the collapsed value. For example, if one element has a bottom margin of –20px and the element below it has a top margin of –10px, the vertical margin between them will collapse to the –20px value.

>> **One margin is negative and the other margin is positive:** The browser collapses the margins and takes the net value between the two margins as the collapsed value. For example, if one element has a bottom margin of 24px and the element below it has a top margin of –8px, the vertical margin between them will be 16px.

### Other margin collapsing scenarios

**TECHNICAL STUFF**

The collapsing of the vertical margin space between two adjacent elements is a head-scratcher and not at all intuitive. However, there are two other scenarios where margins collapse and, believe it or not, these scenarios actually make a bit of sense:

>> **When there's nothing between the tops or bottoms of an element and its containing elements:** Suppose element A contains element B. If there's nothing — no content, padding, or border — between the top margin of element A and the top margin of element B, these margins collapse. Similarly, if there's no content, padding, or border between the bottom margin of element A and the bottom margin of element B, these margins collapse.

>> **When an element is empty:** If an element is empty — that is, it doesn't contain any content, doesn't have any padding or a border, and hasn't had its height or min-height properties set (refer to the next section) — the element's top and bottom margins collapse.

# Styling Element Sizes

When the web browser renders a page, it examines each element and sets the dimensions of that element. For block-level elements such as `<header>` and `<div>`, the browser sets the dimensions as follows:

>> **Width:** Set to the width of the element's containing block. Because by default the width of the `<body>` element is set to the width of the browser's content area, in practice all block-level elements have their widths set to the width of the content area.

>> **Height:** Set just high enough to hold all the element's content.

You alter an element's dimensions by styling its `width` and `height` properties:

```
selector {
    width: width-value;
    height: height-value;
}
```

>> *selector*: A CSS selector that specifies the item (or items) you want to style.

>> *width-value*, *height-value*: One of the following:

- *A number:* Be sure to follow the number with one of the CSS measurement units I talk about in Book 3, Chapter 5 (such as px, em, rem, vw, or vh).

- *A percentage:* The resulting value is the percentage applied to the corresponding dimension of the element's containing block. If you're setting the width, the value is the percentage times the containing element's width; if you're setting the height, the value is the percentage times the containing element's height.

- *A keyword:* For the `width` property, you have three choices here:

  `fit-content`: Sets the width big enough to include all the element's text. If there's more text than can fit into the width of the containing element, the text is wrapped within that container.

  `max-content`: Sets the width big enough to include all the element's text. If there's more text than can fit into the width of the containing element, the text is *not* wrapped. Note that a long text entry may therefore extend beyond its containing element.

  `min-content`: Sets the width to the width of the longest word in the element's text. All the element's text wraps within this width.

For example, if you have an `aside` element that you want to take up only three quarters of the width of its containing element, you use the following rule:

```
aside {
    width: 75%;
}
```

Figure 1-14 shows a page that consists of a main div element that acts as the container for several p elements, each of which tries out a different width value (bk03ch01/example06.html).

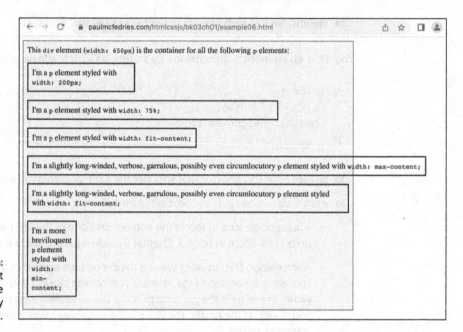

FIGURE 1-14:
Putting different
values of the
width property
to work.

**REMEMBER** Most of the time you'll mess only with an element's width; getting the height right is notoriously difficult because it depends on too many factors: the content, the browser's window size, the user's default font size, and more.

**TIP** Want to turn an element into a perfect circle? Sure you do! Just give the element identical height and width values and then set the border-radius property (which I discuss earlier in the "Rounding your borders" section) to 50%:

```
div {
    border-radius: 50%;
    height: 100px;
    width: 100px;
}
```

# Setting a minimum or maximum height or width

Sometimes (quite often, actually), to make a page design work, you need an element to always be rendered at least at some specified height or width, even if the element's content would normally dictate smaller dimensions. If the element ends up with more content than can fit in the specified height or width, it's okay for the element to expand as needed.

What I'm talking about here is setting a minimum height or width on an element, which you can do just like that by working with the min-height and min-width properties:

```
selector {
    min-height: height-value;
    min-width: width-value;
}
```

» *selector*: A CSS selector that specifies the item (or items) you want to style.

» *width-value*, *height-value*: Use a number (followed by a unit such as px, em, rem, vw, or vh; check out Book 3, Chapter 5), a percentage, or a keyword (max-content, min-content, or auto, which lets the browser decide).

For example, if a section element must be at least 200 pixels high no matter what content it contains, use the following rule:

```
section {
    min-height: 200px;
}
```

The opposite concern is when you don't want an element's height or width to grow beyond a particular value. The element's height or width can be less than that value, but never more than that value, even if it has more content than can fit.

To accomplish this goal, you need to set a maximum height or width on an element, which you can do by working with the max-height and max-width properties:

```
selector {
    max-height: height-value;
    max-width: width-value;
}
```

>> *selector*: A CSS selector that specifies the item (or items) you want to style.

>> *width-value*, *height-value*: Use a number (followed by a unit such as px, em, rem, vw, or vh; refer to Book 3, Chapter 5), a percentage, or a keyword (max-content, min-content, or auto, which lets the browser decide).

For example, if an aside element must be no more than 200 pixels high and no more than 150 pixels wide, no matter what content it contains, use the following rule:

```
footer {
    max-height: 200px;
    max-width: 150px;
}
```

**TIP**

One problem you'll run into using the max-height and max-width properties is content overflowing the box of an element when the maximum height or width is set too small to contain the content. Fortunately, CSS has several properties that enable you to gracefully handle such overflow problems. Download Bonus Chapter 4 from www.dummies.com/go/htmlcss&javascriptaiofd to delve into these properties.

## Making width and height make sense

Width and height seem like such straightforward concepts, but you may as well find out now that CSS has a knack for turning the straightforward into the crooked-sideways. A block element's dimensions are a case in point, because you'd think the "size" of a block element would be the size of its box out to the border: that is, the content, plus the padding, plus the border itself. Nope. By default, the size of a block element's box is just the content part of the box.

That may not sound like a cause for alarm, but it does mean that when you're working with an element's dimensions, you have to take into account its padding widths and border sizes if you want to get things right. Believe me, taking all that into account is no picnic. Fortunately, help is just around the corner. You can avoid all those extra calculations by forcing the web browser to be sensible and define an element's size to include not just the content, but the padding and border as well. A CSS property called box-sizing is the superhero here:

```
selector {
    box-sizing: border-box;
}
```

The declaration `box-sizing: border-box` tells the browser to set the element's height and width to include the content, padding, and border. You could add this declaration to all your block-level element rules, but that's way too much work. Instead, you can use a trick in which you use an asterisk (*) selector, which is a shorthand way of referencing every element on the page:

```
* {
    box-sizing: border-box;
}
```

Put this at the top of your style sheet, and then you never have to worry about it again.

## Magically converting an inline element to a block-level element

Height and width apply only to block-level elements such as `<article>`, `<div>`, and `<p>`, and not to inline elements such as `<span>` and `<a>`. However, it's possible to convert inline elements into blocks. CSS offers two methods for this inline-to-block makeover:

>> **Make it an inline block.** If you want to set an inline element's width, height, or other block-related properties, but still allow the element to flow along with the surrounding text, add the following to the element's CSS declaration:

```
display: inline-block;
```

>> **Make it a true block.** If you want to set an inline element's block-related properties and you no longer want the element to flow with the surrounding text, turn it into an honest-to-goodness block-level element by adding the following to the element's CSS declaration:

```
display: block;
```

IN THIS CHAPTER

» Figuring out parents, children, siblings, and other CSS kinfolk

» Understanding why selectors are so darned important

» Selecting elements by type, class, or id

» Targeting child and sibling elements

» Selecting elements by attribute

Chapter **2**

# Getting to Know the CSS Selectors

*Perhaps the biggest key to understanding CSS is understanding selectors.*

—CHRIS COYIER

I n Book 1, Chapter 1, I mention that one way to add CSS to a page is to insert the style attribute into whatever HTML tag you want to modify. That works, but it's really only workable for the teensiest web pages. If your web projects go even a little beyond putting "Hello World!" in an h1 element, it's light years more efficient to plop your CSS rules inside either an internal stylesheet (using the head section's ‹style› tag) or an external stylesheet (using a separate .css file).

When you go the stylesheet route (be it internal or external), it becomes crucial that each CSS rule applies only to the page elements that you want the rule to style. Ensuring that a CSS rule applies only to a particular element or set of elements is the job of each rule's selector.

In this chapter, you investigate the rich, useful, and incredibly powerful realm of CSS selectors. I take you through not only all the must-know selectors that are part of the coding repertoire of every web designer, but also a satisfyingly extensive tour of the broader selector toolkit. It's not a complete tour, however, because I talk about even more selectors in Book 3, Chapter 3.

# Introducing Yourself to the Web Page Family

One of the key concepts in this chapter — and, indeed, one of the most useful concepts in all of CSS — is the set of relationships that exist between every element in a web page.

To help you understand these relationships, it's useful to have an example to refer to over the next page or two, so here you go (refer to bk03ch02/example00.html in this book's example files):

```
<html lang="en">
    <head>
        <meta charset="UTF-8">
        <title>So Many Kale Recipes</title>
    </head>
    <body>
        <header>
            <h1>Above and Beyond the Kale of Duty</h1>
        </header>
        <main>
            <p>
                Do you love to cook with kale?
            </p>
            <p>
                Do you know the history of kale?
            </p>
            <p>
                Are you obsessed with kale?
            </p>
        </main>
    </body>
</html>
```

As shown in Figure 2-1, one way to look at this code is as a set of nested containers:

>> The html element includes every other element in the page, so its container surrounds everything.

>> Within the html element are two smaller containers: the head and body elements.

>> Within the head element are containers for the meta and title elements.

>> Within the body element are containers for the header and main elements.

>> Within the header element is a container for the h1 element.

>> Within the main element are containers for three p elements.

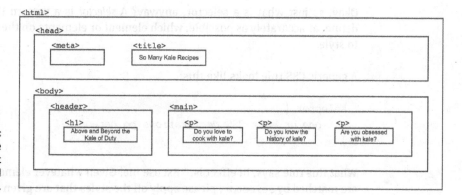

FIGURE 2-1:
The web page
code as a set
of nested
containers.

The key point here is the nesting of these containers because it's the nesting that determines the relationships that each element has to every other element. Here's how it works:

>> If element P contains element C, then element P is said to be the *parent* of element C. In Figure 2-1, for example, the body element is the parent of the header and main elements.

>> If element C is contained in element P, then element C is said to be the *child* of element P. In Figure 2-1, for example, the h1 element is the child of the header element.

>> If both element C1 and C2 are contained in element P, then C1 and C2 are said to be *siblings* of each other. In Figure 2-1, for example, the three p elements in the main element are siblings.

>> If element C is contained in element P, and element D is contained in element C, then element D is said to be a *descendant* of element P, and element P is an *ancestor* of element D. In Figure 2-1, for example, the h1 element is a descendant of the body element. Similarly, the body element is an ancestor of any of the p elements.

I threw a lot of new terminology at you in that list, so don't worry if it hasn't all sunk in just yet. These concepts will quickly become second nature to you as you work with CSS in general and selectors in particular.

# What's All This About a Selector?

Okay, so just what is a selector, anyway? A *selector* is a pattern that you use to define, as accurately as possible, which element or elements on the page you want to style.

A generic CSS rule looks like this:

```
selector {
    one or more CSS declarations go here
}
```

What this rule says, in effect is, "Excuse me! Given whatever element or elements are matched by `selector`, please apply all the styles that are given in the declaration block that follows. Thanks so much."

Any element referenced by a selector is known as the *subject* of the selector.

## Seeing some examples of selectors

What types of subjects are we talking about here? All kinds:

>> Element names (such as header or p)

>> An element that has a specified id

>> Elements that have a particular attribute or attribute value

>> Checkboxes that are currently selected

>> The element over which the user is currently hovering the mouse pointer

>> The children of a particular parent

>> The descendants of a particular ancestor

>> The siblings of a particular element

Given those last three, you can understand why it's important to learn about the relationships between the elements in a page, as I discuss in the previous section.

## Working with selector lists

One of the most powerful aspects of selectors is that you can take a single CSS declaration block and apply it to multiple selectors. For example, you may need to apply exactly the same styling to your page's nav and footer elements.

Applying the same styling to multiple elements isn't a problem because you can create a *selector list* that enables you to add as many selectors as you need instead of creating separate (and identical) CSS rules for each element. In your list, each selector is separated by a comma:

```
selectorA, selectorB, ..., selectorN {
    one or more CSS declarations go here
}
```

For easier reading, most web developers put each selector on its own line, like so:

```
selectorA,
selectorB,
...,
selectorN {
    one or more CSS declarations go here
}
```

Okay, enough theory. It's time to start actually selecting stuff.

**REMEMBER**

In the pages that follow, I provide you with example code for most of the selectors. The problem is that, to make the examples both useful and interesting, I use lots of property names that may be unfamiliar to you. In most cases, you can turn to the following chapters for an explanation:

>> For anything related to padding, borders, margins, and sizes, refer to Book 3, Chapter 1.

>> For anything relate to colors and backgrounds, head for Book 3, Chapter 6.

>> For anything related to text and alignment, turn to Book 3, Chapter 7.

# Learning the Standard Selectors

The happy news about CSS selectors is that, although there are dozens in the CSS standard, there are just a few workhorses that you'll use for most of your CSS rules. In particular, the selectors I cover in the next few sections probably deserve to be tattooed somewhere on your person for easy reference.

## The type selector

The *type selector* matches page items by element name (so it's also sometimes called the *element selector* or the *tag selector*):

```
element {
    property1: value1;
    property2: value2;
    ...
}
```

For example, if you want to put a border around every `aside` element, you use a CSS rule like this (check out bk03ch02/example01.html):

```
aside {
    border: 3px solid black;
}
```

## The class selector (.)

If you master just one CSS selector, make it the class selector, because you'll use it time and again in your web projects. A *class selector* is one that targets its styles at a particular web page class. So, what's a class? I'm glad you asked. A *class* is an attribute assigned to one or more tags that enables you to create a kind of grouping for those tags. Here's the syntax for adding a class to an element:

```
<element class="class-name">
```

>> `element`: The name of the element you're working with.

>> `class-name`: The name you want to assign to the class. The name must begin with a letter, and the rest can be any combination of letters, numbers, hyphens (-), and underscores (_).

Here's an example:

```
<h2 class="subtitle">
```

With your classes assigned to your tags as needed, you're ready to start selecting those classes using CSS. You select a class by preceding the class name with a dot (.) in your style rule:

```
.class-name {
    property1: value1;
    property2: value2;
    . . .
}
```

For example, here's a rule for the subtitle class (bk03ch02/example02.html):

```
.subtitle {
    color: royalblue;
    font-style: italic;
}
```

The advantage here is that you can assign the subtitle class to any tag on the page, and CSS will apply the same style rule to each of those elements.

## Combining type and class selectors

When you use a selector such as .subtitle in a CSS rule, you're asking the browser to match every page element that uses the subtitle class. However, suppose your page uses that class not only in all its h2 elements, but all its h3 elements as well. How can you target just those h3 elements that use the subtitle class? By preceding the class selector with the element name:

```
element.class-name {
    property1: value1;
    property2: value2;
    . . .
}
```

For example, the following rule matches just the h3 elements that have the subtitle class (bk03ch02/example02.html):

```
h3.subtitle {
    border: 2px dashed royalblue;
}
```

## Matching multiple classes

It's possible (in fact, fairly common) for an element to have two or more classes. To add multiple classes to a tag, you still use the class attribute, but in the value, you separate each class name with a space. Here's an example:

```
<h4 class="subtitle aside-title">
```

You can then target any elements that contain both classes by chaining the class selectors together, like so (bk03ch02/example02.html):

```
.subtitle.aside-title {
    color: red;
}
```

# The id selector (#)

In Book 2, Chapter 2, I talk about creating an anchor by adding a unique id attribute to a tag, which enabled you to create a link that targeted the anchor:

```
<element id="id-name">
```

Here's an example:

```
<h1 id="page-title">
```

You can also use the id attribute as a CSS selector, which enables you to target a particular element with extreme precision. You set up this *id selector* by preceding the id value with a hashtag symbol (#) in your CSS rule:

```
#id-name {
    property1: value1;
    property2: value2;
    ...
}
```

For example, here's a rule for the page-title id (bk03ch02/example03.html):

```
#page-title {
    color: maroon;
    font-family: "Times New Roman", serif;
    text-transform: uppercase;
}
```

This isn't as useful as the tag or class selectors because it can target only a single element, which is why web developers use id selectors only rarely.

**WARNING**

You may be considering using the same `id` value on multiple elements to make it easier to apply certain CSS rules. Please, step away from the text editor! Using the same `id` valid for two or more elements in the same HTML document will render your code invalid and could cause no end of unforeseeable CSS woes. A better solution would be to use the same `class` value on each of those elements and then use the class to apply the CSS rules.

## The universal selector (*)

The *universal selector* is a special instance of the type selector because you use it to match every element on the page:

```
* {
    property1: value1;
    property2: value2;
    ...
}
```

Some web developers use the universal selector to perform a simple reset of their CSS:

```
* {
    padding: 0;
    margin: 0;
    box-sizing: border-box;
}
```

To find out more about using a reset in your projects, check out Book 3, Chapter 4.

# Selecting Descendants, Children, and Siblings

One of the most powerful and useful categories of CSS selectors is the collection of so-called *combinators*. These are operators (such as > and ~) that enable you to combine other types of selectors in a way that matches a specific type of relationship between the selectors: descendant, child, or sibling.

**REMEMBER**

The awesome power of the combinators comes from the fact that you can use them with any of the other types of selectors that you learn about in this chapter. This flexibility enables you to create truly useful CSS rules that target just the elements you want to style.

## The descendant combinator ( )

Rather than targeting specific tags, classes, or ids, you may need to target every instance of a particular element that is contained within another element. I'm talking here not just about the children of some parent element, but also the descendants of that element.

To apply styles to all of an ancestor element's descendants, CSS offers the *descendant combinator*. To set up a selector that uses a descendant combinator, you include in your rule the ancestor and the descendant type you want to style, separated by a space:

```
ancestor descendant {
    property1: value1;
    property2: value2;
    ...
}
```

For example, consider the following HTML (bk03ch02/example04.html):

```
<aside>
    <h4>Links:</h4>
    <div>
        <a href="example01.html">The type selector</a><br>
        <a href="example02.html">The class selector</a><br>
        <a href="example03.html">The id selector</a>
    </div>
</aside>
```

Here's a rule that applies a few styles to the `<a>` tags that are descendants of the `<aside>` tag:

```
aside a {
    color: red;
    font-style: italic;
    text-decoration: none;
}
```

# The child combinator (>)

The descendant combinator that I discuss in the previous section is one of the most powerful in the CSS kingdom because it targets all the descendants of a particular type that reside within an ancestor, no matter how many levels down the page hierarchy those descendants live. However, it's often more suitable and more manageable to target only those descendants that reside one level down: in short, the children of some parent element.

To aim some styles at the child elements of a parent, you use the *child combinator*, where you separate the parent and child elements with a greater-than sign (>):

```
parent > child {
    property1: value1;
    property2: value2;
    ...
}
```

For example, here's a rule that targets any h4 element that's a child of an aside element (bk03ch02/example05.html):

```
aside > h4 {
    color: green;
    border-top: 3px solid black;
    border-bottom: 5px double black;
    padding: 4px 0;
    text-transform: uppercase;
}
```

# The subsequent-sibling combinator (~)

One common CSS task is to apply a style rule to a particular subject that meets the following criteria:

>> The target element appears in the HTML after a specified element, which is known as the *reference* element.

>> The target element and the reference element are siblings.

To apply some styles to such a subject, you use the *subsequent-sibling combinator*, where you separate the reference and target elements with a tilde (~):

```
reference ~ target {
    property1: value1;
    property2: value2;
    ...
}
```

For example, here's a rule that targets any ul element that's a subsequent sibling of an h2 element (bk03ch02/example06.html):

```
h2 ~ ul {
    background: lightpink;
    border: 5px outset crimson;
    list-style-type: square;
    padding: 8px 20px;
}
```

## The next-sibling combinator (+)

Rather than target all the siblings that come after some reference element, as does the subsequent-sibling combinator that I discuss in the previous section, you may need to target only the *next* sibling that comes after the reference element.

For example, suppose you have a page full of h2 elements, each of which is followed by multiple p elements, where the first p element is some text that summarizes the p elements that follow. In this case, it makes sense to style those first p elements differently, perhaps by italicizing the text.

To apply a style rule to just the next sibling that comes after some reference element, you use the *next-sibling combinator*, where you separate the reference and target elements with a plus sign (+):

```
reference + target {
    property1: value1;
    property2: value2;
    ...
}
```

For example, here's a rule that targets any p element that's the next sibling of an h2 element (bk03ch02/example07.html):

```
h2 + p {
    font-style: italic;
}
```

# Selecting Elements by Attribute

An *attribute*, as I discuss in Book 1, Chapter 1, is some extra code inserted into a tag that modifies the tag in some way. In an ‹a› tag, for example, the href attribute is set to a string that specifies the address of the link.

Attributes also enable you to differentiate elements in your page. For example, your page may have a bunch of a elements, but only one a element whose href attribute equals https://www.w3.org/.

CSS takes advantage of this differentiability by offering several *attribute selectors* that enable you to target the presence of a specified attribute, the value of a specified attribute, or some subset of that value.

Here's the general syntax for an attribute selector:

```
element[expression] {
    property1: value1;
    property2: value2;
    ...
}
```

>> *element*: The name of the element you want to target

>> *expression*: An expression that specifies the attribute or attribute value in *element* that you want to match

The *expression* part of the syntax is the key here, and it's usually a combination of an attribute name, an operator, and a value. Table 2-1 takes you through the available expression types.

**TABLE 2-1**      CSS Attribute Selectors

| Selector Name | Syntax | What It Matches |
|---|---|---|
| Attribute only | `element[attr]` | Any instance of `element` that includes the attribute named `attr`. The following example styles all abbr elements that have the `title` attribute (bk03ch02/example08.html):<br><br>`abbr[title] {`<br><br>`border: 1px dotted gray;`<br><br>`}` |
| Attribute equals | `element[attr="value"]` | Any instance of `element` with the attribute named `attr`, the value of which is equal to `value`. The following example styles all a elements that have an `href` attribute equal to `https://www.w3.org/` (bk03ch02/example09.html):<br><br>`a[href="https://www.w3.org/"] {`<br><br>`color: green;`<br><br>`}` |
| Attribute begins with | `element[attr^="value"]` | Any instance of `element` with the attribute named `attr`, the value of which starts with `value`. The following example styles all a elements that have an `href` attribute that begins with `http://` (bk03ch02/example10.html):<br><br>`a[href^="http://"] {`<br><br>`color: red;`<br><br>`}` |
| Attribute contains | `element[attr*="value"]` | Any instance of `element` with the attribute named `attr`, the value of which includes `value`. The following example styles all div elements that have an id attribute that includes the string navbar (bk03ch02/example11.html):<br><br>`div[id*="navbar"] {`<br><br>`font-size: 14px;`<br><br>`}` |

| Selector Name | Syntax | What It Matches |
|---|---|---|
| Attribute ends with | element[attr$="value"] | Any instance of element with the attribute named attr, the value of which ends with value. The following example styles all a elements that have an href attribute that ends with .org (bk03ch02/example12.html):<br><br>`a[href$=".org"] {`<br><br>`color: firebrick;`<br><br>`}` |
| Attribute is first | element[attr/="value"] | Any instance of element with the attribute name attr, the value of which is either equal to value or starts with value– (that is, value followed by a hyphen [–]). The following example matches all div elements that have a lang attribute that equals en or starts with en– (bk03ch02/example13.html):<br><br>`div[lang|="en"] {`<br><br>`color: blue;`<br><br>`}` |
| Attribute includes | element[attr~="value"] | Any instance of element with the attribute named attr, the value of which includes value as a whole word. The following example matches all img elements that have an alt attribute that includes photo as a whole word (bk03ch02/example14.html):<br><br>`img[alt~="photo"] {`<br><br>`border: 12px ridge saddlebrown;`<br><br>`}`<br><br>Note that this selector would *not* match alt attributes that include words such as photograph or telephoto (assuming they don't have the whole word photo elsewhere in the alt string). |

Chapter **3**

# Pseudo School: Learning Pseudo-Classes and Pseudo-Elements

*pseudo: adj., almost, approaching, or trying to be.*

—DICTIONARY.COM

When you work with CSS, what you're essentially doing is applying styles to the HTML that you used to build the structure of the page. Your CSS rules deal with real (as far as things like HTML tags can be considered "real," that is) things like headings (h1, h2, and so on), paragraphs (p elements), links (a elements), and images (img elements).

However, your page has a hidden world that's not evident (at least not explicitly) in its HTML code. Has a page visitor selected a checkbox or radio button? Is a user hovering the mouse pointer over an image? Has the user visited one of your links in the past? Is a particular element the first child of its parent element? (Refer to Book 3, Chapter 2 if you're not sure what I mean by the terms *parent* and *child*.)

Okay, maybe you can eyeball that last one, but the point is that first-child-of-its-parent is not something explicit in the HTML. Despite the shadowiness of these states, wouldn't it be nice to be able to target them for styling? Perhaps you'd want to style an image temporarily when the user hovers the mouse over it. Perhaps that first-child-of-its-parent element needs some specific styles.

Happily, CSS *does* enable you to style these states and many more by using pseudo-classes and pseudo-elements. This chapter tells you everything you need to know about two of the most useful and powerful CSS concepts.

# Scratching Your Head Over Pseudo-Classes

You'll spend a surprisingly large chunk of your CSS development time creating classes. At first, these classes will define relatively broad rules that you'll use throughout your page. After a while, however, you'll come up with use cases for classes that are increasingly targeted. For example, if you have an article element that consists of several p child elements, it's common to style the first p element differently because, say, it acts as an introduction to the rest of the article. So, you create a class named intro and apply it to the article's first p element:

```
<article>
    <p class="intro">
```

Say you then you add a second article element and its first paragraph needs the same intro class. Easily done:

```
<article>
    <p class="intro">
    . . .
<article>
    <p class="intro">
```

Then you add an aside element and realize its first div element needs that intro styling, as well. Done:

```
<article>
    <p class="intro">
    . . .
    <aside>
        <div class="intro">
    . . .
```

```
<article>
    <p class="intro">
```

That's all fine, and it works, but what if you or someone you work with adds a paragraph or some other content before any of your tags that have the intro class? Assuming that this new content acts as a new introduction to the article (or whatever), you need to remember to go into your code and move the intro class to the new tag.

## Introducing the pseudo-class

So, here we come to the main problem with classes: They can require a lot of maintenance, especially as your page gets bigger and more sophisticated. That maintenance problem is why the CSS poohbahs came up with the concept of pseudo-classes. A *pseudo-class* is a CSS selector that acts like a class by generically targeting elements that meet some condition.

In my example from the previous section, the "condition" underlying the intro class was that an element had to be the first child of its parent. If an element met that condition, you'd go in and add class="intro" to its tag. However, CSS has a pseudo-class named :first-child that you can use to create a single rule targeting every element that meets the condition of being a first child of its parent. Best of all, you can do that without adding a single class to any tag, so your code is easier to write, easier to read, and easier to maintain. Win, win, win.

## Styling elements with pseudo-classes

All pseudo-classes begin with a colon (:), followed by one or more dash-separated words. You can use a pseudo-class on its own or modified by an element. Here's the general on-its-own syntax:

```
:pseudo-class {
    property1: value1;
    property2: value2;
    ...
}
```

Using a pseudo-class on its own means your rule matches every element that meets the pseudo-class's underlying condition.

The broadest (in a sense) pseudo-class is :root, which selects the parent of everything on the web page (that is, the <html> tag). The :root pseudo-class is most often used with CSS variables, which I talk about in Bonus Chapter 4, which you can download at a www.dummies.com/go/htmlcss&javascriptaiofd.

To style every element that's a first child of its parent element, you use the `:first-child` pseudo-class:

```css
:first-child {
    font-style: italic;
}
```

However, you're more likely to want to apply your rule to first children of a specific element type. You do that by appending the element name before the pseudo-class, like so:

```css
element:pseudo-class {
    property1: value1;
    property2: value2;
    ...
}
```

For example, the following rule applies a style to every p element that's a first child of its parent:

```css
p:first-child {
    font-style: italic;
}
```

You can combine pseudo-classes with other selectors, particularly the combinators. For example, the following rule applies a style to every p element that's a first child of an `article` element:

```css
article > p:first-child {
    font-style: italic;
}
```

Another common way to combine pseudo-classes and selectors is to modify the element name with a class, like so:

```css
element.class:pseudo-class {
    property1: value1;
    property2: value2;
    ...
}
```

For example, the following rule applies a style to every p element that uses the intro class and is a first child of its parent:

```
p.intro:first-child {
    font-style: italic;
}
```

CSS offers several dozen pseudo-classes. Yep, several *dozen*. If that sounds like an alarming amount, don't worry: Many — perhaps even the majority of — pseudo-classes are on the obscure side and are used only occasionally at best, even by professionals. In the sections that follow, I give you the details of the most common pseudo-classes and mention a few other useful ones in passing.

**REMEMBER**

If, in the pages that follow, the example code includes property names that are unfamiliar to you, in most cases you can turn to the following chapters for an explanation:

>> For anything related to padding, borders, margins, and sizes, check out Book 3, Chapter 1.

>> For anything relate to colors and backgrounds, head for Book 3, Chapter 6.

>> For anything related to text and alignment, turn to Book 3, Chapter 7.

## Matching child elements

The pseudo-classes you'll turn to most often in your CSS code are those that match child elements that meet some condition. How is this different from the child combinator (>) that I talk about earlier in this chapter? The child combinator targets *every* element that's a child of the specified parent element. What the child-related pseudo-elements do is give you a way to target specific child elements by position, such as the first, third, or last child.

### :first-child

The :first-child pseudo-class targets any child element that is the first of a parent element's children:

```
element:first-child {
    property1: value1;
    property2: value2;
    ...
}
```

>> *element*: (Optional) The name of the element type you want to target. If you omit *element*, your rule would target everything on the page that's a first child.

For example, in web typography (refer to Book 3, Chapter 7), it's common to indent all paragraphs using the `text-indent` property (for example, `text-indent: 16px`). All paragraphs, that is, except the first one, which should have no indent. Here's a rule that uses `:first-child` to accomplish this (check out bk03ch03/example01.html in this book's example files):

```
p:first-child {
    text-indent: 0;
}
```

When you use `:first-child` on its own (that is, without an element name prefix), you match every element that's the first child of a parent. This is exactly the same as using the universal selector (*) with the pseudo-class: `*:first-child`. This equivalence comes in handy when you want to use a selector such as the following:

```
article :first-child
```

This selector matches every `article` descendant that's a first child. When reading your CSS, you or someone else could easily mistake this selector for the following one:

```
article:first-child
```

This selector matches every `article` element that's a first child, which is completely different! To avoid such confusion, you can make your first selector easier to read by explicitly using the universal selector:

```
article *:first-child
```

## :last-child

The `:last-child` pseudo-class targets any child element that is the last of a parent element's children:

```
element:last-child {
    property1: value1;
    property2: value2;
    ...
}
```

>> *element*: (Optional) The name of the element type you want to target. If you omit *element*, your rule would target everything on the page that's a last child.

For example, one useful design trick is to add some extra whitespace to the bottom of the last paragraph before a heading. Here's a rule that uses `:last-child` to style some extra margin space below every p element that's the last of any parent's children (check out bk03ch03/example02.html):

```
p:last-child {
    margin-bottom: 24px;
}
```

## :nth-child()

The `:nth-child()` pseudo-class selects one or more elements based on their position in a parent element's collection of siblings. Here's the general syntax to use:

```
element:nth-child(n) {
    property1: value1;
    property2: value2;
    ...
}
```

» *element*: (Optional) The name of the element type you want to target. If you omit *element*, your rule would target everything on the page that's an nth-child.

» *n*: A number, expression, or keyword that specifies the position or positions of the child elements you want to match. There are five main ways to specify *n*:

- *A* (an integer): Selects the child element in the *A*th position. For example, `p:nth-child(2)` selects any p element that's the second child of a parent.

- *An* (an integer multiple): Selects every *A*th child element. For example, `p:nth-child(3n)` selects any p element that's in the third, sixth, ninth, and so on, position of a parent's child elements.

- *An+B* (an integer multiple plus an integer offset): Selects every child element that is in the *A*th position, plus *B*. For example, `p:nth-child(3n+2)` selects any p element that's in the second (n=0), fifth (n=1), eighth (n=2), and so on, position of a parent's child elements.

- even (keyword): Selects all the sibling elements that are in even-numbered positions (2, 4, 6, and so on). For example, `p:nth-child(even)` selects any p element that is in an even-numbered position within a parent's child elements. This is equivalent to `p:nth-child(2n)`.

- odd (keyword): Selects all the sibling elements that are in odd-numbered positions (1, 3, 5, and so on). For example, `p:nth-child(odd)` selects any p element that is in an odd-numbered position within a parent's child elements. This is equivalent to `p:nth-child(2n+1)`.

Here's a selector that targets just the even `tr` elements of a parent `table` element (bk03ch03/example03.html):

```css
tr:nth-child(even) {
    background-color: lightgray;
}
```

The rule sets the background color of the matching rows to `lightgray`, which produces the effect shown in Figure 3-1.

paulmcfedries.com/htmlcssjs/bk03ch02/example17.html

Table 1.1 lists five countries that have a goat population that's larger than their human population.

| Country | Goats | People |
|---|---|---|
| Somalia | 20,500,000 | 2,300,000 |
| Mongolia | 5,126,000 | 2,300,000 |
| Mauritania | 3,310,000 | 2,100,000 |
| Namibia | 1,500,000 | 1,400,000 |
| Djibouti | 504,000 | 400,000 |

**FIGURE 3-1:** Using nth-child(even) to style every second row in a table.

**REMEMBER**

When you're counting the child element positions within a parent, you do so regardless of the element type. Consider the following HTML snippet:

```html
<section>
    <p>Some paragraph text</p>
    <aside>Some sidebar text</aside>
    <p>More paragraph text</p>
</section>
```

The parent `section` element has three child elements: a `p` in position 1, then an `aside` in position 2, then another `p` in position 3. A selector such as `p:nth-child(3)` would successfully match the `p` element in position 3, but something like `p:nth-child(even)` would match nothing because there are no `p` elements in even positions within the `section` parent.

The `:nth-child()` pseudo-class has a second syntax that you might find useful:

```
:nth-child(n of list) {
    property1: value1;
    property2: value2;
    ...
}
```

>> *n*: A number, expression, or keyword that specifies the position or positions of the child elements you want to match.

>> *list*: A comma-separated list of selectors.

With this syntax, :nth-child(*n* of *list*) matches the expression *n* only for child elements that match one of the selectors in *list*. For example, the following selector matches those even elements that are h1 or h2:

```
:nth-child(even of h1, h2)
```

## :nth-last-child()

The :nth-last-child() pseudo-class selects one or more elements based on their position in a parent element's collection of siblings, counting from the end. Here's the general syntax to use:

```
element:nth-last-child(n [of list]) {
    property1: value1;
    property2: value2;
    ...
}
```

>> *element*: (Optional) The name of the element type you want to target. If you omit *element*, your rule would target everything that's an nth-last child.

>> *n*: A number, expression, or keyword that specifies the position or positions of the child elements you want to match. You specify *n* using the same methods as I outline in the previous section for the :nth-child() pseudo-class.

>> *list*: (Optional) A comma-separated list of selectors.

In short, :nth-last-child() is the same as :nth-child(), except the positions of the parent's child elements are counted starting from the last child, which is in position 1, the second-last child, which is in position 2, and so on.

## :only-child

The :only-child pseudo-class targets any element that's the only child of a parent element:

```
element:only-child {
    property1: value1;
    property2: value2;
    ...
}
```

>> *element*: (Optional) The name of the element type you want to target. If you omit *element*, your rule would target everything that's an only child.

For example, here's a rule that styles any section element descendant that's an only child (bko3cho3/example05.html):

```
section *:only-child {
    color: plum;
}
```

## Matching child elements by type

One of the quirks of the various child-related pseudo-classes that I yammer on about in the previous section is that they calculate the positions of a parent's child elements without regard to the element type. Here's an example to ponder:

```
<section>
    <p>Some paragraph text</p>
    <aside>Some sidebar text</aside>
    <p>More paragraph text</p>
    <aside>Some sidebar text</aside>
</section>
```

From the point of view of the child-related pseudo-classes, the first p element is in position 1, the aside element is in position 2, the second p element is in position 3, and the second aside element is in position 4. Now consider the following rule, which adds a border around any aside element that's a first child:

```
aside:first-child {
    border: 5px double black;
}
```

That rule won't get applied to the example HTML code because the first `aside` element is not the first child of the `section` element. Sure, you could use `aside:nth-child(2)`, but that breaks if one or more child elements get added before that `aside`. What you really want here is a way of matching the first *instance* of a particular element type. More generally, it's very handy to be able to match elements by position using the subset of a parent's child elements that are of a specified element type. In the preceding code, for example, you may want to work with just the `p` elements or just the `aside` elements. You can do that using the type-related pseudo-classes.

## :first-of-type

The `:first-of-type` pseudo-class targets any child element that's the first of its type in a parent element's children:

```
element:first-of-type {
    property1: value1;
    property2: value2;
    ...
}
```

>> *element*: (Optional) The name of the element type you want to target. If you omit *element*, your rule would target everything that's a first of its type.

For example, consider again this HTML snippet from the previous section:

```
<section>
    <p>Some paragraph text</p>
    <aside>Some sidebar text</aside>
    <p>More paragraph text</p>
    <aside>Some sidebar text</aside>
</section>
```

The following rule successfully targets the `aside` element because it's the first child element of its type (bk03ch03/example06.html):

```
aside:first-of-type {
    border: 5px double black;
}
```

## :last-of-type

The :last-of-type pseudo-class targets any child element that's the last of its type in a parent element's children:

```
element:last-of-type {
    property1: value1;
    property2: value2;
    ...
}
```

» *element*: (Optional) The name of the element type you want to target. If you omit *element*, your rule would target everything that's a last of its type.

Here's an example that targets the last p element of its type in any parent element (bk03ch03/example07.html):

```
p:last-of-type {
    margin-bottom: 24px;
}
```

## :nth-of-type()

The :nth-of-type() pseudo-class selects one or more elements of a specified type based on their position in a parent element's collection of siblings. Here's the general syntax to use:

```
element:nth-of-type(n) {
    property1: value1;
    property2: value2;
    ...
}
```

» *element*: (Optional) The name of the element type you want to target. If you omit *element*, then your rule would target everything that's an nth of its type.

» *n*: A number, expression, or keyword that specifies the position or positions of the child elements you want to match. You specify *n* using the same methods as I outline earlier in the ":nth-child()" section.

Here's a selector that targets every third p element (bk03ch03/example08.html):

```
p:nth-of-type(3n) {
    background-color: gray;
}
```

## :nth-last-of-type()

The :nth-last-of-type() pseudo-class selects one or more elements of a specified type based on their position in a parent element's collection of siblings, counting from the end. Here's the general syntax to use:

```
element:nth-last-of-type(n) {
    property1: value1;
    property2: value2;
    ...
}
```

>> *element*: (Optional) The name of the element type you want to target. If you omit *element*, then your rule would target everything that's an nth-last of its type.

>> *n*: A number, expression, or keyword that specifies the position or positions of the child elements you want to match. You specify *n* using the same methods as I outline earlier in the ":nth-child()" section.

So, :nth-last-of-type() is the same as :nth-of-type(), except that the positions of the parent's child elements are counted starting from the last child, which is in position 1, the second-last child, which is in position 2, and so on. (Check out bk03ch03/example09.html) for some examples.)

## :only-of-type

The :only-of-type pseudo-class targets any element of the specified type that's the only child of a parent element:

```
element:only-of-type {
    property1: value1;
    property2: value2;
    ...
}
```

>> *element*: (Optional) The name of the element type you want to target. If you omit *element*, your rule would target everything that's a first child.

For example, here's a rule that styles any `article` element `div` descendant that's an only child (bk03ch03/example10.html):

```
article div:only-of-type {
    margin: 24px 8px;
}
```

## Matching form elements by state

Form objects — including `input`, `button`, `textarea`, `select`, and `option` elements (refer to Book 2, Chapter 5) — can have various states:

>> The user can interact with the element (the enabled state) or can't interact with it (the disabled state).

>> The user must enter or select an element value (the required state) or can skip the element (the optional state).

>> The user can change the element's value (the read-write state) or can't change the value (the read-only state).

>> The current value of the element is appropriate (for example, is a numeric value when the element's `type` attribute is set to `number`) for that element (the valid state) or inappropriate (the invalid state).

>> The checkbox, radio button, or selection list option is toggled on (the checked state).

>> The current value of the element is within the limits specified by the element's `min` and `max` attributes (the in-range state) or is outside those limits (the out-of-range state).

In all these cases, good user interface design styles a form element in some way based on its current state. For example, a disabled text box may have a gray background and lighter text, whereas an element with an invalid value may have a red border and red text.

You can style a form element's by state with the various CSS pseudo-classes that target each state. Here's the general syntax:

```
form-element:state {
    property1: value1;
    property2: value2;
    ...
}
```

>> *form-element*: (Optional) A selector for the form element or elements you want to target. If you omit *element*, then your rule would target everything that's a first child.

>> *state*: The pseudo-class that represents the state of *form-element* that you want to style.

For example, the following rule uses the :disabled pseudo-class to target the disabled state of any text box:

```
input[type="text"]:disabled {
    background-color: lightgray;
    color: darkgray;
}
```

Table 3-1 lists the most often used pseudo-elements that enable you to target form element states.

**TABLE 3-1**     **Form Element State Pseudo-Classes**

| Pseudo-Class | What It Matches | Example |
|---|---|---|
| :checked | Any instance of a checkbox, radio button, or selection list option that's toggled on (bk03ch03/example11.html). | `input[type="checkbox"]:checked {`<br><br>`  box-shadow: 0 0 10px 3px red;`<br><br>`}`<br><br>`input[type="checkbox"]:checked +`<br>`label {`<br><br>`  color: red;`<br><br>`}` |
| :default* | Any instance of a form element that is in a default state, including a checkbox or radio button with the checked attribute, a selection list option with the selected attribute, or a button element with its type attribute set to submit (bk03ch03/example12.html). | `input[type="radio"]:default {`<br><br>`  box-shadow: 0 0 5px 1px forestgreen;`<br><br>`}`<br><br>`input[type="radio"]:default + label {`<br><br>`  color: forestgreen;`<br><br>`}` |

*(continued)*

**TABLE 3-1** *(continued)*

| Pseudo-Class | What It Matches | Example |
|---|---|---|
| :disabled | Any form element that has the disabled attribute set (bk03ch03/example13.html). | ```button:disabled {`<br>`  cursor: not-allowed;`<br>`  opacity: .5;`<br>`}``` |
| :enabled | Any form element that doesn't have the disabled attribute set (bk03ch03/example14.html). | ```button:enabled {`<br>`  box-shadow: 0 0 5px 3px seagreen;`<br>`  color: seagreen;`<br>`}``` |
| :in-range* | Any form element with a current value that's within the values set by the element's min and max attributes (bk03ch03/example15.html). | ```input[type="range"]:in-range {`<br>`  background-color: lawngreen;`<br>`}``` |
| :invalid | Any form element with a current value that doesn't validate, such as a number field with a text value or an email field with an invalid email address (for example, missing the @ sign) (bk03ch03/example16.html). | ```input[type="email"]:invalid {`<br>`  background: lavenderblush;`<br>`}``` |
| :optional | Any form element that doesn't have the required attribute set (bk03ch03/example17.html). | ```input[type="text"]:optional {`<br>`  background-color: lightgolden rodyellow;`<br>`}``` |
| :out-of-range* | Any form element with a current value that's not within the values set by the element's min and max attributes (bk03ch03/example18.html). | ```input[type="range"]:out-of-range {`<br>`  background-color: tomato;`<br>`}``` |
| :read-only* | Any form element that has the readonly attribute set (bk03ch03/example19.html). | ```textarea:read-only {`<br>`  border: 0;`<br>`  resize: none;`<br>`}``` |

| Pseudo-Class | What It Matches | Example |
|---|---|---|
| :read-write* | Any element that the user can edit, which could be a form element that's editable by default that doesn't have the readonly attribute set, or any element that's not editable by default that has the contenteditable attribute set (check out the sidebar "Editing non-editable content" that appears right after this table) (bk03ch03/example20.html). | `span:read-write {`<br><br>`  background: honeydew;`<br><br>`  caret-color: crimson;`<br><br>`}` |
| :required | Any form element that has the required attribute set (bk03ch03/example21.html). | `input[type="text"]:required {`<br><br>`  background-color: yellow;`<br><br>`}` |
| :valid | Any form element with a current value that validates, such as a number field with a numeric value or an email field with an email address (bk03ch03/example22.html). | `input[type="email"]:valid {`<br><br>`  background: palegreen;`<br><br>`}` |

*Pseudo-class isn't supported by older web browsers such as Internet Explorer 11.*

**TECHNICAL STUFF**

# EDITING NONEDITABLE CONTENT

HTML offers certain *editable* elements — such as textarea and input elements with the type attribute set to text, email, url, password, and search (among others) — with contents that the user can modify. Every other page element that contains text — every div, every blockquote, every span — is *noneditable*, meaning that the user can only read, not modify, the text. That seems reasonable, but every now and then you may want to open up one of those noneditable elements for editing. Why? Perhaps you want to give your page visitors the opportunity to personalize the page in some way. Or perhaps you want to take advantage of the default styling of an element such as blockquote.

Whatever the reason, you can turn any text element into an editable element by adding the contenteditable attribute to the element's tag. You can use any of the following syntaxes:

```
contenteditable = "true"
contenteditable = ""
contenteditable
```

# Matching elements by user action

CSS defines three types of user action that you can target for styling:

- ≫ **Activating an element:** Initiating whatever action is associated with the element, which could be a link, a button, or a form element such as a checkbox. A user activates an element with a mouse by pressing down (but not releasing) the mouse button on the element. Similarly, a user activates an element via touch by pressing down (but not releasing) a finger or stylus on the element. If an element has the focus, a user activates that element from the keyboard by pressing down (but not releasing) the spacebar. The element is active only as long as the mouse button or key is held down; when the user releases, the element is no longer active.

- ≫ **Putting the focus on an element:** Putting the element in a state where it can accept mouse or keyboard input. For elements such as text boxes and selection lists, the user puts the focus on the element either by clicking it or by pressing Tab or Shift+Tab until the element is selected.

- ≫ **Hovering over an element:** Moving the mouse pointer so that it rests within the element's boundaries.

## :active

To style an active element, use the `:active` pseudo-class:

```
element:active {
    property1: value1;
    property2: value2;
    ...
}
```

- ≫ `element`: (Optional) The element you want to target when it's active. If you omit `element`, your rule would target any element that becomes active.

Here's an example that styles a `button` element with a background color, and then changes that background color when the button is active (bk03ch03/example23. html):

```
button {
    background-color: purple;
}
button:active {
    background-color: fuchsia;
}
```

**WARNING**

If you set both the :active pseudo-class and the :hover pseudo-classes (covered shortly) on the same element, be sure to place the :active rule after the :hover rule. Why? Because, by definition, you have to hover over an element before you can activate it, so if your :hover rule comes after your :active rule, the :hover rule will always override the :active rule.

## :focus

To style an element that has the focus, use the :focus pseudo-class:

```
element:focus {
    property1: value1;
    property2: value2;
    ...
}
```

» *element*: (Optional) The element you want to target when it has the focus. If you omit *element*, your rule would target anything that gets the focus.

Here's an example that styles the background color for any input element that has the focus (bko3cho3/example24.html):

```
input:focus {
    background-color: lightsteelblue;
}
```

**TIP**

To match an element that either has the focus itself or has a descendant that has the focus (for example, a fieldset element that has descendant input elements), use the :focus-within pseudo-class instead of :focus. Note, however, that :focus-within is a relatively new pseudo-class, so isn't supported by older browsers such as Internet Explorer 11.

## :hover

To style an element when the user hovers the mouse over the element, use the :hover pseudo-class:

```
element:hover {
    property1: value1;
    property2: value2;
    ...
}
```

>> *element*: (Optional) The element you want to target when the mouse is hovered over it. If you omit *element*, then your rule would target anything that's hovered over.

Here's an example that adds a box shadow when the user hovers over a button element (bk03ch03/example25.html):

```
button:hover {
    box-shadow: 10px 5px 5px grey;
}
```

WARNING

Don't rely on the :hover pseudo-class for crucial styling because many of your site visitors might be using touchscreens, screen readers, or other devices with which hovering isn't possible.

## Matching links

CSS offers several link-related pseudo-classes that you can use to style links without having to resort to complex classes. First, here are some concepts you need to know before you start messing around with styling links:

>> **Link element:** Refers to any element that has an href attribute, particularly the a element, but also the area element.

>> **Visited element:** A link element that points to a web page that the user has already visited. For privacy reasons, all web browsers enable you to work with only a small set of CSS properties for visited links: color, background-color, border-color, border-bottom-color, border-left-color, border-right-color, border-top-color, column-rule-color, outline-color, text-decoration-color, and text-emphasis-color.

>> **Target:** When a user visits a page anchor (refer to Book 2, Chapter 2), the id attribute of the anchor tag is appended to the URL, preceded by a hashtag (#). For example, here's a section element where the anchor id is section1:

```
<section id="section1">
```

When a user follows a link to this anchor, the URL will have #section1 added to the end, something like this:

```
https://www.mysite.com/chapter57.html#section1
```

The page anchor — the <section> tag in this example — is referred to as the *target,* and the part appended to the address is called the *URL fragment.*

Table 3-2 lists the four main link-related pseudo-classes.

**TABLE 3-2**     Link-Related Pseudo-Classes

| Pseudo-Class | What It Matches | Example |
| --- | --- | --- |
| `:any-link*` | Any link element (bk03ch03/example26.html) | `aside a:any-link {`<br><br>   `text-decoration-color: mediumvioletred;`<br><br>   `text-decoration-style: wavy;`<br><br>`}` |
| `:link` | Any link element that the user has not yet visited (bk03ch03/example27.html) | `a:link {`<br><br>   `color: red;`<br><br>   `text-decoration-color: red;`<br><br>`}` |
| `:target` | The element with an id attribute value that matches the fragment of the current URL (bk03ch03/example28.html) | `button:target {`<br><br>   `cursor: not-allowed;`<br><br>   `opacity: .5;`<br><br>`}` |
| `:visited` | Any link element that the user has visited (bk03ch03/example29.html) | `a:visited {`<br><br>   `color: pink;`<br><br>   `text-decoration-color: pink;`<br><br>`}` |

*Pseudo-class isn't supported by older web browsers such as Internet Explorer 11.*

**WARNING**

After a user clicks one of your links, the web browser considers that link to have been "visited" and that state never changes. In other words, when a user clicks one of your links, your `:visited` pseudo-class rule will always apply. That situation can mess up your styles if the `:visited` pseudo-class rule comes after your `:active` and `:hover` pseudo-class rules in your stylesheet. A common rule of thumb is to add your link-related rules in the following order: `:link`, `:visited`, `:hover`, `:active`.

## Working with functional pseudo-classes

As your web projects grow and your work with selectors becomes more complex, you might start to wonder whether CSS offers any shorthand methods that can simplify some of your selector chores. Why, yes, it does! CSS offers several so-called *functional pseudo-classes* that operate not on a single selector, but on a selector list.

## A quick look at selector lists

A *selector list* is a comma-separated collection of selectors. For example, consider the following three rules:

```
h1 {
    margin: 20px 16px;
}
h2 {
    margin: 20px 16px;
}
h3 {
    margin: 20px 16px;
}
```

These rules define identical declaration blocks, so you can simplify the CSS by creating a selector list (h1, h2, h3 in this case):

```
h1, h2, h3 {
    margin: 20px 16px;
}
```

Selector lists are great, but the type shown in the preceding example is known in the CSS trade as an *unforgiving selector list* because if any of the selectors are invalid or unsupported by the browser, the *entire list* is ignored, as it would be in this case:

```
h1, h2, h3% {
    margin: 20px 16px;
}
```

The h3% "selector" is a typo, but the browser throws out the entire rule.

One of the great benefits of functional pseudo-classes is that most of them use *forgiving selector lists*, which means that if any item in the selector list is invalid or unsupported, the browser ignores just that selector and still processes all the rest. Nice.

## :is()

The :is() functional pseudo-class is known as the *matches-any* pseudo-class because it matches any of the selectors in a specified selector list. Here's the syntax:

```
element:is(selector-list) {
    property1: value1;
```

```
        property2: value2;
        ...
}
```

>> *element*: (Optional) The element you want to target with the selector list. If you omit *element*, your rule would target everything that matches something in the selector list.

>> *selector-list*: A comma-separated list of selectors.

When used without the *element* parameter, :is() targets any element that matches at least one item in the selector list. Here's an example (bk03ch03/example30.html):

```
:is(h1, h2, h3) {
    margin: 20px 16px;
}
```

The rule applies the margin styling to any element that's an h1, h2, or h3.

When used with the *element* parameter, :is() targets any element of type *element* that matches at least one item in the selector list. Here's an example (bk03ch03/example30.html):

```
p:is(:first-child, :last-child, :only-child) {
    margin: 24px;
}
```

The rule matches any p element that's a first child, a last child, or an only child.

**REMEMBER**

The :is() pseudo-class uses a forgiving selector list, so even if one or more selectors are invalid or unsupported, the browser still processes the remaining selectors.

**WARNING**

The :is() functional pseudo-class is relatively new, so it's not supported by older web browsers such as Internet Explorer 11.

## :not()

The :not() functional pseudo-class is known as the *matches-none* pseudo-class because it targets elements that don't match any of the selectors in a specified selector list. Here's the syntax:

```
element:not(selector-list) {
    property1: value1;
```

```
    property2: value2;
    ...
}
```

>> *element*: (Optional) The element you want to target with the selector list. If you omit *element*, your rule would target everything that doesn't have a match in the selector list.

>> *selector-list*: A comma-separated list of selectors.

When used without the *element* parameter, :not() targets all elements that don't match any of the items in the selector list. Here's an example (bk03ch03/example31.html):

```
:not(.decorative) {
    font-family: Georgia, serif;
}
```

The rule applies the font-family styling to any element that doesn't use the decorative class.

**WARNING**

You'll want to exercise some caution when using :not() without the *element* parameter because you could end up casting a very wide style net that catches many unintended elements (such as the html or body element).

When used with the *element* parameter, :not() targets any element of type *element* that doesn't match any of the items in the selector list. Here's an example:

```
p:not(:first-child, :last-child, :only-child) {
    margin: 24px;
}
```

The rule matches any p element that's not a first child, a last child, or an only child.

**TIP**

In Book 2, Chapter 6, I mention that not including an alt attribute in each of your <img> tags makes your page not only invalid but also less accessible. However, in the heat of coding battle, it's easy to forget those alt attributes. When I'm in the development stage of my own pages, I make alt-less images stand out by including the following rule in my CSS:

```
img:not(img[alt]) {
    outline: 3px solid red;
}
```

This rule targets img elements that don't have an alt attribute and surrounds them with a red outline.

**REMEMBER**

The :not() pseudo-class uses a unforgiving selector list, so if one or more selectors are invalid or unsupported, the browser discards the entire rule.

## :where()

The :where() functional pseudo-class matches any of the selectors in a specified selector list. Here's the syntax:

```
element:where(selector-list) {
    property1: value1;
    property2: value2;
    ...
}
```

» *element*: (Optional) The element you want to target with the selector list. If you omit *element*, then your rule would target everything that's a first child.

» *selector-list*: A comma-separated list of selectors.

Wait a minute, I hear you say, this is exactly the same as the :is() functional pseudo-class! What's going on here?

First, good eye! Second, the reason that CSS has two functional pseudo-classes that seem to be the same thing is highly technical and won't make even a tiny bit of sense to you until you've read Book 3, Chapter 4 and learned what *specificity* is all about.

For now, let me just say that, yes, :is() and :where() are the same, except for the following:

» The specificity assigned to the :is() pseudo-class is the highest specificity of the selectors in its selector list.

» The specificity assigned to the :where() pseudo-class is always 0.

To learn why this is important, turn to Book 3, Chapter 4's discussion of specificity.

**REMEMBER**

The :where() pseudo-class uses a forgiving selector list, so even if one or more selectors are invalid or unsupported, the browser still processes the remaining selectors.

## :has()

If you took a poll of CSS developers every year since CSS first came on the scene in the late 1990s and you asked which missing feature each developer most wished to have implemented, the top answer every year would arguably be "a parent selector." That is, given an element, a class, or some other selector, what element is the parent (or ancestor) of that selector?

This seems so useful and so obvious that most folks new to CSS were surprised to hear that there's no such thing as a "parent selector" in CSS. That is, there wasn't until the brand-spanking-new :has() functional pseudo-class came along. The :has() pseudo-class is actually designed to do several things:

» Match any element that's a parent of any item in a selector list of child elements. In words, you'd say "Match a parent that *has* a child in this list."

» Match any element that's an ancestor of any item in a selector list of descendant elements. In words, you'd say "Match an ancestor that *has* a descendant in this list."

» Match any element that's a previous sibling of any item in a selector list of sibling elements. In words, you'd say "Match a sibling that *has* a next sibling in this list."

» Match any element that's an earlier sibling of any item in a selector list of sibling elements. In words, you'd say "Match a sibling that *has* a later sibling in this list."

Here's the syntax for :has():

```
element:has(relative-selector-list) {
    property1: value1;
    property2: value2;
    ...
}
```

» *element*: (Optional) The parent, ancestor, or sibling element you want to target with the selector list. If you omit *element*, then your rule would target every parent, ancestor, or sibling element that has something in the selector list.

» *relative-selector-list*: A comma-separated list of items, each of which is a *relative selector*, which is a combinator operator (refer to Book 3, Chapter 2) followed by a selector.

Relative selectors are head-scratchers, for sure, so I unpack them a bit by going through the four use cases for the :has() pseudo-class (bk03ch03/example32.html):

» **Matching a parent:** The relative selector is the child combinator (>) followed by a selector that matches the type of child element you want to match relative to the parent. For example, the relative selector > p matches p elements that are children. To match those p elements relative to, say, an aside element, you'd use aside:has(> p). (That is, match any aside that has at least one p child.) Here's an example:

```
aside:has(> p) {
    border: 1px solid black;
}
```

» **Matching an ancestor:** The relative selector is the descendant combinator (a space, or just omitted altogether) followed by a selector that matches the type of child element you want to match relative to the ancestor. To match div descendant elements relative to, say, an article element, you'd use article:has(div). (That is, match any article that has at least one div descendant.) Here's an example:

```
article:has(div) {
    margin-top: 20px;
}
```

» **Matching a previous sibling:** The relative selector is the next-sibling combinator (+) followed by a selector that matches the type of sibling element you want to match relative to the previous sibling. For example, the relative selector + h2 matches h2 elements that are next siblings. To match those h2 elements relative to, say, an h1 element, you'd use h1:has(+ h2). (That is, match any h1 that has a next-sibling that's an h2.) Here's an example:

```
h1:has(+ h2) {
    margin-bottom: 24px;
}
```

» **Matching a later sibling:** The relative selector is the subsequent-sibling combinator (~) followed by a selector that matches the type of sibling element you want to match relative to the earlier sibling. For example, the relative selector ~ blockquote matches blockquote elements that are subsequent siblings. To match those blockquote elements relative to, say, an h3 element, you'd use h3:has(~ blockquote). (That is, match any h3 that has a subsequent sibling that's a blockquote.) Here's an example:

```
h3:has(~ blockquote) {
    font-style: italic;
}
```

Each of these examples uses a single relative selector, but feel free to use lists that have two or more relative selectors.

**REMEMBER**

The :has() pseudo-class uses a forgiving selector list, so even if one or more selectors are invalid or unsupported, the browser still processes the remaining selectors.

**REMEMBER**

As I write this, the :has() pseudo-class hasn't yet been implemented by all the major browsers. However, overall support is rising very quickly, so by the time you read this, :has() should have excellent support in every modern browser. To keep an eye on the current support level, use the following Can I Use page: https://caniuse.com/css-has. Needless to say, :has() isn't implemented by older browsers such as Internet Explorer 11, so don't use :has() if you need to support those ancient browsers.

# Getting Up to Speed with Pseudo-Elements

As your CSS career progresses, sooner or later (almost always sooner) you'll bump up against two conundrums that have bedeviled web page designers since Day One:

» How can I insert and style content on the fly based on the current state of an element?

» How can I style a specific chunk of an element, such as its first line?

The common thread that runs through both problems is that you want to style something that's not part of the original page's HTML. In the first case, you want to add new content; in the second case, you want to style a chunk that doesn't have an HTML equivalent. In other words, you want to work with page items that are not quite elements, which are known as *pseudo-elements* in the land of CSS.

## Working with pseudo-elements

All pseudo-elements begin with two colons (::), followed by a keyword. Here's the general syntax:

```
element::pseudo-element {
    property1: value1;
    property2: value2;
    ...
}
```

>> *element*: The name of the element type you want to target

>> *pseudo-element*: The name of the pseudo-element

In the sections that follow, I talk about ::after and ::before, which you use to add content on the fly — known as *generated content* — as well as ::first-letter and ::first-line, which you use to style chunks of an element.

## Generating a last child with ::after

You can use the ::after pseudo-element to generate new content for a target element. Although the word "after" implies that the generated content is inserted immediately following the target element (which, if true, would make the new element the next sibling of the target element), that's not the case. Instead, "after" here means "after all the target element's existing child elements." That is, you use ::after to generate a new last child element for some target parent element.

Here's the syntax to use:

```
parent::after {
    content: 'content';
    property1: value1;
    property2: value2;
    ...
}
```

>> *parent*: The parent element in which you want to generate a new last child element.

>> *content*: The content you want to appear in the generated last child. If you don't want any content in the new last child, set the content property to the empty string (" or "").

One very common use case for the ::after pseudo-element is to indicate external links (that is, links to pages outside your site) with a special icon. Sure, you could manually insert the icon's img element after every external link, but that's no one's idea of fun when you're talking more than a few links. No need to go to all that trouble when CSS is happy to do all the work for you (bk03ch03/example33.html):

```
a[href^='http']::after {
    content: url(images/Icon_External_Link.png);
    padding-left: 2px;
}
```

The parent elements here are all the a elements with an href attribute that begins with http, which would be the case for all your external links. For the ::after generated content, the content property is the local address of the image (images/ Icon_External_Link.png). (Head over to Book 3, Chapter 6 to learn more about the CSS url() function.) The rule also uses padding-left: 2px to generate a bit of space between the end of the link text and the image. Figure 3-2 shows the icon added to a few external links.

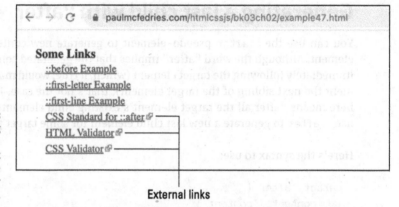

**FIGURE 3-2:**
Using
the ::after
pseudo-element
to generate
icons after
external links.

For elements that can't act as parents, another useful technique is to add an empty <span></span> tag after the element and use that span element to create the generated content. Here's an example for a couple of input elements, the first a text field and the second an email field (bk03ch03/example33.html):

```
<label for="user-name">Name:</label>
<input id="user-name"
       type="text"
       required>
<span></span>

<label for="user-email">Email:</label>
<input id="user-email"
       type="email"
       placeholder="e.g., you@domain.com"
       required>
<span></span>
```

Both fields have the required attribute, so both are invalid when empty. Also, the email field is invalid when it contains an invalid email address. You want to display X (Unicode character 2717) in the span when the field is invalid, and you want to display a checkmark (Unicode character 2713) in the span when the field is valid. Here are some rules that do this (bk03ch03/example33.html):

```
input:invalid + span::after {
    content: '\2717';
    color: red;
}
input:valid + span::after {
    content: '\2713';
    color: green;
}
```

Figure 3-3 shows this rule in action with a regular text field (top), which has a value and therefore is valid; and an email field (bottom), which has only a partial email address and is therefore invalid.

**FIGURE 3-3:**
Using the ::after pseudo-element to generate content based on the current state of an input element.

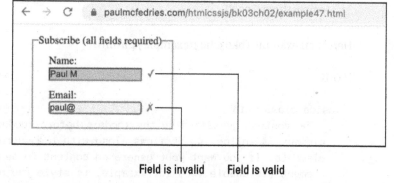

Field is invalid   Field is valid

**TIP**

The content generated by the ::after pseudo-element is inline, so it flows along with the surrounding elements. If you want your generated content to be a block element (to enable you, for example, to style the pseudo-element's width, height, or both), add either display: block or display: inline-block to the pseudo-element's declaration block.

**WARNING**

The ::after pseudo-element is very handy and very fun, but don't use it to generate essential content because many assistive technologies can't read or deal with that content.

## Generating a first child with ::before

You can use the ::before pseudo-element to generate new content for a target element. Here, "before" means "before all the target element's existing child elements." That is, you use ::before to generate a new first child element for some target parent element.

Here's the syntax to use:

```
parent::before {
    content: 'content';
    property1: value1;
    property2: value2;
    ...
}
```

» *parent*: The parent element in which you want to generate a new first child element.

» *content*: The content you want to appear in the generated last child. If you don't want any content in the new last child, set the content property to the empty string (" or "").

Here's an example (bk03ch03/example34.html):

HTML:

```
<aside class="tip">
    The content generated by the <code>::before</code> pseudo-
element is inline, so it flows along with the surrounding
elements. If you want your generated content to be a block
element (to enable you, for example, to style the pseudo-
element's width and/or height), add either <code>display:
block</code> or <code>display: inline-block</code> to the
pseudo-element's declaration block.
</aside>
```

CSS:

```
.tip::before {
    content: 'TIP';
    display: block;
    color: green;
    font-size: 12px;
}
```

The CSS rule uses `::before` to add the text TIP as a block-level element that's the first child of any element that uses the tip class. Figure 3-4 shows this example at work.

Generated content

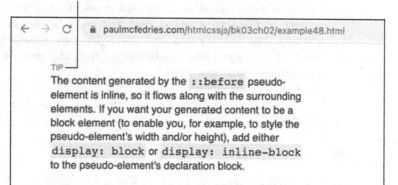

TIP

The content generated by the `::before` pseudo-element is inline, so it flows along with the surrounding elements. If you want your generated content to be a block element (to enable you, for example, to style the pseudo-element's width and/or height), add either `display: block` or `display: inline-block` to the pseudo-element's declaration block.

**FIGURE 3-4:**
Using the
`::before`
pseudo-element
to generate
content.

**WARNING**

Many assistive technologies can't read or deal with `::before` generated content, so don't use `::before` to add essential content.

## Styling the opening letter with ::first-letter

A common design paradigm is to take the first letter of the opening paragraph of an essay or other long-form text and style the letter in some way, often with a font that's a larger size and/or a different color than the regular text.

Yep, you could wrap the letter in a span element and style that element, but CSS offers a more direct and more maintainable route: the `::first-letter` pseudo-element, which targets the first letter of a specified block-level element. Here's the syntax:

```
element::first-letter {
    property1: value1;
    property2: value2;
    ...
}
```

» *element*: A selector that specifies the element that contains the first letter you want to style.

Here's an example (bk03ch03/example35.html):

HTML:

```
<article>
    <h2>Teen Boy's Vocabulary Down to a Single Word</h2>
```

```
    <p>Area teen Dylan Geronimo now communicates with his
    parents and teachers using just the word "whatever." With
    subtle voice inflections, Mr. Geronimo can convey the full
    range of his emotions: sullenness, disgust, exasperation, and
    a seething, nameless rage.
    </p>
...
</article>
```

CSS:

```
h2 + p::first-letter {
    color: crimson;
    font-size: 32px;
}
```

The CSS rule targets the first letter of any p element that's a next sibling of an h2 element. The declaration block styles the letter with a color and a font size. Figure 3-5 shows the result.

← → C    🔒 paulmcfedries.com/htmlcssjs/bk03ch03/example35

**Teen Boy's Vocabulary Down to a Single Word**

Area teen Dylan Geronimo now communicates with his parents and teachers using just the word "whatever." With subtle voice inflections, Mr. Geronimo can convey the full range of his emotions: sullenness, disgust, exasperation, and a seething, nameless rage.

"It was frustrating, at first," said Betty Geronimo, Dylan's mother. "It seemed like he was giving us the same answer to every question. Then we learned the difference between 'whatever' and 'what-EVER'."

The phenomenon is called Adolescent Vocabulary Attrition Syndrome, according to Hans Longwinded, a language chiropractor. "Speaking is quite painful for most male teenagers, so they ease the pain by shedding words."

When asked to comment on this story, Mr. Geronimo said, "WHAT-ever."

**FIGURE 3-5:**
Using the
::first-letter
pseudo-element
to style the
first letter of a
paragraph.

**REMEMBER**

Not all CSS properties are available for your ::first-letter declaration block. You can use all the available padding, border, margin, background, font, and text decoration properties, the color property, and the float property.

# Styling the opening line with ::first-line

In fancier text designs, the first line of some prose is often styled in some way, such as with italics or uppercase letters. (These kinds of styles are particularly common when the first line begins with a styled first letter, such as a drop cap or a raised cap; refer to the previous section.)

But how, I hear you ask, is it possible to know in advance what the first "line" of text will be, given the wildly different screen sizes, display orientations, and default font sizes out there? The short answer is, "You can't." The slightly longer answer is, "You can't and you don't have to because you can use the ::first-line pseudo-element to figure it out for you."

The ::first-line pseudo-element styles the first line of text in a specified block element, however long or short that line ends up being given the display width, page width, font size, and all the other factors that go into web page line lengths. Here's the syntax:

```
element::first-line {
    property1: value1;
    property2: value2;
    ...
}
```

>> *element*: A selector that specifies the element that contains the first line you want to style.

Here's an example (bk03ch03/example36.html):

HTML:

```
<article>
    <h2>Teen Boy's Vocabulary Down to a Single Word</h2>
    <p>Area teen Dylan Geronimo now communicates with his
parents and teachers using just the word "whatever." With
subtle voice inflections, Mr. Geronimo can convey the full
range of his emotions: sullenness, disgust, exasperation, and
a seething, nameless rage.
    </p>
...
</article>
```

CSS:

```
h2 + p::first-line {
    text-transform: uppercase;
}
```

The CSS rule targets the first line of any p element that's a next sibling of an h2 element. The declaration block styles the line text as uppercase letters, as shown in Figure 3-6.

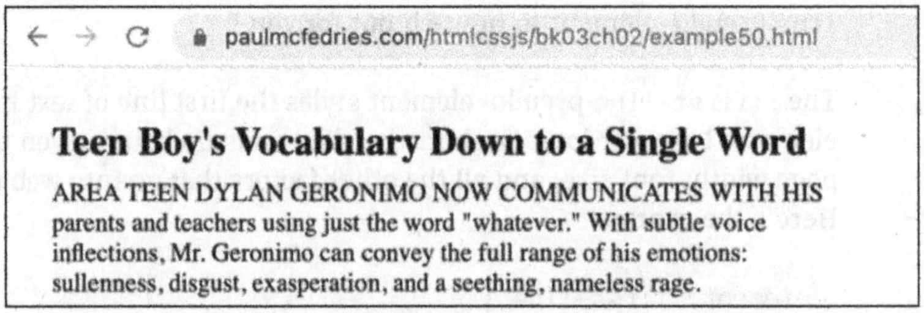

FIGURE 3-6:
Using the
::first-line
pseudo-element
to style the
first line of a
paragraph.

paulmcfedries.com/htmlcssjs/bk03ch02/example50.html

## Teen Boy's Vocabulary Down to a Single Word

AREA TEEN DYLAN GERONIMO NOW COMMUNICATES WITH HIS parents and teachers using just the word "whatever." With subtle voice inflections, Mr. Geronimo can convey the full range of his emotions: sullenness, disgust, exasperation, and a seething, nameless rage.

Not all CSS properties are available for your ::first-line declaration block. You can use all the available background, font, and text decoration properties, and the color property.

REMEMBER

# Chapter **4**

# Making CSS Make Sense

*CSS is hard because its properties interact, often in unexpected ways. Because when you set one of them, you're never just setting that one thing. That one thing combines and bounces off and contradicts a dozen other things, including default things that you never actually set yourself.*

—BRANDON SMITH

C SS is one of those simple-on-the-outside, complex-on-the-inside things. Basic CSS is nothing but a collection of rules, each of which is a set of properties and their values, all applied to a specified selector. At this level, CSS seems almost trivial or, at the very most, resolutely straightforward. Ah, but untold legions of promising CSS careers have foundered on this Rock of Simplicity. Cocky JavaScript programmers routinely wash their hands of CSS with the lament, "This looks right, so why doesn't it work?"

It probably doesn't work because CSS code has a way of multiplying faster than your ability to make sense of it all. It probably doesn't work because CSS is actually quite complex under the hood. It probably doesn't work because no CSS project of even middling ambition will work unless you know how CSS applies its rules.

In this chapter, you investigate a few useful ways to bring CSS to heel in your web projects. You learn how keep even the largest stylesheet comprehensible with judicious comments; how to create a good CSS base with a reset; how to use the browser's development tools to debug your CSS code; and, finally, you pop the hood and explore the various parts of the CSS engine that decide how styles get applied.

# Commenting Your CSS Code

A web project stylesheet — whether it's in a .css file or in a style element — starts off neat and easy to read, but that pristine state never lasts for long. As your project expands, your CSS grows less readable in two ways:

>> You use complex selectors or property values that are difficult to understand (either for another person reading your code or even for yourself a few months from now).

>> You insert new rules either in random places in the stylesheet or either always at the top or always as the bottom. Whichever method you use, finding a particular rule becomes increasingly harder and more frustrating.

You can solve the embarrassing problem of not remembering a few months from now what a particular bit of CSS code is doing by commenting that code. A *comment* is a bit of text that you add to your stylesheet, but that text is ignored by the web browser when it's processing your CSS. You start a comment with the characters /* and end the comment with the characters */:

```
/* This, friends, is a comment. */
```

You're free to extend your comments onto multiple lines, if need be:

```
/* This is the first line of the comment
   and this is the second line. */
```

## Commenting non-obvious code

Whenever you have some CSS where it's not obvious what the code does, go ahead and add a comment just above the rule, like so:

```
/* Add a red outline to images that have no alt text */
img:not(img[alt]) {
    outline: 3px solid red;
}
```

Now, when someone else is reviewing your code or when you return to your code later, the CSS will be much easier to understand. You can also insert comments inside declaration blocks:

```
div {
    /* Set a background color for browsers that don't support
  gradients */
    background-color: white;
    background-image: linear-gradient(to bottom, white 0%,
  crimson 100%);
}
```

## Marking stylesheet sections with comments

The way you tame a large, unruly stylesheet is to organize the code into groups of related rules. The sections you come up with will depend on your page and the CSS you use to style it, but for most sites an organization something like this will apply:

» General or global styles

» Font styles

» Layout styles

» Typography styles

» Styles for specific site features

To make it clear where one section ends and another begins, use a multiline comment to mark the beginning of each section:

```
/*==========================*\
  General styles
\*==========================*/

General rules go here

/*==========================*\
  Font styles
\*==========================*/
```

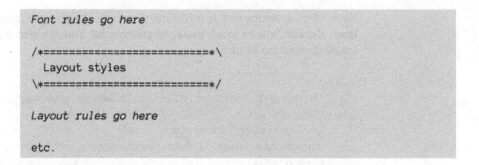

```
Font rules go here

/*===========================*\
  Layout styles
\*===========================*/

Layout rules go here

etc.
```

# Using a CSS Reset

All web browsers ship with an internal set of styles known as the *user agent stylesheet*. I talk about this stylesheet a bit more later (refer to "Popping the Hood: How Styles Get Applied"), but for now it's enough to know that these styles are the defaults that the browser applies to the HTML elements it finds on a page. In other words, even if you don't define a single CSS rule, your page elements will still look okay (if a bit boring) thanks to the margins, padding, and other styles defined by the browser.

For many years, one of the largest bees in the bonnets of CSS developers everywhere were these browser stylesheets. Why? Lots of reasons, but two stood out:

>> Some browsers (Internet Explorer, raise your hand!) made very odd choices for some of their default styles.

>> There were often glaring inconsistencies between the default styles for different browsers, which meant that a page could look noticeably different depending on the browser being used.

Finally, a few CSS mavens decided enough was enough and came up with the idea of the *CSS reset*, which was (usually) an external CSS file that contained rules designed to fix the aforementioned problems:

>> The reset included rules that would override what the developer considered to be bad style choices made by some browsers.

>> The reset included rules that enforced a greater consistency between browsers by overriding certain default browser styles.

These resets were often described as "opinionated" because the choices made by the creators were subjective. Still, most CSS coders embraced resets, and some order was restored to stylesheets the world over.

These days, the situation is far less dire because those problematic older browsers (Internet Explorer, raise your hand yet again!) are either gone or have market share almost too small to measure, and because modern browsers are much more consistent about how they define their default styles. And, in any case, the modern approach is to say that it's cool if there are small differences between how different browsers render a page. After all, it's not like a user surfs your site using Chrome and then says, "Let's check out what this puppy looks like in Safari"!

The upshot is that you can probably get away without a CSS reset these days. Why "probably"? Because although browser defaults are better nowadays, they're not perfect. There are still enough inconsistencies and odd style choices that a CSS reset is recommended.

Okay, which one, because the world seems to have dozens of CSS resets? Fortunately, that's not a hard question to answer because one CSS reset is by far the most popular and is widely considered to have the best balance between fixing problems and retaining useful default styles. And, weighing in at a mere 6KB, it's small enough that it won't slow down your page loading. That reset is called Normalize.css, and you can download it here:

https://necolas.github.io/normalize.css/latest/normalize.css

After you've downloaded the file, move it to your web project's CSS folder and then add a <link> tag to your web page's <head> section *before* any other stylesheet <link> tag and before the <style> tag, if you have one. For example, if you stored normalize.css in a css subfolder that's in the same folder that holds your HTML file, your <link> tag would look like this:

```
<link rel="stylesheet" href="css/normalize.css">
```

**REMEMBER**

Why do I stress that you should put your Normalize.css <link> tag before any other CSS stuff in the <head> section? Because the browser processes CSS sequentially, starting with the first CSS it finds and working its way through the rest in the order the CSS appears in the page. By putting your Normalize.css <link> tag before anything else, you're ensuring that the browser performs the reset first, which is exactly what you want.

**TIP**

One of the great features of Normalize.css is that the code is liberally festooned with comments that explain what each style rule is designed to do. Open the file in your favorite text editor and poke around to learn what the reset does.

# Debugging CSS

CSS is awesome. With just a few rules, you can turn a drab, lifeless page into a work of art that's a pleasure to read and will have your visitors clamoring for more. But CSS is also a pain in the you-know-what. You add what appears to be a straightforward rule to your CSS, save your work, refresh your browser and . . . *nothing changes!* Or maybe things change, but not in the way you expected. Cue the cartoon steam shooting out of your ears.

Let me say at this point that although these kinds of frustrations are the stuff of legend in the CSS community, they do *not* mean, as some folks would have it, that CSS is "illogical" or "stupid" or "broken." A large group of dedicated and very smart people create the CSS standards and, believe me, these folks know what they're doing! It may be a tough pill to swallow, but the truth is that if your CSS seems to be behaving illogically or stupidly or brokenly, it means your code is to blame, not CSS itself.

That's okay, though, because there's a way out of every CSS jam. Perhaps the most important thing you can do is become intimately familiar with how CSS applies its rules, which is the subject of the later section "Popping the Hood: How Styles Get Applied." That will solve a huge percentage of so-called "problems" in CSS.

If you're still having trouble, you can turn to your favorite browser's web development tools (which all the cool kids shorten to *dev tools*); these tools provide plenty of features to help you troubleshoot wonky CSS code.

In the sections that follow, I use the example page (in the book's example files, check out bk03ch04/example01.html) shown in Figure 4-1 which has an awfully crowded top-left corner that I want to debug.

## Displaying the web development tools

Most web developers debug their CSS using Google Chrome, so I focus on that browser in this section. But here's how you open the web development tools in not only Chrome but also the various flavors of Firefox, Microsoft Edge, and Safari:

>> **Chrome for Windows:** Click Customize and Control Google Chrome (the three vertical dots to the right of the address bar) and then select More Tools ⇨ Developer Tools. Shortcut: Ctrl+Shift+I.

>> **Chrome for Mac:** Select View ⇨ Developer ⇨ Developer Tools. Shortcut: Option+⌘+I.

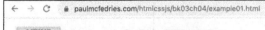

# News of the Word

**Language news you won't find anywhere else (for good reason!)**

Home   What's New   What's Old   What's What   What's *That*?

### Report: Teen Instant Messages Nothing But Gibberish

In a scathing report released today, communications experts have declared that the instant messages teenagers exchange with each other are in reality nothing but gibberish. U.S. Chatmaster General Todd Dood, with technical help from the National Security Agency, examined thousands of instant messages

"None of it made a lick of sense" he said.

It has long been thought that teen instant messages contained abbreviations (such as *LOL* for "laughing out loud" and *MAIBARP* for "my acne is becoming a real problem"), short forms (such as *L8R* for "later" and *R2D2* for "R2D2"), and slang (such as *whassup* for "what's up" and *yo* for "Hello, I am pleased to meet your acquaintance. Do you wish to have a conversation?"). However, the report reveals that this so-called "teenspeak" began to change so fast that kids simply could not keep up. Each teen developed his or her own lingo, and the instant messaging system devolved into anarchy.

"The crazy thing is that teen instant messaging is more popular than ever," said Dood. "They seem not to have noticed that they can't understand a word anyone is texting to them." There seems to be a prestige factor at work here. As one teen quoted in the study said, "If you say you don't understand, then you're just like *so* lame."

**FIGURE 4-1:**
The web page that I'll debug.

>> **Firefox for Windows:** Click Open Application Menu (the three horizontal lines on the far right of the toolbar) and then select More Tools⇨Web Developer Tools. Shortcut: Ctrl+Shift+I.

>> **Firefox for Mac:** Select Tools⇨Browser Tools⇨Web Developer Tools. Shortcut: Option+⌘+I.

>> **Microsoft Edge:** Click Settings and More (the three vertical dots to the right of the address bar) and then select More Tools⇨Developer Tools. Shortcut: Ctrl+Shift+I.

>> **Safari:** Select Develop⇨Show Web Inspector. Shortcut: Option+⌘+I. If the Develop menu isn't around, select Safari⇨Settings, click the Advanced tab, and then select the Show Develop Menu in Menu Bar checkbox.

**TIP**

In all browser development tools, you can configure where the pane appears in relation to the browser window. In Chrome, click the Customize icon (shown in the margin) and then click Dock to Right, Dock to Bottom, or Dock to Left, as shown in Figure 4-2. If you prefer a floating pane that you can move around, click Undock.

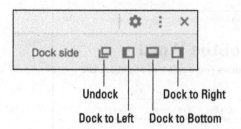

**FIGURE 4-2:**
Choose where
the develop-
ment tools pane
appears in the
browser window.

Dock side

Undock

Dock to Left    Dock to Bottom

Dock to Right

## Inspecting an element

If an element on the page doesn't look right or has gone awry in some other way, the most basic CSS debugging technique is to examine how the web browser has interpreted your CSS code. This is known as *inspecting* the element.

To begin your inspection of any element on a web page, you can use the following techniques:

>> If you don't already have your browser's web development tools open, right-click the element and then click Inspect (or, in Safari, Inspect Element). This opens your browser's development tools, displays the Elements tab (it's called Inspector in Firefox), and highlights the element's HTML.

>> If your browser's web development tools are already open, click the Elements tab (the Inspector tab in Firefox), and then click the tag of the element you want to inspect.

>> If the web development tools are already open, click the Select an Element icon (shown in the margin); then click an element on the rendered page.

Figure 4-3 shows the page from Figure 4-1 with the header's img element selected.

There are two things to note here:

>> The left side of the tab shows the page's HTML code as it was interpreted by the browser.

>> When you hover the mouse pointer over an element, the browser highlights the element in the rendered page and displays the element's dimensions.

…and the browser highlights the element and displays its dimensions

The selected element's style rules appear in the Styles pane

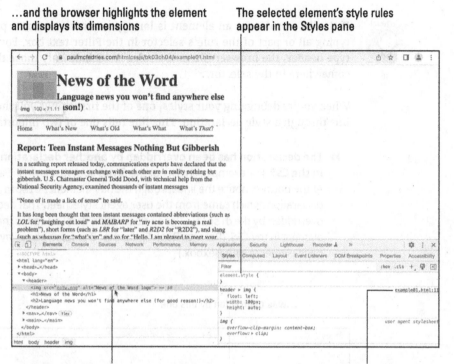

**FIGURE 4-3:**
Inspecting the
img element.

Hover over the element you want to inspect…

The line number where the rule appears in the source code

## Inspecting an element's styles

When you click an element in the HTML code, the Styles subtab on the right shows the style rules that have been applied to the element. (In some browsers, particularly Safari and Firefox, there's a separate Styles pane in the middle.) There are usually two or three types of style rules:

>> The style rules that you created. To the right of each rule, the browser displays the filename of the rule's source code and the line number where the rule appears in that file.

>> Rules from your CSS reset, if you're using one.

>> Rules where the location is user agent stylesheet, which means these are rules applied by the browser.

**REMEMBER**

The order of the rules isn't random, by any means. On the contrary, the browser orders the rules by their relative importance — or *weight*, as CSS types call it — with the most important rules at the top. How does the browser decide which rules are more important than others? Ah, that's a discussion for later in this chapter. Refer to "Popping the Hood: How Styles Get Applied."

Making CSS Make Sense

**TIP**

If the list of rules for an element is long, you can zero in on a particular rule by typing all or part of the rule's selector in the Filter text box. For example, if you type **header**, the browser filters the rules to include only those that have header somewhere in the selector.

When you're debugging your styles, one of the first things you should look for is a line through a style declaration. This line tells one of two important things:

» **The declaration has been overridden by another declaration elsewhere in the CSS.** For example, check out the Styles subtab shown in Figure 4-4. At the bottom, notice the line through the nav element's display: block declaration, which came from the user agent stylesheet. That declaration was overridden by the display: flex declaration that I added to the nav element in my CSS. (Refer to Book 5, Chapter 2 to learn about layout out page elements with Flexbox.)

...was overridden by this one

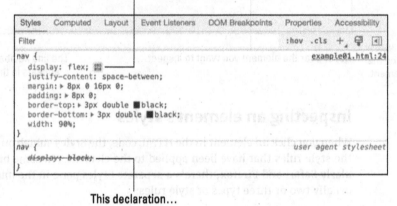

**FIGURE 4-4:**
A line through a declaration tells you it has been overridden by another declaration.

This declaration...

» **The declaration is wrong in some way.** If, besides the line through the declaration, there's also a warning icon to its left, it means the web browser couldn't process the declaration, either because the browser doesn't support the property or value or because the property or value is invalid. For example, in the Styles subtab shown in Figure 4-5, one of the a element declarations has a line through it and a warning icon next to it. Why? Upon closer inspection, you can read that the property name is font-varaint, but it's supposed to be font-variant.

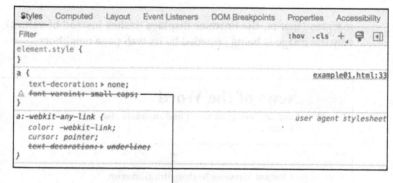

**FIGURE 4-5:**
The browser
displays a
warning icon and
a crossed-out
declaration for
unsupported or
invalid properties
or values.

A misspelled property name is the culprit here

## Inspecting an element's box model

If the spacing within or around an element isn't what you were expecting, some kind of problem with the box model — that is, the element's padding, border, margin, width, or height — should be your first suspect. Click the element you want to inspect and then click the Layout tab.

The browser shows the element's box model abstractly as a series of concentric rectangles (check out Figure 4-6), where the innermost rectangle is the content box, and then successive rectangles represent the padding, the border, and finally the margin. The content box shows the width and height of the element, with each of the other rectangles showing the four values (top, right, bottom, and left) for the corresponding box model component.

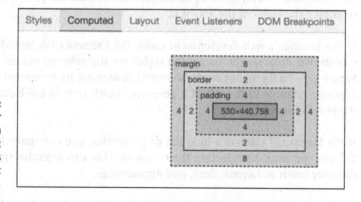

**FIGURE 4-6:**
The browser
displays an
element's box
model as a series
of concentric
rectangles.

How does all this help for debugging? Viewing the actual values that the browser is using for padding and margin, in particular, can help you solve spacing problems. For example, back in Figure 4-1, notice that the header image in the upper-left corner has no space around it. To understand why, I can inspect the img element. Lo and behold, as shown in the Figure 4-7, that element has *no* padding or margins (that is, the browser displays dashes instead of values), which explains why the image is being crowded by its web page neighbors.

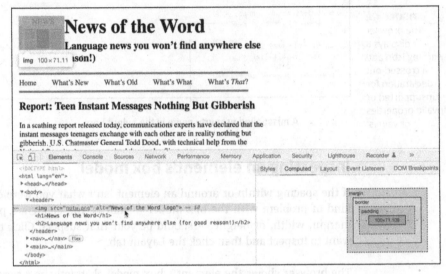

FIGURE 4-7:
The img element's box model tells us that it has no margin or padding set.

## Inspecting an element's computed styles

An element's *computed styles* are the final property values calculated by the browser after weighing all the available CSS rules (such as the default user agent styles, your CSS reset, and the styles you define). If an element isn't displaying the way you thought it would, its computed styles can at least tell you why the browser is rendering the element the way it is.

In the browser's web development tools, the Elements tab includes a Computed subtab that displays the computed styles for the selected element, as shown in Figure 4-8. To figure out where the web browser got its computed value, click the exposure triangle to the left of a property, which reveals the location of the rule the browser is using.

**TIP**

If the Computed tab has a long list of properties, you can make it easier to find the one you want by selecting the Group checkbox to organize the properties by category (such as Layout, Text, and Appearance).

**TIP**

By default, the Computed tab shows only those properties where the browser calculated values that are different than the browser defaults. To inspect every property, including the unchanged default values, select the Show All checkbox.

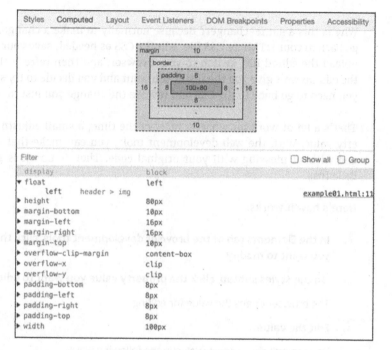

**FIGURE 4-8:**
The Computed tab shows the selected element's computed styles.

## Inspecting an element's layout

The final feature of the Elements tab that you may find useful for troubleshooting CSS is the Layout tab, which offers tools for visualizing layouts that use the following technologies:

» **CSS Grid:** Enables you to add an overlay that shows the grid and its track numbers. You can also optionally view track sizes, named areas, and extended grid lines. Refer to Book 5, Chapter 3 to learn not only how to lay out a page using CSS Grid, but also the details of inspecting a grid.

» **Flexbox:** Enables you to add a simple overlay to help you visualize your flex container and its items. Refer to Book 5, Chapter 2 to learn how to lay out a page using Flexbox and how to use the overlay to inspect a flex layout.

## Editing a property value

If the web development tools were just about inspecting CSS, they'd be useful, for sure, but hardly game-changing. Fortunately, your browser's development tools enable you to not only view the current CSS but also *change it*. That is, you can make temporary, on-the-fly adjustments to just about any property value. As soon as you edit an existing property value, the browser automatically updates the rendered page to reflect the change.

Why is this a game-changer? Because normally to make a change, you'd have to go back to your HTML or CSS file, edit the CSS as needed, save your work, possibly upload the edited file, switch to your browser, and then refresh the page. And if the edit doesn't give you the result you want and you decide to try something else, you need to go back to the CSS and reverse the change you just made.

That's a lot of work for what is, most of the time, a small adjustment to a property value. With the web development tools, you can make that change quickly and without messing with your original code. There's no muss and not even a little fuss.

Here's how it works:

1. **In the Elements tab of the browser development tools, click the element you want to modify.**

2. **On the Styles subtab, click the property value you want to edit.**

   The browser opens the value for editing.

3. **Edit the value.**

   You can edit the property value in the following ways:

   - To replace the entire value, just type the new value. This works because when you first click the property value, the browser selects the entire entry, so your typing replaces that selection.

   - To select a new value from a list, press Delete to remove the current value, and then click the new value from the list the browser displays. Note that this technique works only for property values that accept a defined set of keywords as values.

   - To edit only part of the property value, click the value a second time to place an insertion point cursor inside the field; then make your edits.

   - To increment the current numeric value, press the Up arrow key; to decrement the current numeric value, press the Down arrow key.

4. **When you're done with your changes, press Enter or Return.**

For a box model property, you can also edit the values directly on the box model representation (shown earlier in Figure 4-6) in the Computed tab. Here's how it works:

1. **In the Elements tab of the browser development tools, click the element you want to modify.**

2. **Click the Computed tab.**

**3.** **In the box model, double-click the value you want to edit.**

In the content box, double-click either the width or the height to edit those values. Otherwise, in the padding, border, or margin rectangles, double-click the existing top, right, bottom, or left value.

The browser opens the value for editing.

**4.** **Type the new value and then press Enter or Return.**

## Disabling a declaration

A useful "what-if" question to ask yourself when you're debugging CSS is, "What if declaration A wasn't in rule B?" In other words, how would the browser render an element differently if that element's rule didn't include a particular declaration?

No need to go back to your CSS source code and comment out that declaration. Instead, your browser's web development environment makes it a snap to disable any rule that's not a default user agent stylesheet rule. Here's how:

**1.** **In the Elements tab of the browser development tools, click the element you want to modify.**

**2.** **On the Styles subtab, hover your mouse pointer over the rule that contains the declaration you want to disable.**

The browser displays a checkbox to the left of each declaration in the rule, as shown in Figure 4-9.

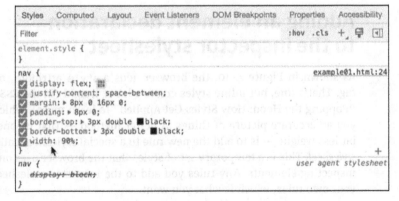

**FIGURE 4-9:** Hovering the mouse pointer over a rule adds checkboxes beside each declaration.

**3.** **Deselect the checkbox for the declaration you want to disable.**

When you're ready to enable the declaration again, repeat Steps 1 and 2 and then select the checkbox.

# Adding an inline declaration to an element

Rather than have you disable an existing declaration, as I describe in the previous section, your CSS troubleshooting chores may also require you to add a new declaration to an element. Happily, as with disabling a declaration, you don't need to modify your existing CSS to add a declaration because you can perform this task within the convenient confines of the web development tools.

Here are the steps to follow to add a declaration:

1. **In the Elements tab of the browser development tools, click the element you want to modify.**

2. **On the Styles subtab, click the element.style rule (it's at the top of the list of styles, just below the Filter box).**

   The browser creates an empty CSS declaration and places the cursor in the property field, just before the colon (:).

3. **Start typing the CSS property you want to use. In the list of properties that match what you've typed, click the property when it appears; then press Tab.**

   The browser moves the cursor to the empty value field.

4. **Either type the property value you want to use or select the value from the list (if any) that appears.**

   The browser adds a new inline declaration to the element's tag and updates the rendered element with the new property value, as shown in Figure 4-10.

## Adding an element declaration to the inspector stylesheet

As shown in Figure 4-10, the browser adds a style attribute to the element's tag. That's fine, but inline styles create a lot of weight (in the CSS sense; refer to "Popping the Hood: How Styles Get Applied" to learn more), which may not give you an accurate picture of things. A better method — that is, one that creates a bit less weight — is to add the new rule to a special stylesheet called the *inspector stylesheet*. This is a temporary set of styles that the browser uses only while you're inspecting elements. Any rules you add to the inspector stylesheet will override your own rules, which is what you want.

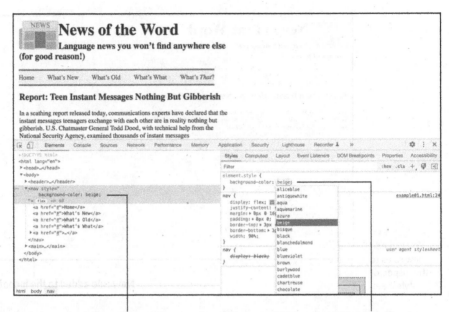

FIGURE 4-10:
You can add new
declarations to an
element.

...the browser adds a style attribute to the element    When you add a declaration here...

Here are the steps to follow to add a new rule to the inspector stylesheet:

1. **In the Elements tab of the browser development tools, click the element you want to modify.**

2. **On the Styles subtab toolbar, click the New Style Rule icon (shown in the margin).**

   The browser starts a new rule using the element selector that has the highest importance. It also opens the selector field for editing.

3. **Modify the rule's selector as needed; then press Tab.**

   The browser creates an empty CSS declaration and places the cursor in the property field, just before the colon (:).

4. **Start typing the CSS property you want to use. In the list of properties that match what you've typed, click the property when it appears; then press Tab.**

   The browser moves the cursor to the empty value field.

5. **Either type the property value you want to use or select the value from the list (if any) that appears.**

   The browser adds the new rule to the inspector stylesheet and updates the rendered element with the new declaration, as shown in Figure 4-11.

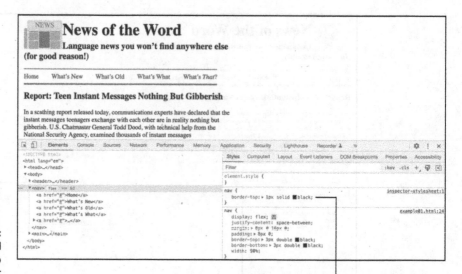

**FIGURE 4-11:**
You can add new rules to the inspector stylesheet.

New rule added to the inspector stylesheet

**TIP**

You can edit the inspector stylesheet by clicking the inspector-stylesheet link that appears to the right of your new rule. After you have the inspector stylesheet open for editing, feel free to add new rules at will using any selector you like. This includes adding new class rules, which you can then add to the element, as I describe in the next section.

## Adding a class to an element

Another useful "what-if" question to ask when debugging a recalcitrant element is, "What if I applied a class to that element?" That is, if a particular class is already defined somewhere in your CSS, would adding that class to the element — that is, inserting the class name into the tag's class attribute — solve the problem? Good question!

To add an existing class — that is, one where a rule that uses that class as the selector, which could be in your own CSS, a third-party CSS file, or the inspector stylesheet — to an element, follow these steps:

1. **In the Elements tab of the browser development tools, click the element you want to modify.**

2. **On the Styles subtab toolbar, click the .cls button.**

   The browser displays the Add New Class text box.

3. **Type the name of the class and then press Enter or Return.**

As shown in Figure 4-12, the browser adds a `class` attribute to the element (if that attribute wasn't already there) and adds the class name as the value. The browser also adds a checkbox for the class to the Styles subtab, which enables you to quickly disable and enable the class.

FIGURE 4-12:
You can add a class to the element.

The browser adds the class name to the tag

The browser creates a check box for the class

## Simulating a pseudo-class state

In Book 3, Chapter 3, I talk long and loud about pseudo-classes and how useful they are as selectors. Several pseudo-classes deal with user behavior, such as the user hovering the mouse pointer over an element, the user putting the focus on an element, and the user clicking a button.

One conundrum you may come across when debugging your CSS is that your pseudo-class rules don't show up in the Styles pane of your browser's web development tools. That's a pain because what if you want to try out new or modified values in your pseudo-class rules?

Fear not, dear debugger, because your web development tools have got you covered with a feature that enables you to quickly toggle several element states on and off. When you toggle on a state such as hover, the browser adds your `:hover` pseudo-class rule to the Styles pane and you can play around with that rule as needed.

Click the element you want to work with. (For example, if you're following along using bk03ch04/example02.html, click any `a` element within the `nav` element.) Then, on the Styles subtab toolbar, click the :hov button. The browser displays the collection of checkboxes shown in Figure 4-13. Each checkbox corresponds to a pseudo-class: `:active`, `:hover`, `:focus`, and so on. To simulate a particular state and therefore display whatever rule uses that pseudo-class as its selector, select the checkbox. Deselect the checkbox to deactivate the element state.

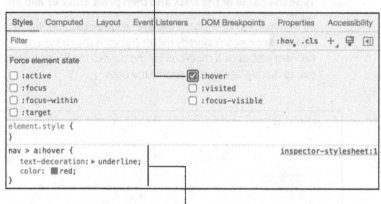

Select a pseudo-class state...

...and the browser displays the pseudo-class rule

**FIGURE 4-13:**
You can simulate pseudo-class states such as :active and :hover.

# Popping the Hood: How Styles Get Applied

I close this chapter with a look at three important concepts that you need to drill into your brain if you want to write good CSS and troubleshoot the inevitable CSS problems that will crop up in your web development career: inheritance, the cascade, and specificity.

## Unravelling inheritance

If a parent element is styled with a property/value declaration, in many cases its child and descendant elements will also be styled with the same property and value. For example, consider the following rule:

```
section {
    color: navy;
}
```

This rule styles section text with the color navy (refer to Book 3, Chapter 6 to learn about colors in CSS). Now consider the following HTML:

```
<section>
    <p>
        What color am I?
    </p>
</section>
```

The p element is a child of the section element, so the p element takes on the section element's color property value, meaning that the p element text will be navy.

This style propagation is known in the CSS game as *inheritance:* Parents "pass along" some of their properties to their children and descendants. Notice, however, that I say "some" properties are inherited. Lots of properties — such as the padding, borders, and margins that I cover in Book 3, Chapter 1 — don't get inherited.

TIP

To give you a flavor of which properties inherit and which don't, check out the table on the following W3C page: https://www.w3.org/TR/CSS2/propidx.html. For each property, the Inherited? column shows either yes (meaning the property inherits) or no (the property doesn't inherit). (This list is a bit out of date, but I couldn't find a newer one that offered the same information.)

## Why some properties don't inherit

Why don't some properties inherit? Usually because otherwise the results would be disastrous. For example, consider the following code (check out bk03ch04/ example03.html):

HTML:

```
<section>
    <p>
        What if the <code>border</code> property inherited?
    </p>
</section>
```

CSS:

```
section {
    border: 3px solid black;
}
```

Here we have a section element styled with a border, a p element that's a child of section, and a code element that's a child of p. The border property doesn't inherit, but if it did, this code would render as shown in Figure 4-14. Mayhem!

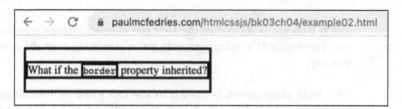

FIGURE 4-14:
If (shudder) the
border property
inherited.

## Forcing inheritance

Through inheritance, properties get passed down from one generation of elements to the next. That's usually what you want, but not always. For example, consider the following code (bk03ch04/example04.html):

HTML:

```
<section>
    <h3>All About Dolphins</h3>
    <p>
        Welcome to All About Dolphins!
    </p>
    <aside>
        <h3>Did You Know?</h3>
        <p>
            Dolphins can sleep with one eye open to watch for
    predators.
        </p>
    </p>
</section>
```

CSS:

```
section {
    color: navy;
}
h3 {
    color: green;
}
```

The section rule colors all the text navy, whereas the h3 rule colors h3 text green. However, what if you don't want the text of the h3 element that's inside the aside element to be green but, instead, to pick up the color defined by the section rule? In other words, how do you force any h3 that's a child of an aside to inherit its text color? That's the job of the inherit property value. In general, when you set a property's value to inherit, it forces the selector to inherit that property from whatever parent or ancestor set it. Here's a rule that enables any h3 that's a child of an aside to inherit its text color:

```
aside > h3 {
    color: inherit;
}
```

# Flowing along with the cascade

For properties that can get passed down from a parent element to a child element to a descendant element, that propagation is the inheritance I speak about in the previous section. Inheritance may seem straightforward, but the browser actually uses quite a complex algorithm to decide how inherited properties get applied. That algorithm is known in the CSS trade as the *cascade*. (Which, yep, is where the "cascading" part of the name *cascading stylesheets* comes from.)

To help you understand the kinds of conundrums the cascade has to solve, check out this code:

HTML:

```
<section>
    <p style="color: salmon">
        What color am I?
    </p>
</section>
```

CSS:

```
section {
    color: navy;
}
```

The section rule styles text with the color navy, which would normally propagate down to the p element, because the color property inherits. However, the <p> tag has a style attribute that sets the color property to salmon. When the browser renders the p element, what color will it use?

Before you can answer that question, you need to know a bit more about how the browser performs its inheritance duties.

# How the cascade works

At its heart, the cascade is a kind of sorting algorithm for property declarations. For each element (or pseudo-element) in the page, the cascade begins by looking through all the page's CSS sources for every property declaration with a selector that matches the element.

If a given property declaration occurs only once for the element, then the cascade applies that declaration to the element, no questions asked. However, it's often the case that a particular property has multiple declarations for the same element and that two or more of those declared property values are different. When there are multiple possible values to apply to an element property, the algorithm must figure out which of those declarations to use. To decide which declaration gets applied, the cascade assigns a *weight* — which is essentially a measure of relevance — to each declaration and styles the element using the declaration that has the greatest weight.

To figure out the declaration with the greatest weight, the cascade algorithm works through one or more tiebreaking criteria in the following order:

» The declaration type

» The origin type

» Specificity

» Source code order

The next few sections flesh out the specifics of these tiebreakers.

# Understanding declaration types

CSS includes a kind of Get Out of Jail Free card that enables a property declaration to climb to the top (or close to the top) of the cascade's relevance hierarchy. That miraculous mechanism is the !important annotation, which you add to a declaration just after the end of the property value:

```
color: navy !important;
```

**REMEMBER**

Be sure to include a space between the value and the !important annotation.

A declaration that includes the !important annotation is said to be using the *important* declaration type, whereas all other declarations are said to be using the *normal* declaration type.

**WARNING**

It's tempting to trot out the !important annotation any time you have a problem getting the cascade to do what you want. Every now and then you may have a good reason to go this route. However, it's almost always better to understand why the cascade is doing what it's doing and come up with a solution — for example, a more relevant selector — before launching the "nuclear option" of the !important annotation.

## Understanding origin types

The source of a particular CSS declaration is known as its *origin*. This is important because the cascade algorithm takes the origin into account when it decides which declarations to use when rendering the page. I get to that in a moment, but for now here's a quick summary of the major *origin types*:

>> **User agent stylesheet:** The list of default styles that the web browser applies to certain HTML tags.

>> **User stylesheet:** The styles that the web browser user has configured, such as a new default type size.

>> **Author stylesheets:** The styles that you create or that a third-party developer has created (such as a CSS reset). Author stylesheets come in three varieties:

- **External stylesheets:** The style rules that reside in separate .css files.

- **Internal stylesheets:** The style rules you add between the <style> and </style> tags in the head section of the HTML file.

- **Inline styles:** The style declarations you add to a tag's style attribute.

What do the origin types have to do with the cascade algorithm, exactly? Friend, it's all about weight.

## Declaration type, origin type, and weight

The two declaration types (normal and important) combine with the different origin types to define a built-in hierarchy of weight. That is, for a given declaration, the cascade assigns a weight based on the declaration's type and origin. When two or more declarations for the same property are competing to be applied to an element, the cascade first uses the declaration type/origin type hierarchy in Table 4-1 (listed from lowest weight to highest weight) to decide which declaration gets applied.

**TABLE 4-1**    The Declaration Type/Origin Type Weight Hierarchy

| Weight Ranking (lowest to highest) | Origin Type | Declaration Type |
|---|---|---|
| 1 | User agent stylesheet | Normal |
| 2 | User stylesheet | Normal |
| 3 | Author stylesheets: Internal or external | Normal |
| 4 | Author stylesheets: Inline | Normal |
| 5 | Author stylesheets: Internal or external | Important |
| 6 | Author stylesheets: Inline | Important |
| 7 | User stylesheet | Important |
| 8 | User agent stylesheet | Important |

So, for example, a normal property declaration in any author stylesheet (weight ranking 3 or 4 in Table 4-1) always overrides the same normal property declaration in the user agent stylesheet (weight ranking 1 in Table 4-1) because author stylesheets are given more weight. Similarly, an inline normal property declaration (weight ranking 4) overrides the same normal property declaration in an external or internal stylesheet (weight ranking 3) because inline styles are given more weight.

Weight ranking enables you to answer the question posed by the following code:

HTML:

```
<section>
    <p style="color: salmon">
        What color am I?
    </p>
</section>
```

CSS:

```
section {
    color: navy;
}
```

The p element's text color will be salmon because the inline declaration `color: salmon` has a higher weight than the `color: navy` declaration.

As a final note about origin type, declaration type, and weight, note in Table 4-1 that the important declaration types essentially reverse the weight ranking of the normal declaration types. That is, when the `!important` annotation is added to a declaration, the user stylesheet origin is given more weight than the author stylesheet origins, and the user agent stylesheet origin is given the highest possible weight.

**TECHNICAL STUFF**

Table 4-1 is incomplete because the CSS standard defines two other origin types. The first involves declarations associated with CSS transitions (refer to Bonus Chapter 2), which have the greatest weight of all, and the second involves CSS animation declarations, (refer to Bonus Chapter 3), which have a rank one notch higher than normal inline author stylesheet declarations. You can download these bonus chapters at www.dummies.com/go/htmlcss&javascriptaiofd.

## Figuring out specificity

What happens when two or more property declarations with the same declaration type and the same origin type target the same element? The declarations will have the same weight ranking from Table 4-1, so you have to turn to the cascade's next tiebreaking mechanism: *specificity*.

Specificity is a kind of score that aims to differentiate between two kinds of selector:

» **Broad:** A selector that targets a large range of elements. For example, the following rule targets every element in the body of the page:

```
body {
    color: slateblue;
}
```

» **Narrow:** A selector that targets a small range of elements. For example, the following rule targets just the element that has the `id` value of `subtitle`:

```
#subtitle {
    color: dodgerblue;
}
```

To understand why this distinction between broad and narrow selectors is important, picture a crowded lecture hall with a group of four panelists on stage in front of the audience. Imagine that each panelist wants to get the attention of the same person in the crowd. Here are some possible strategies each panelist may use:

| Panelist Action | Most Likely Result |
| --- | --- |
| Panelist A yells "Hey!" | Panelist A gets the attention of many people. |
| Panelist B says "Yoo-hoo!" and looks in the general direction of the person. | Panelist B gets the attention of several people along the panelist's line of sight. |
| Panelist C shouts the person's first name. | Unless the person's first name is unique in the audience, Panelist C gets the attention of everyone else with the same first name. |
| Panelist D shouts the person's first and last name and points at the person. | Panelist D gets the person's attention. |

The panelists are, in a sense, competing for the person's attention, and their strategies for doing so run from broad (Panelist A) to narrow (Panelist D). In this analogy, each strategy is like a CSS rule, where the panelist action is the selector and the person in the crowd is the targeted page element.

Most crucially for your purposes here is a CSS concept called *specificity*, which is a measure of whether a particular selector is broad, narrow, or something in between. That is, a selector that targets a broad range of elements is said to have *low specificity*, whereas a selector that targets a narrow range of elements is said to have *high specificity*.

The general idea is that, from the cascade's point of view, the more narrowly a selector targets an element, the more likely it is that the CSS developer's intention was to have the rule apply to the element. Therefore, the more specific a selector, the higher its specificity score and the more weight the cascade gives to the selector's declaration block.

(Let me stress here that the preceding is from the point of view of the *cascade*, which gives preference to selectors with the highest specificity. That doesn't mean that *you* must always prefer high-specificity selectors. Sometimes a broad selector will get the job done; sometimes a narrow selector will do. *You* get to decide the specificity of your selectors, but you must choose your selectors knowing that, for a given property declaration, the cascade will give preference to the selector with the highest specificity.)

Specificity is calculated as a kind of score that examines the components of a given selector and plops them into one of the following three buckets, which for easy memorization I've labeled I, C, and E:

>> **I:** Score one point for each ID selector (that is, a selector that begins with #).

>> **C:** Score one point for each class, pseudo-class, or attribute selector.

>> **E:** Score one point for each element (type) or pseudo-element selector.

You then take the total for each category — each *ICE bucket*, as I like to say — and arrange the scores in the following general way:

I-C-E

For example, if a selector has one ID selector, two class selectors, and four element selectors, the specificity is as follows:

1-2-4

Similarly, a selector with no ID selectors, three class selectors, and two element selectors would have the following specificity:

0-3-2

How does the cascade decide which of these has the higher specificity? It compares each bucket, reading them from left to right:

1. Compare the I (ID) buckets of selector A and selector B:

   • If one selector has a higher I score, that selector has the higher specificity, so skip the rest of the steps.

   • If both selectors have the same score, continue with Step 2.

2. Compare the C (class, pseudo-class, attribute) buckets of selector A and selector B:

   • If one selector has a higher C score, that selector has the higher specificity, so skip the rest of the steps.

   • If both selectors have the same C score, continue with Step 3.

3. Compare the E (element, pseudo-element) buckets of selector A and selector B:

   • If one selector has a higher E score, that selector has the higher specificity.

   • If both selectors have the same E score, it means the selectors have the same specificity, so the cascade moves on to the next tiebreaker (which is source code order; head for the section "The ultimate tiebreaker: source code order," later in this chapter).

So, in the preceding specificity scores, 1-2-4 has a higher specificity than 0-3-2.

TIP

It often helps to view specificity scores as numbers, such as by viewing 1-2-4 as 124 and 0-3-2 as 32. In this example, the number 124 is obviously higher than the number 32, so 1-2-4 has the higher specificity. However, this is a slightly dangerous practice because, at least in theory, it's possible for a particular bucket to have a score of 10 or more, so a specificity along the lines of 1-14-3 doesn't have a numeric equivalent.

To help you get a feel for converting selectors into specificity scores, the following table offers a few examples.

| Selector | I Bucket | C Bucket | E Bucket | Specificity (I-C-E) |
|---|---|---|---|---|
| #title | #title | | | 1-0-0 |
| #title > h2 | #title | | h2 | 1-0-1 |
| .warning | | .warning | | 0-1-0 |
| section | | | section | 0-0-1 |
| header > nav > a:hover | | :hover | header, nav, a | 0-1-3 |
| p.intro + aside | | .intro | p, aside | 0-1-2 |
| footer > div.social::before | | .social | footer, div, ::before | 0-1-3 |
| #nav-header li.external > span | #nav | .external | p, li, span | 1-1-3 |

In practice, you can use specificity to figure out why a particular element has styles that don't seem right. Quite often, the problem turns out to be that the browser is applying some other style rule that has a selector with a higher specificity.

REMEMBER

The universal selector (*) has a specificity value of 0, so you can ignore it when calculating your specificity scores.

REMEMBER

If you use either the :nth-child() or :nth-last-child() pseudo-element with the of list parameter, the specificity is 0-1-0 for the pseudo-class itself, plus the highest specificity of the selectors in list. For example, if list contains only type selectors, the specificity is 0-0-1, so the total specificity for the element is 0-1-1.

TIP

Rather than calculate the specificity yourself, you can let one of the several online calculators handle that chore for you. Here's a good one: https://polypane.app/css-specificity-calculator/.

# Specificity and :is(), :where(), :not(), and :has()

Specificity is arguably the most confusing topic in all of CSS, so don't worry if things are a bit fuzzy right now. Just keep thinking in terms of the ICE buckets, calculate selector specificity as often as you can, and it will all sink in eventually.

Of course, it's not going to help matters one bit that I'm about to add yet another complicating factor into the specificity calculation! I'm talking about the functional pseudo-classes :is(), :where(), :not(), and :has(). Because these are pseudo-classes, you may be tempted to add them to the C bucket when tallying up the I-C-E scores for a selector. That's an eminently reasonable assumption, but not a correct one. Here's how you factor the functional pseudo-classes into your specificity scores:

>> The :is(), :where(), :not(), and :has() pseudo-classes themselves don't add anything to the specificity.

>> The specificity of the :is(), :not(), and :has() pseudo-classes is given by the highest specificity score of the selectors in their respective selector lists.

>> The specificity of the :where() pseudo-class is always 0, no matter which selectors it has in its selector list.

The specificity of the :is(), :not(), and :has() pseudo-classes is a bit brow-furrowing, so here's a breakdown. Suppose you have the following selector:

```
is(#subtitle, nav:first-child, h1.title > h2)
```

There are three selectors in the selectors list, which, from left to right, have ICE specificity scores of 1-0-0, 0-1-1, and 0-1-2. The first of these (1-0-0) is the highest, so that's the specificity applied to the entire :is() selector.

# The ultimate tiebreaker: source code order

If two or more property declarations have the same declaration type, the same origin type weight ranking, and the same selector specificity, the cascade has one last tiebreaking strategy it can fall back on: source code order. That is, given multiple property declarations with equal weight, the declaration that appears latest in the source code is declared the winner.

Just to be clear (because this tiebreaker is crucial to figuring out what the cascade is doing and to solving cascade problems), here's what I mean by "latest" in the source code:

» If the declarations all reside in the same internal or external stylesheet, "latest" means the declaration that's closest to the bottom of the stylesheet. Consider the following code:

```css
p {
    color: darkorchid;
}
...
div, aside, p {
    color: indigo;
}
```

Text in the p element will be colored indigo because that declaration appears later in the source code.

» If the declarations reside in different external stylesheets, "latest" means the external stylesheet <link> tag that's closest to the bottom of the HTML file head section. Consider the following:

```html
<head>
    <meta charset="utf-8">
    <title>Wither MySpace?</title>
    <link rel="stylesheet" href="yourstyles.css">
    <link rel="stylesheet" href="mystyles.css">
</head>
```

» If both external stylesheets have a property declaration with equal weight, the declaration in the mystyles.css files will be the one the browser applies.

**REMEMBER**

Lots of CSS developers think that if a selector has declarations for the same property in both an external stylesheet and an internal stylesheet, the internal stylesheet declaration always wins. That's usually the case, but only because in most HTML files, the <link> tag comes before the <style> tag. If you were to put the <link> tag for your external stylesheet *after* the <style> tag, the external stylesheet declaration would be the winner.

## Putting it all together: the cascade algorithm

Okay, now I can combine all the stuff about declaration types, origin types, specificity, and source code order to explain just how the cascade goes about choosing which property declarations to apply to an element.

The cascade calculates declaration weights by running through the following steps:

1. Sort the property declarations based on the declaration type/origin type weight ranking, from highest (most weight) to lowest.

2. Check for the property declaration that has the highest ranking. One of two things can happen here:

   - If just one declaration has the top ranking, apply that declaration and then skip the rest of the steps.

   - If two or more declarations are tied at the top of the ranking, discard all the other declarations and proceed to Step 3.

3. For the property declarations that are tied with the highest declaration type/origin type weight ranking, calculate the specificity of each of the declarations' selectors and sort the declarations from highest specificity to lowest.

4. Check for the property declaration with the highest specificity. Again, there are two things that can happen now:

   - If one declaration has the highest specificity, apply that declaration and then skip the rest of the steps.

   - If two or more declarations are tied with the highest specificity, discard all the other declarations and proceed to Step 5.

5. For the declarations that are tied with the highest specificity, sort the declarations by their order of appearance in the CSS source code.

6. Apply whichever property declaration appears latest in the code.

IN THIS CHAPTER

» **A brief overview of measuring CSS things**

» **Understanding the CSS absolute measurements**

» **Becoming acquainted with CSS relative measurements**

» **Figuring out what viewport measurements are all about**

» **How to calculate stuff with CSS**

# Chapter **5**

# Taking the Measure of CSS

*Measure what is measurable, and make measurable what is not so.*

— GALILEO GALILEI

With its close ties to design, CSS feels more than a little like the artistic side of web development. And it's certainly true that CSS offers plenty of ways to give your right-brain a good workout: colors, backgrounds, and gradients (refer to Book 3, Chapter 6); fonts, alignment, and other typographical tidbits (Book 3, Chapter 7); fancy page layouts (Book 5); and eye-popping, grin-inducing animations (Bonus Chapters 1-3, downloadable at www.dummies.com/go/htmlcss&javascriptaiofd).

But CSS also has a side that's more likely to warm the cockles of an engineer's heart than an artist's. This is the part of CSS where you measure things: What dimensions should I use for that button? What thickness would look best for the border around that aside element? What's the right type size for my page text? How much space do I want between the page paragraphs?

These questions may seem unimportant, even trivial, but getting these and many other measurements right is a major part of the page design process and one of the key factors in creating web pages that look good and work well.

In this chapter, you replace your artist's beret with your engineer's hard hat and dive into the world of CSS measurement units. Happily, although CSS seems to support an endless number of units, you learn in this chapter that for your everyday CSS needs, there are just a few units that you need to be familiar with.

# Getting Comfy with CSS Measurement Units

Many CSS properties require a value that's a measure of some kind. For example, a border takes a length value that determines the width of that border. Similarly, a block element can take a dimensional value that sets the block's width or height. Values such as length or dimension are called *measurement values,* and they're essential not only to box model components such as padding, borders, margins, width, and height, but also for many other CSS features, including font sizes, shadow widths, and line spacing.

Almost every measurement value requires a *measurement unit,* which is a short code that specifies which unit you want the browser to apply to a measure. (I lead that previous sentence with "almost" because some properties — such as line-height; refer to Book 3, Chapter 7 — take unitless values.) So far in this book, I've talked about measures expressed in pixels, which are designated by the px unit:

```
footer {
    max-height: 200px;
    max-width: 150px;
}
```

However, CSS offers quite a few more measurement units. Most of them are hopelessly obscure or niche, so over the next few sections, I tell you which measurements you need to know.

# Checking Out the Absolute Measurement Units

An *absolute* measurement unit is one that has a fixed size. For example, the px (pixel) unit is defined as 1/96 of an inch. Some web designers prefer absolute measures because they feel it gives them more control over their designs. However, as I explain next, in the "Getting to Know the Relative Measurement Units" section, many web developers are moving away from absolute measurement units because they're too rigid.

Table 5-1 lists all the CSS absolute measurement units.

**TABLE 5-1**

## CSS Absolute Measurement Units

| Unit | Name | Equals |
|------|------|--------|
| px | pixels | 1/96 of an inch |
| pt | points | 1/72 of an inch |
| cm | centimeters | 37.8px or about 0.4in |
| mm | millimeters | 1/10 of a cm; about 3.8px |
| Q | quarter-millimeter | 1/40 of a cm; about 1px |
| in | inches | 96px; about 2.54cm |
| pc | picas | 1/6 of an inch; 16px |

Of these units, px is by far the most used, with a few designers employing pt and cm on occasion when they're writing CSS for documents that will be printed. If you're going to use absolute measurements and you're writing your CSS only for documents that will display on a screen, stick with px.

My recommendations:

>> It's fine to use px for very small lengths such as those used with most borders and outlines because it makes sense for these widths to be absolute values.

>> Don't use px (or any absolute measurement unit) for anything else.

>> Never, ever use px for font sizes. Why not? Because you make your web page less accessible to people with visual impairments that require them to pump up their web browser's default font size. If they customize the default font size

to, say, 32px, and you add a declaration such as font-size: 12px to your html element, you're preventing those folks from experiencing your page text as they wish. Sure, the user can zoom the page, but why would you force them to do that? If you care about a11y (and I know you do), shun pixel-based font sizes like the plague that they are. (Head over to Book 2, Chapter 6 for more about a11y.)

**TECHNICAL STUFF**

Is px *really* a fixed-size unit? Plenty of web design nerds argue that it's not, because the meaning of a measure such as 1px depends on the size and characteristics of the screen used by the reader. The W3C defines the CSS *reference pixel* as "the visual angle of one pixel on a device with a pixel density of 96dpi and a distance from the reader of an arm's length." Devices with pixel densities of 96dpi (dots per inch) refer to those huge CRT displays people used in the previous century. Today's devices use much higher dpi values, which means that a CSS pixel unit becomes smaller to compensate (for some screens, it's about 1/160 of an inch). So, for example, a 96px-by-96px button that would have measured 1 inch by 1 inch in, say, 1995 now appears a bit smaller than that on today's smartphones.

# Getting to Know the Relative Measurement Units

A *relative* unit is one that doesn't have a fixed size. Instead, the size depends on — that is, is relative to — something else. Occasionally that something else is the size of the viewport, a case that I put off until the later section, "Here's Looking at View(port Measurement Units)." The rest of the time, relative unit sizes are measured as outlined in Table 5-2.

**TABLE 5-2**    **CSS Relative Measurement Units**

| Unit | Name | Measured Relative to |
| --- | --- | --- |
| % | percentage | A quantity defined on the same element or an ancestor element. (The specific quantity depends on the CSS property you're working with.) |
| em | M-width | The element's inherited or defined font size. The term *em* comes from print typography, where it referred to the width of the capital letter *M*. |
| ex | x-height | The x-height of the element's font. The *x-height* refers to the height of the lowercase *x* in a specified font. |
| ch | 0-width | The width of the number 0 in the element's font. |
| rem | root em | The font size of the root element of the web page. |

Of these, I only recommend spending any time with %, em, and rem, which I cover in more detail in the sections that follow.

## Using percentages

One quick way to get your page elements to behave nicely on screens of different sizes is to express CSS lengths as percentage values. Percentages work well because they're usually calculated relative to the same property in an element's parent. For example, by default a child block element takes up the full width of its parent block. If you want that child element to use only half its parent's width, you set up a rule like this:

```
child {
    width: 50%;
}
```

This is a screen-friendly approach because as the parent block's size changes (say, because the user is resizing the browser window or changing the screen orientation), the child element's width changes along with it to maintain that 50 percent ratio.

One gotcha to watch out for when using percentages is that sometimes what the percentage is relative to is not what you'd expect. For example, when setting padding-top, padding-bottom, margin-top, or margin-bottom, you'd think that these vertical-spacing values would be relative to the parent container's height. Nope. They're actually calculated relative to the parent's *width*, which can lead to some unexpected behavior if you don't allow for this in your declarations.

## Getting a handle on the em unit

To understand the em measurement unit, you first need to know that CSS uses the font-size property to set the type size for an element. Here's an example:

```
article {
    font-size: 24px;
}
```

**REMEMBER**

(I'm using an absolute value here, which is bad CSS practice, as I explain earlier in this chapter, in the "Checking Out the Absolute Measurement Units" section.)

Second, you also need to bear in mind that font-size is an inherited property so, unless specified otherwise, a child element will always use the same font-size value as its parent.

With those preliminaries out of the way, I can tell you that the em unit takes its value relative to the calculated font size of whatever element you're working with. (This is why em is described as a *font-relative* unit.) Here, *calculated* means the font size that the cascade algorithm (refer to Book 3, Chapter 4) finally applied after calculating the weights of all the font-size property declarations in the various CSS origin types (user agent stylesheet, user stylesheet, and author stylesheets) for those selectors that targeted the element.

That calculated font size will be either of the following:

» **A font size inherited by the element:** The inherited font size will be the value of the font-size property defined on the element's closest ancestor that has a font-size declaration. If no ancestor element has a font-size declaration, the inherited font size will be the default font size. (That is, the default size specified by the web browser or the customized default size set by the user.)

» **A font size defined on the element:** The defined font size is the value of a font-size declaration that targets the element directly.

So, which of these calculated font sizes does the em unit use? Just to thoroughly confuse us all, it depends on what CSS property you're working with! There are, mercifully, just two possibilities:

» If you're working with an element's font-size property (and a few other typography-related properties, such as text-indent), the em unit is relative to the element's inherited font size. In this case, you can interpret the em unit to mean "the font-size value of this element's parent."

» If you're working with any other property (such as width, margin, or padding), the em unit is relative to the element's defined font size. In this case, you can interpret the em unit to mean "the font-size value of this element."

In theory, these possibilities make some sense. For example, if you want some child element to use a slightly smaller font size than its parent, you can set up a rule along these lines:

```
child {
    font-size: 0.75em;
}
```

Similarly, it makes sense for properties such as width and padding to scale up or down along with the font size of the element.

In practice, however, em units can be tricky in the extreme. For example, suppose you have a section element and you want its text to be slightly bigger than the default text. You think "1.25em ought to do it." Now suppose your code looks like this (in this book's example files, check out bk03ch05/example01.html):

HTML:

```
<body>
    <main>
        <article>
            <section>
                What font size am I?
            </section>
        </article>
    </main>
</body>
```

CSS:

```
article {
    font-size: 1.5em;
}
section {
    font-size: 1.25em;
}
```

What font size does the text in the section element use? This is a two-step calculation:

1. **Calculate the font size of the section element's parent, which is the article element.**

   Assuming that the article element has inherited the default font size of 16px, the em unit will be relative to that default, so here's the font size that article uses after applying the font-size declaration:

   1.5em = 1.5 * 16px = 24px

2. **Calculate the font size of the section element itself.**

   The em unit will be relative to the font size of the parent article element, which is 24px from Step 1. Therefore, here's the font size that section uses after applying the font-size declaration:

   1.25em = 1.25 * 24px = 30px

Surprisingly, the text in the section element is not only bigger than the default 16px text, it's nearly *twice* as big. Welcome to the em unit!

Note, as well, that my example here assumes that only the parent article element's font-size property was set. Imagine if there were also em-based font-size declarations on the ancestor elements main and body. Now your calculations have to take *four* levels of inheritance into account! When working with em units, things can get nasty very quickly.

Another way the em unit can surprise you is when you use it with properties other than font-size. Consider the following code (check out bk03ch05/example02. html):

HTML:

```
<article>
    <section>
        How wide am I?
    </section>
</article>
```

CSS:

```
article {
    font-size: 1.5em;
    width: 600px;
}
section {
    font-size: 1.25em;
    width: 25em;
}
```

How wide is the section element? For the width property, the em unit is relative to the element's font size, which per the earlier calculation is 30px. Therefore, here's the calculation that determines the width value for the section element:

25em = 25 * 30px = 750px

The child is now substantially wider than its parent!

So, should you avoid using the em unit in your CSS code? As you've learned, em can be very volatile and slippery because the calculated value could be subject to multiple levels of compounding thanks to inheritance. However, you can often put that inheritance to work for you. For example, it's not uncommon to have a child element whose font size you want to change as the font size of its parent changes. To accomplish this without incurring multiple levels of compounding, you can do the following:

>> Style the parent font size with a unit that doesn't incur inheritance compounding, such as the rem unit discussed in the next section.

>> Style the child font size using em. This way, when the font size of the parent changes, the child font size changes along with it, but in a completely predictable way.

In other words, it's best to use em units only in local components of your web page.

## Meeting your CSS measurement best friend: the rem unit

All the hairy and math-heavy shenanigans of the em unit disappear completely when you use the rem unit instead. Why? Because although the rem unit is also font-relative, the value of rem is relative to just one thing: the font size of the html — also called the *root* — element. What is root font size? It can be any one of the following (in ascending order of weight):

>> The default font size as specified by the web browser. In all modern browsers, that default size is 16px.

>> The custom font size that the user has modified via the web browser's settings. For example, if the user changes Chrome's Font Size setting to 24px, as shown in Figure 5-1, the root font size becomes 24px.

>> The font-size value that your CSS code sets on the html element.

Your defined font-size value for the html element takes precedence over any custom value set by the user, so the accessibility-friendly thing to do is to either not include a font-size declaration in the html element or, as is common practice nowadays, set the font-size to 100% to ensure that you're starting with the user's preferred size:

```
html {
    font-size: 100%;
}
```

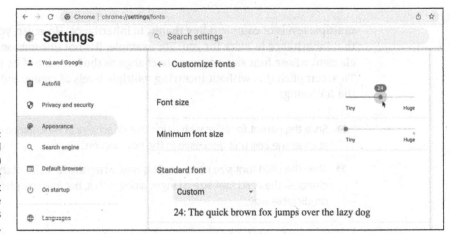

**FIGURE 5-1:**
Users can (and very often do) modify the default font size in the web browser's settings.

To demonstrate the difference between em and rem, here's the same code that I used earlier, except I've substituted rem units for em units in the font-size declarations (bk03ch05/example03.html):

HTML:

```
<body>
    <main>
        <article>
            <section>
                What font size am I?
            </section>
        </article>
    </main>
</body>
```

CSS:

```
article {
    font-size: 1.5rem;
}
section {
    font-size: 1.25rem;
}
```

What font size does the text in the section element use now? Assuming that the default font size is 16px, no complex calculation is required:

1.25rem = 1.25 * 16px = 20px

This calculation will be true no matter which element has the declaration `font-size: 1.25rem` and no matter what font size is used by the element's parent or ancestors (except, of course, for the ultimate ancestor: the `html` element).

What if the user has set the default font size to something other than 16px? The use of the `rem` unit ensures that your text will scale accordingly. For example, if the default font size is now 24px, the calculation becomes the following:

1.25rem = 1.25 * 24px = 30px

And this scaling applies to not just the `font-size` property but also any property that uses a length measure, such as the margins. For example, if the default font size is 24px, the following code means that the margins around the `aside` element will also be 24px:

```
aside {
    margin: 1rem;
}
```

So, does this mean that you should always use `rem` units? Not necessarily. Here are my recommendations:

>> Except for the `html` element (where you should declare `font-size: 100%`), use `rem` units for all other font sizes.

>> Use `rem` for all properties that create whitespace on your page, such as `margin` and `padding`. Doing so will give your page a consistent look throughout.

>> Assume that the user will change the default font size and plan accordingly, which means doing two things:

• If it makes sense for a particular length measurement (such as an element's margins) to scale along with the change in the default font size, declare that measurement with `rem` units.

• If you don't want a particular length measurement to scale along with the default font size, declare that measurement with any unit that isn't font-relative (such as px, %, or one of the viewport units I discuss in the next section).

>> If you want a child element's properties that use font-based values to scale along with changes in the parent's font size, use em units for the child properties. Then, to minimize the effect of compounding due to inheritance, declare the parent element's font size using `rem` units.

# Here's Looking at View(port Measurement Units)

From a CSS perspective, the *viewport* is the rectangle (known officially as the *initial containing block*) defined by the html (root) element, which by definition extends the full width and height of the browser window, minus the browser's *chrome* — that is, its user interface features such as the toolbar, address bar, and bookmarks bar. The viewport, in other words, is that part of the browser window through which the visible part of the current web page appears.

CSS includes several so-called *viewport-percentage* units, which are relative to some dimension of the viewport, as shown in Table 5-3.

**TABLE 5-3**

## CSS Viewport Measurement Units

| Unit | Name | Measured Relative to |
|------|------|----------------------|
| vw | viewport width | 1/100 of the viewport width |
| vh | viewport height | 1/100 of the viewport height |
| vmin | viewport minimum | 1/100 of the viewport's smaller dimension |
| vmax | viewport maximum | 1/100 of the viewport's larger dimension |

Here's an example:

```
article {
    width: 75vw;
}
```

Here, the width of the article element takes up three-quarters of the width of the viewport.

Viewport-based measures look a lot like percentages (because, say, 1vw is defined as one percent of the viewport width), but viewport units are more straightforward to use because they're relative to just one thing: a viewport dimension. A percentage, by contrast, is usually applied relative to some aspect of the parent element, such as its width. This can lead to unintuitive results such as an element's top and bottom padding changing if the parent element's width changes.

The other advantage of viewport units is that they automatically scale along with the changing viewport size. If the user changes the size of the browser window or rotates their device to a different orientation, a property that uses a viewport-based unit will automatically scale to match the new viewport width or height.

I talk more about viewport units when I discuss responsive layouts in Book 5, Chapter 4.

# Calculating with CSS

All the CSS examples in this chapter (and, indeed, so far in this book) have set some property to a fixed value, such as 100% or 1.25rem or 75vw. Computer geeks call these *literal* values because they are what they are. However, there's a powerful class of CSS values that are derived not from literals, but from *calculations*. These CSS features are called *functions*, and there are four that you can use to specify measurement-related property values: calc(), min(), max(), and clamp().

## Calculating with calc()

The calc() function takes two or more literal values, performs one or more arithmetic operations on those values, and then returns the result of that calculation, which is then assigned to whatever property you're working with. Here's the syntax:

```
property: calc(expression);
```

>> *property*: The CSS property to which you want to assign the calc() result.

>> *expression*: Two or more CSS measurement values — called the *operands* of the expression — with each pair interspersed with a symbol — known as an *operator* — that defines the type of calculation to perform:

- *operand*: This is usually a literal value such as 50px or 10rem, but it can also be a CSS variable (refer to Bonus Chapter 4) or even another calc() function. You can mix measurement units. (You can download Bonus Chapter 4 at www.dummies.com/go/htmlcss&javascriptaiofd.)

- *operator*: The calc() function supports four operations: addition (which uses the + operator), subtraction (−), multiplication (∗), and division (/). If you use multiple operators in the expression, note that multiplication and division are normally performed before addition and subtraction. You can force calc() to perform a particular operation first by putting parentheses () around the operation.

Here are a few `calc()` functions with some example expressions:

```
calc(50vw + 10px)
calc(100vh - 5rem)
calc(10% * 3)
calc(100% / 8)
calc(100vw - (5rem + 10px))
```

In the last example, `calc()` performs the addition `5rem + 10px` first because it's in parentheses, and then `calc()` performs the subtraction.

**REMEMBER**

A space on either side of the + and – operators is required. A space on either side of the * and / operators is optional but highly recommended for readability.

When you use a percentage, the browser calculates the percentage from whatever property you're using for your declaration. For example, suppose you have an `article` element and an `aside` element side by side. The `aside` element is `15rem` wide, and you want the article element to take up the rest of the available width. Here's a rule that would do the job (bk03ch05/example04.html):

```
article {
    width: calc(100% - 15rem);
}
```

This calculation takes `100%` of the available `article` element width, subtracts `15rem`, and sets the result as the `width` value.

## Finding the smallest value with min()

If you want to set an upper bound on a property value, use the `min()` function, which takes a list of values and returns the smallest of them:

```
property: min(list);
```

>> *property*: The CSS property to which you want to assign the `min()` result.

>> *list*: A comma-separated list of CSS measurement values, which can include arithmetic expressions and `calc()` functions.

Here's an example (bk03ch05/example05.html):

```
article {
    width: min(75vw, 1200px);
}
```

If the viewport is wider than 1600px, 75vw will be more than 1200px, so min() returns 1200px. If the viewport width falls below 1600px, 75vw falls below 1200px, so min() returns 75vw. In other words, this min() function sets an upper bound of 1200px on the article element's width property.

## Finding the largest value with max()

If you want to set a lower bound on a property value, use the max() function, which takes a list of values and returns the largest of them:

```
property: max(list);
```

» *property*: The CSS property to which you want to assign the max() result.

» *list*: A comma-separated list of CSS measurement values, which can include arithmetic expressions and other CSS functions, such as calc().

Here's an example (bk03ch05/example06.html):

```
article {
    width: max(75vw, 450px);
}
```

If the viewport width is less than 600px, 75vw will be less than 450px, so max() returns 450px. If the viewport widens beyond 600px, 75vw becomes greater 450px, so max() returns 75vw. In other words, this max() function sets a lower bound of 450px on the article element's width property.

## Setting bounds with clamp()

One very common web design conundrum is figuring out a way to prevent some dynamic measurement from getting either too large or too small. For example, when setting regular page text, lines that are too short are annoying to read, and lines that are too long are hard to follow across the page. If you're styling, say, the text in an article element and you're using calc() to set the width property dynamically, it would be nice to have a way to prevent the width value from becoming either too small or too large.

Allow me to present a solution to this conundrum in the form of the clamp() function:

```
property: clamp(min, expression, max);
```

>> *property*: The CSS property to which you want to assign the clamp() result.

>> *min*: The lowest value that can be assigned to *property*.

>> *expression*: The preferred value that you want assigned to *property*. This can be a literal value, an expression, or a CSS function, such as calc().

>> *max*: The highest value that can be assigned to *property*.

The idea behind clamp() is that the browser evaluates the *expression* parameter and then assigns a value to the property as follows:

>> If the *expression* value is between *min* and *max*, the browser uses the *expression* result as the property value.

>> If the *expression* value is less than *min*, the browser uses *min* as the property value.

>> If the *expression* value is greater than *max*, the browser uses *max* as the property value.

Here's an example (bk03ch05/example07.html):

```
article {
    width: clamp(450px, calc(100% – 15rem), 1200px);
}
```

This rule uses calc(100% – 15rem) to calculate the width but sets 450px as the lower bound and 1200px as the upper bound.

Chapter **6**

# Fancifying Pages with Colors and Backgrounds

*Color is free on the web . . . Using different colors not only adds a bit of drama to the page, but also creates hierarchies for the content.*

—ERIK SPIEKERMANN

*love* black-and-white photography. There's just something compelling and beautiful that rises to the surface when an image thumbs its nose at all the world's reds, greens, and blues. It's a brave and risky choice to present your art with such a stark palette.

However, I definitely do *not* love black-and-white web pages! Any site that offers nothing more than black text on a white background (or white text on a black background) tells me something important: That the page designer either didn't care (or was too lazy) to put something beautiful on the web. Because that's what colors do: They make a web page more beautiful, more vivid, and more interesting. Colors aren't mere eye candy; they're an integral part of web design. And after you know how to apply colors, it takes only a little more work to convert a page from something drab and lifeless to a colorful and vibrant expression of your creative side.

In this chapter, you investigate the amazing world of CSS colors. You learn various ways to specify colors, and then you put that newfound know-how to work right away using color to style your text. From there you learn how to set a page background color or image, how to create crowd-pleasing gradients, how to set border colors, and how to style your images. It's a veritable feast for the eyes, so dive right in.

# Specifying Colors in CSS

When rendering the page using their default styles, browsers don't do much with colors, other than show link text in a default and familiar blue. But CSS offers a ton of properties, keywords, and functions that enable you to add a splash (or even a torrent, if that's your thing) of color to your pages.

The next few sections take you through the main ways that CSS offers to specify a color as a property value.

## Papayawhip, peachpuff, and more: color keywords

If you're not a color nerd, you probably don't want to mess around with specifying a color value based on its components (red, green, and blue). (If you *are* a color nerd, don't worry: I get to the geeky stuff after this section.) CSS offers a couldn't-be-easier method for specifying a color value: *color keywords.* These are predefined terms, each of which corresponds to a specific color.

CSS defines more than 140 color keywords, which is more than enough to satisfy anyone who just wants to add a dollop of color to a web page. Some of the keywords are straightforward and readily grasped, such as red, yellow, and purple. Others are, well, a bit whimsical (and hunger-inducing): lemonchiffon, blanchedalmond, and mintcream. My WebDev Workshop lists them all, as shown in part in Figure 6-1 (surf over to https://webdevworkshop.io/ck).

REMEMBER

The CSS color keywords are case insensitive, so the values red, RED, and even ReD all refer to the same color.

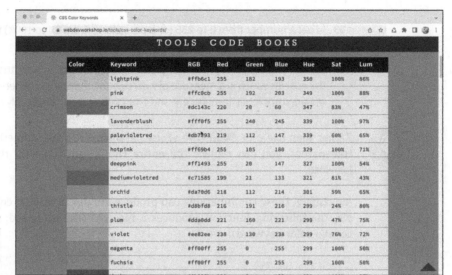

**FIGURE 6-1:**
Go to my WebDev Workshop to check out a full list of the CSS color keywords.

# Rolling your own colors with the rgb() function

You may know that you can specify just about any color in the rainbow by mixing three hues: red, green, and blue. Here are some examples:

- » Mixing pure red and pure green produces yellow
- » Mixing pure green and pure blue produces cyan
- » Mixing pure red and pure blue produces magenta
- » Mixing all three pure colors produces white

In CSS, you indicate the "pureness" of a color with a number between 0 and 255, where 255 represents the color at its highest intensity (most pure) and 0 represents the color at its lowest intensity (least pure).

To specify any color by mixing red, green, and blue, you can use the rgb() function:

```
rgb(red green blue / alpha)
```

- » *red*: A number from 0 to 255 (or a percentage from 0% to 100%) that specifies the intensity of the red portion of the final color.
- » *green*: A number from 0 to 255 (or a percentage from 0% to 100%) that specifies the intensity of the green portion of the final color.

» *blue*: A number from 0 to 255 (or a percentage from 0% to 100%) that specifies the intensity of the blue portion of the final color.

» *alpha*: A number from 0 to 1 or a percentage from 0% to 100% that specifies the *opacity*, which is a measure of how opaque the color is (where 0 or 0% means completely transparent and 1 or 100% means completely opaque).

**TIP**

Rather than use 0 or 0% for the *alpha* parameter to make something completely transparent, you can replace the entire rgb() function with the transparent keyword.

Amazingly, these combinations can produce around 16 million colors. For example, the following function produces a nice red (the same red, actually, as the tomato color keyword):

```
rgb(255 99 71)
```

If you want a bit of whatever's behind the element to show through the color, you can add an opacity value, like so:

```
rgb(255 99 71 / 90%)
```

**REMEMBER**

Until recently, the rgb() function required commas between the red, green, and blue parameters and didn't accept the alpha parameter. In the olden days, you specified opacity using the rgba() function, which used the syntax rgba(red, green, blue, alpha). These older syntaxes are still common, so you'll almost certainly come across them when you're checking out the source code of other sites.

## Specifying colors nerd-style: RGB codes

An *RGB code* is a hash symbol (#) followed by a six-digit value that takes the form *rdgrbl*, where *rd* is a two-digit value that specifies the red component of the color, *gr* is a two-digit value that specifies the green component, and *bl* is a two-digit value that specifies the blue component.

Sounds reasonable, am I right? Not so fast. These two-digit values are, in fact, *hexadecimal* — that is, base 16 — values, which run from 0 to 9 and then from a to f. As two-digit values, the decimal values 0 through 255 are represented as 00 through ff in hexadecimal.

For example, the following RGB code produces the same red as the function rgb(255 99 71):

```
#ff6347
```

**TIP**

If the digits in each two-digit hexadecimal code are the same, you can shorten the code to a three-digit version that gets rid of the repeated digits. For example, the following two RGB codes are equivalent (and produce a rather nice blue):

```
#3388cc
#38c
```

# Going pro with the hsl() function

If you read the previous two sections, you may now be thinking, "Wow, there's *nothing* intuitive about any of this!" I couldn't agree more. RGB codes are pure High Geekery, and even the mixing of red, green, and blue using the rgb() function is tough to fathom unless you've got a great sense of how color mixing works.

The unintuitive nature of the RGB method of specifying colors has led many CSS developers — amateurs and pros alike — to embrace a different color model that's based on three attributes:

» **hue:** The color or, more specifically, the position on the color wheel (shown in Figure 6-2), where red is defined as 0 degrees and the colors progress around the wheel to yellow (60 degrees), green (120 degrees), cyan (180 degrees), blue (240 degrees), and magenta (300 degrees), and, of course, everything in between.

» **saturation:** The purity of the hue, where full saturation means the hue is a pure color and no saturation means the hue is part of the grayscale.

» **lightness:** How light or dark the hue is, where full lightness produces white and no lightness produces black.

(As an aside, the color wheel shown in Figure 6-2 is made of pure CSS goodness! To check out the code, refer to bk03ch06/example01.html in this book's example files.)

This is the HSL color model and it's much more intuitive because you specify a color with a single value (hue) based on a familiar (or at least comprehensible) mechanism: the color wheel. You then adjust the saturation and lightness to get the color you want.

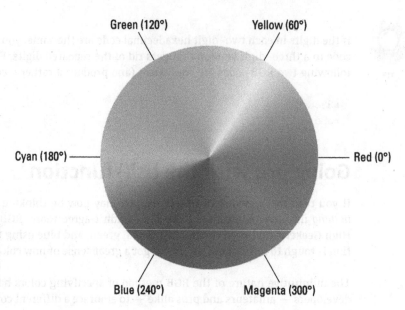

Green (120°)    Yellow (60°)

Cyan (180°) ——————    —————— Red (0°)

Blue (240°)    Magenta (300°)

**FIGURE 6-2:**
In the HSL color
model, hue
refers to a color's
position on the
color wheel.

Even better, the HSL model enables you to easily choose harmonious colors because everything you need is right there on the color wheel:

>> **Complementary colors:** For a given color, its complementary color is the one that lies on the opposite side of the color wheel (that is, 180 degrees away).

>> **Analogous colors:** For a given color, an analogous color is the one that lies plus or minus 30 degrees on the color wheel.

>> **Triadic colors:** For a given color, its triadic colors are the two colors that lie 120 degrees one way and 120 degrees the other way on the color wheel.

>> **Split complementary colors:** For a given color, you determine its split complementary colors by finding the opposite color and then using the colors that are 30 degrees on either side of that opposite (that is, 150 degrees and 210 degrees from the given color).

To work with the HSL color model in CSS, you use the hsl() function:

```
hsl(hue saturation lightness / alpha)
```

>> *hue:* The position on the color wheel of the hue you want to use as the basis of the color, using one of the following angle units:

• deg: An angle in degrees, usually from 0 to 359, but negative values and values of 360 or more are legal. For example, the negative value –60deg is the same as 300deg, and the value 480deg is the same as 120deg. This is the default unit, so if you leave it off, the browser interprets your value as an angle in degrees.

- rad: An angle in radians, usually from 0 to 6.2832 (that is, 2π), but any positive or negative value is allowed.

- grad: An angle in gradians. A complete circle is 400grad.

- turn: An angle in number of turns around the color wheel. A complete circle is 1turn; halfway around (180 degrees) is 0.5turn, and so on.

>> *saturation*: A percentage from 0% to 100% that specifies how much of the *hue* is present in the final color, with 100% meaning completely saturated and 0% meaning completely unsaturated (in which case you get a color on the grayscale).

>> *lightness*: A percentage from 0% to 100% that specifies how light or dark the final color will be, with 100% producing white, 0% producing black, and 50% producing the normal *hue*.

>> *alpha*: A number from 0 to 1 or a percentage from 0% to 100% that specifies the *opacity*, which is a measure of how opaque the color is (where 0 or 0% means completely transparent and 1 or 100% means completely opaque).

**TIP**

If you need an element to be completely transparent, instead of using 0 or 0% for the *alpha* parameter, you can replace the entire hsl() function with the keyword transparent.

Here's the hsl() equivalent of the tomato and rgb(255 99 71) color values that I used as earlier examples:

```
hsl(9deg 100% 64%)
```

To get the split complementary colors, I need only add 150deg and 210deg to the *hue* value:

```
hsl(159deg 100% 64%)
hsl(219deg 100% 64%)
```

**REMEMBER**

Not that long ago, the hsl() function required commas between the hue, saturation, and lightness parameters and didn't accept the alpha parameter. In the before times, you specified opacity using the hsla() function, which used the syntax hsla(hue, saturation, lightness, alpha). These older syntaxes are still prevalent, so you'll likely stumble upon them when you're looking at the source code of other sites.

# Using Color to Spruce Up Your Text

CSS offers properties that enable you to color not only your page text but also the text background, the text decoration (such as a link underline), and the text drop shadow. The next few sections tell you all you need to know about applying color to these elements.

## Applying a text color

To apply a CSS color to some text, you use the color property:

```
color: value;
```

>> *value*: A color keyword, rgb() function, RGB code, or hsl() function.

The following example (check out bk03ch06/example02.html) sets the text color of the aside element to the dark blue given by hsl(209deg 50% 30%):

```
aside {
    color: hsl(209deg 50% 30%);
}
```

## Setting the text decoration color

In Book 3, Chapter 7, you learn various properties for styling link underlines, which in CSS-speak are known as *text decorations*. Refer to that chapter for a full discussion, but for now let me just say that you can style the color of your link underlines using the text-decoration-color property:

```
text-decoration-color: value;
```

>> *value*: A color keyword, rgb() function, RGB code, or hsl() function.

For example, the following rule styles all links with a red underline (bk03ch06/example03.html):

```
a {
    text-decoration-color: red;
}
```

# Creating a text shadow

For a fancy effect, you can style your text with a shadow, which is an exact copy of the text with three characteristics:

>> The copy is offset slightly from the original.

>> The copy is blurred a bit.

>> The copy has its own color.

For example, a *drop shadow* is offset slightly down and to the right, which makes the original text look raised up from the page.

To create a text shadow, use the text-shadow property:

```
text-shadow: offset-x offset-y blur-radius color;
```

>> *offset-x*: A length value that specifies how much the shadow copy is shifted horizontally with respect to the original text.

>> *offset-y*: A length value that specifies how much the shadow copy is shifted vertically with respect to the original text.

>> *blur-radius*: A length value that specifies the amount of blurring to be applied to the shadow copy; the bigger the value you use for blur-radius, the more the shadow text is blurred.

>> *color*: The color you want to apply to the shadow copy; use a color keyword, rgb() function, RGB code, or hsl() function.

Shadows get lost on small text (and make that text harder to read), so reserve your shadows for big text, and the bigger the better. Here's an example (bk03ch06/example04.html) that creates the drop-shadow effect shown in Figure 6-3:

```
div {
    color: steelblue;
    font-size: 15vw;
    text-shadow: 7px 7px 5px cornflowerblue;
}
```

FIGURE 6-3:
Some big text
with a drop
shadow.

**TIP**

The text-shadow property can accept multiple shadow definitions, each separated by a comma, which can create some interesting effects. Here's a simple example:

```
text-shadow:
    7px 7px 5px cornflowerblue,
    9px 9px 5px darkblue;
```

For a more elaborate take, bk03ch06/example05.html.

# Styling an Element's Background

For every HTML element, the *background* is the layer of the element's box model upon which everything else is displayed, including text and images (which together comprise the *foreground*). For each element, the background includes the content box and extends to the outer edge of the element's border.

By default, every element is given a transparent background. (This is true even of the body element. So why are page backgrounds white by default? That whiteness is built into the browser itself.) However, CSS comes with a slew of background-related properties that enable you to perk up that default nothingness with either a color or even an image. The next couple of sections take you through the details.

## Applying a coat of background color

For some extra page pizazz, try adding a color to the background of an element. You do this in CSS by using the background-color property:

```
background-color: value;
```

>> *value*: A color keyword, rgb() function, RGB code, or hsl() function.

The following example (bk03ch06/example06.html) displays the `aside` element with white text on a black background:

```css
aside {
    background-color: hsl(0, 0%, 0%);
    color: hsl(0 0% 100%);
}
```

When you're messing around with text and background colors, make sure you leave enough contrast between the text and background to ensure that your page visitors can still read the text without shaking their fists at you. For more on color contrast and accessibility, refer to the section "Choosing accessible colors," later in this chapter.

But I should also warn you that too much contrast isn't conducive to easy reading, either. For example, using pure white for text and pure black for a background (as I did in the preceding code, tsk, tsk) isn't great because there's too much contrast. Darkening the text a shade and lightening the background a notch makes all the difference:

```css
aside {
    background-color: hsl(0, 0%, 10%);
    color: hsl(0 0% 90%);
}
```

**TIP**

You can apply a bit of color to checkboxes and radio buttons (also range and progress elements) by using the `accent-color` property. For example, to show the background of a checkbox as green when the checkbox is selected, you use the following rule:

```css
input[type="checkbox"] {
    accent-color: green;
}
```

## Wallpapering an element with a background image

To give your element backgrounds a bit more oomph, you can cover them with an image by setting the element's `background-image` property:

```css
background-image: image;
```

» *image*: The image you want to display as the element background. You have multiple ways to specify the image, but the following two are the most common:

- **Image file:** Use `url("file")`, where *file* is the filename of the image, including the directory path if the file doesn't reside in the same directory as the file where your CSS code lives.

- **Gradient:** Specify the gradient using a gradient function such as `linear-gradient()` or `radial-gradient()`. (Head over to "Impressing Your Friends with Color Gradients" to learn how to work with gradients.)

Here's an example (bk03ch06/example07.html) that adds a background image to a `div` element:

HTML:

```
<body>
    <div>
    </div>
</body>
```

CSS:

```
div {
    background-image: url("images/webdev-workshop.png");
    border: 1px solid black;
    height: 75vh;
    width: 75vw;
}
```

Figure 6-4 shows the result. Notice that when the image is smaller than the dimensions of the target element, the browser repeats — or *tiles* — the image to fill the background.

**WARNING**

When you use an image as the background of an element that contains text, make sure the image isn't so busy that it makes the element text hard to decipher. Also, make sure there's sufficient contrast between the colors used in the image and the color of your text.

FIGURE 6-4:
The browser tiles
smaller images to
fill the element's
background.

Here's another example of using an image as the background of the body element
(bk03ch06/example08.html):

```
body {
    margin: 0;
    font-size: 100%;
    background-image: url("images/ant-on-a-flower.jpg");
    height: 100vh;
    width: 100vw;
}
```

As shown in Figure 6-5, when you use an image that's larger than the element's
dimensions, the browser uses the image to fill the entire background and then
lops off the rest of the image.

To control background image characteristics such as how (and whether) a smaller
image tiles and how a larger image fits its element's background, CSS offers an
alarming number of properties related to background images. Here's a look at
most of them:

>> background-position: *x y*: Specifies the starting position of the background
image, where *x* is the horizontal starting position and *y* is the vertical starting
position. Both *x* and *y* can be a keyword (top, right, bottom, left, or center),
a percentage, or a length value (such as 50px or 5rem). The default value is left
top. Bk03ch06/example09.html.

**FIGURE 6-5:**
The browser uses
only enough of a
larger image to
fill the element
background.

>> background-size: *width height* | *keyword*: Specifies the size of the
background image. Both *width* and *height* can be a percentage or a length
value (such as 250px or 15rem). You can also specify just the *width* value and
the browser adjusts the height automatically to keep the image's initial aspect
ratio. Alternatively, you can specify a *keyword*, which can be either of the
following:

- contain: Scales the image until it reaches the full width or height of the
element (whichever happens first). If space is still left in the other dimension, the browser tiles the image until the space is filled.

- cover: Scales the image until it covers the full width and height of the
element. If the image is larger than the element's background, the browser
crops the rest of the image.

The default value is auto auto (which means that the browser automatically
sets the width and height according to the image's intrinsic dimensions).
Check out bk03ch06/example10.html.

>> background-repeat: *horizontal vertical*: Specifies whether and how the
background image repeats (tiles) when the image is smaller than the element
background. Both *horizontal* and *vertical* can take any of the following
keywords:

- repeat: The image repeats along the specified axis (that is, horizontally or
vertically) until it fills the available area. If needed, the last repetition of the
image will be clipped if there's not enough room to fit the entire image.

- space: The image repeats along the specified axis without clipping. If there's
extra space, the first and last repetitions of the image are pinned to the end

of the axis (for example, the left and right ends for the *horizontal* parameter) and the extra space is distributed evenly between the rest of the image repetitions.

- round: The image repeats along the specified axis without clipping. If there's extra space, the image repetitions are stretched in the axis direction to fill that space.

- no-repeat: The image does not repeat along the specified axis.

You can use any of these keywords just once and the browser applies the keyword to both dimensions (for example, background-repeat: space is the same as background-repeat: space space). You can also use the following single-value keywords:

- repeat-x: The image repeats only along the horizontal axis. This is the same as using repeat no-repeat.

- repeat-y: The image repeats only along the vertical axis. This is the same as using no-repeat repeat.

The default value is repeat. Check out bk03ch06/example11.html (shown in Figure 6-6).

» background-clip: *keyword*: Specifies to which part of the element's box model the background image extends. The possibilities for *keyword* are content-box, padding-box, or border-box. The default value is border-box. Check out bk03ch06/example12.html.

» background-origin: *keyword*: Specifies where within the element's box model the background image begins. The possibilities for *keyword* are content-box (that is, the image starts at the upper-left corner of the element's content box), padding-box (that is, the upper-left corner of the element's padding box), or border-box (that is, the upper-left corner of the element's border box). The default value is border-box. Check out bk03ch06/example13.html.

» background-attachment: *keyword*: Specifies whether the background image scrolls along with the content or remains in place. For *keyword*, use one of the following values:

- local: The image scrolls along with the content.

- scroll: The image is fixed relative to the element.

- fixed: The image is fixed relative to the viewport.

The default value is scroll. Check out bk03ch06/example14.html.

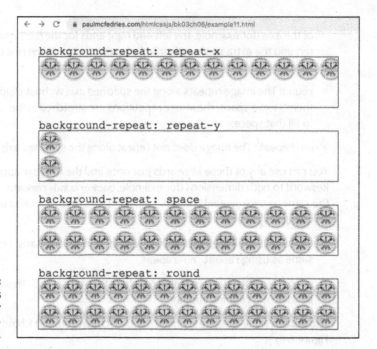

**FIGURE 6-6:** The various values for background-repeat.

**WARNING**

Screen readers and other assistive technologies ignore background images, so don't use a background to convey important or useful information.

## Taking advantage of the background shorthand property

By my count, in the previous two sections I covered no less than *eight* background-related properties. Here they are in alphabetical order:

- » background-attachment
- » background-clip
- » background-color
- » background-image
- » background-origin
- » background-position
- » background-repeat
- » background-size

That's a lot of lines to add to a rule, so CSS offers an alternative shorthand property called background that enables you to set some or all of the preceding background properties in one shot. Here's the syntax recommended by the W3C:

```
background: image position / size repeat attachment origin clip
    color;
```

Here's an example:

```
background: url("images/webdev-workshop.png") center / 50px
    space local content-box content-box red;
```

Some notes:

» For each parameter, use any value that's appropriate for the property, such as url("my-image.png") for the image parameter, repeat-x for the repeat parameter, and any color value for the color parameter.

» You don't have to specify all the parameters; feel free to skip any properties you don't need to set.

» If you do skip a property, bear in mind that the browser will set that property to its default value.

» If you skip the size parameter, be sure to also take out the leading backslash (/).

» If you include just one of the origin and clip parameters, the browser sets both to your specified value.

The background property also supports multiple background definitions, which enables you to layer one background on top of another. To set this up, separate each background definition with a comma. Note that the first definition will be on the top layer, the second definition will go underneath on the second layer, and so on. Also note that you can specify a color only on the final layer.

Here's an example (bk03ch06/example15.html and Figure 6-7) that defines two background layers — a logo on top and a photo underneath it:

```
div {
    background:
        url("images/webdev-workshop.png") bottom right / 150px
    no-repeat,
        url("images/ant-on-a-flower.jpg") top left / cover;
    border: 1px solid black;
    height: 50vh;
    width: 50vw;
}
```

**FIGURE 6-7:**
One background
(the logo) layered
on top of another
(the photo).

# Impressing Your Friends
# with Color Gradients

Coloring an element is a great way to add visual interest to your web page. But if what you want to add to your page is something closer to *pizzazz*, look no farther than the color gradient. A *gradient* is a set of two or more colors where one color gradually transitions into the next color, which gradually transitions in the next, and so on. When used judiciously and with harmonious colors, the gradient is one of the all-time great web page effects.

Before getting to the details, let me point out two general things about gradients:

>> You can apply gradients only as backgrounds.

>> A gradient is actually an image created by the web browser on the fly based on your specifications.

## Applying a linear gradient

A *linear gradient* is one where the color transitions happen in a straight line. For example, the color transition may run from the top of the element to the bottom, or from the upper-left corner to the bottom-right corner. To create a linear gradient, you use the linear-gradient() function:

```
linear-gradient(angle, color1 stop1%, color2 stop2%,..., colorN
   stopN%)
```

» *angle*: The direction of the linear gradient. You can use a value between
0deg and 359deg. Alternatively, you can use the keyword to followed by the
keyword for a vertical direction (top or bottom), a horizontal direction (left
or right), or a diagonal direction (top left, top right, bottom left, or
bottom right).

» *color1*, *color2*, ..., *colorN*: The colors that you want to use in the linear
gradient. Use any of the color values that I discuss earlier in the chapter.

» *stop1*, *stop2*, ..., *stopN*: The color stops for the linear gradient, where a
*color stop* is a percentage that specifies the transition position where the
previous color stops and the next color begins. The first color default stop is
0% (that is, it starts at the beginning) and the last color default stop is 100%
(that is, it stops at the end), so you don't need to enter these values.

Here's an example that applies a linear gradient to a div element's background
(bk03ch06/example16.html and Figure 6-8):

```
div {
    background: linear-gradient(to bottom right, yellow,
    greenyellow 50%, darkgreen);
    border: 1px solid black;
    height: 50vh;
    width: 50vw;
}
```

**FIGURE 6-8:**
A linear gradient
applied to a
div element
background.

# Applying a radial gradient

A *radial gradient* is one where the color transitions happen in the shape of an ellipse or circle. Here's the syntax:

```
radial-gradient(shape, size at position, color1 stop1%, color2
    stop2%,..., colorN stopN%)
```

» *shape*: The gradient's overall shape, which you can set to either `circle` or `ellipse`. (This is the default, so you can omit it.)

» *size*: The size of the *ending shape,* which is the outermost ellipse or circle created by the second-last color stop. (The last color stop just fills in the rest of the element background and is considered to be infinite, at least potentially!) You have several choices here:

- A single length value (such as `15rem`) defines the radius of the ending shape as a circle.

- Two length values (such as `15rem 10rem`) define the horizontal radius and vertical radius, respectively, of the ending shape as an ellipse.

- `closest-side`: For a circle, defines the radius of the ending shape to be the distance from *position* to whichever side of the element's box is closest to *position*. For an ellipse, defines the horizontal radius of the ending shape to be the horizontal distance from *position* to the left or right side of the element's box, whichever is closest to *position*, and it defines the vertical radius of the ending shape to be the vertical distance from *position* to the top or bottom side of the element's box, whichever is closest to *position*.

- `farthest-side`: For a circle, defines the radius of the ending shape to be the distance from *position* to whichever side of the element's box is farthest from *position*. For an ellipse, defines the horizontal radius of the ending shape to be the horizontal distance from *position* to the left or right side of the element's box, whichever is farthest from *position*, and it defines the vertical radius of the ending shape to be the vertical distance from *position* to the top or bottom side of the element's box, whichever is farthest from *position*.

- `closest-corner`: For a circle, defines the radius of the ending shape to be the distance from *position* to whichever corner of the element's box is closest to *position*. For an ellipse, defines the horizontal radius and vertical radius of the ending shape such that the shape just touches whatever corner is closest to *position*.

- `farthest-corner`: For a circle, defines the radius of the ending shape to be the distance from *position* to whichever corner of the element's box is farthest from *position*. For an ellipse, defines the horizontal radius and vertical radius of the ending shape such that the shape just touches whatever corner is farthest from *position*.

The default value for *size* is farthest-corner.

» *position*: Specifies the center point for the shape (that is, the starting point for the gradient). You can specify either a set of x-y points (for example, 45px 100px) or a keyword pair that combines a vertical position (top, center, or bottom) with a horizontal position (left, center, or right). The default *position* value is center center.

» *color1*, *color2*,...,*colorN*: The colors that you want to use in the radial gradient. Use any of the color values that I discuss earlier in the chapter.

» *stop1*, *stop2*,...,*stopN*: The color stops for the radial gradient (that is, the percentages where the previous color stops and the next color begins). The first color default stop is 0% (that is, it starts at the beginning) and the last color default stop is 100% (that is, it stops at the end), so you don't need to enter these values.

Here's an example that applies an ellipse radial gradient to a div element's background (bk03ch06/example17.html and Figure 6-9):

```
div {
    background: radial-gradient(closest-corner at 250px 100px,
    yellow, darkgreen);
    border: 1px solid black;
    height: 50vh;
    width: 50vw;
}
```

FIGURE 6-9:
A radial gradient applied to a div element background.

# Applying a conic gradient

A *conic gradient* is one where the color transitions rotate around a central point. To create a conic gradient, you use the `conic-gradient()` function:

```
conic-gradient(from angle at x y, color1, color2,..., colorN)
```

» *angle*: The initial clockwise rotation of the conic gradient. You can use a value between 0deg and 359deg.

» *x y*: The center of the conic gradient, where *x* is the horizontal starting position and *y* is the vertical starting position. Both *x* and *y* can be a keyword (top, right, bottom, left, or center), a percentage, or a length value (such as 50px or 5rem). The default value is center.

» *color1, color2, ..., colorN*: The colors that you want to use in the conic gradient. Use any of the color values that I discuss earlier in the chapter.

Here's the `conic-gradient()` function I used to create the color wheel shown earlier in Figure 6-2 (bk03ch06/example01.html):

```
#color-wheel {
    width: 33vw;
    height: 33vw;
    background: conic-gradient(
        from 90deg,
        hsl(0 100% 50%),
        hsl(330 100% 50%),
        hsl(300 100% 50%),
        hsl(270 100% 50%),
        hsl(240 100% 50%),
        hsl(210 100% 50%),
        hsl(180 100% 50%),
        hsl(150 100% 50%),
        hsl(120 100% 50%),
        hsl(90 100% 50%),
        hsl(60 100% 50%),
        hsl(30 100% 50%),
        hsl(0 100% 50%)
    );
    clip-path: circle(50%);
}
```

# Setting Border Colors

If you add a border to an element, you may want to give that border a bit of color. CSS is happy to comply and gives you a long list of properties that you can wield to set border colors:

» border: *width style color*: Enables you to set the color of the entire border while defining the border.

» border-color: *top right bottom left*: A shorthand property that enables you to specify individual colors for the border's *top, right, bottom,* and *left* sides.

» border-top: *color*: Sets the color of the top border.

» border-right-color *color*: Sets the color of the right border.

» border-bottom-color *color*: Sets the color of the bottom border.

» border-left-color *color*: Sets the color of the left border.

**TIP**

A little surprisingly, if you add a border around an element but don't specify the border color, the border inherits the element's text color.

# Playing with Colors in the Dev Tools

Your web browser's development tools (refer to Book 3, Chapter 4) have a fistful of features that can make experimenting with and applying colors much easier. Each browser offers a different set of color tools, but most offer some or all of the Google Chrome color tools that I describe below.

First, for an element on which you've applied a color property, open the dev tools by right-clicking that element and then clicking Inspect. The Styles pane (shown in Figure 6-10) shows your color declaration, which includes a small swatch on the left that shows the color being applied.

**FIGURE 6-10:**
In the browser dev tools, element colors include swatches that show the applied color.

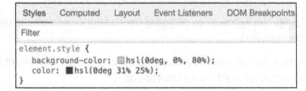

# Changing the color

If you want to change the color format (for example, if the color is currently an RGB code, you may prefer to use an hsl() function). To do so, hold down the Shift key and click the color swatch. With each click of the swatch, the browser displays the color in a different format (hsl(), rgb(), RGB code, and so on).

If you want to try out a different color, besides editing the property value directly, you can click the color swatch to open the color picker, shown in Figure 6-11.

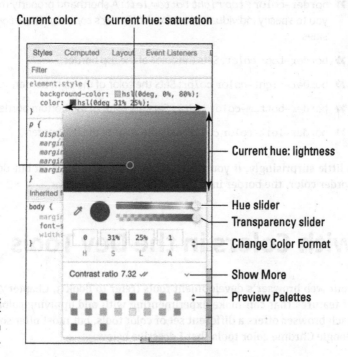

The large swatch at the top of the color picker shows the current hue, with the current saturation and lightness values represented by a small circle. The color picker offers the following tools to modify the color:

>> In the large swatch at the top of the color picker, you can:

- Change the lightness by dragging the current color circle up (lighter) or down (darker).

- Change the saturation by dragging the current color circle left (less saturation) or right (more saturation).

- » Drag the hue slider to select a different hue.

- » Drag the transparency slider to make the color more transparent (left) or more opaque (right).

- » Click Change Color Format to cycle through the available color formats.

- » Use the provided text boxes to change the color parameters. For example, if you're using the hsl() function, you get text boxes for the hue (H), saturation (S), lightness (L), and opacity (A, for alpha channel).

- » Use the color palette at the bottom of the color picker to click a color swatch. You can change to a different palette by clicking Preview Palettes and then clicking a palette from the list that appears.

- » To change the color to an existing color that appears anywhere on your device screen, click the Color Picker button (shown in the margin), hover the mouse over the color you want to choose, and then click the color.

When you're done, click outside the color picker to close it.

## Choosing accessible colors

The *contrast ratio* between two colors is calculated by dividing the relative brightness (which has a technical meaning that you can safely ignore) of the lighter color by the relative brightness of the darker color. The Web Content Accessibility Guidelines (WCAG) define two levels of acceptable color contrast – level AA is the minimum acceptable value and level AAA is the you-get-a-gold-star value — as outlined in the following table:

| Text | Minimum (Level AA) | Enhanced (Level AAA) |
|------|--------------------|-----------------------|
| Body text | At least 4.5 | At least 7 |
| Headings and other large text | At least 3 | At least 4.5 |

How can you figure out the contrast ratio of your text? One possibility is the WebAIM (Web Accessibility In Mind) Contrast Checker: https://webaim.org/resources/contrastchecker/. However, it's often easier to check the contrast using your browser's dev tools because (as I write this), Chrome, Firefox, and Edge all show the contrast ratio of text.

For any element on which you've applied the color property, inspect the element to open the dev tools, and then click the swatch to the left of the color property. The color picker shows a Contrast Ratio value, which tells you the contrast ratio between the current element's text and background colors. The browser also displays an icon that shows the general level of contrast (two check marks for AAA level; one check mark for AA level; or the universal "not" symbol for a ratio that's too low).

Click the Show More icon (pointed out earlier in Figure 6-11) to display more contrast tools (as shown in Figure 6-12):

» The white lines that now appear in the large hue swatch at the top of the color picker represent the different contrast ratio levels. Any color above the top line is too low; any color between the two lines is AA level; and any color below the bottom line is AAA level.

» If your contrast is too low, you can click the color swatch that appears to the right of the AA or AAA level to automatically choose a text color that gets you to that level.

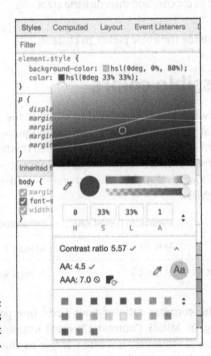

**FIGURE 6-12:**
The color picker's extra contrast ratio tools.

IN THIS CHAPTER

» **Choosing and applying fonts**

» **The three properties that can make you a typography star**

» **Making your page text look amazing**

» **Styling links**

» **Aligning your text just so**

# Chapter **7**

# Taking Your Text Up a Notch with Web Typography

*90 percent of design is typography.*

—JEFFREY ZELDMAN

The next time you come across a web page that you find visually appealing, ask yourself where that appeal comes from. Does it come from the images used? Maybe, but most sites use generic images, so it's likely not that. Is it the colors? Sure, colors play a big part in making a page look good, but the vast majority of web pages either don't bother with color or use it poorly.

No, my guess is that most of the appeal comes from something you may barely notice: the page's typography, which means the way the page uses fonts, spacing, and alignment. The best typography invites you into the page while at the same time not drawing attention to itself. When a page has great typography, it creates a kind of ease in your mind and makes reading a real pleasure. Happily, creating the same kind of ease and pleasure on your own pages is possible for you by learning just a few aspects of typography as it applies to the web.

In this chapter, you explore the awesome world of web typography. You learn just enough about typefaces and fonts to be dangerous; how to use beautiful fonts on your web pages; how learning just three CSS properties can make you a web typography master; how to style links, lists, and other text tricks; and how to fussily align your text just so.

# Taking Care of Your Text

All web browsers display page text and headings using default styles that are, at best, serviceable. I'm assuming that you're not reading this rather large book because you're the type of person who'll settle for "serviceable." To that end, you can make a huge difference in the overall look and appeal of your web pages by paying attention to the look and appeal of the text itself. This is the beginning of all things typographical, and it's the one thing you need to get right with your page design.

## Getting to know typefaces (and fonts, too)

A *typeface* is a particular design applied to all letters, numbers, symbols, and other characters. The most fundamental difference between two typefaces is whether there are small cross-strokes at the extremities of certain characters. These cross-strokes are called *serifs* in the typography game, and Figure 7-1 demonstrates the difference between a character that has serifs and one that doesn't.

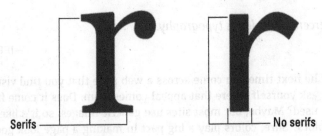

**FIGURE 7-1:**
The letter on the left has serifs; the letter on the right does not.

Serifs ———      ——— No serifs

Typefaces that are decorated with serifs are called — no surprises here — *serif* typefaces, whereas those that lack serifs are called *sans-serif* typefaces (*sans* being a French word that means "without"). So, what does this mean for you when it comes to deciding between one style of typeface and the other? I could probably devote this entire chapter to answering that question, but it really comes down to this:

» Serifs have a traditional, elegant look, so they're great for more formal web pages or pages trying to project an air of gravity or earnestness.

» Sans-serifs have a modern, minimalist feel, so they're great for more informal pages or pages looking to project a sense of fun or simplicity.

» If you've ever been told to use serifs for body text and sans-serifs for headings, forget it. These days, you can switch that advice around or use one kind of typeface for everything on your page.

» The bottom line is that you should pick a typeface you like, that's readable (many are not!), and that matches the personality of your website.

Okay, you may be asking, if that's a typeface, then what's font? Great question! Many people, even many experienced designers, use the terms interchangeably, but there *is* a difference. A typeface is the overall design used on a set of characters, whereas a *font* is a specific instance or implementation of that typeface. Helvetica is a typeface; 16-point, bold Helvetica is a font.

## All in the font family: Applying a typeface

Even though the entire design world uses the term *typeface* to refer to the general design of a set of characters, the CSS powers that be decided to use the term *font family*. Therefore, the property you use to set text in a specific typeface is named font-family:

```
font-family: name;
```

Here, *name* is the name of the typeface, which needs to be surrounded by quotation marks if the name contains spaces, numbers, or punctuation marks other than a hyphen (-):

```
font-family: "Arial Black";
```

## Introducing the font stack

Feel free to list multiple typefaces — thus creating what's known in the trade as a *font stack* — as long as you separate each name with a comma. What's the point of listing multiple typefaces? It gives you more options as a designer. When you list two or more font families, the browser reads the list from left to right, and uses the first font family that's available either on the user's system or in the browser itself.

This left-to-right testing of typeface availability means you can use the following font stack strategy:

```
font-family: ideal, safe, default;
```

» *ideal*: This is the name of the font family you'd prefer to use.

» *safe*: This is the name of a font family that resembles *ideal*, but has a very high chance of being installed on most users' devices.

» *default*: This is the name of a font family that's similar to *ideal* and *safe*, but is guaranteed to exist, usually because it's part of the web browser itself.

Here's an example font stack:

```
font-family: "Gill Sans", Verdana, sans-serif;
```

When it comes to specifying the families you want to include in your font stack, you have three choices: generic, system, and web.

## Generic font families

A *generic* font family is one that's implemented by the browser itself and set by using one of the following five keywords:

» serif: A serif typeface.

» sans-serif: A sans-serif typeface.

» cursive: A typeface designed to look like it was written by hand.

» fantasy: A decorative font that, depending on the browser, can have some extreme elements (such as wild flourishes).

» monospace: A so-called *fixed-width* typeface because it gives equal space to each character, so thin letters such as *i* and *l* take up as much space as wider letters such as *m* and *w*.

Figure 7-2 shows each of these generic fonts in action.

As far as your font stack strategy goes, a generic font is perfect for the last font family in the list because you know that it will always be available. So, for example, if your ideal and safe font families are sans-serifs, you include the sans-serif keyword at the end of your font stack.

FIGURE 7-2:
Generic fonts
are implemented
by all web
browsers and
come in five
flavors: serif,
sans-serif,
cursive,
fantasy, and
monospace.

Generic font family: serif

Generic font family: sans-serif

*Generic font family: cursive*

*Generic font family: fantasy*

`Generic font family: monospace`

## System font families

A *system* font family is a typeface that's installed on the user's computer. Almost all system fonts are much nicer than the browser's generic fonts, and you get a wider variety. You also don't take a performance hit because the font is already available for the browser to use.

How can you possibly know what fonts are installed on each user's system? You can't. Instead, you have two choices. One possibility is to use a system font that's installed universally. Examples include Georgia and Times New Roman (serifs), Verdana and Tahoma (sans serifs), and Courier New (monospace). The other way to go is to use your font stack to list two (or more) system fonts, knowing that the browser will use the first one that's implemented on the user's device. Here's a serif example:

```
font-family: "Big Caslon", Georgia, serif;
```

Some system fonts are installed on at least 90 percent of both Macs and Windows PCs. For sans serif, you can use Arial, Arial Black, Tahoma, Trebuchet MS, or Verdana. For serif, you can use Georgia or Times New Roman. For monospace, it's Courier New. To get the installation percentages for many popular system fonts, surf over to www.cssfontstack.com.

**TIP**

If you want to give your users the familiar feel of their operating system font, use `font-family: system-ui`, which tells the browser to use the operating system's default font.

**TIP**

A fantastic resource for easily and quickly incorporating system fonts into your page designs is Modern Font Stacks (`https://modernfontstacks.com/`), which offers a collection of system font stacks in various historical typeface classifications (Old Style, Industrial, Antique, and so on). Find a stack you like, copy the `font-family` declaration, paste it into your CSS, and then cross "Add system font stack" off your to-do list.

## Web font families

System fonts are awesome because they're free and available immediately to the browser, *assuming* that they're installed on the user's device. That's a big assumption, however. If you want to take full control over your web page's typographical destiny, you need to get into *web* font families, which are hosted on the web, and you use a special CSS directive to use them in your code.

You have two ways to use web fonts: linking and self-hosting.

### Linking to a web font family

There are quite a few third-party font family providers out there that offer fonts you can link to. Most of these require a license fee. However, if you already have an Adobe account, you have access to Adobe Fonts (`https://fonts.adobe.com`), which offers tons of typefaces.

However, the majority of web designers get their web font families via Google Fonts, which offers access to hundreds of free and well-crafted fonts that you can use on your site. Here's how to choose a font family from Google Fonts:

1. **Surf to** `https://fonts.google.com`.

   Figure 7-3 shows the main page of Google Fonts.

2. **Use the Categories list to select the type of font family you want (such as Serif or Monospace).**

3. **Use the other drop-downs and controls to filter the list as needed.**

4. **When you come across a font family you like, click it to show the details of the typeface, which includes a list of the available fonts.**

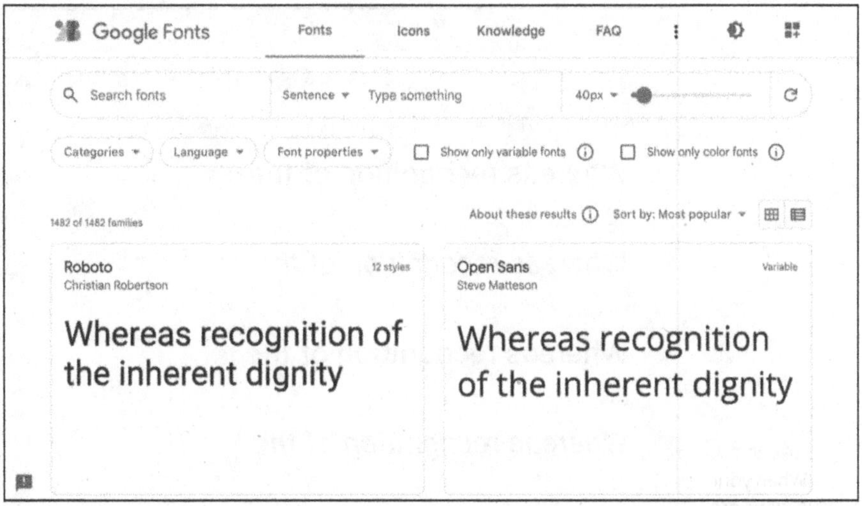

**FIGURE 7-3:**
Google Fonts is
by far the most
popular font
provider.

**5.** **Click the Select link for each font you want. You'll almost always want just three:**

- Regular 400 (this is regular body text with no italics or bold applied)

- Regular 400 Italic (regular text with italics)

- Bold 700 (bold text)

(Refer to "Styling the text weight," later in this chapter, to learn what numbers such as 400 and 700 mean.) Google Fonts displays a sidebar that lists the choices you've made.

> **WARNING**
>
> You may be tempted to select every available font, but that's a bad idea because the more fonts you select, the longer it takes to retrieve them all and the slower your web page will load. Unless you have very specific design requirements, you should need only the regular, italic, and bold fonts for a given font family.

**6.** **When you're done with your choices, make sure that the <link> radio button is selected, and then use the Copy icon to copy the code that appears in the box below that radio button (as shown in Figure 7-4).**

**7.** **Paste the copied code into your HTML file, somewhere in the <head> section (before your <style> tag, if you're using an internal stylesheet, or before your CSS <link> tag, if you're using an external stylesheet).**

**8.** **Return to Google Fonts, scroll down the sidebar until you get to the CSS Rules to Specify Families section, copy that font-family declaration, and then paste that code into each CSS rule where you want to use the font family.**

FIGURE 7-4:
When your
selections are
complete, click
Copy to copy the
`<link>` code.

Copy

Here's an example head section (check out bk03ch07/example03.html in this book's example files) that links to the Google fonts selected in Figure 7-4:

```
<head>
    <meta charset="utf-8">
    <title>Link to a web font family</title>
    <link rel="preconnect" href="https://fonts.googleapis.com">
    <link rel="preconnect" href="https://fonts.gstatic.com"
crossorigin>
    <link href="https://fonts.googleapis.com/css2?
family=Roboto:ital,wght@0,400;1,400;1,700&display=swap"
rel="stylesheet">
    <style>
        body {
            font-family: Roboto, Tahoma, sans-serif;
        }
    </style>
</head>
```

In case you're wondering, the first two `<link>` tags enable the browser to fetch the font files right away, so your page loads quicker.

**TECHNICAL STUFF**

# CHOOSING A WEB FONT FAMILY

The thing with web font families is that there are a lot of them. I mean, a *lot*. Thousands. Even after you've narrowed down your choices to a few typefaces that you think may suit your content, how do you go about choosing your final typeface? Fortunately, you can use a few criteria to help weed out unsuitable typefaces. These criteria are all about readability and legibility.

First, though, you need a quick primer on some typeface anatomy. The following figure points out a few useful parts and the list that follows tells you how to use these parts to choose a good web font family.

- The *baseline* is the notional horizontal line upon which the letters appear to rest. In a well-designed web font, letters with rounded bottoms such as *e*, *c*, and *o* actually sit slightly below the baseline, which improves readability.

- The *x-height* is the height above the baseline of the typeface's lowercase letter *x*. On the web, you generally want a large x-height for readability. However, if a font family you like has a small x-height, it's okay to increase the font size to compensate.

- A *counter* is the round part of lowercase letters such as *o*, *b*, and *d*. (The curved stroke that encloses the counter is called the *bowl*.) A good web typeface has generous counters that are circular (or close to it). Oval counters — that is, counters that are either tall and narrow or short and wide — are okay for large headings but are too hard to read to be used as regular text.

- An *eye* is a special case of a counter, and it refers to the enclosed area at the top of the lowercase *e*. A good web font has a decent-sized eye.

- An *aperture* is the non-enclosed space in lowercase letters such as *a*, *c*, and *e*. When test driving web font families, look for ones that have open apertures.

*(continued)*

(continued)

Tight apertures almost appear to be closed, making each *a* and *e* look alike, and especially making each *c* look too much like an *o*.

- An *ascender* is a stroke that extends above the x-height in lowercase letters such as *b*, *d*, and *f*. A good web font has nice, tall ascenders for legibility.

- A *descender* is a stroke or bowl that extends below the baseline in lowercase letters such as *g*, *p*, and *y*. A good web font has long stroke descenders and open bowl descenders.

When trying out different web font families, don't settle for the example text provided by the font service, and don't just paste in some "lorem ipsum . . ." gibberish. If possible, try to test each typeface using actual content from your page.

## Self-hosting a web font family

Using a font provider such as Google is by far the simplest way to stop settling for generic and system font families. With such a wide range of typefaces available, you're sure to find something that makes your pages gleam.

However, you may feel a bit antsy relying on a third-party for such a crucial part of your web design. Most folks have two main concerns here:

>> **The font provider may not provide the font:** Sure, some glitch may cause your provider to fail to deliver the font. However, with a major provider such as Google or Adobe, such failures are extremely rare. And if a glitch does happen, hopefully you've chosen a good system font that will shoulder the typography load.

>> **Delivering a font from the web must be very slow:** This concern seems reasonable because getting anything from a remote server always takes time. However, all font providers have extensive, worldwide delivery networks that serve font files remarkably quickly. And the best of them (such as Google) have come up with ways that, in a sense, preload remote font files, so they're delivered with very little lag time.

The simplicity, reliability, and speed of modern font providers are why most web developers link to remote font files. However, you can also download the necessary font files and host them on your server along with your HTML, CSS, and other files. Hosting your own font files is reliable and fast, but is it simple? Nope, not even close! Here are some things to consider if you're thinking about self-hosting font files:

>> **Typeface licensing:** Almost every commercial typeface either comes with a built-in restriction that prevents the typeface from being used on the web, or requires you to purchase a license that allows web use. Alternatively, you can search the following typeface collections for free or open source typefaces that allow web use:

- Font Space (www.fontspace.com/category/open)

- Font Spring (www.fontspring.com/free)

- Font Squirrel (www.fontsquirrel.com)

- The League of Moveable Type (www.theleagueofmoveabletype.com)

- Open Font Library (fontlibrary.org)

>> **File format:** There are tons of font file formats, but these days you have to worry about only one: WOFF2 (Web Open Font Format, version 2), which offers terrific file compression to keep those font files as small as possible.

>> **Getting WOFF2 files:** Unfortunately, when you download a font file from a provider, you won't get WOFF2 files. Instead, you'll likely get either TTF (TrueType Font) or OTF (OpenType Font) files. You could use those, I suppose, but they tend to be five or six times the size of WOFF2 files, so you'd be really slowing down your page load times. Instead, you can use either of the following methods to get WOFF2 files:

- **Google Fonts:** For reasons known only to the Google gods, Google Fonts doesn't offer a simple way to download WOFF2 files. Fortunately, a developer named Mario Ranftl has created a tool called google-webfonts-helper (https://gwfh.mranftl.com/fonts) that enables you to search for a Google font, select the styles you want, and then download a .zip file that contains the WOFF2 files. (It also includes WOFF files, which was the original version of the WOFF type.) In the CSS part of the tool, be sure to click Modern Browsers to get the correct CSS code (more on that code coming up).

- **Font Squirrel:** If you've already downloaded a TTF or OTF file, you can use a Font Squirrel service called the Webfont Generator (www.fontsquirrel.com/tools/webfont-generator), which takes your downloaded font file and automatically creates a package that includes the WOFF2 file format (plus the WOFF file, too). The Webfont Generator package also includes the necessary CSS code to use the fonts on your site.

Okay, so assuming that you now have your WOFF2 files, how do you get them into your CSS? You use the CSS code @font-face (this is a special type of CSS rule called an *at-rule*), and the general syntax takes the following form:

```
@font-face {
    font-family: 'name';
    font-style: style;
    font-weight: weight;
    src: url('filename.woff2') format('woff2')
;
}
```

>> *name*: The name of the typeface.

>> *style*: The style of the font, which is usually *normal* or *italic*.

>> *weight*: The weight number of the font, such as 400 for regular text and 700 for bold.

>> *filename*.woff2: The filename of the WOFF2 font file.

You create a @font-face at-rule for each style and weight you downloaded. Here's an example (bk03ch07/example04.html) that sets up three @font-face at-rules for the Roboto typeface:

```
@font-face {
    font-display: swap;
    font-family: 'Roboto';
    font-style: normal;
    font-weight: 400;
    src: url('roboto-regular.woff2') format('woff2')
;
}
@font-face {
    font-display: swap;
    font-family: 'Roboto';
    font-style: italic;
    font-weight: 400;
    src: url('roboto-italic.woff2') format('woff2')
;
}
```

```
@font-face {
    font-display: swap;
    font-family: 'Roboto';
    font-style: normal;
    font-weight: 700;
    src: url('roboto-700.woff2') format('woff2')
;
}
```

I can then use this in a stylesheet, like so:

```
body {
    font-family: Roboto, Tahoma, sans-serif;
}
```

**TIP**

For best performance, put your @font-face rules in your HTML file's head section, at the beginning of your <style> tag.

**TECHNICAL STUFF**

What's up with the font-display: swap declaration in each @font-face rule? The font-display property tells the web browser what to do if the font file doesn't load right away. What you want to avoid is having the browser stop loading the page while it waits for the font file to arrive. The swap value tells the browser to wait very briefly for the font file and, if it doesn't show in that period, to go ahead and use the next available fallback font. Then, when the font file does show up, the browser can swap out the fallback font for the real font.

The preceding examples assume that you've stored the font files in the same directory as your HTML or CSS file. If you've placed those files in a separate directory, you need to add the correct path information to the url() value:

>> If the font files reside in a subdirectory of the location where the CSS (or HTML) file is stored, precede the filename with the directory name and a backslash (/). For example:

```
url('fonts/roboto-regular.woff2')
```

>> If the font files reside in a subdirectory of the site's root directory, precede the filename with a backslash (/), the directory name, and then another backslash (/). For example:

```
url('/fonts/roboto-regular.woff2')
```

# The Typographic Trinity: Setting Type Size, Line Height, and Line Length

Take a look at the page shown in Figure 7-5 (bk03ch07/example05.html). To my eye, this page has four main problems, typographically speaking:

» The typeface is lackluster.

» The type size is a too small for comfortable reading.

» The lines of type are a bit too close together, which creates a distraction because as you scan along one line, the lines above and/or below are in your field of vision.

» The lines are also way too long for comfortable reading.

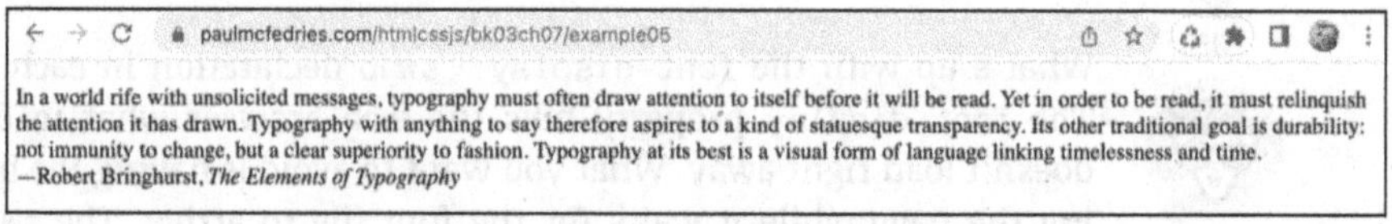

**FIGURE 7-5:**
A typographically terrible web page.

In a world rife with unsolicited messages, typography must often draw attention to itself before it will be read. Yet in order to be read, it must relinquish the attention it has drawn. Typography with anything to say therefore aspires to a kind of statuesque transparency. Its other traditional goal is durability: not immunity to change, but a clear superiority to fashion. Typography at its best is a visual form of language linking timelessness and time.
—Robert Bringhurst, *The Elements of Typography*

Of these qualities, the typeface is an easy fix because right now the page is just using the browser's default serif typeface. I love the universal system font Georgia, so I modified the page with the following font stack (refer to Figure 7-6 and bk03ch07/example05a.htmartclel):

```
p {
    font-family: Georgia, serif;
}
```

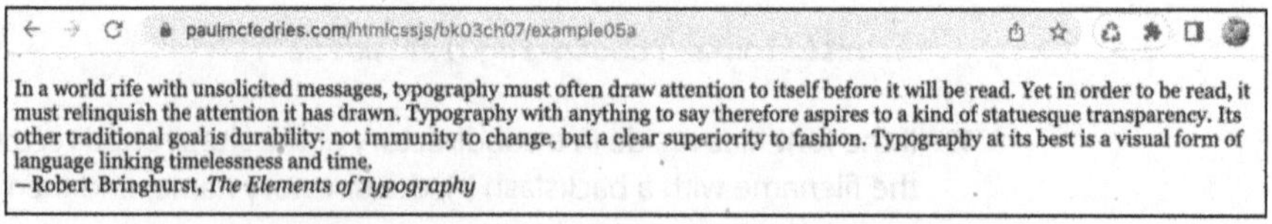

**FIGURE 7-6:**
The example page with an upgraded typeface.

In a world rife with unsolicited messages, typography must often draw attention to itself before it will be read. Yet in order to be read, it must relinquish the attention it has drawn. Typography with anything to say therefore aspires to a kind of statuesque transparency. Its other traditional goal is durability: not immunity to change, but a clear superiority to fashion. Typography at its best is a visual form of language linking timelessness and time.
—Robert Bringhurst, *The Elements of Typography*

The other three qualities — type size, vertical spacing between lines in the same paragraph, and line length — are what I call the typographical troublemakers because they're the source of almost all typographical problems on the web. However, I also refer to these qualities as the typographical trinity because if you can get just these aspects of your web pages right, you'll be well on your way to a beautifully designed site that will be a pleasure to read. The next few sections take you through the details.

# Setting the type size

The biggest problem with typography on the web is that most page text is too small. Why is this problem so widespread? I think there are two main reasons:

>> Most web designers just go with the browser's default text size, which is 16px on all modern browsers. The text in Figure 7-5 uses that default 16px size, and it's just too small, especially when seen on a desktop monitor that's a foot or two away from your eyes.

>> Print design still has a major influence on web design, which is why I still come across web design gurus recommending that we set our page text at 12px or 14px! Those sizes work fine in print, but they're disastrously small on a web page.

Fortunately, you have total control over the size of your page text via the font-size property:

```
font-size: value;
```

>> value: The font size in whatever CSS length measurement unit suits your needs, such as rem or em. You can also use a percentage, which sets the font size to be a percentage of the element's inherited font size.

**WARNING**

Remember never to use px for font sizes because doing so reduces your page's accessibility by overriding the user's custom font size. Always use a relative unit for the font-size value.

Besides using 16px as the default font size for regular page text, modern browsers also use the following default sizes for headings:

| Heading | Default font-size Value |
|---------|-------------------------|
| h1 | 2em |
| h2 | 1.5em |
| h3 | 1.17em |
| h4 | 1em |
| h5 | 0.83em |
| h6 | 0.67em |

**TECHNICAL STUFF**

Bizarrely, the font-size value of the h1 element varies depending on whether the h1 is nested within an article, aside, nav, or section element. If the h1 is nested within any of these elements, its new default size becomes 1.5em (the same as the default for the h2 element). If the h1 is nested two levels deep (say, in a section element that's in an article element), the new default size becomes 1.17em (the same as the default for the h3 element). Nested three levels deep, the h1 size becomes 1em; four levels deep, it becomes 0.83em; and five levels deep, it becomes 0.67em. This unexpected behavior is all the more reason to use just a single h1 at the top of your page and to use h2 through h6 for all the rest of your headings. Note that this font size foolishness does *not* apply to nested h2 through h6 elements. Whew!

You can and should override the default browser sizes. For example, I can modify the p element that contains the text shown earlier in Figure 7-5 to bump up the font-size to 1.25rem:

```
p {
    font-size: 1.25rem;
}
```

Figure 7-7 (bk03ch07/example06.html) shows the result, which is already a marked improvement over the original.

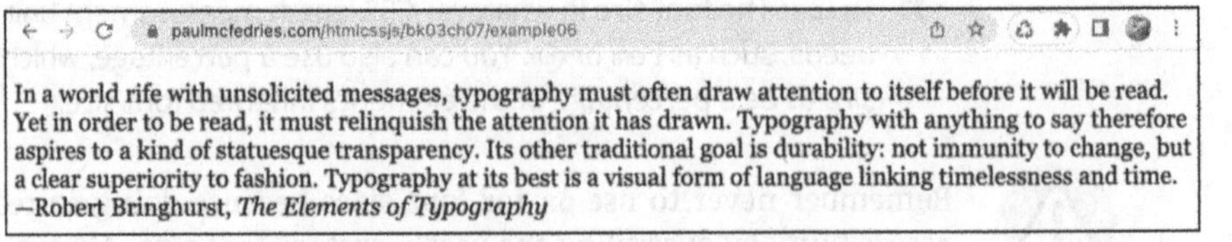

**FIGURE 7-7:**
The example page with font-size set to 1.25rem.

> In a world rife with unsolicited messages, typography must often draw attention to itself before it will be read. Yet in order to be read, it must relinquish the attention it has drawn. Typography with anything to say therefore aspires to a kind of statuesque transparency. Its other traditional goal is durability: not immunity to change, but a clear superiority to fashion. Typography at its best is a visual form of language linking timelessness and time.
> —Robert Bringhurst, *The Elements of Typography*

One way to set your font sizes is to use a *modular scale*, where you begin with a base font size and use a fixed factor to derive all the font sizes you need that are larger and smaller than your base.

For font sizes bigger than your base, you multiply the base by the factor to derive the first larger size, multiply that result by the factor to derive the second larger size, and so on. For example, if your base is 1.25rem and your factor is 1.5, here's the modular scale that results for three larger font sizes:

| Starting Value | Calculation | Result | Apply To |
|---|---|---|---|
| 1.25rem | None (base) | 1.25rem | Regular text, h4 |
| 1.25rem | 1.25rem * 1.5 | 1.875rem | h3 |

| Starting Value | Calculation | Result | Apply To |
|---|---|---|---|
| 1.875rem | 1.875rem * 1.5 | 2.813rem | h2 |
| 2.813rem | 2.813rem * 1.5 | 4.219rem | h1 |

For font sizes smaller than your base, you divide the base by the factor to derive the first smaller size, divide that result by the factor to derive the second smaller size, and so on. For example, if your base is 1.25rem and your factor is 1.5, here's the modular scale that results for two smaller font sizes:

| Starting Value | Calculation | Result | Apply To |
|---|---|---|---|
| 1.25rem | None (base) | 1.25rem | Regular text, h4 |
| 1.25rem | 1.25rem / 1.5 | 0.833rem | h5 |
| 0.833rem | 0.833rem / 1.5 | 0.556rem | h6 |

Why go to this trouble? The modular scale brings several significant advantages to the web design table:

>> **You get a reasonable set of font sizes to use in your pages.** These six sizes should be all you really need for most page elements. And if you find that you need even larger sizes, you can extend the scale as needed.

>> **You restrict the number of font sizes used in your pages.** Without a set of font sizes to work with, I guarantee that any reasonably complex web project will multiply font sizes without end, to the point where maintenance of at least the font size portion of your CSS becomes impossible.

>> **Your font sizes are all related to each other thanks to the factor.** Without a scale, you may pick font sizes based on what looks good, your intuition, or what you had for breakfast that morning. That haphazard approach is sure to result in bad typography. The modular scale, on the other hand, creates harmony, as demonstrated in Figure 7-8, where I've applied each modular scale font-size value to a series of capital Os (bk03ch07/example07.html).

**FIGURE 7-8:** The modular scale at work.

**TIP**

Why bother with the really small font sizes in the modular scale? These can be useful for incidental text such as captions and footnotes and for "unimportant" text such as copyright notices and legalese.

**TIP**

Working with a modular scale becomes an order of magnitude easier when you use CSS variables. Refer to Bonus Chapter 4 to learn how to wield the awesome power of CSS variables (download the chapter at www.dummies.com/go/htmlcss&javascriptaiofd).

## Setting the line height

The *line height* is the amount of vertical space allotted to each line of text. In desktop digital typography, line height is defined as the distance from the baseline of a given line to the baseline of an adjacent line. In CSS, line height is defined as the element's font-size value plus the following (refer to Figure 7-9):

>> One half of the distance between the ascender line of the current line and the descender line of the line above the current line.

>> One half of the distance between the descender line of the current line and the ascender line of the line below.

**FIGURE 7-9:**
The line height as it's used in CSS.

Line height

Ascender line

Descender line

x-height

You can control the line height of your text using the line-height property:

```
line-height: value;
```

>> *value*: A numeric value without a unit. The browser calculates the line height by multiplying this value by the element's font-size. The larger the *value*, the greater the line height.

Getting the line height right is a bit of an art and depends on various factors (which I talk about later, in the "How the typographical trinity are related" section). For now, check out Figure 7-10 (bk03ch07/example08.html), where the left paragraph is set with `line-height: 1` and the right paragraph is set with `line-height: 2`.

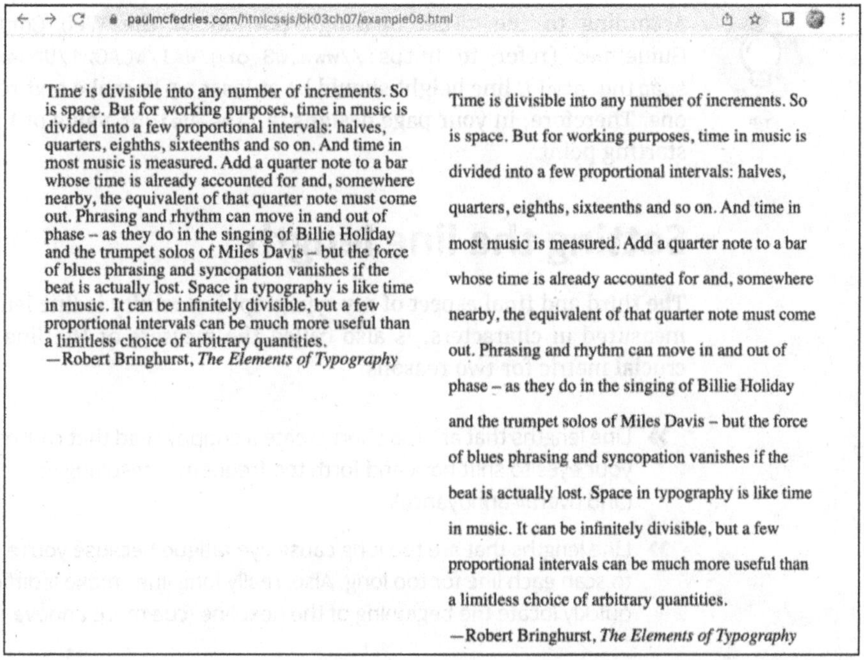

paulmcfedries.com/htmlcssjs/bk03ch07/example08.html

Time is divisible into any number of increments. So is space. But for working purposes, time in music is divided into a few proportional intervals: halves, quarters, eighths, sixteenths and so on. And time in most music is measured. Add a quarter note to a bar whose time is already accounted for and, somewhere nearby, the equivalent of that quarter note must come out. Phrasing and rhythm can move in and out of phase – as they do in the singing of Billie Holiday and the trumpet solos of Miles Davis – but the force of blues phrasing and syncopation vanishes if the beat is actually lost. Space in typography is like time in music. It can be infinitely divisible, but a few proportional intervals can be much more useful than a limitless choice of arbitrary quantities.
—Robert Bringhurst, *The Elements of Typography*

Time is divisible into any number of increments. So is space. But for working purposes, time in music is divided into a few proportional intervals: halves, quarters, eighths, sixteenths and so on. And time in most music is measured. Add a quarter note to a bar whose time is already accounted for and, somewhere nearby, the equivalent of that quarter note must come out. Phrasing and rhythm can move in and out of phase – as they do in the singing of Billie Holiday and the trumpet solos of Miles Davis – but the force of blues phrasing and syncopation vanishes if the beat is actually lost. Space in typography is like time in music. It can be infinitely divisible, but a few proportional intervals can be much more useful than a limitless choice of arbitrary quantities.
—Robert Bringhurst, *The Elements of Typography*

**FIGURE 7-10:**
Line height values of 1 (left) and 2 (right).

The lines in the left paragraph are practically touching each other (at least where descenders brush up against ascenders), and the whole things feels cramped and uninviting. The lines in the right paragraph are so far apart that they've lost the normal cohesion of a paragraph and seem to be individual lines drifting in in space.

Looking back at the typographically suspect page in Figure 7-5, one of the problems is that the lines are set too close together. That happens because, for unknown reasons, all web browsers have a disappointingly small default `line-height` value, usually between 1.15 and 1.2. These values render text in a tightly packed bunch that's hard to read for people with normal eyesight, much less for those with poor vision, dyslexia, or other sight problems. Figure 7-11 (bk03ch07/example09.html) shows the text with `line-height` set to `1.5` (and the same `font-size` value of `1.25rem` that I set in the previous section). Things are looking much better!

**FIGURE 7-11:**
The example page with `line-height` set to 1.5.

In a world rife with unsolicited messages, typography must often draw attention to itself before it will be read. Yet in order to be read, it must relinquish the attention it has drawn. Typography with anything to say therefore aspires to a kind of statuesque transparency. Its other traditional goal is durability: not immunity to change, but a clear superiority to fashion. Typography at its best is a visual form of language linking timelessness and time.
—Robert Bringhurst, *The Elements of Typography*

**TIP**

According to the "Text Spacing" portion of the Web Content Accessibility Guidelines (refer to `https://www.w3.org/WAI/WCAG21/Understanding/text-spacing.html`), line height should be at least 1.5 to make text readable for everyone. Therefore, in your page designs, a `line-height` value of 1.5 should be your starting point.

## Setting the line length

The third and final aspect of my typographical trinity is line length, which, when measured in characters, is also called the *measure* of the line. Line length is a crucial metric for two reasons:

>> Line lengths that are too short create a choppy read that causes your eyes to shift back and forth too frequently, resulting in eyestrain (and overall annoyance).

>> Line lengths that are too long cause eye fatigue because you're required to scan each line for too long. Also, really long lines make it difficult to quickly locate the beginning of the next line (cue more annoyance!).

Figure 7-12 illustrates both problems with a too-short line length on the left and a too-long line length on the right.

**FIGURE 7-12:**
Some text with a line length that's too short (left) and too long (right).

Anything from 45 to 75 characters is widely regarded as a satisfactory length of line for a single-column page set in a serifed text face in a text size. The 66-character line (counting both letters and spaces) is widely regarded as ideal.
—Robert Bringhurst, *The Elements of Typography*

Anything from 45 to 75 characters is widely regarded as a satisfactory length of line for a single-column page set in a serifed text face in a text size. The 66-character line (counting both letters and spaces) is widely regarded as ideal.
—Robert Bringhurst, *The Elements of Typography*

Naively, we may try to control line lengths using the `max-width` property, as in this example:

```
p {
    max-width: 40rem;
}
```

That's a reasonable solution, but it doesn't take the *current* paragraph font size into account. Using the `em` unit, instead, is problematic because, thanks to the cascade (check out Book 3, Chapter 4) it's hard to predict what font size the paragraph will inherit (check out Book 3, Chapter 5).

Also, using a length measure such as `rem` or `em` isn't very intuitive. What we know (from empirical studies and a few hundred years of typographical experience) is that line lengths of a certain number of characters — usually no less than 45 and no more than 75 — are ideal for readability. Notice that I'm talking here about *characters*, not width. That is, it doesn't really make sense to try to control your line lengths by, say, setting a maximum width using a unit such a `rem` (or, worse, `px`).

Here you have a rare opportunity to take advantage of the `ch` measurement unit, which is the width of the character `0` (zero) in the element's current font size. Rather than hang your line lengths off the font size of the parent (`em`) or the root (`rem`), why not cut to the chase by setting the maximum width to a `ch` value? Take a look:

```
p {
    max-width: 65ch;
}
```

Now *that* makes intuitive sense! In Figure 7-13 (bk03ch07/example11.html), I've applied this rule to the problematic example first shown in Figure 7-5. Now *that* is a nice-looking piece of text!

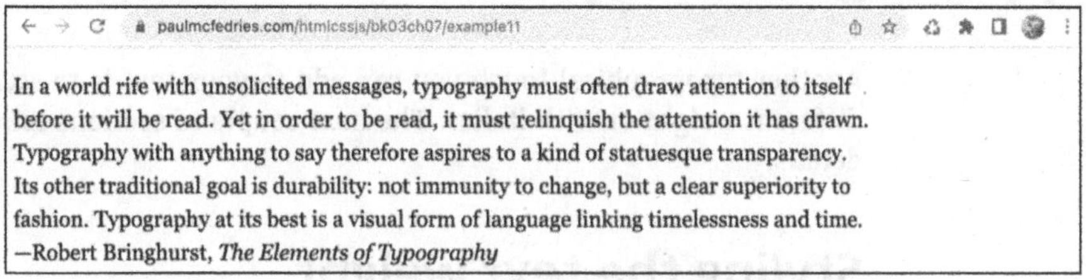
paulmcfedries.com/htmlcssjs/bk03ch07/example11
In a world rife with unsolicited messages, typography must often draw attention to itself before it will be read. Yet in order to be read, it must relinquish the attention it has drawn. Typography with anything to say therefore aspires to a kind of statuesque transparency. Its other traditional goal is durability: not immunity to change, but a clear superiority to fashion. Typography at its best is a visual form of language linking timelessness and time.
—Robert Bringhurst, The Elements of Typography

**FIGURE 7-13:** The example page with `max-width` set to 65ch. Beautiful!

# How the typographical trinity are related

In the past three sections, I describe the type size, line height, and line length as separate typographical qualities, but in the real world these three measures are intimately and intricately related. If you have design constraints on one of these values, you'll need to adjust the others to keep your typography harmonious and balanced. Here's how it works:

>> **Type size:** The size of your type affects the line height and line length as follows:

- With larger type sizes, you can get away with bigger line heights and longer line lengths.
- With smaller type sizes, you can use smaller line heights and shorter line lengths.

>> **Line height:** The height of your lines affects the type size and line length as follows:

- With bigger line heights, you can get away with larger type sizes and longer line lengths.
- With smaller line heights, you can use smaller type sizes and shorter line lengths.

>> **Line length:** The length of your lines affects the type size and line height as follows:

- With longer line lengths, you can get away with larger type sizes and bigger line heights.
- With shorter line lengths, you can use smaller type sizes and shorter line heights.

# Applying Text Styles

Another typographical touch you can add to your text is to style it with either a different weight or with italics. The next couple of sections take you through the details.

## Styling the text weight

In CSS, the relative thickness of the strokes that make up a character is called the *weight* of that character. You can control the weight of some page text by applying the font-weight property:

```
font-weight: value;
```

>> *value*: A unitless numeric value or keyword that specifies the desired weight:

- **Numeric value:** Use one of the following: 100, 200, 300, 400, 500, 600, 700, 800, or 900. As shown in Figure 7-14, these numbers apply weights that run from very thin (100) to very thick (900). The labels applied to each weight in Figure 7-14 (Thin, Light, Bold, Black, and so on) are the names you typically come across when examining typeface styles at a font provider. Note that not all typefaces support all the aforementioned values. If a typeface doesn't support a particular weight, the browser will use the closest available weight.

---

← → C 🔒 paulmcfedries.com/htmlcssjs/bk03ch07/example12.html

Thin (100)
Extra Light (200)
Light (300)
Regular (400)
Medium (500)
Semi Bold (600)
**Bold (700)**
**Extra Bold (800)**
**Black (900)**

**FIGURE 7-14:**
The font-weight
numeric values as
rendered by the
browser.

---

- **Keyword:** You can use bold instead of 700 and normal instead of 400. To set the weight relative to the parent element's weight, use either lighter (to make the element one weight lighter than the parent; only the weights 100, 400, and 700 are possible with this keyword) or bolder (to make the element one weight heavier than the parent; only the weights 400, 700, and 900 are possible with this keyword).

**WARNING**

Don't rely on the font-weight property to apply bold to important text or keywords that you want to stand out. In Book 2, Chapter 2, I talk about how the <strong> and <b> tags have semantic definitions (important text and keywords, respectively), so you should always use those tags to help visitors using assistive technologies. If you want, you can target the `strong` or `b` element in your CSS and use `font-weight` to adjust the weight of those elements.

**WARNING**

Users with poor or low vision may have trouble reading text with a weight of `100` or `200`. If you use these lower weights, consider bumping up the font size to make the text easier to read.

## Styling text with italics

In Book 2, Chapter 2, I mention that the `<em>` and `<i>` tags have semantic significance (emphasis and alternative text, respectively), but you may have text that should get rendered in italics, but not with emphasis or as alternative text. Examples of such text can include subtitles, captions, table column headings, and footnotes. No problem: Get CSS on the job by adding the `font-style` property to your rule:

```
font-style: italic;
```

As an alternative to the `italic` value, you can also specify `oblique` to slant the regular text.

```
font-style: oblique
```

However, because oblique text is just regular text rendered at an angle, oblique text tends to be less attractive than italic text, which is usually a specially designed font.

## Getting more styles with variable fonts

Whether you link to a remote font or self-host your font files, you face one major restriction: You can't use more than three or at most four fonts. Beyond that number, your page performance suffers in two ways:

» **Bandwidth served:** All those font files add up to quite a large download for the user's browser.

» **Loading time:** Each font file is loaded using a separate request to the server, and those requests add up to a significant amount of your page's loading time.

If you self-host, WOFF2 fonts are super-compressed, so they can help with the bandwidth issue, but loading a ton of fonts still means lots of trips to and from the server.

Because most site designs are just fine with three fonts (regular, italic, and bold), they don't suffer from these performance issues. But what if your site really, really, really needs thin (font-weight: 100), light (font-weight: 300), medium (font-weight: 500), and black (font-weight: 900) fonts, plus some or all of their italic counterparts?

If that's the case, forget using so-called *static* fonts that offer a single font style per file. Instead, you need to check out *variable* fonts that package multiple fonts into a single file. From a performance angle, deciding whether to use variable fonts is a trade-off:

» **Pro:** You serve only a single file instead of several files.

» **Con:** Variable font file sizes tend to be huge.

This trade-off means that if you plan to use only standard fonts such as regular, italic, bold, and maybe bold italic, stick with static fonts because they're smaller and you don't need the full capabilities of a variable font. On the other hand, if your page design requires that you use a large number of fonts — say, a half dozen or more — you're better off with a variable font.

Most font providers include at least some variable fonts. In Google Fonts, for example, you can select the Show Only Variable Fonts checkbox to filter the font list to display only variable fonts (about 300 fonts as I write this). You can also check out these sites that specialize in showcasing variable fonts:

» **Axis-Praxis:** https://www.axis-praxis.org/

» **Font Playground:** https://play.typedetail.com/

» **Variable Fonts:** https://v-fonts.com/

Variable fonts are a complex topic that would require several chapters to do them justice. So here I just want to give you a taste of the variable font world by showing you how to use Google Fonts to use a remote variable font that gives you both regular and italic text in a range of weights.

Here are the steps to follow:

1. **In Google Fonts** (https://fonts.google.com), **select the Show Only Variable Fonts checkbox.**

2. **Click the variable font you want to use.**

**3.** **In the list of available font styles, select the following**

- The lightest version of regular text you want to use.

- The lightest version of italic text you want to use.

- The boldest version of regular text you want to use.

- The boldest version of italic text you want to use.

**4.** **Copy the `<link>` tags and then paste them into your HTML file's head section, before any other `<link>` tags or `<style>` tags.**

**5.** **Find the third `<link>` tag, the one that connects to `fonts.googleapis.com`. Here's an example:**

```
<link href="https://fonts.googleapis.com/css2?family=Montse
    rrat:ital,wght@0,100;0,900;1,100;1,900&display=swap"
    rel="stylesheet">
```

**6.** **Inside that `href` attribute, find the part of the string that looks like this:**

```
0,100;0,900;1,100;1,900
```

These values refer to individual fonts: `0,100` is regular text at weight 100; `0,900` is regular text at weight 900; `1,100` is italic text at weight 100; and `1,900` is italic text at weight 900.

Edit the string so that it looks like this:

```
0,100..900;1,100..900
```

The double dots (`..`) indicate a range, so what you're telling Google here is that you want the all the weights of regular text between 100 and 900 and all the weights of italic text between 100 and 900.

**7.** **Save your work.**

Here's what the example `<link>` tag looks like after these changes:

```
<link href="https://fonts.googleapis.com/css2?family=Montserrat:
    ital,wght@0,100..900;1,100..900&display=swap"
    rel="stylesheet">
```

You're all set to use (in this case) Montserrat as a variable font! For an interactive demo, load bk03ch07/example13.html, shown in Figure 7-15. Drag the slider to and fro to change the weight and use the checkbox to toggle italics.

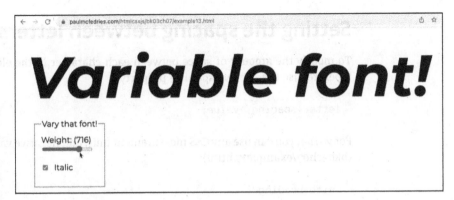

paulmcfedries.com/htmlcssjs/bk03ch07/example13.html

**Variable font!**

Vary that font!
Weight: (716)
☑ Italic

**FIGURE 7-15:**
Use this example page to change the weight of a variable font's regular or italic text on the fly.

# More Typographical Trickery

After you've set the typeface, the type size, the line height, and the line length, you could probably declare your typographical chores complete and move on to the next item in your page-making to-do list. That's not to say that I've exhausted all the typographical tricks that CSS has up its digital sleeve. Far from it. To give you a taste of what else CSS can do for your text, the next few sections offer a quick look at some properties you may find useful.

## Controlling capitalization

To modify the capitalization of an element's text, use the `text-transform` property:

```
text-transform: keyword;
```

Here are the most commonly used values for *keyword* (bk03ch07/example14.html):

>> `capitalize`: Transforms the text so that the first letter of each word is capitalized.

>> `lowercase`: Transforms the text so that every letter is converted to lowercase.

>> `uppercase`: Transforms the text so that every letter is converted to uppercase.

Here's an example:

```
p {
    text-transform: uppercase;
}
```

# Setting the spacing between letters

To modify the amount of space between each character in the element's current typeface, use the letter-spacing property:

```
letter-spacing: value;
```

For *value*, you can use any CSS measurement unit, and negative values are allowed (bk03ch07/example15.html):

```
.site-heading {
    letter-spacing: -5px;
}
```

When would you use this property? I can think of two common use cases:

» If you have a heading that's short but uses a very large font size, you can make that heading look a bit nicer if you reduce the letter spacing by a few pixels.

» If your text includes runs of uppercase letters, small caps, or numbers, increasing the letter spacing by a few pixels improves the readability of those characters.

**TIP**

A similar property is font-stretch, which takes advantage of the built-in ability of some typefaces to display condensed or expanded versions of their characters. You can set font-stretch to a percentage (use less than 100% to condense the text, more than 100% to expand the text) or to one of the following keywords: ultra-condensed, extra-condensed, condensed, semi-condensed, normal, semi-expanded, expanded, extra-expanded, or ultra-expanded.

# Displaying text as small caps

Small capital letters — *small caps*, for short — are uppercase letters shrunk down to lowercase-letter size. To specify whether (and how) an element's text appears as small caps, use the font-variant-caps property:

```
font-variant-caps: keyword;
```

You have three values for *keyword* (bk03ch07/example16.html):

» normal: Displays the text without any small caps.

» small-caps: Displays the lowercase letters of the element's text as uppercase letters that are reduced to the size of lowercase letters. The element's uppercase letters are unaffected.

>> all-caps: Displays all the letters of the element's text as uppercase letters that are reduced to the size of lowercase letters.

Here's an example:

```
.subtitle {
    font-variant-caps: small-caps;
}
```

**WARNING**

Very few typefaces come with small caps, so when you set font-variant-caps to small-caps or all-caps, the browser generates the small caps for you (basically by scaling existing uppercase letters down to lowercase size), resulting in so-called *faux small caps* that usually don't look very good. That's fine if you use small caps only occasionally. However, if your design uses small caps extensively, either look for a typeface that comes with small caps (very rare) or use a font family that comes with small caps only (these usually have "SC" in the name, such as Alegreya Sans SC and Playfair Display SC on Google Fonts).

**TECHNICAL STUFF**

You may be wondering how to know whether a given font supports a feature such as small caps, as well as other OpenType features such as kerning (automatically adjusting the relative positions of certain letters so that words display better), ligatures (single glyphs that are used in place of double-letter combos such as *ff* and *fi*), and alternate numeric glyphs (described in the next section). Unfortunately, this isn't easy information to find out, especially if you use Google Fonts. However, a tool with the whimsical name Wakamai Fondue (https://wakamaifondue.com/) can help. Drag and drop your font file on the site, and this tool will tell you all the features supported by the typeface. (As I write this, the site includes a beta feature that enables you to check typefaces from Google Fonts.)

## Using alternative numeric glyphs

If the typeface you're using supports it, you can add some style to your ordinals (1st, 2nd, 3rd, and so on), numbers, and fractions using the font-variant-numeric property:

```
font-variant-numeric: keyword;
```

For *keyword*, you have the following choices (bk03ch07/example17.html):

>> ordinal: Displays the letters associated with each ordinal (for example, the *st* in *1st*) in a special way, usually as superscripts.

>> slashed-zero: Displays the number 0 with an internal slash or dot (which helps differentiate the number *0* from the uppercase *O*).

» `lining-nums`: Displays all numbers so that their bottoms align with the baseline.

» `oldstyle-nums`: Displays numbers so that some — usually 3, 4,5, 7, and 9 — have descenders.

» `proportional-nums`: Displays numbers so that each number takes up only as much space as needed.

» `tabular-nums`: Displays numbers so that they all take up the same amount of horizontal space.

» `diagonal=fractions`: Displays fractions whose numerator and denominator are smaller and separated by a slash (/).

» `stacked-fractions`: Displays fractions whose numerator and denominator are smaller and separated by a horizontal line.

## The font shorthand property

CSS offers the `font` shorthand property, which enables you to specify values for all the following properties in a single declaration: `font-family`, `font-size`, `font-stretch`, `font-style`, `font-variant`, `font-weight`, and `line height`:

```
font: size/line-height stretch style variant weight family;
```

Here are a few notes to bear in mind when using this shorthand:

» Besides the exceptions below, you can put the values in any order.

» Only the `font-family` and `font-size` property values are required. Remember, though, that if you skip a property in the shorthand, the browser resets that property to its initial value.

» The `line-height` value must come immediately after the `font-size` value, with the two separated by a slash (/).

» The `font-stretch` value can only be a keyword.

» The `font-variant` value can only be `small-caps` or `normal`.

» The `font-family` value must be the last value specified.

# Giving Your Links a Makeover

When you add a link to the page, the web browser displays the link text in a different color (usually blue) and underlined. This styling may not fit at all with the rest of your page design, so go ahead and adjust the link styling as needed.

You can apply any text style to a link, including changing the font size, the typeface, adding bold or italics, and changing the color.

One common question web coders ask is "Links: underlined or not?" Not everyone is a fan of underlined text, and if you fall into that camp, you can use the following rule to remove the underline from your links:

```
a {
    text-decoration-line: none;
}
```

**WARNING**

Creating a custom style for links is standard operating procedure for web developers, but a bit of caution is in order because a mistake made by many new web designers is to style links too much like regular text (particularly when they've removed underlining from their links). Your site visitors should be able to recognize a link from ten paces, so be sure to make your links stick out from the regular text in some way.

Rather than risk the slightly dangerous practice of removing link underlines, why not keep them and jazz them up a bit? You can style the link underline using the following three properties (bk03ch07/example18.html):

>> `text-decoration-color`: *color*: The color of the underline.

```
text-decoration-color: hsl(250, 100%, 75%);
```

>> `text-decoration-style`: *keyword*: The style of the underline: `solid`, `double`, `dotted`, `dashed`, or `wavy`.

```
text-decoration-style: dotted;
```

>> `text-decoration-thickness`: *value*: The size of the underline, specified using any CSS length measurement.

```
text-decoration-thickness: 3px;
```

**TIP**

CSS also offers the `text-decoration` shorthand property, which enables you to specify values for `text-decoration-line`, `text-decoration-color`, `text-decoration-style`, **and** `text-decoration-thickness`:

```
text-decoration: line color style thickness;
```

You can specify the values in any order and include all or just some of the values:

```
text-decoration: underline tomato wavy 2px;
```

Remember, though, that if you skip a property in the shorthand, the browser resets that property to its initial value.

# Messing with Alignment

When you think about typography (you *do* think about typography, right?), it's natural to think mostly of typefaces and type sizes and type styles. I mean, *type* is right there (sort of) in the word *typography*. That's all great stuff, but I think of these type-related aspects as the *trees* of typography. But there's also a whole *forest* of typography that looks at the bigger picture of the web page. This forest view is, mostly, about aligning things in a satisfying way. Fortunately, CSS comes with a few properties that give you quite a bit of control over how your text lines up.

## Aligning text

By default, the text inside your page's block-level elements lines up nice and neat along the left edge of the content block. Nothing wrong with that, but what if you want things to align along the right edge, instead? Or perhaps you want to center something within its container. Wouldn't that be nice? You can do all that and more by pulling out the `text-align` property:

```
text-align: keyword;
```

>> *keyword*: The alignment you want to apply. You can use `left` (the default), `right`, `center`, or `justify` (which aligns the element's text with both the left and right margin).

Figure 7-16 shows the `text-align` property at work, with paragraphs styled as, from left to right, `left`, `right`, `center`, and `justify` (bk03ch07/example19.html)

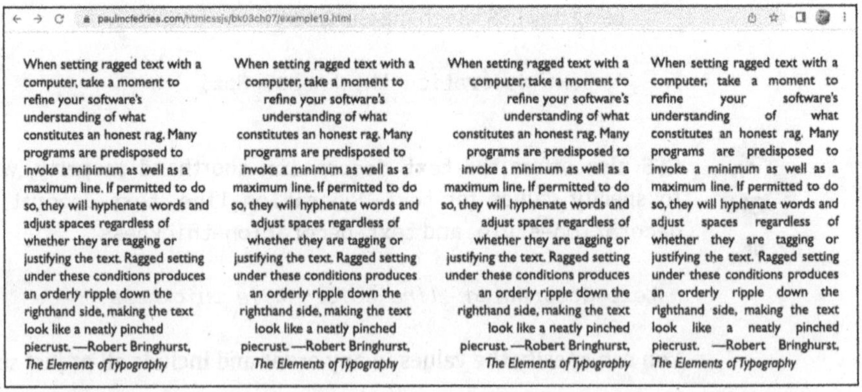

**FIGURE 7-16:** The text-align property doing its thing (left to right): left-aligning, centering, right-aligning, and justifying.

# Hyphenating text

In Figure 7-16, consider the paragraph on the far right that's styled with `text-align: justify`. This paragraph contains yawning chasms of open space, particularly on the third and fourth lines. Alas, most web browsers aren't very good at justifying text, so these unsightly gaps often occur, especially with shorter line lengths.

You could simply not justify your text, but if you really like the otherwise neat look of justified text, you can give the browser a bit of help justifying the text by letting it hyphenate words as needed. You do that by styling the element with the `hyphens` **property**:

```
hyphens: keyword;
```

>> *keyword*: The type of hyphenation you want the browser to use. The default is none, but you can tell the browser to go ahead and break words as needed by using the `auto` keyword. (A third option, `manual`, enables you to specify your own word-break suggestions by inserting `&shy;`, which is the HTML code for a soft hyphen.)

Figure 7-17 shows two paragraphs: the one on the left uses `text-align: justify` with no hyphenation, whereas the paragraph on the right uses both `text-align: justify` and `hyphens: auto` (bk03ch07/example20.html). Letting the browser hyphenate words makes a big difference in both the look and the readability of the text.

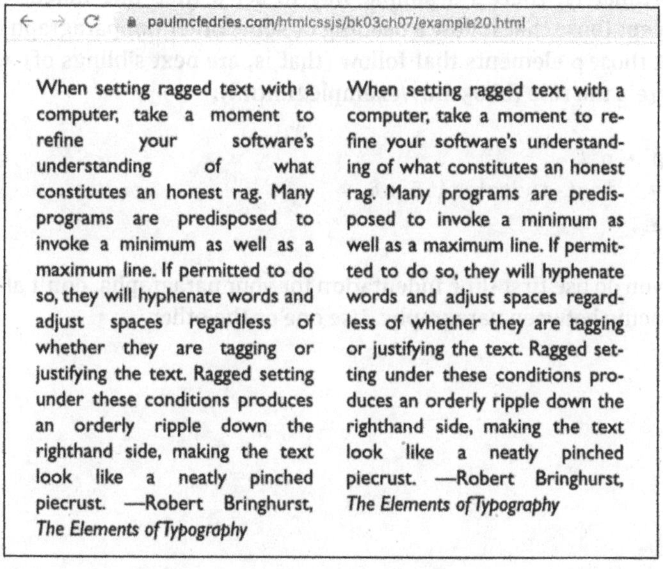

**FIGURE 7-17:**
A justified, unhyphenated paragraph (left) and a justified, hyphenated paragraph (right).

When setting ragged text with a computer, take a moment to refine your software's understanding of what constitutes an honest rag. Many programs are predisposed to invoke a minimum as well as a maximum line. If permitted to do so, they will hyphenate words and adjust spaces regardless of whether they are tagging or justifying the text. Ragged setting under these conditions produces an orderly ripple down the righthand side, making the text look like a neatly pinched piecrust. —Robert Bringhurst, *The Elements of Typography*

When setting ragged text with a computer, take a moment to refine your software's understanding of what constitutes an honest rag. Many programs are predisposed to invoke a minimum as well as a maximum line. If permitted to do so, they will hyphenate words and adjust spaces regardless of whether they are tagging or justifying the text. Ragged setting under these conditions produces an orderly ripple down the righthand side, making the text look like a neatly pinched piecrust. —Robert Bringhurst, *The Elements of Typography*

## Indenting a paragraph's first line

If your page includes long stretches of text divided into paragraphs, you need to help the reader by offering some kind of visual clue that shows where one paragraph ends and the other begins. Setting a top or bottom margin on each paragraph is the most common way of visually separating paragraphs:

```
p {
    margin 1rem auto;
}
```

An alternative method is to indent each paragraph's first line using the text-indent property:

```
text-indent: value;
```

>> value: The length of the indent using your preferred CSS measurement unit. The default value is 0.

Set the indent to at least the same size as the paragraph's font or to at most the paragraph's line height. For example, if the paragraph's font size is 1rem and the line height is 1.5, set the indent to between 1rem and 1.5rem.

**REMEMBER**

Note that it's considered good typographical practice to never indent the first line of any paragraph that immediately follows a heading, an aside, or a page element such as an image or video.

Fortunately, there's a simple way to set a first-line indent on all p elements except those that follow a heading or some other nonparagraph element: just target those p elements that follow (that is, are next siblings of) another p element. Here's the rule (bk03ch07/example21.html):

```
p + p {
    text-indent: 1.5rem;
}
```

If you do use first-line indentation for your paragraphs, don't also include vertical spacing between paragraphs. Use one or the other.

**REMEMBER**

# 4

# Building Dynamic Pages with JavaScript

# Contents at a Glance

Chapter **1**

# JavaScript: The Bird's-Eye View

*Most of the good programmers do programming not because they expect to get paid or get adulation by the public, but because it is fun to program.*

—LINUS TORVALDS

HTML (which I cover in Book 2) and CSS (which I cover in Book 3) are awesome technologies, and you can use them to create pages that look amazing. But after you funnel your page to your web server and look at it a few (dozen) times, you may notice a subtle feeling of disappointment creeping in. Why? It can be hard to pin down, but that hint of dismay comes from a stark fact: Your web page just kind of sits there.

Sure, you probably have a link or three to click, but most likely those links just take you to more of your pages that also just kind of sit there. Or maybe a link takes you to another site altogether, one that feels dynamic and alive and interactive. Ah, engagement! Ooh, excitement!

What's the difference between a page that does nothing and another that seems to be always dancing? One word: JavaScript. With some notable exceptions (check out my coverage of CSS animation in Bonus Chapters 1 through 3 at www.dummies.com/go/htmlcss&javascriptaiofd), HTML and CSS create static pages. If you want your pages to be dynamic and interactive, you need a bit of behind-the-scenes JavaScript to make it so.

I introduce some JavaScript basics in Book 1, Chapter 1, but now it's time to code for real. Don't worry if you've never programmed before. Over the next few chapters, I take you through everything you need to know, step by step, nice and easy. As you're about to find out, it really is fun to program.

# What Is Web Coding?

When people talk about web coding, what they're really talking about is JavaScript. Yep, you need HTML and CSS to create a web page, and you need tools such as PHP and MySQL to convince a web server to give your page some data, but the glue — and sometimes the duct tape — that binds all these technologies together is JavaScript. The result is that JavaScript is now (and has been for a while) the default programming language for web development. If you want to control a page using code (and I know you do), you must use JavaScript to do it.

**TIP**

I don't cover the server side of things — particularly PHP and MySQL — in this book. If that side of the web interests you, please refer to my companion book *Web Coding and Development All-in-One For Dummies* (Wiley).

It also means that JavaScript is (and has been for a while) universal on the web. Sure, you find plenty of bare-bones home pages out there that are nothing but HTML and a sprinkling of CSS, but everything else — from humble personal blogs to fancy-pants designer portfolios to big-time corporate ecommerce operations — relies on JavaScript to make things look good and work the way they're supposed to (most of the time, anyway).

So, when it comes to the care and feeding of your web development education, JavaScript is one of the most important — arguably *the* most important — of all the topics you need to learn.

# What Is a Programming Language?

JavaScript is a programming language. Okay, fine, but what does it mean to call something a "programming language"? To understand this term, you need look no further than the language you use to speak and write. At its most fundamental level, human language is composed of two things — words and rules:

» The words are collections of letters that have a common meaning among all the people who speak the same language. For example, the word *book* denotes a type of object; the word *heavy* denotes a quality; and the word *read* denotes an action.

» The rules are the ways in which words can be combined to create coherent and understandable concepts. If you want to be understood by other speakers of the language, you have only a limited number of ways to throw two or more words together. "I read a heavy book" is an instantly comprehensible sentence, but "book a I read heavy" is gibberish.

The key goal of human language is being understood by someone else who is listening to you or reading something you wrote. If you use the proper words to refer to things and actions, and if you combine words according to the rules, the other person will understand you.

A programming language works in more or less the same way. That is, it, too, has words and rules:

» The words are a set of terms that refer to the specific things that your program works with or the specific ways in which those things can be manipulated. They're known as *reserved words* or *keywords*.

» The rules are the ways in which the words can be combined to produce the desired effect. In the programming world, these rules are known as the language's *syntax*.

In JavaScript, many of the words you work with are very straightforward. Some refer to aspects of the browser, others refer to parts of the web page, and some are used internally by JavaScript. For example, in JavaScript, the word document refers to a specific object (the web page as a whole), and the word write() refers to a specific action (writing data to the page).

The crucial concept here is that just as the fundamental purpose of human language is to be understood by another person, the fundamental purpose of a programming language is to be understood by whatever machine is processing the language. With JavaScript, that machine is the page-reading machine: the web browser.

You can make yourself understood by the page-reading machine by using the proper JavaScript words and by combining them using the proper JavaScript syntax. For example, JavaScript's syntax rules tell you that you can combine the words document and write() like so: document.write(). If you use write().document or document write() or any other combination, the page-reading machine won't understand you.

The key, however, is that being "understood" by the page-reading machine really means being able to *control* the machine. That is, your JavaScript "sentences" are actually commands that you want the machine to carry out. For example, if you want to add the text "Hello World!" to a web page using JavaScript, you include the following statement in your code:

```
document.write("Hello World!");
```

When the page-reading machine trudges through the HTML file and comes upon this statement, it will go right ahead and insert it into the page.

# Is JavaScript Hard to Learn?

I think there's a second reason why many folks get jazzed about creating web pages: It's not that hard. HTML sounds like it's a hard thing, and certainly if you look at the source code of a typical web page without knowing anything about HTML, the code appears about as intimidating as anything you can imagine.

However, I've found that anyone can learn HTML as long as they start with the basic tags, examine lots of examples of how they work, and slowly work their way up to more complex pages. It's just a matter of creating a solid foundation and then building on it.

I'm convinced that JavaScript can be approached in much the same way. I'm certainly not going to tell you that JavaScript is as easy to learn as HTML. That would be a bald-faced lie. However, I will tell you that there is nothing inherently difficult about JavaScript. Using our language analogy, it just has a few more words to know and a few more rules to learn. But I believe that if you begin with the basic words and rules, study tons of examples to learn how they work, and then slowly build up to more complex scripts, you can learn JavaScript programming. I predict here and now that by the time you finish this book, you'll even be a little bit amazed at yourself and at what you can do.

# What You Can Do with JavaScript

The people I've taught to create web pages are a friendly bunch who enjoy writing to me to tell me how their pages are coming along. In many cases, they tell me they've hit the web page equivalent of a roadblock. That is, there's a certain thing they want to do, but they don't know how to do it in HTML. So, I end up getting lots of questions like these:

>> How do I display one of those pop-up boxes?

>> How do I add content to the page on the fly?

>> How can I make something happen when a user clicks a button?

>> How can I make an image change when the mouse hovers over it?

>> How can I calculate the total for my order form?

For each question, the start of the answer is always this: "Sorry, but you can't do that using HTML; you have to use JavaScript instead." I then supply them with a bit of code that they can "cut and paste" into their web pages and then get on with their lives.

If you're just getting started with JavaScript, my goal in this book is to help you to move from "cut and paste" to "code and load." That is, you'll end up being able to create your own scripts to solve your own unique HTML and web-page problems. I hope to show you that learning JavaScript is worthwhile because you can do many other things with it:

>> Add, modify, or remove page text, HTML tags, and even CSS properties.

>> Display messages to the user and ask the user for info.

>> "Listen" for and then perform actions based on events such as a visitor clicking their mouse or pressing a key.

>> Send the user's browser to another page.

>> Validate the values in a form before submitting it to the server. For example, you can make sure that certain fields are filled in.

>> Collect, save, and retrieve data for each of your users, such as site customizations.

In this book, you learn how to do all these things and many more.

# What You Can't Do with JavaScript

JavaScript is good, but it's not that good. JavaScript can do many things, but there's a long list of things that it simply can't do. Here's a sampling of what it can't do:

» Write data permanently to an existing file. For example, you can't take the data from a guest book and add it to a file that stores the messages.

» Access files on the server.

» Glean any information about the user, including email or IP addresses.

» Submit credit card-based purchases for authorization and payment.

» Create multiplayer games.

» Get data directly from a server database.

» Handle file uploads.

JavaScript can't do most of these things because it's what is known in the trade as a *client-side* programming language, which means that it runs on the user's browser (which programming types like to call a *client*).

There are so-called *server-side* JavaScript tools that can do some of these things, but they're super-sophisticated and therefore beyond this book's scope. Fortunately, there are so many things that client-side JavaScript can do that you'll have no trouble being as busy as you want to be.

# What Do You Need to Get Started?

One of the nicest things about HTML and CSS is that the hurdles you have to leap to get started are not only short but few in number. In fact, you really need only two things, both of which are free: a text editor to enter the text, tags, and properties; and a browser to view the results. (You'll also need a web server to host the finished pages, but the server isn't necessary when you're creating the pages.) Yes, there are high-end text editors and fancy graphics programs, but these fall into the "Bells and Whistles" category; you can create perfectly respectable web pages without them.

The basic requirements for JavaScript programming are exactly the same as for HTML: a text editor and a browser. Again, programs are available to help you write and test your scripts, but you don't need them.

To learn more about text editors and using web browsers to test your code, check out Book 1, Chapter 2.

# Dealing with a Couple of Exceptional Cases

In this book, I make a couple of JavaScript assumptions related to the people who'll be visiting the pages you post to the web:

» Those people have JavaScript enabled in their web browser.

» Those people are using a relatively up-to-date version of a modern web browser, such as Chrome, Edge, Safari, or Firefox.

These are pretty safe assumptions, but it pays to be a bit paranoid and wonder how you may handle the teensy percentage of people who don't pass one or both tests.

## Handling browsers with JavaScript turned off

You don't have to worry about web browsers not being able to handle JavaScript, because all modern browsers have supported JavaScript for a very long time. You may, however, want to worry about people who don't support JavaScript. Although rare, some folks have turned off their browser's JavaScript functionality. Why would someone do such a thing? Many people disable JavaScript because they're concerned about security, they don't want cookies written to their hard drives, and so on.

To handle these iconoclasts, place the <noscript> tag within the body of the page:

```
<noscript>
    <p>
        Hey, your browser has JavaScript turned off!
    </p>
    <p>
        Okay, cool, perhaps you'll prefer this <a href="no-js.
    html">non-JavaScript version</a> of the page.
    </p>
</noscript>
```

If the browser has JavaScript enabled, the browser doesn't display any of the text within the <noscript> tag. However, if JavaScript is disabled, the browser displays the text and tags within the <noscript> tag to the user.

To test your site with JavaScript turned off, here are the techniques to use in some popular browsers:

>> **Chrome (desktop):** Open Settings, click Privacy and Security, click Site Settings, click JavaScript, and then select the Don't Allow Sites to Use JavaScript option, as shown in Figure 1-1.

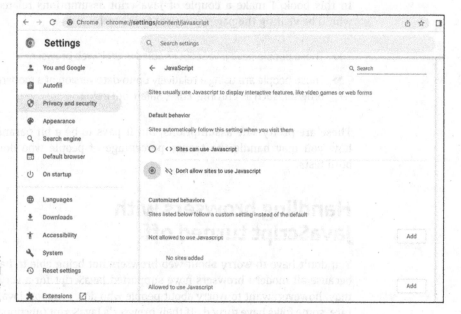

**FIGURE 1-1:**
JavaScript turned off in Google Chrome.

>> **Chrome (Android):** Open Settings, tap Site Settings, tap JavaScript, and then tap the JavaScript switch to off.

>> **Edge:** Open Settings, click the Settings menu, click Cookies and Site Permissions, click JavaScript, and then click the Allowed switch to off.

>> **Safari (macOS):** Open Settings, click the Advanced tab, select the Show Develop Menu in Menu Bar, and then close Settings. Choose Develop ⇨ Disable JavaScript.

>> **Safari (iOS or iPadOS):** Open Settings, tap Safari, tap Advanced, and then tap the JavaScript switch to off.

>> **Firefox (desktop):** In the Address bar, type **about:config** and press Enter or Return. If Firefox displays a warning page, click Accept the Risk and Continue to display the Advanced Preferences page. In the Search Preference Name box, type **javascript**. In the search results, look for the `javascript.enabled` preference. On the far right of that preference, click the Toggle button to turn the value of the preference from `true` to `false`, as shown in Figure 1-2.

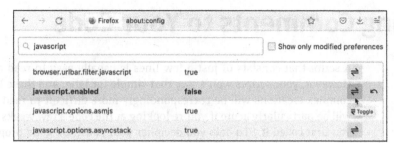

**FIGURE 1-2:**
JavaScript turned
off in Firefox.

# Handling very old browsers

In this book, you learn the version of JavaScript called ECMAScript 2015, also known as ECMAScript 6, or just ES6. Why this version, in particular, and not any of the later versions? Two reasons:

» ES6 has excellent browser support, with more than 98 percent of all current browsers supporting the features released in ES 6. Later versions of JavaScript have less support.

» ES6 has everything you need to add all kinds of useful and fun dynamic features to your pages. Unless you're a professional programmer, the features released in subsequent versions of JavaScript are way beyond what you need.

Okay, so what about that couple of percent of browsers that don't support ES6?

First, know that the number of browsers that choke on ES6 features is getting smaller every day. Sure, it's two percent now (about 1.7 percent, actually), but it will be one percent in six months, a half a percent in a year, and so on until the numbers just get too small to measure.

Second, the percentage of browsers that don't support ES6 varies by region (it's higher in many countries in Africa, for example) and by environment. Most of the people running browsers that don't fully support ES6 are using Internet Explorer 11, and most of those people are in situations in which they can't upgrade (some corporate environments, for example).

If luck has it that your web pages draw an inordinate share of these older browsers, you may need to eschew the awesomeness of ES6 in favor of the tried-and-true features of ECMAScript 5. To that end, as I introduce each new JavaScript feature, I point out those that arrived with ES6 and let you know if there's a simple fallback or workaround (known as a polyfill in the JavaScript trade) if you prefer to use ES5.

# Adding Comments to Your Code

A script that consists of just a few lines is usually easy to read and understand. However, your scripts won't stay that simple for long, and these longer and more complex creations will be correspondingly more difficult to read. (This difficulty will be particularly acute if you're looking at the code a few weeks or months after you first coded it.) To help you decipher your code, it's good programming practice to make liberal use of comments throughout the script. A *comment* is text that describes or explains a statement or group of statements. Comments are ignored by the browser, so you can add as many as you deem necessary.

For short, single-line comments, use the double-slash (//). Put the // at the beginning of the line, and then type your comment after it. Here's an example:

```
// Display the date and time the page was last modified
document.write("This page was last modified on " + document.
  lastModified);
```

You can also use // comments for two or three lines of text, as long as you start each line with //. If you have a comment that stretches beyond that, however, you're better off using multiple-line comments that begin with the /* characters and end with the */ characters. Here's an example:

```
/*
This script demonstrates JavaScript's ability
to write text to the web page by using the
document.write() method to display the date and time
the web page file was last modified.

This script is Copyright Paul McFedries.
*/
```

**WARNING**

Although it's fine to add quite a few comments when you're just starting out, you don't have to add a comment to everything. If a statement is trivial or its purpose is glaringly obvious, forget the comment and move on.

# Creating External JavaScript Files

In Book 1, Chapter 1, I talk about adding JavaScript code to a web page by inserting the ⟨script⟩ and ⟨/script⟩ tags into the page header (that is, between the ⟨head⟩ and ⟨/head⟩ tags), or sometimes into the page body (that is, between the ⟨body⟩ and ⟨/body⟩ tags). You then write your code between the ⟨script⟩ and ⟨/script⟩ tags.

Putting a script inside the page in this way isn't a problem if the script is relatively short. However, if your script (or scripts) take up dozens or hundreds of lines, your HTML code can look cluttered. Another problem you may run into is needing to use the same code on multiple pages. Sure, you can just copy the code into each page that requires it, but if you make changes down the road, you need to update every page that uses the code.

The solution to both problems is to move the code out of the HTML file and into an external JavaScript file. Moving the code reduces the JavaScript presence in the HTML file to a single line (as you'll learn shortly) and means that you can update the code by editing only the external file.

Here are some things to note about using an external JavaScript file:

>> The file must use a plain text format.

>> Use the . js extension when you name the file.

>> Don't use the <script> tag within the file. Just enter your statements exactly as you would within an HTML file.

>> The rules for when the browser executes statements within an external file are identical to those used for statements within an HTML file. That is, statements outside of functions are executed automatically when the browser comes across your file reference, and statements within a function aren't executed until the function is called. (Not sure what a "function" is? You get the full scoop in Book 4, Chapter 5.)

To let the browser know that an external JavaScript file exists, add the src attribute to the <script> tag. For example, if the external file is named myscripts.js, your <script> tag is set up as follows:

```
<script src="myscripts.js">
```

This example assumes that the myscripts.js file is in the same directory as the HTML file. If the file resides in a different directory, adjust the src value accordingly. For example, if the myscripts.js file is in a subdirectory named scripts, you use this:

```
<script src="scripts/myscripts.js">
```

You can even specify a file from another site (presumably your own!) by specifying a full URL as the src value:

```
<script src="http://www.host.com/myscripts.js">
```

As an example, the following code shows a one-line external JavaScript file named `footer.js`:

```
document.write("This page is Copyright " + new Date().
    getFullYear());
```

This statement writes the text "Copyright" followed by the current year. (I know: This code looks like some real gobbledygook right now. Don't sweat it, because you'll learn exactly what's going on here when I discuss the JavaScript Date object in Book 4, Chapter 8.)

The following code shows an HTML file that includes a reference for the external JavaScript file (check out bk04ch01/example01.html in this book's example files):

```
<!DOCTYPE html>
<html lang="en">
    <head>
        <meta charset="utf-8">
        <title>Using an External JS File</title>
    </head>
    <body>
        <p>
            Regular page doodads go here.
        </p>
        <hr>
        <footer>
            <script src="footer.js">
            </script>
        </footer>
    </body>
</html>
```

When you load the page, the browser runs through the HTML line by line. When it gets to the `<footer>` tag, it notices the external JavaScript file that's referenced by the `<script>` tag. The browser loads that file and then runs the code within the file, which writes the Copyright message to the page, as shown in Figure 1-3.

**FIGURE 1-3:**
This page uses an external JavaScript file to display a footer message.

paulmcfedries.com/htmlcssjs/bk04ch01/example01

Regular page doodads go here.

This page is Copyright 2023

# Chapter **2**

# Understanding Variables

*One man's constant is another man's variable.*

—ALAN PERLIS

You may have heard about — or perhaps even know — people who, through mishap or misfortune, have lost the ability to retain short-term memories. If you introduce yourself to one of these folks, they'll be asking you your name again five minutes later. They live in a perpetual present, experiencing the world anew every minute of every day.

What, I'm sure you're asking yourself by now, can any of the above possibly have to do with coding? Just that, by default, your JavaScript programs also live a life without short-term memory. The web browser executes your code one statement at a time until there are no more statements left to process. It all happens in the perpetual present. Ah, but notice that I refer to this lack of short-term memory as the "default" state of your scripts. It's not the only state, so that means things can be different. You have the power to give your scripts the gift of short-term memory, and you do that by using handy little chunks of code called variables. In this chapter, you delve into variables, which is a fundamental and crucial programming topic. You investigate what variables are, what you can do with them, and how to wield them in your JavaScript code.

# Understanding Variables

Why would a script need short-term memory? Because one of the most common concepts that crops up when coding is the need to store a temporary value for use later on. In most cases, you want to use that value a bit later in the same script. However, you may also need to use it in some other script, to populate an HTML form, or as part of a larger or more complex calculation.

For example, your page may have a button that toggles the page text between a larger font size and the regular font size, so you need some way to "remember" that choice. Similarly, if your script performs calculations, you may need to set aside one or more calculated values to use later. For example, if you're constructing a shopping cart script, you may need to calculate taxes on the order. To do that, you must first calculate the total value of the order, store that value, and then later take a percentage of it to work out the tax.

In programming, the way you save a value for later use is by storing it in a variable. A *variable* is a small chunk of computer memory that's set aside for holding program data. The good news is that the specifics of how the data is stored and retrieved from memory happen well behind the scenes, so it isn't something you ever have to worry about. As a coder, working with variables involves just three things:

>> Creating (or *declaring*) variables

>> Assigning values to those variables

>> Including the variables in other statements in your code

The next three sections fill in the details.

## Declaring a variable with let

The process of creating a variable is called *declaring* in programming terms. All declaring really means is that you're supplying the variable with a name and telling the browser to set aside a bit of room in memory to hold whatever value you end up storing in the variable. To declare a variable in JavaScript, you use the let keyword, followed by a space, the name of the variable, and the usual line-ending semicolon. For example, to declare a variable named interestRate, you use the following statement:

```
let interestRate;
```

REMEMBER

Here are a few things to bear in mind when you're declaring variables in your scripts:

>> **Declare a variable only once:** Although you're free to use a variable as many times as you need to within a script, you declare the variable only once. Trying to declare a variable more than once will cause an error.

>> **Use a comment to describe each variable:** Variables tend to proliferate to the point where it often becomes hard to remember what each variable represents. You can make the purpose of each variable clear by adding a comment right after the variable declaration, like so:

```
let interestRate; // Annual interest rate for loan
    calculation
```

>> **Declare each variable before you use it:** If you use a variable before you declare it, you'll get an error.

REMEMBER

In the first two items here, when I say that you'll "get an error," I don't mean that an error message will pop up on the screen. The only thing you'll notice is that your script doesn't run. To read the error message, you need to access your browser's web development tools, a task I go into in satisfying detail in Book 4, Chapter 10.

>> **Declare each variable right before you first use it:** You'll make your programming and debugging (refer to Book 4, Chapter 10) life much easier if you follow this one simple rule: Declare each variable just before (or as close as possible to) the first use of the variable.

TECHNICAL STUFF

The let keyword was introduced in ECMAScript 2015 (ES6). If you need to support really old browsers — I'm looking at *you*, Internet Explorer 11 and earlier — then use the var keyword instead.

## Storing a value in a variable

After your variable is declared, your next task is to give it a value. You use the assignment operator — the equals (=) sign — to store a value in a variable, as in this general statement:

```
variableName = value;
```

Here's an example that assigns the value 0.06 to a variable named interestRate:

```
interestRate = 0.06;
```

Understanding Variables

Note, too, that if you know the initial value of the variable in advance, you can combine the declaration and initial assignment into a single statement, like this:

```
let interestRate = 0.06;
```

It's important to remember that, given a variable declared with the `let` keyword, you're free to change that variable's value any time you want. For example, if the value you assign to the `interestRate` variable is an annual rate, later on your code may need to work with a monthly rate, which is the annual rate divided by 12. Rather than calculate that by hand, just put it in your code using the division operator (`/`):

```
interestRate = 0.06 / 12;
```

As a final note about using a variable assignment, take a look at a variation that often causes some confusion among new programmers. Specifically, you can set up a statement that assigns a new value to a variable by changing its existing value. Here's an example:

```
interestRate = interestRate / 12;
```

If you've never come across this kind of statement before, it probably looks a bit illogical. How can something equal itself divided by 12? The secret to understanding such a statement is to remember that the browser always evaluates the right side of the statement — that is, the expression to the right of the equals sign (`=`) — first. In other words, it takes the current value of `interestRate`, which is `0.06`, and divides it by 12. The resulting value is what's stored in `interestRate` when all is said and done. For a more in-depth discussion of operators and expressions, head over to Book 4, Chapter 3.

**REMEMBER**

Because of this evaluate-the-expression-and-*then*-store-the-result behavior, JavaScript assignment statements shouldn't be read as "variable *equals* expression." Instead, it makes more sense to think of them as "variable *is set to* expression" or "variable *assumes the value given by* expression." Reading assignment statements this way helps to reinforce the important concept that the expression result is being stored in the variable.

## Checking out another way to declare a variable: const

The word *variable* implies that the value assigned to a variable is allowed to *vary*, which is the case for most variables you declare. Most, but not all. Sometimes your scripts will need to use a value that remains constant. For example, suppose you're building a calculator that converts miles to kilometers. The conversion factor is 1.60934, and that value will remain constant throughout your script.

It's good programming practice to store such values in a variable for easier reading. However, if you use let for this declaration, you run the risk of accidentally changing the value somewhere in your code because variables declared with let can change.

To avoid accidentally changing a value that you want to remain constant, you can declare the variable using the const keyword instead. Here's the general syntax:

```
const variableName = value;
```

Note that, unlike with let, you must assign a value to the variable when you declare it with const. Here's an example that declares a variable named milesTo-Kilometers and assigns it the value 1.60934:

```
const milesToKilometers = 1.60934;
```

**REMEMBER**

Are there any real advantages to using const over let in cases where a variable's value must never change? Yep, there are two pretty good ones:

>> Using the const keyword is a reminder that you're dealing with a nonchanging value, which helps you to remember not to assign the variable a new value.

>> If you do try to change the value of a variable declared with const, you'll generate an error, which is another way to remind you that the variable's value is not to be messed with.

**TIP**

Given these advantages, many JavaScript programmers declare every variable with const and use let only for the variables that they know will change. As your code progresses, if you find that a const variable needs to change, you can go back and change const to let.

## Using variables in statements

With your variable declared and assigned a value, you can then use that variable in other statements. When the browser comes across the variable, it goes to the computer's memory, retrieves the current value of the variable, and then substitutes that value into the statement. The following code presents an example (check out bk04ch02/example01.html in this book's example files):

```
let interestRate = 0.06;
interestRate = interestRate / 12;
document.write(interestRate);
```

This code declares a variable named interestRate with the value 0.06; it then divides that value by 12 and stores the result in the variable. The document.write() statement then displays the current value of the variable, as shown in Figure 2-1.

**FIGURE 2-1:**
The browser substituting the current value of a variable.

The following code shows a slightly different example (check out bk04ch02/example02.html):

```
let firstName;
firstName = prompt("Please tell me your first name:");
document.write("Welcome to my website, " + firstName);
```

This script uses the prompt() method (explained shortly) to ask the user to enter their first name, as shown in Figure 2-2. When the user clicks OK, their name is stored in the firstName variable. The script then uses a document.write() statement to display a personalized welcome message using the value of the firstName variable, as shown in Figure 2-3.

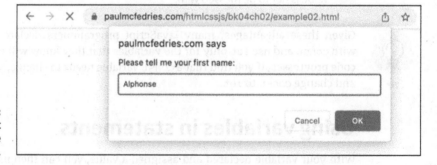

**FIGURE 2-2:**
The script first prompts for the user's first name.

**FIGURE 2-3:**
The script then uses the name to display a personalized welcome message.

**REMEMBER**

When you need to get data from the user, run the prompt() method:

```
prompt(string, default);
```

>> *string:* A string that instructs the user what to enter into the prompt box.

>> *default:* An optional string that specifies the initial value that appears in the prompt box.

The prompt() method always returns a value:

>> If the user clicks OK, prompt() returns the value entered into the prompt text box.

>> If the user clicks Cancel, prompt() returns null.

# Naming Variables: Rules and Best Practices

If you want to write clear, easy-to-follow, and easy-to-debug scripts (and who doesn't?), you can go a long way toward that goal by giving careful thought to the names you use for your variables. This section helps by running through the rules you need to follow and by giving you some tips and guidelines for creating good variable names.

## Rules for naming variables

JavaScript has only a few rules for variable names:

>> The first character must be a letter or an underscore (_). You can't use a number as the first character.

>> The rest of the variable name can include any letter, any number, or the underscore. You can't use any other characters, including spaces, symbols, and punctuation marks.

>> As with the rest of JavaScript, variable names are case sensitive. That is, a variable named InterestRate is treated as an entirely different variable than one named interestRate.

>> There's no limit to the length of the variable name.

>> You can't use one of JavaScript's *reserved words* as a variable name (such as let, const, var, alert, or prompt). All programming languages have a supply of words that are used internally by the language and that can't be used for variable names, because doing so would cause confusion (or worse). Check out "JavaScript's Reserved Words," later in this chapter, for a complete list.

## Ideas for good variable names

The process of declaring a variable doesn't take much thought, but that doesn't mean you should just type in any old variable name that comes to mind. Take a few extra seconds to come up with a good name by following these guidelines:

REMEMBER

>> **Make your names descriptive.** Sure, using names that are just a few characters long makes them easier to type, but I guarantee you that you won't remember what the variables represent when you look at the script down the road. For example, if you want a variable to represent an account number, use accountNumber or accountNum instead of, say, acnm or accnum.

>> **Mostly avoid single-letter names.** Although it's best to avoid single-letter variable names, such short names are accepted in some places, such as when constructing loops, as described in Book 4, Chapter 4.

>> **Use multiple words with no spaces.** The best way to create a descriptive variable name is to use multiple words. However, because JavaScript doesn't take kindly to spaces in names, you need some way of separating the words to keep the name readable. The two standard conventions for using multi-word variable names are *camelCase*, where you cram the words together and capitalize all but the first word (for example, lastName), or to separate each word with an underscore (for example, last_name). I prefer the former style, so I use it throughout this book.

>> **Use separate naming conventions.** Use one naming convention for JavaScript variables and a different one for HTML identifiers and CSS classes. For example, if you use camelCase for JavaScript variables, use dashes for id values and class names.

>> **Differentiate your variable names from JavaScript keywords.** Try to make your variable names look as different from JavaScript's keywords and other built-in terms (such as alert) as possible. Differentiating variable names helps avoid the confusion that can arise when you look at a term and you can't remember if it's a variable or a JavaScript word.

>> **Don't make your names too long.** Although short, cryptic variable names are to be shunned in favor of longer, descriptive names, that doesn't mean you should be using entire sentences. Extremely long names are inefficient because they take so long to type, and they're dangerous because the longer the name, the more likely you are to make a typo. Names of 2 to 4 words and 8 to 20 characters should be all you need.

# Understanding Literal Data Types

In programming, a variable's *data type* specifies what kind of data is stored within the variable. The data type is a crucial idea because it determines not only how two or more variables are combined (for example, mathematically), but also whether they can be combined at all. *Literals* are a special class of data type, and they cover those values that are fixed (even if only temporarily). For example, consider the following variable assignment statement:

```
let todaysQuestion = "What color is your parachute?";
```

Here, the text "What color is your parachute?" is a literal string value. Java-Script supports three kinds of literal data types: numeric, string, and Boolean. The next three sections discuss each type.

## Working with numeric literals

Unlike many other programming languages, JavaScript treats all numbers the same, so you don't have to do anything special when working with the two basic numeric literals, which are integers and floating-point numbers:

>> **Integers:** These are numbers that don't have a fractional or decimal part. So, you represent an integer using a sequence of one or more digits, as in these examples:

```
0
42
2001
-20
```

>> **Floating-point numbers:** These are numbers that do have a fractional or decimal part. Therefore, you represent a floating-point number by first writing the integer part, followed by a decimal point, followed by the fractional or decimal part, as in these examples:

```
0.07
3.14159
-16.6666667
7.6543e+21
1.234567E-89
```

## Exponential notation

The last two floating-point examples require a bit more explanation. These two use *exponential notation,* which is an efficient way to represent really large or really small floating-point numbers. Exponential notation uses an e (or E) followed by the *exponent,* which is a number preceded by a plus sign (+) or a minus sign (–).

You multiply the first part of the number (that is, the part before the e or E) by 10 to the power of the exponent. Here's an example:

```
9.87654e+5;
```

The exponent is 5, and 10 to the power of 5 is 100,000. So, multiplying 9.87654 by 100,000 results in the value 987,654.

Here's another example:

```
3.4567e-4;
```

The exponent is -4, and 10 to the power of -4 is 0.0001. So, multiplying 3.4567 by 0.0001 results in the value .00034567.

JavaScript has a ton of built-in features for performing mathematical calculations. To get the details on these, head for Book 4, Chapter 8.

**TECHNICAL STUFF**

My earlier mention that JavaScript treats all numeric literals the same really means that JavaScript treats the numeric literals as floating-point values. This is fine (after all, there's no practical difference between 2 and 2.0), but it does put a limit on the maximum and minimum integer values that you can work with safely. The maximum is 9007199254740992 and the minimum is -9007199254740992. If you use numbers outside this range (unlikely, but you never know), JavaScript won't be able to maintain accuracy. One solution is to use BigInt values, either by appending n to the end of a large integer value or by using BigInt(*value*), where *value* is a variable containing a large integer value.

## Hexadecimal integer values

You'll likely deal with the usual decimal (base-10) number system throughout most of your JavaScript career. However, just in case you have cause to work with hexadecimal (base-16) numbers, this section shows you how JavaScript deals with them.

```
The hexadecimal number system uses the digits 0 through 9 and
    the letters A through F (or a through f), where these letters
    represent the decimal numbers 10 through 15. So, what in the
    decimal system would be 16 is actually 10 in hexadecimal. To
    specify a hexadecimal number in JavaScript, begin the number
    with a 0x (or 0X), as shown in the following examples:0x23;
0xff;
0X10ce;
```

# Working with string literals

A *string literal* is a sequence of one or more letters, numbers, or punctuation marks, enclosed either in double quotation marks (") or single quotation marks ('). Here are some examples:

```
"HTML, CSS, and JavaScript";
'August 23, 1959';
"";
"What's the good word?";
```

**REMEMBER**

The string "" (or ' ' — two consecutive single quotation marks) is called the *null string*. It represents a string that doesn't contain any characters.

## Using quotation marks within strings

The final example in the previous section shows that it's okay to insert one or more instances of one of the quotation marks (such as ') inside a string that's enclosed by the other quotation mark (such as "). Being able to nest quotation marks comes in handy when you need to embed one string inside another, which is very common (particularly when using bits of JavaScript within HTML tags). Here's an example:

```
onsubmit="processForm('testing')";
```

However, it's illegal to insert in a string one or more instances of the same quotation mark that encloses the string, as in this example:

```
"This is "illegal" in JavaScript.";
```

## Understanding escape sequences

What if you must include, say, a double quotation mark within a string that's enclosed by double quotation marks? Having to nest the same type of quotation mark is rare, but it is possible if you precede the double quotation mark with a backslash (\), like this:

```
"The double quotation mark (\") encloses this string.";
```

The \" combination is called an *escape sequence.* You can combine the backslash with a number of other characters to form other escape sequences, and each one enables the browser to represent a character that, by itself, would be illegal or not representable otherwise. Table 2-1 lists the most commonly used escape sequences.

**TABLE 2-1** ## Common JavaScript Escape Sequences

| Escape Sequence | Character It Represents |
| --- | --- |
| \' | Single quotation mark |
| \" | Double quotation mark |
| \b | Backspace |
| \f | Form feed |
| \n | New line |
| \r | Carriage return |
| \t | Tab |
| \\ | Backslash |

The following code shows an example script that uses the \n escape sequence to display text on multiple lines with an alert box.

```
alert("This is line 1.\nSo what. This is line 2.");
```

Figure 2-4 shows the result.

To learn how to combine two or more string literals, check out Book 4, Chapter 3. Also, JavaScript has a nice collection of string manipulation features, which I discuss in Book 4, Chapter 8.

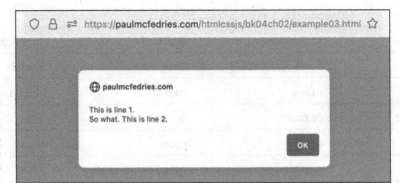

This is line 1.
So what. This is line 2.

OK

## Working with Boolean literals

Booleans are the simplest of all the literal data types because they can assume only one of two values: true or false. That simplicity may make it seem as though Booleans aren't particularly useful, but the capability to test whether a particular variable or condition is true or false is invaluable in JavaScript programming.

You can assign Boolean literals directly to a variable, like this:

```
taskCompleted = true;
```

Alternatively, you can work with Boolean values implicitly using expressions:

```
currentMonth === "August"
```

The comparison expression currentMonth === "August" asks the following: Does the value of the currentMonth variable equal the string "August"? If it does, the expression evaluates to the Boolean value true; if it doesn't, the expression evaluates to false. I discuss much more about comparison expressions in Book 4, Chapter 3.

# JavaScript Reserved Words

As mentioned earlier, JavaScript has a bunch of reserved words that you need to avoid when naming your variables. Table 2-2 presents a list of the JavaScript reserved words. It's illegal to use any of these words as variable or function names.

TABLE 2-2

## JavaScript's Reserved Words

| | | | |
|---|---|---|---|
| abstract | arguments | await | boolean |
| break | byte | case | catch |
| char | class | const | continue |
| debugger | default | delete | do |
| double | else | enum | eval |
| export | extends | false | final |
| finally | float | for | function |
| goto | if | implements | import |
| in | instanceof | int | interface |
| let | long | native | new |
| null | package | private | protected |
| public | return | short | static |
| super | switch | synchronized | this |
| throw | throws | transient | true |
| try | typeof | var | void |
| volatile | while | with | yield |

# JavaScript and HTML Keywords

Table 2-3 presents the complete list of keywords used in JavaScript and HTML that you should avoid using for variable and function names. It's not illegal to use these words, but using them outside their natural habitat could cause confusion.

**TABLE 2-3**      **JavaScript and HTML Keywords**

| | | | |
|---|---|---|---|
| alert | all | anchor | anchors |
| area | Array | assign | blur |
| button | checkbox | clearInterval | clearTimeout |
| clientInformation | close | closed | confirm |

| | | | |
|---|---|---|---|
| constructor | crypto | Date | decodeURI |
| decodeURIComponent | defaultStatus | document | element |
| elements | embed | embeds | encodeURI |
| encodeURIComponent | escape | eval | event |
| fileUpload | focus | form | forms |
| frame | frameRate | frames | function |
| hasOwnProperty | hidden | history | image |
| images | Infinity | innerHeight | innerWidth |
| isFinite | isNaN | isPrototypeOf | layer |
| layers | length | link | location |
| Math | mimeTypes | name | NaN |
| navigate | navigator | Number | Object |
| offscreenBuffering | onblur | onclick | onerror |
| onfocus | onkeydown | onkeypress | onkeyup |
| onload | onmousedown | onmouseover | onmouseup |
| onsubmit | open | opener | option |
| outerHeight | outerWidth | packages | pageXOffset |
| pageYOffset | parent | parseFloat | parseInt |
| password | pkcs11 | plugin | prompt |
| propertyIsEnum | prototype | radio | reset |
| screenX | screenY | scroll | secure |
| select | self | setInterval | setTimeout |
| status | String | submit | taint |
| text | textarea | top | toString |
| undefined | unescape | untaint | valueOf |
| window | | | |

# Chapter **3**

# Building Expressions

*You might not think that programmers are artists, but programming is an extremely creative profession. It's logic-based creativity.*

—JOHN ROMERO

A surprising amount of JavaScript coding involves making little calculations: Add 5 to this number; multiply these two items together; is the value of variable A greater than the value of variable B?; given a collection of Boolean values, is at least one of them true?

These examples are all English-language equivalents of a JavaScript feature known as the expression. When coding in JavaScript, you use expressions constantly, so it's vital to understand what they are and to get comfortable with the types of expressions that are available to you. Every JavaScript coder is different, but I can say without fear of contradiction that every *good* JavaScript coder is fluent in expressions.

This chapter takes you through everything you need to know about expressions. You discover some expression basics and then explore a number of techniques for building powerful expressions using numbers, strings, and Boolean values.

# Understanding Expression Structure

To be as vague as I can be, an *expression* is a collection of symbols, words, and numbers that performs a calculation and produces a result. That's a nebulous definition, I know, so I'll make it more concrete.

When your check arrives after a restaurant meal, one of the first things you probably do is take out your smartphone and use the calculator to figure out the tip amount. The service and food were good, so you're thinking 20 percent is appropriate. With phone in hand, you tap in the bill total, tap the multiplication button, tap 20%, and then tap Equals. *Voilà!* The tip amount appears on the screen and you're good to go.

A JavaScript expression is something like this kind of procedure because it takes one or more inputs, such as a bill total and a tip percentage, and combines them in some way — for example, by using multiplication. In expression lingo, the inputs are called *operands*, and they're combined by using special symbols called *operators*.

>> **operand:** An input value for an expression. It is, in other words, the raw data that the expression manipulates to produce its result. It could be a number, a string, a variable, a function result (refer to Book 4, Chapter 5), or an object property (refer to Book 4, Chapter 6).

>> **operator:** A symbol that represents a particular action performed on one or more operands. For example, the * operator represents multiplication, and the + operator represents addition. I discuss the various JavaScript operators throughout this chapter.

For example, here's an expression that calculates a tip amount and assigns the result to a variable:

```
tipAmount = billTotal * tipPercentage;
```

The expression is everything to the right of the equals sign (=). Here, bill Total and tipPercentage are the operands, and the multiplication sign (*) is the operator.

**TECHNICAL STUFF**

Expression results always have a particular data type — numeric, string, or Boolean. So, when you're working with expressions, always keep in mind what type of result you need and then choose the appropriate operands and operators accordingly.

**REMEMBER**

Another analogy I like to use for operands and operators is a grammatical one — that is, if you consider an expression to be a sentence, the operands are the nouns (the things) of the sentence, and the operators are the verbs (the actions) of the sentence.

# Building Numeric Expressions

Calculating a tip amount on a restaurant bill is a mathematical calculation, so you may be thinking that JavaScript expressions are going to be mostly mathematical. If I was standing in front of you and I happened to have a box of gold stars on me, I'd certainly give you one because, yes, math-based expressions are probably the most common type you'll come across.

In JavaScript, a mathematical calculation is called a *numeric expression*, and it combines numeric operands and arithmetic operators to produce a numeric result. This section discusses all the JavaScript arithmetic operators and shows you how best to use them to build useful and handy numeric expressions.

## A quick look at the arithmetic operators

JavaScript's basic arithmetic operators are more or less the same as those found in your smartphone's calculator app or on the numeric keypad of your computer's keyboard, plus a couple of extra operators for more advanced work. Table 3-1 lists the basic arithmetic operators you can use in your JavaScript expressions. (In subsequent sections, I discuss each one in more detail.)

**TABLE 3-1**     **The JavaScript Arithmetic Operators**

| Operator | Name | Example | Result |
|----------|------|---------|--------|
| + | Addition | 10 + 4 | 14 |
| ++ | Increment | 10++ | 11 |
| – | Subtraction | 10 – 4 | 6 |
| – | Negation | –10 | –10 |
| –– | Decrement | 10–– | 9 |
| * | Multiplication | 10 * 4 | 40 |
| / | Division | 10 / 4 | 2.5 |
| % | Modulus | 10 % 4 | 2 |

JavaScript also comes with a few extra operators that combine some of the arithmetic operators and the assignment operator, which is the humble equals sign (=) that assigns a value to a variable. Table 3-2 lists these so-called *arithmetic assignment* operators.

**TABLE 3-2**

## The JavaScript Arithmetic Assignment Operators

| Operator | Example | Equivalent |
|----------|---------|------------|
| += | x += y | x = x + y |
| -= | x -= y | x = x - y |
| *= | x *= y | x = x * y |
| /= | x /= y | x = x / y |
| ^= | x ^= y | x = x ^ y |
| %= | x %= y | x = x % y |

## Using the addition (+) operator

You use the addition operator (+) to calculate the sum of two operands. The operands are usually of the numeric data type, which means they can be numeric literals, variables that store numeric values, or methods or functions that return numeric values. Here's an example (check out bk04ch03/example01.html in this book's example files):

```
widthMax = widthContent + widthSidebar + 100;
```

You could use such an expression in a web app when you need to know the maximum width to assign the app's container. In this case, you take the width of the app's content (represented by the widthContent variable), add the width of the app's sidebar (the widthSidebar variable), and then add the literal value 100 (which may be a value in pixels).

## Using the increment (++) operator

One of the most common programming operations involves adding 1 to an existing value, such as a variable. This operation is called *incrementing* the value, and the standard way to write such a statement is as follows:

```
someVariable = someVariable + 1;
```

However, JavaScript offers a much more compact alternative that uses the increment operator (++), which you place immediately after the variable name (check out bk04ch03/example02.html):

```
let someVariable = 0;
someVariable++;
```

After these two statements are executed, the value of someVariable will be 1.

**WARNING**

It is now considered bad programming practice to use the increment operator. Why? Most of the reasons are fairly technical, but the main reason is that this operator is a tad cryptic and makes code hard to read. Almost all modern code gurus recommend using the addition assignment operator (+=), instead of the increment operator (refer to "Using the arithmetic assignment operators," later in this chapter).

That is, instead of this:

```
someVariable++;
```

use this:

```
someVariable += 1;
```

## Using the subtraction and negation (-) operators

The subtraction operator (-) subtracts the numeric value to the right of the operator from the numeric value to the left of the operator. For example, consider the following statements (bk04ch03/example03.html):

```
const targetYear = 2025;
const birthYear = 1985;
const yearsDifference = targetYear - birthYear;
```

The third statement subtracts 1985 from 2025, and the result — 40 — is stored in the yearsDifference variable.

# THE PRE- AND POST-INCREMENT OPERATORS

For the record, there are two other ways that JavaScript coders use the ++ operator. Again, I don't recommend using these methods, but I think you should at least know about them just in case you come across them in someone else's code.

The first alternative use of ++ is to increment a variable and then assign this new value to another variable:

```
someVariable = ++anotherVariable;
```

This is exactly the same as the following two statements:

```
anotherVariable = anotherVariable + 1;
someVariable = anotherVariable;
```

Because the ++ appears before the variable, it is often called the *pre-increment operator*.

The second alternative use of ++ is called the *post-increment operator*:

```
someVariable = anotherVariable++;
```

In this case, the ++ operator appears after the variable. Big whoop, right? Actually, there is a subtle but crucial difference. Take a look at the following two statements that do exactly the same thing as the post-increment operator:

```
someVariable = anotherVariable;
anotherVariable = anotherVariable + 1;
```

The first variable is set equal to the second variable and then the second variable is incremented.

The negation operator (–) is the same symbol, but it works in a totally different way. You use it as a kind of prefix by appending it to the front of an operand. The result is a new value that has the opposite sign of the original value. In other words, applying the negation operator to an operand is exactly the same as multiplying the operand by –1. This means that the following two statements are identical:

```
negatedValue = -originalValue;
negatedValue = originalValue * -1;
```

# Using the decrement (--) operator

Another common programming operation is subtracting 1 from an existing variable or other operand. This operation is called *decrementing* the value, and the usual way to go about this is with a statement like this one:

```
thisVariable = thisVariable - 1;
```

However (you just knew there was going to be a however), JavaScript offers a much more svelte alternative that takes advantage of the decrement operator (--), which you place immediately after the variable name (bk04ch03/example04. html):

```
let thisVariable = 1;
thisVariable--;
```

After these two statements are executed, the value of thisVariable will be 0.

**WARNING**

As with the increment operator, these days it's also frowned upon to use the decrement operator. Instead, your code will read better if you use the subtraction assignment operator (-=), instead of the decrement operator (refer to "Using the arithmetic assignment operators," later in this chapter).

That is, instead of this:

```
thisVariable--;
```

use this:

```
thisVariable -= 1;
```

# Using the multiplication (*) operator

The multiplication operator (*) multiplies two operands together. Here's an example (bk04ch03/example05.html):

```
const columns = 8;
const columnWidth = 100;
const totalWidth = columns * columnWidth;
```

You might use this code when you want to calculate the width taken up by a web page layout that uses multiple columns. This code assigns literal numeric values to the variables columns and columnWidth. It then uses a numeric expression to multiply these two values together and assign the result to the totalWidth variable.

## THE PRE- AND POST-DECREMENT OPERATORS

There are two other ways that JavaScript programmers use the −− operator. I don't recommend using these methods, but you should know about them just in case you trip over them in someone else's code.

The first alternative use of −− is to decrement a variable and then assign this new value to another variable, which is called the *pre-decrement* form:

```
thisVariable = --thatVariable;
```

This is the same as the following two statements:

```
thatVariable = thatVariable - 1;
thisVariable = thatVariable;
```

The second alternative use of −− is to assign the value of a variable to another variable and then decrement the first variable, which is called the *post-decrement* form:

```
thisVariable = thatVariable--;
```

Again, the following two statements do exactly the same thing:

```
thisVariable = thatVariable;
thatVariable = thatVariable - 1;
```

The first variable is set equal to the second variable and then the second variable is decremented.

## Using the division (/) operator

The division operator (/) divides one numeric value by another. You can show off at parties by remembering that the number to the left of the slash (/) is called the *dividend*, and the number to the right of the / is called the *divisor*:

```
dividend / divisor
```

Here's an example (bk04ch03/example06.html):

```
const contentWidth = 600;
const windowWidth = 1200;
const contentRatio = contentWidth / windowWidth;
```

You can use this code to calculate the portion of the browser's window width that the page content is currently using. In this code, the variables contentWidth and windowWidth are assigned literal numeric values, and then a numeric expression divides the first of the values by the second, the result of which is stored in the contentRatio variable.

**WARNING**

Whenever you use the division operator, you must guard against cases where the divisor is 0. If that happens, your script will produce an Infinity result, which is almost certain to wreak havoc on your calculations. Before performing any division, your script should use an if() statement (refer to Book 4, Chapter 4) to check whether the divisor is 0 and, if it is, to cancel the division or perform some kind of workaround.

## Using the modulus (%) operator

The modulus operator (%) divides one number by another and then returns the remainder as the result:

```
dividend % divisor
```

For example, the following code stores the value 1 in the variable named myRemainder because 5 (the myDivisor value; also known as the *modulus*) divides into 16 (the myDividend value) three times and leaves a remainder of 1 (bk04ch03/example07.html):

```
const myDividend = 16;
const myDivisor = 5;
const myRemainder = myDividend % myDivisor;
```

On a more practical level, suppose that you're trying to come up with a web-page color scheme and you want to use two colors that are complements of each other. *Complementary* means that the two hues are on the opposite side of the color wheel, so one way to calculate the second color is by adding 180 to the first color's hue value. That approach works when the hue of the first color is between 0 and 179, which gives the second color hue values between 180 and 359. However, an initial hue of 180, 181, and so on produces a second hue of 360, 361, and so on, which are illegal values. You can work around that issue by using a modulus expression like this (bk04ch03/example07.html):

```
complementaryColor = (originalColor + 180) % 360;
```

This statement adds 180 to the original color, but then uses % 360 to return the remainder when divided by 360 to avoid illegal values.

## Using the arithmetic assignment operators

Your web coding scripts will often update the value of a variable by adding to it the value of some other operand. Here's an example:

```
totalInterestPaid = totalInterestPaid + monthlyInterestPaid
```

Coders are an efficiency-loving bunch, so the fact that the totalInterestPaid variable appears twice in that statement is like chewing tin foil to your average programmer. The JavaScript brain trust hates that kind of thing, too, so they came up with the addition assignment operator (+=), which you use like so (bk04ch03/example08.html):

```
totalInterestPaid += monthlyInterestPaid
```

Yep, this statement does exactly the same thing as the first one, but it does it with 19 fewer characters. Sweet!

If you need to subtract one operand from another, again you can do it the old-fashioned way:

```
principleOwing = principleOwing - monthlyPrincipalPaid
```

To avoid other coders laughing behind your back at your inefficiency, use the subtraction assignment operator (-=), which works like this (bk04ch03/example08.html):

```
principleOwing -= monthlyPrincipalPaid
```

**REMEMBER**

Like the increment and decrement operators, the arithmetic assignment operators are designed to save wear and tear on your typing fingers and to reduce the size of your scripts, particularly if you use long variable names.

# Building String Expressions

A string expression is one where at least one of the operands is a string, and the result of the expression is another string. String expressions are straightforward in the sense that there is only one operator to deal with: *concatenation* (+). You use this operator to combine (or *concatenate*) strings within an expression. For example, the expression "Java" + "Script" returns the string "JavaScript". Note, however, that you can also use strings with the comparison operators discussed in the next section.

# BREAKING UP LONG STATEMENTS

**TIP**

All your JavaScript statements should appear on a single line (refer to Book 4, Chapter 1). An exception to that rule is any statement that contains a long expression, which you can break into multiple lines as long as the break occurs immediately before or after an operator. For example, you can write a string expression in multiple lines as long as the break occurs immediately before or after the + operator, as in the following examples:

```
const message1 = "How did the fool and his money " +
                 "get together in the first place?";
const message2 = "Never put off until tomorrow that which you "
                 + "can put off until the day after tomorrow.";
```

It's unfortunate that the concatenation operator is identical to the addition operator because this similarity can lead to some confusion. For example, the expression 2 + 2 returns the numeric value 4 because the operands are numeric. However, the expression "2" + "2" returns the string value 22 because the two operands are strings.

To further complicate matters, JavaScript will often convert numbers into strings depending on the context:

» If the first operand in an expression is a string, JavaScript converts any number in the expression to a string. For example, the following expression returns the string 222:

```
"2" + 2 + 2
```

» If the first two or more operands in an expression are numbers and the rest of the expression contains a string, JavaScript handles the numeric part of the expression first and then converts the result into a string. For example, the following expression returns the string 42 because the result of 2 + 2 is 4, which is then concatenated as a string to "2":

```
2 + 2 + "2"
```

As an example of how this conversion can be a problem, consider the script in the following code (bk04ch03/example09.html):

```
const preTipTotal = 10.00;
const tipAmount = preTipTotal * 0.15;
const message1 = "Your tip is ";
```

```
const message2 = "<br>Your total bill is ";
document.write(message1 + tipAmount +
    message2 + preTipTotal + tipAmount);
```

The preTipTotal variable stores a total for a restaurant bill, and the tipAmount variable stores 15 percent of the total. The variables message1 and message2 are initialized with strings, and then the results are written to the page. In particular, the expression preTipTotal + tipAmount is included in the document.write() method to display the total bill. However, as shown in Figure 3-1, the "total" displayed is actually 101.5 instead of 11.5 (10 plus 1.5 for the tip).

What happened here is that because the first part of the expression in the document.write() method was a string, JavaScript converted the preTipTotal and tipAmount values to strings and concatenated them instead of adding them.

**FIGURE 3-1:**
Concatenating instead of adding the preTipTotal and tipAmount values.

← → C    🔒 paulmcfedries.com/htmlcssjs/bk04ch03/example01.html    ⬆ ☆

Your tip is 1.5
Your total bill is 101.5

To fix this problem, you could perform the addition in a separate statement and then use only this sum in the document.write() expression. The following code demonstrates this approach (bk04ch03/example10.html):

```
const preTipTotal = 10.00;
const tipAmount = preTipTotal * 0.15;
const totalBill = preTipTotal + tipAmount;
const message1 = "Your tip is ";
const message2 = "<br>Your total bill is ";
document.write(message1 + tipAmount + message2 + totalBill);
```

A new variable named totalBill is declared and is used to store the preTip Total + tipAmount sum. totalBill is then used to display the sum in the document.write() expression, which, as shown in Figure 3-2, now displays the correct answer.

**FIGURE 3-2:**
Calculating preTipTotal and tipAmount separately fixes the problem.

← → C    🔒 paulmcfedries.com/htmlcssjs/bk04ch03/example02.html    ⬆ ☆

Your tip is 1.5
Your total bill is 11.5

# Building Comparison Expressions

You use comparison expressions to compare the values of two or more numbers, strings, variables, properties, or function results. If the expression is true, the expression result is set to the Boolean value true; if the expression is false, the expression result is set to the Boolean value false. You'll use comparisons with alarming frequency in your JavaScript code, so it's important to understand what they are and how you use them.

## The comparison operators

Table 3-3 summarizes JavaScript's comparison operators.

**TABLE 3-3**

### The JavaScript Comparison Operators

| Operator | Name | Example | Result |
|----------|------|---------|--------|
| == | Equality | 10 == 4 | false |
| != | Inequality | 10 != 4 | true |
| > | Greater than | 10 > 4 | true |
| < | Less than | 10 < 4 | false |
| >= | Greater than or equal | 10 >= 4 | true |
| <= | Less than or equal | 10 <= 4 | false |
| === | Strict equality | "10" === 10 | false |
| !== | Strict inequality | "10" !== 10 | true |

## Using the equality (==) operator

You use the equality operator (==) (often also called the equals operator) to compare the values of two operands. If both have the same value, the comparison returns true; if the operands have different values, the comparison returns false.

For example, in the following statements the variables booksRead and weeksPassed contain the same value, so the expression booksRead == weeksPassed returns true (check out Figure 3-3 and bk04ch03/example11.html):

```
const booksRead = 48;
const weeksPassed = 48;
```

```
const bookAWeek = booksRead == weeksPassed;
document.write("Me: I'm averaging a book a week, amirite?<br>");
document.write("JavaScript: " + bookAWeek);
```

**FIGURE 3-3:**
The expression
booksRead ==
weeksPassed
returns true.

```
←  →  C    🔒 paulmcfedries.com/htmlcssjs/bk04ch03/example11
```

Me: I'm averaging a book a week, amirite?
JavaScript: true

**WARNING**

One of the most common mistakes made by beginning and experienced JavaScript programmers alike is to use = instead of == in a comparison expression. If your script isn't working properly or is generating errors, one of the first things you should check is that your equality operator has two equal signs.

**REMEMBER**

It's important to understand here that the equality operator returns true when the two operands have the same value *even if* the two operands have different data types. (For an explanation of why this happens, check out "The comparison operators and data conversion," later in this chapter.) For example, in the following code, the bookAWeek variable winds up with the value true:

```
const booksRead = 48;
const weeksPassed = "48";
const bookAWeek = booksRead == weeksPassed;
```

This may be what you want, but you're more likely to want the comparison to return false. For that, you need to use the strict equality operator (===), discussed later in this section.

## Using the inequality (!=) operator

You use the inequality operator (!=) to compare the values of two operands, but in the opposite sense of the equality operator. That is, if the operands have different values, the comparison returns true; if both operands have the same value, the comparison returns false.

In the following statements, for example, the variables currentFontSize and defaultFontSize contain different values, so the expression currentFontSize!=defaultFontSize returns true (bk04ch03/example12.html):

```
const currentFontSize = 19;
const defaultFontSize = 16;
const usingCustomFontSize = currentFontSize != defaultFontSize;
```

**REMEMBER**

The inequality operator returns `false` (meaning the two operands have the same value) *even if* the two operands have different data types. This may be what you want, but you're more likely to want the comparison to return `true`. For that you need to use the strict inequality operator (`!==`), discussed later in this section.

## Using the greater than (>) operator

You use the greater than operator (`>`) to compare two operands to determine whether the operand to the left of `>` has a greater value than the operand to the right of `>`. If it does, the expression returns `true`; otherwise, it returns `false`.

In the statements below, the value of the `contentWidth` variable is more than that of the `windowWidth` variable, so the expression `contentWidth > windowWidth` returns `true` (bk04ch03/example13.html):

```
const contentWidth = 1000;
const windowWidth = 800;
const tooBig = contentWidth > windowWidth;
```

## Using the less than (<) operator

You use the less than operator (`<`) to compare two operands to determine whether the operand to the left of `<` has a lesser value than the operand to the right of `<`. If it does, the expression returns `true`; otherwise, it returns `false`.

For example, in the statements that follow, the values of the `kumquatsInStock` and `kumquatsSold` variables are the same, so the expression `kumquatsInStock < kumquatsSold` returns `false` (check out Figure 3-4 and bk04ch03/example14. html):

```
const kumquatsInStock = 3;
const kumquatsSold = 3;
const backordered = kumquatsInStock < kumquatsSold;
document.write("Are kumquats on back order? " + backordered);
```

**FIGURE 3-4:**
The expression
kumquats
InStock <
kumquatsSold
returns false.

← → C 🔒 paulmcfedries.com/htmlcssjs/bk04ch03/example14

Are kumquats on back order? false

## Using the greater than or equal (>=) operator

You use the greater than or equal operator (>=) to compare two operands to determine whether the operand to the left of >= has a greater value than or an equal value to the operand to the right of >=. If either or both of those comparisons get a thumbs up, the expression returns true; otherwise, it returns false.

In the following statements, for example, the value of the score variable is more than that of the prize1Minimum variable and is equal to that of the prize2Minimum variable. Therefore, both the expressions score >= prize1Minimum and score >= prize2Minimum return true (bk04ch03/example15.html):

```
const score = 90;
const prize1Minimum = 80;
const prize2Minimum = 90;
const getsPrize1 = score >= prize1Minimum;
const getsPrize2 = score >= prize2Minimum;
```

## Using the less than or equal (<=) operator

You use the less than or equal operator (<=) to compare two operands to determine whether the operand to the left of <= has a lesser value than or an equal value to the operand to the right of <=. If either or both of those comparisons get a nod of approval, the expression returns true; otherwise, it returns false.

For example, in the following statements, the value of the defects variable is less than that of the defectsMaximumA variable and is equal to that of the defects MaximumB variable. Therefore, both the expressions defects <= defectsMaximumA and defects <= defectsMaximumB return true (bk04ch03/example16.html):

```
const defects = 5;
const defectsMaximumA = 10;
const defectsMaximumB = 5;
const getsBonus = defects <= defectsMaximumA;
const getsRaise = defects <= defectsMaximumB;
```

## The comparison operators and data conversion

In the examples in previous sections, I use only numbers to demonstrate the various comparison operators. However, you can also use strings and Boolean values.

These comparisons are straightforward if your expressions include only operands of the same data type; that is, if you compare two strings or two Booleans. (However, refer to my discussion in the section "Using strings in comparison expressions," a bit later in this chapter.)

**TECHNICAL STUFF**

Things become less straightforward if you mix data types within a single comparison expression. In this case, you need to remember that JavaScript always attempts to convert each operand into a number before running the comparison. Here's how it works:

» If one operand is a string and the other is a number, JavaScript attempts to convert the string into a number. For example, in the following statements, the string "5" gets converted to the number 5, so the comparison value1 == value2 returns true:

```
const value1 = "5";
const value2 = 5;
const result = value1 == value2;
```

If the string can't be converted to a number (for example, the string "rutabaga" can't be converted to a number), the comparison always returns false.

The null string ("") gets converted to 0.

**REMEMBER**

» If one operand is a Boolean and the other is a number, JavaScript converts the Boolean to a number, as follows:

• true — This value is converted to 1.

• false — This value is converted to 0.

For example, in the following statements, the Boolean true gets converted to the number 1, so the comparison value1 == value2 returns true:

```
const value1 = true;
const value2 = 1;
const result = value1 == value2;
```

» If one operand is a Boolean and the other is a string, JavaScript converts the Boolean to a number, as in the previous item, and attempts to convert the string into a number. For example, in the following statements, the Boolean false is converted to the number 0 and the string "0" is converted to the number 0, so the comparison value1 == value2 returns true:

```
const value1 = false;
const value2 = "0";
const result = value1 == value2;
```

If the string can't be converted to a number, the comparison always returns false.

## Using the strict equality (===) operator

The strict equality operator (===) checks whether two operands are identical, which means that it checks not only that the operands' values are equal but also that the operands are of the same data type. (Which is why the strict equality operator is also sometimes called the *identity operator*.)

For example, in the following statements, variable albumName contains a string and variable albumReleaseDate contains a number. These values are of different data types, so the expression albumName === albumReleaseDate returns false (bk04ch03/example17.html):

```
const albumName = "1984";
const albumReleaseDate = 1984;
const result = albumName === albumReleaseDate;
```

By comparison, if instead you used the equality operator (==), which doesn't check the operand data types, the expression albumName == albumReleaseDate would return true.

**REMEMBER**

So, when should you use equality (==) and when should you use strict equality (===)? Many pro JavaScript coders ignore this question entirely and just use the strict equality operator all the time. You should, too.

## Using the strict inequality (!==) operator

The strict inequality operator (!==) performs (sort of) the opposite function of the strict equality operator. That is, it checks not only whether the values of two operands are different but also whether the operands are of different data types. (Which is why the strict inequality operator is also sometimes called the *non-identity operator*.)

In the following statements, the variable hasBugs contains the Boolean value true and the variable totalBugs contains a number. These values are of different data types, so the expression hasBugs !== totalBugs returns true (bk04ch03/example18.html):

```
const hasBugs = true;
const totalBugs = 1;
const result = hasBugs !== totalBugs;
```

# Using strings in comparison expressions

Comparison expressions involving only numbers hold few surprises, but comparisons involving only strings can sometimes raise an eyebrow or two. The comparison is based on alphabetical order, as you may expect, so "A" comes before "B" and "a" comes before "b." Ah, but this isn't your father's alphabetical order. In JavaScript's world, all the uppercase letters come before all the lowercase letters, which means that, for example, "B" comes before "a," so the following expression would return `false`:

```
"a" < "B"
```

Another thing to keep in mind is that most string comparisons involve multiple-letter operands. In these situations, JavaScript compares each string letter by letter. For example, consider the following expression:

```
"Smith" < "Smyth"
```

The first two letters in each string are the same, but the third letters are different. The internal value of the `i` in `Smith` is less than the internal value of the `y` in `Smyth`, so the preceding comparison would return `true`. (Notice, too, that after a point of difference is found, JavaScript ignores the rest of the letters in each string.)

---

**TECHNICAL STUFF**

## UNICODE STRING VALUES (OR, WHY *A* ISN'T LESS THAN *B*)

In the "a" < "B" returning `false` example, what does it mean to say that all the uppercase letters "come before" all the lowercase letters? The story here is that a technology called Unicode keeps track of (give or take) every possible character, nearly 150,000 of them as I write this. Each of those characters is given a unique numeric value. For example, the asterisk (*) has the value 42, whereas the digit *5* has the value 53.

For some reason, Unicode lists the uppercase Latin letters before the lowercase letters. The letter *A* is given the value 65, *B* is 66, and so on to *Z*, which has the value 90. The lowercase Latin letters start with *a*, which is given the value 97, *b* has 98, and so on up to *z*, which has the value 122.

When you use a comparison operator to compare two letters, what JavaScript is actually comparing are the letters' Unicode values. That's why the string "a" (value 97) is actually greater than the string "B" (value 66).

Also, a space is a legitimate character for comparison purposes, and its internal value comes before all other letters and printable symbols. (If you read the "Unicode string values [or, why *a* isn't less than *B*]" sidebar, I can tell you that the Unicode value for the space character is 32.) Consider, then, the following comparison:

```
"Marge Simpson" > "Margerine"
```

The expression returns false because the sixth "letter" of the left operand is a space, whereas the sixth letter of "Margerine" is r.

## Using the ternary (?:) operator

Knowing the comparison operators also enables you to use one of my favorite expression tools, a complex but oh-so-handy item called the *ternary operator* (?:). Here's the basic syntax for using the ternary operator in an expression:

```
expression ? result_if_true : result_if_false
```

The *expression* is a comparison expression that results in a true or false value. In fact, you can use any variable, function result, or property that has a true or false Boolean value. The *result_if_true* is the value that the expression returns if the *expression* evaluates to true; the *result_if_false* is the value that the expression returns if the *expression* evaluates to false.

In JavaScript, by definition, the following values are the equivalent of false:

» 0 (the number zero)

» "" (the empty string)

» null

» undefined (which is, say, the "value" of an uninitialized variable)

Everything else is the equivalent of true.

Here's an example (bk04ch03/example19.html):

```
const screenWidth = 768;
const maxTabletWidth = 1024;
const screenType = screenWidth > maxTabletWidth ? "Desktop!" :
    "Tablet!";
```

The variable `screenWidth` is initialized to 768, the variable `maxTabletWidth` is initialized to 1024, and the variable `screenType` stores the value returned by the conditional expression. For the latter, `screenWidth > maxTabletWidth` is the comparison expression, `"Desktop!"` is the string that is returned given a `true` result, and `"Portable!"` is the string that is returned given a `false` result. Because `screenWidth` is less than `maxTabletWidth`, the comparison will be `false`, so `"Tablet!"` will be the result.

# Building Logical Expressions

You use logical expressions to combine or manipulate Boolean values, particularly comparison expressions. For example, if your code needs to test whether two different comparison expressions are both `true` before proceeding, you can do that with a logical expression.

## The logical operators

Table 3-4 lists JavaScript's logical operators.

**TABLE 3-4**     **The JavaScript Logical Operators**

| Operator | Name | General Syntax | Returned Value |
|---|---|---|---|
| && | AND | *expr1* && *expr2* | true if both *expr1* and *expr2* are true; false otherwise. |
| \|\| | OR | *expr1* \|\| *expr2* | true if one or both of *expr1* and *expr2* are true; false otherwise. |
| ! | NOT | !*expr* | true if *expr* is false; false if *expr* is true. |

## Using the AND (&&) operator

You use the AND operator (&&) when you want to test two Boolean operands to determine whether they're both `true`. For example, consider the following statements (bk04ch03/example20.html):

```
const finishedDinner = true;
const clearedTable = true;
const getsDessert = finishedDinner && clearedTable;
```

Because both finishedDinner and clearedTable are true, the logical expression finishedDinner && clearedTable evaluates to true.

On the other hand, consider these statements:

```
const haveWallet = true;
const haveKeys = false;
const canGoOut = haveWallet && haveKeys;
```

In this example, because haveKeys is false, the logical expression haveWallet && haveKeys evaluates to false. The logical expression would also return false if just haveWallet was false or if both haveWallet and haveKeys were false.

Table 3-5 lists the various operands you can enter and the results they generate (this is called a *truth table*).

**Truth Table for the AND (&&) Operator**

| left_operand | right_operand | left_operand && right_operand |
| --- | --- | --- |
| true | true | true |
| true | false | false |
| false | true | false |
| false | false | false |

## Using the OR (||) operator

You use the OR (||) operator when you want to test two Boolean operands to determine whether at least one of them is true. For example, consider the following statements (bk04ch03/example21.html):

```
const hasFever = true;
const hasCough = false;
const missSchool = hasFever || hasCough;
```

Because hasFever is true, the logical expression hasFever || hasCough evaluates to true because only one of the operands needs to be true. You get the same result if only hasCough is true or if both operands are true.

On the other hand, consider these statements:

```
const salesOverBudget = false;
const expensesUnderBudget = false;
const getsBonus = salesOverBudget || expensesUnderBudget;
```

In this example, because both salesOverBudget and expensesUnderBudget are false, the logical expression salesOverBudget || expensesUnderBudget evaluates to false.

Table 3-6 displays the truth table for the various operands you can enter.

**TABLE 3-6**

## Truth Table for the OR ( || ) Operator

| left_operand | right_operand | left_operand || right_operand |
|---|---|---|
| true | true | True |
| true | false | True |
| false | true | True |
| false | false | False |

# Using the NOT (!) Operator

The NOT (!) operator is the logical equivalent of the negation operator (−) I covered earlier in this chapter. In this case, NOT returns the opposite Boolean value of an operand. For example, consider the following statements (bk04ch03/example22.html):

```
const dataLoaded = false;
const waitingForData = !dataLoaded;
```

dataLoaded is false, so !dataLoaded evaluates to true.

Table 3-7 displays the truth table for the various operands you can enter.

**TABLE 3-7**

## Truth Table for the NOT ( ! ) Operator

| Operand | !Operand |
|---|---|
| true | false |
| false | true |

## Advanced notes on the && and || operators

I mentioned earlier that JavaScript defines various values that are the equivalent of false — including 0 and "" — and that all other values are the equivalent of true. These equivalences mean that you can use both the AND operator and the OR operator with non-Boolean values. However, if you plan on using non-Booleans, you need to be aware of exactly how JavaScript evaluates these expressions.

I'll begin with an AND expression:

1. Evaluate the operand to the left of the AND operator.

2. If the left operand's value is false or is equivalent to false, return that value and stop; otherwise, continue with Step 3.

3. If the left operand's value is true or is equivalent to true, evaluate the operand to the right of the AND operator.

4. Return the value of the right operand.

This is quirky behavior, indeed, and there are two crucial concepts you need to bear in mind:

» If the left operand evaluates to false or its equivalent, the right operand is *never* evaluated.

» The logical expression returns the result of either the left or right operand, which means the expression might *not* return true or false; instead, it might return a value that's equivalent to true or false.

To try out these concepts, use the following code (bko4cho3/example23.html):

```
const v1 = true;
const v2 = 10;
const v3 = "testing";
const v4 = false;
const v5 = 0;
const v6 = "";
const leftOperand =
    eval(prompt("Enter the left operand (a value or
  expression):", true));
const rightOperand =
    eval(prompt("Enter the right operand (a value or
  expression):", true));
const result = leftOperand && rightOperand;
document.write(result);
```

The script begins by declaring and initializing six variables. The first three (v1, v2, and v3) are given values equivalent to true, and the last three (v4, v5, and v6) are given values equivalent to false. The script then prompts for a left operand and a right operand, which are then entered into an AND expression. The key here is that you can enter any value for each operand, or you can use the v1 through v6 variables to enter a comparison expression, such as v2 > v5. The use of eval() on the prompt() result ensures that JavaScript uses the expressions as they're entered.

Table 3-8 lists some sample inputs and the results they generate.

**TABLE 3-8**

## Some Sample Results for the Previous Code

| left_operand | right_operand | left_operand && right_operand |
|---|---|---|
| true | true | true |
| true | false | false |
| 5 | 10 | 10 |
| false | "Yo" | false |
| v2 | v5 | 0 |
| true | v3 | testing |
| v5 | v4 | 0 |
| v2 > v5 | v5 == v4 | true |

Like the AND operator, the logic of how JavaScript evaluates an OR expression is strange and needs to be understood, particularly if you'll be using operands that are true or false equivalents:

1. Evaluate the operand to the left of the OR operator.

2. If the left operand's value is true or is equivalent to true, return that value and stop; otherwise, continue with Step 3.

3. If the left operand's value is false or is equivalent to false, evaluate the operand to the right of the AND operator.

4. Return the value of the right operand.

# Understanding Operator Precedence

Your JavaScript code will often use expressions that are blissfully simple: just one or two operands and a single operator. Alas, "often" here doesn't mean "mostly," because many expressions you use will have a number of values and operators. In these more complex expressions, the order in which the calculations are performed becomes crucial. For example, consider the expression 3+5*2. If you calculate from left to right, the answer you get is 16 (3+5 equals 8, and 8*2 equals 16). However, if you perform the multiplication first and then the addition, the result is 13 (5*2 equals 10, and 3+10 equals 13). In other words, a single expression can produce multiple answers depending on the order in which you perform the calculations.

To control this ordering problem, JavaScript evaluates an expression according to a predefined *order of precedence*. This order of precedence lets JavaScript calculate an expression unambiguously by determining which part of the expression it calculates first, which part second, and so on.

## The order of precedence

The order of precedence that JavaScript uses is determined by the various expression operators that I've covered so far in this chapter. Table 3-9 summarizes the complete order of precedence used by JavaScript.

For example, Table 3-9 tells you that JavaScript performs multiplication before addition. Therefore, the correct answer for the expression 3+5*2 (just discussed) is 13.

Notice, as well, that some operators in Table 3-9 have the same order of precedence (for example, multiplication and division). Having the same precedence means that the order in which JavaScript evaluates these operators doesn't matter. For example, consider the expression 5*10/2. If you perform the multiplication first, the answer you get is 25 (5*10 equals 50, and 50/2 equals 25). If you perform the division first, you also get an answer of 25 (10/2 equals 5, and 5*5 equals 25).

However, JavaScript does have a predefined order for these kinds of expressions, which is what the Order of Evaluation column tells you. A value of L -> R means that operations with the same order of precedence are evaluated from left-to-right; R -> L means the operations are evaluated from right-to-left.

**TABLE 3-9**

## The JavaScript Order of Precedence for Operators

| Operator | Operation | Order of Precedence | Order of Evaluation |
|---|---|---|---|
| ++ | Increment | First | R -> L |
| -- | Decrement | First | R -> L |
| - | Negation | First | R -> L |
| ! | NOT | First | R -> L |
| *, /, % | Multiplication, division, modulus | Second | L -> R |
| +, - | Addition, subtraction | Third | L -> R |
| + | Concatenation | Third | L -> R |
| <, <= | Less than, less than or equal | Fourth | L -> R |
| >, >= | Greater than, greater than or equal | Fourth | L -> R |
| == | Equality | Fifth | L -> R |
| != | Inequality | Fifth | L -> R |
| === | Strict equality | Fifth | L -> R |
| !== | Strict inequality | Fifth | L -> R |
| && | AND | Sixth | L -> R |
| \|\| | OR | Sixth | L -> R |
| ?: | Ternary | Seventh | R -> L |
| = | Assignment | Eighth | R -> L |
| +=, -=, etc. | Arithmetic assignment | Eighth | R -> L |

# Controlling the order of precedence

Sometimes you want to take control of the situation and override the order of precedence. That may seem like a decidedly odd thing to do, so perhaps an example is in order. As you probably know, you calculate the total cost of a retail item by multiplying the retail price by the tax rate and then adding that result to the retail price:

```
Total Price = Retail Price + Retail Price * Tax Rate
```

However, what if you want to reverse this calculation? That is, suppose you know the final price of an item and, given the tax rate, you want to know the original (that is, pre-tax) price. Applying a bit of algebra to the preceding equation, it turns out that you can calculate the original price by dividing the total price by 1 plus the tax rate. So, if the total price is $11.00 and the tax rate is 10 percent, you divide 11 by 1.1 and get an answer of $10.00.

Okay, now I'll convert this calculation to JavaScript code. A first pass at the new equation may look something like this:

```
retailPrice = totalPrice / 1 + taxRate;
```

The following code implements this formula, and Figure 3-5 shows the result (bk04ch03/example24.html):

```
const totalPrice = 11.00;
const taxRate = .1;
const retailPrice = totalPrice / 1 + taxRate;
document.write("The pre-tax price is " + retailPrice);
```

FIGURE 3-5:
The result of
a first stab at
calculating the
pre-tax cost
of an item.

The pre-tax price is 11.1

As Figure 3-3 shows, the result is incorrect. What happened? Well, according to the rules of precedence, JavaScript performs division before addition, so the totalPrice value first is divided by 1 and then is added to the taxRate value, which isn't the correct order.

To get the correct answer, you have to override the order of precedence so that the addition 1 + taxRate is performed first. You override precedence by surrounding that part of the expression with parentheses, as shown in the following code. Using this revised script, you get the correct answer, as shown in Figure 3-6 (bk04ch03/example25.html):

```
const totalPrice = 11.00;
const taxRate = .1;
const retailPrice = totalPrice / (1 + taxRate);
document.write("The pre-tax price is " + retailPrice);
```

FIGURE 3-6:
The revised
script calculates
the pre-tax cost
correctly.

The pre-tax price is 10

**WARNING**

One of the most common mistakes when using parentheses in expressions is to forget to close a parenthetical term with a right parenthesis. To make sure you've closed each parenthetical term, count all the left parentheses and count all the right parentheses. If these totals don't match, you know you've left out a parenthesis.

In general, you can use parentheses to control the order that JavaScript uses to calculate expressions. Terms inside parentheses are always calculated first; terms outside parentheses are calculated sequentially (according to the order of precedence). To gain even more control over your expressions, you can place parentheses inside one another; this is called *nesting* parentheses, and JavaScript always evaluates the innermost set of parentheses first.

Using parentheses to determine the order of calculations allows you to gain full control over JavaScript expressions. This way, you can make sure that the answer given by an expression is the one you want.

Building Expressions

IN THIS CHAPTER

» **Understanding how you control the flow of JavaScript**

» **Setting up your code to make decisions**

» **Understanding code looping**

» **Setting up code loops**

» **Avoiding the dreaded infinite loop**

Chapter **4**

# Controlling the Flow of JavaScript

*A good programmer is someone who always looks both ways before crossing a one-way street.*

—DOUG LINDER

f left to its own devices, the web browser will process HTML and JavaScript code in its default way. Nothing is inherently wrong with that default, but if you stand back and just let the browser do its standard thing, the result will be a standard-issue web page.

The secret to producing beautiful and lively web pages is to wrest control from the web browser and take matters into your own hands. You learn how to break out of the browser's default layout flow in Book 5. Here, I'm talking JavaScript, so you need to learn how to break out of the browser's default script-processing flow.

The default script flow means that the browser processes the code inside a `script` element or an external JavaScript file one statement at a time. The browser reads and then executes the first statement, reads and then executes the second statement, and so on until it has no more JavaScript left to read and execute.

That statement-by-statement flow seems reasonable, but it's extremely limited. What if you want your code to test some condition and then branch to a specific chunk of code depending on the result of that test? What if you want your code to repeat some statements multiple times, with some change occurring in each repetition? Code that runs tests and code that repeats itself all fall under the rubric of controlling the flow of JavaScript. In this chapter, you explore this fascinating and powerful subject.

# Making True/False Decisions
# with if Statements

A smart script performs tests on its environment and then decides what to do next based on the results of each test. For example, suppose you've declared a variable that you later use as a divisor in an expression. You should test the variable before using it in the expression to make sure that the variable's value isn't 0.

The most basic test is the simple true/false decision (which could also be thought of as a yes/no or an on/off decision). In this case, your program looks at a certain condition, determines whether it's currently true or false, and acts accordingly. Comparison and logical expressions (covered in Book 4, Chapter 3) play a big part here because they always return a true or false result.

In JavaScript, simple true/false decisions are handled by the if statement. You can use either the *single-line* syntax:

```
if (expression) statement;
```

or the *block* syntax:

```
if (expression) {
    statement1;
    statement2;
    ...
}
```

In both cases, *expression* is a comparison or logical expression that returns true or false, and *statement(s)* represent the JavaScript statement or statements to run if *expression* returns true. If *expression* returns false, JavaScript skips over the statements.

**TIP**

This is a good place to note that JavaScript defines the following values as the equivalent of `false`: `0`, `""` (that is, the empty string), `null`, and `undefined`. Everything else is the equivalent of `true`.

**REMEMBER**

This is the first time you've encountered JavaScript's braces (`{` and `}`), so take a second to understand what they do because they come up a lot. The braces surround one or more statements that you want JavaScript to treat as a single entity. This entity is a kind of statement itself, so the whole caboodle — the braces and the code they enclose — is called a *block statement*. Also, any JavaScript construction that consists of a statement (such as `if`) followed by a block statement is called a *compound statement*. And, just to keep you on your toes, note that the lines that include the braces don't end with semicolons.

Whether you use the single-line or block syntax depends on the statements you want to run if the *expression* returns a `true` result. If you have only one statement, you can use either syntax. If you have multiple statements, use the block syntax.

**TECHNICAL STUFF**

## A QUICK LOOK AT BLOCK SCOPE

Now that you've been introduced to JavaScript blocks, I'd like to take a brief foray in a concept called block scope. I get into this in much more detail in Book 4, Chapter 5, but for now just know that *scope* specifies where a variable is accessible to other statements in your code. When a variable has *block scope*, it means that the variable is accessible only to other statements within that block. When does a variable have block scope? When the variable is declared using `let` or `const` within a block statement.

For example, consider this section's example code once again, with an extra `document.write` statement tacked on:

```
if (totalSales != 0) {
    const grossMargin = (totalSales - totalExpenses) /
    totalSales;
}
document.write(grossMargin);
```

Here you see that the variable `grossMargin` is declared using `const` within the `if` statement's block. This means that `grossMargin` is *not* accessible outside the block. Therefore, the browser doesn't run the `document.write` statement because it doesn't know what to do with this "undefined" `grossMargin` variable.

Consider the following example (check out bk04ch04/example01.html in this book's example files):

```
if (totalSales != 0) {
    const grossMargin = (totalSales - totalExpenses) /
  totalSales;
}
```

This code assumes that earlier, the script has calculated the total sales and total expenses, which are stored in the totalSales and totalExpenses variables, respectively. The code now calculates the gross margin, which is defined as gross profit (that is, sales minus expenses) divided by sales. The code uses if to test whether the value of the totalSales variable is not equal to zero. If the total-Sales != 0 expression returns true, the grossMargin calculation is executed; otherwise, nothing happens. The if test in this example is righteous because it ensures that the divisor in the calculation — totalSales — is never zero.

## Branching with if. . .else Statements

Using the if statement to make decisions adds a powerful new weapon to your JavaScript arsenal. However, the simple version of if suffers from an important limitation: A false result only bypasses one or more statements; it doesn't execute any of its own. This is fine in many cases, but there will be times when you need to run one group of statements if the condition returns true and a different group if the result is false. To handle these scenarios, you need to use an if... else statement:

```
if (expression) {
    statements-if-true
} else {
    statements-if-false
}
```

The *expression* is a comparison or logical expression that returns true or false. *statements-if-true* represents the block of statements you want JavaScript to run if *expression* returns true, and *statements-if-false* represents the block of statements you want executed if *expression* returns false.

As an example, consider the following code (check out bk04ch04/example02. html):

```
let discountRate;
if (currMonth === "December") {
```

```
        discountRate = 0.2;
    } else {
        discountRate = 0.1;
    }
    const discountedPrice = regularPrice * (1 - discountRate);
```

This code calculates a discounted price of an item, where the discount depends on whether the current month is December. The code assumes that earlier, the script set the value of the current month (currMonth) and the item's regular price (regularPrice). After declaring the discountRate variable, an if...else statement checks whether currMonth equals December. If it does, discountRate is set to 0.2; otherwise, discountRate is set to 0.1. Finally, the code uses the discount-Rate value to calculate discountedPrice.

**TIP**

if...else statements are much easier to read when you indent the statements within each block, as I've done in my examples. This indentation lets you easily identify which block will run if there is a true result and which block will run if the result is false. I find that an indent of four spaces does the job, but many programmers prefer either two spaces or a tab.

The if...else statements are very similar to the ternary operator (?:) that I discuss in Book 4, Chapter 3. In fact, for a very specific subset of if...else statements, the two are identical.

The ?: operator evaluates a comparison expression and then returns one value if the expression is true, or another value if it's false. For example, if you have a variable named currentHour that contains the hour part of the current time of day, consider the following statement:

```
let greeting = currentHour < 12 ? "Good morning!" : "Good day!";
```

If currentHour is less than 12, the string "Good morning!" is stored in the greeting variable; otherwise, the string "Good day!" is stored in the variable. This statement does exactly the same thing as the following if...else statements:

```
let greeting;
if (currentHour < 12) {
    greeting = "Good morning!";
} else {
    greeting = "Good day!";
}
```

The ternary operator version is clearly more efficient, both in terms of total characters typed and total lines used. So any time you find yourself testing a condition only to store something in a variable depending on the result, use a ternary operator statement instead of if...else.

# Making Multiple Decisions

The if...else control structure makes only a single decision. The if part calculates a single logical result and performs one of two actions. However, plenty of situations require multiple decisions before you can decide which action to take.

For example, to calculate the pre-tax price of an item given its total price and its tax rate, you divide the total price by the tax rate plus 1. In real-world web coding, one of your jobs as a developer is to make sure you're dealing with numbers that make sense. What makes sense for a tax rate? Probably that it's greater than or equal to 0 and less than 1 (that is, 100 percent). That's two things to test about any tax rate value in your code, and JavaScript offers multiple ways to handle this kind of thing.

## Using the AND (??) and OR (||) operators

One solution to a multiple-decision problem is to combine multiple comparison expressions in a single if statement. As I discuss in Book 4, Chapter 3, you can combine comparison expressions by using JavaScript's AND (??) and OR (||) operators.

The following code shows an example if statement that combines two comparison expressions using the && operator (bk04ch04/example03.html):

```
if (taxRate >= 0 && taxRate < 1) {
    const retailPrice = totalPrice / (1 + taxRate);
    document.write(retailPrice);
} else {
    document.write("Please enter a tax rate between 0 and 1.");
}
```

The key here is the if statement:

```
if (taxRate >= 0 && taxRate < 1);
```

This tells the browser that only if the taxRate value is greater than or equal to 0 and less than 1 should the statements in the true block be executed. If either one is false (or if both are false), the browser writes the message in the false block instead.

# Stringing together multiple if statements

There is a third syntax for the `if...else` statement that lets you string together as many logical tests as you need using a *multi-block statement* (so-called because it contains multiple `if`/`else` blocks):

```
if (expression1) {
    statements-if-expression1-true
} else if (expression2) {
    statements-if-expression2-true
}
etc.
else {
    statements-if-false
}
```

JavaScript first tests *expression1*. If *expression1* returns `true`, JavaScript runs the block represented by *statements-if-expression1-true* and skips over everything else. If *expression1* returns `false`, JavaScript then tests *expression2*. If *expression2* returns `true`, JavaScript runs the block represented by *statements-if-expression2-true* and skips over everything else. Otherwise, if all the `if` tests return `false`, JavaScript runs the block represented by *statements-if-false*.

The following code shows a script that strings together several `if` statements (bko4cho4/example04.html):

```
let greeting;
if (currentHour < 12) {
    greeting = "Good morning!";
} else if (currentHour < 18) {
    greeting = "Good afternoon!";
} else {
    greeting = "Good evening!";
}
document.write(greeting);
```

The code assumes that earlier in the script, the current hour value was stored in the `currentHour` variable. The first `if` checks whether `currentHour` is less than 12. If so, the string `"Good morning!"` is stored in the `greeting` variable; if not, the next `if` checks whether `currentHour` is less than 18 (that is, less than 6:00 p.m.). If so, `greeting` is assigned the string `"Good afternoon!"`; if not, `greeting` is assigned `"Good evening"`, instead.

# Using the switch statement

Performing multiple tests with `if...else if` is a handy technique — it's a Java-Script tool you'll reach for quite often. However, it quickly becomes unwieldy as the number of tests you need to make gets larger. It's okay for two or three tests, but any more than that makes the logic harder to follow.

For situations in which you need to make a whole bunch of tests (say, four or more), JavaScript's `switch` statement is a better choice. The idea is that you provide an expression at the beginning and then list a series of possible values for that expression. For each possible result — called a *case* — you provide one or more JavaScript statements to execute should the case match the expression. Here's the syntax:

```
switch(expression) {
    case Case1:
        Case1 statements
        break;
    case Case2:
        Case2 statements
        break;
    etc.
    default:
        Default statements
}
```

The *expression* is evaluated at the beginning of the structure. It must return a value (numeric, string, or Boolean). *Case1*, *Case2*, and so on are possible values for *expression*. JavaScript examines each case value to determine whether one matches the result of *expression*. If *expression* returns the *Case1* value, the code represented by *Case1* `statements` is executed, and the `break` statement tells JavaScript to stop processing the rest of the `switch` statement. Otherwise, if *expression* returns the *Case2* value, the code represented by *Case2* `statements` is executed, and JavaScript stops processing the rest of the `switch` statement. Finally, the optional `default` statement is used to handle situations where none of the cases matches *expression*, so JavaScript executes the code represented by *Default* `statements`.

If you do much work with dates in JavaScript, your code is likely to eventually need to figure out how many days are in any month. No built-in JavaScript property or method tells you this, so you need to construct your own code, as shown here (bk04ch04/example05.html):

```javascript
let daysInMonth;
switch(monthName) {
    case "January":
        daysInMonth = 31;
        break;
    case "February":
        if (yearValue % 4 === 0) {
            daysInMonth = 29;
        }
        else {
            daysInMonth = 28;
        }
        break;
    case "March":
        daysInMonth = 31;
        break;
    case "April":
        daysInMonth = 30;
        break;
    case "May":
        daysInMonth = 31;
        break;
    case "June":
        daysInMonth = 30;
        break;
    case "July":
        daysInMonth = 31;
        break;
    case "August":
        daysInMonth = 31;
        break;
    case "September":
        daysInMonth = 30;
        break;
    case "October":
        daysInMonth = 31;
        break;
    case "November":
        daysInMonth = 30;
        break;
    case "December":
        daysInMonth = 31;
}
```

This code assumes that the variable monthName is the name of the month you want to work with, and yearValue is the year. (You need the latter to know when you're dealing with a leap year.) The switch is based on the name of the month:

```
switch(monthName)
```

Then case statements are set up for each month. For example:

```
case "January":
    daysInMonth = 31;
    break;
```

If monthName is "January", this case is true and the daysInMonth variable is set to 31. All the other months are set up the same, with the exception of February:

```
case "February":
    if (yearValue % 4 === 0) {
        daysInMonth = 29;
    }
    else {
        daysInMonth = 28;
    }
    break;
```

Here you need to know whether you're dealing with a leap year, so the modulus (%) operator checks to determine whether yearValue is divisible by four. If so, it's a leap year, so daysInMonth is set to 29; otherwise, it's set to 28.

**TECHNICAL STUFF**

Time geeks will no doubt have their feathers ruffled by my assertion that a year is a leap year if it's divisible by four. In fact, that works only for the years 1901 to 2099, which should take care of most people's needs. The formula doesn't work for 1900 and 2100 because, despite being divisible by 4, these years aren't leap years. The general rule is that a year is a leap year if it's divisible by 4 and it's not divisible by 100, unless it's also divisible by 400.

# Understanding Code Looping

There are some who would say that the only real goal of the programmer should be to get the job done. As long as the code produces the correct result or performs the correct tasks in the correct order, everything else is superfluous. Perhaps, but *real* programmers know that the true goal of programming is not only to get the job done, but to get it done *as efficiently as possible*. Efficient scripts run faster, take less time to code, and are usually (not always, but usually) easier to read and troubleshoot.

One of the best ways to introduce efficiency into your coding is to avoid reinventing too many wheels. For example, consider the following code fragment:

```
let sum = 0;
let num = prompt("Type a number:", 1);
sum += Number(num);
num = prompt("Type a number:", 1);
sum += Number(num);
num = prompt("Type a number:", 1);
sum += Number(num);
document.write("The total of your numbers is " + sum);
```

This code first declares a variable named sum. The code prompts the user for a number (using the prompt method with a default value of 1) that gets stored in the num variable, adds that value to sum, and then repeats this prompt-and-sum routine two more times. (Note my use of the Number function, which ensures that the value returned by prompt is treated as a number rather than a string.) Finally, the sum of the three numbers is displayed to the user.

Besides being a tad useless, this code just reeks of inefficiency because most of the code consists of the following two lines appearing three times:

```
num = prompt("Type a number:", 1);
sum += Number(num);
```

Wouldn't it be more efficient if you put these two statements just once in the code and then somehow get JavaScript to repeat these statements as many times as necessary?

Why, yes, it would, and the good news is that not only is it possible to do this, but JavaScript also gives you a number of different methods to perform this so-called *looping*. I spend the rest of this chapter investigating each of these methods.

# Using while Loops

The most straightforward of the JavaScript loop constructions is the while loop, which uses the following syntax:

```
while (expression) {
    statements
}
```

Here, *expression* is a comparison or logical expression (that is, an expression that returns true or false) that, as long as it returns true, tells JavaScript to keep executing the *statements* within the block.

Essentially, JavaScript interprets a while loop as follows: "Okay, as long as *expression* remains true, I'll keep running through the loop statements, but as soon as *expression* becomes false, I'm out of there."

Here's a closer look at how a while loop works:

1. Evaluate the *expression* in the while statement.

2. If *expression* is true, continue with Step 3; if *expression* is false, skip to Step 5.

3. Execute each of the statements in the block.

4. Return to Step 1.

5. Exit the loop (that is, execute the next statement that occurs after the while block).

The following code demonstrates how to use while to rewrite the inefficient code shown in the previous section (bk04ch04/example06.html):

```
let sum = 0;
let counter = 1;
let num;
while (counter <= 3) {
    num = prompt("Type a number:", 1);
    sum += Number(num);
    counter += 1;
}
document.write("The total of your numbers is " + sum);
```

To control the loop, the code declares a variable named counter and initializes it to 1, which means that the expression counter <= 3 is true, so the code enters the block, does the prompt-and-sum thing, and then increments counter. This is repeated until the third time through the loop, when counter is incremented to 4, at which point the expression counter <= 3 becomes false and the loop is done.

TIP

To make your loop code as readable as possible, always use a two- or four-space indent for each statement in the while block. The same applies to the for and do...while loops that I talk about later in this chapter.

The while statement isn't the greatest loop choice when you know exactly how many times you want to run through the loop. For that, use the for statement, described in the next section. The best use of the while statement is when your script has some naturally occurring condition that you can turn into a comparison expression. A good example is when you're prompting the user for input values. You'll often want to keep prompting the user until they click the Cancel button. The easiest way to set that up is to include the prompt inside a while loop, as shown here (bk04ch04/example07.html):

```
let sum = 0;
let num = prompt("Type a number or click Cancel:", 1);
while (num != null) {
    sum += Number(num);
    num = prompt("Type a number or click Cancel:", 1);
}
document.write("The total of your numbers is " + sum);
```

The first prompt method displays a dialog box like the one shown in Figure 4-1 to get the initial value, and stores it in the num variable.

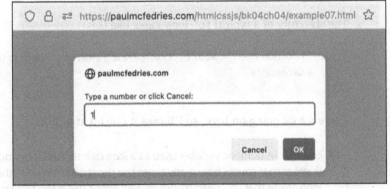

FIGURE 4-1:
Set up your
while expression
so that the
prompting stops
when the user
clicks the Cancel
button.

Then the while statement checks the following expression:

```
num != null
```

Two things can happen here:

» If the user enters a number, this expression returns true and the loop continues. In this case, the value of num is added to the sum variable, and the user is prompted for the next number.

» If the user clicks Cancel, the value returned by prompt is null, so the expression becomes false and the looping stops.

# Using for Loops

Although while is the most straightforward of the JavaScript loops, the most common type by far is the for loop. This fact is slightly surprising when you consider (as you will shortly) that the for loop's syntax is a bit more complex than that of the while loop. However, the for loop excels at one thing: looping when you know exactly how many times you want to repeat a group of statements. This is extremely common in all types of programming, so it's no wonder for is so often used in scripts.

The structure of a typical for loop looks like this:

```
for (let counter = start; counterExpression; counterUpdate) {
    statements
}
```

There's a lot going on here, so I'll take it one bit at a time:

» *counter*: A numeric variable used as a *loop counter*. The loop counter is a number that counts how many times the procedure has gone through the loop. (Note that you need to include let only if this is the first time you've used the variable in the script.)

» *start*: The initial value of *counter*. This value is usually 1, but you can use whatever value makes sense for your script.

» *counterExpression*: A comparison or logical expression that determines the number of times through the loop. This expression usually compares the current value of *counter* to some maximum value.

» *counterUpdate*: An expression that changes the value of *counter*. This expression is evaluated after each turn through the loop. Most of the time, you'll increment the value of counter with the expression *counter* += 1.

» *statements*: The statements you want JavaScript to execute each time through the loop.

When JavaScript stumbles upon the for statement, it changes into its for-loop outfit and follows this seven-step process:

1. Set *counter* equal to *start*.

2. Evaluate the *counterExpression* in the for statement.

3. If *counterExpression* is true, continue with Step 4; if *counterExpression* is false, skip to Step 7.

4. Execute each of the statements in the block.

5. Use *counterUpdate* to increment (or whatever) *counter*.

6. Return to Step 2.

7. Exit the loop (that is, execute the next statement that occurs after the for block).

As an example, the following code shows how to use for to rewrite the inefficient code shown earlier in this chapter (bk04ch04/example08.html):

```
let sum = 0;
let num;
for (let counter = 1; counter <= 3; counter += 1) {
    num = prompt("Type a number:", 1);
    sum += Number(num);
}
document.write("The total of your numbers is " + sum);
```

This is the most efficient version yet because the declaring, initializing, and incrementing of the counter variable all take place within the for statement.

**REMEMBER**

To keep the number of variables declared in a script to a minimum, always try to use the same name in all your for loop counters. The letters i through n traditionally are used for counters in programming. For greater clarity, you may prefer full words, such as count or counter.

**TECHNICAL STUFF**

It's not obvious, but any variable you declare in the for statement (particularly the counter variable) has scope only within the for block.

Here's a slightly more complex example (bk04ch04/example09.html):

```javascript
let sum = 0;
for (let counter = 1; counter < 4; counter += 1) {
    let num;
    let ordinal;
    switch (counter) {
        case 1:
            ordinal = "first";
            break;
        case 2:
            ordinal = "second";
            break;
        case 3:
            ordinal = "third";
    }
    num = prompt("Enter the " + ordinal + " number:", 1);
    sum += Number(num);
}
document.write("The average is " + sum / 3);
```

The purpose of this script is to ask the user for three numbers and then to display the average of those values. The for statement is set up to loop three times. (Note that counter < 4 is the same as counter <= 3.) The first thing the loop block does is use switch to determine the value of the ordinal variable: If counter is 1, ordinal is set to "first"; if counter is 2, ordinal becomes "second"; and so on. These values enable the script to customize the prompt message with each pass through the loop (check out Figure 4-2). With each loop, the user enters a number, and that value is added to the sum variable. When the loop exits, the average is displayed.

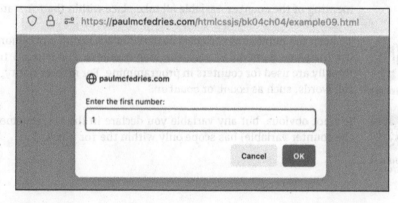

FIGURE 4-2:
This script uses the current value of the counter variable to customize the prompt message.

It's also possible to use for to count down. You do this by using the subtraction assignment operator instead of the addition assignment operator:

```
for (let counter = start; counterExpression; counter -= 1) {
    statements
}
```

In this case, you must initialize the *counter* variable to the maximum value you want to use for the loop counter, and use the *counterExpression* to compare the value of *counter* to the minimum value you want to use to end the loop.

In the following example (bk04ch04/example10.html), I use a decrementing counter to ask the user to rank, in reverse order, their top three CSS colors (refer to Book 3, Chapter 6 for the details on using colors):

```
for (let rank = 3; rank >= 1; rank -= 1) {
    let ordinal;
    let color;
    switch (rank) {
        case 1:
            ordinal = "first";
            break;
        case 2:
            ordinal = "second";
            break;
        case 3:
            ordinal = "third";
    }
    color = prompt("What is your " + ordinal + "-favorite CSS
    color?", "");
    document.write(rank + ". " + color + "<br>");
}
```

The for loop runs by decrementing the rank variable from 3 down to 1. Each iteration of the loop prompts the user to type a favorite CSS color, and that color is written to the page, with the current value of rank being used to create a reverse-ordered list, as shown in Figure 4-3.

FIGURE 4-3:
The
decrementing
value of the rank
variable is used to
create a reverse-
ordered list.

←  →  C        ○ 🔒 ⇌ https://paulmcfedries.com/htmlcssjs/bk04ch04/example10.html

3. papayawhip
2. lemonchiffon
1. chocolate

**TIP**

There's no reason why the `for` loop counter has to be only incremented or decremented. You're actually free to use any expression to adjust the value of the loop counter. For example, suppose you want the loop counter to run through only the odd numbers 1, 3, 5, 7, and 9. Here's a `for` statement that will do that:

```
for (let counter = 1; counter <= 9; counter += 2)
```

The expression `counter += 2` uses the addition assignment operator to tell JavaScript to increase the `counter` variable by 2 each time through the loop.

# Using do...while Loops

JavaScript has a third and final type of loop that I've left until the last because it isn't one that you'll use all that often. To understand when you might use it, consider this code snippet:

```
let sum = 0;
let num = prompt("Type a number or click Cancel:", 1);
while (num != null) {
    sum += Number(num);
    num = prompt("Type a number or click Cancel:", 1);
}
```

The code needs the first `prompt` statement so that the `while` loop's expression can be evaluated. The user may not feel like entering *any* numbers, and they can avoid it by clicking Cancel in the first prompt box so that the loop will be bypassed.

That seems reasonable enough, but what if your code requires that the user enter at least one value? The following presents one way to change the code to ensure that the loop is executed at least once:

```
let sum = 0;
let num = 0;
while (num !== null || sum === 0) {
    num = prompt("Type a number; when you're done, click
  Cancel:", 1);
    sum += Number(num);
}
document.write("The total of your numbers is " + sum);
```

The changes here are that the code initializes both `sum` and `num` as 0. Initializing both to 0 ensures that the `while` expression — num !== null || sum === 0 — returns `true` the first time through the loop, so the loop will definitely execute at least once. If the user clicks Cancel right away, sum will still be 0, so the while expression — num !== null || sum === 0 — still returns true and the loop repeats once again.

This approach works fine, but you can also turn to JavaScript's third loop type, which specializes in just this kind of situation. It's called a do...while loop, and its general syntax looks like this:

```
do {
    statements
}
while (expression);
```

Here, statements represents a block of statements to execute each time through the loop, and expression is a comparison or logical expression that, as long as it returns true, tells JavaScript to keep executing the statements within the loop.

This structure ensures that JavaScript executes the loop's statement block at least once. How? Take a closer look at how JavaScript processes a do...while loop:

1. Execute each of the statements in the block.

2. Evaluate the expression in the while statement.

3. If expression is true, return to Step 1; if expression is false, continue with Step 4.

4. Exit the loop.

For example, the following shows you how to use do...while to restructure the prompt-and-sum code I showed you earlier (bk04ch04/example11.html):

```
let sum = 0;
let num;
do {
    num = prompt("Type a number; when you're done, click
  Cancel:", 1);
    sum += Number(num);
}
while (num !== null || sum === 0);
document.write("The total of your numbers is " + sum);
```

This code is very similar to the while code I show earlier in this section. All that's really changed is that the while statement and its expression have been moved after the statement block so that the loop must be executed once before the expression is evaluated.

# Controlling Loop Execution

Most loops run their natural course, and then the procedure moves on. Sometimes, however, you may want to exit a loop prematurely or skip over some statements and continue with the next pass through the loop. You can handle each situation with, respectively, the break and continue statements.

## Exiting a loop using the break statement

You use break when your loop comes across some value or condition that would either prevent the rest of the statements from executing properly, or that satisfies what the loop was trying to accomplish. The following code demonstrates break with a simple example (bk04ch04/example12.html):

```
let sum = 0;
for (let counter = 1; counter <= 3; counter += 1) {
    let num = prompt("Type a positive number:", 1);
    if (num < 0) {
        sum = 0;
        break;
    }
    sum += Number(num);
}
if (sum > 0) {
    document.write("The average of your numbers is " + sum / 3);
}
```

This script sets up a for loop to prompt the user for positive numbers. For the purposes of this section, the key code is the if test:

```
if (num < 0) {
    sum = 0;
    break;
}
```

If the user enters a negative number, the sum variable is reset to 0 (to prevent the message from being written to the page later in the script). Also, a break statement tells JavaScript to bail out of the loop altogether.

Here's a more complex example (bk04ch04/example13.html):

```
const numberToGuess = Math.ceil(Math.random() * 10);
let promptMessage = "Guess a number between 1 and 10:";
```

```
let totalGuesses = 1;
do {
    const guess = Number(prompt(promptMessage, ""));
    if (guess === 0) {
        break;
    } else if (guess === numberToGuess) {
        document.write ("You guessed it in " + totalGuesses +
            (totalGuesses === 1 ? " try." : " tries."));
        break;
    } else if (guess < numberToGuess) {
        promptMessage = "Sorry, your guess was too low. Try
again:";
    } else {
        promptMessage = "Sorry, your guess was too high. Try
again:";
    }
    totalGuesses += 1;
}
while (true);
```

This script is a game in which a number between 1 and 10 is generated and the user
has to try and guess what it is. The first four lines set up some variables. The head-
scratcher here is the expression for the numberToGuess variable. This expression
uses a couple of methods of the Math object, which I discuss in Book 4, Chapter 8.
For now, suffice it to say that this expression generates a random integer between
(and including) 1 and 10.

Then a do...while loop is set up with the following structure:

```
do {
    statements
}
while (true);
```

This tells JavaScript to run the loop without bothering with a comparison expression. As you'll learn, the loop itself will take care of exiting the loop by using the
break statement.

Next the user is prompted to enter a guess, which is stored in the guess variable.
The script then checks whether guess equals 0, which would mean that the user

clicked Cancel. (Clicking Cancel returns `null`, but the `Number` function converts `null` to 0.) If so, `break` is used to stop the game by exiting the loop:

```
const guess = Number(prompt(promptMessage,""));
if (guess === 0) {
    break;
}
```

Otherwise, a series of `if` statements tests the guessed number against the actual number. The first one checks whether they're the same. If so, a message is written to the page and then another `break` statement exits the loop because the game is finished:

```
else if (guess === numberToGuess) {
    document.write("You guessed it in " + totalGuesses +
        (totalGuesses === 1 ? " try." : " tries."));
    break;
}
```

**TIP**

Notice that the `document.write` statement contains a ternary operator expression:

```
totalGuesses === 1 ? " try." : " tries."
```

This illustrates an extremely common programming situation: You have to display a word to the user, but that word may be either singular or plural depending on the value of some variable or expression. In this case, if `totalGuesses` equals 1, you want to display the word `try` (as in 1 try); if `totalGuesses` is more than 1, you want to display the word `tries` (as in 2 tries). This is what the ternary operator does in the previous code.

The other two tests check whether the guess was lower or higher than the actual number, and a message to that effect is displayed, as shown in Figure 4-4.

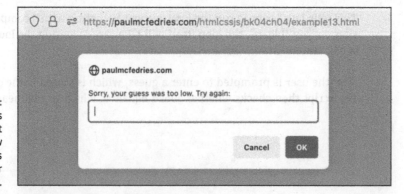

**FIGURE 4-4:**
If you guess wrong, the script lets you know if your guess was too high or too low.

# Bypassing loop statements using the continue statement

The continue statement is similar to break, but instead of exiting a loop entirely, continue tells JavaScript to bypass the rest of the statements in the loop block and begin a new iteration of the loop.

A good use for continue is when you want the user to enter one or more values no matter what. If they click Cancel in the prompt box, you want the script to keep on looping until the user enters the correct number of values. The following code shows one way to do this (bk04ch04/example14.html):

```javascript
let counter = 0;
let sum = 0;
while (counter < 3) {
    const num = prompt("Type a number:", 1);
    if (num === null) {
        continue;
    }
    sum += Number(num);
    counter += 1;
}
document.write("The average of your numbers is " + sum / 3);
```

Because you don't know in advance how many times the code will have to run through the loop, a while loop is a better choice than a for loop. You need to count the number of values entered, however, so a variable named counter is initialized for that purpose. The script requires three numbers, so the while statement is set up to continue looping as long as counter is less than 3. The prompt result is stored in the num variable, which is then tested:

```javascript
if (num === null) {
    continue;
}
```

If the user enters a number, the if expression returns false and the rest of the loop executes: sum is updated and counter is incremented.

However, if the user clicks Cancel, num equals null, so the if expression returns true. What you want here is to keep looping, but you don't want the rest of the loop statements to execute. That's exactly what the continue statement accomplishes.

# Avoiding Infinite Loops

Whenever you use a while, for, or do...while loop, there's always the danger that the loop will never terminate. This is called an *infinite loop*, and it has been the bugbear of programmers for as long as people have been programming. Here are some notes to bear in mind to help you avoid infinite loops:

» The statements in the for block should never change the value of the loop counter variable. If they do, your loop may either terminate prematurely or end up in an infinite loop.

» In while and do...while loops, make sure you have at least one statement within the loop that changes the value of the comparison variable (that is, the variable you use in the loop's comparison statement). Otherwise, the statement may always return true and the loop will never end.

» In while and do...while loops, never rely on the user to enter a specific value to end the loop. They may cancel the prompt box or do something else that prevents the loop from terminating.

» If you have an infinite loop and you're not sure why, insert one or more debugger and console.log statements within the loop statement block to enable you to step through the script one statement at a time and to display the current value of the counter or comparison variable. (Wondering what the heck "debugger" and "console.log" may be? I cover them in Book 4, Chapter 10.) This process enables you to learn what happens to the variable with each pass through the loop.

# Chapter 5

# Harnessing the Power of Functions

*The ability to simplify means to eliminate the unnecessary so that the necessary may speak.*

—HANS HOFMANN

**W**ay back in Book 1, Chapter 1, I introduce two methods: alert() and document.write(). Although not part of the JavaScript standard (they come from separate Web APIs; refer to Book 4, Chapter 6), web browsers make them available so that you can use them in your JavaScript code. Both alert() and document.write() are examples of ready-to-run features that you can use without having to know anything about how they work internally.

When you combine all the built-in JavaScript features with all the Web APIs, you end up with hundreds of actions that perform tasks ranging from the indispensable to the obscure. That might sound like enough to cover every possible action your code may take, but it's not even close. Almost every JavaScript project beyond the simplest scripts will require one or more (usually a lot more) tasks or calculations that aren't part of the JavaScript language or any Web API. What's a coder to do? You roll up your sleeves and then roll your own code that accomplishes the task or runs the calculation.

This chapter shows you how to create such do-it-yourself code. In the pages that follow, you explore the powerful and infinitely useful realm of custom functions, where you craft reusable code that performs tasks that out-of-the-box JavaScript can't do.

# What Is a Function?

A *function* is a group of JavaScript statements that are separate from the rest of the script and that perform a designated task. (Technically, a function can perform any number of chores, but as a general rule it's best to have each function focus on a specific task.) When your script needs to perform that task, you tell it to run — or *execute*, in the vernacular — the function.

Functions are also useful for those times when you need to control exactly when a particular task occurs (if ever). If you just enter some statements between your web page's <script> and </script> tags, the browser runs those statements automatically when the page loads. However, the statements within a function aren't executed by the browser automatically. (There are actually some exceptions to that rule that I mention briefly later in this chapter.) Instead, the function doesn't execute until either your code asks the function to run or some event occurs — such as the user clicking a button — and you've set up your page to run the function in response to that event.

# The Structure of a Function

The basic structure of a function looks like this:

```
function functionName([arguments]) {
    JavaScript statements
}
```

Here's a summary of the various parts of a function:

>> `function`: Identifies the block of code that follows it as a function.

>> *functionName*: A unique name for the function. The naming rules and guidelines that I outline for variables in Book 4, Chapter 2 also apply to function names.

>> *arguments*: One or more values that are passed to the function and that act as variables within the function. Arguments (or *parameters,* as they're sometimes called) are typically one or more values that the function uses as the raw materials for its tasks or calculations. You always enter arguments between parentheses after the function name, and you separate multiple arguments with commas. If you don't use arguments, you must still include the parentheses after the function name.

>> *JavaScript statements*: This is the code that performs the function's tasks or calculations.

**TIP**

Notice how the *JavaScript statements* line in the example is indented slightly from the left margin. This is a standard and highly recommended programming practice because it makes your code easier to read. This example is indented four spaces, which is enough to do the job but isn't excessive. Some programmers use two spaces, and others indent using a single tab.

Note, too, the use of braces ({ and }). These are used to enclose the function's statements within a block, which tells you (and the browser) where the function's code begins and ends. There are only two rules for where these braces appear:

>> The opening brace must appear after the function's parentheses and before the first function statement.

>> The closing brace must appear after the last function statement.

No set-in-stone rule exists that specifies exactly where the braces appear. The positions used in the previous function syntax are the traditional ones, but you're free to try other positions if you want. For example:

```
function functionName([arguments])
{
    JavaScript statements
}
```

# Where Do You Put a Function?

For most applications, it doesn't matter where you put your functions, as long as they reside within a `<script>` block. However, one of the most common uses of functions is to handle events when they're triggered. A particular event may fire when the page is loading, and if that happens before the browser has parsed the corresponding function, you could get strange results or an error. To prevent that possibility, good practice is to place the script containing all your functions within the page's header section (or within an external JavaScript file).

Note, as well, that you can add as many functions as you want within a single `<script>` block, but make sure that each function has a unique name. In fact, all the functions that exist in or are referenced by a page must have unique names.

# Calling a Function

After your function is defined, you'll eventually need to tell the browser to execute — or *call* — the function. There are three main ways to do this:

>> When the browser parses the `<script>` tag

>> After the page is loaded

>> In response to an event, such as the user clicking a button

The next three sections cover each of these scenarios.

## Calling a function when the `<script>` tag is parsed

The simplest way to call a function is to include in your script a statement consisting of only the function name, followed by parentheses (assuming for the moment that your function uses no arguments.) The following code (check out bk04ch05/exaample01.html in this book's example files) provides an example. (I've listed the entire page to show you where the function and the statement that calls it appear in the page code.)

```
<!DOCTYPE html>
<html lang="en">
<head>
    <meta charset="utf-8">
```

```
    <title>Calling a function when the &lt;script&gt; tag is
parsed</title>
    <script>
        function displayGreeting() {
            const currentHour = new Date().getHours();
            if (currentHour < 12) {
                console.log("Good morning!");
            } else {
                console.log("Good day!");
            }
        }
        displayGreeting();
    </script>
</head>
<body>
</body>
</html>
```

The `<script>` tag includes a function named `displayGreeting`, which determines the current hour of the day and then writes a greeting to the console (check out Figure 5-1) based on whether it's currently morning. The function is called by the `displayGreeting` statement that appears just after the function.

**REMEMBER**

The console is part of each web browser's developer tools. You use the console to display messages (as in this section's example), run JavaScript code on the fly, and look for script error messages. You learn all about the console in Book 4, Chapter 10.

**TIP**

To display the console in most web browsers, right-click the web page, click Inspect (or press Ctrl+Shift+I in Windows or Option+⌘+I in macOS), and then click the Console tab.

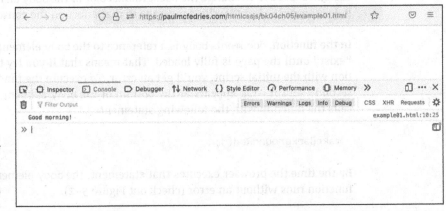

**FIGURE 5-1:**
An example of calling a function when the `<script>` tag is parsed.

# Calling a function after the page is loaded

If your function references a page element, then calling the function from within the page's head section won't work because when the browser parses the script, the rest of the page hasn't loaded yet, so your element reference will fail.

To work around this problem, place another <script> tag at the end of the body section, just before the closing </body> tag, as shown here (check out bk04ch05/example02.html):

```html
<!DOCTYPE html>
<html lang="en">
<head>
    <meta charset="utf-8">
    <title>Calling a function after the page is loaded</title>
    <script>
        function makeBackgroundRed() {
            document.body.style.backgroundColor = "red";
            console.log("The background is now red.");
        }
    </script>
</head>
<body>
    <!-- Other body elements go here -->

    <script>
        makeBackgroundRed();
    </script>
</body>
</html>
```

The makeBackgroundRed function does two things: It uses document.body.style.backgroundColor to change the background color of the body element to red, and it uses console.log to write a message to that effect on the console.

In the function, document.body is a reference to the body element, which doesn't "exist" until the page is fully loaded. That means that if you try to call the function with the initial script, you'll get an error. To execute the function properly, a second <script> tag appears at the bottom of the body element, and that script calls the function with the following statement:

```
makeBackgroundRed();
```

By the time the browser executes that statement, the body element exists, so the function runs without an error (check out Figure 5-2).

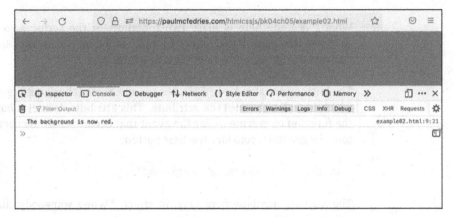

FIGURE 5-2:
An example of
calling a function
after the page
has loaded.

The background is now red.                                    example02.html:9:21

## Calling a function in response to an event

One of the most common ways that JavaScript functions are called is in response to some event. Events are is such an important topic that I devote a big chunk of Book 4, Chapter 6 to them. For now, check out a relatively straightforward application: executing the function when the user clicks a button. The following code shows one way to do it (bk04ch05/example03.html):

```
<!DOCTYPE html>
<html lang="en">
<head>
    <meta charset="utf-8">
    <title>Calling a function in response to an event</title>
    <script>
        function makeBackgroundRed() {
            document.body.style.backgroundColor= "red";
        }

        function makeBackgroundWhite() {
            document.body.style.backgroundColor= "white";
        }
    </script>
</head>
<body>
    <button onclick="makeBackgroundRed()">
        Make Background Red
    </button>
    <button onclick="makeBackgroundWhite()">
        Make Background White
    </button>
</body>
</html>
```

What I've done here is place two functions in the script: makeBackgroundRed changes the page background to red, as before, and makeBackgroundWhite changes the background color back to white.

The buttons are standard HTML button elements (check out Figure 5-3), each of which includes the onclick attribute. This attribute defines a *handler* — that is, the function to execute — for the event that occurs when the user clicks the button. For example, consider the first button:

```
<button onclick="makeBackgroundRed()">
```

The onclick attribute here says, in effect, "When somebody clicks this button, call the function named makeBackgroundRed."

**WARNING**

The example I've used here is a tad old-fashioned in that it defines the event handler inside an HTML tag, which is now considered bad programming practice. The modern way is to set up an event listener using JavaScript. I show you a revised version of this example that uses an event listener later in this chapter (that would be the section "Getting Your Head around Anonymous Functions"). I talk more about event listeners in Book 4, Chapter 6.

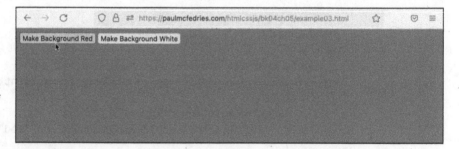

**FIGURE 5-3:**
An example of calling a function in response to an event.

# Passing Values to Functions

One of the main reasons to use functions is to gain control over when some chunk of JavaScript code gets executed. The previous section, for example, discusses how easy it is to use functions to set things up so that code doesn't run until the user clicks a button.

However, there's another major reason to use functions: to avoid repeating code unnecessarily. To understand what I mean, consider the two functions from the previous section:

```
function makeBackgroundRed() {
    document.body.style.backgroundColor= "red";
}
function makeBackgroundWhite() {
    document.body.style.backgroundColor= "white";
}
```

These functions perform the same task — changing the background color — and the only difference between them is that one changes the color to red and the other changes it to white. Whenever you end up with two or more functions that do essentially the same thing, you know that your code is inefficient.

So how do you make the code more efficient? That's where the arguments mentioned earlier come into play. An *argument* is a value that is "sent" — or *passed*, in programming terms — to the function. The argument acts just like a variable, and it automatically stores whatever value is sent.

## Passing a single value to a function

As an example, you can take the previous two functions, reduce them to a single function, and set up the color value as an argument. Here's a new function that does just that:

```
function changeBackgroundColor(newColor) {
    document.body.style.backgroundColor = newColor;
}
```

The argument is named newColor and is added between the parentheses that occur after the function name. JavaScript declares newColor as a variable automatically, so you don't need a separate let or const statement. The function then uses the newColor value to change the background color. So how do you pass a value to the function? The following code presents a sample file that does so (bk04ch05/example04.html):

```
<!DOCTYPE html>
<html lang="en">
<head>
    <meta charset="utf-8">
    <title>Passing a single value to a function</title>
    <script>
        function changeBackgroundColor(newColor) {
            document.body.style.backgroundColor = newColor;
        }
```

```
        </script>
    </head>
    <body>
        <button onclick="changeBackgroundColor('red')">
            Make Background Red
        </button>
        <button onclick="changeBackgroundColor('white')">
            Make Background White
        </button>
    </body>
</html>
```

The key here is the `onclick` attribute that appears in both `<button>` tags. For example:

```
onclick="changeBackgroundColor('red')"
```

The string `'red'` is inserted into the parentheses after the function name, so that value is passed to the function itself. The other button passes the value `'white'`, and the function result changes accordingly.

**WARNING**

In the two `onclick` attributes in the example code, notice that the values passed to the function are enclosed in single quotation marks ('). This is necessary because the `onclick` value as a whole is enclosed in double quotation marks (").

## Passing multiple values to a function

For more complex functions, you may need to use multiple arguments so that you can pass different kinds of values. If you use multiple arguments, separate each one with a comma, like this:

```
function changeColors(newBackColor, newForeColor) {
    document.body.style.backgroundColor = newBackColor;
    document.body.style.color = newForeColor;
}
```

In this function, the `document.body.style.color` statement changes the foreground color (that is, the color of the page text). The following code shows a revised page where the buttons pass two values to the function (bk04ch05/example05. html):

```
<!DOCTYPE html>
<html lang="en">
```

```
<head>
    <meta charset="utf-8">
    <title>Passing multiple values to a function</title>
    <script>
        function changeColors(newBackColor, newForeColor) {
            document.body.style.backgroundColor = newBackColor;
            document.body.style.color = newForeColor;
        }
    </script>
</head>
<body>
    <h1>Passing Multiple Values to a Function</h1>
    <button onclick="changeColors('red', 'white')">
        Red Background, White Text
    </button>
    <button onclick="changeColors('white', 'red')">
        White Background, Red Text
    </button>
</body>
</html>
```

**WARNING**

If you define a function to have multiple arguments, you must always pass values for each of those arguments to the function. If you don't, the "value" undefined is passed, instead, which can cause problems.

**TECHNICAL
STUFF**

If you use a variable to pass data to a function, only the current value of that variable is sent, not the variable itself. Therefore, if you change the value of the argument within the function, the value of the original variable isn't changed. Here's an example:

```
let passThis = 10;
function sendMe(acceptThis) {
    acceptThis = 5;
}
sendMe(passThis);
console.log(passThis);
```

The variable passThis starts off with a value of 10. The function sendMe is defined to accept an argument named acceptThis and to change the value of that argument to 5. sendMe is called and the value of the passThis variable is passed to it. Then a console.log statement displays the value of passThis. If you run this code, the displayed value will be 10, the original value of passThis. In other words, changing the value of acceptThis within the function had no effect on the value of the passThis variable.

## A QUICK LOOK AT REST PARAMETERS

Most of the time you'll know exactly how many arguments a function requires, but every now and then you'll need a bit more flexibility. For example, a function may take two arguments most of the time, but in certain situations, your script may need to pass three, four, or even a dozen arguments. How can you handle these scenarios? By applying the rest operator (. . .) to the last function argument:

```
function myFunction(argA, argB, ...moreArgs) {
    JavaScript statements
}
```

Now consider the following function calls:

```
myFunction("eeny", "meeny");
myFunction("eeny", "meeny", "miney", "mo");
```

In the first call, the two passed values are stored as expected in the function's argA and argB parameters. In the second call, the first two passed values are stored in the argA and argB parameters, but the next two are stored in the moreArgs parameter as an array (refer to Book 4, Chapter 7 to find out how to work with arrays).

Note that rest parameters came into JavaScript with ECMAScript 2015 (ES6), so don't use them if you're in the unfortunate position of having to support ancient web browsers (such as Internet Explorer 11).

## Making an argument optional

In most of your functions, the arguments will be required and the function will fail in some way if it's called without including all the arguments. However, making an argument optional is not unusual. Your function may still require some kind of value to produce the correct result, but you can specify a default value to use if the argument isn't included in the function call.

For example, consider the following function that calculates a tip:

```
function calculateTip(preTip, tipPercent) {
    const tipResult = preTip * tipPercent;
    return tipResult;
}
```

And here's an example call:

```
calculateTip(100, 0.15);
```

If you usually tip 15 percent, it would be nice if you didn't have to always specify the tipPercent argument with each function call. You can set that up — that is, you can make the tipPercent argument optional — by setting the tipPercent argument to a default value, like so:

```
function calculateTip(preTip, tipPercent = 0.15) {
    const tipResult = preTip * tipPercent;
    return tipResult;
}
```

Now you can call this function like so:

```
calculateTip(100);
```

JavaScript notices the missing tipPercent argument, so it uses the default value of 0.15 for the calculation.

TIP

If your function has multiple optional arguments, how do you skip one of the middle arguments when you call the function? Excellent question! Here's an example of such a function where the second and third arguments are optional:

```
function addEmUp(argA, argB = 10, argC = 15) {
    return argA + argB + argC;
}
```

How do you skip just the second argument in a function call? You pass the value undefined, like this:

```
addEmUp(100, undefined, 200);
```

REMEMBER

Specifying a default value to make a function argument optional is an ES6 (ECMAScript 2015) feature, so avoid it if you have to support way-past-their-prime browsers such as Internet Explorer 11.

# Returning a Value from a Function

So far, I've outlined two major advantages of using functions:

>> You can use them to control when code is executed.

>> You can use them to consolidate repetitive code into a single routine.

The third major benefit that functions bring to the JavaScript table is that you can use them to perform calculations and then return the result. As an example, here's a function that calculates the tip on a restaurant bill (bko4cho5/example06.html):

```
function calculateTip(preTip, tipPercent) {
    const tipResult = preTip * tipPercent;
    return tipResult;
}

const preTipTotal = 100.00;
const tipPercentage = 0.15;
const tipCost = calculateTip(preTipTotal, tipPercentage);
const totalBill = preTipTotal + tipCost;
document.write("Your total bill is $" + totalBill);
```

The function named `calculateTip` takes two arguments: `preTip` is the total of the bill before the tip, and `tipPercent` is the percentage used to calculate the tip. The function then declares a variable named `tipResult` and uses it to store the calculation — `preTip` multiplied by `tipPercent`. The key for this example is the second line of the function:

```
return tipResult;
```

The `return` statement is JavaScript's way of sending a value *back* to the statement that called the function. That statement comes after the function:

```
tipCost = calculateTip(preTipTotal, tipPercentage);
```

This statement first passes the value of `preTipTotal` (initialized as `100.00` earlier in the script) and `tipPercentage` (initialized as `0.15` earlier) to the `calculateTip` function. When that function returns its result, the entire expression `calculateTip(preTipTotal, tipPercentage)` is replaced by that result, meaning that it gets stored in the `tipCost` variable. Then `preTipTotal` and `tipCost` are added together, the result is stored in `totalBill`, and a `document.write` statement displays the final calculation (check out Figure 5-4).

FIGURE 5-4:
The output
includes the
return value
of the custom
function
calculation.

https://paulmcfedries.com/htmlcssjs/bk04ch05/example06.html

Your total bill is $115

# Getting Your Head around Anonymous Functions

Here's another look at the function syntax from earlier in this chapter:

```
function functionName([arguments]) {
    JavaScript statements
}
```

This version of function syntax creates a so-called *named function* because — you guessed it — the function has a name.

However, creating a function that doesn't have a name is also possible:

```
function ([arguments]) {
    JavaScript statements
}
```

This variety of function syntax creates a so-called *anonymous function* because — that's right — the function has no name.

Why use anonymous functions? Well, first, you don't have to if you don't want to. Second, the main reason to use anonymous functions is to avoid creating a named object when you don't need to. Every large web project has a huge *namespace*, which refers to the full collection of identifiers you assign to things like variables and functions. The larger the namespace, the greater the chance of a *namespace collision*, where you use the same identifier for two different things. Bad news!

**REMEMBER**

Anonymous functions were introduced in ES6, so don't use them if you need to support very old browsers, such as Internet Explorer 11.

If you have a function that will be used only once in your project, it's considered good modern programming practice to make that an anonymous function so that you have one less identifier in your namespace.

Okay, I hear you thinking, earlier you said we invoke a function by using the function name. If an anonymous function has no name, how are we supposed to run it? Excellent question! There are two main methods to look at:

» Assigning the function to a variable

» Replacing a function call with the function itself

## Assigning an anonymous function to a variable

Once again, here's the example code from the previous section:

```
const preTipTotal = 100.00;
const tipPercentage = 0.15;

function calculateTip(preTip, tipPercent) {
    const tipResult = preTip * tipPercent;
    return (tipResult);
}

const tipCost = calculateTip(preTipTotal, tipPercentage);
const totalBill = preTipTotal + tipCost;
document.write("Your total bill is $" + totalBill);
```

This code defines the named function calculateTip() and later uses the tipCost variable to store the function result. This is a perfect example of when a named function is not needed because you only ever use the named function to calculate the tipCost value. Adding an identity to the namespace when you don't have to is called *polluting* the namespace, and it's a big no-no in modern JavaScript programming.

You can rewrite this code to use an anonymous function instead (bk04ch05/ example07.html):

```
const preTipTotal = 100.00;
const tipPercentage = 0.15;

// Declare tipCost using an anonymous function
const tipCost = function (preTip, tipPercent) {
    const tipResult = preTip * tipPercent;
    return (tipResult);
}
```

```
const totalBill = preTipTotal + tipCost(preTipTotal,
    tipPercentage);
document.write("Your total bill is $" + totalBill);
```

The big change here is that now I declare the value of the `tipCost` variable to be an anonymous function. That anonymous function is the same as the `calculate Tip()` named function from before, just without the name. In the second-last statement, I invoke the anonymous function by using `tipCost(preTipTotal, tipPercentage)`.

# Replacing a function call with an anonymous function

One of the most common uses for anonymous functions is when you need to pass a function as an argument to another function. The passed function is known as a *callback* function.

First, here's an example that uses named functions (bk04ch05/example08.html):

```
<body>
    <button id="bgRed">
        Make Background Red
    </button>
    <button id="bgWhite">
        Make Background White
    </button>
    <script>
        function makeBackgroundRed() {
            document.body.style.backgroundColor= 'red';
        }

        function makeBackgroundWhite() {
            document.body.style.backgroundColor= 'white';
        }
        document.getElementById('bgRed').addEventListener(
            'click',
            makeBackgroundRed
        );
        document.getElementById('bgWhite').addEventListener(
            'click',
            makeBackgroundWhite
        );
    </script>
</body>
```

The script declares two named functions: makeBackgroundRed() and makeBackgroundWhite(). The code then creates two event listeners. One of them listens for clicks on the button that has the id value bgRed and, when a click is detected, runs the makeBackgroundRed() callback function. The other event listener listens for clicks on the button that has the id value bgWhite and, when a click is detected, runs the makeBackgroundWhite() callback function. Refer to Book 4, Chapter 6 to get the details on the document object and the getElementById() and addEventListener() methods.

Again, you have two functions that don't need to be named, so you can remove them from the namespace by replacing the callbacks with anonymous functions. Here's the revised code (bk04ch05/example09.html):

```
<body>
    <button id="bgRed">
        Make Background Red
    </button>
    <button id="bgWhite">
        Make Background White
    </button>
    <script>
        document.getElementById('bgRed').addEventListener(
            'click',
            function() {
                document.body.style.backgroundColor= 'red';
            }
        );
        document.getElementById('bgWhite').addEventListener(
            'click',
            function() {
                document.body.style.backgroundColor= 'white';
            }
        );
    </script>
</body>
```

# Moving to Arrow Functions

As you progress in JavaScript, you'll find yourself using anonymous functions constantly. When you get to that stage, you'll be happy to know that ES6 also offers a simpler anonymous function syntax. That is, instead of using this:

```
function ([arguments]) {
    JavaScript statements
}
```

you can use this:

```
([arguments]) => {
    JavaScript statements
}
```

All I've done here is remove the function keyword and replaced it with the characters = and › between the arguments and the opening brace. The characters => look like an arrow (JavaScripters call it a *fat arrow*), so this version of the syntax is known as an *arrow function*.

**REMEMBER**

Arrow functions are an ES6 invention, so don't use them if you need to support very old browsers, such as Internet Explorer 11.

For example, here's an anonymous function from a bit earlier (the "Assigning an anonymous function result to a variable" section):

```
// Declare tipCost using an anonymous function
const tipCost = function (preTip, tipPercent) {
    const tipResult = preTip * tipPercent;
    return (tipResult);
}
```

You can rewrite this using an arrow function (bk04ch05/example10.html):

```
// Declare tipCost using an arrow function
const tipCost = (preTip, tipPercent) => {
    const tipResult = preTip * tipPercent;
    return (tipResult);
}
```

If your anonymous function consists of a single statement, you can take advantage of an arrow function feature called *implicit return*:

```
([arguments]) => statement
```

Here, JavaScript assumes that a single-statement function means that the function returns right after executing the statement, so you can leave out the braces and the `return` keyword. Here's an example:

```javascript
// Declare tipCost using an arrow function with implicit return
const tipCost = (preTip, tipPercent) => preTip * tipPercent;
```

Similarly, here's one of the anonymous callback functions from the previous section:

```javascript
document.getElementById('bgRed').addEventListener(
    'click',
    function() {
        document.body.style.backgroundColor= 'red';
    }
);
```

You can rewrite this code as follows to use an arrow function with implicit return (bk04ch05/example11.html):

```javascript
document.getElementById('bgRed').addEventListener(
    'click',
    () => document.body.style.backgroundColor= 'red'
);
```

# Running Functions in the Future

In the scripts I've presented so far in this book, the code has executed in one of three ways:

>> Automatically when the page loads

>> When your script calls a function

>> In response to some event, such as the user clicking a button

JavaScript also offers a fourth execution method that's based on time. There are two possibilities:

>> Have some code run once after a specified number of milliseconds. This is called a *timeout*.

>> Have some code run after a specified number of milliseconds, and then repeat each time that number of milliseconds expires. This is called an *interval*.

The next couple of sections show you how to set up both procedures.

## Using a timeout to perform a future action once

To set up a JavaScript timeout, use the setTimeout() method:

```
setTimeout(function, delay, arg1, arg2, ...)
```

>> *function:* The anonymous or named function that you want JavaScript to run when the timeout expires. Instead of a function, you can also use a JavaScript statement, surrounded by quotation marks.

>> *delay:* The number of milliseconds that JavaScript waits before executing *function*.

>> *arg1, arg2, ...:* Optional arguments to pass to *function*.

Note that setTimeout() returns a value that uniquely identifies the timeout. You can store this value just in case you want to cancel the timeout (as described later in this section).

Here's some code that shows how setTimeout() works (bk04ch05/example12. html):

```
// Create a message
const str = "Hello World!";

// Set the timeout
const timeoutId = setTimeout(function (msg) {
    document.write(msg);
}, 5000, str);
```

The script begins by creating a message string and storing it in the str variable. Then the setTimeout() method tells JavaScript to run an anonymous function after five seconds (5,000 milliseconds) have elapsed, and to pass the str variable to that function. The anonymous function takes the msg argument and displays it on the page with document.write().

If you've set up a timeout and then decide that you don't want the code to execute after all for some reason, you can cancel the timeout by running the clearTimeout() method:

```
clearTimeout(id)
```

>> *id:* The name of the variable that was used to store the setTimeout() method's return value

For example, suppose you set a timeout with the following statement:

```
const timeoutId = setTimeout(function (msg) {
    document.write(msg);
}, 5000, str);
```

You'd cancel the timeout using the following statement:

```
clearTimeout(timeoutId);
```

## Using an interval to perform a future action repeatedly

Running code once after a specified number of seconds is only an occasionally useful procedure. A much more practical skill is being able to repeat code at a specified interval. Doing so enables you to set up countdowns, timers, animations, image slide shows, and more. To set up an interval, use the setInterval() method:

```
setInterval(function, delay, arg1, arg2, ...)
```

>> *function:* The anonymous or named function that you want JavaScript to run at the end of each interval. Instead of a function, you can also use a JavaScript statement, surrounded by quotation marks.

>> *delay:* The number of milliseconds in each interval, after which JavaScript executes *function.*

>> *arg1, arg2, ...:* Optional arguments to pass to *function.*

As with setTimeout(), the setInterval() method returns a value that uniquely identifies the interval. You use that value to cancel the interval with the clearInterval() method:

```
clearInterval(id);
```

>> *id:* The name of the variable that was used to store the setInterval() method's return value

For example, suppose you set an interval with the following statement:

```
const intervalId = setInterval(countdown, 5000);
```

You'd cancel the interval using the following statement:

```
clearInterval(intervalId);
```

Note that although the clearTimeout() method is optional with setTimeout(), you should always use clearInterval() with setInterval(). Otherwise, the interval will just keep executing.

The following code demonstrates both setInterval() and clearInterval() (bk04ch05/example13.html):

```
let counter = 10;

// Set the interval
const intervalId = setInterval(function () {

    // Display the countdown and then decrement the counter
    document.open();
    document.write(counter);
    counter -= 1;

    // Cancel the interval after we hit 0
    if (counter < -1) {
        clearInterval(intervalId);
        document.open();
        document.write("All done!");
    }
}, 1000);
```

The purpose of this script is to display a countdown from 10 to 0 on the page. The script begins by declaring a variable named counter and initializing it to 10. Then the setInterval() method sets up an anonymous function to run at intervals of one second (1,000 milliseconds). The anonymous function clears the page using document.open, displays the current value of counter on the page, and decrements counter. Then an if test checks the value of counter. If it's negative, it means that counter was just 0, so it's done. The clearInterval() method cancels the interval, and then a final message is written to the page.

# Understanding Variable Scope

In programming, the *scope* of a variable defines where in the script a variable can be used and where it can't be used. To put it another way, a variable's scope determines which statements and functions can access and work with the variable. There are two main reasons you need to be concerned with scope:

» **You may want to use the same variable name in multiple functions.** If these variables are otherwise unrelated, you'll want to make sure that there is no confusion about which variable you're working with. In other words, you'll want to restrict the scope of each variable to the block or function in which it is declared.

» **You may need to use the same variable in multiple blocks or functions.** For example, a function may use a variable to store the results of a calculation, and other functions may also need to use that result. In this case, you'll want to set up the scope of the variable so that it's accessible to multiple functions.

JavaScript lets you establish three types of scope for your variables:

» Block scope

» Function scope

» Global scope

The next three sections describe each type in detail.

## Working with block scope

When a variable has *block scope*, it means that the variable was declared using let or const inside a statement block — that is, between a set of braces: { and } — and the only statements that can access the variable are the ones within that same block. Statements outside the block and statements in other blocks can't access the variable (bk04ch05/example14.html):

```
if (true) {
    const myMessage = "I'm in the scope!";
    console.log("Inside the if block: " + myMessage);
}
console.log("Outside the if block: " + myMessage);
```

This code uses an `if` construction to create a statement block. Inside that block, the code declares a variable named `myMessage`, sets its value to a text string, and uses JavaScript's `console.log()` method to display the string in the console.

After the `if` block, another `console.log` statement attempts to display the `myMessage` variable. However, as shown in Figure 5-5, JavaScript generates an error that says `myMessage is not defined`. Why? Because the scope of the `myMessage` variable extends only to the `if` block. Statements outside that block can't "see" the `myMessage` variable, so it has nothing to display. In fact, after the `if` statement finishes executing, JavaScript removes the `myMessage` variable from memory entirely, so that's why the `myMessage` variable referred to the final line is undefined.

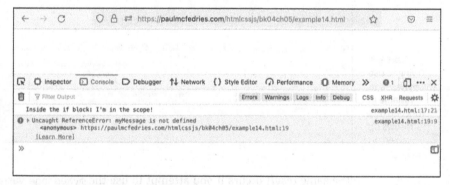

FIGURE 5-5: Attempting to display the myMessage variable outside the if block results in an error.

# Working with function scope

When a variable has *function scope* (often also known as *local* scope), it means that the variable was declared inside a function and the only statements that can access the variable are the ones in that same function. Statements outside the function and statements in other functions can't access the variable.

The following code demonstrates function scope (bk04ch05/example15.html):

```
function A() {
    const myMessage = "I'm in the scope!";
    console.log("Function A: " + myMessage);
```

```
}
function B() {
    console.log("Function B: " + myMessage);
}
A();
B();
```

There are two functions here, named A() and B(). Function A() declares a variable named myMessage, sets its value to a text string, and uses JavaScript's console.log() method to display the string in the console.

Function B() also uses console.log to attempt to display the myMessage variable. As shown in Figure 5-6, JavaScript generates an error that says myMessage is not defined. Why? Because the scope of the myMessage variable extends only to function A(); function B() can't "see" the myMessage variable, which was removed from memory as soon as function A() finished executing.

FIGURE 5-6:
Trying to use
the myMessage
variable in
function B()
throws up
an error.

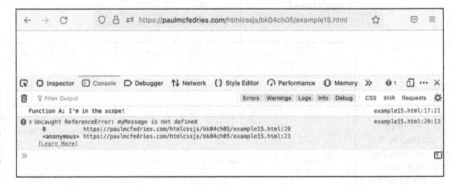

The same result occurs if you attempt to use the myMessage variable outside any function, as in the following code:

```
function A() {
    const myMessage = "I'm in the scope!";
    console.log("Function A: " + myMessage);
}
A();
// The following statement generates an error:
console.log(myMessage);
```

# Working with global scope

What if you want to use the same variable in multiple functions or even in multiple script blocks within the same page? In that case, you need to use *global* scope, which makes a variable accessible to any statement or function on a page. (That's why global scope is also called *page-level* scope.) To set up a variable with global scope, declare it outside any block or function. The following code gives this a whirl (bk04ch05/example16.html):

```
const myMessage = "I've got global scope!";

if (true) {
    console.log("Inside the if block: " + myMessage);
}
function C() {
    console.log("Function C: " + myMessage);
}
C();
console.log("Outside any block or function: " + myMessage);
```

The script begins by declaring the myMessage variable and setting it equal to a string literal. Then an if block uses a console.log statement to attempt to display the myMessage value. Next, a function named C() is created and displays a console message that attempts to display the value of myMessage. After the function is called, another console.log statement attempts to display the myMessage value outside any block or function. Figure 5-7 shows the results: All three console.log statements display the value of myMessage without a problem.

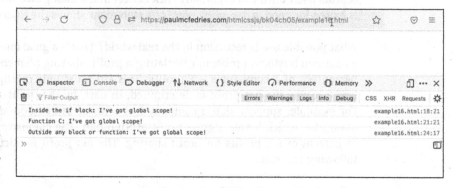

**FIGURE 5-7:**
When you declare a global variable, you can access its value both inside and outside any block or function.

# Using Recursive Functions

One of the stranger things you can do with a function is to have it execute itself. That is, you place a statement within the function that calls the function. This is called *recursion*, and such a function is called a *recursive function*.

Before trying out a practical example, here's a simple script that demonstrates the basic procedure (bk04ch05/example17.html):

```
let counter = 0;
addOne();

function addOne() {
    counter += 1;
    if (confirm("counter is now " + counter + ". Add another
  one?")) {
        addOne();
    }
}

document.write("Counter ended up at " + counter);
```

The script begins by declaring a variable named counter and initializing it to 0. Then a function named addOne() is called. This function increments the value of counter. It then displays the current value of counter and asks if you want to add another. If you click OK, the addOne() function is called again, but this time it's called from within addOne() itself! This just means that the whole thing repeats itself until you eventually click Cancel in the dialog box. After the function is exited for good, a document.write() statement shows the final counter total.

What possible use is recursion in the real world? That's a good question. Consider a common business problem: calculating a profit-sharing plan contribution as a percentage of a company's net profits. This isn't a simple multiplication problem, because the net profit is determined, in part, by the profit-sharing figure. For example, suppose that a company has sales of $1,000,000 and expenses of $900,000, which leaves a gross profit of $100,000. The company also sets aside 10 percent of net profits for profit sharing. The net profit is calculated with the following formula:

```
Net Profit = Gross Profit - Profit Sharing Contribution;
```

That looks straightforward enough, but it's really not because the Profit Sharing Contribution value is derived with the following formula:

```
Profit Sharing Contribution = Net Profit * 10%;
```

In other words, the Net Profit value appears on both sides of the equation, which complicates things considerably.

One way to solve the Net Profit formula is to guess at an answer and calculate how close you come. For example, because profit sharing should be 10 percent of net profits, a good first guess may be 10 percent of *gross* profits, or $10,000. If you plugged this number into the Net Profit formula, you get a value of $90,000. This wouldn't be right, however, because you'd end up with a profit sharing value — 10 percent of $90,000 — of $9,000. Therefore, the original profit-sharing guess would be off by $1,000.

So, you can try again. This time, use $9,000 as the profit-sharing number. Plugging this new value into the Net Profit formula returns a value of $91,000. This number translates into a profit-sharing contribution of $9,100. This time, you're off by only $100, so you're getting closer.

If you continue this process, your profit-sharing guesses will get closer to the calculated value. (This process is called *convergence*.) When the guesses are close enough (for example, within a dollar), you can stop and pat yourself on the back for finding the solution.

This process of calculating a formula and then continually recalculating it using different values is what recursion is all about, so now I show you how to go about writing a script that runs recursively. Check out the following code (bk04ch05/example18.html):

```
const profitSharingPercent = 0.1;
const grossProfit = 100000;
let netProfit;

// Here's the initial guess
let profitSharing = grossProfit * profitSharingPercent;

calculateProfitSharing(profitSharing);

function calculateProfitSharing(guess) {

    // First, calculate the new net profit
    netProfit = grossProfit - guess;
```

```
    // Now use that to guess the profit-sharing value again
    profitSharing = Math.ceil(netProfit * profitSharingPercent);

    // Do we have a solution?
    if ((netProfit + profitSharing) != grossProfit) {
        // If not, plug it in again
        calculateProfitSharing(profitSharing);
    }
}
// Write the solution
document.write("Gross Profit: " + grossProfit +
    "<br>Net Profit: " + netProfit +
    "<br>Profit Sharing: " + profitSharing);
```

The grossProfit variable is initialized at 100000, the netProfit variable is declared, the profitSharingPercent variable is set to 0.1 (10 percent), and the profitSharing variable is set to the initial guess of 10 percent of gross profits. Then the calculateProfitSharing function is called, and the profitSharing guess is passed as the initial value of the guess argument.

The function first calculates the netProfit and then uses that value to calculate the new profitSharing number. Remember that your goal here is to end up with the sum of netProfit and profitSharing being equal to grossProfit. The if statement tests that, and if the sum is not equal to grossProfit, the calculateProfitSharing() function is called again (here's the recursion), and this time the new profitSharing value is passed. When the correct values are finally found, the function exits and displays the results, as shown in Figure 5-8.

REMEMBER

Note that all the variables in previous example are declared as globals. That's because if you declared them within the calculateProfitSharing() function, they would get wiped out and reset with each call, which is not what you want when doing recursion.

← → C ⟳    ○ 🔒 ⇄ https://paulmcfedries.com/htmlcssjs/bk04ch05/example18.html

**FIGURE 5-8:**
Using recursion
to calculate
a profit
sharing value.

Gross Profit: 100000
Net Profit: 90909
Profit Sharing: 9091

# AVOIDING INFINITE RECURSION

**TECHNICAL
STUFF**

If you're trying to call a function recursively, you may get error messages such as Stack overflow or Too much recursion. These error messages indicate that you have no "brakes" on your recursive function so, if not for the errors, it would call itself forever. This is called *infinite recursion*, and the actual maximum number of recursive calls depends on the browser, your operating system, and how much memory your device has installed.

In any case, it's important to build in some kind of test to ensure that the function will stop calling itself after a certain number of calls:

- The addOne() function in the previous section avoided infinite recursion by asking the user if they wanted to continue or stop.

- The calculateProfitSharing() function in the previous section avoided infinite recursion by testing the sum of netProfit and profitSharing to determine if this sum was equal to grossProfit. (Although note that you may not know in advance whether the calculation converges, so some other way of limiting the recursion may be needed at first. For example, you could declare a global counter variable that gets incremented with each recursive function call and is tested within the function to ensure it doesn't exceed some maximum value.)

If you don't have a convenient or obvious method for stopping the recursion, you can set up a counter that tracks the number of function calls. When that number hits a predetermined maximum, the script should bail out of the recursion process. The following code presents such a script (bk04ch05/example19.html):

```
let currentCall = 1;
const maximumCalls = 3;

recursionTest();

function recursionTest() {
    if (currentCall <= maximumCalls) {
        console.log(currentCall);
        currentCall += 1;
        recursionTest();
    }
}
```

*(continued)*

(continued)

The currentCall variable is the counter, and the maximumCalls variable specifies the maximum number of times the recursive function can be called. In the function, the following statement compares the value of currentCall and maximumCalls:

```
if (currentCall <= maximumCalls)
```

If currentCall is less than or equal to maximumCalls, all is well and the script can continue. In this case, a console message displays the value of currentCall, that value is incremented, and the recursionTest() function is called again. When currentCall becomes greater than maximumCalls, the function exits and the recursion is done.

IN THIS CHAPTER

» **Understanding objects**

» **Messing with object properties and methods**

» **Taking a deep dive into the Document Object Model**

» **Figuring out events**

» **Handling mouse clicks, keypresses, and more**

# Chapter **6**

# Playing with the Document Object Model

*The programmer, like the poet, works only slightly removed from pure thought-stuff. He builds his castles in the air, from air, creating by exertion of the imagination. Few media of creation are so flexible, so easy to polish and rework, so readily capable of realizing grand conceptual structures.*

—FRED BROOKS

've talked a lot of JavaScript over the past few chapters, but in a very real sense all that has been just the programming equivalent of noshing on a few appetizers. Now it's time to sit down for the main course: programming the Document Object Model. I explain what that is shortly, but for now it's enough to know that it means taking control over every aspect of the web page. Want to change some web page text on the fly? JavaScript can do that. Want to add an element to the page? JavaScript's up to the task. Want to modify an element's CSS? JavaScript's all over that. Want to perform some action based on the user clicking something or pressing a key combination? JavaScript raises its hand and says, "Ooh, ooh, pick me, pick me!"

In this chapter, you explore the fascinating world of the Document Object Model. You learn lots of powerful coding techniques that enable you to make your web pages do almost anything you want them to do. You learn, too, that this is where web coding becomes fun and maybe just a little addictive (in a good way, I promise).

# Working with Objects

Before I talk about the Document Object Model, you need to get familiar with what is arguably the most important word in that name: *object*. Over the next few pages, you learn what objects are, what you can do with them, and why they're important.

## What is an object, anyway?

Only the simplest JavaScript programs do nothing but assign values to variables and calculate expressions. To go beyond these basic programming beginnings — that is, to write truly useful scripts — you have to do what JavaScript was designed to do from the start: manipulate the web page that it's displaying. That's what JavaScript is all about, and that manipulation can come in many different forms:

>> Add text and HTML attributes to an **element**.

>> Modify a CSS **property** of a class or other selector.

>> Store some data in the browser's internal **storage**.

>> Validate a **form's** data before submitting it.

The bold items in this list are examples of the "things" that you can work with, and they're special for no other reason than they're programmable. In JavaScript parlance, these "programmable things" are called *objects*.

You can work with objects in JavaScript in any of the following three ways:

>> You can read and make changes to the object's *properties*.

>> You can make the object perform a task by activating a *method* associated with the object.

>> You can define a procedure that runs whenever a particular *event* happens to the object.

To help you understand objects and their properties, methods, and events, I'll put things in real-world terms. Specifically, consider your computer as though it were an object:

>> If you wanted to describe your computer as a whole, you'd mention things like the name of the manufacturer, the price, the size of the hard drive, and the amount of RAM. Each of these items is a *property* of the computer.

>> You also can use your computer to perform tasks such as writing letters, crunching numbers, and coding web pages. These are the *methods* associated with your computer.

>> A number of things happen to the computer that cause it to respond in predefined ways. For example, when the On button is pressed, the computer runs through its Power On Self-Test, initializes its components, and so on. The actions to which the computer responds automatically are its *events*.

All these properties, methods, and events give you an overall description of your computer.

But your computer is also a collection of objects, each with its own properties, methods, and events. The hard drive, for example, has various properties, including its speed and data-transfer rate. The hard drive's methods are actions such as storing and retrieving data. A hard drive event may be a scheduled maintenance task, such as checking the drive for errors.

In the end, you have a complete description of the computer: how it appears (its properties), how you interact with it (its methods), and to what actions it responds (its events).

## Manipulating object properties

All JavaScript objects have at least one property, and some of them have a couple of dozen or more. What you do with these properties depends on the object, but you generally use them for the following tasks:

>> **Gathering information about an object's current settings:** With an element object (such as a div or p element), for example, you can use the textContext property to get whatever text is currently in the element.

>> **Changing an object's current settings:** For example, you can use the document object's location property to send the web browser to a different URL.

>> **Changing an object's appearance:** With an element's style object, for example, you can use the fontSize property to change the size of the element's text.

## Referencing a property

Whatever the task, you refer to a property by using the syntax in the following generic expression:

```
object.property
```

>> *object:* The object that has the property.

>> *property:* The name of the property you want to work with.

The dot ( . ) in between is called the *property access operator.*

For example, consider the following expression:

```
document.location
```

This expression refers to the document object's location property, which holds the address of the document currently displayed in the browser window. (In conversation, you'd pronounce this expression as "document dot location.") The following code shows a simple one-line script that displays this property in the console, as shown in Figure 6-1.

```
console.log(document.location);
```

**TIP**

To display the console in most web browsers, right-click the web page, click Inspect (or press Ctrl+Shift+I in Windows or Option+⌘+I in macOS), and then click the Console tab.

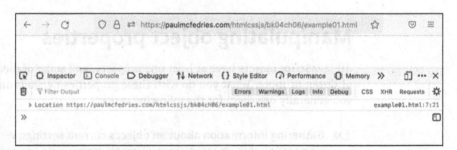

**FIGURE 6-1:**
This script displays the document. location property in a console message.

Because the property always contains a value, you're free to use property expressions in just about any type of JavaScript statement and as an operand in a JavaScript expression. (To find out what an operand is, refer to Book 4, Chapter 3.)

For example, the following statement assigns the current value of the document.
location property to a variable named currentUrl:

```
const currentUrl = document.location;
```

Similarly, the following statement includes document.location as part of a string
expression:

```
const message = "The current address is " + document.location
    + ".";
```

## Some properties are objects

Just to keep you on your toes, when you're working with objects, you'll constantly
come across a common but mystifying notion: Some properties pull double-duty
as full-fledged objects! This is one of the most confusing aspects of the relationship between objects and properties, but it's also one of the most important, so I'll
dive into this a bit deeper to make sure you understand what's going on.

The basic idea is that the value returned by a property is usually a literal (which
is programmer-speak for "it is what it is") such as a string or number, but often
it's an object. An example of the latter is the document object's location property,
which actually returns a Location object. Because location is an object, it also has
its own properties. For example, it has a hostname property that references just
the host name part of the address (for example, paulmcfedries.com). To work
with this property, you extend the expression syntax accordingly:

```
document.location.hostname
```

## Changing the value of a property

Some properties are "read only," which means your code can only read the current value and can't change it. However, many properties are "read/write," which
means you can also change their values. To change the value of a property, use the
following generic syntax:

```
object.property = value
```

>> *object:* The object that has the property

>> *property:* The name of the property you want to change

>> *value:* A literal value (such as a string or number) or an expression that
returns the value to which you want to set the property

Here's an example:

```
const newAddress = prompt("Enter the address you want to surf
    to:");
document.location = newAddress;
```

This script prompts the user for a web page address and stores the result in the newAddress variable. This value is then used to change the document.location property, which in this case tells the browser to open the specified address.

## Working with object methods

Every JavaScript object has at least one or two methods that you can wield to make the object do something. These actions generally fall into the following categories:

>> **Simulate a user's action:** For example, the form object's submit() method submits a form to the server just as though the user clicked the form's submit button.

>> **Perform a calculation:** For example, the Math object's sqrt() method calculates the square root of a number.

>> **Manipulate an object:** For example, the String object's toLowercase() method changes all of a string's letters to lowercase.

To run a method, begin with the simplest case, which is a method that takes no arguments:

```
object.method()
```

>> *object:* The object that has the method you want to work with

>> *method:* The name of the method you want to execute

For example, consider the following statement:

```
history.back();
```

This runs the history object's back() method, which tells the browser to go back to the previously visited page. The following code shows this method at work:

```
const goBack = confirm("Do you want to go back?");
if (goBack === true) {
    history.back();
}
```

The user is first asked whether they want to go back. If the user clicks OK, the Boolean value `true` is stored in the `goBack` variable and the comparison expression `goBack === true` becomes `true`, so the `history.back()` method runs.

I mention in Book 4, Chapter 5 that you can define a function so that it accepts one or more arguments, and these arguments are then used as input values for whatever calculations or manipulations the function performs. Methods are similar in that they can take one or more arguments and use those values as raw data.

If a method requires arguments, you use the following generic syntax:

```
object.method (argument1, argument2, ...)
```

For example, consider the `confirm()` method, used in the following statement, which takes a single argument — a string that specifies the text to display to the user:

```
confirm("Do you want to go back?")
```

Finally, as with properties, if the method returns a value, you can assign that value to a variable (as I do with the `confirm()` method in the earlier example) or you can incorporate the method into an expression.

## Rolling your own objects

Although you'll mostly deal with prefab objects such as those that are built into JavaScript or that are exposed by a Web API (refer to the next section), you can also create your own objects. Why would you ever want to do that? There are lots of reasons, but for your purposes here, the biggest reason is that a custom object enables you to store multiple, related values in a single data structure.

For example, suppose your script needs to work with the following user preferences for the styles that get applied to your page when the user visits: background color, text color, text size, and typeface. You could store these preferences in separate variables:

```
const userBgColor = "darkolivegreen";
const userTextColor = "antiquewhite";
const userTextSize = "1.25em";
const userTypeface = "Comic Sans";
```

This approach isn't terrible, but it feels a bit unwieldy, and it would *definitely* get unwieldy if the number of preferences you had to store increased to 10 or 15 or more. Hey, it can happen!

A much easier and more flexible way to deal with such a collection of related data is to pour everything into a custom object using the following syntax:

```
const objectName = {
    propertyName1: value1,
    propertyName2: value2,
    ...
    propertyNameN: valueN
}
```

>> *objectName*: The variable name of the object.

>> *propertyName1* through *propertyNameN*: The names of the object's properties.

>> *value1* through *valueN*: The values assigned to the properties. Each value can be a literal value (such as a string, number, or Boolean), an array, a function result, a variable name (assuming the variable has already been declared and initialized), or even another object literal.

This data structure is called an *object literal*. Here's how you'd use an object literal to store the user preferences from earlier:

```
const userPrefs = {
    bgColor: "darkolivegreen",
    textColor: "antiquewhite",
    textSize: "1.25em",
    typeface: "Comic Sans"
};
```

You can then reference a property's value using the standard *property.value* syntax:

```
document.body.style.backgroundColor = userPrefs.bgColor;
```

You can also change a property value in the usual way:

```
userPrefs.textColor = "papayawhip";
```

**REMEMBER**

Wait, what!? I declared userPrefs with const and then I changed a property value? How is this possible? This is a common question, and it strikes at the heart of what it really means to declare a variable with const. In this case, what const is doing is binding userPrefs to a particular object, and you can't change that binding. However, you're free to change the *contents* of that object.

What about custom object methods? Yep, you can add them as well:

```
const objectName = {
    propertyName1: value1,
    propertyName2: value2,
    ...
    propertyNameN: valueN,
    methodName: function(arguments) {
        code
    }
};
```

>> *methodName*: The name of the method

>> *arguments*: An optional (comma-separated) list of the arguments taken by the method

>> *code*: The JavaScript code to run when the method is invoked

Here's an example (see bk04ch06/example00.html in this book's example files):

```
const userPrefs = {
    bgColor: "darkolivegreen",
    textColor: "antiquewhite",
    textSize: "1.25em",
    typeface: "Comic Sans",
    resetDefaults: function() {
        document.body.style.backgroundColor = 'white';
        document.body.style.color = 'black';
        document.body.style.fontSize = '1em';
        document.body.style.fontFamily = 'initial';
    }
};
```

This code defines a resetDefaults() method that, when run, resets the background color, text color, text size, and typeface to their default values. Your code would invoke this method as follows:

```
userPrefs.resetDefaults();
```

## The Web APIs: Some special objects

JavaScript has its own set of built-in objects, including the String, Date, and Math objects that are the subject of Book 4, Chapter 8. However, a huge collection of objects exists outside of JavaScript and these objects are available to your scripts.

This collection consists of the Web Application Programming Interfaces, or Web APIs, for short.

To understand how the Web APIs work, consider your car (if you have one; if not, consider someone else's car). The engine inside the car is a monumentally complex piece of engineering, but you don't have to worry about any of that to start the car. Instead, all you have to do is insert the key (or fob, or whatever) into the ignition and turn (or push the button, or whatever). The complexity of the engine and its startup process is hidden from you and is reduced to putting the key (or fob or whatever) into the ignition.

From a programming point of view, the car engine is an object and the ignition is what's known as an *interface:* that is, a way of accessing the properties and methods of the object (such as the "method" of starting the engine).

In the simplest terms, an *application programming interface* (API) is a way for your JavaScript code to access a hidden (and presumably complex) object by exposing that object's properties and methods. Fortunately, many Web APIs are built right into the web browser, so your JavaScript code can access many sophisticated objects right out of the box.

A good example is the Web Storage API, which enables your JavaScript code to store and retrieve data within the user's web browser. It's an extremely handy API, which is why I devote an entire chapter to it (refer to Book 4, Chapter 9).

Other Web APIs enables you to access a device's battery state (Battery API), the clipboard (Clipboard API), server data (Fetch API), geolocation data (Geolocation API), audio (Web Audio API), and notifications (Web Notifications).

However, for this chapter's purposes (and, indeed, for pretty much the rest of this book), the Big Kahuna API is the Document Object Model, which I turn to next.

# Getting to Know the Document Object Model

Here's some source code for a simple web page:

```
<html lang="en">
    <head>
        <title>So Many Kale Recipes</title>
    </head>
```

```
<body>
    <header>
        <h1>Above and Beyond the Kale of Duty</h1>
    </header>
    <main>
        <p>
            Do you love to cook with <a href="kale.
    html">kale</a>?
        </p>
    </main>
</body>
</html>
```

One way to examine this code is hierarchically. That is, the html element is, in a sense, the topmost element because every other element is contained within it. The next level down in the hierarchy contains the head and body elements. The head element contains a title element, which contains the text So Many Kale Recipes. Similarly, the body element contains a header element and a main element. The header element contains an h1 element with the text Above and Beyond the Kale of Duty, while the main element contains a p element with the text Do you love to cook with kale?.

Hierarchies are almost always more readily grasped in visual form, so Figure 6-2 graphs the page elements hierarchically.

**REMEMBER**

When speaking of object hierarchies, if object P contains object C, object P is said to be the *parent* of object C, and object C is said to be the *child* of object P. In Figure 6-2, the arrows represent parent-to-child relationships. Also, elements on the same level — such as the header and main elements — are known as *siblings*.

You have several key points to consider here:

>> Every box in Figure 6-2 represents an object.

>> Every object in Figure 6-2 is one of three types: element, text, or attribute.

>> Every object in Figure 6-2, regardless of its type, is called a *node*.

>> The page as a whole is represented by the document object.

Therefore, this hierarchical object representation is known as the Document Object Model, or the DOM as it's usually called. The DOM is a Web API that enables your JavaScript code to access the complete structure of an HTML document. This access is the source of one of JavaScript's most fundamental features: the capability it offers you as a web developer to read and change the elements of a web page,

Playing with the Document Object Model

CHAPTER 6 **Playing with the Document Object Model** 523

even after the page is loaded. To that end, this section presents you with a quick tour of some extremely useful and powerful JavaScript techniques for dealing with the DOM and the document object.

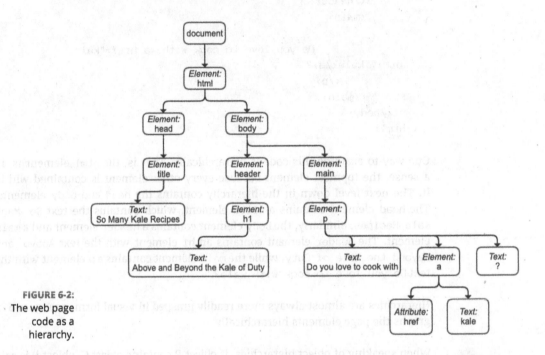

To get you started, Table 6-1 describes a few common properties of the document object.

### TABLE 6-1    Useful Properties of the document Object

| Property | What it Does |
|---|---|
| activeElement | Returns an object that represents the element that currently has the focus on the current web page |
| body | Returns an object that represents the current web page's body element |
| childElementCount | Returns the number of child elements in the current web page |
| children | Returns a collection that contains all the current web page's elements |
| forms | Returns a collection that contains all the current web page's form elements |
| head | Returns an object that represents the current web page's head element |

| Property | What it Does |
|---|---|
| images | Returns a collection that contains all the current web page's img elements |
| lastModified | Returns the date and time the current web page was last changed |
| links | Returns a collection that contains all the current web page's a element |
| location | Returns an object that represents the URL of the current web page |
| title | Returns an object that represents the current web page's title element |
| URL | Returns a string that contains the URL of the current web page |

# Specifying Elements

Elements represent the tags in a document, so you'll be using them constantly in your code. This section shows you several methods for referencing one or more elements.

## Specifying an element by id

If it's a specific element you want to work with in your script, you can reference the element directly by first assigning it an identifier using the id attribute:

```
<div id="kale-quotations">
```

With that done, you can then refer to the element in your code by using the document object's getElementById() method:

```
document.getElementById(id)
```

>> *id:* A string representing the id attribute of the element you want to work with

For example, the following statement returns a reference to the previous <div> tag (the one that has id=" kale-quotations"):

```
document.getElementById("kale-quotations")
```

**WARNING** When you're coding the document object, don't put your <script> tag in the web page's head section (that is, between the <head> and </head> tags). If you place your code there, the web browser will run the code before it has had a chance to create the document object, which means your code will fail, big time. Instead, place your <script> tag at the bottom of the web page, just before the </body> tag.

## Specifying elements by tag name

Besides working with individual elements, you can also work with collections of elements. One such collection is the set of all elements in a page that use the same tag name. For example, you could reference all the <a> tags or all the <div> tags. This is a handy way to make large-scale changes to these tags (such as by changing all the target attributes in your links).

The mechanism for returning a collection of elements that have the same tag is the getElementsByTagName() method:

```
document.getElementsByTagName(tag)
```

>> *tag:* A string representing the HTML name used by the tags you want to work with

This method returns an array-like collection that contains all the elements in the document that use the specified tag. (Refer to Book 4, Chapter 7 to find out how arrays work. Also check out "Working with collections of elements," later in this chapter.) For example, to return a collection that includes all the div elements in the current page, you'd use the following statement:

```
const divs = document.getElementsByTagName("div");
```

## Specifying elements by class name

Another collection you can work with is the set of all elements in a page that use the same class. The JavaScript tool for returning all the elements that share a specific class name is the getElementsByClassName() method:

```
document.getElementsByClassName(class)
```

>> *class:* A string representing the class name used by the elements you want to work with

This method returns an array-like collection that contains all the elements in the document that use the specified class name. The collection order is the same as the order in which the elements appear in the document. Here's an example:

```
const keywords = document.getElementsByClassName("keyword");
```

# Specifying elements by selector

In Book 3, Chapters 2 and 3, I discuss CSS selectors, including the id, tag, class, descendant, and child selectors. You can use those same selectors in your JavaScript code to reference page elements by using the document object's query Selector() and querySelectorAll() methods:

```
document.querySelector(selector)
document.querySelectorAll(selector)
```

> » *selector:* A string representing the selector for the element or elements you want to work with

The difference between these methods is that querySelectorAll() returns a collection of all the elements that match your selector, whereas querySelector() returns only the first element that matches your selector.

For example, the following statement returns the collection of all section elements that are direct children of an article element:

```
const articles = document.querySelectorAll("article > section");
```

**REMEMBER**

Rather than use three distinct document object methods to reference page elements by id, tag, and class — that is, getElementById(), getElementsBy TagName(), and getElementsByClassName() —, many web developers prefer the more generic approach offered by querySelector() and querySelectorAll().

# Working with collections of elements

The getElementsByTagName(), getElementsByClassName(), and querySelector All() methods each return an array-like collection that contains all the elements in the document that use the specified tag, class, or selector, respectively. The collection order is the same as the order in which the elements appear in the document. For example, consider the following HTML code (check out bk04ch06/ example01.html in this book's example files):

```
<div id="div1">
    This, of course, is div 1.
</div>
<div id="div2">
    Yeah, well <em>this</em> is div 2!
</div>
<div id="div3">
    Ignore those dudes. Welcome to div 3!
</div>
```

Now consider the following statement:

```
divs = document.getElementsByTagName("div");
```

In the resulting collection, the first item (divs[0]) will be the <div> element with id equal to div1; the second item (divs[1]) will be the <div> element with id equal to div2; and the third item (divs[2]) will be the <div> element with id equal to div3.

You can also refer to elements directly using their id values. For example, the following statements are equivalent:

```
const firstDiv = divs[0];
const firstDiv = divs.div1;
```

To learn how many items are in a collection, use the length property:

```
const totalDivs = divs.length;
```

To perform one or more operations on each item in the collection, you can use a for...of loop to run through the collection one item at a time. In the JavaScript trade, this is known as *iterating* over the collection. Here's the syntax to use:

```
for (const item of collection) {
    statements
}
```

>> *item*: A variable that holds an item in the collection. The first time through the loop, *item* is set to the first element in the collection; the second time through the loop, *item* is set to the second element; and so on.

>> *collection*: The collection of elements you want to iterate over.

>> *statements*: The JavaScript code you want to use to manipulate (or view, or whatever) *item*.

For example, here's some code that iterates over the preceding div elements and displays each item's id value in the console (refer to Book 4, Chapter 10 for details on the console), as shown in Figure 6-3 (check out bk04ch06.example01.html):

```
divs = document.getElementsByTagName("div");
for (const d of divs) {
    console.log(d.id);
}
```

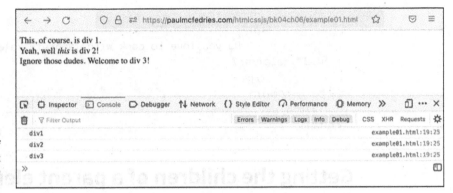

**FIGURE 6-3:**
The output of
the script that
iterates over the
div elements.

**WARNING**

The for...of loop is an ECMAScript 2015 (ES6) addition. If you need to support ancient browsers such as Internet Explorer 11, you can use a regular for loop, instead:

```
for (var i = 0; i < collection.length; i += 1) {
    statements
    // Use collection[i] to refer to each item
}
```

# Traversing the DOM

One common task in JavaScript code is working with the children, parent, or siblings of some element in the page. This is known as *traversing the DOM*, because you're using these techniques to move up, down, and along the DOM hierarchy.

In the sections that follow, I use the following HTML code for each example technique (bk04ch06/example02.html):

```
<html lang="en">
    <head>
        <title>So Many Kale Recipes</title>
    </head>
    <body>
        <header id="page-banner">
            <h1>Above and Beyond the Kale of Duty</h1>
        </header>
        <main id="page-content">
```

```
        <p>
            Do you love to cook with <a href="kale.
html">kale</a>?
        </p>
    </main>
</body>
</html>
```

# Getting the children of a parent element

When you're working with a particular element, it's common to want to perform one or more operations on that element's children. Every parent element offers several properties that enable you to work with all or just some of its child nodes:

>> All the child nodes

>> The first child node

>> The last child node

## Getting all the child nodes

To return a collection of all the child nodes of a parent element, use the child-Nodes property:

```
parent.childNodes
```

>> *parent*: The parent element you're working with

For example, the following statement stores all the child nodes of the body element in a variable:

```
const bodyChildren = document.body.childNodes;
```

The result is a NodeList object, which is a collection of nodes. If you were to use the console (refer to Book 4, Chapter 10) to display the value of bodyChildren, you'd get the output shown in Figure 6-4.

**TIP**

If you need to iterate over a NodeList collection, you can use the for...of loop that I talk about earlier in this chapter (head back to "Working with collections of elements").

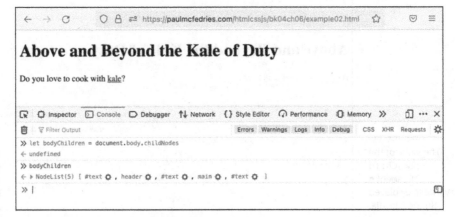

**FIGURE 6-4:**
The value of the
bodyChildren
variable displayed
in the console.

Here's the output shown in the console:

```
NodeList(5) [ #text, header, #text, main, #text ]
```

The (5) part tells you there are five items in the NodeList, and from the values within the square brackets, you know that the nodes consist of the header and main elements, as expected, but also three text nodes. Where did those text nodes come from? They represent (in this example) the white space between the elements. For example, the first text node is the carriage return and eight spaces that appear between the end of the <body> tag and the start of the <header> tag. The other text nodes represent the white space between the </header> and <main> tags and between the </main> and </body> tags.

If what you really want is the collection of child nodes that are elements, you need to turn to a different property:

```
parent.children
```

**»** *parent*: The parent element

For example, the following statement stores the all the child element nodes of the body element in a variable:

```
const bodyChildElements = document.body.children;
```

The result is an HTMLCollection object, which is an array-like collection of element nodes. If you were to use the console (refer to Book 4, Chapter 10) to display the value of bodyChildElements, you'd get the output shown in Figure 6-5.

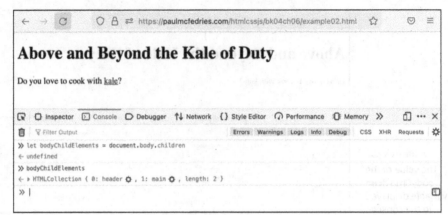

Here's the output:

```
HTMLCollection { 0: header, 1: main, length: 2 }
```

The numbers 0 and 1 are the index numbers of each child. For example, you could use bodyChildElements[0] to refer to the first element in the collection, which in this example is the header element.

## Getting the first child node

If you use a parent element's childNodes or children property to return the parent's child nodes, as I describe in the previous section, you can refer to the first item in the resulting collection by tacking [0] on to the collection's variable name. For example:

```
bodyChildren[0]
bodyChildElements[0]
```

However, the DOM offers a more direct route to the first child node:

```
parent.firstChild
```

>> *parent*: The parent element

For example, suppose you want to work with the first child node of the main element from the HTML example at the beginning of this section. Here's some code that'll do the job (bk04ch06/example03.html):

```
const content = document.getElementById("page-content");
const firstContentChildNode = content.firstChild;
```

In this example, the resulting node is a text node (the white space between the `<main>` and `<p>` tags). If you want the first child element node, use the `first ElementChild` property, instead:

```
parent.firstElementChild
```

» *parent*: The parent element

To get the first child element node of the `main` element from the code at the beginning of this section, you'd do something like this (bk04ch06/example04.html):

```
const content = document.getElementById("page-content");
const firstContentChildElement = content.firstElementChild;
```

In this example, this code returns the p element.

## Getting the last child node

If your code needs to work with the last child node, use the `lastChild` property of the parent element:

```
parent.lastChild
```

» *parent*: The parent element

For example, suppose you want to work with the last child node of the p element from the HTML example at the beginning of this section. Here's some code that'll do the job (bk04ch06/example05.html):

```
const para = document.querySelector("main > p");
const lastParaChildNode = para.lastChild;
```

In this example, the resulting node is a text node representing the question mark (?) and the white space to the `</p>` tag. If you want the last child element node, use the `lastElementChild` property, instead:

```
parent.lastElementChild
```

» *parent*: The parent element

To get the last child element node of the p element from the code at the beginning of this section, you could do this (bko4ch06/example06.html):

```
const para = document.querySelector("main > p");
const lastParaChildElement = para.lastElementChild;
```

In the example, this code returns the a element.

## Getting the parent of a child element

If your code needs to work with the parent of a child element, use the child element's parentNode property:

```
child.parentNode
```

>> *child*: The child element

For example, suppose you want to work with the parent element of the h1 element from the HTML example at the beginning of this section. Here's some code that'll do the job (bko4ch06/example07.html):

```
const childElement = document.querySelector("h1");
const parentElement = childElement.parentNode;
```

## Getting the siblings of an element

It's often important to work with an element's siblings in your code. Recall that an element's *siblings* are those elements in the DOM that share the same parent element.

A parent's child nodes appear in the DOM in the same order in which they appear in the HTML code, which means the siblings also appear in the order they appear in the HTML. Therefore, for a given child element, there are two sibling possibilities:

>> **Previous sibling:** This is the sibling that appears in the DOM immediately before the child element you're working with. If the child element is the first sibling, it will have no previous sibling.

>> **Next sibling:** This is the sibling that appears in the DOM immediately after the child element you're working with. If the child element is the last sibling, it will have no next sibling.

### Getting the previous sibling

To return the previous sibling of a particular element, use the `previousElement Sibling` property:

```
element.previousElementSibling
```

> **»** `element`: The element you're working with

For example, the following statement stores the previous sibling of the `main` element in a variable (bk04ch06/example08.html):

```
const currElement = document.querySelector("main");
const prevSib = currElement.previousElementSibling;
```

### Getting the next sibling

To return the next sibling of a particular element, use the `nextElementSibling` property:

```
element.nextElementSibling
```

> **»** `element`: The element you're working with

For example, the following statement stores the next sibling of the `header` element in a variable (bk04ch06/example09.html):

```
const currElement = document.querySelector("header");
const nextSib = currElement.nextElementSibling;
```

# Manipulating Elements

After you've got a reference to one or more elements, you can then use code to manipulate those elements in various ways, as shown in the next few sections.

## Adding an element to the page

One of the most common web development chores is to add elements to a web page on the fly. When you add an element, you always specify the parent element to which it will be added, and then you decide whether you want the new element added to the end or to the beginning of the parent's collection of children.

To add an element to the page, you follow three steps:

1. **Create an object for the type of element you want to add.**
2. **Add the new object from Step 1 as a child element of an existing element.**
3. **Insert some text and tags into the new object from Step 1.**

## Step 1: Creating the element

For Step 1, you use the document object's createElement() method:

```
document.createElement(elementName)
```

> » *elementName:* A string containing the HTML element name for the type of the element you want to create

This method creates the element and then returns it, which means you can store the new element in a variable. Here's an example:

```
const newArticle = createElement("article");
```

## Step 2: Adding the new element as a child

With your element created, Step 2 is to add it to an existing parent element. You have four choices:

> » **Append the new element to the end of the parent's collection of child elements:** Use the append() method:
>
> ```
> parent.append(child)
> ```
>
> - *parent:* A reference to the parent element to which the new element will be appended.
> - *child:* A reference to the child element you're appending. Note that you can append multiple elements at the same time by separating each element with a comma. The *child* parameter can also be a text string.

> » **Prepend the new element to the beginning of the parent's collection of child elements:** Use the prepend() method:
>
> ```
> parent.prepend(child)
> ```
>
> - *parent:* A reference to the parent element to which the new element will be prepended.

- *child:* A reference to the child element you're prepending. Note that you can prepend multiple elements at the same time by separating each element with a comma. The *child* parameter can also be a text string.

» **Insert the new element just after an existing child element of the parent:** Use the after() method:

```
child.after(sibling)
```

- *child:* A reference to the child element after which the new element will be inserted.

- *sibling:* A reference to the new element you're inserting. Note that you can insert multiple elements at the same time by separating each element with a comma. The *sibling* parameter can also be a text string.

» **Insert the new element just before an existing child element of the parent:** Use the before() method:

```
child.before(sibling)
```

- *child:* A reference to the child element before which the new element will be inserted.

- *sibling:* A reference to the new element you're inserting. Note that you can insert multiple elements at the same time by separating each element with a comma. The *sibling* parameter can also be a text string.

Here's an example that creates a new article element and then appends it to the main element (bk04ch06/example10.html):

```
const newArticle = document.createElement("article");
document.querySelector("main").append(newArticle);
```

Here's an example that creates a new nav element and then prepends it to the main element:

```
const newNav = document.createElement("nav");
document.querySelector("main").prepend(newNav);
```

## Step 3: Adding text and tags to the new element

With your element created and appended to a parent, the final step is to add some text and tags using the innerHTML property:

```
element.innerHTML = text
```

>> *element:* A reference to the new element within which you want to add the text and tags

>> *text:* A string containing the text and HTML tags you want to insert

**WARNING**

Whatever value you assign to the innerHTML property completely overwrites an element's existing text and tags, so use caution when wielding innerHTML. Check out the next section to learn how to insert text and tags rather than overwrite them.

In this example, the code creates a new nav element, prepends it to the main element, and then adds a heading (bk04ch06/example10.html):

```
const newNav = document.createElement("nav");
document.querySelector("main").prepend(newNav);
newNav.innerHTML = "<h2>Navigation</h2>";
```

## Inserting text or HTML into an element

You can use an element's innerHTML property to overwrite that element's tags and text, as I describe in the previous section. However, it's often the case that you want to keep the element's existing tags and text and insert new tags and text. Each element offers a couple of methods that enable you do to do this:

>> **To insert just text into an element:** Use the insertAdjacentText() method:

```
element.insertAdjacentText(location, text)
```

- *element:* A reference to the element into which the new text will be inserted.

- *location:* A string specifying where you want the text inserted. I outline your choices here shortly.

- *text:* A string containing the text you want to insert.

>> **To insert tags and text into an element:** Use the insertAdjacentHTML() method:

```
element.insertAdjacentHTML(location, data)
```

- *element:* A reference to the element into which the new tags and text will be inserted.

- *location*: A string specifying where you want the tags and text inserted. I outline your choices here shortly.

- *data:* A string containing the tags and text you want to insert.

For both methods, you can use one of the following strings for the *location* argument:

**»** "beforebegin": Inserts the data outside of and just before the element

**»** "afterbegin": Inserts the data inside the element, before the element's first child

**»** "beforeend": Inserts the data inside the element, after the element's last child

**»** "afterend": Inserts the data outside of and just after the element

For example, suppose your document has the following element:

```
<h2 id="nav-heading">Navigation</h2>
```

If you want to change the heading to Main Navigation, the following code will do the job (bko4cho6/example11.html):

```
const navHeading = document.getElementById("nav-heading");
navHeading.insertAdjacentText("afterbegin", "Main ");
```

## Removing an element

If you no longer require an element on your page, you can use the element's remove() method to delete it from the DOM:

```
element.remove()
```

For example, the following statement removes the element with an id value of temp-div from the page:

```
document.getElementById("temp-div").remove();
```

# Modifying CSS with JavaScript

Although you specify your CSS rules in a static stylesheet (.css) file, that doesn't mean that the rules themselves have to be static. With JavaScript on the job, you can modify an element's CSS in a number of ways. You can

» Read the current value of a CSS property

» Change the value of a CSS property

» Add or remove a class

» Toggle a class on or off

Why would you want to make these changes to your CSS? You already know that a big part of a well-designed web page is a strong CSS component that uses typography, colors, and spacing to create a page that's easily readable, sensibly navigable, and pleasing to the eye. But all that applies to the initial page displayed to the user. In the sorts of dynamic web apps that you're learning how to build, your page will change in response to some condition changing, such as the user clicking a button or pressing a key. This dynamic behavior needs to be matched with dynamic changes to the page, including changes to the CSS to highlight or reflect what's happening.

## Changing an element's styles

Most HTML tags can have a style attribute that you use to set inline styles. Because standard attributes all have corresponding element object properties (as I explain a bit later in the "Tweaking HTML Attributes with JavaScript" section), you won't be surprised to learn that most elements also have a style property that enables you to get and modify a tag's styles. It works like this: The style property actually returns a style object that has properties for every CSS property. When referencing these style properties, you need to keep two things in mind:

» For single-word CSS properties (such as color and visibility), use all-lowercase letters.

» For multiple-word CSS properties, drop the hyphen and use uppercase for the first letter of the second word and for each subsequent word if the property has more than two. For example, the font-size and border-left-width CSS properties become the fontSize and borderLeftWidth style object properties.

Here's an example (bko4cho6/example12.html):

```
const pageTitle = document.querySelector("h1");
pageTitle.style.fontSize = "64px";
pageTitle.style.color = "maroon";
pageTitle.style.textAlign = "center";
pageTitle.style.border = "1px solid black";
```

This code gets a reference to the page's first <h1> element. With that reference in hand, the code then uses the style object to style four properties of the heading: fontSize, color, text-align, and border.

## Adding a class to an element

If you have a class rule defined in your CSS, you can apply that rule to an element by adding the class attribute to the element's tag and setting the value of the class attribute equal to the name of your class rule.

First, you can get a list of an element's assigned classes by using the classList property:

```
element.classList
```

>> *element:* The element you're working with

The returned list of classes is an array-like object that includes an add() method that you can use to add a new class to the element's existing classes:

```
element.classList.add(class)
```

>> *element:* The element you're working with.

>> *class:* A string representing the name of the class you want to add to *element*. You can add multiple classes by separating each class name with a comma.

Here's an example (bko4cho6/example13.html), and Figure 6-6 shows the result.

CSS:

```
.my-class {
    display: flex;
    justify-content: center;
```

```
        align-items: center;
        border: 6px dotted black;
        font-family: Verdana, serif;
        font-size: 2rem;
        background-color: lightgray;
    }
```

HTML:

```
<div id="my-div">
    Hello World!
</div>
```

JavaScript:

```
document.getElementById('my-div').classList.add('my-class');
```

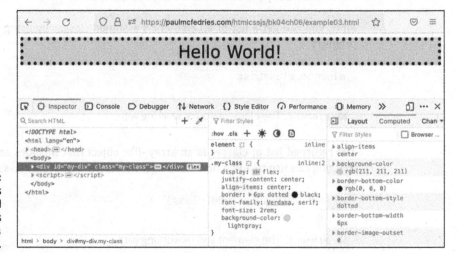

FIGURE 6-6:
This code uses
the add() method
to add the class
named my-class
to the <div> tag.

REMEMBER

If the class attribute doesn't exist in the element, the addClass() method inserts it into the tag. So in the previous example, after the code executes, the <div> tag now appears like this:

```
<div id="my-div" class="my-class">
```

## Removing a class

To remove a class from an element's class attribute, the classList object offers the remove() method:

```
element.classList.remove(class)
```

>> *element:* The element you're working with.

>> *class:* A string representing the name of the class you want to remove from *element*. You can remove multiple classes by separating each class name with a comma.

Here's an example:

```
document.getElementById('my-div').classList.remove('my-class');
```

## Toggling a class

One very common web development scenario is switching a web page element between two different states. For example, you may want to change an element's styles depending on whether a check box is selected or deselected, or you may want to alternate between showing and hiding an element's text when the user clicks the element's heading.

One way to handle this is to use the classList object's add() method to add a particular class when the element is in one state (for example, the user clicks the element's header for the first time) and then use the remove() method to remove that class when the element is in the other state (for example, the user clicks the element's header for a second time).

That approach would work, but it would mean that your code would somehow have to check the element's current state, using something like this pseudo-code:

```
if (the element has the class applied) {
    remove the class
} else {
    add the class
}
```

That's a lot of extra work, but fortunately it isn't work you have to worry about because your old friend the classList object has got your back on this one. The toggle() method does the testing for you. That is, it checks the element for the specified class; if the class is there, JavaScript removes it; if the class isn't there, JavaScript adds it. Sweet! Here's the syntax:

```
element.classList.toggle(class)
```

» *element:* The element you're working with

» *class:* A string representing the name of the class you want to toggle for *element*

Here's an example:

```
document.getElementById('my-div').classList.toggle('my-class');
```

# Tweaking HTML Attributes with JavaScript

One of the key features of the DOM is that each tag on the page becomes an element object. You may be wondering, do these element objects have any properties? Yep, they have tons. In particular, if the tag included one or more attributes, those attributes become properties of the element object.

For example, consider the following `<img>` tag:

```
<img id="header-image"
     src="mangosteen.png"
     alt="Drawing of a mangosteen">
```

This tag has three attributes: `id`, `src`, and `alt`. In the DOM's representation of the `<img>` tag, these attributes become properties of the `img` element object. Here's some JavaScript code that references the `img` element (bk04ch06/example14.html):

```
const headerImage = document.getElementById("header-image");
```

The `headerImage` variable holds the `img` element object, so your code could now reference the `img` element's attribute values with any of the following property references:

```
headerImage.id
headerImage.src
headerImage.alt
```

However, the DOM doesn't create properties either for custom attributes or for attributes added programmatically. Fortunately, each element object also offers methods that enable you to read any attribute, as well as add, modify, or remove the element's attributes. The next few sections tell all.

# Reading an attribute value

If you want to read the current value of an attribute for an element, use the element object's `getAttribute()` method:

```
element.getAttribute(attribute)
```

>> *element:* The element you want to work with

>> *attribute:* The name of the attribute you want to read

Here's an example that gets the `src` attribute of the element with an `id` value of `header-image`:

```
const headerImage = document.getElementById("header-image");
const srcHeaderImage = headerImage.getAttribute("src");
```

# Setting an attribute value

To set an attribute value on an element, use the element object's `setAttribute()` method:

```
element.setAttribute(attribute, value);
```

>> *element:* The element you want to work with

>> *attribute:* The name of the attribute you want to set

>> *value:* The string value you want to assign to *attribute*

If the attribute already exists, `setAttribute` overwrites the attribute's current value; if the attribute doesn't exist, `setAttribute` adds it to the element.

Here's an example that sets the `alt` attribute for the element with an `id` value of `header-image`:

```
const headerImage = document.getElementById("header-image");
headerImage.setAttribute("alt", "Lithograph of a mangosteen");
```

## Removing an attribute

To remove an attribute from an element, use the element object's removeAttribute() method:

```
element.removeAttribute(attribute);
```

>> *element:* The element you want to work with

>> *attribute:* A string specifying the name of the attribute you want to remove from the element

Here's an example:

```
const headerImage = document.getElementById("header-image");
headerImage.removeAttribute("id");
```

# Building Reactive Pages with Events

When you buy a car, no matter how much you paid for it or how technologically advanced it is, the car just sits there unless you do something. (If you're reading this in a future in which all the cars are autonomous, my apologies.) Having a car just sitting there may be fine if it's a good-looking car, but you're likely to want the car to do something, anything. Here's a short list of actions you can take to achieve that goal:

>> Start the car.

>> Put the transmission into gear.

>> Press the accelerator.

>> Turn on the radio.

The common denominator for all these actions is that they set up a situation to which the car must respond in some way: turning on, engaging the gears, moving, playing sounds. Approached from this angle, the car is a machine that responds to external stimuli, or, in a word, to events.

Somewhat surprisingly, a web page is also a machine that responds to external stimuli. Read on to learn what I mean.

# What's an event?

In web development, an *event* is an action that occurs in response to some external stimulus. A common type of external stimulus is when a user interacts with a web page. Here are some examples:

>> Surfing to or reloading the page

>> Clicking a button

>> Pressing a key

>> Scrolling the page

How can your web page possibly know when any of these actions occur? The secret is that JavaScript was built with events in mind. As the computer science professors would say, JavaScript is an *event-driven* language.

So why don't web pages respond to events automatically? Why do they just sit there? Because web pages are *static* by default, meaning that they ignore the events that are firing all around them. Your job as a web developer is to change that behavior by making your web pages "listen" for particular events to occur. You do that by setting up special chunks of code called *event handlers* that say, in effect, "Be a dear and watch out for event X to occur, will you? When it does, be so kind as to execute the code that I've placed here for you. Thanks so much." An event handler consists of two parts:

>> **Event listener:** An instruction to the web browser to watch out ("listen") for a particular event occurring on a particular element.

>> **Callback function:** The code that the web browser executes when it detects that the event has occurred.

In the rest of this chapter, I talk about how to use JavaScript to build your own event handlers and take your scripts to a more interactive level.

# Understanding the event types

There are dozens of possible events your web page can respond to, but luckily for you, only a small subset of these events are needed in most day-to-day web development. I break these down into the following five categories:

>> **Document:** Events that fire in relation to the loading of the document object. The only event you need to worry about here is DOMContentLoaded, which fires when the document object has completed loading.

>> **Mouse:** Events that fire when the user does something with the mouse (or a similar device, such as a trackpad or touchscreen). The most important events in this category are click (the user clicks the mouse); dblclick (the user double-clicks the mouse); and mouseover (the user moves the mouse pointer over an element).

>> **Keyboard:** Events that fire when the user interacts with the keyboard. The main event in this category is keypress, which is fired when the user presses a key.

>> **Form:** Events associated with web page forms. The important ones are focus (an element gains the focus, for example, when the user tabs to a form control); blur (an element loses the focus); change (the user changes the value of a form control); and submit (the user submits the form). Check out Book 4, Chapter 11 to learn about forms and form events.

>> **Browser window:** Events that fire when the user interacts with the browser window. The two main events here are scroll, which fires when the user scrolls the window vertically or horizontally, and resize, which fires when the user changes the window width or height.

You configure your code to listen for and react to an event by setting up an event handler using the element object's addEventListener() method. Here's the syntax:

```
element.addEventListener(event, callback);
```

>> *element:* The web page element to be monitored for the event. The event is said to be *bound* to the element.

>> *event:* A string specifying the name of the event you want the browser to listen for. For the main events I mention in the previous section, use one of the following, enclosed in quotation marks: DOMContentLoaded, click, dblclick, mouseover, keypress, focus, blur, change, submit, scroll, or resize.

>> *callback:* The callback function that JavaScript executes when the event occurs. The callback can be an anonymous function or a reference to a named function.

Here's an example (bk04ch06/example15.html):

HTML:

```
<div id="my-div"></div>
<button id="my-button">Click to add some text, above</button>
```

JavaScript:

```javascript
const myButton = document.getElementById('my-button');
myButton.addEventListener('click', function() {
    const myDiv = document.getElementById('my-div');
    myDiv.innerHTML = '<h1>Hello Click World!</h1>';
});
```

The HTML sets up an empty `div` element and a `button` element. The JavaScript code attaches a `click` event listener to the button, and the callback function adds the HTML string `<h1>Hello Click World!</h1>` to the `div`. Figure 6-7 shows the resulting page after the button has been clicked.

Playing with the Document Object Model

FIGURE 6-7:
The `click` event callback function adds some HTML and text to the `div` element.

**TIP**

If you want to run some code after the web page document has loaded, add an event handler to the `document` object that listens for the `DOMContentLoaded` event (bk04ch06/example16.html):

```javascript
document.addEventListener('DOMContentLoaded', function() {
    console.log('We are loaded!');
});
```

## Getting data about the event

When an event fires, the DOM creates an `Event` object, the properties of which contain info about the event, including the following:

>> `target`: The web page element to which the event occurred. For example, if you set up a `click` handler for a `div` element, that `div` is the target of the click.

>> `which`: A numeric code that specifies the key that was pressed during a keypress event.

>> `pageX`: The distance (in pixels) that the mouse pointer was from the left edge of the browser's content area when the event fired.

>> pageY: The distance (in pixels) that the mouse pointer was from the top edge of the browser's content area when the event fired.

>> metaKey: A Boolean value that equals true if the user had the Windows key (⊞) or the Mac Command key (⌘) held down when the event fired.

>> shiftKey: A Boolean value that equals true if the user had the Shift key held down when the event fired.

To access these properties, you insert a name for the Event object as an argument in your event handler's callback function:

```
element.addEventListener(event, function(e) {
    This code runs when the event fires
});
```

>> e: A name for the Event object that the DOM generates when the event fires. You can use whatever name you want, but most coders use e (although evt and event are also common).

For example, when handling the keypress event, you need access to the which property to find out the code for the key the user pressed. Here's an example page that can help you determine which code value to use (bk04ch06/example17.html):

HTML:

```
<div>
    Type a key:
</div>
<input id="key-input" type="text">
<div>
    Here's the code of the key you pressed:
</div>
<div id="key-output">
</div>
```

JavaScript:

```
const keyInput = document.getElementById('key-input');
keyInput.addEventListener('keypress', function(e) {
    const keyOutput = document.getElementById('key-output');
    keyOutput.innerHTML = e.which;
});
```

The HTML sets up an ⟨input⟩ tag to accept a keystroke, and a ⟨div⟩ tag with id="key-output" to use for the output. The JavaScript code adds a keypress event listener to the input element, and when the event fires, the callback function writes e.which to the output div. Figure 6-8 shows the page in action.

← → C    ○ 🔒 🖾 https://paulmcfedries.com/htmlcssjs/bk04ch06/example07.html

Type a key:

a

Here's the code of the key you pressed:

97

## Preventing the default event action

TIP

Some events come with default actions that they perform when the event fires. For example, a link's click event opens the target URL, whereas a form's submit event sends the form data to a script on the server. Most of the time, these default actions are exactly what you want, but that's not always the case. For example, you may want to intercept a link click to perform some custom action, such as displaying a menu. Similarly, rather than let the browser submit a form, you may prefer to massage the form data and then send the data via your script.

For these and many similar situations, you can tell the web browser not to perform an event's default action by running the Event object's preventDefault() method:

```
event.preventDefault();
```

» *event:* A reference to the Event object that the DOM creates when an event fires

For example, examine the following code (bk04ch06/example18.html):

HTML:

```
<a href="https://wiley.com/">Wiley</a><br>
<a href="https://262.ecma-international.org/6.0/">ECMAScript
    2015 Spec</a><br>
<a href="https://webdev.mcfedries.com/tools/workbench/">WebDev
    Workbench</a>
```

```
<div id="output">
    Link URL:
<div>
```

JavaScript:

```
const links = document.getElementsByTagName('a')
for (const link of links) {
    link.addEventListener('click', function(e) {
        e.preventDefault();
        strURL = e.target.href;
        document.getElementById('output').innerHTML = 'Link URL:
  ' + strURL;
    })
}
```

The HTML defines three links (styled as inline blocks, which I haven't shown here) and a `div` element. The JavaScript uses a `for...of` loop to set up a `click` event listener for all the `a` elements, and the callback function does three things:

- It uses the `e.preventDefault()` method to tell the browser not to navigate to the link address.
- It uses `e.target.href` to get the URL of the link.
- It displays that URL in the `div` element. Figure 6-9 shows an example.

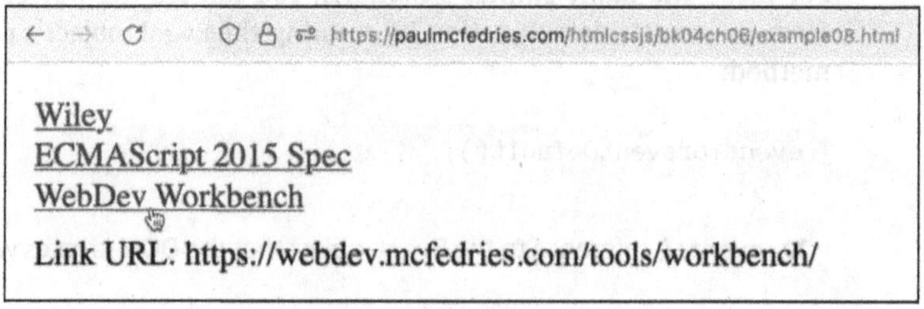
https://paulmcfedries.com/htmlcssjs/bk04ch06/example08.html
Wiley
ECMAScript 2015 Spec
WebDev Workbench
Link URL: https://webdev.mcfedries.com/tools/workbench/

**FIGURE 6-9:** You can use `e.preventDefault()` to stop the browser from navigating to the link URL.

# Chapter **7**

# Working with Arrays

*The disorder of the desk, the floor; the yellow Post-It notes everywhere; the whiteboards covered with scrawl: all this is the outward manifestation of the messiness of human thought. The messiness cannot go into the program; it piles up around the programmer.*

—ELLEN ULLMAN

've talked quite a bit about efficient programming in this book because I believe (okay, I know) that efficient scripts run faster and take less time to program and debug. Efficiency in programming really means eliminating unnecessary repetition, whether it's consolidating statements into a loop that can be repeated as often as required (refer to Book 4, Chapter 4) or moving code into a function that can be called as often as you need (refer to Book 4, Chapter 5).

In this chapter, you take your coding efficiency to an even higher level by exploring one of JavaScript's most important concepts: the array. Arrays are important not only because they're extremely efficient and very powerful but also because after you know how to use them, you'll think of a thousand and one uses for them. To make sure you're ready for your new array-filled life, this chapter explains what they are and why they're so darn useful, and then explores all the fantastic ways that arrays can make your coding life easier.

# What Is an Array?

One common source of unnecessary code repetition involves variables. For example, consider the following declarations (check out bk04ch07/example01.html in this book's example files):

```
const dog1 = "dog-1";
const dog2 = "dog-2";
const dog3 = "dog-3";
const dog4 = "dog-4";
const dog5 = "dog-5";
```

These are string variables, and they store the names of some dog photos.

This code may not seem outrageously inefficient, but what if instead of five images you actually had to take 10, 20, or even 100 images into account? I'm sure the idea of typing 100 const declarations isn't your idea of a good time.

To understand the solution to this problem, first understand that the variables dog1 through dog5 all contain related values. That is, each variable holds part of the filename of a dog photo, which in turn is part of the full URL for that image. In JavaScript (or, indeed, in just about any programming language), whenever you have a collection of variables with related data, you can group them together into a single variable called an *array*. You can enter as many values as you want into the array, and JavaScript tracks each value by the use of an *index number*. For example, the first value you add is given the index 0. (For obscure reasons, programmers since time immemorial have started numerical lists with 0 instead of 1.) The second value you put into the array is given the index 1; the third value gets 2; and so on. You can then access any value in the array by specifying the index number you want.

The next couple of sections flesh out this theory with the specifics of creating and populating an array.

# Declaring an Array

Because an array is a type of variable, you need to declare it before using it. In fact, unlike regular numeric, string, or Boolean variables that don't really need to be declared (but always should be), JavaScript insists that you declare an array in advance. You use the const (or let) statement again, but this time with a slightly different syntax. Actually, there are four syntaxes you can use. Here's the syntax that's the most informative:

```
const arrayName = new Array();
```

Here, *arrayName* is the name you want to use for the array variable.

In JavaScript, an array is actually an object, so what the new keyword is doing here is creating a new Array object. The Array() part of the statement is called a *constructor* because its job is to construct the object in memory. For example, to create a new array named dogPhotos, you'd use the following statement:

```
const dogPhotos = new Array();
```

The second syntax is useful if you know in advance the number of values (or *elements*) you'll be putting into the array:

```
const arrayName = new Array(num);
```

>> *arrayName:* The name you want to use for the array variable

>> *num:* The number of values you'll be placing into the array

For example, here's a statement that declares a new dogPhotos array with five elements:

```
const dogPhotos = new Array(5);
```

If you're not sure how many elements you need, don't worry about it, because JavaScript is happy to let you add elements to and delete elements from the array as needed, and it will grow or shrink the array to compensate. I talk about the other two array declaration syntaxes in the next section.

# Populating an Array with Data

After your array is declared, you can start populating it with the data values you want to store. Here's the general syntax for doing this:

```
arrayName[index] = value;
```

>> *arrayName:* The name of the array variable

>> *index:* The array index number where you want the value stored

>> *value:* The value you're storing in the array

JavaScript is willing to put just about any type of data inside an array, including numbers, strings, Boolean values, and even other arrays! You can even mix multiple data types within a single array.

**TIP**

You most commonly add new elements to the end of the array. Happily, the Array object has a special method for doing just that. It's called push( ), and I talk about it later in this chapter (specifically, the section "Adding elements to the end of an array: push()").

As an example, here are a few statements that declare a new array named dog Photos and then enter five string values into the array:

```
const dogPhotos = new Array(5);
dogPhotos[0] = "dog-1";
dogPhotos[1] = "dog-2";
dogPhotos[2] = "dog-3";
dogPhotos[3] = "dog-4";
dogPhotos[4] = "dog-5";
```

To reference an array value (say, to use it within an expression), you specify the appropriate index:

```
strURL + dogPhotos[3]
```

The following code offers a complete example (check out bk04ch078/example02. html):

HTML:

```
<div id="output">
</div>
```

JavaScript:

```
// Declare the array
const dogPhotos = new Array(5);

// Initialize the array values
dogPhotos[0] = "dog-1";
dogPhotos[1] = "dog-2";
dogPhotos[2] = "dog-3";
dogPhotos[3] = "dog-4";
dogPhotos[4] = "dog-5";

// Display an example
document.getElementById('output').innerHTML = '<img
    src="images/' + dogPhotos[0] + '.png" alt="">';
```

# Declaring and populating an array at the same time

Earlier, I mentioned that JavaScript has two other syntaxes for declaring an array. Both enable you to declare an array *and* populate it with values by using just a single statement.

The first method uses the `Array()` constructor in the following general format:

```
const arrayName = new Array(value1, value2, ...);
```

» *arrayName:* The name you want to use for the array variable

» *value1, value2, ...:* The initial values with which you want to populate the array

Here's an example:

```
const dogPhotos = new Array("dog-1", "dog-2", "dog-3", "dog-4",
    "dog-5");
```

JavaScript also supports the creation of *array literals*, which are similar to string, numeric, and Boolean literals. In the same way that you create, say, a string literal by enclosing a value in quotation marks, you create an array literal by enclosing one or more values in square brackets. Here's the general format:

```
const arrayName = [value1, value2, ...];
```

» *arrayName:* The name you want to use for the array variable

» *value1, value2, ...:* The initial values with which you want to populate the array

An example:

```
const dogPhotos= ["dog-1", "dog-2", "dog-3", "dog-4", "dog-5"];
```

**REMEMBER**

Including values in the declaration of an array literal is optional, which means that you can declare an empty array using the following statement:

```
const arrayName = [];
```

Most JavaScript programmers prefer this syntax over using the `Array` constructor.

# Using a loop to populate an array

So far, you probably don't think arrays are all that much more efficient than using separate variables. That's because you haven't yet learned about the single most powerful aspect of working with arrays: using a loop and some kind of counter variable to access an array's index number programmatically.

For example, here's a `for()` loop that replaces the six statements used earlier to declare and initialize the dogPhotos array:

```
const dogPhotos = [];
for (let counter = 0; counter < 5; counter += 1) {
    dogPhotos[counter] = "dog-" + (counter + 1);
}
```

The statement inside the `for()` loop uses the variable counter as the array's index. For example, when counter is 0, the statement looks like this:

```
dogPhotos[0] = "dog-" + (0 + 1);
```

In this case, the expression to the right of the equals sign evaluates to `"dog-1"`, which is the correct value. The following code shows this loop technique at work (bk04ch078/example03.html):

HTML:

```
<div id="output">
</div>
```

JavaScript:

```
// Declare the array
const dogPhotos = [];

// Initialize the array values using a loop
for (let counter = 0; counter < 5; counter += 1) {
    dogPhotos[counter] = "dog-" + (counter + 1);
}

// Display an example
document.getElementById('output').innerHTML = '<img
  src="images/' + dogPhotos[0] + '.png" alt="">';
```

Using a loop to insert data into an array works best in two situations:

>> When the array values can be generated using an expression that changes with each pass through the loop

>> When you need to assign the same value to each element of the array

**REMEMBER**

If you declare your array with a specific number of elements, JavaScript doesn't mind at all if you end up populating the array with more than that number.

# How Do I Iterate Thee?
# Let Me Count the Ways

The real problem with using a large number of similar variables isn't so much declaring them but working with them in your code. Here's an example (bk04ch07/example01.html):

```
const dog1 = "dog-1";
const dog2 = "dog-2";
const dog3 = "dog-3";
const dog4 = "dog-4";
const dog5 = "dog-5";
const promptNum = prompt("Enter the dog you want to see
   (1-5):", "");

if (promptNum !== "" && promptNum !== null) {
    const promptDog = "dog-" + promptNum;
    if (promptDog === dog1) {
        document.body.style.backgroundImage = "url('images/" +
dog1 + ".png')";
    } else if (promptDog === dog2) {
        document.body.style.backgroundImage = "url('images/" +
dog2 + ".png')";
    } else if (promptDog === dog3) {
        document.body.style.backgroundImage = "url('images/" +
dog3 + ".png')";
    } else if (promptDog === dog4) {
        document.body.style.backgroundImage = "url('images/" +
dog4 + ".png')";
```

```
    } else if (promptDog === dog5) {
        document.body.style.backgroundImage = "url('images/" +
    dog5 + ".png')";
    }
}
```

In this example, the script has to use five separate if() tests to check the input value against all five variables.

Arrays can really help make your code more efficient by enabling you to reduce these kinds of long-winded procedures to a much shorter routine that fits inside a function. These routines are iterative methods of the Array object, where iterative means that the method runs through the items in the array, and for each item, a function (called a callback) performs some operation on or with the item.

The Array object actually has fourteen iterative methods. I don't cover them all, but over the next few sections I talk about the most useful methods.

## Iterating an array: forEach()

The Array object's forEach() method runs a callback function for each element in the array. That callback takes up to three arguments:

» *value*: The value of the element

» *index*: (Optional) The array index of the element

» *array*: (Optional) The array being iterated

You can use any of the following syntaxes:

```
array.forEach(namedFunction);
array.forEach(function (value, index, array) { code });
array.forEach((value, index, array ) => { code });
```

» *array*: The Array object you want to iterate over.

» *namedFunction*: The name of an existing function. This function should accept the *value* argument and perhaps also the optional *index* and *array* arguments.

» *code*: The statements to run during each iteration.

Here's an example (bk04ch07/example04.html):

```
// Declare the array
const dogPhotos= ["dog-1", "dog-2", "dog-3", "dog-4", "dog-5"];

// Iterate through the array
dogPhotos.forEach((value, index) => {
    console.log("Element " + index + " has the value " + value);
});
```

After declaring the array, the code uses `forEach()` to iterate the array. During each iteration, `console.log()` (refer to Book 4, Chapter 10) displays a string that includes the `index` and `value` parameters. Figure 7-1 shows the results.

**TIP**

To display the console in most web browsers, right-click the web page, click Inspect (or press Ctrl+Shift+I in Windows or Option+⌘+I in macOS), and then click the Console tab.

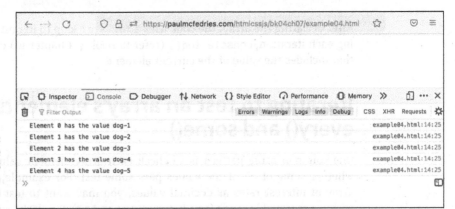

**FIGURE 7-1:**
The console messages displayed with each iteration using forEach().

## Iterating an array: for...of

Although you'll usually iterate an array with the `forEach()` method, you'll sometimes need to use a more traditional loop to run through each array element. That loop type is the `for...of` loop:

```
for (element of array) {
    code
}
```

>> *array*: The Array object you want to iterate over

>> *element*: The current array element during each pass through the loop

>> *code*: The statements to run during each iteration

**REMEMBER**

The for . . . of loop was introduced in ECMAScript 2015 (ES6), so don't use it if you need to support ancient browsers, such as Internet Explorer 11.

Here's an example (bk04ch07/example04a.html):

```
// Declare the array
const dogPhotos= ["dog-1", "dog-2", "dog-3", "dog-4", "dog-5"];

// Iterate through the array
for (const currentPhoto of dogPhotos) {
    console.log("The current element has the value " +
  currentPhoto);
}
```

After declaring the array, the code uses a for . . . of loop to iterate the array. During each iteration, console.log() (refer to Book 4, Chapter 10) displays a string that includes the value of the current element.

## Iterating to test an array's elements: every() and some()

One common array pattern is to check each array element value to determine whether some or all of the values pass some test. For example, if you have an array of interest rates as decimal values, you may want to test that they're all within a reasonable range (say, between 0.01 and 0.1). Similarly, suppose you have an array of numbers that at some point in your script will be used as divisors in a calculation. Before getting that far, you may want to determine whether at least one of the numbers in the array is zero and, if so, your script would bypass the calculation.

### Testing whether all elements pass a test: every()

To check whether all the elements in an array pass some test, use the Array object's every() method. There are three syntaxes you can use:

```
array.every(namedFunction);
array.every(function (value, index, array) { code });
array.every((value, index, array ) => { code });
```

>> *array*: The Array object with the values you want to test.

>> *namedFunction*: The name of an existing function that performs the test on each array value. This function should accept the *value* argument and perhaps also the optional *index* and *array* arguments.

>> *code*: The statements to run during each iteration to test each value.

In the *namedFunction* or *code*, use a return statement to send the result of the test back to the every() method. If all the array elements pass the test, every() returns true; otherwise, it returns false.

Here's an example (bk04ch07/example05.html):

```
// Declare an array of interest rates
const rates = [0.02, 0.025, 0.03, 0.035, 0.04, 0.045, 0.5];

// Test each rate
const legitRates = rates.every(currentValue => {
    return currentValue >= 0.01 && currentValue <= 0.1;
});

// Output the result
console.log(legitRates);
```

This code declares an array of interest rates (as decimal values). Then the every() method iterates over the rates array and with each pass tests whether the current array element value (stored in the currentValue parameter) is between (or equal to) 0.01 and 0.1. The final result is stored in the legitRates variable, the value of which is then displayed in the console, as shown in Figure 7-2.

**REMEMBER**

The every() method isn't a true iterative method because it stops iterating when it comes across the first array element value that doesn't pass the test.

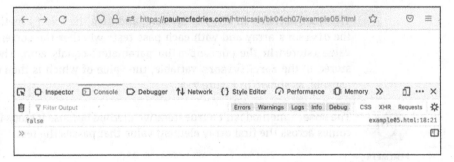

**FIGURE 7-2:**
The final result (false, in this case) of the every() method.

## Testing whether some elements pass a test: some()

To check whether at least one of the elements in an array passes some test, use the Array object's some() method. There are three syntaxes you can use:

```
array.some(namedFunction);
array.some(function (value, index, array) { code });
array.some((value, index, array ) => { code });
```

>> *array*: The Array object with the values you want to test.

>> *namedFunction*: The name of an existing function that performs the test on each array value. This function should accept the *value* argument and perhaps also the optional *index* and *array* arguments.

>> *code*: The statements to run during each iteration to test each value.

In the *namedFunction* or *code*, use a return statement to send the result of the test back to the some() method. If at least one the array elements passes the test, some() returns true; otherwise, it returns false.

Here's an example (bk04ch07/example06.html):

```
// Declare an array of divisors
const divisors = [27, 53, 6, 0, 17, 88, 32];

// Test each divisor
const zeroDivisors = divisors.some(currentValue => {
    return currentValue === 0;
});

// Output the result
console.log(zeroDivisors);
```

This code declares an array of divisors, and then the some() method iterates over the divisors array and with each pass tests whether the current array element value (stored in the currentValue parameter) equals zero. The final result is stored in the zeroDivisors variable, the value of which is then displayed in the console, as shown in Figure 7-3.

The some() method isn't a true iterative method because it stops iterating when it comes across the first array element value that passes the test.

FIGURE 7-3:
The final result
(true, in this
case) of the
some( ) method.

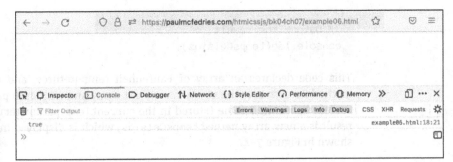

# Iterating to create a new array: map()

When you iterate over an array, it's common to apply some operation to each element value. In some cases, however, you want to preserve the original array values and create a new array that contains the updated values.

The easiest way to create a new array that stores updated values of an existing array is to use the Array object's map( ) method. There are three syntaxes you can use:

```
array.map(namedFunction);
array.map(function (value, index, array) { code });
array.map((value, index, array ) => { code });
```

>> *array*: The Array object with the values you want to use.

>> *namedFunction*: The name of an existing function that performs the operation on each array value. This function should accept the *value* argument and perhaps also the optional *index* and *array* arguments.

>> *code*: The statements to run during each iteration to perform the operation on each value.

The map( ) method returns an Array object that contains the updated values, so be sure to store the result in a variable.

Here's an example (bk04ch07/example07.html):

```
// Declare an array of Fahrenheit temperatures
const tempsFahrenheit = [-40, 0, 32, 100, 212];

// Convert each array value to Celsius
const tempsCelsius = tempsFahrenheit.map(currentTemp => {
    return (currentTemp - 32) * 0.5556;
});
```

```
// Output the result
console.log(tempsCelsius);
```

This code declares an array of Fahrenheit temperatures, and then the `map()` method iterates over the `tempsFahrenheit` array and with each pass converts the current Fahrenheit value (stored in the `currentTemp` parameter) to Celsius. The result is a new array named `tempsCelsius`, which is displayed in the console, as shown in Figure 7-4.

**FIGURE 7-4:**
The `map()`
method creates
a new array
by applying an
operation to
each value in the
original array.

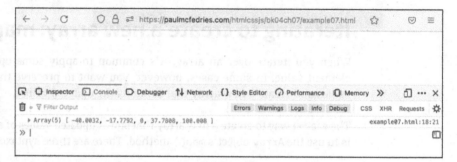

## Iterating an array down to a value: reduce()

One common iteration pattern is to perform a cumulative operation on every element in an array to produce a value. For example, you may want to know the sum of all the values in the array.

Iterating an array in this way to produce a value is the job of the `Array` object's `reduce()` method. There are three syntaxes you can use:

```
array.reduce(namedFunction, initialValue);
array.reduce(function (accumulator, value, index, array) { code
    }, initialValue);
array.reduce((accumulator, value, index, array) => { code },
    initialValue);
```

>> *array*: The Array object with the values you want to reduce.

>> *namedFunction*: The name of an existing function that performs the reducing operation on each array value. This function should accept the *accumulator* and *value* arguments and perhaps also the optional *index* and *array* arguments.

>> *code*: The statements to run during each iteration to perform the reducing operation on each value.

>> *initialValue*: The starting value of *accumulator*. If you omit *initialValue*, JavaScript uses the value of the first element in *array*.

Here's an example (bk04ch07/example08.html):

```
// Declare an array of product inventory
const unitsInStock = [547, 213, 156, 844, 449, 71, 313, 117];

// Get the total units in stock
const initialUnits = 0;
const totalUnits = unitsInStock.reduce((accumulatedUnits,
  currentInventoryValue) => {
    return accumulatedUnits + currentInventoryValue;
}, initialUnits);

// Output the result
console.log("Total units in stock: " + totalUnits);
```

This code declares an array of product inventory and declares `initialUnits` with a value of 0. Then the `reduce()` method (using `initialUnits` as the starting value of the accumulator) iterates over the `unitsInStock` array and with each pass adds the current product inventory value (stored in the `currentInventoryValue` parameter) to the accumulator (stored in the `accumulatedUnits` parameter). The resulting total is stored in the `totalUnits` variable, which is then displayed in the console, as shown in Figure 7-5.

**FIGURE 7-5:**
The `reduce()` method iterates an array's values down to a single value.

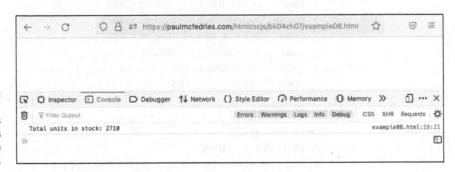

# Iterating to locate an element: find()

To search within an array for the first element that matches some condition, use the Array object's find() method. There are three syntaxes you can use:

```
array.find(namedFunction);
array.find(function (value, index, array) { code });
array.find((value, index, array ) => { code });
```

>> *array*: The Array object with the values in which you want to search.

>> *namedFunction*: The name of an existing function that applies the condition to each array value. This function should accept the *value* argument and perhaps also the optional *index* and *array* arguments.

>> *code*: The statements to run during each iteration to apply the condition to each value.

In the *namedFunction* or *code*, you set up a logical condition that tests each element in the array and use a return statement to send the result of the test back to the find() method. The final value returned by find() is the first element for which the test is true, or undefined if the test is false for all the array elements.

Here's an example (bk04ch07/example08a.html):

```
// Declare an array of product objects
const products = [
    { name: 'doodad', units: 547 },
    { name: 'gizmo', units: 213 },
    { name: 'gimcrackery', units: 156 },
    { name: 'knickknack', units: 844 },
    { name: 'bric-a-brac', units: 449 },
    { name: 'thingamajig', units: 71 },
    { name: 'watchamacallit', units: 313 },
    { name: 'widget', units: 117 }
];

// Query the array
const strQuery = "gizmo";
const stock = products.find((currentProduct) => {
    return currentProduct.name === strQuery;
});

// Output the result
if (stock) {
```

```
      console.log("Product " + stock.name + " has " + stock.units
   + " units in stock.");
} else {
   console.log("Product " + strQuery + " not found.");
}
```

This code declares an array of object literals. Then the find() method iterates over the products array and with each pass checks whether the name property of the current array element value (passed to the callback function using the current Product parameter) is equal to whatever value is stored in the strQuery variable. The result is stored in the stock variable. An if test checks the result: If stock is defined, the product name and inventory are displayed in the console; otherwise, a message saying the product was not found is displayed.

**TIP**

If you want to know the index number of the array item that matches the condition, use findIndex() instead of find().

# Creating Multidimensional Arrays

A *multidimensional array* is one where two or more values are stored within each array element. For example, if you wanted to create an array to store user data, you may need each element to store a first name, a last name, a username, a password, and more. The bad news is that JavaScript doesn't support multidimensional arrays. The good news is that you can use a trick to simulate a multidimensional array.

The trick is to populate your array in such a way that each element is itself an array. To understand how such an odd idea may work, first recall the general syntax for an array literal:

```
[value1, value2, ...]
```

Now recall the general syntax for assigning a value to an array element:

```
arrayName[index] = value;
```

In a one-dimensional array, the *value* is usually a string, number, or Boolean. Now imagine, instead, that *value* is an array literal. For a two-dimensional array, the general syntax for assigning an array literal to an array element looks like this:

```
arrayName[index] = [value1, value2];
```

As an example, say you want to store an array of background and foreground colors. Here's how you may declare and populate such an array:

```
const colorArray = [];
colorArray[0] = ['white', 'black'];
colorArray[1] = ['aliceblue', 'midnightblue'];
colorArray[2] = ['honeydew', 'darkgreen'];
```

Alternatively, you can declare and populate the array using only the array literal notation:

```
const colorArray = [
    ['white', 'black'],
    ['aliceblue', 'midnightblue'],
    ['honeydew', 'darkgreen']
];
```

Either way, you can then refer to individual elements using double square brackets, as in these examples:

```
colorArray[0][0]; // Returns 'white'
colorArray[0][1]; // Returns 'black'
colorArray[1][0]; // Returns 'aliceblue'
colorArray[1][1]; // Returns 'midnightblue'
colorArray[2][0]; // Returns 'honeydew'
colorArray[2][1]; // Returns 'darkgreen'
```

The number in the left set of square brackets is the index of the overall array, and the number in the right set of square brackets is the index of the element array.

# Manipulating Arrays

Like any good object, Array comes with a large collection of properties and methods that you can work with and manipulate. The rest of this chapter takes a look at a few of the most useful of these properties and methods.

## The length property

The Array object has just a couple of properties, but the only one of these that you'll use frequently is the length property:

```
array.length
```

The `length` property returns the number of elements that are currently in the specified array. This is very useful when looping through an array because it means you don't have to specify a literal as the maximum value of the loop counter. For example, consider the following `for` statement:

```
for (let counter = 0; counter < 5; counter += 1) {
    dogPhotos[counter] = "dog-" + (counter + 1);
}
```

This statement assumes that the `dogPhotos` array has five elements, which may not be the case. To enable the loop to work with any number of elements, replace 5 with `dogPhotos.length`:

```
for (let counter = 0; counter < dogPhotos.length; counter
   += 1) {
    dogPhotos[counter] = "dog-" + (counter + 1);
}
```

Note, too, that the loop runs while the `counter` variable is *less than* `dogPhotos.length`. That's because array indexes run from 0 to the array's `length` value minus 1. In other words, the previous `for` loop example is equivalent to the following:

```
for (let counter = 0; counter <= dogPhotos.length - 1; counter
   += 1)
```

## Concatenating to create a new array: concat()

The `concat()` method takes the elements of one or more existing arrays and concatenates them to an existing array to create a new array:

```
array.concat(array1, array2, ...)
```

>> *array:* The name of the array you want to work with.

>> *array1*, *array2*, ...: The arrays you want to concatenate to *array*. These can also be values.

Note that the original array remains unchanged. The following code (bk04ch07/example09.html) demonstrates using concat() to concatenate two arrays into a third array, each element of which is printed to the page, as shown in Figure 7-6.

```
// Declare the arrays
const array1 = ["One", "Two", "Three"];
const array2 = ["A", "B", "C"];

// Concatenate them
const array3 = array1.concat(array2);

// Display the concatenated array
console.log(array3);
```

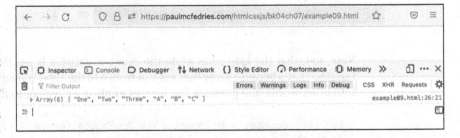

**TECHNICAL STUFF**

# A QUICK LOOK AT THE SPREAD OPERATOR (. . .)

When applied to an array, the *spread operator* (. . .) expands the array reference to include all the elements of the array. Here's the syntax for an array:

```
...arrayName
```

For example, instead of using the concat() method, you can combine two arrays using the spread operator, like so (bk04ch07/example09a.html):

```
// Declare the arrays
const array1 = ["One", "Two", "Three"];
const array2 = ["A", "B", "C"];

// Combine them with the spread operator
const array3 = [...array1, ...array2];
```

```
// Display the concatenated array
console.log(array3);
```

The spread operator is also useful if you want to use an array's elements as the arguments for a function. Consider the following function:

```
function volumeOfPrism(length, width, height) {
    return length * width * height;
}
```

If you have an array that consists of a particular length, width, and height, you can apply the spread operator to use the array's individual elements as the function's arguments:

```
const myPrism = [5, 8, 10];
const myPrismVolume = volumeOfPrism(...myPrism);
```

The spread operator is an ECMASCript 2015 (ES6) innovation, so don't use it if you have to support very old browsers (such as Internet Explorer 11).

## Creating a string from an array's elements: join()

The join() method enables you to take the existing values in an array and concatenate them together to form a string. Check out the syntax:

```
array.join(separator)
```

>> *array:* The name of the array you want to work with.

>> *separator:* An optional character or string to insert between each array element when forming the string. If you omit this argument, a comma is inserted between each element.

In the following code (bk04ch07/example10.html), three arrays are created and then join() is applied to each one using a space as a separator, and then the null string (""), and then no separator. Figure 7-7 shows the resulting page output.

HTML:

```
<div id="output">
</div>
```

JavaScript:

```javascript
// Declare the arrays
const array1 = ["Make", "this", "a", "sentence."];
const array2 = ["antid", "isest", "ablis", "hment", "arian",
    "ism"];
const array3 = ["John", "Paul", "George", "Ringo"];

//Join them to strings
const string1 = array1.join(" ");
const string2 = array2.join("");
const string3 = array3.join();

// Display the results
document.getElementById('output').innerHTML = string1 + '<br>' +
    string2 + '<br>' + string3;
```

Make this a sentence.
antidisestablishmentarianism
John,Paul,George,Ringo

**FIGURE 7-7:**
Joining the arrays
with a space, null
string (""), and
default comma.

**REMEMBER**

The Array object's toString() method performs a similar function to the join() method. Using *array*.toString() takes the values in *array*, converts them all to strings, and then concatenates them into a single, comma-separated string. In other words, *array*.toString() is identical to *array*.join(","), or just *array*.join().

**TIP**

You can use the Array object's from() method to perform the opposite operation: create an array from a string, where the array elements are the individual string characters:

```javascript
Array.from("Boo!") // Returns ["B", "o", "o", "!"]
```

# Removing an array's last element: pop()

The pop() method removes the last element from an array and returns the value of that element. Here's the syntax:

```javascript
array.pop()
```

For example, consider the following statements:

```
const myArray = ["First", "Second", "Third"];
const myString = myArray.pop();
```

The last element of myArray is "Third", so myArray.pop() removes that value from the array and stores it in the myString variable.

**REMEMBER**

After you run the pop() method, JavaScript reduces the value of the array's length property by one.

## Adding elements to the end of an array: push()

The push() method is the opposite of pop(): It adds one or more elements to the end of an array. Here's the syntax to use:

```
array.push(value1, value2, ...)
```

>> *array:* The name of the array you want to work with.

>> *value1, value2, ...:* The values you want to add to the end of *array*. This can also be another array.

push() differs from the concat() method in that it doesn't return a new array. Instead, it changes the existing array by adding the new values to the end of the array. For example, consider the following statements:

```
const myArray = ["First", "Second", "Third"];
const pushArray = ["Fourth", "Fifth", "Sixth"];
for (let i = 0; i < pushArray.length; i += 1) {
    myArray.push(pushArray[i]);
}
```

After these statements, myArray contains six values: "First", "Second", "Third", "Fourth", "Fifth", and "Sixth". Why didn't I just add the entire pushArray in one fell swoop? That is, like so:

```
myArray.push(pushArray);
```

That's perfectly legal, but it would mean myArray would contain the following four elements: "First", "Second", "Third", and pushArray, which means you've created a kind of hybrid multidimensional array, which is probably not what you want in this situation.

After you run the push() method, JavaScript increases the value of the array's length property by the number of new elements added.

## Reversing the order of an array's elements: reverse()

The reverse() method takes the existing elements in an array and reverses their order: The first moves to the last, the last moves to the first, and so on. The syntax takes just a second to show:

```
array.reverse()
```

The following code (bk04ch07/example11.html) puts the reverse() method to work, and Figure 7-8 shows what happens.

```
const myArray = ["Show", "Place", "Win"];
myArray.reverse();
console.log(myArray);
```

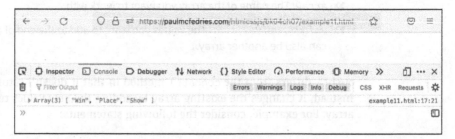

**FIGURE 7-8:**
Use the reverse() method to reverse the order of elements in an array.

## Removing an array's first element: shift()

The shift() method removes the first element from an array and returns the value of that element:

```
array.shift()
```

For example, consider the following statements:

```
const myArray = ["First", "Second", "Third"];
const myString = myArray.shift();
```

The first element of myArray is "First", so myArray.shift() removes that value from the array and stores it in the myString variable.

**REMEMBER**

After you run the `shift()` method, JavaScript reduces the value of the array's `length` property by one.

# Returning a subset of an array: slice()

The `slice()` method returns a new array that contains a subset of the elements in an existing array. Here's the syntax:

```
array.slice(start, end);
```

> » *array:* The name of the array you want to work with.

> » *start:* A number that specifies the index of the first element in *array* that you want to include in the subset. If this number is negative, the subset starting point is counted from the end of *array* (for example, -1 is the last element of the array). If you leave out this value, JavaScript uses 0 (that is, the first element of the array).

> » *end:* An optional number that specifies the index of the element in *array* *before which* you want the subset to end. If you leave out this value, the subset includes all the elements in *array* from *start* to the last element. This value can be negative.

**TIP**

A quick way to make a copy of an array is to use `slice()` without any parameters:

```
const thisArray = ["alpha", "beta", "gamma"];
const thatArray = thisArray.slice();
// thatArray() is ["alpha", "beta", "gamma"];
```

**TIP**

You can also quickly copy an array by using the spread operator (. . .), as described earlier in the sidebar, "A quick look at the spread operator (. . .)":

```
const thisArray = ["alpha", "beta", "gamma"];
const thatArray = [...thisArray];
// thatArray() is ["alpha", "beta", "gamma"];
```

The following code (bk04ch07/example12.html) defines an array and then tries out various values for the `slice()` arguments. The results are shown in Figure 7-9.

HTML:

```
<div id="output">
</div>
```

JavaScript:

```javascript
const myArray = ["A", "B", "C", "D", "E", "F"];
const array1 = myArray.slice(0, 4);
const array2 = myArray.slice(3);
const array3 = myArray.slice(-3, -1);
let str = "array1: " + array1 + "<br>";
str += "array2: " + array2 + "<br>";
str += "array3: " + array3;
document.getElementById('output').innerHTML = str;
```

**FIGURE 7-9:**
The slice()
method creates
a new array
from a subset of
another array.

← → C    ○ 🔒 ⇄ https://paulmcfedries.com/htmlcssjs/bk04ch07/example12.html    ☆    ⊙  ≡

array1: A,B,C,D
array2: D,E,F
array3: D,E

## Ordering array elements: sort()

The sort() method is an easy way to handle a common programming problem: rearranging an array's elements to put them in alphabetical, numerical, or some other order. There are four syntaxes you can use:

```javascript
array.sort()
array.sort(namedFunction)
array.sort(namedFunction (a, b) { code });
array.sort((a, b) => { code });
```

» *array:* The name of the array you want to sort

» *namedFunction:* The name of an existing function that performs the sorting operation by comparing the array items two at a time, where the first array item in the comparison is passed as argument *a* and the second array item in the comparison is passed as argument *b*

» *code:* The statements to run during each iteration to perform the sorting operation on each value

Using sort() without an argument gives you a straightforward alphabetical sort:

```javascript
myArray.sort();
```

If you want to sort the array based on some other criterion, you need to create a function to define the sort order. Your function must be set up as follows:

>> The function must accept two arguments, which represent two array values to be compared so that they can be sorted relative to each other. For the purposes of this list, I'll call these arguments a and b.

>> Using these arguments, the function must define an expression that returns a numeric value.

>> For those cases where you want a sorted before b, the function must return a negative value.

>> For those cases where you want a sorted after b, the function must return a positive value.

>> For those cases where you want a and b to be treated equally, the function must return zero.

The following code (bk04ch07/example13.html) shows a function named numericSort that you can use if you want a numeric sort from lowest to highest. Figure 7-10 displays the original array and then the sorted array.

HTML:

```
<div id="output">
</div>
```

JavaScript:

```
// This function sorts numbers from highest to lowest
function numericSort(a, b) {
    return b - a;
}

const myArray = [3, 5, 1, 6, 2, 4];

// Write the array before sorting it
let str = "myArray (before sorting): " + myArray + "<br>";

// Sort the array
myArray.sort(numericSort);

// Write the array after sorting it
str+= "myArray (after sorting): " + myArray;

document.getElementById('output').innerHTML = str;
```

**TIP**

To get a numeric sort from lowest to highest, either use sort() without an argument or use the following return expression:

```
return a - b;
```

FIGURE 7-10:
Using sort()
and a function
to sort items
numerically from
highest to lowest.

```
←  →  C    🔒 paulmcfedries.com/htmlcssjs/bk04ch07/example13
```

myArray (before sorting): 3,5,1,6,2,4
myArray (after sorting): 6,5,4,3,2,1

**TIP**

What if you want a reverse alphabetical sort? Just chain sort() with reverse():

```
myArray.sort().reverse();
```

# Removing, replacing, and inserting elements: splice()

The splice() method is a complex function that comes in handy in all kinds of situations. First, here's the syntax:

```
array.splice(start, elementsToDelete, value1, value2, ...)
```

» *array:* The name of the array you want to work with.

» *start:* A number that specifies the index of the element where the splice takes place.

» *elementsToDelete:* An optional number that specifies how many elements to delete from *array* beginning at the *start* position. If you don't include this argument, elements are deleted from *start* to the end of the array.

» *value1, value2, ...:* Optional values to insert into *array* beginning at the *start* position.

With splice() at your side, you can perform one or more of the following tasks:

» **Deletion:** If *elementsToDelete* is greater than zero or unspecified and no insertion values are included, splice() deletes elements beginning at the index *start*. The deleted elements are returned in a separate array.

>> **Replacement:** If *elementsToDelete* is greater than zero or unspecified and one or more insertion values are included, splice( ) first deletes elements beginning at the index *start*. It then inserts the specified values at index *start*.

>> **Insertion:** If *elementsToDelete* is 0, splice( ) inserts the specified values at index *start*.

The following code (bk04ch07/example14.html) demonstrates all three tasks, and the results are shown in Figure 7-11.

HTML:

```
<div id="output">
</div>
```

JavaScript:

```
const array1 = ["A", "B", "C", "D", "E", "F"];
const array2 = ["A", "B", "C", "D", "E", "F"];
const array3 = ["A", "B", "C", "D", "E", "F"];

// DELETION
// In array1, start at index 2 and delete to the end
// Return the deleted elements to the delete1 array
const delete1 = array1.splice(2);

// Write array1
let str = "array1: " + array1 + "<br>";

// Write delete1
str += "delete1: " + delete1 + "<br>";

// REPLACEMENT
// In array2, start at index 3 and delete 2 elements
// Insert 2 elements to replace them
// Return the deleted elements to the delete2 array
const delete2 = array2.splice(3, 2, "d", "e");

// Write array2
str += "array2: " + array2 + "<br>";

// Write delete2
str += "delete2: " + delete2 + "<br>";
```

```
// INSERTION
// In array3, start at index 1 and insert 3 elements
array3.splice(1, 0, "1", "2", "3")

// Write array3
str += "array3: " + array3;

document.getElementById('output').innerHTML = str;
```

**FIGURE 7-11:**
The splice()
method can
delete, replace,
and insert array
elements.

← → C  ○ 🔒 ⇄ https://paulmcfedries.com/htmlcssjs/bk04ch07/example14.html  ☆  ▽  ≡

array1: A,B
delete1: C,D,E,F
array2: A,B,C,d,e,F
delete2: D,E
array3: A,1,2,3,B,C,D,E,F

## Inserting elements at the beginning of an array: unshift()

The unshift() method is the opposite of the shift() method: It inserts one or more values at the beginning of an array. When it's done, unshift() returns the new length of the array. Here's the syntax:

```
array.unshift(value1, value2, ...)
```

>> *array:* The name of the array you want to work with

>> *value1, value2, ...:* The values you want to add to the beginning of *array*

For example, consider the following statements:

```
const myArray = ["First", "Second", "Third"];
const newLength = myArray.unshift("Fourth", "Fifth", "Sixth");
```

After these statements, myArray contains six values — "Fourth", "Fifth", and "Sixth", "First", "Second", and "Third" — and the value of newLength is 6.

# Chapter **8**

# Manipulating Strings, Dates, and Numbers

*All great programmers learn the same way. They poke the box. They code something and see what the computer does. They change it and see what the computer does. They repeat the process again and again until they figure out how the box works.*

—SETH GODIN

lthough your JavaScript code will spend much of its time dealing with web page knickknacks such as HTML tags and CSS properties, it will also perform lots of behind-the-scenes chores that require manipulating strings, dealing with dates and times, and performing mathematical calculations. To help you through these tasks, in this chapter you explore three of JavaScript's built-in objects: the String object, the Date object, and the Math object. You investigate the most important properties of each object, master the most used methods, and encounter lots of useful examples along the way.

# Manipulating Text with the String Object

I've used dozens of examples of strings so far in this book. These include not only string literals (such as `"HTML, CSS, and JavaScript For Dummies"`) but also methods that return strings (such as the `prompt()` method). So, it should be clear by now that strings play a major role in all JavaScript programming, and it will be a rare script that doesn't have to deal with strings in some fashion.

For this reason, it pays to become proficient at manipulating strings, which includes locating text within a string and extracting text from a string. You'll find out about all that and more in this section.

Any string you work with — whether it's a string literal or the result of a method or function that returns a string — is a `String` object. So, for example, the following two statements are equivalent:

```
const bookName = new String("HTML, CSS, and JavaScript For
    Dummies");
const bookName = "HTML, CSS, and JavaScript For Dummies";
```

This means that you have quite a bit of flexibility when applying the properties and methods of `String` objects. For example, the `String` object has a `length` property that I describe in the next section. The following are all legal JavaScript expressions that use this property:

```
bookName.length;
"HTML, CSS, and JavaScript For Dummies".length;
prompt("Enter the book name:").length;
myFunction().length;
```

The last example assumes that `myFunction()` returns a string value.

## Working with string templates

Before diving in to the properties and methods of the `String` object, take a second to examine a special type of string that's designed to solve three string-related problems that will come up again and again in your coding career:

>> **Handling internal quotation marks:** String literals are surrounded by quotation marks, but what do you do when you need the same type of quotation mark inside the string?

One solution is to use a different type of quotation mark to delimit the string. For example, this is illegal:

```
'There's got to be some better way to do this.'
```

But this is fine:

```
"There's got to be some better way to do this."
```

A second solution is to escape the internal quotation mark with a slash, like so:

```
'There\'s got to be some better way to do this.'
```

These solutions work fine, but *remembering* to use them is harder than you may think!

» **Incorporating variable values:** When you need to use the value of a variable inside a string, you usually end up with something ungainly, such as the following:

```
const adjective = "better";
const lament = "There's got to be some " + adjective + "
    way to do this.";
```

» **Multiline strings:** It's occasionally useful to define a string using multiple lines. However, if you try the following, you'll get a `string literal contains an unescaped line break` error:

```
const myHeader = '
    <nav class="banner">
        <h3 class="nav-heading">Navigation</h3>
        <ul class="nav-links">
            <li>Home</li>
            <li>Away</li>
            <li>In Between</li>
        </ul>
    </nav>'
```

You can solve all three problems by using a *string template* (also called a *template literal*), which is a kind of string literal where the delimiting quotation marks are replaced by back ticks (`` ` ``):

```
`Your string goes here`
```

**REMEMBER**

String templates were introduced as part of ECMAScript 2015 (ES6), so use them only if you don't need to support ancient web browsers such as Internet Explorer 11.

Here's how you can use a string template to solve each of the three problems just described:

» **Handling internal quotation marks:** You're free to plop any number of single or double quotation marks inside a string template:

```
`Ah, here's the better way to do this!`
```

» **Incorporating variable values:** String templates support something called *variable interpolation,* which is a technique for referencing a variable value directly within a string. Here's an example:

```
const adjective = "better";
const paean = `Ah, here's the ${adjective} way to do
   this!`;
```

Within any string template, using ${*variable*} inserts the value of *variable*, no questions asked. Actually, you don't have to stick to just variables. String templates can also interpolate any JavaScript expression, including function results.

» **Multiline strings:** String templates are happy to work error free with strings that are spread over multiple lines:

```
const myHeader = `
    <nav class="banner">
        <h3 class="nav-heading">Navigation</h3>
        <ul class="nav-links">
            <li>Home</li>
            <li>Away</li>
            <li>In Between</li>
        </ul>
    </nav>`
```

## Determining the length of a string

The most basic property of a `String` object is its `length`, which tells you how many characters are in the string:

```
string.length
```

All characters within the string — including spaces and punctuation marks — are counted toward the length. The only exceptions are escape sequences (such as \n), which always count as one character. The following code grabs the length property value for various `String` object types.

```
function myFunction() {
    return "filename.htm";
}
const bookName = "HTML, CSS, and JavaScript For Dummies";

length1 = myFunction().length; // Returns 12
length2 = bookName.length; // Returns 37
length3 = "123\n5678".length; // Returns 8
```

What the `String` object lacks in properties, it more than makes up for in methods. There are dozens, and they enable your code to perform many useful tasks, from converting between uppercase and lowercase letters, to finding text within a string, to extracting parts of a string.

## Searching for substrings

A *substring* is a portion of an existing string. For example, some substrings of the string "JavaScript" would be "Java", "Script", "vaSc", and "v". When working with strings in your scripts, you'll often have to determine whether a given string contains a given substring. For example, if you're validating a user's email address, you should check that it contains an @ symbol.

Table 8-1 lists the several `String` object methods that find substrings within a larger string.

You'll use each of these methods quite often in your scripts, so I take a closer look at them in the sections that follow.

**TABLE 8-1** **String Object Methods for Searching for Substrings**

| Method | What It Does |
| --- | --- |
| *string*.endsWith(*substring*, *start*) | Tests whether *substring* appears at the end of *string* |
| *string*.includes(*substring*, *start*) | Tests whether *substring* appears in *string* |
| *string*.indexOf(*substring*, *start*) | Searches *string* for the first instance of *substring* |
| *string*.lastIndexOf(*substring*, *start*) | Searches *string* for the last instance of *substring* |
| *string*.startsWith(*substring*, *start*) | Tests whether *substring* appears at the beginning of *string* |

## The startsWith(), includes(), and endsWith() methods

If you just want to know whether a particular substring exists within a larger string, use one of the following methods:

```
string.startsWith(substring, position)
string.includes(substring, position)
string.endsWith(substring, position)
```

>> *string:* The string in which you want to search.

>> *substring:* The substring that you want to search for in *string*.

>> *position:* An optional numeric value that defines either the starting character position for the search (for the startsWith() and includes() methods) or the ending character position for the search (for the endsWith() method). If you omit this argument, JavaScript starts the search from the beginning of the string (for the startsWith() and includes() methods) or the end of the string (for the endsWith() method).

The search is case sensitive. These methods return true if they find *substring* in *string*; they return false, otherwise. Here are some examples (check out bk04ch08/example01.html in this book's example files):

```
const bookName = "HTML, CSS, and JavaScript For Dummies";
bookName.startsWith("HTML"); // Returns true
bookName.startsWith("CSS", 6); // Returns true
bookName.includes("JavaScript"); // Returns true
bookName.includes("And"); // Returns false
bookName.endsWith("Dummies"); // Returns true
bookName.endsWith("JavaScript", 25); // Returns true
```

On a more practical note, the following code (check out bk04ch08/example01a. html) presents a simple validation script that uses includes():

```
let emailAddress = "";
do {
    emailAddress = prompt("Enter a valid email address:");
}
while (!emailAddress.includes("@"));
```

The script prompts the user for a valid email address, which is stored in the emailAddress variable. Any valid address will contain the @ symbol, so the while() portion of a do...while() loop checks to determine whether the entered string contains @:

```
while (!emailAddress.includes("@"));
```

If not (that is, if emailAddress.includes("@") returns false), the loop continues and the user is prompted again.

The startsWith(), endsWith(), and includes() methods were introduced as
part of ECMAScript 2015 (ES6), so use them only if you don't need to support
ancient web browsers such as Internet Explorer 11.

## The indexOf() and lastIndexOf() methods

When you want to find the first instance of a substring, use the indexOf() method;
if you need to find the last instance of a substring, use the lastIndexOf() method:

```
string.indexOf(substring, start)
string.lastIndexOf(substring, start)
```

>> *string:* The string in which you want to search.

>> *substring:* The substring that you want to search for in *string*.

>> *start:* An optional character position from which the search begins. If you
   omit this argument, JavaScript starts the search from the beginning of the
   string (for the indexOf() method) or the end of the string (for the last
   IndexOf() method).

Here are some notes you should keep in mind when using indexOf() or
lastIndexOf():

>> Each character in a string is given an index number, which is the same as the
   character's position within the string.

>> Strings, like arrays, are *zero-based,* which means that the first character has
   index 0, the second character has index 1, and so on.

>> Both methods are case sensitive. For example, if you search for B, neither
   method will find any instances of b.

>> If either method finds *substring*, they return the index position of the first
   character of *substring*.

>> If either method doesn't find *substring*, they return -1.

The following code (bk04ch08/example02.html) tries out these methods in a few
different situations:

HTML:

```
<pre>
HTML, CSS, and JavaScript For Dummies
01234567890123456789012345678901234567890123456
</pre>
<div id="output"></div>
```

JavaScript:

```
const bookName = "HTML, CSS, and JavaScript For Dummies";

let str = "\"C\" is at index " + bookName.indexOf("C") + "<br>";
str += "\"v\" is at index " + bookName.indexOf("v") + "<br>";
str += "The first space is at index " + bookName.indexOf(" ") +
    "<br>";
str += "The first \"S\" is at index " + bookName.indexOf("S") +
    "<br>";
str += "The last \"S\" is at index " + bookName.lastIndexOf("S")
    + "<br>";
str += "The first \"a\" after index 12 is at index " +
    bookName.indexOf("a", 12) + "<br>";
str += "The substring \"Script\" begins at index " + bookName.
    indexOf("Script");

document.getElementById("output").innerHTML = str;
```

As shown in Figure 8-1, the numbers show you the index positions of each character in the script.

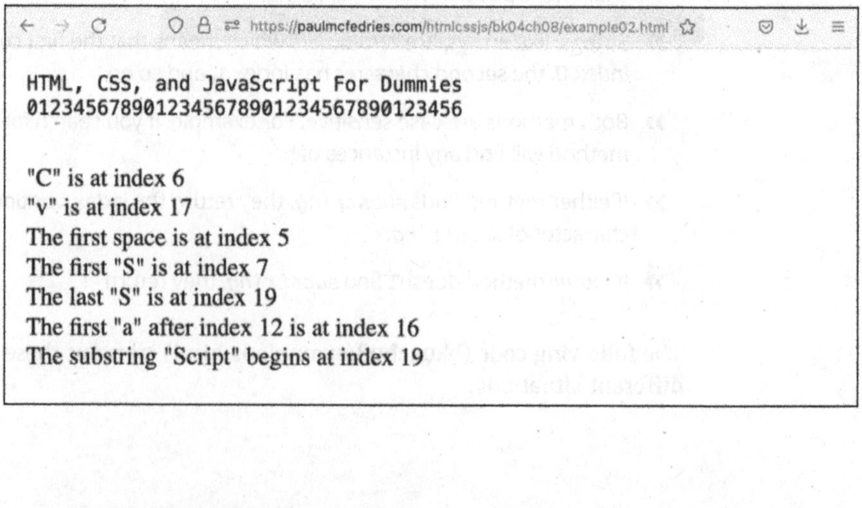

FIGURE 8-1:
The indexOf() and lastIndexOf() methods search for substrings within a string.

The browser window shows:

HTML, CSS, and JavaScript For Dummies
01234567890123456789012345678901234567890123456

"C" is at index 6
"v" is at index 17
The first space is at index 5
The first "S" is at index 7
The last "S" is at index 19
The first "a" after index 12 is at index 16
The substring "Script" begins at index 19

# Methods that extract substrings

Finding a substring is one thing, but you'll often have to extract a substring, as well. For example, if the user enters an email address, you may need to extract just the username (the part to the left of the @ sign) or the domain name (the part to the right of @). For these kinds of operations, JavaScript offers six methods, listed in Table 8-2.

**TABLE 8-2**     **String Object Methods for Extracting Substrings**

| Method | What It Does |
| --- | --- |
| *string*.charAt(*index*) | Returns the character in *string* that's at the index position specified by *index* |
| string.charCodeAt(*index*) | Returns the code of the character in *string* that's at the index position specified by *index* |
| string.slice(*start*, *end*) | Returns the substring in *string* that starts at the index position specified by *start* and ends immediately before the index position specified by *end* |
| string.split(*separator*, *limit*) | Returns an array where each item is a substring in *string*, where those substrings are separated by the *separator* character |
| string.substr(*start*, *length*) | Returns the substring in *string* that starts at the index position specified by *start* and is *length* characters long |
| *string*.substring(start, end) | Returns the substring in *string* that starts at the index position specified by *start* and ends immediately before the index position specified by *end* |

## The charAt() method

You use the charAt() method to return a single character that resides at a specified position within a string:

```
string.charAt(index)
```

>> *string:* The string that contains the character

>> *index:* The position within *string* of the character you want

Here are some notes about this method:

>> To return the first character in *string,* use the following:

```
string.charAt(0)
```

>> To return the last character in *string,* use this:

```
string.charAt(string.length - 1)
```

>> If the *index* value is negative or if it's greater than or equal to *string*.length, JavaScript returns the empty string ("").

The following code presents an example (bk04ch08/example03.html):

HTML:

```
<div id="output"></div>
```

JavaScript:

```
// Set up an array of test strings
const stringArray = [];
stringArray[0] = "Not this one.";
stringArray[1] = "Not this one, either.";
stringArray[2] = "1. Step one.";
stringArray[3] = "Shouldn't get this far.";

// Loop through the array
for (const currentString of stringArray) {

    // Get the first character of the string
    const firstChar = currentString.charAt(0);

    // Is it a number?
    if (!isNaN(firstChar)) {

        // If so, display the string because that's the one
we want
        document.getElementById("output").innerHTML = `Here's
the one: "${currentString}"`;

        // We're done here, so break out of the loop
        break;
    }
}
```

The idea here is to examine a collection of strings and find the one that starts with a number. The collection is stored in the array named stringArray, and a for . . . of loop is set up to run through each item in the array. The charAt() method is applied to each array item (stored in the currentString variable) to return the first character, which is stored in the firstChar variable. In the if test, the logical expression !isNaN(firstChar) returns true if the firstChar value is a number, at which point the correct string is displayed in the web page and the loop breaks.

**TIP**

Each character in a JavaScript string has an index number, where the first character is index 0, the second character is index 1, and so on. You specify a particular character using square bracket notation. For example, the expression myString[5] references the character at index 5 of whatever string is stored in the myString variable.

Therefore, an alternative to using charAt() is to reference the character you want by its index number. For example, the following two expressions reference the same character:

```
currentString.charAt(0)
currentString[0]
```

## The slice() method

Use the slice() method to carve out a piece of a string:

*string*.slice(*start*, *end*)

>> *string:* The string you want to work with.

>> *start:* The position within *string* of the first character you want to extract.

>> *end:* An optional position within *string* immediately after the last character you want to extract. If you leave out this argument, JavaScript extracts the substring that runs from *start* to the end of the string. Also, this argument can be negative, in which case it specifies an offset from the end of the string.

To be clear, slice() extracts a substring that runs from the character at *start* up to, but not including, the character at *end*.

The following code (bk04ch08/example04.html) runs through a few examples (check out Figure 8-2):

HTML:

```
<pre>
HTML, CSS, and JavaScript For Dummies
012345678901234567890123456789012345 6
</pre>
<div id="output"></div>
```

JavaScript:

```javascript
const bookName = "HTML, CSS, and JavaScript For Dummies";

let str = "slice(0, 4) = " + bookName.slice(0, 4) + "<br>";
str += "slice(6, 9) = " + bookName.slice(6, 9) + "<br>";
str += "slice(15) = " + bookName.slice(15) + "<br>";
str += "slice(0, -12) = " + bookName.slice(0, -12);
document.getElementById("output").innerHTML = str;
```

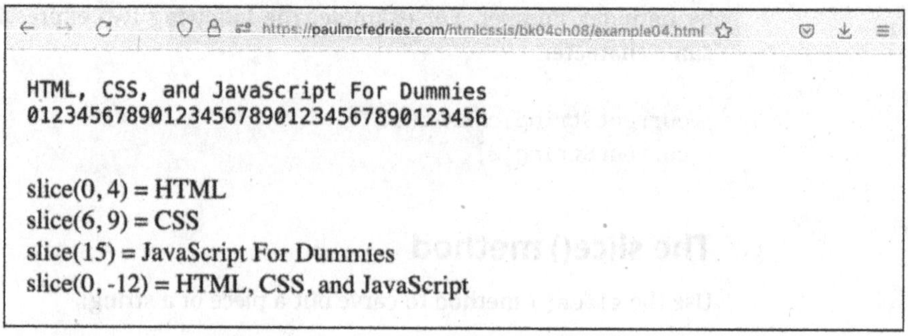

← → C    ⟳ 🔒 ⚏ https://paulmcfedries.com/htmlcssjs/bk04ch08/example04.html ☆    ▽ ↓ ≡

HTML, CSS, and JavaScript For Dummies
01234567890123456789012345678901234567890123456

slice(0, 4) = HTML
slice(6, 9) = CSS
slice(15) = JavaScript For Dummies
slice(0, -12) = HTML, CSS, and JavaScript

**FIGURE 8-2:**
Some examples
of the slice()
method in action.

## The split() method

The split() method breaks up a string and returns an array that stores the pieces:

```javascript
string.split(separator, limit)
```

>> *string:* The string you want to work with.

>> *separator:* The character used to mark the positions at which *string* is split. For example, if *separator* is a comma, the splits will occur at each comma in *string*.

>> *limit:* An optional value that sets the maximum number of items to store in the array. For example, if *limit* is 5, split() stores the first five pieces in the array and then ignores the rest of the string.

TIP

If you want each character in the string stored as an individual array item, use the empty string ("") as the *separator* value.

The split() method is useful for those times when you have a "well-structured" string. This means that the string contains a character that acts as a delimiter between each string piece that you want to set up as an array item. For example, it's common to have to deal with *comma-delimited* strings:

```
string1 = "Sunday,Monday,Tuesday,Wednesday,Thursday,Friday,
  Saturday";
```

Handily, each day in the string is separated by a comma, which makes using the `split()` method a no-brainer:

```
const string1Array = string1.split(",");
```

When you run this statement, `string1Array[0]` will contain `"Sunday"`, `string1Array[1]` will contain `"Monday"`, and so on. Note, too, that JavaScript sets up the array for you automatically. You don't have to declare the array using `new Array()`.

The following code (bk04ch08/example05.html) tries out `split()` with a couple of example strings:

HTML:

```
<div id="output"></div>
```

JavaScript:

```
const string1 = "Sunday,Monday,Tuesday,Wednesday,Thursday,Friday,
  Saturday";
const string2 = "ABCDEF";
let str = "";

const string1Array = string1.split(",");
string1Array.forEach((value, index) => {
    str += `string1Array[${index}] = ${value}<br>`;
});

const string2Array = string2.split("", 4);
string2Array.forEach ((value, index) => {
    str += `string2Array[${index}] = ${value}<br>`;
});

document.getElementById("output").innerHTML = str;
```

After `string1` is split into `string1Array`, that array's `forEach()` method runs through the array and writes the items to the global `str` variable. For `string2`, the empty string is used as the separator and a limit of 4 is placed on the size of the `string2Array`. Again, that array's `forEach()` methods writes the array values to the `str` variable. The script closes by writing `str` to the page. Figure 8-3 shows what happens.

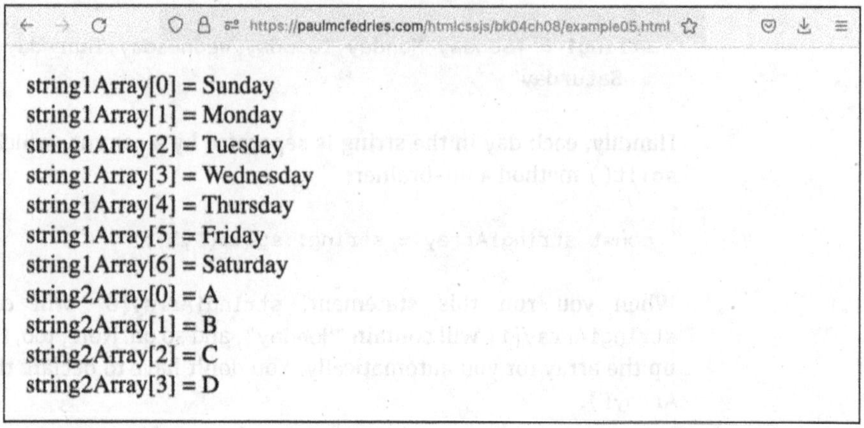

https://paulmcfedries.com/htmlcssjs/bk04ch08/example05.html

```
string1Array[0] = Sunday
string1Array[1] = Monday
string1Array[2] = Tuesday
string1Array[3] = Wednesday
string1Array[4] = Thursday
string1Array[5] = Friday
string1Array[6] = Saturday
string2Array[0] = A
string2Array[1] = B
string2Array[2] = C
string2Array[3] = D
```

**FIGURE 8-3:**
Some examples
of the split()
method.

## The substr() method

If you want to extract a substring and you know how long you want that substring
to be, the substr() method is often the best approach:

*string*.substr(*index*, *length*)

» *string:* The string you want to work with.

» *index:* The position within *string* of the first character you want to extract.

» *length:* An optional value that specifies the length of the substring. If you
omit this argument, JavaScript extracts all the way to the end of the string.

The following code (bk04ch08/example06.html) runs substr() through some
examples; the results appear in Figure 8-4.

HTML:

```
<pre>
HTML, CSS, and JavaScript For Dummies
0123456789012345678901234567890123456
</pre>
<div id="output"></div>
```

JavaScript:

```
const bookName = "HTML, CSS, and JavaScript For Dummies";

let str = "substr(0, 9) = " + bookName.substr(0, 9)+"<br>";
str += "substr(15, 10) = " + bookName.substr(15, 10) + "<br>";
```

```
str += "substr(26) = " + bookName.substr(26);

document.getElementById("output").innerHTML = str;
```

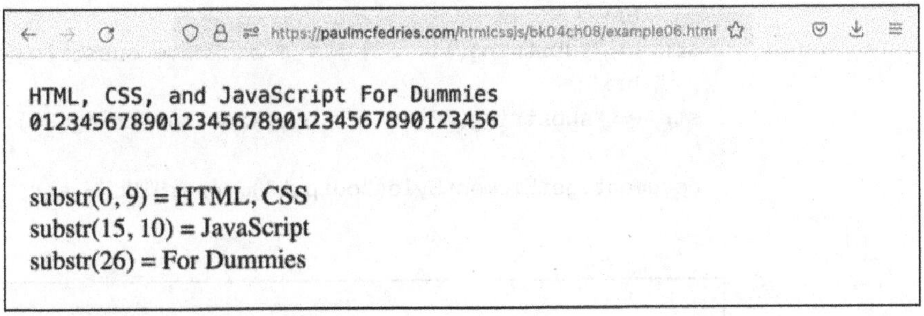

```
←  →  C        ○ 🔒 ⇌ https://paulmcfedries.com/htmlcssjs/bk04ch08/example06.html  ☆        ♡  ↓  ≡

HTML, CSS, and JavaScript For Dummies
012345678901234567890123456789012345

substr(0, 9) = HTML, CSS
substr(15, 10) = JavaScript
substr(26) = For Dummies
```

FIGURE 8-4:
Some examples
of the substr()
method.

## The substring() method

Use the substring() method to extract a substring from a string:

*string*.substring(*start*, *end*)

>> *string:* The string you want to work with.

>> *start:* The position within *string* of the first character you want to extract.

>> *end:* An optional value that specifies the position within *string* immediately after the last character you want to extract. If you leave out this argument, JavaScript extracts the substring that runs from *start* to the end of the string.

The following code (bk04ch08/example07.html) gives the substring() method a whirl, and the results are shown in Figure 8-5.

HTML:

```
<pre>
HTML, CSS, and JavaScript For Dummies
012345678901234567890123456789012345
</pre>

<div id="output"></div>
```

JavaScript:

```javascript
const bookName = "HTML, CSS, and JavaScript For Dummies";

let str = "substring(0, 9) = " + bookName.substring(0, 9) +
    "<br>";
str += "substring(11, 14) = " + bookName.substring(11, 14) +
    "<br>";
str += "substring(30) = " + bookName.substring(30);

document.getElementById("output").innerHTML = str;
```

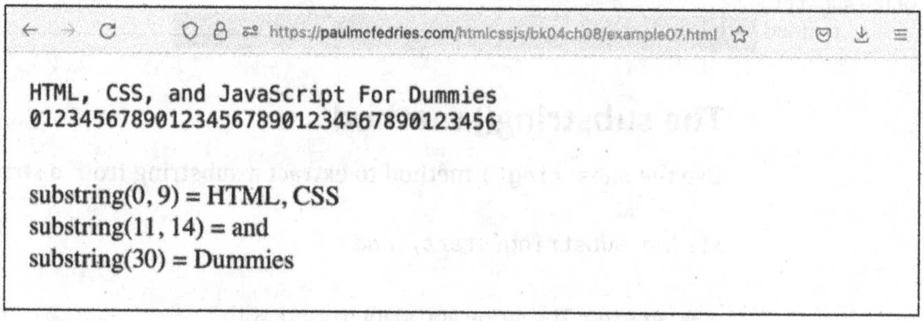

```
←  →  C       O  🔒  ⇄  https://paulmcfedries.com/htmlcssjs/bk04ch08/example07.html  ☆        ♡  ↓  ≡

HTML, CSS, and JavaScript For Dummies
012345678901234567890123456789012456

substring(0, 9) = HTML, CSS
substring(11, 14) = and
substring(30) = Dummies
```

**FIGURE 8-5:**
Some examples of the substring() method.

## Understanding the differences between splice(), substr(), and substring()

The splice(), substr(), and substring() methods are very similar and are often confused by even experienced JavaScript programmers. Here are some notes to help you understand the differences between these three string extraction methods:

» The splice() and substring() methods perform the same task. The only difference is that splice() enables you to use a negative value for the *end* argument. This is handy if you want to leave out a certain number of characters from the end of the original string. For example, if you wanted to extract everything but the last three characters, you'd use this:

```javascript
string.splice(0, -3)
```

» Use either splice() or substring() when you're not sure how long the extracted string will be. This usually means that you'll use the indexOf() and lastIndexOf() methods to find particular characters that mark the starting and ending points of the substring you want. You then use those values as the *start* and *end* arguments of splice() or substring(). For example, suppose you have a string of the form www.domain.com and you want to extract just the domain part. Here's a short routine that will do it:

```
const hostName = "www.domain.com";
const firstDot = hostName.indexOf(".");
const lastDot = hostName.lastIndexOf(".");
const domainName = hostName.substring(firstDot + 1, lastDot);
```

**TIP**

This technique for extracting the domain name is illustrative, but woefully inefficient. Here's a one-liner that takes advantage of the split() method (which I discuss earlier in this chapter; check out "The split() method"):

```
const domainName = hostName.split('.')[1];
```

» On the other hand, if you know in advance exactly how long the extracted string must be, use the substr() method.

# Dealing with Dates and Times

Dates and times seem like the kind of things that ought to be straightforward programming propositions. After all, there are only 12 months in a year, 28 to 31 days in a month, seven days in a week, 24 hours in a day, 60 minutes in an hour, and 60 seconds in a minute. Surely something so set in stone couldn't get even the least bit weird, could it?

You'd be surprised. Dates and times *can* get strange, but they get much easier to deal with if you always keep three crucial points in mind:

» JavaScript time is measured in milliseconds, or thousandths of a second. More specifically, JavaScript measures time by counting the number of milliseconds that elapsed between January 1, 1970 and the date and time in question. So, for example, *you* might come across the date January 1, 2001, and think, "Ah, yes, the start of the new millennium." *JavaScript,* however, comes across that date and thinks "978220800000."

» In the JavaScript world, time began on January 1, 1970, at midnight Greenwich Mean Time. Dates before that have *negative* values in milliseconds.

>> Because your JavaScript programs run inside a user's browser, dates and times are almost always the user's *local* dates and times. That is, the dates and times your scripts will manipulate will *not* be those of the server on which your page resides. This means that you can never know what time the user is viewing your page.

## Arguments used with the Date object

Before getting to the nitty-gritty of the Date object and its associated methods, I'll take a second to run through the various arguments that JavaScript requires for many date-related features. This will save me from repeating these arguments tediously later on. Table 8-3 has the details.

**TABLE 8-3**      **Arguments Associated with the Date Object**

| Argument | What It Represents | Possible Values |
|---|---|---|
| date | A variable name | A Date object |
| yyyy | The year | Four-digit integers |
| yy | The year | Two-digit integers |
| month | The month | The full month name from "January" to "December" |
| mth | The month | Integers from 0 (January) to 11 (December) |
| dd | The day of the month | Integers from 1 to 31 |
| hh | The hour of the day | Integers from 0 (midnight) to 23 (11:00 PM) |
| mm | The minute of the hour | Integers from 0 to 59 |
| ss | The second of the minute | Integers from 0 to 59 |
| ms | The milliseconds of the second | Integers from 0 to 999 |

## Working with the Date object

Whenever you work with dates and times in JavaScript, you work with an instance of the Date object. More to the point, when you deal with a Date object in Java-Script, you deal with a specific moment in time, down to the millisecond. A Date object can never be a block of time, and it's not a kind of clock that ticks along while your script runs. Instead, the Date object is a temporal snapshot that you use to extract the specifics of the time it was taken: the year, month, date, hour, and so on.

## Specifying the current date and time

The most common use of the Date object is to store the current date and time. You do that by invoking the Date() function, which is the constructor function for creating a new Date object. Here's the general format:

```
const dateToday = new Date();
```

## Specifying any date and time

If you need to work with a specific date or time, you need to use the Date() function's arguments. There are five versions of the Date() function syntax (refer to the list of arguments near the beginning of this chapter):

```
const date = new Date("month dd, yyyy hh:mm:ss");
const date = new Date("month dd, yyyy");
const date = new Date(yyyy, mth, dd, hh, mm, ss);
const date = new Date(yyyy, mth, dd);
const date = new Date(ms);
```

The following statements give you an example for each syntax:

```
const myDate = new Date("August 23, 2023 3:02:01");
const myDate = new Date("August 23, 2023");
const myDate = new Date(2023, 8, 23, 3, 2, 1);
const myDate = new Date(2023, 8, 23);
const myDate = new Date(1692763200000);
```

# Extracting information about a date

When your script just coughs up whatever Date object value you stored in the variable, the results aren't particularly appealing. If you want to display dates in a more attractive format, or if you want to perform arithmetic operations on a date, you need to dig a little deeper into the Date object to extract specific information such as the month, year, hour, and so on. You do that by using the Date object methods listed in Table 8-4.

One of the ways you can take advantage of these methods is to display the time or date to the user using any format you want. Here's an example (bk04ch08/example08.html):

HTML:

```
<div id="output"></div>
```

**TABLE 8-4**      **Date Object Methods That Extract Date Values**

| Method Syntax | What It Returns |
| --- | --- |
| *date*.getFullYear() | The year as a four-digit number (1999, 2000, and so on) |
| *date*.getMonth() | The month of the year; from 0 (January) to 11 (December) |
| *date*.getDate() | The date in the month; from 1 to 31 |
| *date*.getDay() | The day of the week; from 0 (Sunday) to 6 (Saturday) |
| *date*.getHours() | The hour of the day; from 0 (midnight) to 23 (11:00 PM) |
| *date*.getMinutes() | The minute of the hour; from 0 to 59 |
| *date*.getSeconds() | The second of the minute; from 0 to 59 |
| *date*.getMilliseconds() | The milliseconds of the second; from 0 to 999 |
| *date*.getTime() | The milliseconds since January 1, 1970 GMT |

JavaScript:

```
const timeNow = new Date();
const hoursNow = timeNow.getHours();
const minutesNow = timeNow.getMinutes();
let message = "It's ";
let hoursText;

if (minutesNow <= 30) {
    message += minutesNow + (minutesNow === 1 ? " minute past "
    : " minutes past ");
    hoursText = hoursNow;
} else {
    message += (60 - minutesNow) + ((60 - minutesNow) === 1 ? "
    minute before " : " minutes before ");
    hoursText = hoursNow + 1;
}

if (hoursNow == 0 && minutesNow <= 30) {
    message += "midnight.";
} else if (hoursNow == 11 && minutesNow > 30) {
    message += "noon.";
} else if (hoursNow < 12) {
    message += hoursText + " in the morning.";
} else if (hoursNow == 12 && minutesNow <= 30) {
    message += "noon.";
```

```
} else if (hoursNow < 18) {
    message += parseInt(hoursText - 12) + " in the afternoon.";
} else if (hoursNow == 23 && minutesNow > 30) {
    message += "midnight.";
} else {
    message += parseInt(hoursText - 12) + " in the evening.";
}
document.getElementById("output").innerHTML = message;
```

This script begins by storing the user's local time in the timeNow variable. Then the current hour is extracted using getHours() and stored in the hoursNow variable, and the current minute is extracted using getMinutes() and stored in the minutesNow variable. A variable named message is initialized and will be used to store the message that's displayed in the web page. The variable hoursText will hold the nonmilitary hour (for example, 4 instead of 16).

Then the value of minutesNow is checked to determine whether it's less than or equal to 30, because this determines the first part of the message, as well as the value of hoursText. Here are two examples of how the message will appear:

```
It's 20 minutes past 10 // minutesNow is less than or equal to
    30 (10:20)
It's 1 minute to 11 // minutesNow is greater than 30 (10:59)
```

Then the script checks the value of hoursNow:

>> If it equals 0 and minutesNow is less than or equal to 30, the string midnight is added to the message.

>> If it equals 11 and minutesNow is greater than 30, the string noon is added to the message.

>> If it's less than 12, the value of hoursText and the string in the morning are added to the message.

>> If it equals 12 and minutesNow is less than or equal to 30, the string noon is added to the message.

>> If it's less than 18 (6:00 PM), the result of hoursText - 12 and the string in the afternoon are added.

>> If it equals 23 and minutesNow is greater than 30, the string midnight is added to the message.

>> Otherwise, hoursText - 12 and the string in the evening are added.

Finally, the result is written to the page, as shown in Figure 8-6.

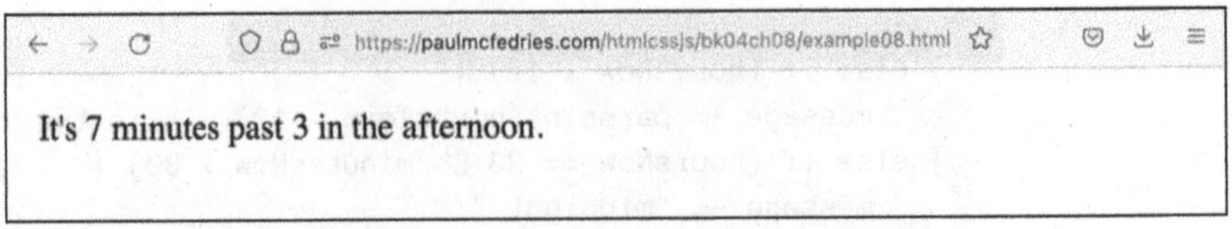

FIGURE 8-6:
The results
of the script.

```
←  →  C        ○ 🔒 ≡ https://paulmcfedries.com/htmlcssjs/bk04ch08/example08.html  ☆      ♡  ↓  ≡
```

It's 7 minutes past 3 in the afternoon.

## Extracting the month name from a date

If you want to use the month in a nicer format than the standard Date object display, you have one problem. The getMonth() method returns a number instead of the actual name of the month: 0 for January, 1 for February, and so on. If you prefer to use the name, you need some way to extract the name from the Date object.

The easiest way to extract the month name from a date is to use the toLocale-DateString() method:

```
date.toLocaleDateString(locale, options)
```

» *date*: The Date object from which you want to extract the month name.

» *locale*: A string specifying the language to use such as en-us. Use default for the current language.

» *options*: A JavaScript object that specifies the method output. To extract just the month name, use the object { month: 'long' }.

Here's an example (bk04ch08/example09.html):

HTML:

```
<div id="output"></div>
```

JavaScript:

```
const dateNow = new Date();
document.getElementById("output").innerHTML =
    `The date is ${dateNow}<br>
    The month name is ${dateNow.toLocaleDateString('default', {
    month: 'long' })}`;
```

## Extracting the day name from a date

You face a similar problem with getDay() as you do with getMonth(): converting the returned number into a "friendly" name such as, in this case, Sunday for 0, Monday for 1, and so on. The solution, as you can imagine, is also similar: Use the toLocaleDateString() method, but this time specify the object { weekday: 'long' } as the *options* parameter. Here's an example (bk04ch08/example10. html):

HTML:

```
<div id="output"></div>
```

JavaScript:

```
const dateNow = new Date();
document.getElementById("output").innerHTML =
    `The date is ${dateNow}<br>
    The month name is ${dateNow.toLocaleDateString('default', {
    weekday: 'long' })}`;
```

## Setting the date

When you perform date arithmetic, you often have to change the value of an existing Date object. For example, an e-commerce script may have to calculate a date that is 90 days from the date that a sale occurs. It's usually easiest to create a Date object and then use an expression or literal value to change the year, month, or some other component of the date. You do that by using the Date object methods listed in Table 8-5.

**TABLE 8-5**     **Date Object Methods That Set Date Values**

| Method Syntax | What It Sets |
|---|---|
| *date*.setFullYear(*yyyy*) | The year as a four-digit number (1999, 2000, and so on) |
| *date*.setMonth(*mth*) | The month of the year; from 0 (January) to 11 (December) |
| *date*.setDate(*dd*) | The date in the month; from 1 to 31 |
| *date*.setHours(*hh*) | The hour of the day; from 0 (midnight) to 23 (11:00 PM) |
| *date*.setMinutes(*mm*) | The minute of the hour; from 0 to 59 |
| *date*.setSeconds(*ss*) | The second of the minute; from 0 to 59 |
| *date*.setMilliseconds(*ms*) | The milliseconds of the second; from 0 to 999 |
| *date*.setTime(*ms*) | The milliseconds since January 1, 1970 GMT |

The following code (bk04ch08/example11.html) tries out some of these methods:

HTML:

```html
<div>
    <label for="user-year">Enter a year:</label>
    <input type="text" id="user-year" size="4" value="2024">
</div>
<div>
    <label for="user-month">Enter a month (1-12):</label>
    <input type="text" id="user-month" size="2" value="1">
</div>
<div>
    <label for="user-day">Enter a day (1-31):</label>
    <input type="text" id="user-day" size="2" value="1">
</div>
<div id="output"></div>
```

JavaScript:

```javascript
// Get the inputs
const inputs = document.querySelectorAll('input');

// Add a `change` event listener to each input
inputs.forEach( input => {
    input.addEventListener('change', makeDate);
});

// Run this function each time an input changes
function makeDate() {

    // Get the year, month (minus 1), and day
    const userYear = document.querySelector('#user-year').value;
    const userMonth = document.querySelector('#user-month').
  value - 1;
    const userDay = document.querySelector('#user-day').value;

    // Create a new Date object
    const userDate = new Date();

    // Set the year, month, and date
    userDate.setFullYear(userYear);
    userDate.setMonth(userMonth);
    userDate.setDate(userDay);
```

```
    // Convert the date info to strings
    const dateString = userDate.toLocaleDateString('default', {
 month: 'long', day: 'numeric', year: 'numeric' });
    const dayName = userDate.toLocaleDateString('default', {
 weekday: 'long' });

    // Display the message
    document.getElementById("output").innerHTML =
        `The date entered is: ${dateString}
        <br>The day of the week is: ${dayName}`;
}

// Run the function as soon as the page loads
makeDate();
```

The HTML defines three input elements that gather the year, month, and day of the month. The JavaScript stores the input elements in the inputs node list and then loops through the elements, adding a change event handler to each element, which defines makeDate as the callback function.

The makeDate callback function stores the value of each input element in a variable to store. Notice that the script subtracts 1 from the month value to get a proper month number for JavaScript to use.

The next four statements are the keys to this example. A new Date object is stored in the userDate variable. Then the script runs the setFullYear(), setMonth(), and setDate() methods.

At this point, the userDate variable contains a new date that corresponds to the supplied date. This means you can use the toLocaleDateString method to convert the date into whatever string you need. The script first defines string (dateString) for the full date and then defines a string (dayName) for just the weekday name. After that's done, the script displays the date and the day of the week that it corresponds to (check out Figure 8-7).

**REMEMBER**

All the "set" methods also return values. Specifically, they return the number of milliseconds from January 1, 1970 GMT to whatever new date is the result of the method. Therefore, you can use the return value of a "set" method to create a new Date object:

```
newDate = new Date(userDate.SetFullYear(userYear))
```

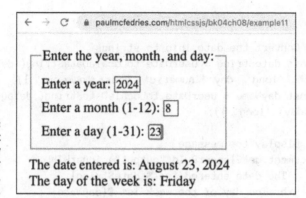

FIGURE 8-7:
The script
displays the day
of the week for
a given a year,
month, and day.

# Performing date calculations

Many of your date-related scripts will need to make arithmetic calculations. For example, you may need to figure out the number of days between two dates, or you may need to calculate the date that's six weeks from today. The methods you've learned so far, and the way JavaScript represents dates internally, serve to make most date calculations straightforward.

The simplest calculations are those that involve whole numbers of the basic JavaScript date and time units: years, months, days, hours, minutes, and seconds. For example, suppose you need to calculate a date that's five years from the current date. Here's a code snippet that will do it:

```
const myDate = new Date();
const myYear = myDate.getFullYear() + 5;
myDate.setFullYear(myYear);
```

You use getFullYear() to get the year, add 5 to it, and then use setFullYear() to change the date.

## Determining a person's age

As a practical example, the following code presents a script that calculates a person's age (bk04ch08/example12.html):

HTML:

```
<label for="date-picker">Select your birth date:</label>
<input type="date" id="date-picker" value="2000-01-01">

<div id="output"></div>
```

JavaScript:

```javascript
// Add a `change` event listener to the date picker
const datePicker = document.querySelector('#date-picker');
datePicker.addEventListener('change', calculateAge);

// Run this function when the date changes
function calculateAge() {

    // Create a new Date object from the date picker value
    const birthDate = new Date(datePicker.value);

    // Store the user's birth year
    const birthYear = birthDate.getFullYear();

    // Make a Date object and set it
    // to the user's birthday this year
    const birthdayDate = new Date();
    birthdayDate.setMonth(birthDate.getMonth());
    birthdayDate.setDate(birthDate.getDate());

    // Store the current date and current year
    const currentDate = new Date();
    const currentYear = currentDate.getFullYear();

    // Calculate the user's age
    let userAge = currentYear - birthYear;

    // Has the birthday occurred yet this year?
    if (currentDate < birthdayDate) {
        // If not, adjust the age down by one year
        userAge -= 1;
    }
    // Output the result
    document.getElementById("output").innerHTML = `You are
${userAge} years old.`;
}
```

The HTML sets up a date picker to get the user's birth date. The JavaScript adds a change event listener to the date picker and runs the calculateAge function each time the date picker changes. The calculateAge function converts the date picker value to a Date object, and then extracts the birth year to the birthyear variable.

The script creates a new `Date` object and stores it in `birthdayDate`. The date is changed using `setMonth()` — which is set to `birthDate.getMonth()` — and `setDate()` — which is set to `birthDate.getDate()` — but *not* `setFullYear()`. This gives you the user's birthday for this year. Then the current date is stored in `currentDate` and the year is stored in `currentYear`.

Now the script calculates the user's age by subtracting `birthYear` from `current Year`. However, that won't be accurate if the user's birthday hasn't occurred yet this year, so the script compares `currentDate` and `birthdayDate`: If `currentDate` is less, it means the user's birthday hasn't happened, so the script subtracts 1 from the user's age.

## Performing complex date calculations

Other date calculations are more complex. For example, you may need to calculate the number of days between two dates. For this kind of calculation, you need to take advantage of the fact that JavaScript stores dates internally as millisecond values. They're stored, in other words, as numbers, and when you're dealing with numeric values, you can use numeric expressions to perform calculations on those values.

The key here is converting the basic date units — seconds, minutes, hours, days, and weeks — into milliseconds. Here's some code that will help:

```
const ONESECOND = 1000;
const ONEMINUTE = ONESECOND * 60;
const ONEHOUR = ONEMINUTE * 60;
const ONEDAY = ONEHOUR * 24;
const ONEWEEK = ONEDAY * 7;
```

**REMEMBER**

In programming, whenever you have variables that are *constants* — that is, they have values that will never change throughout the script — it's traditional to write them entirely in uppercase letters to help differentiate them from regular variables.

Because one second equals 1,000 milliseconds, the `ONESECOND` variable is given the value 1000; because one minute equals 60 seconds, the `ONEMINUTE` variable is given the value `ONESECOND * 60`, or 60,000 milliseconds. The other values are derived similarly.

## Calculating the days between two dates

A common date calculation involves figuring out the number of days between any two dates. The following code presents a function that performs this calculation (bko4ch08/example13.html):

```
function daysBetween(date1, date2) {

    // Convert both dates to milliseconds
    const date1Ms = date1.getTime();
    const date2Ms = date2.getTime();

    // Calculate the difference in milliseconds
    const differenceMs = Math.abs(date1Ms - date2Ms);

    // The number of milliseconds in one day
    const ONEDAY = 1000 * 60 * 60 * 24;

    // Convert to days and return
    return Math.round(differenceMs/ONEDAY);
}
```

This function accepts two Date object arguments — date1 and date2. Note that it doesn't matter which date is earlier or later because this function calculates the absolute value of the difference between them. The constant ONEDAY stores the number of milliseconds in a day, and then the two dates are converted into milliseconds using the getTime() method. The results are stored in the variables date1Ms and date2Ms.

Next, the following statement calculates the absolute value, in milliseconds, of the difference between the two dates:

```
const differenceMs = Math.abs(date1Ms - date2Ms);
```

This difference is then converted into days by dividing it by the ONEDAY constant. Math.round() (which I discuss in the next section) ensures an integer result.

# Working with Numbers: The Math Object

It's a rare JavaScript programmer who never has to deal with numbers. Most of us have to cobble together scripts that process order totals, generate sales taxes and shipping charges, calculate mortgage payments, and perform other number-crunching duties. To that end, it must be said that JavaScript's numeric tools aren't the greatest in the programming world, but they have plenty of features to keep most scripters happy. This section tells you about those features, with special emphasis on the Math object.

The first thing you need to know is that JavaScript likes to keep things simple, particularly when it comes to numbers. For example, JavaScript is limited to dealing with just two numeric data types: *integers* — numbers without a fractional or decimal part, such as 1, 759, and -50 — and *floating-point numbers* — values that have a fractional or decimal part, such as 2.14, 0.01, and -25.3333.

# Converting between strings and numbers

When you're working with numeric expressions in JavaScript, it's important to make sure that all your operands are numeric values. For example, if you prompt the user for a value, you need to check the result to make sure it's not a letter or undefined (the default prompt() value). If you try to use the latter, for example, JavaScript will report that its value is NaN (not a number).

Similarly, if you have a value that you know is a string representation of a number, you need some way of converting that string into its numerical equivalent.

For these situations, JavaScript offers several techniques to ensure that your operands are numeric.

## The parseInt() function

I begin with the parseInt() function, which you use to convert a string into an integer:

```
parseInt(string, base);
```

» *string:* The string value you want to convert.

» *base:* An optional base used by the number in *string*. If you omit this value, JavaScript uses base 10.

Note that if the *string* argument contains a string representation of a floating-point value, parseInt() returns only the integer portion. Also, if the string begins with a number followed by some text, parseInt() returns the number (or, at least, its integer portion). The following table shows you the parseInt() results for various *string* values.

| string | parseInt(string) |
|--------|------------------|
| "5"    | 5                |
| "5.1"  | 5                |
| "5.9"  | 5                |

| string | parseInt(string) |
|--------|------------------|
| "5 feet" | 5 |
| "take 5" | NaN |
| "five" | NaN |

## The parseFloat() function

The parseFloat() function is similar to parseInt(), but you use it to convert a string into a floating-point value:

```
parseFloat(string);
```

Note that if the *string* argument contains a string representation of an integer value, parseFloat() returns just an integer. Also, like parseInt(), if the string begins with a number followed by some text, parseFloat() returns the number. The following table shows you the parseFloat() results for some *string* values.

| string | parseFloat(string) |
|--------|--------------------|
| "5" | 5 |
| "5.1" | 5.1 |
| "5.9" | 5.9 |
| "5.2 feet" | 5.2 |
| "take 5.0" | NaN |
| "five-point-one" | NaN |

## The + operator

For quick conversions from a string to a number, I most often use the + operator, which tells JavaScript to treat a string that contains a number as a true numeric value. For example, consider the following code:

```
const numOfShoes = '2';
const numOfSocks = 4;
const totalItems = +numOfShoes + numOfSocks;
```

By adding + in front of the numOfShoes variable, I force JavaScript to set that variable's value to the number 2, and the result of the addition will be 6.

# The Math object's properties and methods

The Math object is a bit different than most of the other objects you come across in this book. That's because you never create an instance of the Math object that gets stored in a variable. Instead, the Math object is a built-in JavaScript object that you use as is. The rest of this chapter explores some properties and methods associated with the Math object.

## Properties of the Math object

The Math object's properties are all constants that are commonly used in mathematical operations. Table 8-6 lists all the available Math object properties.

**TABLE 8-6**  Some Properties of the Math Object

| Property Syntax | What It Represents | Approximate Value |
|---|---|---|
| Math.E | Euler's constant | 2.718281828459045 |
| Math.LN10 | The natural logarithm of 10 | 2.302585092994046 |
| Math.LN2 | The natural logarithm of 2 | 0.6931471805599453 |
| Math.LOG2E | Base 2 logarithm of E | 1.4426950408889633 |
| Math.LOG10E | Base 10 logarithm of E | 0.4342944819032518 |
| Math.PI | The constant pi | 3.141592653589793 |
| Math.SQRT1_2 | The square root of 1/2 | 0.7071067811865476 |
| Math.SQRT2 | The square root of 2 | 1.4142135623730951 |

## Methods of the Math object

The Math object's methods enable you to perform mathematical operations such as square roots, powers, rounding, trigonometry, and more. Many of the Math object's methods are summarized in Table 8-7.

**TABLE 8-7**     ## Some Methods of the Math Object

| Method Syntax | What It Returns |
|---|---|
| Math.abs(*number*) | The absolute value of *number* (that is, the number without any sign) |
| Math.cbrt(*number*) | The cube root of *number* |
| Math.ceil(*number*) | The smallest integer greater than or equal to *number* (ceil is short for *ceiling*) |
| Math.cos(*number*) | The cosine of *number*; returned values range from -1 to 1 radians |
| Math.exp(*number*) | E raised to the power of *number* |
| Math.floor(*number*) | The largest integer that is less than or equal to *number* |
| Math.log(*number*) | The natural logarithm (base E) of *number* |
| Math.max(*number1*, *number2*) | The larger of *number1* and *number2* |
| Math.min(*number1*, *number2*) | The smaller of *number1* and *number2* |
| Math.pow(*number1*, *number2*) | *number1* raised to the power of *number2* |
| Math.random() | A random number between 0 and 1 |
| Math.round(*number*) | The integer closest to *number* |
| Math.sin(*number*) | The sine of *number*; returned values range from -1 to 1 radians |
| Math.sqrt(*number*) | The square root of *number* (which must be greater than or equal to 0) |
| Math.tan(*number*) | The tangent of *number*, in radians |
| Math.trunc(*number*) | The integer portion of *number* |

IN THIS CHAPTER

» **Getting the hang of the Web Storage API**

» **Taking your first look at JSON**

» **Adding stuff to storage**

» **Getting stuff from storage**

» **Removing stuff from storage**

# Chapter 9

# Storing User Data in the Browser

*Data is like garbage. You'd better know what you are going to do with it before you collect it.*

—MARK TWAIN (ATTRIBUTED)

One of the hallmarks of a bigtime website is that most of what you as a site visitor see is data that has been retrieved from a server. That data has been created and managed by a database specialist, and the code that asks for the required data and then returns that data to the web browser is created by a *back-end* web developer.

Alas, back-end coding is beyond the purview of this book (but it's a big part of my companion book *Web Coding and Development All-in-One For Dummies* [Wiley]). This book is all about *front-end* web development, but does that mean you're out of luck when it comes to working with data?

For example, suppose your web page enables each user to set custom background and text colors. That's just two pieces of data, so setting up a hideously complex back-end edifice to store that data would be like building the Taj Mahal to store a few towels.

Fortunately, you don't have to embark on a major construction job to save small amounts of data for each user. Instead, you can take advantage of a technology called *web storage* that enables you to store data for each user right in that person's web browser. It's all very civilized, and you find out everything you need to know in this chapter.

# Understanding Web Storage

Web storage is possible via a technology called the Web Storage API (application programming interface), which defines two properties of the Window object (the object that references the user's browser window):

>> localStorage: A storage space created within the web browser for your domain (meaning that only your local code can access this storage). Data within this storage can't be larger than 5MB. This data resides permanently in the browser until you delete it.

>> sessionStorage: The same as localStorage, except that the data persists only for the current browser session. That is, the browser erases the data when the user closes the browser window.

**WARNING**

Users can also delete web storage data by using their browser's command for removing website data. If your web page really needs its user data to be permanent (or, at least, completely under your control), you need to store it on the server.

Both localStorage and sessionStorage do double duty as objects that implement several methods that your code can use to add, retrieve, and delete user data. Each data item is stored as a key-value pair as part of a JSON object. What on Earth is a "JSON object" you ask? Read on, dear reader, read on.

# Introducing JSON

Long ago, someone with a tall forehead realized that the JavaScript world needed a straightforward way to move data to and from a script (from and to a web server, say, or from and to a web browser). The format needed to be pure text, have a relatively simple syntax, and be an open standard so that there would be no restrictions on its use.

The result was a data format called *JavaScript Object Notation*, or *JSON* (pronounced like the name Jason), for short. The "JavaScript" part of the name tells you that JSON is part of the JavaScript standard, which includes a JSON object for working with JSON strings. The "Object" part of the name tells you that (as I describe in the next section) JSON's syntax is very much like the syntax used by JavaScript objects.

## Learning the JSON syntax

I talk about JavaScript object literals in several places in this book, and if you know about object literals, then JSON objects will look very familiar. Here's the general syntax:

```
{
    "property1": value1,
    "property2": value2,
    ...
    "propertyN": valueN
}
```

JSON data looks like an object, but it's really just text that consists of one or more property-value pairs with the following characteristics:

>> Each property name is surrounded by double quotation marks (").

>> Each value can be one of the following:

- A number

- A string (in which case the value must be surrounded by double quotation marks)

- A Boolean (true or false)

- null (that is, no value)

- A JavaScript array literal (comma-separated values surrounded by square brackets — [ and ])

- A JavaScript object literal (comma-separated *property*: *value* pairs surrounded by braces — { and })

>> The property-value pairs are separated by commas.

>> The block of property-value pairs is surrounded by braces ({ and}).

Here's an example:

```
{
    "account": 853,
    "name": "Alfreds Futterkiste",
    "supplier": false,
    "recentOrders": [28394,29539,30014],
    "contact": {
        "name": "Maria Anders",
        "phone": "030-0074321",
        "email": "m.anders@futterkiste.com"
    }
}
```

## Declaring and using JSON variables

In the next section, I talk about how useful JSON is for getting data to and from web storage. However, you can also use JSON data in your non-web-storage code. You begin by declaring a JSON variable (check out bk04ch09/example01.html in this book's example files):

```
const customer = {
    "account": 853,
    "name": "Alfreds Futterkiste",
    "supplier": false,
    "recentOrders": [28394,29539,30014],
    "contact": {
        "name": "Maria Anders",
        "phone": "030-0074321",
        "email": "anders@futterkiste.com"
    }
}
```

You can then refer to any property in the JSON data by using the *variable.property* syntax. Here are some examples:

```
customer.account          // Returns 853
customer.name             // Returns "Alfreds Futterkiste"
customer.recentOrders[1]  // Returns 29539
customer.contact.email    // Returns "anders@futterkiste.com"
```

**TIP**

The JSON syntax can be a bit tricky, so it's a good idea to check that your data is valid before using it in your code. The easiest way to do that is to use the JSONLint (`https://jsonlint.com`) validation tool. Copy your JSON code, paste it into the JSONLint text area, and then click Validate JSON.

## Converting a JavaScript object to JSON

Although you can use JSON data directly in your code, you're more likely to store your data in a JavaScript object. If you then need to convert that object to the JSON format, you can *stringify* the object by invoking the `stringify()` method of the JSON object. Here's the simplified syntax to use:

```
JSON.stringify(object, replacer, spaces)
```

>> *object*: The JavaScript object you want to convert to JSON format.

>> *replacer*: A function or array that modifies the stringification process in some way. This parameter is beyond the scope of this book, so in the examples I set this parameter to `null`.

>> *spaces*: An optional value that specifies the number of spaces you want your JSON string to be indented for readability. (If you won't ever look at the resulting JSON string, you can leave off the `null` and *spaces* arguments and use just the *object* argument.)

Here's an example (check out bk04ch09/example02.html):

HTML:

```
<pre id="output">
</pre>
```

JavaScript:

```
// Declare a JavaScript object
const userData = {
    bgColor: "darkolivegreen",
    textColor: "antiquewhite",
    textSize: "1.25em",
    typefaces: ["Georgia", "Verdana", "serif"],
    subscriber: true,
    subscriptionType: 3
};
```

```
// Stringify it
const userDataJSON = JSON.stringify(userData, null, "    ");

// Display the result
document.querySelector('#output').innerHTML = userDataJSON;
```

Figure 9-1 shows the output.

```
{
    "bgColor": "darkolivegreen",
    "textColor": "antiquewhite",
    "textSize": "1.25em",
    "typefaces": [
        "Georgia",
        "Verdana",
        "serif"
    ],
    "subscriber": true,
    "subscriptionType": 3
}
```

**FIGURE 9-1:**
The JavaScript object converted to a JSON string.

# Converting a JSON string to a JavaScript object

When your script receives a JSON string (from the server or, for the purposes of this chapter, from web storage), you'll usually want to convert that string to a good, old-fashioned JavaScript object. You make that conversion by invoking the parse() method of the JSON object:

```
JSON.parse(json)
```

» *json*: The JSON string you want to convert to a JavaScript object.

Here's an example (bk04ch09/example03.html):

```
// Declare a JSON string
const userDataJSON = `{
    "bgColor": "darkolivegreen",
    "textColor": "antiquewhite",
    "textSize": "1.25em",
    "typefaces": [
        "Georgia",
        "Verdana",
```

```
        "serif"
    ],
    "subscriber": true,
    "subscriptionType": 3
}`;

// Parse it
const userData = JSON.parse(userDataJSON);

// Display the result
console.log(userData);
```

Note the use of back tick (`) delimiters in the userDataJSON string, which enable me to display the JSON data on multiple lines for readability. Figure 9-2 shows the output in the console (see Book 4, Chapter 10).

To display the console in most web browsers, right-click the web page, click Inspect (or press Ctrl+Shift+I in Windows or Option+⌘+I in macOS), and then click the Console tab.

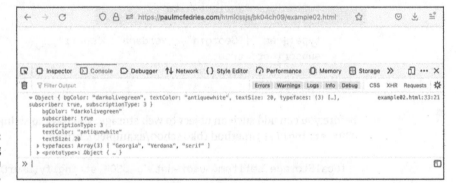

The JSON string converted to a JavaScript object.

# Adding Data to Web Storage

When you want to store data beyond the current browser session with localStorage or just for the current browser session with sessionStorage, you add data to web storage using the setItem() method:

```
localStorage.setItem(key, value)
```

Storing User Data in the Browser

Or:

```
sessionStorage.setItem(key, value)
```

>> *key:* A string that specifies the key for the web storage item.

>> *value:* The value associated with the web storage key. The value can be a string, number, Boolean, or object. Note, however, that web storage can store only strings, so any value you specify will be converted to a string when it's stored.

Here's an example:

```
localStorage.setItem('fave-color', '#ba55d3');
```

It's common to store a collection of related key-value pairs as a JSON string. For example, suppose you collect your data into a JavaScript object:

```
// Declare a JavaScript object
const userData = {
    bgColor: "darkolivegreen",
    textColor: "antiquewhite",
    textSize: 20,
    typefaces: ["Georgia", "Verdana", "serif"],
    subscriber: true,
    subscriptionType: 3
}
```

Before you can add such an object to web storage, you have to stringify it using the JSON.stringify() method (bk04ch09/example04.html):

```
localStorage.setItem('user-data', JSON.stringify(userData));
```

TIP

When you're testing your web page, you may want to check that your data is being stored correctly. You can just try getting the data back from storage, as I describe in the next section. Alternatively, you can open your browser's web development tools (see Book 4, Chapter 10) and then display the Application tab (if you're using Chrome or Edge) or the Storage tab (for Firefox or Safari). The tab includes both Local Storage and Session Storage items where you can check to see whether your data stored correctly (refer to Figure 9-3).

REMEMBER

When you store user data using web storage, that data is available only to the user in the same web browser running on the same device. For example, if you save data for a user running, say, Safari on an iPhone, when that user returns to your site using, say, Chrome on a desktop computer, that data will not be available to the user.

**FIGURE 9-3:**
Viewing local storage data in the web browser's development tools.

# Getting Data from Web Storage

After you've stored some data, you can retrieve an item from web storage by using the getItem() method of either the localStorage or sessionStorage object (use the same storage object that you used to store the data in the first place):

```
localStorage.getItem(key)
```

Or:

```
sessionStorage.getItem(key)
```

> ** *key:* A string that specifies the key for the storage item

Here's an example:

```
const userFaveColor = localStorage.getItem('fave-color');
```

If you stored a JavaScript object as a JSON string, use JSON.parse() to restore the object (bk04ch09/example05.html):

```
const userData = JSON.parse(localStorage.getItem('user-data'));
```

# Removing Data from Web Storage

Web storage is limited, so if you've stored some data you no longer need, it's best to remove it from either the localStorage or sessionStorage object (depending on where you stored the data originally).

To delete some data, use the removeItem() method:

```
localStorage.removeItem(key)
```

Or:

```
sessionStorage.removeItem(key)
```

>> *key:* A string that specifies the key for the storage item

Here's an example:

```
localStorage.removeItem('fave-color');
```

If you want to start fresh and delete everything from web storage, use the clear() method:

```
localStorage.clear()
```

Or:

```
sessionStorage.clear()
```

IN THIS CHAPTER

» Learning JavaScript's error types

» Debugging errors using the Console

» Setting breakpoints

» Watching variable and expression values

» Learning JavaScript's most common errors and error messages

# Chapter **10**

# Debugging Your Code

*Testing proves a programmer's failure. Debugging is the programmer's vindication.*

—BORIS BEIZER

t usually doesn't take too long to get short scripts and functions up and running. However, as your code grows larger and more complex, errors inevitably creep in. In fact, it has been proven mathematically that any code beyond a minimum level of complexity will contain at least one error, and probably quite a lot more than that.

Many of the bugs that creep into your code will consist of simple syntax problems that you can fix quickly, but others will be more subtle and harder to find. For the latter — whether the errors are incorrect values being returned by functions or problems with the overall logic of a script — you need to be able to get "inside" your code to scope out what's wrong. The good news is that JavaScript and modern web browsers offer a ton of top-notch debugging tools that can remove some of the burden of program problem solving. In this chapter, you delve into these tools to explore how they can help you find and fix most programming errors. You also investigate a number of tips and techniques that can go a long way in helping you avoid coding errors in the first place.

# Understanding JavaScript's Error Types

When a problem occurs, the first thing you need to determine is what kind of error you're dealing with. There are three basic types: syntax errors, runtime errors, and logic errors.

## Syntax errors

Syntax errors arise from misspelled or missing keywords or incorrect punctuation. JavaScript almost always catches these errors when you load the page (which is why syntax errors are also known as *load-time errors*). That is, as JavaScript reads the script's statements, it checks each one for syntax errors. If it finds an error, it stops processing the script and displays an error message. Here's an example statement (check out bk04ch10/example01.html in this book's example files) with a typical syntax error (can you spot it?) and Figure 10-1 shows how the error gets flagged in the Firefox Console window.

```
const pageFooter - document.querySelector("footer");
```

**FIGURE 10-1:**
The Firefox
Console window
displaying data
about a typical
syntax error.

## Runtime errors

Runtime errors occur during the execution of a script. They generally mean that JavaScript has stumbled upon a statement that it can't figure out. It may be caused by trying to use an uninitialized variable (that is, a variable that hasn't yet been assigned a value) in an expression or by using a property or method with the wrong object.

If your script has statements that execute as the page loads, and no syntax errors have been found, JavaScript will attempt to run those statements. If it comes across a statement with a problem, it halts execution of the script and displays the error. If your script has one or more functions, JavaScript doesn't look for runtime errors in those functions until you call them.

Here's some code (check out bk04ch10/example02.html) in which I misspelled a variable name in the third line (pagefooter instead of pageFooter), and Figure 10-2 shows the Chrome Console window displaying the runtime error that results.

```
const pageFooter = document.querySelector("footer");
const currDate = new Date();
pagefooter.innerHTML = "Copyright " + currDate.getFullYear() +
    " Logophilia Limited.";
```

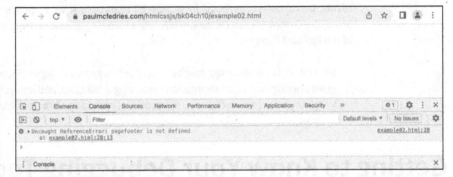

## Logic errors

If your code zigs instead of zags, the cause is usually a flaw in the logic of your script. It may be a loop that never ends or a switch test that doesn't switch to anything.

Logic errors are the toughest to pin down because you don't get any error messages to give you clues about what went wrong and where. What you usually need to do is set up *debugging code* that helps you monitor values and trace the execution of your program. I go through the most useful debugging techniques later in this chapter.

# Getting to Know Your Debugging Tools

All the major web browsers come with a sophisticated set of debugging tools that can make your life as a web developer much easier and much saner. Most web developers debug their scripts using Google Chrome, so I focus on that browser in this chapter. But in this section, I give you an overview of the tools that are available in all the major browsers and how to get at them.

Here's how you open the web development tools in Chrome, Firefox, Microsoft Edge, and Safari:

>> **Chrome for Windows:** Click Customize and Control Google Chrome (the three vertical dots to the right of the address bar) and then select More Tools⇨Developer Tools. Shortcut: Ctrl+Shift+I.

>> **Chrome for Mac:** Select View⇨Developer⇨Developer Tools. Shortcut: Option+⌘+I.

>> **Firefox for Windows:** Click Open Application Menu (the three horizontal lines on the far right of the toolbar) and then select More Tools ⇨Web Developer Tools. Shortcut: Ctrl+Shift+I.

>> **Firefox for Mac:** Select Tools⇨Browser Tools⇨Web Developer Tools. Shortcut: Option+⌘+I.

>> **Microsoft Edge:** Click Settings and More (the three vertical dots to the right of the address bar) and then select More Tools⇨Developer Tools. Shortcut: Ctrl+Shift+I.

>> **Safari:** Select Develop⇨Show Web Inspector. Shortcut: Option+⌘+I. If you don't have the Develop menu, select Safari⇨Settings, click the Advanced tab, and then select the Show Develop Menu in Menu Bar check box.

These development tools vary in the features they offer, but each one provides the same set of basic tools, which are the tools you'll use most often. These basic web development tools include the following:

>> **HTML viewer:** This tab (called Inspector in Firefox and Elements in the other browsers) shows the HTML source code used in the web page. When you hover the mouse pointer over a tag, the browser highlights the element in the displayed page and shows its width and height, as shown in Figure 10-3. When you click a tag, the browser shows the CSS styles applied with the tag, as well as the tag's box dimensions (again, refer to Figure 10-3). Check out Book 3, Chapter 4 to learn much more about inspecting CSS with the development tools.

The selected element is highlighted on the page

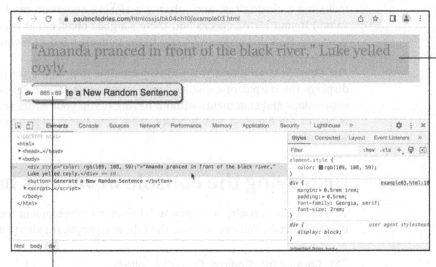

**FIGURE 10-3:** The HTML viewer, such as Chrome's Elements tab, enables you to inspect each element's styles and box dimensions.

The element's width and height

Debugging Your Code

>> **Console:** This tab enables you to view error messages, log messages, test expressions, and execute statements. I cover the Console in more detail in the next section.

>> **Debugging tool:** This tab (called Debugger in Firefox and Sources in the other browsers) enables you to pause code execution, step through your code, watch the values of variables and properties, and much more. This is the most important JavaScript debugging tool, so I cover it in detail later in this chapter.

>> **Network:** This tab tells you how long it takes to load each file referenced by your web page. If you find that your page is slow to load, this tab can help you find the bottleneck.

>> **Web storage:** This tab (called Application in Chrome and Edge and Storage in Firefox and Safari) enables you to examine data stored in the browser using the Web Storage API that I discuss in Book 4, Chapter 9.

# Debugging with the Console

If your web page is behaving strangely — for example, the page is blank or missing elements — you should first check your HTML code to make sure it's correct. (Common HTML errors are not finishing a tag with a greater than sign (>), not including a closing tag, and missing a closing quotation mark for an attribute value.) If your HTML checks out, there's a good chance that your JavaScript code is wonky. How do you know? A trip to the Console window is your first step.

The Console is an interactive browser window that shows warnings and errors, displays the output of console.log() statements, and enables you to execute expressions and statements without having to run your entire script. The Console is one of the handiest web browser debugging tools, so you need to know your way around it.

## Displaying the console in various browsers

To display the Console, open your web browser's development tools and then click the Console tab. You can also use the following keyboard shortcuts:

>> **Chrome for Windows:** Press Ctrl+Shift+J.

>> **Chrome for Mac:** Press Option+⌘+J.

>> **Firefox for Windows:** Press Ctrl+Shift+K.

>> **Firefox for Mac:** Press Option+⌘+K.

# Logging data to the Console

You can use the `console.log()` method of the special `Console` object to print text and expression values in the Console:

```
console.log(output)
```

>> *output:* The expression you want to print in the Console

The *output* expression can be a text string, a variable, an object property, a function result, or any combination of these.

**TIP**

You can also use the handy `console.table()` method to output the values of arrays or objects in an easy-to-read tabular format:

```
console.table(output)
```

>> *output:* The array or object (as a variable or as a literal) you want to view in the Console

For debugging purposes, you most often use the Console to keep an eye on the values of variables, object properties, and expressions. That is, when your code sets or changes the value of something, you insert a `console.log()` (or `console.table()`) statement that outputs the new value. When the script execution is complete, you can open the Console and then check out the logged value or values.

# Executing code in the Console

One of the great features of the Console is that it's interactive, which means that you can not only read messages generated by the browser or by your `console.log()` statements but also type code directly into the Console. That is, you can use the Console to execute expressions and statements. There are many uses for this feature:

>> You can try some experimental expressions or statements to determine their effect on the script.

>> When the script is paused, you can output the current value of a variable or property.

Debugging Your Code

>> When the script is paused, you can change the value of a variable or property. For example, if you notice that a variable with a value of zero is about to be used as a divisor, you can change that variable to a nonzero value to avoid crashing the script.

>> When the script is paused, you can run a function or method to determine whether it operates as expected under the current conditions.

Each browser's Console tab includes a text box (usually marked by a greater-than > prompt) that you can use to enter your expressions or statements.

You can execute multiple statements in the Console by separating each statement with a semicolon. For example, you can test a for . . . loop by entering a statement similar to the following:

```
for (let i=1; i < 10; i += 1){console.log(i**2); console.log(i**3);}
```

If you want to repeat an earlier code execution in the Console, or if you want to run some code that's very similar to code you ran earlier, you can recall statements and expressions that you used in the current browser session. Press the Up Arrow key to scroll back through your previously executed code; press the Down Arrow key to scroll forward through your code.

# Pausing Your Code

Pausing your code midstream lets you examine certain elements such as the current values of variables and properties. It also lets you execute program code one statement at a time so that you can monitor the flow of the script.

When you pause your code, JavaScript enters *break mode*, which means that the browser displays its debugging tool and highlights the current statement (the one that JavaScript will execute next). Figure 10-4 shows a script in break mode in Chrome's debugger (the Sources tab).

## Entering break mode

JavaScript gives you two ways to enter break mode:

>> By setting breakpoints

>> By using a debugger statement

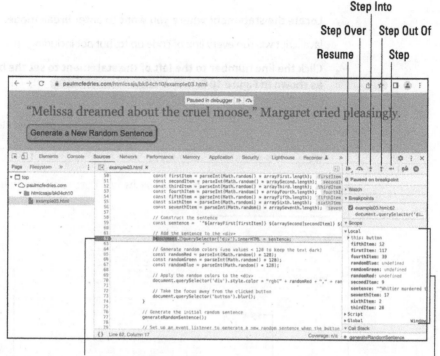

FIGURE 10-4:
When you invoke break mode, the web browser displays its debugging tool and highlights the statement that it will execute next.

The browser pauses on the current statement      The current values of the script's variables

## Setting a breakpoint

If you know approximately where an error or logic flaw is occurring, you can enter break mode at a specific statement in the script by setting up a *breakpoint*. Here are the steps to set up a breakpoint:

1. **Display your web browser's developer tools and switch to the debugging tool (such as the Sources tab in Chrome).**

2. **Open the file that contains the JavaScript code you want to debug.**

   How you do this depends on the browser: in Chrome (and most browsers), you have two choices:

   - In the left pane, click the HTML file (if your JavaScript code is within a `script` element in your HTML file) or the JavaScript (`.js`) file (if your code resides in an external JavaScript file).

   - Press Ctrl+P (Windows) or ⌘+P (macOS) and then click the file in the list that appears.

3. **Locate the statement where you want to enter break mode.**

   JavaScript will run every line of code up to, but not including, this statement.

4. **Click the line number to the left of the statement to set the breakpoint, as shown in Figure 10-5.**

Deactivate Breakpoints

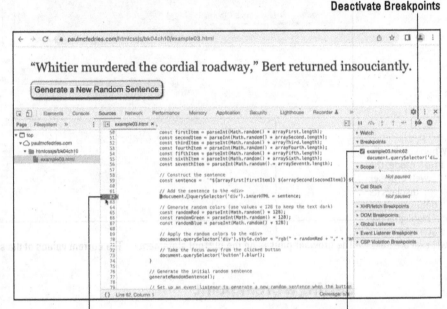

"Whitier murdered the cordial roadway," Bert returned insouciantly.

[ Generate a New Random Sentence ]

FIGURE 10-5:
In the browser's
debugging
tool, click a line
number to set
a breakpoint on
that statement.

Click a line number to set a breakpoint          Deselect to disable the breakpoint

To remove a breakpoint, most browsers give you three choices:

» To disable a breakpoint temporarily, deselect the breakpoint's check box in the Breakpoints list.

» To disable all your breakpoints temporarily, click the Deactivate Breakpoint button. Chrome's version of this button is shown here in the margin. Click this button again to reactivate all the breakpoints.

» To remove a breakpoint completely, click the statement's line number.

## Entering break mode using a debugger statement

When developing your web pages, you'll often test the robustness of a script by sending it various test values or by trying it out under different conditions. In many cases, you'll want to enter break mode to make sure things appear okay. You could set breakpoints at specific statements, but you lose them if you close the file.

For something a little more permanent, you can include a debugger statement in a script. JavaScript automatically enters break mode whenever it encounters a debugger statement.

Here's a bit of code that includes a debugger statement (bk04ch10/example03. html):

```
// Add the sentence to the <div>
document.querySelector('div').innerHTML = sentence;
// Generate random colors (use values < 128 to keep the
   text dark)
const randomRed = parseInt(Math.random() * 128);
const randomGreen = parseInt(Math.random() * 128);
const randomBlue = parseInt(Math.random() * 128);
debugger;
```

### Exiting break mode

To exit break mode, you can use either of the following methods in the browser's debugging tool:

>> **Click the Resume button.** Chrome's version of this button is shown here in the margin.

>> **Press the browser's Resume keyboard shortcut.** In Chrome (and most browsers), either press F8 or press Ctrl+\ (Windows) or ⌘+\ (macOS).

# Stepping Through Your Code

One of the most common (and most useful) debugging techniques is to step through the code one statement at a time. Doing so lets you get a feel for the program flow to make sure that things such as loops and function calls are executing properly. You can use four techniques:

>> Stepping one statement at a time

>> Stepping into some code

>> Stepping over some code

>> Stepping out of some code

# Stepping one statement at a time

The most common way of stepping through your code is to step one statement at a time. In break mode, stepping one statement at a time means two things:

>> You execute the current statement and then pause on the next statement.

>> If the current statement to run is a function call, stepping takes you into the function and pauses at the function's first statement. You can then continue to step through the function until you execute the last statement, at which point the browser returns you to the statement after the function call.

To step through your code one statement at a time, set a breakpoint and then, after your code is in break mode, do one of the following to step through a single statement:

>> **Click the Step button.** Chrome's version of this button is shown here in the margin.

>> **Press the browser's Step keyboard shortcut.** In Chrome (and most browsers, except Firefox, which doesn't support Step as of this writing; use the Step Into button, instead), press F9.

Keep stepping through until the script ends or until you're ready to resume normal execution (by clicking Resume).

# Stepping into some code

In all the major browsers (except Firefox), stepping into some code is exactly the same as stepping through the code one statement at a time. The difference comes when a statement executes asynchronously (that is, it performs its operation after some delay rather than right away).

To understand the difference, consider the following code (I've added line numbers to the left; they're not part of the code; check out bko4ch10/example04.html):

```
1    setTimeout(() => {
2        console.log('Inside the setTimeout() block!');
3    }, 5000);
4    console.log('Outside the setTimeout) block!');
```

This code uses setTimeout() to execute an anonymous function after five seconds. Suppose you enter break mode at the setTimeout() statement (line 1). What happens if you use Step versus Step Into here? Check it out:

>> **Step:** Clicking the Step button doesn't take you to line 2, as you may expect. Instead, because `setTimeout( )` is asynchronous, Step essentially ignores the anonymous function and takes you directly to line 4.

>> **Step Into:** Clicking the Step Into button *does* take you to line 2, but only after the specified delay (five seconds, in this case). You can then step through the anonymous function as needed.

To step into your code, set a breakpoint and then, after your code is in break mode, do one of the following:

>> **Click the Step Into button.** Chrome's version of this button is shown here in the margin.

>> **Press the browser's Step Into keyboard shortcut.** In Chrome (and most browsers), either press F11 or press Ctrl+; (Windows) or ⌘+; (macOS).

**REMEMBER**

My description of Step Into here doesn't apply (at least as I write this) to Firefox. Instead, the Firefox Step Into feature works like the Step feature I describe in the previous section.

## Stepping over some code

Some statements call other functions. If you're not interested in stepping through a called function, you can step over it. Stepping over a function means that JavaScript executes the function normally and then resumes break mode at the next statement *after* the function call.

To step over a function, first either step through your code until you come to the function call you want to step over, or set a breakpoint on the function call and refresh the web page. When you're in break mode, you can step over the function using any of the following techniques:

>> **Click the Step Over button.** Chrome's version of this button is shown here in the margin.

>> **Press the browser's Step Over keyboard shortcut.** In Chrome (and most browsers), either press F10 or press Ctrl+' (Windows) or ⌘+' (macOS).

## Stepping out of some code

I'm always accidentally stepping into functions I'd rather step over. If the function is short, I just step through it until I'm back in the original code. If the function is long, however, I don't want to waste time stepping through every statement. Instead, I invoke the Step Out feature using any of these methods:

>> **Click the Step Out button.** Chrome's version of this button is shown here in the margin.

>> **Press the browser's Step Out keyboard shortcut.** In Chrome (and most browsers), either press Shift+F11 or press Ctrl+Shift+; (Windows) or ⌘+Shift+; (macOS).

JavaScript executes the rest of the function and then reenters break mode at the first line after the function call.

# Monitoring Script Values

Many runtime and logic errors are the result of (or, in some cases, can result in) variables or properties assuming unexpected values. If your script uses or changes these elements in several places, you'll need to enter break mode and monitor the values of these elements to figure out where things go awry. The browser developer tools offer three main ways to keep an eye on your script values:

>> View the current value of a single variable.

>> View the current values of all the variables in both the local and global scopes.

>> View the value of a custom expression or object property.

## Viewing a single variable value

If you just want to eyeball the current value of a variable, the developer tools in Chrome (and all major browsers) make this straightforward:

1. **Enter break mode in the code that contains the variable you want to check.**

2. **If the script hasn't yet set the value of the variable, step through the code until you're past the statement that supplies the variable with a value.**

   If you're interested in how the variable's value changes during the script, step through the script until you're past any statement that changes the value.

3. **Hover the mouse over the variable name.**

   The browser pops up a tooltip that displays the variable's current value. Figure 10-6 shows an example.

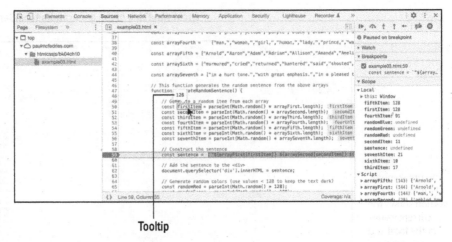

**FIGURE 10-6:**
In break mode, hover the mouse pointer over a variable name to display the variable's current value.

Tooltip

# Viewing all variable values

Most of the values you'll want to monitor will be variables, which come in three flavors (or *scopes*):

>> **Block scope:** These are variables declared within the current statement block and are available only to that block.

>> **Local scope:** These are variables declared in the current function and are available only to that function.

>> **Global scope:** These are variables declared outside of any function, which makes them available to any script or function on the page.

For more detailed coverage of variable scope, refer to Book 4, Chapter 5.

When you're in break mode, the Chrome debugging tool (like all the major browser debuggers) displays a pane on the right that includes a section that shows the current values of all your declared variables. In Chrome, the section is named Scope and includes several lists: Block (for block-scoped variables), Local (for local variables) and Script (for global variables). Confusingly, there's also a Global section that references just the Window object. Chrome's Scope section appears back in Figure 10-4.

In Figure 10-7, notice that some of the local variables show the value undefined. Those variables are undefined because the script hasn't yet reached the point where the variables are assigned a value.

Local variables of the generateRandomSentence() function

**FIGURE 10-7:**
In break mode,
Firefox's Scopes
section shows the
current values
of the local and
global variables.

# Adding a watch expression

Besides monitoring variable values, JavaScript also lets you monitor the results of any expression or the current value of an object property. To do this, you need to set up a *watch expression* that defines what you want to monitor. These watch expressions appear in a special section of the browser's debugging tools. Here's how to add a watch expression in Chrome (the steps in other major browsers are similar):

1. **Put your code into break mode.**

2. **Open the Watch section in the right pane.**

3. **Click Add Watch Expression (+).**

   A blank text box appears.

4. **Type your expression in the text box and then press Enter or Return.**

The browser adds the expression and then displays the current value of the expression to the right. Figure 10-8 shows an example.

Refresh Watch Expression

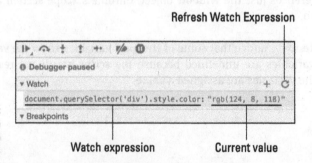

**FIGURE 10-8:**
You can define a
watch expression
for your code.

Watch expression          Current value

You can use the following techniques to work with your watch expressions:

>> **Edit a watch expression.** Double-click the expression, edit it, and then press Enter or Return.

>> **Update the values of your watch expressions.** Click the Refresh Watch Expression button (located in the upper-right corner of Figure 10-8).

>> **Delete a watch expression.** Hover the mouse over the watch expression you want to remove; then click the Delete icon (X) that appears to the right of the expression.

# More Debugging Strategies

Debugging your scripts can be a frustrating job, even for relatively small scripts. Here are a few tips to keep in mind when tracking down programming problems:

>> **Indent your code for readability.** JavaScript code is immeasurably more readable when you indent the code within each statement block. Readable code is that much easier to trace and decipher, so your debugging efforts have one less hurdle to negotiate. How far you indent is a matter of personal style, but two or four spaces is typical:

```
function myFunction() {
    Each statement in this function
    block is indented four spaces.
}
```

If you nest one block inside another, indent the nested block by another four spaces:

```
function myFunction() {
    Each statement in this function
    block is indented four spaces.
    for (const item of someArray) {
        Each statement in this nested for...of
        block is indented another four spaces.
    }
}
```

>> **Break down complex tasks.** Don't try to solve all your problems at one time. If you have a large script or function that isn't working right, test it in small chunks to try to narrow down the problem.

>> **Break up long statements.** One of the most complicated aspects of script debugging is making sense out of long statements (especially expressions). The Console window can help (you can use it to print parts of the statement), but it's usually best to keep your statements as short as possible. After you get things working properly, you can often recombine statements for more efficient code.

>> **Comment out problem statements.** If a particular statement is giving you problems, you can temporarily deactivate it by placing two slashes (//) at the beginning of the line. The slashes tell JavaScript to treat the line as a comment. If you have a number of statements you want to skip, place /* at the beginning of the first statement and */ at the end of the last statement.

>> **Use comments to document your scripts.** Speaking of comments, it's a programming truism that good code — meaning (at least in part) code that uses clear variable and function names and a logical structure — should be self-explanatory. However, almost every piece of nontrivial code contains sections that, when you examine them later, aren't immediately obvious. For those section, it's another programming truism that you can never add enough explanatory comments. The more comments you add to complex and potentially obscure chunks of your code, the easier your scripts will be to debug.

# The Ten Most Common JavaScript Errors

When you encounter a script problem, the first thing you should do is examine your code for the most common errors. To help you do that, here's a list of the ten most common errors made by both beginning and experienced programmers:

>> **JavaScript keywords as variable names.** JavaScript has many reserved words and keywords that are built into the language, so it's common to accidentally use one of these words as a variable or function name. Double-check your names to make sure you're not using any reserved words, or the names of any objects, properties, or methods.

>> **Misspelled variables and other names.** Check your variable and function names to make sure you spell them consistently throughout the script. Also, check the spelling of the objects, properties, and methods you use.

>> **Misused uppercase and lowercase letters.** JavaScript is a *case-sensitive* language, which means that it treats each letter differently depending on whether it's uppercase or lowercase. For example, consider the following two statements:

```
const firstName = "Millicent";
const message = "Welcome " + firstname;
```

The first statement declares a variable named `firstName`, but the second statement uses `firstname`. This code would generate the error `firstname is not defined` (or something similar, depending on the browser) because JavaScript thinks that `firstname` is a different (and uninitialized) variable.

» **Mismatched quotation marks.** In any statement where you began a string literal with a quotation mark (" or '), always check to make sure that you included the corresponding closing quotation mark at the end of the string. Also, check whether you used one or more instances of the same quotation mark within the string. If so, either edit the string to use the proper escape sequence (\" or \') or switch to back ticks (`):

```
// Bad
const myString = "There are no "bad" programs.";

// Better
const myString = "There are no \"bad\" programs.";

// Best
const myString = `There are no "bad" programs.`;
```

» **Mismatched parentheses.** Examine your code for statements that contain a left parenthesis — ( — and make sure there's a corresponding right parentheses: ). This also applies to square brackets — [ and ] — and braces — { and }.

**TIP**

For complex expressions that include three or more sets of parentheses, a quick match-up check is to count the number of left parentheses in the expression, and then count the number of right parentheses. If these numbers don't match, you know you have a mismatch somewhere in the expression.

» **Missed parentheses after function names.** Speaking of parentheses, if your script calls a function or method that doesn't take any arguments, check that you included the parentheses — ( ) — after the name of the function or method:

```
function tryThis() {
    alert("Parentheses travel in pairs!");
}

// This won't work
tryThis;

// This will
tryThis();
```

>> **Improper use of braces.** JavaScript uses braces to mark the start ({) and end (}) of statement blocks associated with functions, tests involving `if` and `switch`, and loops, including `for...of`, `for`, `while`, and `do...while`. It's very easy to miss one or both braces in a block, and it's even easier to get the braces mixed up when nesting one test or loop inside another. Double-check your braces to make sure each block has both an opening and a closing brace.

TIP

One way to ensure that you don't miss any braces is to position them consistently throughout your script. For example, many people prefer to use the traditional style for brace positions:

```
keyword {
    statements
}
```

(Here, *keyword* means the statement — such as `function` or `if` — that defines the block.) If you prefer this style, use it all through your script so that you know exactly where to find each brace.

An easy way to ensure that you never forget a closing brace is to enter it immediately after entering the opening brace. That is, you type {, press Enter twice, and then type }.

Also, use indentation consistently for the statements within the block. Consistent indentation makes it much easier to view the braces, particularly when you have one block nested within another.

>> **Using = or == instead of ===.** The identity operator (===) is one of the least intuitive JavaScript features, because the assignment operator (=) feels so much more natural. The equality operator (==) can cause problems because it often converts the data types before making the comparison. Therefore, check all your comparison expressions to make sure you always use === instead of = or ==.

>> **Conflicts between global variables and block or local variables.** A global variable is available throughout the entire page, even within blocks and functions. So, within a block or function, make sure that you don't declare and use a variable that has the same name as a global variable.

>> **The use of a page element before it's loaded.** JavaScript runs through a page's HTML one line at a time and checks the syntax of each JavaScript statement as it comes to it. If your code refers to an element (such as a form field) that JavaScript hasn't come to yet, it will generate an error. Therefore, if your code deals with an element, always place the script after the element in the HTML file.

# The Ten Most Common JavaScript Error Messages

To help you decipher the error messages that JavaScript throws your way, here's a list of the ten most common errors and what they mean:

» `Syntax error`. This load-time error means that JavaScript has detected improper syntax in a statement. The error message almost always tells you the exact line and character where the error occurs. For example, if you refer back to the error message shown Figure 10-1, notice that to the right of the error message you see the following:

```
example01:17:18
```

This text means that the error occurs in the example01 file, on line 17, at character position 18 (counting from the start of the statement).

» `Expected (` or `Missing (`. These messages mean that you forgot to include a left parenthesis:

```
function changeBackgroundColor newColor) {
```

If you forget a right parenthesis instead, you'll get `Expected )` or `Missing )`:

```
function changeBackgroundColor (newColor{
```

» `Expected {` or `Missing { before function body`. These errors tell you that your code is missing the opening brace for a function:

```
function changeBackgroundColor (newColor)
    statements
}
```

If you're missing the closing brace instead, you'll get the errors `Expected }` or `Missing } after function body`.

» `Unexpected end of input` or `Missing } in compound statement`. These messages indicate that you forgot the closing brace in an `if` block or other compound statement:

```
if (currentHour < 12) {
    console.log("Good morning!");
} else {
    console.log("Good day!");
```

If you forget the opening brace, instead, you'll get a `Syntax error` message that points, confusingly, to the block's closing brace (which is the point where the browser first realizes that there's an error).

» **Missing ; or Missing ; after for-loop initializer|condition.**
These errors mean that a for loop definition is missing a semicolon (;), either
because you forgot the semicolon or because you used some other character
(such as a comma):

```
for (let counter = 1; counter < 5, counter += 1) {
```

» **Unexpected identifier or Missing ; before statement.** These errors
tell you that the previous statement didn't end properly for some reason, or
that you've begun a new statement with an invalid value. In JavaScript,
statements are supposed to end with a semicolon (;), but using a semicolon
is optional. So, if JavaScript thinks you haven't finished a statement properly,
it assumes that a semicolon is missing. For example, this can happen if you
forget to include the opening /* to begin a multiple-line comment:

```
Start the comment (oops!)
Close the comment */
```

» **X is not defined.** This message most often refers to a variable named X
that has not been declared or initialized, and that you're trying to use in an
expression. If that's the case, declare and initialize the variable. Another
possible cause is a string literal that isn't enclosed in quotation marks. Finally,
also check whether you misspelled the variable name:

```
const grossProfit = 100000;
const profitSharing = grossPrifit * profitSharingPercent;
```

» **X is not an object or X has no properties.** These messages mean that
your code refers to an object that doesn't exist, or to a property that doesn't
belong to the specified object. Check whether you misspelled the object or
property or, for the second case, that you're using the wrong object:

```
document.alert("Nope!")
```

» **Unterminated string constant or Unterminated string literal.** Both
messages mean that you began a string literal with a quotation mark, but
forgot to include the closing quotation mark:

```
const greeting = "Welcome to my Web site!
```

» **A script on this page is causing [browser name] to run slowly.
Do you want to abort the script? or Lengthy JavaScript still
running. Continue?.** These errors tell you that your code has probably
fallen into an infinite loop. You don't get any specific information about what's
causing the problem, so you'll need to scour your code carefully for the
possible cause.

IN THIS CHAPTER

» **Coding text boxes**

» **Programming checkboxes and radio buttons**

» **Processing selection lists**

» **Monitoring and triggering form events**

» **Dealing with the form data**

# Chapter **11**

# Processing Form Data

*Programming requires more concentration than other activities. It's the reason programmers get upset about 'quick interruptions' — such interruptions are tantamount to asking a juggler to keep three balls in the air and hold your groceries at the same time.*

—STEVE MCCONNELL

uilding HTML forms (the subject of Book 2, Chapter 5) is awesome and fun, but you may have noticed something more than a little dismaying about your forms: They don't really do very much! Sure, there's a certain satisfaction in toggling a checkbox, selecting a value from a list, and choosing a hue from a color picker, but that satisfaction is short-lived. It's like renovating your kitchen, turning a burner knob on your new oven, and having nothing happen. Why not? No electricity! Why doesn't your HTML form do anything? No JavaScript!

In this chapter, you learn how to "wire up" your HTML forms by plugging them into some JavaScript code. You explore various form-related objects and then get right to work coding text fields, checkboxes, radio buttons, and selection lists. You also dive into the useful world of form events and even learn how to enhance your form controls with keyboard shortcuts. To top it all off, you go hog wild and learn how to store form data using the Web Storage API that I talk about in Book 4, Chapter 9.

# Looking at the HTMLFormElement Object

A form element is an `HTMLFormElement` object that offers a few potentially useful properties (in each case, assume that *form* is a reference to a form element object):

» *form*.action: The value of the form's action attribute

» *form*.elements: Returns a collection (an `HTMLFormControlsCollection` object) of all the form's controls

» *form*.length: The number of controls in the form

» *form*.method: The value of the form's method attribute

» *form*.name: The value of the form's name attribute

» *form*.target: The value of the form's target attribute

# Taking a Peek at the HTMLInputElement Object

Any form field that's based on the input element is an `HTMLInputElement` object that offers quite a few useful properties (in each case, assume that *input* is a reference to an input element object):

» *input*.form: The form (an `HTMLFormElement` object) in which the element resides

» *input*.labels: Returns a NodeList of the label elements associated with the element

» *input*.name: The value of the element's name attribute

» *input*.type: The element's type attribute

» *input*.value: The current value of the element

» *input*.valueAsDate: The current value of the element, interpreted as a date

» *input*.valueAsNumber: The current value of the element, interpreted as a time value, then as a number

# Programming Text Fields

Text-based fields are the most commonly used form elements, and most of them use the `<input>` tag. The `input` element has tons of attributes (refer to Book 2, Chapter 5), but from a coding perspective, you're generally interested in only four:

```
<input id="textId" type="textType" name="textName"
    value="textValue">
```

» *textId:* A unique identifier for the text field

» *textType:* The kind of text field you want to use in your form

» *textName:* The name you assign to the field

» *textValue:* The initial value of the field, if any

## Referencing text fields by field type

One common form-scripting technique is to run an operation on every field of the same type. For example, you may want to apply a style to all the URL fields. Here's the JavaScript selector to use to select all `input` elements of a given type:

```
document.querySelectorAll('input[type=fieldType]')
```

» *fieldType:* The type attribute value you want to select, such as `text` or `url`

Here's an example where the JavaScript returns the set of all `input` elements that use the type `url` (check out bk04ch11/example01.html in this book's example files):

HTML:

```
<label for="url1">
    Site 1:
</label>
<input id="url1" type="url" name="url1" value="https://">
```

```
<label for="url2">
    Site 2:
</label>
<input id="url2" type="url" name="url2" value="https://">

<label for="url3">
    Site 3:
</label>
<input id="url3" type="url" name="url3" value="https://">
```

JavaScript:

```
const urlFields = document.querySelectorAll('input[type=url]');
console.log(urlFields);
```

## Getting a text field value

Your script can get the current value of any text field by using one of the field object's value-related properties:

```
field.value
field.valueAsDate
field.valueAsNumber
```

>> *field:* A reference to the form field object you want to work with

Here's an example (check out bk04ch11/example02.html):

HTML:

```
<label for="search-field">
    Search the site:
</label>
<input id="search-field" name="q" type="search">
```

JavaScript:

```
const searchString = document.getElementById('search-field').
    value;
console.log(searchString);
```

# Setting a text field value

To change a text field value, assign the new string to the field object's `value` property:

```
field.value = value
```

**»** *field:* A reference to the form field object you want to work with

**»** *value:* The string you want to assign to the text field

Here's an example (bk04ch11/example03.html):

HTML:

```
<label for="homepage-field">
    Type your homepage address:
</label>
<input id="homepage-field" name="homepage" type="url"
    value="HTTPS://PAULMCFEDRIES.COM/"">
```

JavaScript:

```
const homepageField = document.getElementById('homepage-field');
const homepageURL = homepageField.value;
homepageField.value = homepageURL.toLowerCase();
```

The HTML defines an `input` element of type `url` where the default value is in all-uppercase letters. The JavaScript code grabs a URL, converts it to all-lowercase characters, and then returns it to the same `url` field. As shown in Figure 11-1, the text box now displays all-lowercase letters.

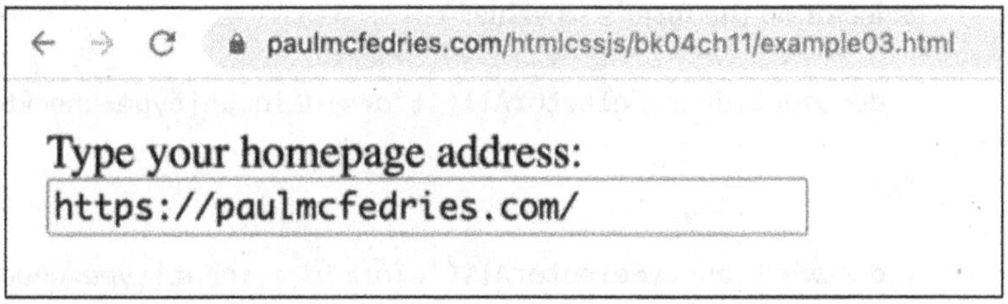

**FIGURE 11-1:**
The script
converts the
input element's
default text to all-
lowercase letters.

paulmcfedries.com/htmlcssjs/bk04ch11/example03.html

Type your homepage address:

https://paulmcfedries.com/

# Coding Checkboxes

You use a checkbox in a web form to toggle a setting on (that is, the checkbox is selected) and off (the checkbox is deselected). You create a checkbox by including in your form the following version of the `<input>` tag:

```
<input id="checkId" type="checkbox" name="checkName"
    value="checkValue" [checked]>
```

» *checkId:* A unique identifier for the checkbox.

» *checkName:* The name you want to assign to the checkbox.

» *checkValue:* The value you want to assign to the checkbox. Note that this is a hidden value that your script can access when the form is submitted; the user never encounters it.

» checked: When this optional attribute is present, the checkbox is initially selected.

REMEMBER

One strange thing about a checkbox field is that it's only included in the form submission if it's selected. If the checkbox is deselected, it's not included in the submission.

## Referencing checkboxes

If your code needs to reference all the checkboxes in a page, use the following selector (bk04ch11/example04.html):

```
document.querySelectorAll('input[type=checkbox]')
```

If you just want the checkboxes from a particular form, use a descendent or child selector on the form's id value:

```
document.querySelectorAll('#formid input[type=checkbox]')
```

Or:

```
document.querySelectorAll('#formid > input[type=checkbox]')
```

# Getting the checkbox state

You have to be a bit careful when discussing the "value" of a checkbox. If it's the value attribute you want to work with, then getting this is no different than getting the value property of a text field by using checkbox object's value property.

However, you're more likely to be interested in whether a checkbox is selected or deselected. This is called the checkbox *state*. In that case, you need to examine the checkbox object's checked property instead:

```
checkbox.checked
```

>> *checkbox:* A reference to the checkbox object you want to work with

The checked property returns true if the checkbox is selected, or false if the checkbox is deselected.

Here's an example (bk04ch11/example05.html):

HTML:

```
<label>
    <input id="autosave" type="checkbox" name="autosave">
    Autosave this project
</label>
```

JavaScript:

```
const autoSaveCheckBox = document.querySelector('#autosave');
if (autoSaveCheckBox.checked) {
    console.log(`${autoSaveCheckBox.name} is checked`);
} else {
    console.log(`${autoSaveCheckBox.name} is unchecked`);
}
```

The JavaScript code stores a reference to the checkbox object in the autoSave-CheckBox variable. Then an if statement examines the object's checked property and displays a different message in the console, depending on whether checked returns true or false.

## Setting the checkbox state

To set a checkbox field to either the selected or deselected state, assign a Boolean expression to the checked property:

```
checkbox.checked = Boolean
```

» *checkbox:* A reference to the checkbox object you want to work with.

» *Boolean:* The Boolean value or expression you want to assign to the checkbox. Use true to select the checkbox; use false to deselect the checkbox.

For example, suppose you have a form with a large number of checkboxes and you want to set up that form so that the user can select at most three checkboxes. Here's some code that does the job (bk04ch11/example06.html):

```
document.querySelector('form').addEventListener('click',
  event => {

    // Make sure a checkbox was clicked
    if (event.target.type === 'checkbox') {

        // Get the total number of selected checkboxes
        const totalSelected = document.querySelectorAll('input
        [type=checkbox]:checked').length;

        // Are there more than three selected checkboxes?
        if (totalSelected > 3) {

            // If so, deselect the checkbox that was just
    clicked
            event.target.checked = false;
        }
    }
});
```

This event handler runs when anything inside the form element is clicked, and it passes a reference to the click event as the parameter event. Then the code uses the :checked selector to return the set of all checkbox elements that have the checked attribute, and the length property tells you how many are in the set. An if test checks whether more than three are now selected. If that's true, the code deselects the checkbox that was just clicked.

# Dealing with Radio Buttons

If you want to offer your users a collection of related options, only one of which can be selected at a time, then radio buttons are the way to go. Form radio buttons congregate in groups of two or more where only one button in the group can be selected at any time. If the user clicks another button in that group, it becomes selected and the previously selected button becomes deselected.

You create a radio button using the following variation of the `<input>` tag:

```
<input id="radioId" type="radio" name="radioGroup"
    value="radioValue" [checked]>
```

» *radioId:* A unique identifier for the radio button.

» *radioGroup:* The name you want to assign to the group of radio buttons. All the radio buttons that use the same name value belong to that group.

» *radioValue:* The value you want to assign to the radio button. If this radio button is selected when the form is submitted, this is the value that's included in the submission.

» checked: When this optional attribute is present, the radio button is initially selected.

## Referencing radio buttons

If your code needs to work with all the radio buttons in a page, use this JavaScript selector:

```
document.querySelectorAll('input[type=radio]')
```

If you want the radio buttons from a particular form, use a descendent or child selector on the form's id value:

```
document.querySelectorAll('#formid input[type=radio]')
```

Or:

```
document.querySelectorAll('#formid > input[type=radio]')
```

If you require just the radio buttons from a particular group, use the following JavaScript selector, where *radioGroup* is the common name of the group:

```
document.querySelectorAll('input[name=radioGroup]')
```

## Getting a radio button state

If your code needs to know whether a particular radio button is selected or deselected, you need to determine the radio button *state*. You do that by examining the radio button's checked attribute, like so:

```
radio.checked
```

» *radio:* A reference to the radio button object you want to work with

The checked attribute returns true if the radio button is selected, or false if the button is deselected.

For example, consider the following HTML (bk04ch11/example07.html):

```
<form>
    <fieldset>
        <legend>
            Select a delivery method
        </legend>
        <label>
            <input type="radio" id="carrier-pigeon"
    name="delivery" value="pigeon" checked>Carrier pigeon
        </label>
        <label>
            <input type="radio" id="pony-express"
    name="delivery" value="pony">Pony express
        </label>
        <label>
            <input type="radio" id="snail-mail" name="delivery"
    value="postal">Snail mail
        </label>
        <label>
            <input type="radio" id="some-punk" name="delivery"
    value="bikecourier">Some punk on a bike
        </label>
    </fieldset>
</form>
```

The following statement stores the state of the radio button with the id value of pony-express:

```
const ponySelected = document.querySelector('#pony-express').
   checked;
```

However, your code is more likely to want to know which radio button in a group is selected. You can do that by applying the :checked selector to the group and then getting the value property of the returned object:

```
const deliveryMethod = document.querySelector('input[name=
   delivery]:checked').value;
```

**TIP**

To get the text of the label associated with a radio button, use the input element's labels property to get a reference to the label element, and then use the innerText property to get the label text:

```
document.querySelector('input[name=delivery]:checked').
   labels[0].innerTextinnerText);
```

## Setting the radio button state

To set a radio button field to either the selected or deselected state, assign a Boolean expression to the checked attribute:

```
radio.checked = Boolean
```

>> *radio:* A reference to the radio button object you want to change.

>> *Boolean:* The Boolean value or expression you want to assign to the radio button. Use true to select the radio button; use false to deselect the radio button.

For example, in the HTML code from the previous section, the initial state of the form group had the first radio button selected. You can reset the group by selecting that button. You could get a reference to the id of the first radio button, but what if later you change (or someone else changes) the order of the radio buttons? A safer way is to get a reference to the first radio button in the group, whatever it may be, and then select that element. Here's some code that does this (bk04ch11/example08.html):

```
const firstRadioButton = document.querySelectorAll('input
   [name=delivery]')[0];
firstRadioButton.checked = true;
```

This code uses `querySelectorAll()` to return a `NodeList` collection of all the radio buttons in the `delivery` group; then it uses `[0]` to reference just the first element in the collection. Then that element's `checked` property is set to `true`.

# Programming Selection Lists

Selection lists are common sights in HTML forms because they enable the web developer to display a relatively large number of choices in a compact control that most users know how to operate.

To create the list container, you use the `<select>` tag:

```
<select id="selectId" name="selectName" size="selectSize"
    [multiple]>
```

» *selectId:* A unique identifier for the selection list.

» *selectName:* The name you want to assign to the selection list.

» *selectSize:* The optional number of rows in the selection list box that are visible. If you omit this value, the browser displays the list as a drop-down box.

» `multiple`: When this optional attribute is present, the user is allowed to select multiple options in the list.

For each item in the list, you add an `<option>` tag between the `<select>` and `</select>` tags:

```
<option value="optionValue" [selected]>
```

» *optionValue:* The value you want to assign to the list option.

» `selected`: When this optional attribute is present, the list option is initially selected.

## Checking out the HTMLSelectElement object

A selection list is an `HTMLSelectElement` object that offers quite a few useful properties (in each case, assume that *select* is a reference to a selection list object):

>> *select*.form: The form (an HTMLFormElement object) in which the selection list resides.

>> *select*.length: The number of option elements in the selection list.

>> *select*.multiple: A Boolean value that returns true if the selection list includes the multiple attribute; otherwise, it returns false.

>> *select*.name: The value of the selection list's name attribute.

>> *select*.options: The option elements (an HTMLOptionsCollection object) contained in the selection list.

>> *select*.selectedIndex: The index of the first selected option element (index values begin at 0 for the first option element). This property returns –1 if no option elements are selected.

>> *select*.selectedOptions: The option elements (an HTMLCollection object) that are currently selected in the selection list.

>> *select*.type: The selection list type: select–one for a regular list or select–multiple for a list with the multiple attribute applied.

>> *select*.value: The value property of the first selected option element. If no option element is selected, this property returns the empty string.

## Checking out the HTMLOptionElement object

Each option element in a selection list is an HTMLOptionElement object. Here are a few useful HTMLOptionElement properties to bear in mind (in each case, assume that *option* is a reference to an option element object):

>> *option*.defaultSelected: A Boolean value that returns true if the option element included the selected attribute by default, and false otherwise

>> *option*.form: The form (an HTMLFormElement object) in which the option element resides

>> *option*.index: The index of the option element within the selection list (index values begin at 0 for the first option element)

>> *option*.selected: A Boolean value that returns true if the option element is currently selected, and false otherwise

>> *option*.text: The text content of the option element

>> *option*.value: The value of the value attribute of the option element

# Referencing selection list options

If your code needs to work with all the options in a selection list, use the selection list object's options property (bk04ch11/example09.html):

```
document.querySelector(list).options
```

>> *list*: A selector that specifies the select element you want to work with

To work with a particular option within a list, use JavaScript's square brackets operator ([]) to specify the index of the option's position in the list (bk04ch11/example09.html):

```
document.querySelector(list).options[n]
```

>> *list*: A selector that specifies the select element you want to work with

>> *n*: The index of the option in the returned NodeList collection (where 0 is the first option, 1 is the second option, and so on)

To get the option's text (that is, the text that appears in the list), use the option object's text property:

```
document.querySelector(list).options[2].text
```

# Getting the selected list option

If your code needs to know whether a particular option in a selection list is selected or deselected, examine the option's selected property, like so:

```
option.selected
```

>> *option:* A reference to the option object you want to work with

The selected attribute returns true if the option is selected, or false if the option is deselected.

For example, consider the following selection list:

```
<select id="hair-color" name="hair-color">
    <option value="black">Black</option>
    <option value="blonde">Blonde</option>
    <option value="brunette" selected>Brunette</option>
```

```
        <option value="red">Red</option>
        <option value="neon">Something neon</option>
        <option value="none">None</option>
</select>
```

The following JavaScript statement stores the state of the first item in the selection list:

```
let black = document.querySelector('#hair-color').options[0].
    selected;
```

However, you'll more likely want to know which option in the selection list is selected. You do that via the list's selectedOptions property:

```
const hairColor = document.querySelector('#hair-color').
    selectedOptions[0];
```

This isn't a multi-select list, so specifying selectedOptions[0] returns the selected option element. In this example, your code could use hairColor.text to get the text of the selected option.

If the list includes the multiple attribute, the selectedOptions property may return an HTMLCollection object that contains multiple elements. Your code needs to allow for that possibility by, say, looping through the collection (bk04ch11/example10.html):

HTML:

```
<select id="hair-products" name="hair-products" size="5"
   multiple>
     <option value="gel" selected>Gel</option>
     <option value="grecian-formula" selected>Grecian
   Formula</option>
     <option value="mousse">Mousse</option>
     <option value="peroxide">Peroxide</option>
     <option value="shoe-black">Shoe black</option>
</select>
```

JavaScript:

```
const selectedHairProducts = document.querySelector('#hair-
    products').selectedOptions;
for (const hairProduct of selectedHairProducts) {
    console.log(hairProduct.text);
}
```

## Changing the selected option

To set a selection list option to either the selected or deselected state, assign a Boolean expression to the option object's `selected` property:

```
option.selected = Boolean
```

» *option:* A reference to the `option` element you want to modify.

» *Boolean:* The Boolean value or expression you want to assign to the option. Use `true` to select the option; use `false` to deselect the option.

Using the HTML code from the previous section, the following statement selects the third option in the list:

```
document.querySelector('#hair-products').options[2].selected =
    true;
```

You can reset the list by deselecting all the options. You do that by setting the selection list object's `selectedIndex` property to –1:

```
document.querySelector('#hair-products').selectedIndex = -1
```

# Handling and Triggering Form Events

With all the clicking, typing, tabbing, and dragging that goes on, web forms are veritable event factories. Fortunately, you can let most of these events pass you by, but a few do come in handy, both in running code when the event occurs and in triggering the events yourself.

Most form events are clicks, so you can handle them by setting `click` event handlers using JavaScript's `addEventListener()` method (which I cover in Book 4, Chapter 6). Here's an example (bk04ch11/example11.html):

HTML:

```
<form>
    <label for="user">Username:</label>
    <input id="user" type="text" name="username">
    <label for="pwd">Password:</label>
    <input id="pwd" type="password" name="password">
</form>
```

JavaScript:

```
document.querySelector('form').addEventListener('click', () => {
    console.log('Thanks for clicking the form!');
});
```

This example listens for clicks on the entire form element, but you can also create click event handlers for buttons, input elements, checkboxes, radio buttons, and more.

## Setting the focus

One simple feature that can improve the user experience on your form pages is to set the focus on the first form field when your page loads. Setting the focus saves the user from having to make that annoying click inside the first field.

To get this done, run JavaScript's focus() method on the element you want to have the focus at startup:

```
field.focus()
```

>> *field:* A reference to the form field you want to have the focus.

Here's an example that sets the focus on the text field with id equal to user at startup (bk04ch11/example12.html):

HTML:

```
<form>
    <label for="user">Username:</label>
    <input id="user" type="text" name="username">
    <label for="pwd">Password:</label>
    <input id="pwd" type="password" name="password">
</form>
```

JavaScript:

```
document.querySelector('#user').focus();
```

## Monitoring the focus event

Rather than set the focus, you may want to monitor when a particular field gets the focus (for example, by the user clicking or tabbing into the field). You can monitor that by setting up a focus event handler on the field:

```
field.addEventListener('focus', () => {
    Focus code goes here
});
```

» *field:* A reference to the form field you want to monitor for the focus event

Here's an example (bk04ch11/example13.html):

```
document.querySelector('#user').addEventListener('focus', () => {
    console.log('The username field has the focus!');
});
```

## Monitoring the blur event

The opposite of setting the focus on an element is *blurring* an element, which removes the focus from the element. You blur an element by running the blur() method on the element, which causes it to lose focus:

```
field.blur()
```

» *field:* A reference to the form field you no longer want to have the focus

However, rather than blur an element, you're more likely to want to run some code when a particular element is blurred (for example, by the user clicking or tabbing out of the field). You can monitor for a particular blurred element by setting up a blur() event handler:

```
field.addEventListener('blur', () => {
    Blur code goes here
});
```

» *field:* A reference to the form field you want to monitor for the blur event

Here's an example (bk04ch11/example14.html):

```
document.querySelector('#user').addEventListener('blur', () => {
    console.log('The username field no longer has the focus!');
});
```

# Listening for element changes

One of the most useful form events is the change event, which fires when the value or state of a field is modified in some way. When this event fires depends on the element type:

>> For a textarea element and the various text-related input elements, the change event fires when the element loses the focus.

>> For checkboxes, radio buttons, selection lists, and pickers, the change event fires as soon as the user clicks the element to modify the selection or value.

You listen for a field's change events by setting up a change() event handler:

```
field.addEventListener('change', () => {
    Change code goes here
});
```

>> field: A reference to the form field you want to monitor for the change event

Here's an example (bk04ch11/example15.html):

HTML:

```
<label for="bgcolor">Select a background color</label>
<input id="bgcolor" type="color" name="bg-color"
    value="#ffffff">
```

JavaScript:

```
document.querySelector('#bgcolor').addEventListener('change',
    (event) => {
        const backgroundColor = event.target.value;
        document.body.bgColor = backgroundColor;
});
```

The HTML code sets up a color picker. The JavaScript code applies the change event handler to the color picker. When the change event fires on the picker, the code stores the new color value in the backgroundColor variable by referencing event.target.value, where event.target refers to the element to which the event listener is bound (the color picker, in this case). The code then applies that color to the body element's bgColor property.

# Creating Keyboard Shortcuts for Form Controls

**REMEMBER**

A web page is very much a click- (or tap-) friendly medium, but that doesn't mean you can't build some keyboard support into your interface. For example, adding the tabindex="0" attribute to any HTML tag automatically makes that element "tabbable" (meaning that a user can set the focus on that element by tapping the Tab key one or more times).

Another good example is a button that you feature on most or all of your pages. In that case, you can set up a keyboard shortcut that enables a user to execute the button by pressing a key or key combination.

You define a keyboard shortcut for a web page by setting up an event handler for the document object's keydown event (which fires when the user presses, but hasn't yet released, a key). Depending on the type of shortcut, you may also be able to define the shortcut using the document object's keyup event (which fires when the user releases a pressed key). Your event handler needs to look for two kinds of keys:

>> **Special keys:** These include the Alt, Ctrl (or Control on a Mac), Shift, and Meta (that is, ⌘ on a Mac) keys. When the user presses a special key, the KeyboardEvent object sets one of the following properties to true: altKey (for Alt), ctrlKey (for Ctrl or Control), shiftKey (for Shift), or metaKey (for Cmd).

>> **Any other key:** This includes the letters, numbers, and symbols on a typical keyboard. In this case, the pressed key is returned as the KeyboardEvent object's key property.

Here's an example (bk04ch11/example16.html):

HTML:

```html
<button type="button">
    Run Me!
</button>
<p>
    Keyboard shortcut: Ctrl+Shift+E
</p>
```

JavaScript:

```javascript
// Add a listener for the button's 'click' event
document
    .querySelector('button')
    .addEventListener('click',
    (event) => {
        // Change the button text
        event.target.innerText = 'Thanks!';

        // Reset the button after 3 seconds
        setTimeout(() => document
            .querySelector('button').innerText = 'Run Me!',
            3000);
    }
);

// Add a listener for the 'keydown' event
document
    .addEventListener('keydown',
    function(event) {
        // Check whether Ctrl+Shift+E are all pressed
        if(event.ctrlKey && event.shiftKey &&
    event.key === 'E') {
            // If so, trigger the button's 'click' event
            document.querySelector('button').click();
        }
    }
);
```

The HTML creates a simple button. The JavaScript sets up an event handler for the button's `click` event, which changes the button text, and then uses `setTimeout()` to change the text back after three seconds. The code also sets up a `keydown` event handler that checks whether the Ctrl, Shift, and E keys were pressed at the same time. If so, the code invokes the button's `click()` method, which fires the `click` event and triggers the `click` event handler.

# Dealing with the Form Data

There's one form event that I didn't cover earlier, and it's a biggie: the `submit` event, which fires when the form data is to be sent to the server.

However, if your scripts deal with form data only locally — that is, you never send the data to a server — then you don't need to bother with submitting the form. Instead, it's more straightforward to add a button to your form and then use that button's `click` event handler to process the form data in whatever way you need.

**TIP**

Submitting form data to the server is beyond the scope of this book. If you're interested, I go into all that in great detail in my companion book, *Web Coding and Development All-in-One For Dummies* (Wiley).

Here's an example (bk04ch11/example17.html):

HTML:

```
<form>
    <fieldset>
        <legend>
            Settings
        </legend>
        <label for="background-color">Select a background
color</label>
        <input id="background-color" type="color" name="bg-
color" value="#ffffff">
        <label for="text-color">Select a text color</label>
        <input id="text-color" type="color" name="text-color"
value="#000000">
        <label for="font-stack">Select a typeface:</label>
        <select id="font-stack" name="font-stack">
            <option value="Georgia, 'Times New Roman', serif"
selected>Serif</option>
            <option value="Verdana, Tahoma, sans-serif">Sans-
serif</option>
            <option value="'Bradley Hand', Brush Script MT,
cursive">Cursive</option>
```

```
            <option value="Luminari">Fantasy</option>
            <option value="Monaco, Courier,
  monospace">Monospace</option>
      </select>
      <button>
          Save Your Settings
      </button>
    </fieldset>
</form>
```

JavaScript:

```
// Listen for changes on the #background-color color picker
document.querySelector('#background-color').
  addEventListener('change', function() {
    const backgroundColor = this.value;
    document.body.style.backgroundColor = backgroundColor;
});

// Listen for changes on the #text-color color picker
document.querySelector('#text-color').addEventListener('change',
  function() {
    const textColor = this.value;
    document.body.style.color = textColor;
});

// Listen for changes on the #font-stack selection list
document.querySelector('#font-stack').addEventListener('change',
  function() {
    const fontStack = this.selectedOptions[0].value;
    document.body.style.fontFamily = fontStack;
});

// Listen for the button being clicked
document.querySelector('button').addEventListener('click',
  () => {

    // Store the form data in a JavaScript object
    const userSettings = {
        backgroundColor: document.querySelector('#background-
    color').value,
        textColor: document.querySelector('#text-color').value,
```

Processing Form Data

```
        fontStack: document.querySelector('#font-stack').
    selectedOptions[0].value
      }

      // Save the settings in local storage
      localStorage.setItem('user-settings',
    JSON.stringify(userSettings));
    });
```

The HTML sets up a form (check out Figure 11-2) to gather some user settings —
background color, text color, and typeface style — as well as a button. The
JavaScript sets up change event handlers for the two color pickers and the selection list. Finally, the code listens for click events on the button, and the handler
stores the form data in a JavaScript object and then saves the data to local storage
(refer to Book 4, Chapter 9).

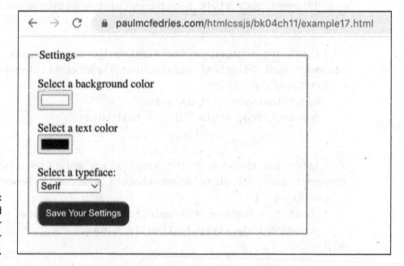

**FIGURE 11-2:**
A form used
to gather user
settings for
the page.

# 5

# Looking Good with Layouts

# Contents at a Glance

# Chapter **1**

# Exploring Some Layout Basics

*To dismiss basic contexts such as link colours, page layouts, navigation systems, and visual hierarchy as 'boring' or 'pedestrian' is akin to laughing at a car's steering wheel as unimaginative.*

—JEFFREY VEEN

Why are some web pages immediately appealing, while others put the "Ugh" in "ugly"? There are lots of possible reasons: colors, typography, image quality, the density of exclamation points. For my money, however, the number one reason why some pages soar while others are eyesores is the overall look and feel of the page. We've all visited enough websites in our lives to have developed a kind of sixth sense that tells us immediately whether a page is worth checking out. Sure, colors and fonts play a part in that intuition, but we all respond viscerally to the "big picture" that a page presents.

That big picture refers to the overall layout of the page, and that's the subject you start to explore here in Book 5. In this chapter, you build a solid foundation by understanding how the web browser lays out a page by default, and then exploring a few basic CSS techniques that enable you to break out of that default layout and take control of your pages. By the time you're done mastering the nitty-gritty of page layout, you'll be in a position to design and build beautiful and functional pages that'll have them screaming for more.

# Getting a Grip on Page Flow

When a web browser renders a web page, one of the really boring things it does is lay out the tags by applying the following rules to each element type:

>> **Inline elements:** Render these from left to right within each element's parent container.

>> **Block-level elements:** Stack these on top of each other, with the first element at the top of the page, the second element below the first, and so on.

**REMEMBER**

These rules assume that the current language is one whose text reads from left to right and top to bottom (such as English). In some languages (such as Hebrew and Arabic), the default text flow is from right to left and top to bottom. In vertical languages, the default text flow is from top to bottom and then either right to left (as in Japanese and Chinese) or left to right (as in Mongolian).

This is called the *page flow*. For example, consider the following HTML code (refer to bk05ch01/example01.html in this book's example files):

```
<header>
    The page header goes here.
</header>
<nav>
    The navigation doodads go here.
</nav>
<section>
    This is the first section of the page.
</section>
<section>
    This is—you got it—the second section of the page.
</section>
<aside>
    This is the witty or oh-so-interesting aside.
</aside>
<footer>
    The page footer goes here.
</footer>
```

This code is a collection of six block-level elements — a header, a nav, two section tags, an aside, and a footer — and Figure 1-1 shows how the web browser renders them as a stack of boxes.

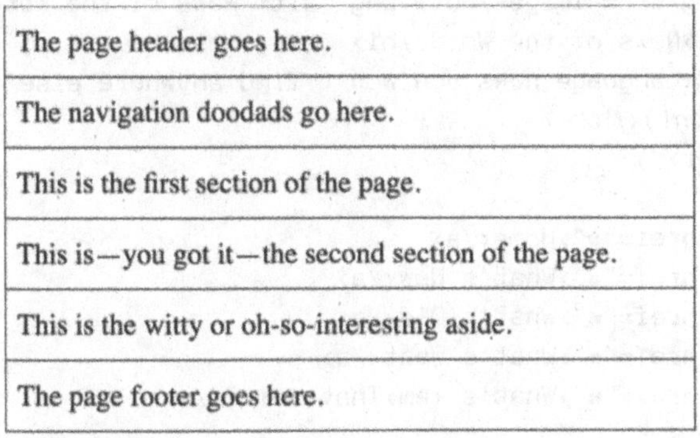

**FIGURE 1-1:**
The web browser
renders the
block-level
elements as a
stack of boxes.

| |
|---|
| The page header goes here. |
| The navigation doodads go here. |
| This is the first section of the page. |
| This is—you got it—the second section of the page. |
| This is the witty or oh-so-interesting aside. |
| The page footer goes here. |

**FIGURE 1-1:**
The web browser
renders the
block-level
elements as a
stack of boxes.

Nothing is inherently wrong with the default page flow, but having your web page render as a stack of boxes lacks a certain flair. Fortunately for your creative spirit, you're not married to the default, one-box-piled-on-another flow. CSS gives you a ton useful methods for breaking out of the normal page flow and giving your pages some pizzazz. In this chapter, you learn about three of those methods: floating, positioning, and stacking.

# Floating Elements

When you *float* an element, the web browser takes the element out of the default page flow. Where the element ends up on the page depends on whether you float it to the left or to the right:

>> **Float left:** The browser places the element as far to the left and as high as possible within the element's parent container.

>> **Float right:** The browser places the element as far to the right and as high as possible within the element's parent container.

In both cases, the nonfloated elements flow around the floated element.

You convince the web browser to float an element by adding the float property:

```
element {
    float: left|right|none;
}
```

For example, consider the following code (check out bk05ch01/example02.html) and its rendering in Figure 1-2:

```
<header>
    <img src="images/notw.png" alt="News of the Word logo">
    <h1>News of the Word</h1>
    <h2>Language news you won't find anywhere else (for good
    reason!)</h2>
</header>
<nav>
    <a href="#">Home</a>
    <a href="#">What's New</a>
    <a href="#">What's Old</a>
    <a href="#">What's What</a>
    <a href="#">What's <em>That</em>?</a>
</nav>
```

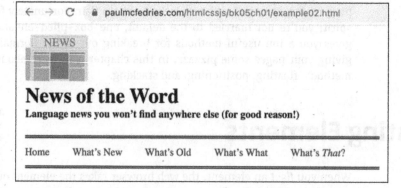

**FIGURE 1-2:**
As usual, the browser displays the block-level elements as a stack of boxes.

In Figure 1-2, note that the web browser is up to its usual page-flow tricks: stacking all the block-level elements on top of each other. However, I think this page would look better if the title and subtitle (the h1 and h2 elements) appeared to the right of the logo. To do that, I can float the img element to the left (bk05ch01/example03.html):

```
header > img {
    float: left;
    margin-right: 2em;
}
```

Figure 1-3 shows the results. With the logo floated to the left, the title and subtitle — the h1 and h2 elements — now flow around (or, really, to the right of) the img element.

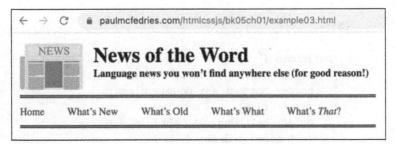

## Example: Creating a pull quote

A *pull quote* is a short excerpt copied ("pulled") from the current page text. The excerpt should be evocative or interesting, and the pull quote is set off from the regular text. A well-chosen and well-designed pull quote can entice an ambivalent site visitor to read (or, at least, start) the article.

You create a pull quote by copying the article excerpt and placing it inside an element such as an `aside`. You then float that element, most often to the right. Style the element as needed to make it stand apart from the regular text and you're done.

Here's an example (bk05ch01/example04.html):

HTML (partial):

```
<p>
    "None of it made a lick of sense" he said.
</p>
<aside class="pullquote">
    They can't understand a word anyone is texting to them.
</aside>
<p>
    It has long been thought that teen instant messages
    contained abbreviations (such as <i>LOL</i> for "laughing out
    loud" and <i>MAIBARP</i> for "my acne is becoming a real
    problem"), short forms (such as <i>L8R</i> for "later" and
    <i>R2D2</i> for "R2D2"), and slang (such as <i>whassup</i> for
    "what's up" and <i>yo</i> for "Hello, I am pleased to meet
    your acquaintance. Do you wish to have a conversation?").
    However, the report reveals that this so-called "teenspeak"
    began to change so fast that kids simply could not keep up.
    Each teen developed his or her own lingo, and the instant
    messaging system devolved into anarchy.
</p>
```

CSS:

```css
.pullquote {
    border-top: 4px double black;
    border-bottom: 4px double black;
    float: right;
    color: hsl(0deg, 0%, 40%);
    font-size: 1.9rem;
    font-style: italic;
    margin: 0 0 0.75rem 0.5rem;
    padding: 8px 0 8px 16px;
    width: 50%;
}
```

Figure 1-4 shows how everything looks.

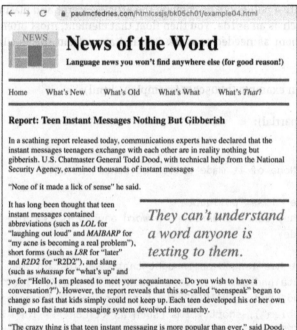

**FIGURE 1-4:**
A pull quote floated to the right of the article text.

# Clearing your floats

The default behavior for nonfloated stuff is to wrap around anything that's floated, which is often exactly what you want. However, you'll sometimes want to avoid having an element wrap around your floats. For example, consider the following code (bk05ch01/example05.html) and how it gets rendered, as shown in Figure 1-5.

```html
<header>
    <h1>Can't You Read the Sign?</h1>
</header>
<nav>
    <a href="/">Home</a>
    <a href="semantics.html">Signs</a>
    <a href="contact.html">Contact Us</a>
    <a href="about.html">Suggest a Sign</a>
</nav>
<article>
    <img src="/images/keep-off-the-grass.jpg"  alt="A sign
  reading Keep Off the Grass beside a well-trodden path running
  across the grass.">
</article>
<footer>
    &copy; Can't You Read?, Inc.
</footer>
```

**FIGURE 1-5:**
When the image is floated left, the footer wraps around it and ends up in a weird place.

With the `<img>` tag floated to the left, the rest of the content flows around it, including the content of the `<footer>` tag, which now appears by the top of the image.

You want your footer to appear at the bottom of the page, naturally, so how can you fix this? By telling the web browser to position the `footer` element so that it *clears* the floated image, which means that it appears after the image in the page flow. You clear an element by adding the `clear` property:

```
element {
    clear: left|right|both|none;
}
```

Use `clear: left` to clear all left-floated elements, `clear: right` to clear all right-floated elements, or `clear: both` to clear everything. When I add `clear: left` to the `footer` element (bk05ch01/example06.html), you can note in Figure 1-6 that the footer content now appears at the bottom of the page.

```
footer {
    clear: left;
}
```

**FIGURE 1-6:** Adding `clear: left` to the footer element causes the footer to clear the left-floated image and appear at the bottom of the page.

# Collapsing containers ahead!

The odd behavior of CSS is apparently limitless, and floats offer yet another example. Consider the following HTML (bk05ch01/example07.html) and its result in Figure 1-7:

```
<article>
    <section>
        An awfully long time ago...
    </section>
    <aside>
        <b>Note:</b> Creating a new word by...
    </aside>
</article>
```

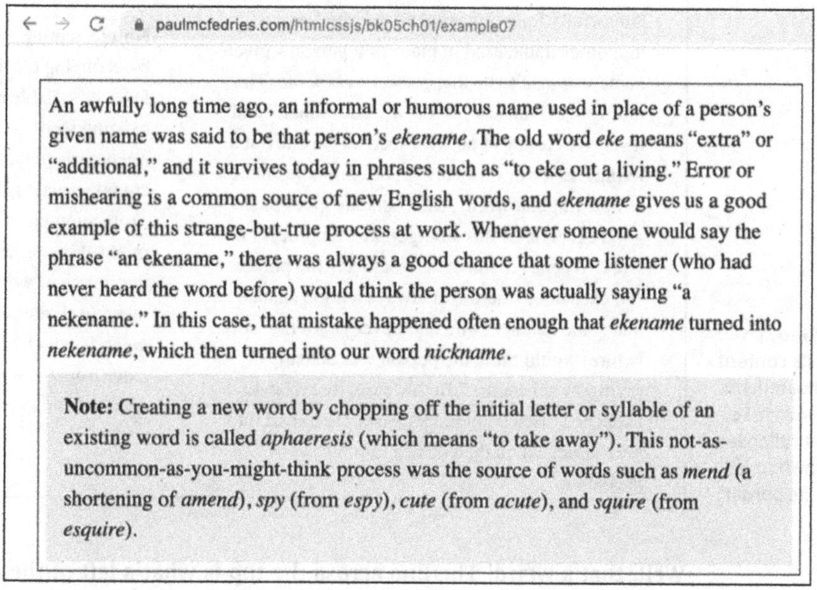

**FIGURE 1-7:**
An <article> tag containing a <section> tag and an <aside> tag, rendered using the default page flow.

Note, in particular, that I've styled the article element with a border.

Rather than the stack of blocks shown in Figure 1-10, you may prefer to have the section and the aside elements appear side by side. Great idea! So, you add width properties to each, and float the section element to the left and the aside element to the right. Here are the rules (bk05ch01/example08.html), and Figure 1-8 shows the result.

```
section {
    float: left;
    width: 25rem;
}
aside {
    float: right;
    width: 16rem;
}
```

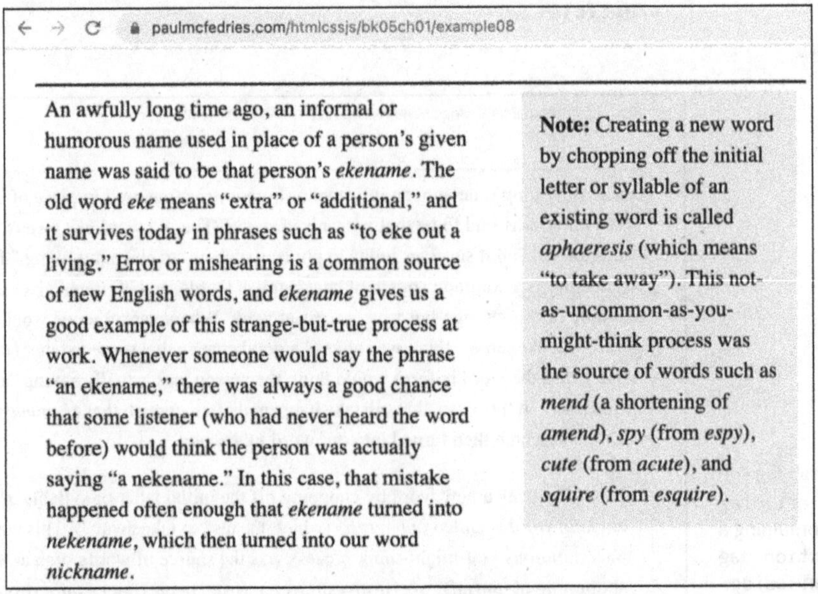

← → C 🔒 paulmcfedries.com/htmlcssjs/bk05ch01/example08

An awfully long time ago, an informal or humorous name used in place of a person's given name was said to be that person's *ekename*. The old word *eke* means "extra" or "additional," and it survives today in phrases such as "to eke out a living." Error or mishearing is a common source of new English words, and *ekename* gives us a good example of this strange-but-true process at work. Whenever someone would say the phrase "an ekename," there was always a good chance that some listener (who had never heard the word before) would think the person was actually saying "a nekename." In this case, that mistake happened often enough that *ekename* turned into *nekename*, which then turned into our word *nickname*.

**Note:** Creating a new word by chopping off the initial letter or syllable of an existing word is called *aphaeresis* (which means "to take away"). This not-as-uncommon-as-you-might-think process was the source of words such as *mend* (a shortening of *amend*), *spy* (from *espy*), *cute* (from *acute*), and *squire* (from *esquire*).

**FIGURE 1-8:**
With its content floated, the
⟨article⟩
element collapses down to just its border.

Well, that's weird! The line across the top is what's left of the article element. What happened? Because I floated both the section and the aside elements, the browser removed them from the page flow, which made the article element behave as though it had no content at all. The result? A CSS bugaboo known as *container collapse*.

To fix this issue, you have to force the parent container to clear its own children.

HTML:

```
<article class="self-clear">
```

CSS:

```
.self-clear::after {
    content: "";
    display: block;
    clear: both;
}
```

The `::after` pseudo-element tells the browser to add an empty string (because you don't want to add anything substantial to the page), and that empty string is displayed as a block that uses `clear: both` to clear the container's children. It's weird, but it works, as shown in Figure 1-9 (bk05ch01/example09.html).

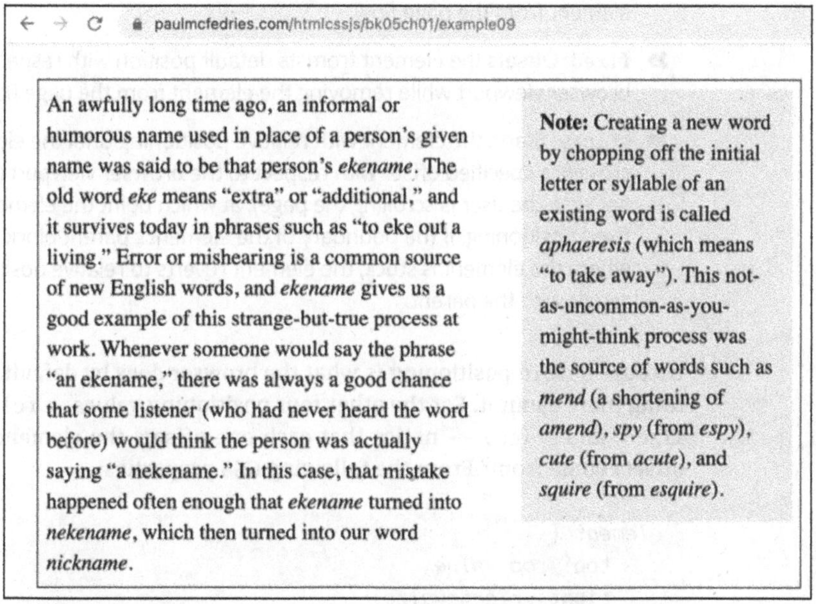
paulmcfedries.com/htmlcssjs/bk05ch01/example09
An awfully long time ago, an informal or humorous name used in place of a person's given name was said to be that person's *ekename*. The old word *eke* means "extra" or "additional," and it survives today in phrases such as "to eke out a living." Error or mishearing is a common source of new English words, and *ekename* gives us a good example of this strange-but-true process at work. Whenever someone would say the phrase "an ekename," there was always a good chance that some listener (who had never heard the word before) would think the person was actually saying "a nekename." In this case, that mistake happened often enough that *ekename* turned into *nekename*, which then turned into our word *nickname*.
**Note:** Creating a new word by chopping off the initial letter or syllable of an existing word is called *aphaeresis* (which means "to take away"). This not-as-uncommon-as-you-might-think process was the source of words such as *mend* (a shortening of *amend*), *spy* (from *espy*), *cute* (from *acute*), and *squire* (from *esquire*).

**FIGURE 1-9:** With the `self-clear` class added to the `<article>` tag, the `article` element now clears its own children and is no longer collapsed.

# Positioning Elements

The second major method for breaking out of the web browser's default "stacked boxes" page flow is to position an element yourself using CSS properties. For example, you could tell the browser to place an image in the top-left corner of the window, no matter where that element's `<img>` tag appears in the page's HTML code. In the CSS world, this is known as *positioning*, and it's a very powerful tool, so much so that most web developers use positioning only sparingly.

The first bit of positioning wizardry you need to know is, appropriately, the `position` property:

```
element {
    position: static|relative|absolute|fixed|sticky;
}
```

>> `static`: Places the element in its default position in the page flow.

>> `relative`: Offsets the element from its default position while keeping the element in the page flow.

>> `absolute`: Offsets the element from its default position with respect to its parent (or sometimes an earlier ancestor) container while removing the element from the page flow.

>> `fixed`: Offsets the element from its default position with respect to the browser viewport while removing the element from the page flow.

>> `sticky`: Starts the element with relative positioning until the element's parent crosses a specified offset with respect to the browser viewport (usually because the user is scrolling the page), at which point the element switches to fixed positioning. If the boundary of the element's parent block then scrolls to where the element is stuck, the element reverts to relative positioning and scrolls with the parent.

Because `static` positioning is what the browser does by default, I won't say anything more about it. For the other four positioning values — `relative`, `absolute`, `fixed`, and `sticky` — notice that each one offsets the element. Where do these offsets come from? From the following CSS properties:

```
element {
    top: top-value;
    right: right-value;
    bottom: bottom-value;
    left: left-value;
}
```

>> `top`: Shifts the element down

>> `right`: Shifts the element from the right

>> `bottom`: Shifts the element up

>> `left`: Shifts the element from the left

In each case, the value you supply is either a number followed by one of the CSS measurement units (such as px, em, rem, vw, or vh) or a percentage.

# Using relative positioning

Relative positioning is a bit weird because not only does it offset an element relative to its parent container, but it still keeps the element's default space in the page flow intact.

Here's an example (bk05ch01/example10.html):

HTML:

```
<h1>
    holloway
</h1>
<div>
    <i>n.</i> A sunken footpath or road; a path that is enclosed
  by high embankments on both sides.
</div>
<img src="/images/holloway1.jpg" alt="Photo of a holloway">
<img src="/images/holloway2.jpg" alt="Photo of a holloway"
    class="offset-image">
<img src="/images/holloway3.jpg" alt="Photo of a holloway">
```

CSS:

```
.offset-image {
    position: relative;
    left: 200px;
}
```

The CSS defines a rule for a class named offset-image, which applies relative positioning and offsets the element from the left by 200px. In the HTML, the offset-image class is applied to the middle image. As shown in Figure 1-10, not only is the middle image shifted from the left, but the space in the page flow where it would have appeared by default remains intact, so the third image's place in the page flow doesn't change. As far as that third image is concerned, the middle image is still right above it.

**FIGURE 1-10:**
The middle image
uses relative
positioning to
shift from the
left, but its place
in the page flow
remains.

## Giving absolute positioning a whirl

*Absolute positioning* not only offsets the element from its default position but also removes the element from the page flow. Sounds useful, but if the element is no longer part of the page flow, from what element is it offset? Good question, and here's the short answer: the closest ancestor element that uses nonstatic positioning.

If that has you furrowing your brow, I have a longer answer that should help. To determine which ancestor element is used for the offset of the absolutely positioned element, the browser goes through a procedure similar to this:

1. Move one level up the page hierarchy to the previous ancestor.

2. Check the position property of that ancestor element.

3. If the position value of the ancestor is static, go back to Step 1 and repeat the process for the next level up the hierarchy; otherwise (that is, if the position value of the parent is anything other than static), offset the original element with respect to the ancestor.

4. If, after going through Steps 1 to 3 repeatedly, you end up at the top of the page hierarchy — that is, at the html element — then use the html element to offset the element, which means in practice that the element is offset with respect to the browser's viewport.

I mention in the previous section that relative positioning is weird because it keeps the element's default position in the page flow intact. However, now that weirdness turns to goodness because if you want a child element to use absolute positioning, you add position: relative to the parent element's style rule. Because you don't also supply an offset to the parent, it stays put in the page flow, but now you have what CSS nerds called a *positioning context* for the child element.

I think an example would be welcome right about now (bk05ch01/example11. html):

HTML:

```
<section>
    <img src="images/new.png" alt="">
    <h1>
        holloway
    </h1>
    <div>
        <i>n.</i> A sunken footpath or road; a path that is
enclosed by high embankments on both sides.
    </div>
    <div>
        There are two main methods that create holloways: By
years (decades, centuries) of constant foot traffic that wears
down the path (a process usually accelerated somewhat by water
erosion); or by digging out a path between two properties and
piling up the dirt on either side.
    </div>
</section>
```

CSS:

```
section {
    position: relative;
    border: 1px double black;
}

img {
    position: absolute;
    top: 0;
    right: 0;
}
```

In the CSS, the section element is styled with the position: relative declaration, and the img element is styled with position: absolute and top and right offsets set to 0. In the HTML, note that the <section> tag is the parent of the <img> tag, so the latter's absolute positioning will be with respect to the former. With top and right offsets set to 0, the image will now appear in the top-right corner of the section element and, indeed, it does, as shown in Figure 1-11.

**WARNING**

Because an absolutely positioned element now resides outside of the normal page flow, the element no longer abides by the default "rule" that no two elements should overlap. Therefore, you need to be careful when absolutely positioning an element to ensure that it doesn't accidentally end up on top of your page text or other elements.

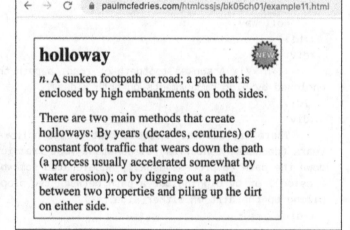

**FIGURE 1-11:**
The img element uses absolute positioning to send it to the top-right corner of the section element.

## Trying out fixed positioning

With *fixed positioning*, the element is taken out of the normal page flow and is then offset with respect to the browser's viewport, which means the element doesn't move, not even a little, when you scroll the page (that is, the element is "fixed" in its new position).

One of the most common uses of fixed positioning is to plop a header at the top of the page and make it stay there while the user scrolls the rest of the content.

Here's an example (bk05ch01/exmple12.html) that shows you how to create such a header:

HTML:

```
<header>
    <img src="images/holloway3.jpg" alt="Photo of a holloway">
    <h1>
        holloway
    </h1>
</header>
<main>
...
</main>
```

CSS:

```
header {
    position: fixed;
    top: 0;
    left: 0;
    width: 100%;
    height: 4rem;
    border: 1px double black;
    background-color: hsl(101, 38%, 63%);
}

main {
    margin-top: 4rem;
}
```

The HTML includes a header element with an image and a heading, followed by a longish main section that I don't include here for simplicity's sake. In the CSS code, the header element is styled with position: fixed, and the offsets top and left set to 0. These offsets fix the header to the top left of the browser's viewport. I also added width: 100% to give the header the entire width of the window. Note, too, that I set the header height to 4rem. To make sure that the main section begins below the header, I styled the main element with margin-top: 4rem. Figure 1-12 shows the results.

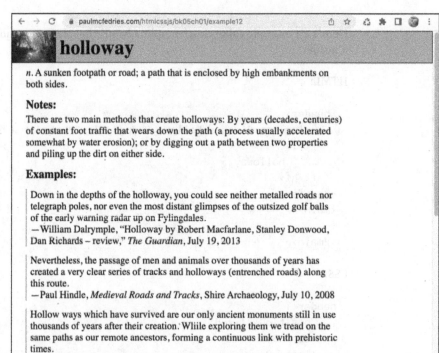

FIGURE 1-12:
A page with the
header element
fixed to the top of
the screen. When
you scroll the rest
of the page, the
header remains
where it is.

## Making elements stick (temporarily)

*Sticky positioning* is a kind of combination of relative and fixed. That is, the element starts off with relative positioning until the element's containing block crosses a specified threshold (usually because the user is scrolling the page), at which point the element switches to fixed positioning. If the opposite edge of the element's containing block then scrolls to where the element is stuck, the element reverts to relative positioning and scrolls with the containing block.

For example, suppose your page has a `section` element, and inside that `section` is an `h2` element that you've positioned as sticky. Here's an abbreviated version of the code (check out bk05ch01/example13.html for the complete version):

HTML:

```
<section>
    <h2>Cat ipsum</h2>
    <p><a href="http://www.catipsum.com/">http://www.catipsum.
com/</a></p>
    <p>Sample:</p>
```

```
<p class="sample-text">
    Cat ipsum dolor sit amet, prance along on top of the
garden fence, annoy the neighbor's dog and make it bark stuff
and things intrigued by the shower. Please stop looking at
your phone and pet me sleep everywhere, but not in my bed get
my claw stuck in the dog's ear and adventure always but drool
yet roll over and sun my belly. Ooh, are those your $250
dollar sandals?
</p>
</section>
```

CSS:

```
h2 {
    position: sticky;
    top: 0;
}
```

In the CSS, notice that for the h2 element, I've set position: sticky. To specify
the threshold at which the element sticks, I've set top: 0, which means this element will stick in place when the top edge of the section element hits the top of
the viewport.

Here's what happens when the user starts scrolling toward the bottom of the
page:

1. At first, the section and h2 elements scroll up together, as shown in Figure 1-13.
   Note that I've added an outline around the section element to make it easier
   for you to visualize its edges.

2. When the top edge of the section element hits the top of the viewport
   (because I set top: 0 as the sticky threshold), the h2 stops scrolling and
   "sticks" in place, as shown in Figure 1-14.

3. As the user keeps scrolling, the section content keeps scrolling up, as shown
   in Figure 1-15.

4. When the bottom edge of the section element reaches the bottom of the
   stuck h2 element, the h2 becomes "unstuck" (that is, it goes back to relative
   positioning) and resumes scrolling up with the section, as shown in
   Figure 1-16.

The h2 element               The scroll direction

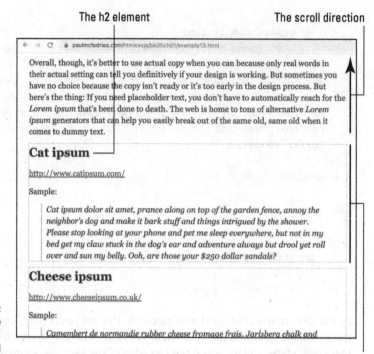

The section element

The top edge of the section element has reached the top edge of the viewport, so…

…the h2 element sticks in place

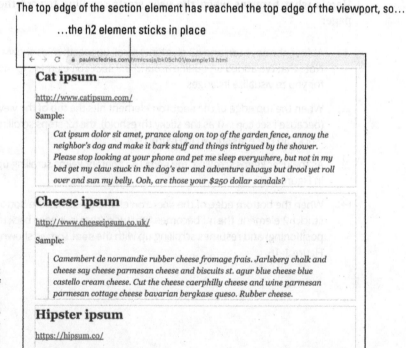

The h2 element remains stuck    The section element continues to scroll

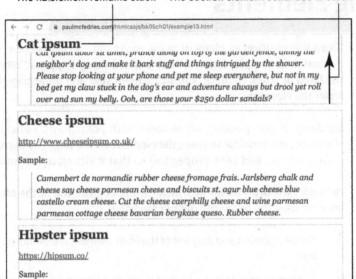

FIGURE 1-15:
As you keep
scrolling,
the section
content keeps
scrolling up.

The bottom edge of the section element has reached
the bottom edge of the h2 element, so...

...the h2 element becomes unstuck and resumes scrolling with the section element

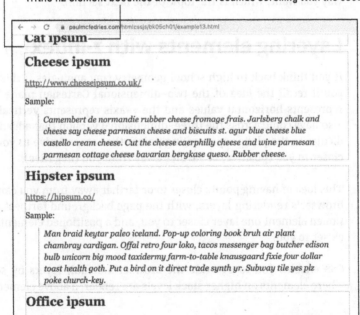

FIGURE 1-16:
When the
section bottom
reaches the stuck
h2 element, the
h2 becomes
"unstuck."

# Stacking Elements

When you position an element using `position: fixed,` or `position: sticky,` as I describe in the previous section, a weird thing happens: When you scroll past the fixed or stuck element, the subsequent text and other page knickknacks slide *under* the element.

Similarly, if you position an element with `position: relative` or `position: absolute`, it's possible to place the element on the page (by manipulating the `top`, `right`, `bottom`, and `left` properties) so that it sits on *top* of some other elements.

How does the browser know which elements go on top of the other elements? The browser uses the following default layering:

1. The background and borders of the `html` element are rendered on the bottom layer.

2. All nonpositioned elements (that is, all elements where the `position` property is `static`) are placed on the next layer.

3. All positioned elements (that is, elements with a `position` value of `relative`, `absolute`, `fixed`, or `sticky`) are placed on subsequent layers in the order they appear in the HTML.

These layers represent the browser defaults, but CSS offers a way to layer stuff the way *you* want, which is the topic of the next section.

## Layering elements with z-index

If you think back to high school geometry (my apologies if this is a painful ask), you'll recall the idea of the two-dimensional Cartesian plane where the x-axis represents horizontal values and the y-axis represents vertical values. You may also have come across the three-dimensional version that added a z-axis perpendicular to the plane representing points that are, relative to you as the observer, closer to you (positive) or farther away from you (negative).

This idea of having points closer to or farther away from you can be applied to the browser's rendering layers, with the page background farthest away, a nonpositioned element one layer closer to you, and a positioned element yet another layer closer to you.

CSS enables you to override the browser's default layers by setting up a *stack*, where elements on higher stack levels are rendered above elements on lower stack levels. You specify an element's stack level by setting the z-index property on a positioned element (z-index has no effect on nonpositioned elements):

```
z-index: value;
```

>> *value*: An integer that specifies the stack level. 0 (or auto) is the default level. A positioned element with a larger z-index value is rendered above a positioned element with a lower z-index value. Negative values are allowed.

Here's an example (bk05ch01/example14.html):

HTML:

```
<body>
    <div id="div1">
        <span>div1</span>
    </div>
    <div id="div2">
        <span>div2</span>
    </div>
</body>
```

CSS:

```
#div1 {
    position: relative;
    z-index: 2;
}
#div2 {
    position: relative;
    bottom: 100px;
    left: 100px;
    z-index: 1;
}
```

The HTML creates two div elements with ids div1 and div2. In the CSS, div2 is positioned relatively and shifted up by 100px and to the left by 100px. Because div2 comes after div1 in the HTML, div2 should appear on top of div1 by default. However, I set z-index: 2 on div1, which is higher than the z-index: 1 declared on div2, so div1 now appears on top of div2, as shown in Figure 1-17.

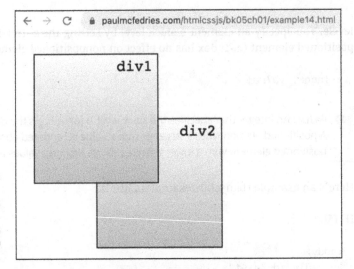

FIGURE 1-17:
The element div1
now appears
on top of div2
because its
z-index value (2)
is higher.

# Getting your head around stacking contexts

The general idea that an element with a higher z-index value gets rendered on top of an element with a lower z-index value seems pretty straightforward. Ah, but here be dragons! To learn how z-index can get mightily weird, here's a look at some code (bk05ch01/example15.html):

HTML:

```
<body>
    <div id="div1">
        <span>div1</span>
    </div>
    <div id="div2">
        <span>div2</span>
        <aside>
            <span>aside</span>
        </aside>
    </div>
</body>
```

CSS:

```
#div1 {
    position: relative;
    z-index: 2;
}
```

```
#div2 {
    position: relative;
    bottom: 100px;
    left: 100px;
    z-index: 1;
}
aside {
    position: relative;
    top: 25px;
    left: 80px;
    z-index: 3;
}
```

This is the same code as in the previous section, except for two things:

>> The HTML adds an aside child to the second div element.

>> The aside CSS positions the element relatively, adds vertical and horizontal offsets, and sets the z-index property to 3.

The aside now has the highest z-index value of the three elements, so you'd expect that the aside would get rendered on top of everything. Figure 1-18 shows what actually happens.

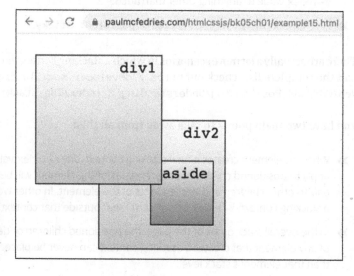

**FIGURE 1-18:**
The new aside
element appears
behind the div1
despite having a
higher z-index
value (3).

Wait, what!? The browser is rendering the `aside` element, which has a `z-index` value of 3, *behind* `div1`, which has a `z-index` value of 2! How can that be?

To understand what's going on here, you need to become fast friends with a concept known as the *stacking context*, which is the ability of a parent element's children to be stacked on top of each other.

The default stacking context is created by the `html` element, and within this stacking context the following rules apply:

>> Nonpositioned elements are rendered at the bottom of the stacking order.

>> Positioned elements are rendered above the nonpositioned elements in stack levels that reflect the order in which the positioned elements appear in the HTML.

>> Positioned elements can use `z-index` to move up or down in the stacking order.

All this would be no big deal if you had just the one stacking context to worry about. Ah, if only life on Planet CSS were that simple! In fact, CSS creates *new* stacking contexts whenever either one of the following is true:

>> An element uses `position: relative` or `position: absolute` and sets its `z-index` value to anything other than `auto`.

>> An element uses `position: fixed` or `position: sticky`.

There are actually a *lot* more scenarios in which a stacking context is created. To eyeball the complete list, check out `https://developer.mozilla.org/en-US/docs/Web/CSS/CSS_Positioning/Understanding_z_index/The_stacking_context`.

**TECHNICAL STUFF**

You have two main points to take away from all this:

>> When an element creates a new stacking context, any `z-index` values you apply to positioned children or descendants of the element will be relative *only* to other children and descendants of the element. In other words, within a stacking context, `z-index` values can't "see" outside that context.

>> In the overall stack order of the page, the positioned children or descendants of any element that creates a stacking context can never be placed higher than that element's stack level.

Take look at the code once again, but now with fresh eyes:

HTML:

```
<body>
    <div id="div1">
        <span>div1</span>
    </div>
    <div id="div2">
        <span>div2</span>
        <aside>
            <span>aside</span>
        </aside>
    </div>
</body>
```

CSS:

```
#div1 {
    position: relative;
    z-index: 2;
}
#div2 {
    position: relative;
    bottom: 100px;
    left: 100px;
    z-index: 1;
}
aside {
    position: relative;
    top: 25px;
    left: 80px;
    z-index: 3;
}
```

The div2 element uses position: relative and z-index: 1, so it creates a stacking context. The aside element is a child of the div2 element, so its declaration of z-index: 3 is relative only within the div2. And because the div2 is declared with z-index: 1, the aside can never go higher than that in the overall page stack order. That's why the aside appears behind the div1 element in Figure 1-18.

# Chapter **2**

# Getting Fancy with Flexbox

*Flexbox is the first CSS layout technique that works for the modern web.*

—PADDI MACDONNELL

Web design geeks use the term *brittle* to describe any page layout system that's so baroque and overengineered that it works under only very constrained conditions and breaks when even some trivial aspect of those conditions changes. The opposite design philosophy can be described as a *rigid* page layout, where everything is coded in a way that nothing can possibly change no matter what device or screen or other variable you throw at the page.

What both brittle and rigid page layout designs lack is the simple and beautiful trait of *flexibility*. Rigid layouts have no flexibility whatsoever, whereas brittle layouts fall to pieces when even a tiny amount of flex is introduced. Web design geeks knew all that, of course, and longed for a technology that would enable them to create flexible layouts that could handle diverse environments without raising a fuss.

That technology arrived a few years back in the form of Flexbox, which was originally hampered by poor and conflicting browser support. These days, however, Flexbox is a mature technology that enjoys near-universal browser support. That's awesome news because Flexbox is a fantastic addition to anyone's page layout toolkit. In this chapter, you explore all that Flexbox has to offer and learn how you can incorporate Flexbox into your overall page layout plan.

# Introducing Flexbox

For many years, the go-to layout technique for most CSS pros was either floating elements or inline blocks (that is, setting a block element's `display` property to `inline-block` so that the element behaves, layout-wise, as an inline element). Both techniques offered numerous banana peels in the path that tripped up many a developer, including forgetting to clear your floats and having containers collapse (check out Book 5, Chapter 1 to learn more about these pitfalls).

However, beyond these mere annoyances, float- or inline-block-based layouts had trouble with a few more important things, making it very hard to

>> Get an element's content centered vertically within the element's container

>> Get elements evenly spaced horizontally across the full width (or vertically across the full height) of their parent container

>> Get a footer element to appear at the bottom of the browser's content area

Fortunately, these troubles vanish if you use a CSS technology called Flexible Box Layout Module, or *Flexbox* for short. The key here is the "flex" part of the name. As opposed to the default page flow and layouts that use floats and inline blocks, all of which render content using rigid blocks, Flexbox renders content using containers that can grow and shrink — I'm talking both width and height here — in response to changing content or browser window size. But Flexbox also offers powerful properties that make it a breeze to lay out, align, distribute, and size the child elements of a parent container.

I get to the Flexbox details in a sec, but first I need to answer what is arguably the most common page layout question these days.

# Do I Still Need Flexbox Now That CSS Grid Is Here?

CSS Grid is a newer page layout tool that you dive into in Book 5, Chapter 3, but for now I can say that it turns your page into a grid that gives you exquisite control over the horizontal and vertical placement of elements within that grid. CSS Grid is much newer than Flexbox, but it already enjoys nearly the same level of browser support as Flexbox. So, if Grid is that good, why bother learning Flexbox?

The answer is that, in a sense, the comparison is not quite apples to apples here. Yep, both Flexbox and Grid are page layout tools, but they focus on different aspects of the page:

>> Flexbox excels at working with page elements that you want to lay out in *one* direction: that is, *either* horizontally *or* vertically.

>> Grid excels at working with page elements that you want to lay out in *two* directions: that is, *both* horizontally *and* vertically.

In most nontrivial web pages, these two aspects can easily coexist. For example, if you have a nav element that contains a list of links you want to lay out across the web page, Flexbox is perfect for that. On that same page, you may also have a complex, but regular, intermingling of text and images. Grid is probably the perfect tool to lay out that content the way you want.

So, happily, the question of Flexbox versus Grid isn't either/or. You can have your Flex and eat Grid, too.

# Setting Up and Configuring Flex Containers

To get started with Flexbox, you need to know right off the bat that Flexbox divides its world into two categories:

>> **Flex container:** This is a block-level element that acts as a parent to the flexible elements inside it.

>> **Flex items:** These are the child elements that reside within the flex container.

I discuss flex items in a satisfying amount of detail later in this chapter (check out "Taking Control of Flex Items"). For now, though, the next few sections show you what flex containers are all about.

## Setting up the flex container

To designate an element as a flex container, you set its `display` property to `flex`:

```
element {
    display: flex;
}
```

With that one declaration, the element's children automatically become flex items, just like that. Sweet!

## Touring the landscape of a flex container

One of the confusing things about Flexbox is the distinction it makes between the directionality and dimensionality of a flex container. Here's what I mean:

>> **Directionality:** A flex container is *one-directional* in the sense that flex items flow within their flex container either horizontally — that is, in a row — or vertically — that is, in a column.

>> **Dimensionality:** A flex container is *two-dimensional* in the sense that, as a block element, it defines two perpendicular axes. First, the flex container's flow direction runs along the *primary axis* (also called the *main axis*). So, for example, if the flow direction is horizontal, the primary axis is also horizontal. Second, the axis that's perpendicular to the primary axis is called the *secondary axis* (also called the *cross axis*). So, for example, if the flow direction is horizontal, the secondary axis will be vertical.

Having both a primary and a secondary axis to work with means you get fine-grained control over how items get arranged with the flex container. I get to that shortly, but first you need to choose a flex direction.

## Setting the flex direction

After you have a flex container, the next item on your Flexbox to-do list is to decide which direction you want the flex items to flow within the container. You specify that direction using the `flex-direction` property:

```
element {
    display: flex;
    flex-direction: row|row-reverse|column|column-reverse;
}
```

>> row: The primary axis is horizontal, and the flex items are arranged from left to right. This is the default value.

>> row-reverse: The primary axis is horizontal, and the flex items are arranged from right to left.

>> column: The primary axis is vertical, and the flex items are arranged from top to bottom.

>> column-reverse: The primary axis is vertical, and the flex items are arranged from bottom to top.

Following is an example. First, here's some HTML and CSS code (check out bk05ch02/example01.html), and Figure 2-1 shows how it appears if you let the browser lay it out:

HTML:

```
<div class="container">
    <div class="item item1">1</div>
    <div class="item item2">2</div>
    <div class="item item3">3</div>
    <div class="item item4">4</div>
    <div class="item item5">5</div>
</div>
```

CSS:

```
.container {
    border: 5px double black;
}
.item {
    font-family: Verdana, sans-serif;
    font-size: 5rem;
    padding: .1rem;
    text-align: center;
}
.item1 {
    background-color: hsl(0, 0%, 94%);
}
```

```
.item2 {
    background-color: hsl(0, 0%, 88%);
}
.item3 {
    background-color: hsl(0, 0%, 82%);
}
.item4 {
    background-color: hsl(0, 0%, 76%);
}
.item5 {
    background-color: hsl(0, 0%, 70%);
}
```

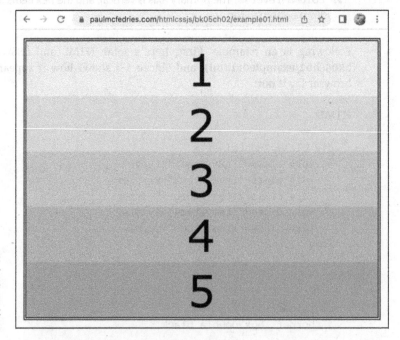

paulmcfedries.com/htmlcssjs/bk05ch02/example01.html

**FIGURE 2-1:**
Let the browser
lay out the
elements and you
get the default
stack of blocks.

The browser does its default thing where it stacks the div blocks on top of each other and makes each one take up the full width of its parent div (the one with the container class), which, in Figure 2-1, has its boundaries marked by the double border.

Now configure the parent div — again, the one with the container class — as a flex container with a horizontal primary axis (check out bk05ch02/example02. html):

```
.container {
    display: flex;
    flex-direction: row;
    border: 5px double black;
}
```

This automatically configures the child div elements — the ones with the item class — as flex items. As shown in Figure 2-2, the flex items are now aligned horizontally and take up only as much horizontal space as their content requires.

**FIGURE 2-2:**
With their parent as a flex container, the child elements become flex items.

## Aligning flex items along the primary axis

Notice in Figure 2-2 that the flex items are bunched together on the left side of the flex container (which has its boundaries shown by the double border). This is the default alignment along the primary axis, but you can change that alignment by modifying the value of the justify-content property:

```
container {
    display: flex;
    justify-content: flex-start|flex-end|center|space-around|
    space-between|space-evenly;
}
```

>> flex-start: Aligns all the flex items with the start of the flex container (where "start" means: left if flex-direction is row; right if flex-direction is row-reverse; top if flex-direction is column; or bottom if flex-direction is column-reverse). This value is the default, so you can leave out the justify-content property if flex-start is the alignment you want.

>> flex-end: Aligns all the flex items with the end of the flex container (where "end" means: right if flex-direction is row; left if flex-direction is row-reverse; bottom if flex-direction is column; or top if flex-direction is column-reverse).

>> center: Aligns all the flex items with the middle of the flex container.

» `space-around`: Assigns equal amounts of space before and after each flex item, where the amount of space is calculated to get the flex items distributed evenly along the primary axis. Actually, the distribution isn't quite even, because the inner flex items (2, 3, and 4 in Figure 2-3) have two units of space between them, whereas the starting and ending flex items (1 and 5, respectively, in Figure 2-3) have only one unit of space to the outside (that is, to the left of item 1 and to the right of item 5).

» `space-between`: Places the first flex item at the start of the flex container, the last flex item at the end of the flex container, and then distributes the rest of the flex items evenly in between.

» `space-evenly`: Assigns equal amounts of space before and after each flex item, where the amount of space is calculated to get the flex items distributed evenly along the primary axis. And, unlike with `space-around`, this time the spacing really is even!

Figure 2-3 (check out bk05ch02/example03.html) demonstrates each of the possible values of the `justify-content` property when the `flex-direction` property is set to `row`.

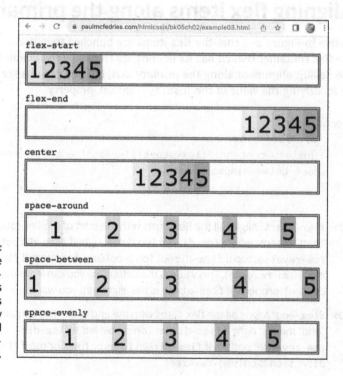

FIGURE 2-3:
How the `justify-content` values align flex items when the primary axis is horizontal (`flex-direction: row`).

# Aligning flex items along the secondary axis

Besides aligning the flex items along the primary axis, you can also align them along the secondary axis. For example, if you've set `flex-direction` to row, which gives you a horizontal primary axis, the secondary axis is vertical, which means you can also align the flex items vertically.

That's odd (I hear you thinking), when I examine the examples in Figure 2-3, there doesn't seem to be any vertical room to do anything, much less align the flex items.

True! By default, the flex items always take up the entire height of the flex container, and if you don't specify a height (as I didn't in the examples shown in Figure 2-3), Flexbox just makes the container high enough to fit its tallest content.

When you do set a height on a flex container that has a vertical secondary axis (or you set a width on a flex container that has a horizontal secondary axis), you can get a different secondary axis alignment by changing the value of the `align-items` property:

```
container {
    display: flex;
    align-items: stretch|flex-start|flex-end|center|baseline;
}
```

» `stretch`: Expands each flex item in the secondary axis direction until it fills the entire height (if the secondary axis is vertical) or width (if the secondary axis is horizontal) of the flex container. This alignment is the default, so you can leave out the `align-items` property if stretch is the alignment you want.

» `flex-start`: Aligns all the flex items with the start of the flex container's secondary axis (where "start" means: top if `flex-direction` is row or row-reverse; or left if `flex-direction` is column or column-reverse).

» `flex-end`: Aligns all the flex items with the end of the flex container's secondary axis (where "end" means: bottom if `flex-direction` is row or row-reverse; or right if `flex-direction` is column or column-reverse).

» `center`: Aligns all the flex items with the middle of the flex container's secondary axis.

» `baseline`: Aligns the flex items along the bottom edges of the item text. (Technically, given a line of text, the *baseline* is the invisible line upon which lowercase characters such as o and x appear to sit.) If the flex items contain multiple lines of text, the flex items are aligned along the baseline of the first lines in each item.

Figure 2-4 (check out bk05ch02/example04.html) demonstrates each of the possible values of the `align-items` property when the secondary axis is vertical (that is, in this case, the `flex-direction` property is set to `row`) and each flex container is given a height of `30vh` (the edges of each container are given a double border). To make the `baseline` example useful, I added random amounts of top and bottom padding to each flex item.

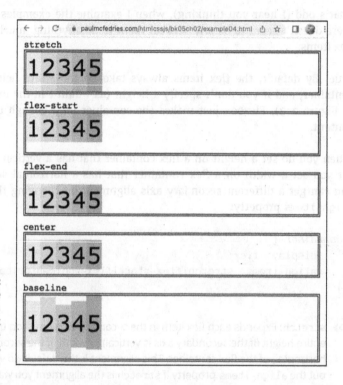

**FIGURE 2-4:**
How the `align-items` values align flex items when the secondary axis is vertical.

**TIP**

If you want to set a secondary axis alignment for an individual flex item, you can use the `align-self` property, which accepts the same values as `align-items`, but applies the value only to the specified flex item:

```
item {
    align-self: stretch|flex-start|flex-end|center|baseline;
}
```

# Centering an element horizontally and vertically

In the olden days of CSS, centering an element both horizontally and vertically within its parent was notoriously difficult. Style wizards stayed up until late at night coming up with ways to achieve this feat. They succeeded, but their techniques were obscure and convoluted. Then Flexbox came along and changed everything by making it almost ridiculously easy to plop something smack dab in the middle of the page:

```
container {
    display: flex;
    justify-content: center;
    align-items: center;
}
```

Yes, that's all there is to it. Here's an example (check out bk05ch02/example05. html):

HTML:

```
<div class="container">
    <div class="item">Look, ma, I'm centered!</div>
</div>
```

CSS:

```
.container {
    border: 5px double black;
    display: flex;
    justify-content: center;
    align-items: center;
    height: 50vh;
}
.item {
    font-family: Georgia, serif;
    font-size: 2rem;
}
```

As shown in Figure 2-5, the flex item sits smack dab in the middle of its flex container.

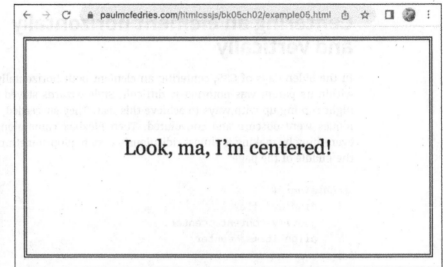

← → C 🔒 paulmcfedries.com/htmlcssjs/bk05ch02/example05.html

Look, ma, I'm centered!

## Allowing flex items to wrap

By default, a flex container is either a single row (if you've set flex-direction to row or row-reverse) or a single column (if you've set flex-direction to column or column-reverse). If the flex items are too big to fit into the container's row or column, Flexbox shrinks the flex items along the primary axis just enough to get them to fit. If, for some reason, Flexbox can't shrink one or more items enough to make them fit (for example, an item may have a min-width value or its content may force a minimum width), the items will overflow along the primary axis.

Letting Flexbox shrink flex items can lead to problems such as too-narrow widths or the overflow scenario I just mentioned. Rather than let Flexbox shrink items to make them fit, you can instead ask the browser to wrap the container's items to multiple rows (if the primary axis is horizontal) or to multiple columns (if the primary axis is vertical). You enable wrapping by using the container's flex-wrap property:

```
element {
    display: flex;
    flex-wrap: nowrap|wrap|wrap-reverse;
}
```

>> nowrap: Doesn't wrap the container's items. This is the default behavior.

>> wrap: Wraps the items to as many rows (if the primary axis is horizontal) or columns (if the primary axis is vertical) as needed.

>> wrap-reverse: Wraps the items starting at the end of the secondary axis.

Here's an example (check out bk05ch02/example06.html):

HTML:

```
<div class="container">
    <div class="item item1">1</div>
    <div class="item item2">2</div>
    <div class="item item3">3</div>
    <div class="item item4">4</div>
    <div class="item item5">5</div>
</div>
<div><code>wrap</code></div>
<div class="container wrap">
    <div class="item item1">1</div>
    <div class="item item2">2</div>
    <div class="item item3">3</div>
    <div class="item item4">4</div>
    <div class="item item5">5</div>
</div>
<div><code>wrap-reverse</code></div>
<div class="container wrap-reverse">
    <div class="item item1">1</div>
    <div class="item item2">2</div>
    <div class="item item3">3</div>
    <div class="item item4">4</div>
    <div class="item item5">5</div>
</div>
```

CSS:

```
.container {
    border: 5px double black;
    display: flex;
    flex-direction: row;
    align-items: flex-start;
    height: 40vh;
    width: 85vw;
}
.wrap {
    flex-wrap: wrap;
}
.wrap-reverse {
    flex-wrap: wrap-reverse;
}
```

```
.item {
    height: 50%;
    width: 25vw;
}
```

The flex container (the `container` class) is set up with a height and width, as is each flex item (the `item` class). I also use the `wrap` and `wrap-reverse` classes to apply the corresponding `flex-wrap` values to the respective flex items. Figure 2-6 shows the results.

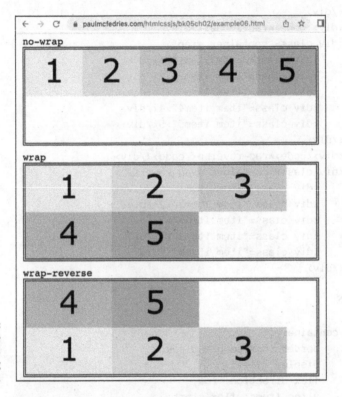

FIGURE 2-6:
The three
flex-wrap
values doing
their thing.

## Aligning rows or columns along the secondary axis

After you've got multiple rows or columns inside a flex container, you need to decide how you want those rows or columns aligned along the secondary axis. This is akin to aligning individual flex items along the primary axis using the `justify-content` property, except that now you're working with entire rows or columns of items.

To align entire rows or columns along the secondary axis, use the flex container's `align-content` property:

```
element {
    display: flex;
    align-content: stretch|center|flex-start|flex-end|
    space-around|space-between|space-evenly;
}
```

>> `stretch`: Expands the rows or columns along the secondary axis to fill the container height or width. This is the default value.

>> `center`: Aligns the rows or columns with the middle of the secondary axis.

>> `flex-start`: Aligns the rows or columns with the beginning of the secondary axis.

>> `flex-end`: Aligns the rows or columns with the end of the secondary axis.

>> `space-around`: Distributes most of the rows or columns evenly within the container by supplying each with a set amount of space on either side, but the first item gets half that space before it and the last item gets half that space after it.

>> `space-between`: Places the first row or column at the beginning of the secondary axis, the last row or column at the end, and distributes the rest of the rows or columns evenly in between.

>> `space-evenly`: Distributes the rows or columns evenly within the container by supplying each row or column the same amount of space before and after.

Figure 2-7 (check out bk05ch02/example07.html) demonstrates each of the possible values of the `align-content` property when the secondary axis is vertical.

**TIP**

You can combine the `align-content` and `justify-content` properties into a single declaration by using the `place-content` property:

```
place-content: align-value [justify-value];
```

Replace *align-value* with the `align-content` value you want to use; replace *justify-value* with the `justify-content` value you want to use. If you specify just one value, the browser uses it for both `align-content` and `justify-content`.

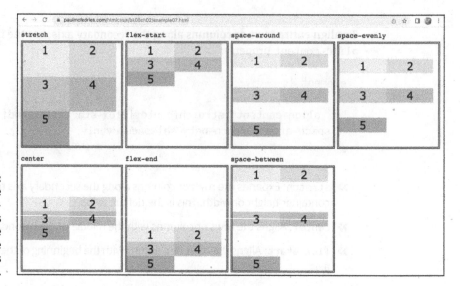

FIGURE 2-7:
How the align-content values align multiple rows when the secondary axis is vertical.

# Adding gaps between items

By default, when you use alignment values such as stretch, flex-start, flex-end, and center, Flexbox scrunches all the flex items together. That may be just the effect you want, but sometimes you'll prefer to have some daylight between your flex items. Adding margins is one way to create a bit of breathing space between items, but if you don't want to worry about fussing with margins, you can let Flexbox do the work for you by automatically creating gaps — often called *gutters* — between the rows, columns, or both. Here are the properties you can use:

```
row-gap: row-gap-value;
column-gap: column-gap-value;
gap: row-gap-value [column-gap-value];
```

» *row-gap-value*: A length value that specifies the space between each row of items in the flex container

» *column-gap-value*: A length value that specifies the space between each column of items in the flex container

REMEMBER

When you use the gap shorthand property, if you specify only *row-gap-value*, Flexbox applies the value to both rows and columns.

Here's an example (check out bk05ch02/example08.html):

```css
.container {
    border: 5px double black;
    display: flex;
    flex-direction: row;
    flex-wrap: wrap;
    gap: 1rem;
    height: 50vh;
    width: 50vw;
}
```

This code uses the gap property to apply 1rem of space between both the rows and columns of the flex container, as shown in Figure 2-8.

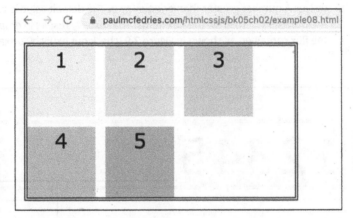

FIGURE 2-8:
Use the gap property to give your flex container's rows and columns some personal space.

# Taking Control of Flex Items

So far, this Flexbox journey has been about the big picture of controlling aspects of the flex container such as direction, alignment, and wrapping. But a flex container is nothing without its flex items, so there's a whole "small picture" Flexbox world where you deal with individual flex items. The rest of this chapter takes you through the various properties that Flexbox offers to control flex items.

# Allowing flex items to grow

By default, when you set the `justify-content` property to `flex-start`, `flex-end`, or `center`, the flex items take up only as much room along the primary axis as they need for their content, as shown earlier in Figure 2-3. This is admirably egalitarian, but it does often leave a bunch of empty space in the flex container. Interestingly, one of the meanings behind the "flex" in Flexbox is that you can make one or more flex items grow to fill that empty space.

You configure a flex item to grow by setting the `flex-grow` property on the item:

```
item {
    flex-grow: value;
}
```

>> *value*: A number greater than or equal to 0. The default value is 0, which tells the browser not to grow the flex items. That usually results in empty space in the flex container, as shown in Figure 2-9 (check out bk05ch02/example09.html).

FIGURE 2-9:
By default, all
flex items have a
`flex-grow` value
of 0, resulting in
empty space.

Empty space in the flex conginer

For positive values of `flex-grow`, you have three scenarios to consider:

>> **You assign a positive `flex-grow` value to just one flex item.** The flex item grows until the flex container has no more empty space. For example, here's a rule that sets `flex-grow` to 1 for the element with class `item1`, and Figure 2-10 shows that item 1 has grown until there is no more empty space in the flex container (check out bk05ch02/example10.html):

```
.item1 {
    flex-grow: 1;
}
```

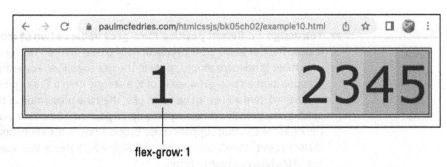

FIGURE 2-10:
With
flex–grow: 1,
an item grows
until the
container
has no more
empty space.

flex-grow: 1

>> **You assign the same positive `flex–grow` value to two or more flex items.** The flex items grow equally until there is no more empty space in the flex container. For example, here's a rule that sets `flex–grow` to 1 for the elements with the classes `item1`, `item2`, and `item3`, and Figure 2-11 shows that items 1, 2, and 3 have grown until the flex container has no more empty space (check out bk05ch02/example11.html):

```
.item1,
.item2,
.item3 {
    flex-grow: 1;
}
```

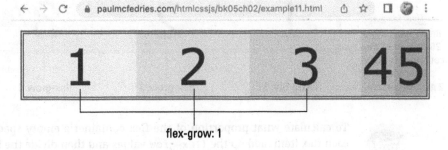

FIGURE 2-11:
When items 1, 2,
and 3 are
styled with
flex–grow: 1,
the items
grow equally.

flex-grow: 1

>> **You assign a different positive `flex-grow` value to two or more flex items.** The flex items grow proportionally based on the `flex-grow` values until there is no more empty space in the flex container. For example, if you give one item a `flex-grow` value of 1, a second item a `flex-grow` value of 2, and a third item a `flex-grow` value of 1, then the proportion of the empty space given to each will be, respectively, 25 percent, 50 percent, and 25 percent. Here's some CSS that supplies these proportions to the elements with the classes `item1`, `item2`, and `item3`, and Figure 2-12 shows the results (check out bk05ch02/example12.html):

```css
.item1 {
    flex-grow: 1;
}
.item2 {
    flex-grow: 2;
}
.item3 {
    flex-grow: 1;
}
```

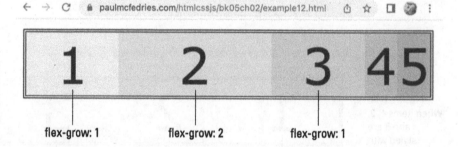

**FIGURE 2-12:**
Items 1 and 3 get
25 percent of the
container's empty
space, and item
2 gets 50 percent.

**TECHNICAL STUFF**

To calculate what proportion of the flex container's empty space is assigned to each flex item, add up the `flex-grow` values and then divide the individual `flex-grow` values by that total. For example, values of 1, 2, and 1 add up to 4, so the percentages are 25 percent (1/4), 50 percent (2/4), and 25 percent (1/4), respectively.

## Allowing flex items to shrink

The flexibility of Flexbox means not only that flex items can grow to fill a flex container's empty space but also that they can shrink if the flex container doesn't have enough space to fit the items. Shrinking flex items to fit inside their container is the default Flexbox behavior, but you gain a measure of control over which items shrink and by how much by using the `flex-shrink` property on a flex item:

```
item {
    flex-shrink: value;
}
```

>> *value*: A number greater than or equal to 0. The default value is 1, which tells the browser to shrink all the flex items equally to get them to fit inside the flex container.

For example, consider the following code:

HTML:

```
<div class="container">
    <div class="item item1">1</div>
    <div class="item item2">2</div>
    <div class="item item3">3</div>
    <div class="item item4">4</div>
    <div class="item item5">5</div>
</div>
```

CSS:

```
.container {
    display: flex;
    width: 600px;
    border: 5px double black;
}
.item {
    width: 200px;
}
```

The flex container (the `container` class) is 600px wide, but each flex item (the item class) is 200px wide. To get everything to fit, the browser shrinks each item equally, and the result is shown in Figure 2-13 (check out bk05ch02/example13. html).

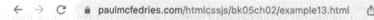

FIGURE 2-13:
By default, the browser shrinks the items equally along the primary axis until they fit.

flex-shrink: 1

TECHNICAL STUFF

The browser shrinks each flex item truly equally (that is, by the same amount) only when each item has the same size along the primary axis (for example, the same width when the primary axis is horizontal). If the flex items have different sizes, the browser shrinks each item roughly in proportion to its size: larger items shrink more, whereas smaller items shrink less. I use the word "roughly" here because in fact the calculations that the browser uses to determine the shrinkage factor are brain-numbingly complex. If you want to learn more (don't say I didn't warn you!), check out `https://madebymike.com.au/writing/understanding-Flexbox`.

You have three ways to control the shrinkage of a flex item:

>> **Assign the item a `flex-shrink` value between 0 and 1.** The browser shrinks the item less than the other flex items. For example, here's a rule that sets `flex-shrink` to `0.5` for the element with class `item1`, and Figure 2-14 shows that item 1 has shrunk less than the other items in the container (check out bk05ch02/example14.html):

```
.item1 {
    flex-shrink: 0.5;
}
```

FIGURE 2-14:
Styling item 1 with `flex-shrink: 0.5` shrinks it less than the other items.

flex-shrink: 0.5

>> **Assign the item a** `flex-shrink` **value greater than 1.** The browser shrinks the item more than the other flex items. For example, the following rule sets `flex-shrink` to 2 for the element with class `item1`, and Figure 2-15 shows that item 1 has shrunk more than the other items in the container (check out bk05ch02/example15.html):

```
.item1 {
    flex-shrink: 2;
}
```

paulmcfedries.com/htmlcssjs/bk05ch02/example15.html

**FIGURE 2-15:** Styling item 1 with `flex-shrink: 2` shrinks the item more than the others.

flex-shrink: 2

>> **Assign the item a** `flex-shrink` **value of 0.** The browser doesn't shrink the item. The following rule sets `flex-shrink` to 0 for the element with class `item1`, and Figure 2-16 shows that the browser doesn't shrink item 1 (check out bk05ch02/example16.html):

```
.item1 {
    flex-shrink: 0;
}
```

**WARNING**

If a flex item is larger along the primary axis than its flex container, and you set `flex-shrink: 0` on that item, ugliness ensues. That is, the flex item breaks out of the container and, depending on where it sits within the container, may take one or more other items with it. If you don't want a flex item to shrink, make sure the flex container is large enough to hold it.

FIGURE 2-16:
Styling item 1
with flex-
shrink: 0
doesn't shrink
the item.

flex-shrink: 0

## Suggesting a flex item size

Flex items have an *initial main size* (the Flexbox standard calls it the *hypothetical main size*), which is the amount of space along the primary (main) axis that the item would consume naturally based on its content. When you declare flex-grow: 1 and flex-shrink: 1 on an item, that item grows or shrinks from this initial main size.

**REMEMBER**

To reduce the verbosity in this section, I assume flex-direction: row, so the primary axis is horizontal, and the initial main size is the item's width. However, if flex-direction: column is declared on the container, the primary axis is vertical, and the initial main size is the item's height. So, throughout this section, change each instance of "width" to "height" if your container's primary axis is vertical.

You can suggest a different initial main size for an item by setting the flex-basis property:

```
item {
    flex-basis: value;
}
```

>> *value:* A length or percentage value for the initial main size. You can also use one of the following keywords:

- auto: Sets the initial main size to the item's width value. If the item doesn't have a declared width, auto sets the initial main size to the size of the item's content. (The auto keyword is the default value for flex-basis.)

- content: Sets the initial main size based on the item's content. This keyword overrides the item's declared width value (if any).

- `max-content`: Sets the initial main size to the widest value that will fit the content without wrapping (or to the maximum width available in the flex container, whichever is smaller).

- `min-content`: Sets the initial main size based on the item's smallest possible width.

- `fit-content`: Sets the initial main size between `max-content` and `min-content` based on the item's content.

REMEMBER

Except for the `auto` keyword, any value you set on the `flex-basis` property overrides whatever `width` value you've applied to the same item.

The CSS Flexible Box Layout Module standard (check out https://www.w3.org/TR/css-flexbox-1/) calls `flex-basis`, `flex-grow`, and `flex-shrink` the "components of flexibility." And no wonder, because these three properties are intimately related:

>> `flex-basis` creates a new initial main size for an item. Note, however, that the `flex-basis` value (or the `width` value) is just a suggested width.

>> `flex-grow` enables the item size to expand from the minimum of the initial main size to the maximum of the initial main size plus the available space along the main axis.

>> `flex-shrink` enables the item size to contract from the maximum of the initial main size to the minimum possible size based on the content.

To help you get your head around the `flex-basis` property, here are four common scenarios:

>> **You want a flex item to have a minimum width.** Set `flex-basis` to whatever you want to use as the minimum width; set `flex-grow` to a positive value to enable the item to grow beyond the `flex-basis` value when there's space available; and declare `flex-shrink: 0` to prevent the item from shrinking below the `flex-basis` value. Here's an example (check out Figure 2-17 and bk05ch02/example17.html):

```
.item1 {
    flex-grow: 1;
    flex-shrink: 0;
    flex-basis: 200px;
}
```

In a narrow container, the item width never falls below 200px

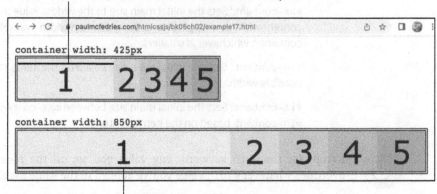

FIGURE 2-17:
Styling item 1
to have a
minimum width.

In a wide container, the item width expands as much as it can

» **You want a flex item to have a maximum width.** Set flex-basis to whatever you want to use as the maximum width; set flex-grow: 0 to prevent the item from growing beyond the flex-basis value; and declare flex-shrink: to a non-zero value to allow the item to shrink below the flex-basis value. Here's an example (check out Figure 2-18 and bk05ch02/example18.html):

```
.item1 {
    flex-grow: 0;
    flex-shrink: 1;
    flex-basis: 200px;
}
```

In a wide container, the item never expands beyond 200px

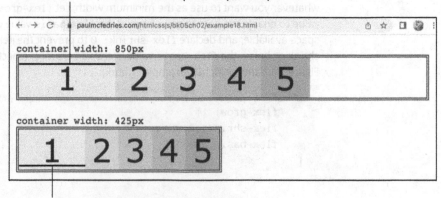

FIGURE 2-18:
Styling item 1
to have a
maximum width.

In a narrow container, the item shrinks as needed

**»** **You want a flex item to have an unchanging width.** Set flex-basis to whatever you want to use as the unchanging width; set flex-grow: 0 to prevent the item from growing beyond the flex-basis value; and declare flex-shrink: 0 to prevent the item from shrinking below the flex-basis value. Here's an example (check out Figure 2-19 and bk05ch02/example19.html):

```css
.item1 {
    flex-grow: 0;
    flex-shrink: 0;
    flex-basis: 200px;
}
```

In a narrow container, the item is 200px wide

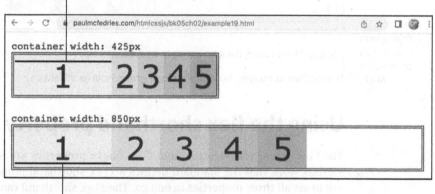

FIGURE 2-19: Styling item 1 to have an unchanging width.

In a wide container, the item is still 200px wide

**»** **You want a flex item to have minimum and maximum widths.** Set flex-basis to whatever you want to use as the main initial width; set flex-grow to a positive value to allow the item to grow beyond the flex-basis value; declare flex-shrink to a non-zero value to allow the item to shrink below the flex-basis value; set min-width to whatever you want to use as the minimum width; and set max-width to whatever you want to use as the maximum width. Here's an example (check out Figure 2-20 and bk05ch02/example19a.html):

```css
.item1 {
    flex-grow: 1;
    flex-shrink: 1;
    flex-basis: 300px;
    min-width: 200px;
    max-width: 400px
}
```

In a narrow container, the item shrinks to its minimum size

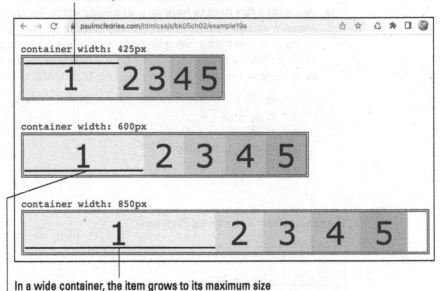

container width: 425px

1  2 3 4 5

container width: 600px

1  2  3  4  5

container width: 850px

1  2  3  4  5

FIGURE 2-20:
Styling item
1 to have an
unchanging
width.

In a wide container, the item grows to its maximum size

In a medium container, the item shrinks or grows from its initial size

## Using the flex shorthand property

The flex-grow, flex-shrink, and flex-basis properties are so fundamental to Flexbox work that the standard defines a flex shorthand property that you can use to set all three properties in one go. The flex shorthand can take one, two, or three values, and I spell out each of these syntaxes in Table 2-1.

REMEMBER

When you use the flex shorthand, it's crucial to remember that if you specify only one or two values, Flexbox applies default values for the missing property or properties. For example, consider the following code:

```
.item1 {
    flex-shrink: 0;
    flex-basis: 10rem;
    flex: 1;
}
```

**TABLE 2-1** The `flex` Shorthand Property

| Syntax | Description | Example | Equivalent |
|---|---|---|---|
| `flex: grow;` | Sets flex–grow to grow; sets flex–shrink to 1 and flex–basis to 0 | `flex: 2;` | `flex-grow: 2;` `flex-shrink: 1;` `flex-basis: 0;` |
| `flex: basis;` | Sets flex–basis to basis; sets flex–grow to 1 and flex–shrink to 1 | `flex: 10rem;` | `flex-grow: 1;` `flex-shrink: 1;` `flex-basis: 10rem;` |
| `flex: grow basis;` | Sets flex–grow to grow; sets flex–basis to basis; sets flex–shrink to 1 | `flex: 2 12vw;` | `flex-grow: 2;` `flex-shrink: 1;` `flex-basis: 12vw;` |
| `flex: grow shrink basis;` | Sets flex–grow to grow; sets flex–shrink to shrink; sets flex–basis to basis | `flex 0 0 200px;` | `flex-grow: 0;` `flex-shrink: 0;` `flex-basis: 200px;` |

At first glance, this code appears to be setting a minimum size of 10rem on item. However, by using the flex: 1 shorthand, Flexbox applies default values for flex–shrink and flex–basis, so the preceding code is equivalent to the following:

```
.item1 {
    flex-shrink: 0;
    flex-basis: 10rem;
    flex-grow: 1;
    flex-shrink: 1;
    flex-basis: 0;
}
```

The last two declarations override the first two, so if you're not aware of the defaults applied by the flex shorthand, you may be flummoxed when your flex item doesn't behave the way you expect it to.

## Laying out content columns with Flexbox

Flexbox works best when you use it to lay out components along one dimension, but that doesn't mean you can't use it to lay out an entire page. As long as the page structure is relatively simple, Flexbox works great for laying out elements both horizontally and vertically.

A good example is the classic page layout: a header and navigation bar across the top of the page; a main section with an article and a sidebar beside it; and a footer across the bottom of the page. Here's some Flexbox code that creates this layout, which is shown in Figure 2-21 (check out bk05ch02/example20.html):

HTML:

```
<body>
    <header>
        Header
    </header>
    <nav>
        Navigation
    </nav>
    <main>
        <article>
            Article
        </article>
        <aside>
            Aside
        </aside>
    </main>
    <footer>
        Footer
    </footer>
</body>
```

CSS:

```
html {
    height: 100%
}
body {
    display: flex;
    flex-direction: column;
    gap: 1rem;
    height: 100%;
    width: 75vw;
}
main {
    flex: 1;
    display: flex;
    flex-wrap: wrap;
    gap: 1rem;
}
```

```
article {
    flex: 1 0 15rem;
}
aside {
    flex: 0 0 10rem;
}
```

← → C  🔒 paulmcfedries.com/htmlcssjs/bk05ch02/example20.html

Header

Navigation

Article                                    Aside

Footer

FIGURE 2-21:
A classic
page layout,
Flexbox-style.

Here's what's happening in this code:

>> The <body> tag is set up as a flex container, and that container is styled with
flex-direction: column to create a vertical primary axis for the page
as a whole.

>> The body element has its height property set to 100%, which makes the flex
container take up the entire height of the browser's viewport.

>> The main element is styled with flex: 1, which tells the browser to grow the
main element vertically until it uses up the empty space in the flex container.
This also ensures that the footer element appears at the bottom of the
content area even if there isn't enough content to fill the main element.

» The main element is also a flex container styled with flex-direction: row to create a horizontal primary axis. This container also declares flex-wrap: wrap, which allows the aside element to wrap under the article element on smaller screen sizes.

» Inside the main flex container, the article element is given flex: 1 0 15rem, so it grows as needed to take up the remaining width of the main element (that is, after the width of the aside element is taken into account), but doesn't get any narrower than 15rem.

» To get a fixed-width sidebar, the aside element's rule uses flex: 0 0 10rem.

## Changing the order of flex items

One final trick for messing around with flex items is that you can change the order that the browser renders the flex items within their container. That may sound like a weird thing to do, but it's surprisingly handy.

For example, when I talk about responsive layouts in Book 5, Chapter 4, one of the keys to supporting mobile browsers is to make sure that your page's main content appears on the initial screen presented to mobile users. If the desktop version of your page shows other content first, rather than restructuring everything for mobile, you could create a media query (more on that in Book 5, Chapter 4) that uses Flexbox to change the content order.

A similar idea is that accessibility best practices require that a page's main content appear as close to the top of the page as possible. Why? Because you don't want people using assistive technologies to have to traverse ads or other nonessential content before they get to the main part of the page. If your design has, say, a left sidebar that normally appears first in the HTML code, you can use Flexbox to render the sidebar's code after the main content.

You customize the order of a flex item with the order property:

```
item {
    order: value;
}
```

>> *value*: By default, a flex container's items are assigned an order value of 0. You change the item order like so:

- The higher a flex item's order value, the later the item appears in the flex container.

- The flex item with the highest order value appears last in the flex container.

- The flex item with the lowest order value appears first in the flex container.

- Negative order values are cool, so you can move a flex item to the front of its flex container by setting its order value to –1.

Here's an example (check out bk05ch02/example21.html):

```
.item1 {
    order: 1;
}
```

In this example, by declaring order: 1 on the item with class item1, the browser moves that item to the end of the container, as shown in Figure 2-22.

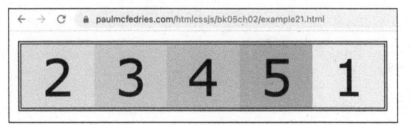

FIGURE 2-22: By setting order: 1 on item 1, that item moves to the end of its flex container.

IN THIS CHAPTER

» **Getting acquainted with CSS Grid**

» **Setting up a grid container**

» **Carving up the grid into rows and columns**

» **Creating grid gaps**

» **Aligning grid items**

# Chapter **3**

# Laying Out a Page with CSS Grid

*If you haven't learned CSS Grid yet (and you are a person who writes CSS), you are seriously missing out.*

— JEN SIMMONS

Perhaps I'm dating myself, but back when I started crafting web pages, the exciting new technique for laying out a page was to create a giant table element and slot the various parts of the page into one or more table cells. This enabled us to line up our content like bootcamp recruits, which was great, but our pages looked as rigid and uninviting as a bootcamp sergeant, which wasn't so great.

Ever since then, web developers have dreamed of a CSS solution that would give us control over layout but still allow for some flexibility and creativity. That goal was partially realized a while back with Flexbox (check out Book 5, Chapter 2), which made it a breeze to lay out web page elements in one dimension. But web pages are resolutely two-dimensional creatures, so although we loved Flexbox, we also knew we weren't quite there yet.

Finally, the dream of a modern, full-page layout method that was both precise and flexible came true a few years ago in the form of CSS Grid. Oh, the web development nerds were all aflutter! But they were also impatient because it took some time for the browsers to implement the large and complex Grid specifications. But now Grid enjoys near-universal browser support and is ready for you to take your page layout to a higher level. In this chapter, I introduce you to CSS Grid and help you explore all that it has to offer.

# Introducing CSS Grid

CSS Grid Layout Module Level 1 — a mouthful of an official moniker that I refer to in this chapter as either CSS Grid or just Grid — gives you a straightforward way to divide a container into one or more column and one or more rows — that is, as a *grid* — and then optionally assign the container's elements to specific sections of the grid. With CSS Grid, you can give the web browser instructions such as the following:

>> Set up the `<body>` tag as a grid with four rows and three columns.

>> Place the header element in the first row and make it span all three columns.

>> Place the nav element in the second row and make it span all three columns.

>> Place the article element in the third row, columns 1 and 2.

>> Place the aside element in the third row, column 3.

>> Place the footer element in the fourth row and make it span all three columns.

Before you learn how to do all this and more, you need to know that a Grid uses two categories of elements:

>> **Grid container:** This is a block-level element that acts as a parent to the elements inside it and that you configure with a set number of rows and columns.

>> **Grid items:** These are the elements that reside within the grid container and that you assign (or the browser assigns automatically) to specific parts of the grid.

# Setting Up the Grid Container

To designate an element as a grid container, you set its `display` property to `grid`:

```
container {
    display: grid;
}
```

With that first step complete, the element's children automatically become grid items.

Check out this code (which you can find in bk05ch03/example01.html in this book's example files):

HTML:

```
<div class="container">
    <div class="item item1">1</div>
    <div class="item item2">2</div>
    <div class="item item3">3</div>
    <div class="item item4">4</div>
    <div class="item item5">5</div>
    <div class="item item6">6</div>
</div>
```

CSS:

```
.container {
    border: 5px double black;
    display: grid;
    text-align: center;
}
.item {
    font-family: Verdana, sans-serif;
    font-size: 3rem;
}
.item1 {
    background-color: hsl(0, 0%, 94%);
}
.item2 {
    background-color: hsl(0, 0%, 88%);
}
.item3 {
    background-color: hsl(0, 0%, 82%);
}
```

```
.item4 {
    background-color: hsl(0, 0%, 76%);
}
.item5 {
    background-color: hsl(0, 0%, 70%);
}
.item6 {
    background-color: hsl(0, 0%, 64%);
}
```

Figure 3-1 shows the result.

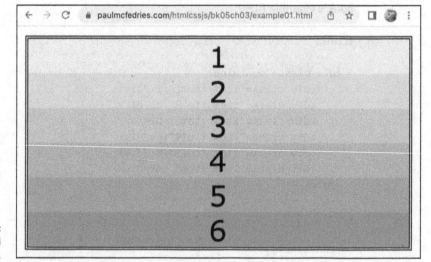

FIGURE 3-1:
A basic grid
container.

# Specifying the Grid Rows and Columns

The result shown in Figure 3-1 is a bit disappointing, isn't it? Here I am talking up Grid as this major evolution in web page design, and it just looks like the browser has laid out the child `div` elements using its default one-block-on-top-of another flow.

However, that's not the case. What you're really looking at here is a grid layout consisting of one column and six rows. This is known as an *implicit grid* because it was created automatically by the browser. Implicit grids are a major benefit of CSS Grid because they reduce the amount of work you have to do. I talk about implicit grids in more detail a bit later (check out "Letting the browser do some of the work: the implicit grid"). For now, keep reading to find out how you go about creating your own rows and columns.

# Setting your own columns and rows: the explicit grid

When you tell the browser exactly how many columns and rows you want in your grid, you're creating an *explicit grid*. You do that by creating a *grid template*, which specifies the number of columns and the number of rows you want in your grid. You set up your template by adding the `grid-template-columns` and `grid-template-rows` properties to your grid container:

```
container {
    display: grid;
    grid-template-columns: column-values;
    grid-template-rows: row-values
}
```

» `column-values`: A space-separated list of the sizes you want to use for each column in your grid.

» `row-values`: A space-separated list of the sizes you want to use for each row in your grid.

In the simplest case, the column and row sizes can be numbers expressed in any of the standard CSS measurement units (px, em, rem, vw, vh, and so on) or as a percentage.

Here's an example (check out bk05ch03/example02.html), and Figure 3-2 shows the result:

HTML:

```
<div class="container">
    <div class="item item1">1</div>
    <div class="item item2">2</div>
    <div class="item item3">3</div>
    <div class="item item4">4</div>
    <div class="item item5">5</div>
    <div class="item item6">6</div>
</div>
```

CSS:

```
.container {
    display: grid;
```

```
    grid-template-columns: 100px 300px 200px;
    grid-template-rows: 100px 200px;
}
```

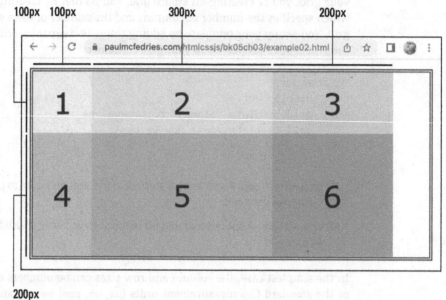

100px 100px  300px  200px

paulmcfedries.com/htmlcssjs/bk05ch03/example02.html

FIGURE 3-2:
A basic grid
created by setting
just three
properties:
display,
grid-template-
columns,
and grid-
template-rows.

## Letting a column or row grow or shrink as needed

Notice in Figure 3-2 that the two rows don't take up the entire width of the grid container. That's because I set rigid pixel values for the column widths and those values didn't add up to the grid container width. If the grid container was smaller than the combined column widths, the columns would have overflowed the container on the right.

All of which is good reason not to always size your columns and rows with pixels. Often a better way to go is to specify a column or row size using a new unit called fr, which is specific to Grid and represents a fraction of the free space available in the grid container, either horizontally (for columns) or vertically (for rows). For example, here's the CSS code from the previous section, with the third column's original value of 200px replaced by 1fr (bk05ch03/example03.html):

```
.container {
    display: grid;
    grid-template-columns: 100px 300px 1fr;
    grid-template-rows: 100px 200px;
}
```

As shown in Figure 3-3, the third column now expands to fill up the available grid container space on the right.

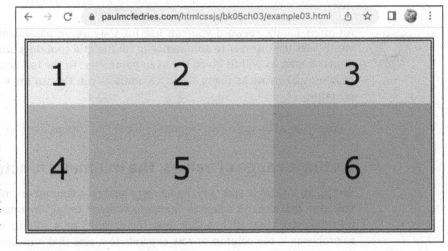

1    2    3

4    5    6

**FIGURE 3-3:** By changing the third column size to 1 fr, that column expands to fill the rest of the container space.

If you assign fractional sizes to multiple columns (or rows), the browser assigns the free space proportionally. For example, if you assign one column 1 fr of space and another column 2 fr, the browser gives one third of the horizontal free space to the first column and two thirds of the horizontal free space to the second column.

## De-drudgifying Grid: the repeat() function

Depending on the layout you want, you may end up specifying consecutive rows or columns that all use the same size. Here's an example:

```
grid-template-columns: 250px 1fr 1fr 1fr 1fr 1fr 1fr 1fr
    1fr 300px;
```

This declaration creates a 250-pixel column on the left, a 300-pixel column on the right, and eight fractionally sized columns in between. All those instances of 1 fr are not only a pain to type but also make it hard to know at-a-glance how many total columns you're defining. An easier and clearer way to write such a declaration is to replace the repeated values with, appropriately enough, the repeat() function:

```
repeat(number, size)
```

>> *number*: The number of times you want the browser to repeat *size*.

>> *size*: The column or row size you want repeated.

So, instead of the preceding declaration, you could use the following (bk05ch03/example04.html):

```
grid-template-columns: 250px repeat(8, 1fr) 300px;
```

**TIP**

An often-handy keyword you can use for the *number* parameter is auto-fill, which asks the browser to automatically fill the grid container with as many columns or rows as will fit given the size parameter. In the following example, the browser will create as many 100px columns as can fit into the width of the grid container:

```
grid-template-columns: repeat(auto-fill, 100px);
```

## Setting a range of values: the minmax() function

Setting an inflexible size (say, by using pixels) on a column or row creates a rigid structure that doesn't adapt to changing content. Going the opposite route with a flexible size (that is, one that uses the fr unit) on a column or row can lead to problems if the column or row expands to a size that's much larger than the content.

I mention in the next section some keywords that can solve this problem, but another solution is to set a range of size values using the minmax() function:

```
minmax(min, max)
```

>> *min*: The minimum size to which the column or row is allowed to shrink

>> *max*: The maximum size to which the column or row is allowed to expand

For example, in the following declaration, the third column can be no less than 200px wide and no more than 500px wide (bk05ch03/example05.html):

```
grid-template-columns: 150px 200px minmax(200px, 500px);
```

In the following example, the first column can expand to fill the available space, but it can never be less than 250px wide (bk05ch03/example06.html):

```
grid-template-columns: minmax(250px, 1fr) repeat(5, 10vw);
```

## Sizing with the auto keyword

You can set a grid-template-columns or grid-template-rows size using the auto keyword. The auto keyword sends the following instructions to the web browser:

>> **For a column:** It's okay to shrink the column, but no smaller than the smallest possible width (which is usually the length of the longest word in the column). Also, it's okay to expand the column, but no larger than the largest possible width (which, if there's room, is usually the length of the longest unwrapped entry in the column). If the container has extra horizontal space, it's okay to expand the column to fill up the extra space (so in this scenario, auto acts the same as 1fr).

>> **For a row:** It's okay to shrink the row, but no smaller than the tallest entry in the row. Also, it's okay to expand the row, but no larger than the tallest content in the row.

Here's an example that uses the auto keyword (bk05ch03/example07.html):

```
grid-template-columns: repeat(3, auto);
grid-template-rows: auto auto;
```

# Letting the browser do some of the work: the implicit grid

Working with the explicit grid — that is, specifying the grid-template-columns and grid-template-rows properties on a grid container — means that you're doing all the heavy lifting when it comes to defining your grid layout. Most of the time, that'll be what you want because the explicit grid gives you, well, explicit control over the grid structure.

Sometimes, however, you can take a more hands-off approach and let the web browser pick up some of the slack. For example, if you leave out the grid-template-columns and grid-template-rows properties, the browser creates a one-column grid with as many rows as there are child items in the grid container (for an example, check out "Setting Up the Grid Container," earlier in this chapter). That's an example of the *implicit grid*, where the web browser automatically sets up the grid structure in the absence of one or more of the grid template properties.

You won't need to go completely without a grid template all that often, but sometimes your design may require that you specify just the column or row template.

## Leaving out the grid rows template

If you specify the grid-template-columns property and leave out the grid-template-rows property, the browser automatically does two things:

>> Creates as many rows as are needed to fit all the grid container's child elements into the column template

>> Configures the row heights with the value auto (check out "Sizing with the auto keyword"), which usually means setting each row height to the height of the tallest element in the row

Here's an example (bk05ch03/example08.html):

HTML:

```
<div class="container">
    <div class="item item1">1</div>
    <div class="item item2">2</div>
    <div class="item item3">3</div>
    <div class="item item4">4</div>
    <div class="item item5">5</div>
    <div class="item item6">6</div>
    <div class="item item7">7</div>
    <div class="item item8">8</div>
</div>
```

CSS:

```
.container {
    border: 5px double black;
    display: grid;
    grid-template-columns: 1fr 3fr 2fr;
}
```

This example only sets up a three-column grid without specifying a row template. As shown in Figure 3-4, the browser automatically creates the required number of rows to fit all the child div elements (with a blank final cell in the third row).

## Leaving out the grid columns template

If you specify the grid-template-rows property and leave out the grid-template-columns property, the browser automatically does two things:

>> Creates a single column for all the grid container's child elements

>> Configures the column width with the value auto (check out "Sizing with the auto keyword")

FIGURE 3-4:
Without a row
template, the
browser creates
as many rows as
are needed to
fit all the child
elements.

Here's an example (check out Figure 3-5 and bk05ch03/example09.html):

HTML:

```
<div class="container">
    <div class="item item1">1</div>
    <div class="item item2">2</div>
    <div class="item item3">3</div>
    <div class="item item4">4</div>
    <div class="item item5">5</div>
    <div class="item item6">6</div>
    <div class="item item7">7</div>
    <div class="item item8">8</div>
</div>
```

CSS:

```
.container {
    border: 5px double black;
    display: grid;
    grid-template-rows: repeat(8, auto);
}
```

You may be wondering why, if the column width in Figure 3-5 defaults to auto, the column isn't only as wide as its widest item. That's because the default alignment for grid columns is stretch, which causes the columns to take up all the available horizontal space in the grid container. To learn how to control column and row alignment, check out "Getting Your Grid Ducks in a Row (or a Column): Aligning Things," later in this chapter.

**FIGURE 3-5:**
Without a column template, the browser creates a single column that spans the width of the grid container.

## Specifying a size for implicit rows or columns

When you omit the `grid-template-rows` or `grid-template-columns` property, the browser sizes the implicit columns or rows (respectively) with the keyword `auto`. If these automatic sizes don't work for your design, you can override them with the following properties:

```
grid-auto-rows: value;
grid-auto-columns: value;
```

>> *value*: A length, percentage, or `minmax()` function that specifies the size you prefer

For example (check out bk05ch03/example10.html), here's an update to the implicit rows code (check out "Leaving out the grid rows template") that instructs the browser to apply a height of 100px to each row (as shown in Figure 3-6).

```
.container {
    border: 5px double black;
    display: grid;
    grid-template-columns: 1fr 3fr 2fr;
    grid-auto-rows: 100px;
}
```

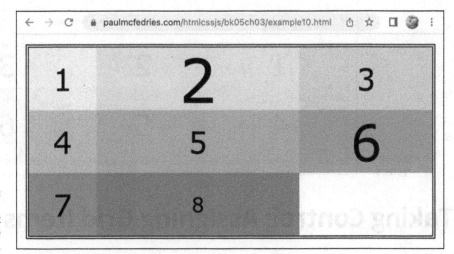

**FIGURE 3-6:** Using grid-auto-rows to set a height for the implicit rows.

## Creating grid gaps

By default, the browser doesn't include any *gutters*: horizontal space between each column or vertical space between each row. If you'd prefer some daylight between your grid items, you can add the following properties to your grid container:

```
row-gap: row-gap-value;
column-gap: column-gap-value;
gap: row-gap-value [column-gap-value];
```

>> *row-gap-value*: A length value that specifies the space between each row of items in the grid container.

>> *column-gap-value*: A length value that specifies the space between each column of items in the grid container.

**REMEMBER**

When you use the gap shorthand property, if you specify only *row-gap-value*, Grid applies the value to both rows and columns.

In all three properties, the value is a number expressed in any of the standard CSS measurement units (px, em, rem, vw, or vh). Here's an example (check out bk05ch03/example11.html and Figure 3-7):

```
.container {
    display: grid;
    grid-template-columns: repeat(3, 1fr);
    grid-template-rows: 1fr 2fr;
    gap: 1vw;
}
```

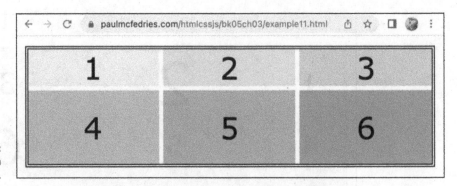

FIGURE 3-7:
A grid with
gutters.

# Taking Control: Assigning Grid Items

One of the most important concepts in Grid World is the *grid cell*, which is the intersection of a grid column and a grid row. Grid cells are crucial because it's at the cell level that the browser positions the grid items.

For example, whether you set up an explicit grid by specifying the `grid-template-columns` and `grid-template-rows` properties on a grid container, or you set up an implicit grid by omitting one or both of these properties, the browser populates the grid by assigning each grid item — that is, each child element — to a single cell in the grid container.

Rather than let the web browser populate the grid automatically with its default one-item-per-cell algorithm, you can take control of the process and assign the grid items yourself. This is where Grid gets insanely useful, because now you have exquisite control over not only where your items reside within the grid, but also over the number of cells over which a given item can span. For example, in a three-column grid, you can make a `header` element in the first row span all three cells of that row.

CSS Grid gives you two ways to assign grid items:

» Assigning items to specific columns and rows

» Assigning items to named grid areas

The next few sections provide all the details you need.

## Assigning grid items to columns and rows

Perhaps the more obvious route to breaking out of the browser's default one-item-per-cell grid layout algorithm is to assign a grid item to whatever rectangular collection of columns and rows your design requires. Why did I insert the word *rectangular* in that last sentence? Because nonrectangular assignments are verboten in CSS Grid. For example, you can't assign a grid item to an L-shaped collection of cells or to a collection of noncontiguous cells.

For example, take a look at the grid design shown in Figure 3-8, where A, B, and C represent grid items.

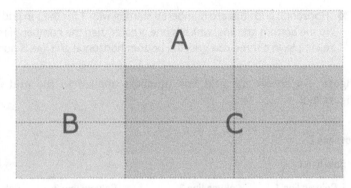

**FIGURE 3-8:**
A three-column,
three-row grid
design.

You may think that implementing this design would involve assignments something like these:

» Assign item A to columns 1, 2, and 3 in row 1.

» Assign item B to column 1, rows 2 and 3.

» Assign item C to columns 2 and 3 and rows 2 and 3.

That design would make intuitive sense, but for some reason, that intuitive path was not the road taken by the CSS Grid specification. To get your head around what the standard does instead, you need to understand the difference between rows and columns on the one hand, and tracks and lines on the other.

## Figuring out grid lines, tracks, and axes

In the CSS specification, a grid container isn't divided into columns and rows, as you may expect. Instead, the grid container is divided into a series of vertical and horizontal lines known as *grid lines*. In Figure 3-8, each dashed line represents a grid line. In every grid container, grid lines have the following characteristics:

» A *grid track* is the generic term for a grid column or a grid row and is defined as the space between two consecutive grid lines.

>> A vertical grid track — a column to you and me — is bounded by a vertical grid line on the left and a vertical grid line on the right.

>> A horizontal grid track — a row — is bounded by a horizontal grid line above and a horizontal grid line below.

>> Vertical grid lines are numbered starting with 1 for the leftmost grid line, up to the farthest right grid line, which is one greater than the number of columns (for example, in a three-column grid, the rightmost vertical grid line is number 4).

>> Horizontal grid lines are numbered starting with 1 for the top grid line, down to the bottom grid line, which is one greater than the number of rows (for example, in a three-row grid, the bottom horizontal grid line is number 4).

Figure 3-9 shows the grid line numbers applied to the grid container from Figure 3-8.

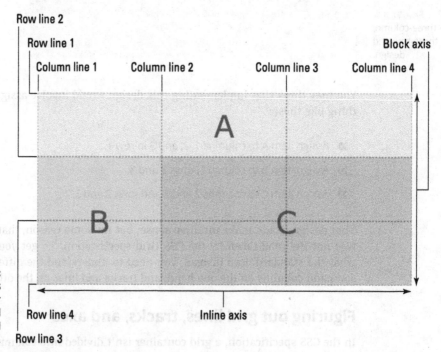

**FIGURE 3-9:**
CSS grid divides the grid container by numbered vertical and horizontal lines.

So, the column- and row-specific item assignments I proposed in the previous section should in fact be *column-line-* and *row-line*-specific assignments:

>> Assign item A to span from column line 1 to column line 4 and from row line 1 to row line 2.

>> Assign item B to span from column line 1 to column line 2 and from row line 2 to row line 4.

>> Assign item C to span from column line 2 to column line 4 and from row line 2 to row line 4.

Given that CSS Grid is a two-dimensional layout mechanism, you won't be in the least surprised to learn that a grid container has two axes:

>> **Block axis:** The vertical axis along which the grid container's column grid lines run

>> **Inline axis:** The horizontal axis along which the grid container's row grid lines run

**REMEMBER**

These definitions assume that the current language is one where text reads horizontally and top to bottom (such as English). In vertical languages (such as Japanese and Chinese), the block axis is horizontal and the inline axis is vertical).

If you're thinking to yourself, "Wow, there's nothing very intuitive about *that*," know that I agree with you wholeheartedly! The good news is that CSS Grid does offer a much more intuitive way to assign grid items (check out "Assigning grid items to named grid areas"); the bad news is that first I should finish telling you about the line number assignment method, which is the task of the next section.

## Assigning grid items using line numbers

To position a grid item anywhere within the grid container, you specify the starting and ending column line numbers and the starting and ending row line numbers. So, for each grid item, you set four property values:

```
item {
    grid-column-start: column-start-value;
    grid-column-end: column-end-value;
    grid-row-start: row-start-value;
    grid-row-end: row-end-value;
}
```

>> grid-column-start: A number that specifies the column line where you want the item to begin.

>> grid-column-end: A number that specifies the column line where you want the item to end. For example, if grid-column-end is set to 4, the grid item ends in column 3. Some notes:

- If you omit this property, the item uses only the starting column.

- The value –1 always refers to the rightmost column line. So, when you declare `grid-column-end: -1`, the item spans from its starting column line through to the rightmost column in the grid (even if you subsequently add more columns to the grid).

- You can use the keyword `span` followed by a space and then a number that specifies the number of columns you want the item to span across the grid. For example, the following two sets of declarations are equivalent:

```
grid-column-start: 1;
grid-column-end: 4;

grid-column-start: 1;
grid-column-end: span 3;
```

» `grid-row-start`: A number that specifies the row line where you want the item to begin.

» `grid-row-end`: A number that specifies the row line where you want the item to end. For example, if `grid-row-end` is set to 3, the grid item ends in row 2. Some notes:

- If you omit this property, the item uses only the starting row.

- The value –1 always refers to the bottom row line. So, when you declare `grid-row-end: -1`, the item spans from its starting row line through to the bottom row in the grid (even if you later add more rows to the grid).

- You can use the keyword `span` followed by a space and then a number that specifies the number of rows you want the item to span down the grid. For example, the following two sets of declarations are equivalent:

```
grid-row-start: 2;
grid-row-end: 4;

grid-row-start: 2;
grid-row-end: span 2;
```

Here's an example (bk05ch03/example12.html), and the results are shown in Figure 3-10:

HTML:

```
<div class="container">
    <div class="item item1">1</div>
    <div class="item item2">2</div>
```

```
    <div class="item item3">3</div>
    <div class="item item4">4</div>
    <div class="item item5">5</div>
    <div class="item item6">6</div>
</div>
```

CSS:

```css
.container {
    display: grid;
    grid-template-columns: 15vw repeat(3, 1fr) 20vw;
    grid-template-rows: 15vh 1fr 1fr;
    height: 100%;
}
.item1 {
    grid-column-start: 1;
    grid-row-start: 1;
}
.item2 {
    grid-column-start: 2;
    grid-column-end: span 4;
    grid-row-start: 1;
}
.item3 {
    grid-column-start: 1;
    grid-row-start: 2;
    grid-row-end: -1;
}
.item4 {
    grid-column-start: 2;
    grid-column-end: 5;
    grid-row-start: 2;
    grid-row-end: -1;
}
.item5 {
    grid-column-start: 5;
    grid-row-start: 2;
}
.item6 {
    grid-column-start: 5;
    grid-row-start: 3;
}
```

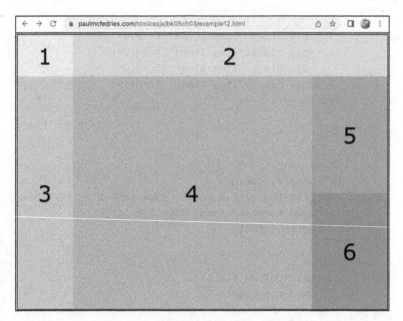

FIGURE 3-10:
Some grid items
assigned to
different columns
and rows
in the grid.

TIP

CSS Grid also offers two shorthand properties that you can use to make the process of assigning items to column and row lines a bit more streamlined:

```
item {
    grid-column: column-start-value / column-end-value;
    grid-row: row-start-value / row-end-value;
}
```

## Displaying grid line numbers in the browser dev tools

The more complex your grid, the harder it is to keep track of the column and row line numbers. Not to worry, though, because your web browser has your back on this one. Specifically, the browser's web development tools offer a feature that overlays the column and row line numbers on your grid container so that you can easily visualize what's happening.

Here are the steps to follow in Google Chrome (the steps are similar in all the major browsers) to inspect a grid container's line numbers in the dev tools:

1. **Right-click anywhere inside the grid container and then click Inspect.**

   The web development tools open.

2. **In the Elements tab, click the Layout sub-tab.**

3. **In the Grid section's Overlay Display Settings area, make sure Show Line Numbers is selected in the drop-down list.**

4. **In the Grid Overlays list, select the checkbox beside your grid container.**

   The browser overlays the line numbers on your grid container, as shown in Figure 3-11.

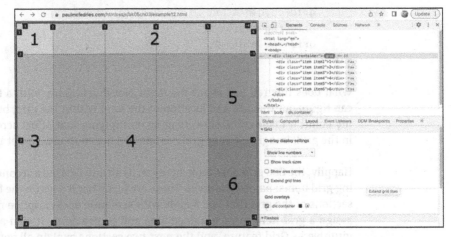

Laying Out a Page with CSS Grid

**FIGURE 3-11:**
Visualizing the grid container's column and row line numbers using the Chrome dev tools.

## Assigning grid items to named grid areas

CSS Grid suffers from an intuition problem. That is, although the basics of Grid are readily grasped, what your code is actually doing is often harder to wrap your head around. For example, consider the grid container definition from the previous section:

```
.container {
    display: grid;
    grid-template-columns: 15vw repeat(3, 1fr) 20vw;
    grid-template-rows: 15vh 1fr 1fr;
}
```

When first presented with code like this, you may be able to get a general sense of what it does, but chances are that general sense won't look anything like the finished product shown in Figure 3-10.

Speaking of the grid in Figure 3-10, you can probably intuit more or less what each grid item may be used for: item 1 may be a site logo; item 2 may be a header; item 3 may be a navigation area; item 4 may be the main content; and items 5 and 6 may be sidebars or ads.

Taking item 3 as a for instance, now take a look at the assignment code from the previous section:

```
.item3 {
    grid-column-start: 1;
    grid-row-start: 2;
    grid-row-end: -1;
}
```

What does this tell you about the item? Not much! Sure, with a bit of effort you can figure out the size and location of the item within the grid, but that's kind of my point: it takes *effort*. Now imagine multiplying that effort across all six items in the grid. Imagine if your grid contained a dozen items. Forget it!

Happily, the CSS grandees took mercy on us all and devised a second way of assigning grid items: *named grid areas*. These are just what it says on the box: rectangular sections of the grid that you supply with semantic or descriptive names. You then assign a grid item to each named area and you're done. It's an awesome — and intuitive — Grid feature, and the next two sections explain all you need to know.

## Setting up named grid areas

Your first chore when using named grid areas is to do the actual naming. With your grid template in place, you then apply the grid-template-areas property to the grid container:

```
grid-template-areas:
    "first row named areas"
    "second row named areas"
    etc.
    "bottom row named areas";
```

» *row named areas*: For each cell in the row, provide a name, keeping the following guidelines in mind:

- Each quotation-surrounded line in the value represents a row in your grid.

- If a named area spans across *X* columns, repeat the name *X* times in that row's string.

- If the named area spans across *X* rows, repeat the name *X* times in consecutive row strings.

- For easy visualization of the grid structure, type each row's named areas on their own line in the declaration.

- To leave a cell empty, use a dot ( . ) instead of a name.

- Enter a name (or a dot) for every cell in the grid.

- You can define only rectangular named areas.

- If you define a named area in one part of the grid, you can't use the same name elsewhere in the grid.

Named grid areas are tricky to explain in the abstract, but are readily grasped in practice. To that end, here's how I'd name the grid areas for the grid shown earlier in Figure 3-10:

```
.container {
    display: grid;
    grid-template-columns: 15vw repeat(3, 1fr) 20vw;
    grid-template-rows: 15vh 1fr 1fr;
    grid-template-areas:
        "logo header header header header"
        "nav content content content sidebar"
        "nav content content content ad";
}
```

Here's what going on in the `grid-template-area` value:

>> **First row:** The first cell is an area named *logo;* the next four cells comprise an area named *header.*

>> **Second row:** The first cell is part of an area named *nav;* the next three cells are part of an area named *content;* the rightmost cell is an area named *sidebar.*

>> **Third row:** The first cell is the second part of the area named *nav;* the next three cells form the rest of the area named *content;* the rightmost cell is an area named *ad.*

Next, you assign each item to a named area.

## Assigning the items to the area

With your named areas defined, your final task is to assign each grid item to one of those named areas using the `grid-area` property:

```
item {
    grid-area: name;
}
```

>> *name*: The named area you want to assign to the item. This name must be one of the names you specified in the `grid-template-areas` property of the grid container.

For example (check out bk05ch03/example13.html), the following code assigns six grid items to the named areas from the previous section:

```
.item1 {
    grid-area: logo;
}
.item2 {
    grid-area: header;
}
.item3 {
    grid-area: nav;
}
.item4 {
    grid-area: content;
}
.item5 {
    grid-area: sidebar;
}
.item6 {
    grid-area: ad;
}
```

I think you'll agree that this code is light years more readable than assigning items using column lines and row lines.

## Displaying named areas in the browser dev tools

Named grid areas are a refreshingly intuitive way to set up your grid. However, the more complex your grid, the easier it is to introduce problems into the structure of your named area. When that happens, or if you just want to check that your named areas are working the way you want, you can use your web browser's development tools to overlay the named areas on your grid container so that you can visualize the layout.

Follow these steps in Google Chrome (the steps are more or less the same in all the major browsers) to overlay a grid container's named areas in the dev tools:

1. **Right-click anywhere inside the grid container and then click Inspect.**

   The dev tools open.

2. **In the Elements tab, click the Layout sub-tab.**

3. **In the Grid section's Overlay Display Settings area, choose Hide Line Labels in the drop-down list.**

4. **Select Show Area Names.**

5. **In the Grid Overlays list, select the checkbox beside your grid container.**

   The browser overlays the named areas on your grid container, as shown in Figure 3-12.

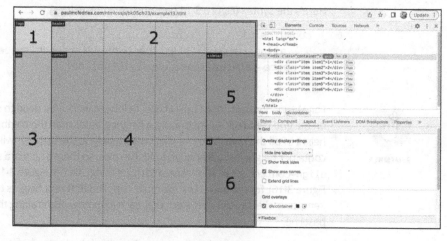

**FIGURE 3-12:** Eyeballing a grid container's named areas using the Chrome dev tools.

# Getting Your Grid Ducks in a Row (or a Column): Aligning Things

CSS Grid offers several properties that you can use to align stuff in your grid. Grid's alignment properties fall into two general categories:

» **Direction:** Refers to the axis along which the alignment is performed:
   - **Justify:** Sets the alignment along the grid container's inline axis.
   - **Align:** Sets the alignment along the grid container's block axis.

>> **Target:** Refers to the part of the grid to which the alignment is applied:

- **Content:** Sets the alignment on all the columns or all the rows in the grid.

- **Items:** Sets the alignment on individual grid items within their assigned grid areas.

Given the preceding categories, CSS Grid defines four alignment properties:

>> justify-content: Sets the alignment along the inline axis of all grid's columns. Here's the syntax (Figure 3-13 demonstrates each value):

```
container {
    justify-content: start|center|end|stretch|space-around|
    space-between|space-evenly;
}
```

>> align-content: Sets the alignment along the block axis of all grid's rows. Here's the syntax (Figure 3-14 demonstrates the values):

```
container {
    align-content: start|center|end|stretch|space-around|
    space-between|space-evenly|baseline;
}
```

**REMEMBER**

For align-content (or align-items, below) to work, you need to set a height on the grid container — specifically, a height greater than the combined natural height of all the rows. Without that custom height, the browser will set the container height just tall enough to fit the rows, so there's no extra space for align-content (or align-items) to do its thing. Also, in Figure 3-14 (and Figure 3-16), for the baseline example, I applied different heights to the grid items to make it easier to discern that each item now aligns along the text baseline.

>> justify-items: Sets the alignment along the inline axis of each grid item within its grid area. Here's the syntax (Figure 3-15 shows each value at work):

```
container {
    justify-items: start|center|end|stretch;
}
```

>> align-items: Sets the alignment along the block axis of each grid item within its grid area. Here's the syntax (Figure 3-16 tries out each value):

```
container {
    align-items: start|center|end|stretch|baseline;
}
```

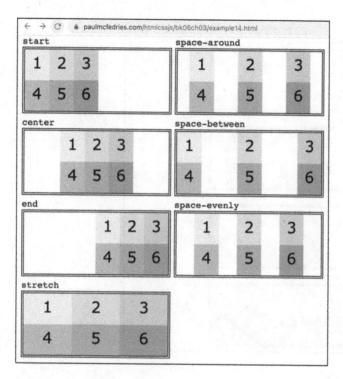

**FIGURE 3-13:** The justify-content property values in action.

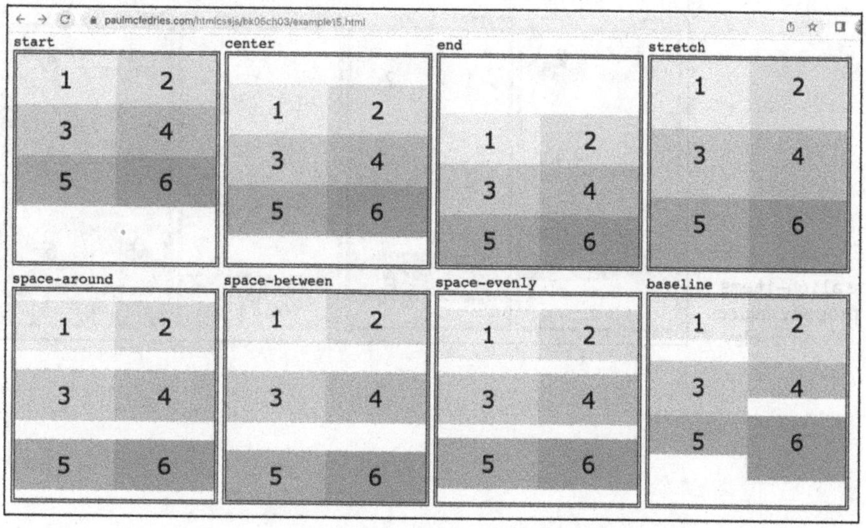

**FIGURE 3-14:** The align-content property values on parade.

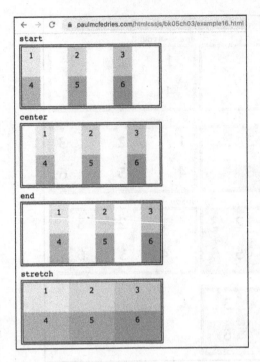

**FIGURE 3-15:**
The justify-items property values in the wild.

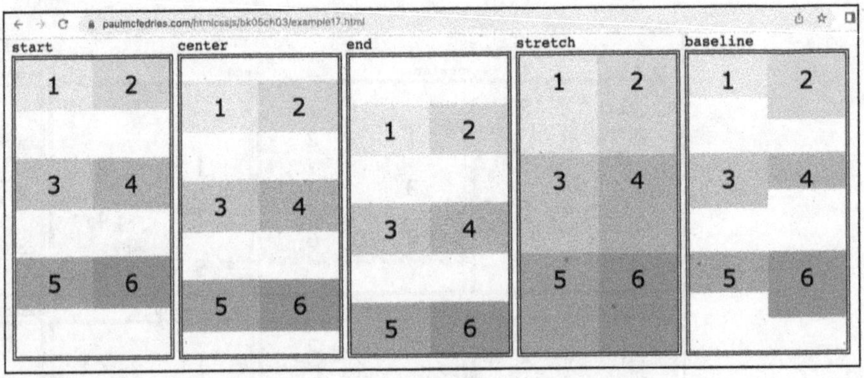

**FIGURE 3-16:**
The align-items property values on display.

IN THIS CHAPTER

» Using Flexbox, Grid, and viewport units for fluid layouts

» Using media, container, and user preference queries for adaptive layouts

» Making your page typography responsive

» Delivering images responsively

» Getting to know the mobile-first approach to layout

# Chapter **4**

# Creating Responsive Layouts

*We can design for an optimal viewing experience, but embed standards-based technologies into our designs to make them not only more flexible, but more adaptive to the media that renders them. In short, we need to practice responsive web design.*

— ETHAN MARCOTTE

Chances are, you do all or most of your web page coding on a relatively large screen, either using a full-size desktop monitor or a notebook screen. Nothing wrong with that, of course, except that it can (and all too often does) lead to a big problem: You end up building your web page so that it looks good and works properly only on larger screens. Why is that a problem? For the simple reason that your page's visitors will be using a wide range of device sizes, from 60-inch smart TVs, to 27-inch desktop monitors, to 17-inch notebook displays, all the way down to 2.5-inch smartphones. On the modern web, one size definitely does not fit all, so you need to build your page so that its *user experience* (*UX*, to the cognoscenti) — that is, what visitors encounter and/or interact with — is positive for everyone.

In this chapter, you investigate the rich world of responsive web design. You learn how to use Flexbox and/or Grid to make your layouts fluid with just a few properties; how to use queries to make your layouts adaptive; how to deliver images with responsiveness in mind; and you dive into the biggest trend in page layout: the mobile-first approach.

# What is a Responsive Layout?

To make your web page look good and operate well on any size screen, you need to plan your page with responsiveness in mind. A *responsive* web page is one that changes its layout, styling, and often also its content to ensure that the page works on whatever screen size or device type the reader is using.

To understand why you need to code responsively from the start of your web page, consider the two main nonresponsive layouts you could otherwise use:

>> **Fixed-width:** A layout in which the width of the content is set to a fixed size. In this case, if the fixed width is greater than the width of the screen, most of the time the user must scroll horizontally to get to all the content, as shown in Figure 4-1 (check out bk05ch04/example01.html in this book's example files).

>> **No-width:** A layout in which the width of the content has no set width. You may think that having no width would enable the text and images to wrap nicely on a small screen, and you'd be right. However, the problem is on larger screens, where your text lines expand to fill the browser width and, as shown in Figure 4-2 (check out bk05ch04/example02.html), those lines can become ridiculously long, to the point where scanning the lines becomes just about impossible.

You could describe both of the preceding scenarios as "don't-care" layouts, because neither one concerns itself with what device or screen size is being used. If you don't want to be a "don't-care" developer, you need to build "care" into your web pages right from the start. How do you do that? By taking all (not some, *all*) of the following into account with each line of code you write:

FIGURE 4-1:
When a page has a fixed width, users with small screens must scroll horizontally to get to all the content.

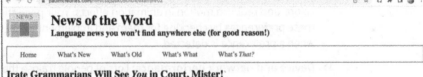

FIGURE 4-2:
When a page has no maximum width, the lines of text can become too long for comfortable reading.

» **Device type:** These days, people who surf to your page may be using a phone, tablet, notebook computer, desktop computer, or any of the various "smart" devices now available: TV, watch, refrigerator, lawn mower, and so on. All these devices have different screen sizes, and your goal should be to design your page so that it looks good and works well on every screen size.

>> **Browser window size:** Not every computer user who visits your page will do so with their browser window maximized. Some people prefer a relatively small window; others choose to use their operating system's split-screen feature; still others may dynamically resize the browser window depending on your page content. The point is that you can't design your page with the idea that your visitors will use only a few common viewport sizes.

>> **Screen orientation:** Smartphone and tablet users can easily switch their devices from portrait to landscape orientation, and some "swivel" (or "rotating") monitors can also make the same switch. Your page needs to gracefully handle the change from one orientation to another without breaking a sweat.

>> **User zoom level:** Some folks navigate the web with their browser's zoom level cranked up. That is, instead of the default 100% zoom level, some people use 125%, 150%, or even 200%. Your page should still be readable and usable even when the user cranks the zoom level to 11.

>> **User default font size:** Rather than (or sometimes in addition to) raising the zoom level, some people amp up the default font size from 16px to 20px, 24px, 32px, or even higher. Your page should not only honor that change (by not styling your font sizes using an absolute unit, such as pixels) but should also look okay and work properly at these higher font sizes.

>> **User preferences:** Many of the people who visit your page will have customized their operating system to use settings such as dark mode, high-contrast colors, and reduced motion in animation effects. Your page should honor these preferences by checking for them and implementing the necessary CSS when a preference is detected.

>> **Device and network performance:** Lots of people traipse the web using underpowered devices, slow network connections, and limited bandwidth. Your page shouldn't leave these people behind by burdening them with unnecessary data or features.

TIP

You can use your browser's dev tools to simulate slower network speeds. In Chrome (and most other browsers are similar), open the dev tools (for example, by right-clicking the page and then clicking Inspect), click the Network tab, click the Throttling list (it says No Throttling, by default), and then select a network speed: Fast 3G, Slow 3G, or even Offline. You can also click Add to create a custom throttling profile. To simulate a slower device CPU, click the Performance tab, click Capture Settings (the gear icon), and then use the CPU list to select a slowdown option (4x Slowdown or 6x Slowdown). You can now reload your page to test its performance with these simulated slowdowns in place.

A responsive web page is one that successfully handles all these different scenarios. That may sound like a daunting task, but modern CSS is powerful enough that you can get all or most of the way to your responsive goal by adopting one of the following approaches:

>> **Fluid layout:** A layout that adjusts smoothly in response to small changes in the browser environment, such as a changing viewport size.

>> **Adaptive layout:** A layout that adjusts only when certain predefined criteria are met, such as the viewport width crossing a specified threshold.

**REMEMBER**

Note that these are not either/or choices. Relatively simple pages may use only fluid or only adaptive techniques, but more complex pages may combine elements of both techniques.

The next two sections explain fluid and adaptive layouts in more detail.

# Going with the Flow: Fluid Layouts

The early days of responsive design were all about desktop versus mobile users, to the point where CSS designers were required to build *two* entirely separate sites: one site that worked fine on desktops and another site that was optimized for mobile users.

That strategy was madness, for sure, but there remains a lingering odor of the desktop/mobile dyad in modern web development circles where it's common to use responsive techniques (usually media queries; check out the section "Querying Your Way to Responsiveness: Adaptive Layouts," later in this chapter) to make sure a page looks good on mobile device screens and in browser windows maximized on desktop monitors, but that's it. But I guarantee that a large percentage of your users will visit your page using a browser window that's in between those sizes.

To ensure that your page looks good and works the way it should no matter what size browser window the user has, or even when the user changes the window size on the fly, you need to build your page using fluid-layout techniques. What is a fluid layout, anyway? It's a big subject, but for this section's purposes, I can narrow it down to the following:

>> Block-level elements naturally fill the space available.

>> Block-level elements expand as the viewport expands and shrink as the viewport shrinks.

> » Block-level elements wrap onto multiple rows (or columns) naturally as the viewport gets smaller.

> » Large text (not body text) expands and contracts along with the viewport.

> » Image sizes expand and contract along with the viewport.

In the ideal fluid layout, you use CSS to give the web browsers a few guidelines about how you want your layout to work, but then you leave it up to the browser to figure out the rest.

## How Flexbox makes a page fluid

The best strategy you can use to create a fluid layout is to deploy Flexbox for one-dimensional layouts and CSS Grid for two-dimensional layouts. I discuss CSS Grid in the next section, but here I focus on the inherent responsiveness of Flexbox-based layouts. (Check out Book 5, Chapter 2 for all the Flexbox details.)

First, you can get flex items to naturally fill the space available in the flex container *and* expand and contract along with the viewport by adding a single declaration to each flex item:

```
flex: 1;
```

This is equivalent to setting the following three declarations:

```
flex-grow: 1;
flex-shrink: 1;
flex-basis: 0;
```

flex-grow: 1 enables the items to expand along the primary axis as the viewport size changes; flex-shrink: 1 enables the items to contract along the primary axis as the viewport size changes; and flex-basis: 0 sets no restriction on the size of the items (except for not shrinking any smaller than the minimum content size).

If all your flex items have similar content and similar box model properties (padding, and so on), then setting flex: 1 on each item means you end up with equal-size columns (if you're using flex-direction: row) or rows (if you're using flex-direction: column).

Setting flex: 1 on all flex items means you're not particular about the item sizes in the main axis direction (such as width for flex-direction: row). However, for many layouts, you'll want some control over item sizes, such as setting minimum widths for an `article` element and an `aside` element. If these elements normally lay out side by side, you'll have an overflow problem when the viewport width shrinks below the combined minimum widths of the two elements. To fix that problem fluidly, tell the browser to wrap the flex items when there isn't enough room to display them side by side:

```
flex-wrap: wrap;
```

For example, check out the following code (bk05ch04/example03.html):

HTML (abbreviated version):

```
<header>
   ...
</header>
<nav>
   ...
</nav>
<main>
    <article>
        <h2>
            Irate Grammarians Will See <em>You</em> in Court,
    Mister!
        </h2>
        <p>
            KALAMAZOO, Michigan—A group of disgruntled
    grammarians calling themselves "Mad, We Are, As Hell" has
    filed a number of civil lawsuits over the past few weeks. The
    targets of these suits are writers, raconteurs, and
    professional man-in-the-street interviewees who, they claim,
    are inveterate violators of the rules of grammar.
        </p>
        etc.
    </article>
    <aside>
        <h3>Related Stories</h3>
        <p>
            It's Official: Teen Instant Messages Nothing But
    Gibberish
        </p>
        etc.
    </aside>
</main>
```

CSS:

```
body {
    max-width: 60rem;
}
main {
    display: flex;
    flex-wrap: wrap;
}
article {
    flex: 3;
    min-width: 22rem;
}
aside {
    flex: 1;
    min-width: 16rem;
}
```

This main element is a two-column flex container: an article element on the left and an aside element on the right. The body element has a maximum width of 60rem that's inherited by the main element, so by setting flex: 3 on the article element and flex: 1 on the aside element, these columns take up the full width of the container, as shown in the desktop screen in Figure 4-3.

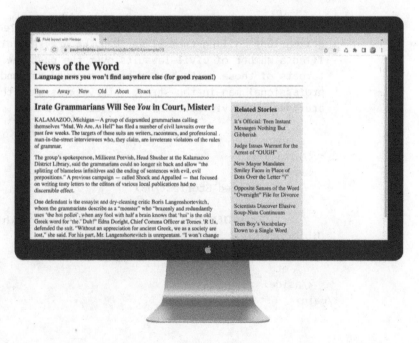

FIGURE 4-3:
The web page as
it appears in a
desktop browser
viewport.

The code also sets minimum widths on the article element (22rem) and the aside element (16rem), so when the browser viewport width drops below 38rem (the combined minimum widths of the two elements), the main element's flex-wrap: wrap declaration kicks in, and the aside element wraps, so now you have a single-column layout, as shown in Figure 4-4.

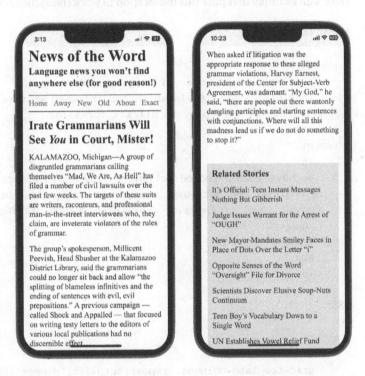

**FIGURE 4-4:**
In a smaller viewport, the main element becomes a single column (left) because the aside element has wrapped (right).

## How CSS Grid makes a page fluid

Depending on your page content, CSS Grid can be a great choice for turning a static layout into a fluid one. (Check out Book 5, Chapter 3 to learn how CSS Grid works.) Grid has many options for building in responsiveness, but the following three techniques will get you there in most cases:

» Use fr units to allow grid items to fill the available space in the grid container.

» Let the browser do some of the work for you by specifying only a column or a row template (not both).

» In your template, use the auto-fit keyword to let the browser perform the column-width or row-height calculations automatically.

For example, the following declaration tells the browser to automatically fit the container width with equal-sized (1 fr) columns that are no less than 15rem wide:

```
grid-template-columns: repeat(auto-fit, minmax(15rem, 1fr));
```

Here's an example that puts this declaration to work (bk05ch04/example04.html):

HTML (abbreviated):

```
<header>
    <h1>The Vibrant Edges of Language</h1>
    <p class="subtitle">In which our intrepid writers let loose
  with talk of word play in all its forms</p>
</header>
<main>
    <p>
    We have a deep-rooted delight in the comic effect of words
  in English, and not just in advertising jingles but at the
  highest level of endeavor. <br>—BILL BRYSON, <i>The Mother
  Tongue</i>, 1990
    </p><p>
    etc.
</main>
```

CSS:

```
main {
    display: grid;
    grid-template-columns: repeat(auto-fit, minmax(15rem, 1fr));
    gap: 2rem;
}
main > p:nth-child(even) {
    background: hsl(208deg 50% 80%);
}
```

On a larger screen, the main element is a four-column grid, as shown in Figure 4-5.

Reduce the width of the viewport a bit and the layout automatically switches to a three-column grid, as shown in Figure 4-6.

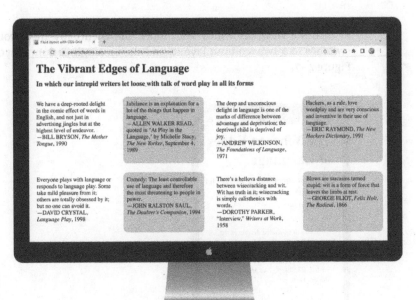

**FIGURE 4-5:**
The grid layout as it appears in a desktop browser viewport.

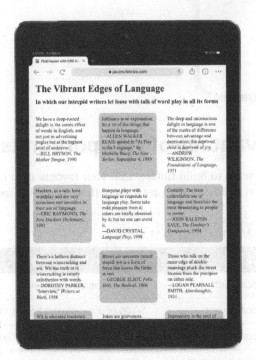

**FIGURE 4-6:**
The grid layout as it appears in a tablet viewport.

Reduce the viewport width even more and eventually the layout automatically switches to a two-column layout, and then a single-column layout, as shown in Figure 4-7.

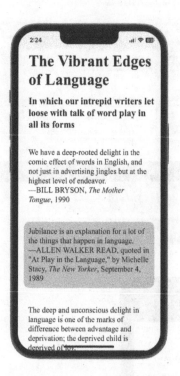

**FIGURE 4-7:**
The grid layout as it appears in a smartphone viewport.

# Taking advantage of viewport units

One of the easiest ways to build fluidity into your layouts is to use the viewport units that I mention in Book 3, Chapter 5. Here they are again (see Table 4-1):

**TABLE 4-1**     ## CSS Viewport Measurement Units

| Unit | Name | Measured Relative to |
|------|------|----------------------|
| vw | viewport width | 1/100 of the viewport width |
| vh | viewport height | 1/100 of the viewport height |
| vmin | viewport minimum | 1/100 of the viewport's smaller dimension |
| vmax | viewport maximum | 1/100 of the viewport's larger dimension |

I should also mention a few new viewport units that have been available in most major browsers for a little while, but don't yet have universal support. These viewport units were created to handle the inconvenient fact that most mobile browsers hide their user interface (UI) features (such as the toolbar and address/search bar) when you scroll down the page, and then show those features when you scroll back up. This means you're really dealing with three viewports:

>> **Small viewport:** This is the viewport that's available when the browser UI is shown. This viewport is "small" because the browser UI takes up a portion of the screen.

>> **Large viewport:** This is the viewport that's available when the browser UI is hidden. This viewport is "large" because the browser UI no longer takes up a portion of the screen.

>> **Dynamic viewport:** This is the browser viewport that's currently displayed, which could be small or large depending on the user's scrolling behavior.

Given these viewports, Table 4-2 lists the new units that are based on these sizes:

**TABLE 4-2**     **New CSS Viewport Measurement Units**

| Unit | Name | Measured Relative to |
|------|------|----------------------|
| svw | small viewport width | 1/100 of the small viewport width |
| svh | small viewport height | 1/100 of the small viewport height |
| svmin | small viewport minimum | 1/100 of the small viewport's smaller dimension |
| svmax | small viewport maximum | 1/100 of the small viewport's larger dimension |
| lvw | large viewport width | 1/100 of the large viewport width |
| lvh | large viewport height | 1/100 of the large viewport height |
| lvmin | large viewport minimum | 1/100 of the large viewport's smaller dimension |
| lvmax | large viewport maximum | 1/100 of the large viewport's larger dimension |
| dvw | dynamic viewport width | 1/100 of the dynamic viewport width |
| dvh | dynamic viewport height | 1/100 of the dynamic viewport height |
| dvmin | dynamic viewport minimum | 1/100 of the dynamic viewport's smaller dimension |
| dmax | dynamic viewport maximum | 1/100 of the dynamic viewport's larger dimension |

**TIP**

As I write this, these new viewport units have just under 87 percent browser support. To keep an eye on this support level, use the following Can I Use page: https://caniuse.com/viewport-unit-variants.

The advantage of viewport units is that they automatically scale along with the changing viewport size, so they're fluid by default. If the user changes the size of the browser window or rotates their device to a different orientation, a property that uses a viewport-based unit will automatically scale to match the new viewport width or height.

For example, if you're using a grid layout and you've set gaps with the row-gap and column-gap properties, you may want those gaps to grow and shrink along with the viewport. Here's one way to accomplish this (bk05ch04/example05. html):

```
column-gap: 2vw;
row-gap: 2vh;
```

## Making typography fluid

Although many developers use viewport units for features such as grid gaps, padding, margins, and even element widths and heights, by far the most common use case for viewport units is fluid typography. That is, by setting your font-size properties to values that use viewport units, your type will scale along with the viewport size.

Note that this doesn't mean doing something like this:

```
font-size: 1.5vmax;
```

The problem is that this isn't an accessible approach because it overrides the user's custom font size setting. A better way to go is to combine a rem unit (for accessibility) and a viewport unit (for fluidity) using calc():

```
font-size: calc(0.75rem + 1vmax);
```

A calculation like this is suitable for regular text. For headings, you'll need to experiment a bit to figure out what suits your page. For example, an h1 element may use the following declaration:

```
font-size: calc(1.75rem + 2vmax);
```

## Introducing your best fluid friend: clamp()

The problem with using viewport units for lengths and font sizes is that you lose some control over the final value of whatever property you're working with. That's by design, of course, because part of the value proposition for a fluid layout is to cede some control to the browser and let it do more of the responsive heavy lifting.

However, viewport-based sizes, although they can look fine at intermediate screen sizes, can become unreadably small at the smallest viewport widths and comically large when faced with the largest viewports. Fortunately, you can turn to the powerful clamp() function (check out Book 3, Chapter 5) to set minimum and maximum values for your fluid calculations.

For example, if the smallest size you want for your regular text is 1.25rem and the largest size is 1.75rem, the following clamp() function will do the job (bk05ch04/example06.html):

```
font-size: clamp(1.25rem, 0.75rem + 1vmax, 1.75rem);
```

# Querying Your Way to Responsiveness: Adaptive Layouts

In Book 4, Chapter 4, I talk about controlling JavaScript using if...else statements where a script runs one block of code if a specified expression is true and a different block of code if that expression is false.

CSS has something similar called a *query*, where you test for a particular condition and, if that condition is true, the browser applies one or more styles; if the condition is false, the browser just skips over those styles. (So, a query is like a JavaScript if statement without the else part.)

CSS offers quite a few query types, but for your purposes here, you can consider just the following three:

>> **Media query:** A query that interrogates some aspect of the screen, usually the viewport width

>> **Container query:** A query that examines some feature of a parent or ancestor element, such as the element's width or orientation

>> **User preference query:** A special type of media query that checks whether the user has declared a preference for a particular feature, such as dark mode

In each case, the point is to use the query to create an *adaptive layout*, which is a layout that changes depending on the result of the query. In each case, you can specify a declaration block that the browser applies if the query is true. This makes adaptive layouts more powerful than fluid layouts because you can apply just about any CSS rule you want when a query is true:

» You can hide a displayed element or show a hidden element.

» You can modify an existing layout, such as changing a three-column grid to a one- or two-column grid.

» You can switch to an entirely different layout type, such as from Grid to Flexbox.

» If you're using Flexbox, you can change the order of the elements.

» You can modify any CSS property, such as font-size, width, and margin.

The next three sections take you through the specifics of each query type.

## Interrogating the screen with media queries

By far the most common type of adaptive layout uses a CSS feature called a *media query*, which is the @media at-rule, an expression that evaluates to either true or false, and a code block consisting of one or more style rules. The expression interrogates some feature of the viewport, usually its width. If that expression is true for the current device, the browser applies the media query's style rules; if the expression is false, the browser ignores the media query's rules. Here's the syntax:

```
@media (expression) {
    declarations
}
```

» *expression:* A property-value pair that the browser uses to test the current device viewport

» *declarations:* The style declarations that the browser applies if *expression* is true

There are lots of different possibilities for *expression*, but the vast majority of media queries test for a viewport width that's either less than or equal to some value or greater than or equal to some value.

To test for a viewport width that's greater than or equal to some value, use the `min-width` property:

```
@media (min-width: value) {
    declarations
}
```

>> *value:* A length value using any of the standard CSS measurement units

To test for a viewport width that's less than or equal to some value, use the `max-width` property:

```
@media (max-width: value) {
    declarations
}
```

>> *value:* A length value using any of the standard CSS measurement units.

Here's an example (bk05ch04/example07.html):

HTML:

```
<header>
    <img src="images/notw.png" alt="News of the Word logo"
  class="site-logo">
    <h1>News of the Word</h1>
    <p class="subtitle">Language news you won't find anywhere
  else (for good reason!)</p>
</header>
```

CSS:

```
@media (max-width: 40rem) {
    .site-logo {
        display: none;
    }
}
```

This media query looks for a viewport width of 40rem or less. When that's true, the rule inside the media query block runs, which sets the display property to none for the header image (which uses the class site-logo). As shown in Figure 4-8, the logo appears in a tablet-sized viewport, but not in the smartphone-sized viewport shown in Figure 4-9.

**FIGURE 4-8:**
The header
logo appears in
a tablet-sized
viewport.

**FIGURE 4-9:**
On a
smartphone-
sized
viewport, the
media query
expression is
true, so the
header logo
is hidden.

**TIP**

You can specify multiple expressions in your media queries. For example, if you separate expressions with the keyword and, the browser applies the style rules only if all the expressions are true:

```
@media (expression1) and (expression2) {
    declarations
}
```

Similarly, if you separate expressions with the keyword or, then the browser applies the style rules if one or more of the expressions are true:

```
@media (expression1) or (expression2) {
    declarations
}
```

For example, if you wanted to target viewport sizes between 40rem and 60rem, you'd do this:

```
@media (min-width: 40rem) and (max-width: 60rem) {
    declarations
}
```

## Laying out trees instead of forests with container queries

The media queries that I talk about in the previous section have been a staple of CSS layout since at least 2009 and are even supported by Internet Explorer 9 and later. The chief advantage of media queries over the fluid techniques I talk about earlier (check out "Going with the Flow: Fluid Layouts") is that when a media query expression is true, you can write very specific style rules for the browser to apply to one or more elements.

But media queries, although still useful and relevant, are starting to show their age a bit for two reasons:

>> Media queries almost always interrogate the size of the entire viewport.

>> Modern web design is focused on the idea of the *component,* which is a standalone collection of elements, particularly one that gets reused in different contexts.

For example, a component for a product may have a photo of the product, a header with the product name, some body text describing the product, and some action buttons related to the product. Here are some example contexts where this component may get used:

>> On the product landing page, this component may take up most of the viewport.

>> On the site home page, the product may be featured with a large card.

>> On the product catalog page, the component may be a medium-sized card.

>> In the site's navigation sidebar, the component may be a small card, perhaps without the image.

These different contexts require different layouts for the component. Media queries don't work well in this scenario because they examine only the size of the whole viewport and in each of the preceding contexts, the viewport size may not change.

So, it's no wonder the entire CSS community is abuzz with excitement over a new adaptive layout technology called *container queries*. These queries enable you to examine the width (and a few other properties) of a parent element (that's the container that gives these queries their name) and then apply style rules to the child and descendant elements whenever that width (or whatever) meets your specified criteria.

So, for example, assuming that your product component is wrapped in a parent element, such as a div, then a container query would examine, say, the width of that div and apply different styles to the child and descendant elements — the image, the heading, the text, and the links — depending on the result.

**WARNING**

As I write this, container queries have only recently become supported by all the major browsers, so they're not quite ready for production use. However, there's a good chance container queries will have near-universal support (say, over 90 percent) by the time you read this, so check out the following Can I Use page to find out where things stand: https://caniuse.com/css-container-queries.

## Setting up the query container

To work with container queries, you first set up an element as the query container. This will be the parent or ancestor of the child or descendant elements you want to style. To set up an element as a query container, use the container-type property:

```
element {
    container-type: value;
}
```

» *element*: The parent or ancestor of the elements you want to style.

» *value*: Use `inline-size` if in your container query you want to interrogate only the container's width (assuming a horizontal inline direction). Use `size` instead if you want to interrogate width and/or height in your container query.

Here's an example (bk05ch04/example08.html) that sets up the default layout for a product card:

HTML:

```
<div class="card-container">
    <div class="card-wrapper">
        <img class="card-image" src="images/inflatable-
    dartboard.png" alt="Inflatable dartboard product photo">
        <div>
            <h3 class="card-title">Inflatable Dartboard</h3>
            <p class="card-description">
                Yes, it's the world-famous inflatable dartboard!
    No hassle setup! Comes with an easy-to-use inflation tube.
    Just take a deep breath and blow. And blow. Keep going.
    Anyway, within a few hours, you'll be ready to play darts. Now
    only $1,999! Patch kit sold separately.
            </p>
            <div class="card-actions">
                <button class="card-button learn-more">Learn
    more</button>
                <button class="card-button add-to-cart">Add to
    cart</button>
            </div>
        </div>
    </div>
</div>
```

CSS:

```
.card-container {
    container-type: inline-size;
}
.card-wrapper {
```

```
    display: grid;
    gap: 1.5rem;
    grid-template-columns: auto auto;
    grid-template-rows: auto;
}
.card-image {
    min-width: auto;
    height: auto;
    object-fit: cover;
    object-position: center;
    overflow: hidden;
}
.card-title {
    text-align: left;
}
.card-actions {
    display: flex;
    gap: 1rem;
    justify-content: flex-start;
}
```

Of particular interest is the parent `div` with class `card-container`. That `div` is styled in the CSS as a query container:

```
.card-container {
    container-type: inline-size;
}
```

Figure 4-10 shows the default card.

**FIGURE 4-10:**
A product card in
its default layout.

**TIP**

I should point out that if you want to have multiple query containers on your page, you need to name each container by adding the `container-name` property to the container element:

```
element {
    container-type: value;
    container-name: name;
}
```

## Querying the container

With your query container set up, you're ready to query it using the `@container` at-rule:

```
@container (expression) {
    declarations
}
```

» *expression:* An expression that the browser uses to test some property of the container, such as its width

» *declarations:* The style declarations that the browser applies if *expression* is true

For example, here's a container query for the product card from the previous section that applies its style rules when the container's width is less than 25rem:

```
@container (width < 25rem) {
    .card-wrapper {
        align-items: center;
        display: block;
        padding: 1rem;
    }
    .card-image {
        display: none;
    }
    .card-title {
        margin-top: 0;
    }
}
```

Figure 4-11 shows the resulting card when its container is less than 25rem wide.

**FIGURE 4-11:**
The product card
layout when the
parent element
is less than
25rem wide.

As with media queries, you can also use multiple expressions in your container queries. Separate expressions with and to apply the rules only when every expression is true; separate expressions with or to apply the rules only when at least one of the expressions is true.

Here's a container query for the product card from the previous section that applies its style rules when the container's width is greater than 25rem and less than 35rem:

```
@container (width > 25rem) and (width < 35rem) {
    .card-wrapper {
            grid-template-columns: auto;
            grid-template-rows: auto auto;
    }
    .card-image {
      width: 100%;
      height: 10rem;
    }
    .card-title {
        text-align: center;
    }
    .card-actions {
        justify-content: center;
    }
}
```

Figure 4-12 shows the resulting card layout when the container is between 25rem and 35rem wide.

**FIGURE 4-12:**
The product card
layout when the
parent element is
between 25rem
and 35rem wide.

## Working with container query units

After you've set up an element as a query container, you're free to size that element's children and descendants using *container query units*, which are measurement units that are relative to the dimensions of the query container. Table 4-3 lists the available container query units you can use.

**TABLE 4-3**

### CSS Container Query Measurement Units

| Unit | Name | Measured Relative to |
|------|------|----------------------|
| cqw | container width | 1/100 of the container width |
| cqh | container height | 1/100 of the container height |
| cqmin | container minimum | 1/100 of the container's smaller dimension |
| cqmax | container maximum | 1/100 of the container's larger dimension |

# Respecting your visitors with user preference queries

Through their operating system's settings, users can express certain preferences related to how their device looks and operates. For example, many people choose to use either a light color scheme or a dark color scheme, as shown in Figure 4-13.

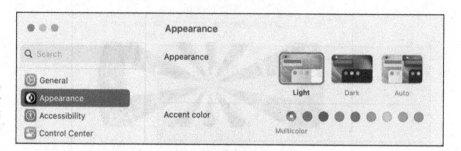

**FIGURE 4-13:**
Choosing either
a light or a dark
color scheme in
macOS.

You can use a CSS media query to detect some of these user preferences and style your page accordingly. Here's the general syntax:

```
@media (preference: value) {
    declarations
}
```

» *preference:* A keyword that specifies which preference you're detecting

» *value:* The preference setting your query is looking for

» *declarations:* The style declarations that the browser applies if *preference* matches *value*

Although more preferences are in the offing, for now you can detect three. Here are the associated keywords and values:

» prefers-color-scheme: Detects whether the user has set a preference for the color scheme. The two values you can query are dark or light. The usual procedure here is to set up your page assuming the light color scheme, and then use something like the following to apply darker colors if the dark color scheme preference is detected:

```
@media (prefers-color-scheme: dark) {
    /* Dark color scheme colors go here */
}
```

**TIP**

If you use the hsl() function for your colors, one easy way to convert a light color to a dark variant is to subtract the lightness value from 100 while keeping the hue and saturation values the same. For example, if the light color is hsl(180deg 50% 80%), the corresponding dark mode color will be hsl(180deg 50% 20%).

» prefers-contrast: Detects whether the user has set a preference for higher or lower contrast colors to be used. The values you can query are no-preference (the user hasn't set a contrast preference), more (the user prefers higher contrast), less (the user prefers lower contrast), or custom (the user has set a custom contrast level). Most users who set this preference prefer higher-contrast colors, which you can detect as follows:

```
@media (prefers-contrast: more) {
    /* Higher-contrast colors go here */
}
```

» prefers-reduced-motion: Detects whether the user has set a preference for a reduced level of animation effects and similar nonessential motion on the screen. The values you can query are no-preference (the user hasn't set a reduced motion preference) or reduced (the user prefers reduced motion). Here's a media query that detects whether the user prefers reduced motion and, if so, sets all animations to their minimums:

```
@media (prefers-reduced-motion: reduce) {
    *,
    ::after,
    ::before {
        animation-duration: 0.01ms;
        animation-iteration-count: 1;
        transition-duration: 0.01ms;
        scroll-behavior: auto;
    }
}
```

**TIP**

You can use the browser dev tools to test these preferences without having to toggle them in your operating system's settings app. In Chrome, open the dev tools, click the Customize and Control Dev Tools icon (shown in the margin), choose More Tools ⇨ Rendering, and then use the controls that emulate each user preference.

# Working with Images Responsively

When planning a web page, you always need to consider the impact of images, both on your design and on your users.

# Making images responsive

On the design side, you need to ensure that your images scale responsively, depending on the screen width or height. For example, if the user's screen is 1,024 pixels wide, an image that's 800 pixels wide will fit with no problem, but that same image will overflow a 400-pixel-wide screen. You create responsive images with the following CSS rule:

**REMEMBER**

```
image {
    max-width: 100%;
    height: auto;
}
```

Here, *image* is a selector that references the image or images you want to be responsive. Setting `max-width: 100%` enables the image width to scale smaller or larger as the viewport (or the image's container) changes size, but also mandates that the image can't scale larger than its original width. Setting `height: auto` cajoles the browser into maintaining the image's original aspect ratio by calculating the height automatically based on the image's current width.

**TIP**

Occasionally, you'll want the image height instead of its width to be responsive. To do that, you use the following variation on the preceding rule:

```
image {
    max-height: 100%;
    width: auto;
}
```

# Delivering images responsively

On the user side, delivering images that are far larger than the screen size can be a major problem. Sure, you can make the images responsive, but you're still sending a massive file down the tubes, which won't be appreciated by those mobile surfers using slow connections with limited data plans.

Instead, you need to deliver to the user a version of the image file that's appropriately sized for the device screen. For example, you may deliver the full-size image to desktop users, a medium-sized version to tablet folk, and a small-sized version to smartphone users. That sounds like a complex bit of business, but HTML5 lets you handle everything from the comfort of the `<img>` tag. The secret? The `sizes` and `srcset` attributes.

The `sizes` attribute is a collection of *expression-width* pairs:

>> The *expression* part specifies a screen feature, such as a minimum or maximum width, surrounded by parentheses.

>> The *width* part specifies how wide you want the image displayed on screens that match the expression.

For example, to specify that on screens up to 600 pixels wide, you want an image displayed with a width of 90vw, you'd use the following expression-width pair:

```
(max-width: 600px) 90vw
```

A typical `sizes` attribute is a collection of expression-width pairs, separated by commas. Here's the general syntax to use:

```
sizes="(expression1) width1,
       (expression2) width2,
       etc.,
       widthN"
```

Notice that the last item doesn't specify an expression. This tells the web browser that the specified width applies to any screen that doesn't match any of the expressions.

Here's an example:

```
sizes="(max-width: 600px) 90vw,
       (max-width: 1000px) 60vw,
       30vw"
```

The `srcset` attribute is a comma-separated list of image file locations, each followed by the image width and letter `w`. Here's the general syntax:

```
srcset="location1 width1w,
        location2 width2w,
        etc.">
```

This gives the browser a choice of image sizes, and it picks the best one based on the current device screen dimensions and the preferred widths you specify in the `sizes` attribute. Here's a full example, and Figure 4-14 shows how the browser serves up different images for different screen sizes:

```
<img src="/images/img-small.jpg" alt=""
     sizes="(max-width: 600px) 90vw,
```

```
                (max-width: 1000px) 60vw,
                30vw"
       srcset="/images/img-small.jpg 450w,
              /images/img-medium.jpg 900w,
              /images/img-large.jpg 1350w">
```

**FIGURE 4-14:**
With the `<img>`
tag's `sizes` and
`srcset` attributes
on the job, the
browser serves
up different
versions of
the image
for different
screen sizes.

**WARNING**

The `sizes` and `srcset` attributes don't always work the way you may expect. For example, if the browser finds that, say, the large version of the image is already stored in its cache, it will usually decide that it's faster and easier on the bandwidth to just grab the image from the cache and scale it instead of going back to the server to download a more appropriately sized file for the current screen.

# Exploring the Principles of Mobile-First Development

If you've been hanging around the web for a while, you probably remember the days when you'd surf to a site using a small screen such as a smartphone or sim- ilar portable device, and instead of getting the regular version of the site, you'd get the "mobile" version. In rare cases, this alternate version would be optimized for mobile viewing and navigation, but more likely it was just a poor facsimile of the regular site with a few font changes and all the interesting and useful features removed.

From the web developer's viewpoint, the poor quality of those mobile sites isn't all that surprising. After all, who wants to build and maintain two versions of the same site? Fortunately, the days of requiring an entirely different site to support mobile users are long gone. Yes, using responsive web design enables you to create a single site that looks and works great on everything from a wall-mounted display to a handheld device. But in modern web development, there's a strong case to be made that all web pages should be built from the ground up as though they were going to be displayed only on mobile devices. In the rest of this chapter, you explore the principles and techniques behind this mobile-first approach to web development.

## What is mobile-first web development?

As I discuss earlier in this chapter, when you develop a web page to look good and work well on a desktop-sized screen, you can employ a number of responsive tricks to make that same code look good and work well on a mobile device screen:

>> Set up a Flexbox or Grid layout that automatically adjusts to any size screen.

>> Use viewport units, particularly with font sizes.

>> Use media queries to remove elements when the screen width falls below a specified threshold.

**REMEMBER**

That third technique — the one where you remove stuff that doesn't fit on a smaller screen — is known in the web coding trade as *regressive enhancement* (*RE*). RE has ruled the web development world for many years, but lately there's been a backlash against it. Here's why:

>> RE relegates mobile screens to second-class web citizenship.

>> RE leads to undisciplined development because coders and designers inevitably stuff a desktop-sized screen with content, widgets, and all the web bells and whistles.

**REMEMBER**

What's the solution? You've probably guessed it by now: *progressive enhancement*, which means starting with content that fits on the smallest screen size that you need to support and then adding components as the screen gets bigger. When that original content represents what's essential about your page, and when that base screen width is optimized for mobile devices — especially today's most popular smartphones — then you've got yourself a *mobile-first* approach to web development.

Let me be honest right off the top: Mobile-first web development is daunting because if you're used to having the giant canvas of a desktop screen to play with, starting instead with a screen that's a mere 360- or 400-pixels across can feel a tad claustrophobic. However, I can assure you that it seems that way only because of the natural tendency to wonder how you're possibly going to shoehorn your massive page into such a tiny space. Mobile-first thinking takes the opposite approach by ignoring (at least at the beginning) large screens and focusing instead on what works best for mobile screens which, after all, represent the majority of your page visitors. Thinking the mobile-first way isn't hard: It just means keeping a few key design principles in mind.

## Mobile first means content first

One of the biggest advantages of taking a mobile-first approach to web development is that it forces you to prioritize. That is, a mobile-first design means that you include in the initial layout only those page elements that are essential to the user's experience of the page. This essential-stuff-only idea is partly a response to having a smaller screen size in which to display that stuff, but it's also a necessity for many mobile users who are surfing with sluggish Internet connections and limited data plans. It's your job — no, scratch that, it's your *duty* as a conscientious web developer — to make sure that those users aren't served anything superfluous, frivolous, or in any other way nonessential.

That's all well and good, I hear you thinking, but define "superfluous" and "frivolous." Good point. The problem, of course, is that one web developer's trivial appetizer is another's essential meat and potatoes. Only you can decide between what's inconsequential and what's vital, depending on your page goals and your potential audience.

So, the first step toward a mobile-first design is to decide what's most important in the following content categories:

**REMEMBER**

» **Text:** Decide what words are essential to get your page's message across. Usability expert Steve Krug tells web designers to "Get rid of half the words on each page, then get rid of half of what's left." For a mobile-first page, you may need to halve the words once again. Be ruthless. Does the user really need that message from the CEO or your "About Us" text? Probably not.

» **Images:** Decide what images are essential for the user, or whether any images are needed at all. The problem with images is that, although everyone likes a bit of eye candy, that sweetness comes at the cost of screen real estate and bandwidth. If you really do need to include an image or two in your mobile-first page, at least serve up smaller images to your mobile visitors. To learn how to do that, check out "Working with images responsively," earlier in this chapter.

» **Navigation:** All users need to be able to navigate your site, but the recent trend is to create gigantic menus that include links to every section and page on the site. Decide which of those links is truly important for navigation and just include those in your mobile-first layout.

» **Widgets:** Modern web pages are festooned with widgets for social media, content scrollers, photo light boxes, automatic video playback, and, of course, advertising. Mobile users want content first, so consider ditching the widgets altogether. If there's a widget you really want to include, and you're sure it won't put an excessive burden on either the page's load time or the user's bandwidth, push the widget to the bottom of the page.

## Pick a testing width that makes sense for your site

**REMEMBER**

For most websites, testing a mobile-first layout should begin with the smallest devices, which these days means smartphones with screens that are 360 pixels wide. However, you don't necessarily have to begin your testing with a width as small as 360px. If you have access to your site analytics, they should tell you what devices your visitors use. If you find that all or most of your mobile users are on devices that are at least 400 pixels wide, then that's the initial width you should test for your mobile-first layout.

# Get your content to scale with the device

For your mobile-first approach to be successful, it's paramount that you configure each page on your site to scale horizontally with the width of the device screen. You do that by adding the following `<meta>` tag to the head section of each page:

**TIP**

```
<meta name="viewport" content="width=device-width,
   initial-scale=1.0">
```

This instructs the web browser to do two things:

>> Set the initial width of the page content to the width of the device screen.

>> Set the initial zoom level of the page to 1.0, which means that the page is neither zoomed in nor zoomed out.

# Build your CSS the mobile-first way

When you're ready to start coding the CSS for your page, understand that the style definitions and rules that you write will be your page defaults — that is, these are the styles the browser will display on all devices, unless you've defined one or more media queries (or container queries) to override these defaults. You shouldn't have to write any special rules as long as you follow a few basic tenets of responsive web design:

**REMEMBER**

>> Use the viewport units for measures such as width and padding.

>> Use the rem units for font sizes.

>> Make all your images responsive.

>> Use Grid or Flexbox for the page layout. If you're using Flexbox, be sure to apply `flex-wrap: wrap` to any flex container.

It's also important to make sure that your mobile-first layout renders the content just as you want it to appear on the mobile screen. This means avoiding any tricks such as using the Flexbox `order` property to mess around with the order of the page elements.

Finally, and perhaps most important, be sure to hide any unnecessary content by styling that content with `display: none`.

In the end, your mobile-first CSS should be the very model of simplicity and economy.

# Pick a "non-mobile" breakpoint that makes sense for your content

Your mobile-first CSS code probably includes several elements that you've hidden with `display: none`. I assume you want to show those elements eventually (otherwise, you'd have deleted them altogether), so you need to decide when you want them shown. Specifically, you need to decide what the minimum screen width is that will show your content successfully.

Notice I didn't say that you should decide when to show your hidden content based on the width of a target device. For example, for years developers considered a screen to be "wide enough" when it was at least as wide as an iPad screen in portrait mode, which for the longest time was 768 pixels. Fair enough, but although iPad minis still use that width, newer iPads are now much wider (for example, the iPad Pro is 1,024 pixels wide in portrait mode).

TIP

Devices change constantly, and it's a fool's game to try to keep up with them. Forget all that. Instead, decide what minimum width is best for your page when the hidden content is made visible. How can you do that? Here's one easy way:

1. **Load your page into the Chrome web browser.**

2. **Display Chrome's developer tools.**

   Press either Ctrl+Shift+I (Windows) or ⌘+Shift+I (Mac).

3. **Use your mouse to adjust the size of the browser window:**

   - If the developer tools are below or undocked from the browser viewport, drag the right or left edge of the browser window.

   - If the developer tools are docked to the right or left of the browser viewport, drag the vertical bar that separates the developer tools from the viewport.

4. **Read the current viewport dimensions, which Chrome displays in the upper-right corner of the viewport.**

   The dimensions appear as width x height, in pixels.

5. **Narrow the window to your mobile-first testing width (such as 360px).**

6. **Increase the width and, as you do, watch how your layout changes.**

   In particular, watch for the width where the content first looks the way you want it to appear in larger screens. Make a note of that width.

**REMEMBER**

The width where your full content looks good is the basis for a CSS media query breakpoint that you'll use to display the elements that were hidden in the mobile-first layout. For example, say that your mobile-first layout hides the `aside` element and that you found that your full content looks right at a width of 742px. You then can set up the following media query (using 750px for a round number):

```
@media (min-width: 750px) {
    aside {
        display: block;
    }
}
```

This media query tells the browser that when the screen width is 750px or more, display the `aside` element.

# Index

## SYMBOLS

+ (addition operator), 430, 613–614

& (ampersand), 109

&& (AND operator), 447–448, 450–451, 462

* (asterisk), 233, 243

\ (backslash), 17, 102, 422

` (back ticks), 585, 623

{ } (braces), 27, 459, 483, 646

: (colon), 253

+ (concatenation), 436–437

–– (decrement operator), 433

/ (division operator), 434–435

. (dot), 240–242, 516

:: (double colon), 278

" (double quotation marks), 421

// (double-slash), 408

– (em dash), 108–109

== (equality operator), 439–440, 646

= (equals sign), 413

>= (greater than or equal operator), 442

> (greater-than symbol), 82, 109, 245, 441

# (hashtag symbol), 104, 242–243

– (hyphen), 104

=== (identity operator), 444, 646

++ (increment operator), 430–431

!= (inequality operator), 440–441

<= (less than or equal operator), 442

< (less-than symbol), 82, 109

– (minus sign), 420

% (modulus operator), 324, 435

* (multiplication operator), 433

! (NOT operator), 449

|| (OR operator), 448–449, 450–451, 462

+ (plus sign), 246–247, 420

; (semicolon), 36, 109

' (single quotation marks), 421

/ (slash), 17

. . . (spread operator), 572–573

[ ] (square brackets operator), 662

=== (strict equality operator), 444

!== (strict inequality operator), 444

– (subtraction and negation operators), 431–432

?: (ternary operator), 446–447

~ (tilde), 245–246

_ (underscore), 104, 417

## NUMBERS

0-width (ch), 324

## A

<a> tag, 102–103, 128

<abbr> tag, 110

absolute measurement units, 323–324

absolute positioning, 688–690

accessibility semantics, 191–198

adding form field labels, 192

ARIA roles, 192–198

Accessible Rich Internet Applications (ARIA) roles, 192–198

accordions, 166

:active pseudo-class, 268–269

activeElement property, 524

ad requirements, 51

adaptive layouts, 779–791

container queries, 783–789

media queries, 780–783

user preference queries, 789–791

add() method, 541

addEventListener() method, 664

addition operator (+), 430, 613–614

<address> tag, 110–111

administration interface, 51

Adobe Fonts, 368

::after pseudo-element, 279–281, 685

age, 608–610

alert() method, 36, 481

align-content property, 762

aligning, 394–396

flex containers

centering element horizontally and vertically, 713–714

# T

tab order
  adding element to, 199
  removing element from, 200
tabindex="0" attribute, 668
table footer, 152–154
tables, 143–162
  adding more rows, 148
  elements, 149–154
    captions, 150–151
    header column, 151–152
    header row, 149–150
    table footer, 152–154
  one-row table, 146–147
  overview, 143–145
  styling, 154–162
    aligning text within cells, 154–158
    borders, 159–161
    location of captions, 162
    padded cells, 161–162
tabs, 22
tags
  attributes, 17–18
  defined, 15–17
  specifying elements by name of, 526
target, 270
:target pseudo-class, 271
<td> tag, 147
tech support, 52
tel type, 169
templates
  grid, 741
  string, 584–586
ternary operator (?:), 446–447
testing code, 59–75
  cross-browser testing, 60–62
    browser market share, 60–61
    testing online, 61–62
    testing suite, 61

testing suite, 61
testing width, 797
text
  adding, 21–23
  adding color to, 344–346
    color property, 344
    text decorations, 344
    text shadow, 345–346
  aligning within table cells, 154–158
  inserting into element, 538–539
  mobile-first design, 797
  web accessibility, 188–189
  writing to pages, 37
text decorations, 344
text editors, 10–11
  choosing, 42–45
  validating code
    CSS, 72
    HTML, 67–69
    JavaScript, 74–75
text fields, 651–653
  getting value of, 652
  referencing by field type, 651–652
  setting value of, 653
text files, 11
text processing, 43
text styles, 384–389
  italics, 386
  text weight, 384–386
  variable fonts, 386–389
text tags, 98–101, 109–121
  <abbr> tag, 110
  adding quotations, 100–101
  <address> tag, 110–111
  <cite> tag, 111–112
  <code> tag, 112–113
  <dfn> tag, 113–114
  <dl> tag, 114–115
  emphasizing text, 98–99

<kbd> tag, 116
<mark> tag, 116–117
marking important text, 99
nesting tags, 100
<pre> tag, 117–118
<s> tag, 118–120
<sub> tag, 120
<sup> tag, 120–121
text type, 168
<textarea> tag, 170
text-based fields, 168–171
TextEdit, 11, 42
text-transform property, 389
<tfoot> tag, 152–153
<th> tag, 149, 151–152
tilde (~), 245–246
time, 601. *see also* dates and times
time type, 169
timeout, 501–502
title property, 525
<title> tag, 20–21
titles, web page, 20–21
top value, 130
Torvalds, Linus, 2
<tr> tag, 146–147
<track> tag, 191
tracks, grid, 751–753
traversing DOM, 529–535
  getting children of parent element, 530–534
  getting parent of child element, 534
  getting siblings of element, 534–535
true/false decisions, 458–460
truth table, 448, 449
two-directional containers, 706
type attribute, 136, 141, 168–170
type selector, 240
typefaces, 364–365

width attribute, 135

Windows
  Notepad on, 11
  web browsers, 13
  web development tools for, 292–293

WOFF2 files, 373

World Wide Web Consortium (W3C), 62

wrapping flex items, 714–716

writing, text to pages, 37

writing mode, 219

# X

x-height (ex), 324, 371

# Y

YouTube, 132

yy argument, 600

yyyy argument, 600

# Z

z-index property, 696–698

Zoom command, 186

zoom level, 768

## About the Author

*Information appears to stew out of me naturally, like the precious ottar of roses out of the otter. —Mark Twain*

Paul McFedries is a technical writer who spends his days writing books just like the one you're holding in your hands. In fact, Paul has written more than one hundred such books that have sold over four million copies worldwide. Paul invites everyone to drop by his personal website at paulmcfedries.com, or to follow him on Twitter (@paulmcf) or Facebook (facebook.com/PaulMcFedries).

## Dedication

To Karen, my lobster

## Authors' Acknowledgments

Each time I complete a book, the publisher sends me a heavy box filled with a few so-called "author" copies. Opening that box, lifting out a book, feeling the satisfying weight of something that has up to now been weightlessly digital, and seeing my name printed on the cover, well, it's a pretty fine feeling, let me tell you. That's pretty cool, but you know what's *really* cool? That I've done that over a hundred times in my writing career and seeing my name on the cover *never* gets old.

But just because mine is the only name you see on the cover, it doesn't mean this book was a one-man show. Far from it. Sure, I did write this book's text and take its screenshots, but those represent only a part of what constitutes a "book." The rest of it is brought to you by the dedication and professionalism of Wiley's editing, graphics, and production teams, who toiled long and hard to turn my text and images into an actual book.

I offer my heartfelt thanks to everyone at Wiley who made this book possible, but I'd like to extend some special thank-yous to the folks I worked with directly: Executive Editor Steve Hayes, Project and Copy Editor Susan Christophersen, and Technical Editor Rod Stephens.

## Publisher's Acknowledgments

**Executive Editor:** Steve Hayes

**Project Manager and Copy Editor:**
  Susan Christophersen

**Technical Editor:** Rod Stephens

**Production Editor:** Pradesh Kumar

**Cover Image:** © FreshSplash/Getty Images;
  Screenshot courtesy of Paul McFedries